Something about
the Author *was named
an "Outstanding
Reference Source,"
the highest honor given
by the American
Library Association
Reference and Adult
Services Division.*

SOMETHING ABOUT THE AUTHOR®

ISSN 0276-816X

SOMETHING ABOUT THE AUTHOR®

**Facts and Pictures about Authors
and Illustrators of Books for Young People**

VOLUME 116

GALE GROUP

*Detroit
New York
San Francisco
London
Boston
Woodbridge, CT*

Library of Congress Catalog Card Number 72-27107

ISBN 0-7876-4034-4
ISSN 0276-816X

Printed in the United States of America

10 9 8 7 6 5 4 3 2 1

Contents

Authors in Forthcoming Volumes

Below are some of the authors and illustrators that will be featured in upcoming volumes of *SATA*. These include new entries on the swiftly rising stars of the field, as well as completely revised and updated entries (indicated with *) on some of the most notable and best-loved creators of books for children.

Ian Bone: Australian author Bone enjoyed a career in filmmaking and children's television, producing, directing, and developing various programs, before pursuing a career in writing in 1993. He is the author of "The Wiggles" series and the "Bananas in Pyjamas" books, as well as stand-alone fictional works.

*Emma Chichester Clark: Born in England and raised in Ireland, Chichester Clark is a popular and prolific author and illustrator. She has been compared to such well-respected figures as Beatrix Potter and Tony Ross, and has provided the illustrations for more than forty books by writers such as Roald Dahl and Diana Wynne Jones. Chichester Clark is also the author and illustrator of a dozen critically acclaimed picture books.

*Tessa Duder: Duder, a native of New Zealand, is the author of short stories, novels, and plays. She is perhaps most well-known in the United States for her "Alex" novels, which feature a young girl's struggle to balance the demands of her succesful swimming career with her private life.

Mary Dobson: Primarily a researcher and lecturer on the history of medicine, Dobson, who hails from England, has recently turned to the arena of children's literature to relay her fascination with the history of smells to readers. Books such as *Victorian Vapours, Reeking Royals,* and *Greek Grime* feature scratch-and-sniff panels that simulate the odors of each era.

Kaye Gibbons: The author of a string of best-selling novels, Gibbons has been praised for the strength and character of her female protagonists. She has written six novels, all set in the South and told in the simple vernacular of that region.

*Margaret Moore Hodges: Hodges, whose works number over fifty and include fiction, biographies, and retellings of myths and folktales, is the recipient of dozens of prestigious awards for her works. She has recently released a biography of Joan of Arc and *Up the Chimney,* a retelling of an English folktale.

Barry B. Longyear: Science fiction author Longyear burst onto the literary scene in the late seventies and early eighties, winning a Nebula Award, a Hugo Award, and a Locus Award for his novella "Enemy Mine," and a John W. Campbell Award for best new writer.

Todd McFarlane: A former comic artist for Marvel and DC, Canadian author/illustrator McFarlane has worked on such popular titles as *The Incredible Hulk, Batman,* and *Spider-Man.* He is most widely recognized, however, for his own creation, *Spawn,* which is a top-selling comic in the United States and several European countries, and which has "spawned" animated television episodes, a film, and a line of action figures.

*Patricia McKissack: A celebrated author of historical fiction and biographies for children, McKissack has acquired an impressive array of awards, including a Newbery, a Caldecott, an Image Award, and numerous Coretta Scott King Awards. She has authored over one hundred books, alone and with her husband, that focus primarily on religious and African-American themes.

Anna Pomaska: Born in Scotland to Polish refugees, Pomaska immigrated to the United States as a child. She is the author of over one hundred books and projects for children, and she also works in fine photographic/drawing art.

John Winch: Winch is an author and illustrator whose picture books celebrate life in the Australia "bush" where he resides. Also an artist, Winch works in printmaking, sculpture, ceramics, and painting.

Introduction

Something about the Author (*SATA*) is an ongoing reference series that examines the lives and works of authors and illustrators of books for children. *SATA* includes not only well-known writers and artists but also less prominent individuals whose works are just coming to be recognized. This series is often the only readily available information source on emerging authors and illustrators. You'll find *SATA* informative and entertaining, whether you are a student, a librarian, an English teacher, a parent, or simply an adult who enjoys children's literature.

What's Inside SATA

SATA provides detailed information about authors and illustrators who span the full time range of children's literature, from early figures like John Newbery and L. Frank Baum to contemporary figures like Judy Blume and Richard Peck. Authors in the series represent primarily English-speaking countries, particularly the United States, Canada, and the United Kingdom. Also included, however, are authors from around the world whose works are available in English translation. The writings represented in *SATA* include those created intentionally for children and young adults as well as those written for a general audience and known to interest younger readers. These writings cover the entire spectrum of children's literature, including picture books, humor, folk and fairy tales, animal stories, mystery and adventure, science fiction and fantasy, historical fiction, poetry and nonsense verse, drama, biography, and nonfiction.

Obituaries are also included in *SATA* and are intended not only as death notices but also as concise overviews of people's lives and work. Additionally, each edition features newly revised and updated entries for a selection of *SATA* listees who remain of interest to today's readers and who have been active enough to require extensive revisions of their earlier biographies.

New Autobiography Feature

Beginning with Volume 103, *SATA* features three or more specially commissioned autobiographical essays in each volume. These unique essays, averaging about ten thousand words in length and illustrated with an abundance of personal photos, present an entertaining and informative first-person perspective on the lives and careers of prominent authors and illustrators profiled in *SATA*.

Two Convenient Indexes

In response to suggestions from librarians, *SATA* indexes no longer appear in every volume but are included in alternate (odd-numbered) volumes of the series, beginning with Volume 57.

SATA continues to include two indexes that cumulate with each alternate volume: the Illustrations Index, arranged by the name of the illustrator, gives the number of the volume and page where the illustrator's work appears in the current volume as well as all preceding volumes in the series; the Author Index gives the number of the volume in which a person's biographical sketch, autobiographical essay, or obituary appears in the current volume as well as all preceding volumes in the series.

These indexes also include references to authors and illustrators who appear in Gale's *Yesterday's Authors of Books for Children, Children's Literature Review,* and *Something about the Author Autobiography Series.*

Easy-to-Use Entry Format

Whether you're already familiar with the *SATA* series or just getting acquainted, you will want to be aware of the kind of information that an entry provides. In every *SATA* entry the editors attempt to give as complete a picture of the person's life and work as possible. A typical entry in *SATA* includes the following clearly labeled information sections:

- *PERSONAL:* date and place of birth and death, parents' names and occupations, name of spouse, date of marriage, names of children, educational institutions attended, degrees received, religious and political affiliations, hobbies and other interests.

- *ADDRESSES:* complete home, office, electronic mail, and agent addresses, whenever available.

- *CAREER:* name of employer, position, and dates for each career post; art exhibitions; military service; memberships and offices held in professional and civic organizations.

- *AWARDS, HONORS:* literary and professional awards received.

- *WRITINGS:* title-by-title chronological bibliography of books written and/or illustrated, listed by genre when known; lists of other notable publications, such as plays, screenplays, and periodical contributions.

- *ADAPTATIONS:* a list of films, television programs, plays, CD-ROMs, recordings, and other media presentations that have been adapted from the author's work.

- *WORK IN PROGRESS:* description of projects in progress.

- *SIDELIGHTS:* a biographical portrait of the author or illustrator's development, either directly from the biographee—and often written specifically for the *SATA* entry—or gathered from diaries, letters, interviews, or other published sources.

- *FOR MORE INFORMATION SEE:* references for further reading.

- *EXTENSIVE ILLUSTRATIONS:* photographs, movie stills, book illustrations, and other interesting visual materials supplement the text.

How a SATA Entry Is Compiled

A *SATA* entry progresses through a series of steps. If the biographee is living, the *SATA* editors try to secure information directly from him or her through a questionnaire. From the information that the biographee supplies, the editors prepare an entry, filling in any essential missing details with research and/or telephone interviews. If possible, the author or illustrator is sent a copy of the entry to check for accuracy and completeness.

If the biographee is deceased or cannot be reached by questionnaire, the *SATA* editors examine a wide variety of published sources to gather information for an entry. Biographical and bibliographic sources are consulted, as are book reviews, feature articles, published interviews, and material sometimes obtained from the biographee's family, publishers, agent, or other associates.

Entries that have not been verified by the biographees or their representatives are marked with an asterisk (*).

Contact the Editor

We encourage our readers to examine the entire *SATA* series. Please write and tell us if we can make *SATA* even more helpful to you. Give your comments and suggestions to the editor:

BY MAIL: Editor, *Something about the Author,* The Gale Group, 27500 Drake Rd., Farmington Hills, MI 48331-3535.

BY TELEPHONE: (800) 877-GALE

BY FAX: (248) 699-8054

Acknowledgments

Grateful acknowledgment is made to the following publishers, authors, and artists whose works appear in this volume.

ADAMS, DOUGLAS. From a cover of *The Hitchhiker's Guide to the Galaxy,* by Douglas Adams. Ballantine Books, 1995. Reproduced by permission of Random House, Inc./ Adams, Douglas, photograph by Frank Capri. Archive Photos, Inc. © Frank Capri/SAGA. Reproduced by permission.

AGEE, JON. Agee, Jon, illustrator. From an illustration in his *The Incredible Painting of Felix Clousseau.* Farrar, Straus and Giroux, 1988. Copyright © 1988 by Jon Agee. Reproduced by permission of Farrar, Straus and Giroux, LLC./ Agee, Jon, illustrator. From an illustration in his *The Return of Freddy Legrand*. Farrar, Straus and Giroux, 1992. Copyright © 1992 by Jon Agee. Reproduced by permission of Farrar, Straus and Giroux, LLC./ Agee, Jon, illustrator. From an illustration in his *So Many Dynamos! and Other Palindromes.* Farrar, Straus and Giroux, 1994. Copyright © 1994 by Jon Agee. Reproduced by permission of Farrar, Straus and Giroux, LLC./ Agee, Jon, photograph. © 2000 Steven Borns/ www.stevenborns.com. Reproduced by permission.

ANDREW, IAN. Andrew, Ian (Peter), illustrator. From an illustration in *Back to the Blue,* by Virginia McKenna. The Millbrook Press, Inc., 1998. Design and illustration © 1997 by The Templar Company plc. Reproduced by permission./ Andrew, Ian, photograph. *The Dorking Advertiser.* Reproduced by permission.

ARNOLD, TEDD. From a cover of *No More Water in the Tub!,* by Tedd Arnold. Puffin Books, 1995. Copyright © 1995 by Tedd Arnold. Personius-Warne Studio. Reproduced by permission./ Arnold, Tedd, photograph. Personius-Warne Studio. Reproduced by permission of Tedd Arnold.

BIAL, RAYMOND. Bial, Raymond, Photographer. From a photograph in his *Cajun Home.* Houghton Mifflin, 1998. Copyright © 1998 by Raymond Bial. Reproduced by permission of Houghton Mifflin Company./ Bial, Raymond, photographer. From a photograph in his *Corn Belt Harvest.* Houghton Mifflin, 1991. Copyright © 1991 by Raymond Bial. Reproduced by permission of Houghton Mifflin Company./ Bial, Raymond, Photographer. From a photograph in his *Portrait of a Farm Family.* Houghton Mifflin, 1995. Copyright © 1995 by Raymond Bial. Reproduced by Permission of Houghton Mifflin Company. / Bial, Raymond, photograph by Sarah Bial. Reproduced by permission./ Bial, Raymond (wearing light plaid shirt), photograph. *The Champaign-Urbana News Gazette.* Reproduced by permission.

BLOCK, FRANCESCA LIA. Block, Francesca Lia, photograph by Claudia Kunin. Reproduced by permission of Francesca Lia Block.

BLY, STEPHEN A. Brown, Dan, illustrator. From a cover of *Miss Fontenot,* by Stephen Bly. Crossway, 1999. Copyright © 1999 by Stephen Bly. Reproduced by permission of Good News Publishers./ Brown, Dan, illustrator. From a cover of *Sweet Carolina,* by Stephen Bly. Crossway Books, 1998. Reproduced by permission of Good News Publishers./ Schofield, Den, illustrator. From the cover of *Standoff at Sunrise Creek,* by Stephen Bly. Crossway Books, 1993. Reproduced by permission of Good News Publishers./ From a cover of *Where the Deer and the Antelope Play,* by Stephen Bly. G. K. Hall & Co., 1995. Copyright © 1995 by Stephen Bly./ Bly, Stephen, photograph. Mary Steiger Studio, Lewiston, Idaho. Reproduced by permission of Stephen Bly.

BUCHANAN, PAUL. Buchanan, Paul, photograph. Reproduced by permission of Paul Buchanan.

DRAGISIC, PATRICIA. Dragisic, Patricia, photograph. Reproduced by permission of Patricia Dragisic.

GADD, JEREMY. Gadd, Jeremy, photograph by Pauline Green. Reproduced by permission of Jeremy John Gadd.

GOLDEN, CHRISTIE. Caldwell, Clyde, illustrator. From a cover of *Vampire of the Mists,* by Christie Golden. TSR, 1991. Copyright © 1991 TSR. All rights reserved. Reproduced by permission./ Golden, Christie, photograph. Wizards of the Coast, Inc. Reproduced by permission.

GRIESSMAN, ANNETTE. Griessman, Annette, photograph. Reproduced by permission of Annette Griessman.

GROENING, MATT. *The Simpsons,* cast of, photograph. AP/Wide World Photos. Reproduced by permission./ Groening, Matt, photograph. AP/Wide World Photos. Reproduced by permission.

HALL, MELANIE. Hall, Melanie, illustrator. From an illustration in *In Our Image: God's First Creatures,* by Nancy Sohn Swartz. Jewish Lights Publishing, 1998. Illustrations copyright © 1998 by Melanie W. Hall. Reproduced by permission./ Hall, Melanie, illustrator. From an illustration in *On Passover,* by Cathy Goldberg Fishman. Aladdin Paperbacks, 1997. Illustrations copyright © 1997 by Melanie W. Hall. Reproduced by permission of Simon & Schuster Macmillan./ Hall, Melanie, photograph. Reproduced by permission of Melanie Hall.

Wright, Cornelius and Ying-Hwa Hu, illustrators. From an illustration in *Zora Hurston and the Chinaberry Tree,* by William R. Miller. Lee & Low Books, Inc., 1994. Illustrations copyright © 1994 by Cornelius Van Wright and Ying-Hwa Hu. Reproduced by permission./ Miller, William, photograph by Teresa Rowe/Everlasting Images. Reproduced by permission.

MORTIMER, ANNE. Mortimer, Anne, photograph. Reproduced by permission of Anne Mortimer.

NAMIOKA, LENSEY. Namioka, Lensey with her mother, Buwei, holding infant sister, Bella, older sisters Xinna and Rulan, and father, Yuen Ren, (outside in yard of their home), Beijing, China, photograph. Reproduced by permission./ Namioka, Lensey (outside, wearing velvet dress), 1931, photograph. Reproduced by permission./ Namioka, Lensey (her sister Rulan, with Xinna and Bella), photograph. Reproduced by permission./ Namioka, Lensey (posing for graduation photo), photograph. Reproduced by permission./ Namioka, Lensey and Isaac (holding hands behind their backs), photograph. Reproduced by permission./ Namioka, Isaac with brother, Sheigo, and parents, Saburo and Evelyn, photograph. Reproduced by permission./ Namioka, Lensey (wearing sports coat) seated with family, photograph. Reproduced by permission./ Namioka, Lensey and Isaac (holding hands), Himeji Castle, photograph. Reproduced by permission./ Namioka, Michi and Aki, photograph. Reproduced by permission./ Namioka, Lensey's granddaughter, Leila with father, Jim, photograph. Reproduced by permission.

OTFINOSKI, STEVE. Kennedy, Kelly, illustrator. From a cover of *The Kid's Guide to Money,* by Steve Otfinoski. Scholastic Inc., 1996. cover design by Karen Hudson. Copyright (c) 1996 by Scholastic Inc. Reproduced by permission./ From a cover of *Nations in Transition: Bulgaria,* by Steven Otfinoski. Facts on File, Inc., 1998. Copyright (c) 1999 by Steven Otfinoski. Reproduced by permission.

OWENS, BRYANT. Owens, Bryant, photograph. Reproduced by permission of Bryant Owens.

PACKER, KENNETH L. From a cover of *HIV Infection: The Facts You Need To Know,* by Kenneth L. Packer. Franklin Watts, 1998. Copyright (c) 1998 by Kenneth L. Packer. All rights reserved. Reproduced by permission.

PARSONS, MARTIN. Parsons, Martin, photograph. Reproduced by permission of Martin Parsons.

PEGUERO, LEONE. Peguero, Adrian and Gerard, illustrators. From a cover of *Lionel and Amelia,* by Leone Peguero. Mondo Publishing, 1996. Illustrations copyright © 1988 by Multimedia International, (UK) Ltd. Reproduced by permission./ Peguero, Leone Iris, photograph. Reproduced by permission of Leone Iris Peguero.

REECE, COLLEEN L. From a cover of *Mysterious Monday,* by Colleen L. Reece. Barbour & Company, 1997. Illustrations copyright © MCMXCVII by Barbour & Co., Inc. Reproduced by permission.

REED, KIT. Lerner, Judith, artist, *Summer Day.* From a cover of *J. Eden,* by Kit Reed. University Press of Hanover, 1996. Copyright © 1998 by Kit Reed. Reproduced by permission of University Press of New England./ Reed, Joseph, illustrator. From a cover of *Weird Women, Wired Women*, by Kit Reed. Wesleyan University Press, 1998. Copyright © 1998 by Kit Reed. Reproduced by permission of University Press of New England./ Reed, Kit, photograph. © Jerry Bauer. Reproduced by permission.

RENDON, MARIA. Rendon, Maria, Illustrator. From an illustration in *Touching the Distance: Native American Riddle-Poems,* by Brian Swann. Browndeer Press, 1998. Illustrations copyright © 1998 by Maria Rendon. Reproduced by permission of Harcourt, Inc.

RICHARDSON, SANDY. Richardson, Sandy, photograph. Reproduced by permission of Sandy Richardson.

ROOP, CONSTANCE. Hanson, Peter E., illustrator. From the cover of *Buttons for General Washington,* by Peter and Connie Roop. Carolrhoda Books, Inc., 1986. Copyright © 1986 by Carolrhoda Books, Inc. Reproduced by permission./ Arnsteen, Katy Keck, illustrator. From a jacket of *Let's Celebrate Halloween,* by Peter and Connie Roop, by Peter and Connie Roop. The Millbrook Press, 1997. Illustration copyright © 1997 Katy Keck Arnsteen. Reproduced by permission.

ROOP, PETER. Farnsworth, Bill, illustrator. From a cover of *The Buffalo Jump,* by Peter Roop. Rising Moon, 1999. Illustration copyright © 1996 by Bill Farnsworth. Reproduced by permission./ Pritchett, Shelley, illustrator. From a cover of *Pilgrim Voices: Our First Year in the New World,* edited by Connie and Peter Roop. Walker and Company, 1995. Illustrations © 1995 by Shelley Pritchett. Reproduced by permission.

ROSSI, JOYCE. Rossi, Joyce, photograph. Reproduced by permission of Joyce Rossi.

RUBINSTEIN, GILLIAN. Rubinstein, Gillian (with her dog), photograph. Reproduced by permission of Gillian Rubinstein./ Rubinstein, Gillian (as an infant, with older sister), photograph. Reproduced by permission of Gillian Rubinstein./ Rubinstein, Gillian (with her father and older sister), photograph. Reproduced by permission of Gillian Rubinstein./ Rubinstein, Gillian (in school play), photograph. Reproduced by permission of Gillian Rubinstein./ Rubinstein, Gillian (Rubinstein's mother Margaret Jocelyn Wigg), photograph. Reproduced by permission of Gillian Rubinstein./ Rubinstein, Gillian (her daughter Tessa with her horse), photograph. Reproduced by permission of Gillian Rubinstein./ Rubinstein, Gillian (her daughter Suzy on a horse), photograph. Reproduced by permission of Gillian Rubinstein./ Rubinstein, Gillian (with her son Matt), photograph. Reproduced by permission of Gillian Rubinstein./ Rubinstein, Gillian (her husband Philip with their dog), photograph. Reproduced by permission of Gillian Rubinstein./ Rubinstein, Gillian (in costume as the Duchess), photograph. Reproduced by permission of Gillian Rubinstein.

sOMEThING ABOUT ThE AUThOR

ADAMS, Douglas (Noel) 1952-

Personal

Born March 11, 1952, in Cambridge, England; son of Christopher Douglas (a management consultant) and Janet (a nurse; maiden name, Donovan, present surname, Thrift) Adams; married Jane Elizabeth Belson, 1991; children: Polly Jane Rocket. *Education:* St. John's College, Cambridge, B.A. (with honors), 1974, M.A. *Hobbies and other interests:* Purchasing equipment for recreations he would like to take up.

Addresses

Home—London, England. *Agent*—Ed Victor Ltd., 6 Bayley St., London WCIB 3HB, England.

Career

British Broadcasting Corporation (BBC), London, producer and scriptwriter for "Hitchhiker's Guide to the Galaxy" radio and television series, beginning 1978, script editor for television series "Doctor Who," 1978-80; writer, 1978—.

Awards, Honors

Best Books for Young Adults List, American Library Association (ALA), 1980, and Golden Pen Award, 1983, for *The Hitchhiker's Guide to the Galaxy.*

Writings

"THE HITCHHIKER'S GUIDE TO THE GALAXY" SERIES

The Hitchhiker's Guide to the Galaxy, Pan Books (London), 1979, Harmony (New York City), 1980.
The Restaurant at the End of the Universe, Pan Books, 1980, Harmony, 1982.
Life, the Universe and Everything, Harmony, 1982.
So Long, and Thanks for All the Fish, Pan Books, 1984, Harmony, 1985.
The Hitchhiker's Trilogy (omnibus volume), Harmony, 1984.
The Original Hitchhiker's Radio Scripts, edited with an introduction by Geoffrey Perkins, Harmony, 1985.
The Hitchhiker's Quartet (omnibus volume), Harmony, 1986.
More Than Complete Hitchhiker's Guide, Longmeadow Press (New York City), 1987, revised edition published as *More Than Complete Hitchhiker's Guide Fifty-One Point Eighty,* 1989, unabridged edition, 1994.
Mostly Harmless, Crown (New York City), 1992.
The Illustrated Hitchhiker's Guide to the Galaxy, Crown, 1994.
The Ultimate Hitchhiker's Guide, unabridged and complete version, Wings Books (New York City), 1996.

OTHER

(With others) *Not 1982: Not the Nine O'Clock News Rip-Off Annual,* Faber (London), 1981.
(With John Lloyd) *The Meaning of Liff,* Pan Books, 1983, Harmony, 1984.

1

Douglas Adams

(Editor with Peter Fincham) *The Utterly Utterly Merry Comic Relief Christmas Book,* Fontana (London), 1986.

Dirk Gently's Holistic Detective Agency (novel), Simon & Schuster (New York City), 1987.

The Long Dark Tea-Time of the Soul (novel), Heinemann, 1988, Simon & Schuster, 1989.

(With Mark Carwardine) *Last Chance to See* (nonfiction), Crown, 1990.

(With Lloyd) *The Deeper Meaning of Liff: A Dictionary of Things There Aren't Words for Yet—But There Ought to Be,* Crown, 1990.

Two Complete Novels (*Dirk Gently's Holistic Detective Agency* [and] *The Long Dark Tea-Time of the Soul*), Wings Books, 1994.

Dirk Gently's Holistic Detective Agency: Two Complete Novels (contains *Dirk Gently's Holistic Detective Agency* and *The Long Dark Tea-Time of the Soul*), Random House (New York City), 1995.

Also author of scripts for the "Hitchhiker's Guide to the Galaxy" radio and television programs, BBC-TV; author, with Steve Meretzky, of interactive computer program.

Contributor to *The Great Ape Project: Equality Beyond Humanity,* edited by Peter Singer, St. Martin's, 1993. Also author of episodes of "Doctor Who" for BBC-TV; co-author of interactive computer program, "Bureaucracy" and designer of a CD-ROM adventure game, "Starship Titanic," 1997.

Adaptations

The Hitchhiker's Guide to the Galaxy has been produced as a stage play, as a television series for BBC-TV and PBS-TV, 1983, as a computer game, Infocom, 1984, as an abridged audio-cassette, Listen for Pleasure, 1986, and unabridged audio-cassette, Minds Eye, 1988; producer Ivan Reitman holds the movie rights to the *Hitchhiker* trilogy; *The Restaurant at the End of the Universe* was adapted for cassette by Listen for Pleasure; *Life, the Universe and Everything* was adapted for cassette by Listen for Pleasure, and for a comic book by John Carnell; *So Long, and Thanks for All the Fish* was adapted for cassette by Listen for Pleasure, 1985; *Dirk Gently's Holistic Detective Agency* was adapted for cassette by Simon & Schuster, 1987. Adams's "Starship Titanic" video game has spawned a spin-off novel, *Douglas Adams's Starship Titanic,* by Terry Jones, 1997, and *Douglas Adams's Starship Titanic: The Official Strategy Guide,* by Neil Richards, 1998.

Work in Progress

A novel, *The Chaos Engineer;* possible sixth installment in the "Hitchhiker" series.

Sidelights

"Every particle of the universe ... affects every other particle, however faintly or obliquely. Everything interconnects with everything. The beating of a butterfly's wings in China can affect the course of an Atlantic hurricane. If I could interrogate this table leg in a way that made sense to me, or to the table leg, then it would provide me with the answer to any question about the universe." Or so Douglas Adams's offbeat private detective, Dirk Gently, supposes in *The Long Dark Tea-Time of the Soul.* At another point in that same novel, Gently contends that the impossible has "integrity," while the improbable is quite commonplace. The themes of universal questions to be asked—if not answered—of the interconnectedness of all things and the vitality of the improbable play throughout all the works of Douglas Adams with silly gusto.

Improbable is a word that quite well describes Adams's own meteoric rise to popularity and an odd sort of fame. It all started with Adams lying drunk on his back in a field. This took place in Innsbruck on a hitchhiking trip around Europe before he entered university. "I sort of laid down on the ground and stared up at the stars," Adams told Susan Adamo of *Starlog* in a 1981 interview, "and it occurred to me then that somebody ought to write a hitchhiker's guide to the galaxy. The thought didn't come back to me for years afterward." When it did, after Douglas had been writing scripts for England's BBC radio for several years, it returned with the resounding thud of the planet Earth being destroyed, and one Arthur Dent being propelled into space to become the first Earth-born galactic hitchhiker.

Adams's quirky idea for a radio program spawned a multimedia blitz for the young writer: a series of five novels in the "Hitchhiker" group (the first one of which sold 100,000 copies in less than a month and ultimately sold more than two million in England alone); a stage play; a television series; and a computer game. Adams became a loopy cultural hero for the young; his tongue-in-cheek antics in the formerly strictly non-humorous precincts of outer space and sci fi earned him a legion of eager fans around the globe. Adams has gone on to write of a "film-*blanc*" private eye, endangered species, and a galaxy of objects, actions, and feelings for which no words exist. The production of video games has taken up much of his working time in the 1990s, but fans hope for a sixth instalment in the "Hitchhiker" series twenty years after publication of the first. As Marc Conly summed up in *Bloomsbury Review*, "Douglas Adams is a dismayed idealist in jester's clothing. His portrayal of modern society, and his unrelenting dissection of the modern style of self-centeredness, make us think, make us laugh, and make us look forward to his next book."

Adams was born in Cambridge, the son of a theology teacher and management consultant, Christopher Douglas Adams, and a nurse, Janet Donovan Adams. Adams stayed in his hometown for his university training, attending prestigious Cambridge University, where he majored in English literature. But more importantly, Adams spent nearly every free moment at school writing sketches for Cambridge Footlights, a college theatrical club that has long proved a breeding ground for actors, comedians, and writers alike. "It's not so much that being a member of Footlights gives you a guaranteed entree into show business, which a lot of people kind of assume simply because so many people have come out of it," Adams told D. C. Denison of the *Boston Globe* in a 1985 interview. "The reason why so many people of that type have come out of it is because they've gone into it. Certainly in my experience, when I was deciding on what kind of university career I was going to have, I wanted to go to Cambridge because I wanted to do Footlights—mainly because I knew I had a reasonable opportunity to meet people of like mind.... It's just sort of a rallying flag." Some of those like-minded people included core members of what would later become the Monty Python group: John Cleese, Eric Idle, and Graham Chapman.

After graduation, while trying to start a writing career, Adams toiled at a series of menial jobs, including hospital reporter, barn builder, chicken shed cleaner, and bodyguard for the royal family of Qatar, work for which his 6'5—", 210-pound frame—if not his disposition—suited him well. During this same period, he also worked with Chapman, later of Python fame, on numerous unsuccessful projects. Finally Adams began writing scripts for BBC radio and TV, among them for the long-running "Doctor Who" sci-fi series. Then he recalled the inebriated night in Innsbruck and his idea for a guide of a very different stripe.

Adams presented his idea for a radio show to BBC Radio 4 and received pocket change as up-front money to develop a pilot script. Adams sketched out the basic premises of his story: clueless Englishman Arthur Dent

and his alien friend Ford Prefect hitch rides across the galaxy after Earth is destroyed in order to make room for an intergalactic highway. What started out as an experiment—almost a write-off—on radio soon garnered loyal fans who loved the send-up humor and piercing glances at contemporary life. Adams and the producers of the show revolutionized the way BBC radio did things, by taking days to record each segment, using stereo sound effects, and occupying studio after studio. "We wanted the sound to be the verbal equivalent of a rock album," Adams told James Brown of the *Los Angeles Times* in a 1982 interview.

By 1978, the BBC radio series was so popular that Pan Books in England asked Adams to novelize the story. "I never set out to be a novelist," Adams once said "because I thought I was just a scriptwriter." But with his novelization for Pan, Adams went beyond simply filling in "he said" in the proper places in radio scripts.

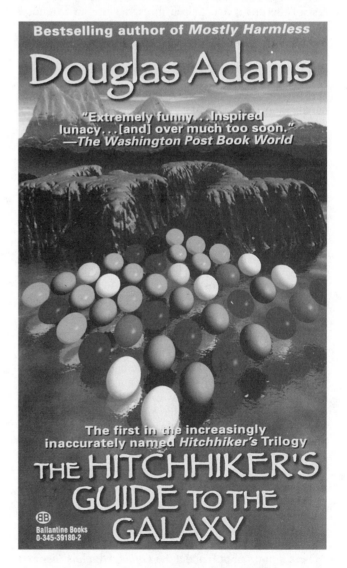

Adams's witty science-fiction adventure book begins with the destruction of Earth to make way for an express route in hyper space and follows several characters as they try to decipher the seemingly nonsensical answer to the meaning of life.

Instead, he rewrote the entire story. The published book was an instant success, reaching the top of British best-seller lists.

The first of what has become five books in the "Hitchhiker" series, begins with Earth destroyed to make way for an express route in hyperspace. Ford Prefect, a researcher for a guide to hitchhiking the galaxies, manages to rescue low-keyed Arthur Dent just as the planet disintegrates. They end up on a spaceship operated by Zaphod Beeblebrox, a two-headed adventurer and sort of cousin to Ford. Others aboard the spacecraft are Zaphod's girlfriend, Trillian, and a robot, Marvin, who is forever depressed. Together they make their way to Magrathea where custom-made planets are manufactured. There Slartibartfast, who helped design Earth, informs the crew that the planet was part of a project to come up with the meaning of life, the universe and everything, and that the answer is forty-two. The rest of the novel and indeed the series are an extended and hilarious faux-sci-fi adventure to discover the question for which forty-two is the answer. Plot, it becomes rapidly obvious, plays second place to witty dialogue and outlandish characterizations.

Michael Adams, writing in *Dictionary of Literary Biography Yearbook: 1983,* noted, "One of Adams's main virtues is his gift for characterization. The adventures of Arthur and his friends are entertaining not only for all the last-second escapes from disaster but for how the characters respond to the whims of fate." Adams told James Brown of the *Los Angeles Times* that Dent, the putative main character, was something of an autobiographical rendering, and that in moving "from one astonishing event to another without fully comprehending what's going on," he is an Everyman. Using the literary devices of science fiction, Adams, in fact, managed to spoof most of the sacred cows of contemporary society: technology, health fads, literary critics, and rock 'n' roll. Most of society's shibboleths provided grist for the Adams irony mill.

Critics on both sides of the Atlantic applauded Adams's antic wit. The *Listener*'s Peter Kemp called the first volume "a sardonically funny exercise in galactic globe-trotting," and noted that what makes the book "almost unputdownable is its surreal, comic creativity." Kemp concluded that "for most of the book, the characters zoom exuberantly through other worlds." In the United States, a critic for *Kirkus Reviews* called Adams's book an attempt at science fiction "Monty Python style," concluding that "fans of absurd deadpan-parody will happily flip through this likable send-up in order to extract a couple of dozen fine giggles." Reviewer Lisa Tuttle noted in the *Washington Post Book World,* "There's nothing dull about the *Guide,* which is inspired lunacy that leaves hardly a science fictional cliche alive." And Gerald Jonas commented in the *New York Times Book Review* that while humorous sci fi usually has "notoriously limited audiences," Adams's novel "is a delightful exception."

Critics have noted Adams's debt to earlier authors including Jonathan Swift, Lewis Carroll, Kurt Vonnegut, and the antics of Monty Python. Adams himself has also credited the British humorist, P. G. Wodehouse. Michael Adams noted in *Dictionary of Literary Biography Yearbook* that the "human characters [in *Hitchhiker's Guide*] are space-age variations on Wodehouse's Bertie Wooster and all his eccentric friends and relatives, and know-it-all Marvin is a neurotic version of Jeeves." The same critic went on to note that while the characters of Slartibartfast and Trillian are underdeveloped, "Marvin [the chronically depressed robot] delightfully complements Arthur, Ford, and Zaphod in Adams's satire of Me-generation manifestations." Indeed, many critics agree that satire is Adams's main goal in the novels.

To date, Adams has written four more "Hitchhiker" novels. The immediate sequel to the first book appeared in 1980 with *The Restaurant at the End of the Universe,* in which Ford Prefect and his friends continue their ultimate road adventures. The restaurant in question is the fabled Milliways, where the clients can witness the end of the cosmos. Adams himself in *Dictionary of Literary Biography Yearbook* pronounced the novel to be "the [series's] most entertaining satire." As Philip Howard noted in the *Times* of London, the story "has attracted a cult even among those normally impervious to the mechanical charms of science fiction." Howard went on to note that a "summary of the plot [of the sequel] would read like case notes of a nervous breakdown" involving "a sequence of episodic disasters and hilarities." *Kirkus Reviews* concluded that Adams's second venture into hyperspace was "[s]ometimes lame, limp, or just plain silly—but, at its best, very funny indeed." Claudia Morner noted in *School Library Journal* that Adams's sequel "is both an entertaining, silly story and a successful satire of the worst of S. F. novels." Morner concluded that it "maintains the disrespectful, crazy tone [of the first] and should be popular."

In the third instalment, *Life, the Universe and Everything,* Dent and Ford "find themselves caught up in the malevolent plan of the rulers of the planet Krikkit to destroy everything that isn't cricket and to seize the Golden Bail that will give them great power," according to Richard Brown writing in *Times Literary Supplement.* Featured here is the computer Deep Thought which came up with the answer to the mystery of the universe as being the number forty-two. Arthur Dent is also still bumbling along, attempting to discover the Ultimate Question to Life. As Richard Brown explained, "Much of the comedy arises from a variety of pseudo-high-tech mis-information." Tom Hutchinson pointed out in the *Times* of London: "There is a serious undertow to all this, of course, a Vonnegut-appreciation of the universe's futility which allows Mr. Adams to slip in some moments of sly terror so that the smile freezes on our faces like ancient winter." Michael Brown noted in *Dictionary of Literary Biography Yearbook* that the "strongest satire comes with the attack on war, imperialism, and xenophobia."

Most reviewers, and Adams himself, felt the fourth volume of the "Hitchhiker" chronicles was a mistake. *So Long, and Thanks for All the Fish* is set back on earth. Arthur Dent is in love with the beautiful Frenchurch who is the only earthling to remember that the planet was once destroyed. As Robert Reilly commented in *Twentieth-Century Science Fiction Writers,* despite the changed venue, this fourth novel "proves to be too much of the same thing. The freshness which lent such force to *Hitchhiker* is gone; the joke has been carried too far."

For nearly a decade Adams steered away from further forays into the "Hitchhiker" realm, busying himself with other book projects as well as computer games, which continue to occupy much of his creativity. The "Hitchhiker's Guide" computer game was released in the mid-1980s, and as Adams told Denison of the *Boston Globe,* "I've just become totally engrossed [with computers], and now there seem to be more things to do than I can possibly encompass." His "Starship Titanic" came out on CD-ROM in 1997, the product of several years of work by his London-based production company, Digital Village.

In 1992 the fifth book in the "Hitchhiker" series appeared, *Mostly Harmless,* a book that again won praise for the concept as a whole. Ford Prefect discovers a Vogon plot to take over the imprint of *The Hitchhiker's Guide to the Galaxy* and notifies Arthur Dent, now a resident Sandwich Maker on the isolated world of Lamuella. There are Grebulons galore colonizing a new planet and a daughter for Arthur who comes from a time distant in space. Writing in *Locus,* Carolyn Cushman observed that "This time, [Adams] sinks his teeth into a basic human problem [looking for a purpose in life] and uses it as a theme, giving *Mostly Harmless* a coherence lacking in the other novels in the series. And it's funny to boot." A reviewer for *Analog Science Fiction and Fact* noted that Adams's new novel was "a bit of bubbly seltzer in a dour, dour world," adding that "Adams's cock-eyed logic is bound to make you smile."

Adams took a rest from Dent and Ford with a pair of nonsense dictionaries inspired by more youthful inebriation—this time with a group of friends in Greece in 1978. The basis of that game was to come up with new words or phrases or existing words to be used in a new sense. These neologisms, which were scribbled on sheets of scrap paper, filled a drawer and later became the core of *The Meaning of Liff* and *The Deeper Meaning of Liff.* A reviewer for the London publication *Observer* called the latter book "One of that rarest of things, a good, original idea for a funny book."

Another fictional turn came in the companion volumes *Dirk Gently's Holistic Detective Agency* and *The Long Dark Tea-Time of the Soul,* both featuring the private detective Dirk Gently and his adventures with strange supernatural forces. Dirk is usually most competent with missing cat cases, but takes on the murder of a computer executive in the first of the novels. Adams assembles his usual zany cast of characters and incidents to propel the plot: a time machine, a spaceship, an Electric Monk, and the ghost of Samuel Taylor Coleridge. While reviewer Christopher Farley of the *Chicago Tribune* faulted the novel for "too much" plot, others found the book on a par with Adams's earlier work. H. J. Kirchoff stated in the Toronto *Globe and Mail* that it was Adams's "best novel." Kirchoff felt the author's characters were "more fully delineated ... the settings more credible and the plot more ... well, linear." John Nicholson concluded in the *Times* of London that "what signifies here is the quality of the writing, the asides and allusions, and—above all—the jokes. Mr Adams scores very high on all counts."

"In *The Long Dark Tea-Time of the Soul,* Adams has thrown a smattering of Norse mythology, a pinch of detective fiction, and a good helping of fantasy into a stew of satire and sardonic observation that the fans of *Hitchhiker's Guide to the Galaxy* ... will easily recognize," according to Marc Conly of *Bloomsbury Review.* This second Dirk Gently novel was not meant as a sequel, but as the ongoing adventures of an unlikely detective. Gently is trying to get to the bottom of the murder of his only client and the explosion at an airport check-in counter. These are apparently unrelated crimes, but holistic Dirk Gently sees a connection and teams up with Kate, the American with an attitude, to investigate Thor, the Norse god of Thunder, who is none too pleased with Odin. Along the way Adams shoots barbs at religion and modern mores. Conly noted that Adams's "social awareness and the accuracy of his barbs keep the narrative ... from becoming too frothy." Cathleen Schine concluded in the *New York Times Book Review* that Adams's "humor, crisp and intelligent, and his prose—elegant, absurdly literal-minded understatements or elegant, absurdly literal-minded overstatements—are a pleasure to read."

More of a departure for Adams was his 1990 *Last Chance to See,* co-authored with zoologist Mark Carwardine. Traveling to Indonesia, China, New Zealand, and Mauritius, the two authors chronicle endangered species around the world, and provide a droll travelogue at the same time. Jack Beatty observed in the *Atlantic* that Douglas Adams was not a sanctimonious type of nature writer. "He smokes, he drinks, he has unflinching things to say about certain representative people of the Third World, a type often treated as a protected species, and he is an Englishman, which means that he would rather be clever than profound any day. Above all," Beatty continued, "he packs his irony with his shaving kit." The book is an episodic narrative of several of Adams's and Carwardine's travel-adventures, research journeys as originally planned for a series of radio programs on endangered species. "Don't expect any great insights here" commented Beth Levine in *New York Times Book Review,* "but *Last Chance to See* is enjoyable and accessible, and its details on the heroic efforts being made to save these animals are inspirational." Reviewer Melissa Greene of *Washington Post Book World* hailed Adams's *Last Chance to See* as a "rambunctious ... and moving travel book, a kind of catalogue of the civilization that exists at the fringes of civilization." Greene went on to conclude that "despite the backdrop of ecological disaster and colossal human stupidity, the book is funny and a sort of rollicking good read, and the animals themselves are among the most wonderful characters in it."

Adams took a hiatus from book publishing through much of the 1990s, putting aside a Dirk Gently book that went haywire to concentrate instead on his Digital Village projects. Adams participates not only in writing the computer-game adventures, but also in the overall production phase as well. As Brad Stone noted in *Newsweek,* "Adams, who applies a sort of comical Murphy's Law toward technology in the 'Hitchhiker' books, has also become something of a new media guru. Companies like Dell and Canon pay to hear his humorous take on our digital future and the power of new technologies." Stone went on to note, "But [Adams] also has a serious message: 'If you approach the future pessimistically, then you can be pretty certain the things you most fear are going to happen.'" Stone goes on to quote Adams as saying, "I would never claim technology is going to make the world better, but it certainly makes it more and more interesting."

Works Cited

Adamo, Susan, "Douglas Adams," *Starlog,* June, 1981.

Adams, Douglas, *The Long Dark Tea-Time of the Soul,* Simon and Schuster, 1989.

Adams, Michael, "Douglas Adams," *Dictionary of Literary Biography Yearbook: 1983,* Gale, 1983, pp. 175-78.

Beatty, Jack, review of *Last Chance to See, Atlantic,* March, 1991, p. 267.

Brown, James, "Thumbs Up for the Hitchhiker," *Los Angeles Times,* April 4, 1982.

Brown, Richard, "Posh-School SF," *Times Literary Supplement,* September 24, 1982, p. 1032.

Conly, Marc, "Ruminations on the State of the Universe," *Bloomsbury Review,* May-June, 1989. p. 16.

Cushman, Carolyn, review of *Mostly Harmless, Locus,* October, 1992, p. 37.

Review of *The Deeper Meaning of Liff, Observer,* December 2, 1990, p. 64.

Denison, D. C., "Twenty One: Douglas Adams," *Boston Globe,* January 20, 1985.

Farley, Christopher, review of *Dirk Gently's Holistic Detective Agency, Chicago Tribune,* August 25, 1987.

Greene, Melissa, review of *Last Chance to See, Washington Post Book World,* March 24, 1991, p. 4.

Review of *The Hitchhiker's Guide to the Galaxy, Kirkus Reviews,* July 15, 1980, p. 941.

Howard, Philip, review of *The Restaurant at the End of the Universe, Times* (London), February 7, 1981, p. 9.

Hutchinson, Tom, "Hitching Another Hike to the Stars," *Times* (London), September 9, 1982, p. 7.

Jonas, Gerald, review of *The Hitchhiker's Guide to the Galaxy, New York Times Book Review,* January 25, 1981, pp. 24-25.

Kemp, Peter, "Wise-Guy-Sci-Fi," *Listener,* December 18 & 25, 1980, p. 866.

Kirchoff, H. J., review of *Dirk Gently's Holistic Detective Agency, Globe and Mail* (Toronto), April 14, 1987.

Levine, Beth, review of *Last Chance to See, New York Times Book Review,* March 17, 1991, p. 22.

Morner, Claudia, review of *The Restaurant at the End of the Universe, School Library Journal,* April 15, 1982, p. 87.

Review of *Mostly Harmless, Analog Science Fiction and Fact,* September, 1993, pp. 164-65.

Nicholson, John, review of *Dirk Gently's Holistic Detective Agency, Times* (London), June 18, 1987.

Reilly, Robert, "Adams, Douglas," *Twentieth-Century Science Fiction Writers,* St. James Press, 1986, pp. 1-2.

Review of *The Restaurant at the End of the Universe, Kirkus Reviews,* December 1, 1981, p. 1490.

Schine, Cathleen, review of *The Long Dark Tea-Time of the Soul, New York Times Book Review,* March 12, 1989, p. 11.

Stone, Brad, "The Unsinkable Starship," *Newsweek,* April 13, 1998, p. 78.

Tuttle, Lisa, "As Other Worlds Turn," *Washington Post Book World,* November 23, 1980, p. 6.

For More Information See

BOOKS

Bestsellers 89, Issue 3, Gale, 1989.

PERIODICALS

Bloomsbury Review, December, 1982.

Chicago Tribune, October 28, 1982; March 13, 1985; March 17, 1985; March 31, 1989.

Chicago Tribune Book World, October 12, 1980.

Globe and Mail (Toronto), June 27, 1987.

London Times, December 13, 1984; November 5, 1988.

Los Angeles Times, April 19, 1985; June 13, 1987; March 17, 1989.

Los Angeles Times Book Review, December 7, 1980; February 3, 1991, p. 4.

Magazine of Fantasy and Science Fiction, February, 1982.

Newsweek, November 15, 1982.

People, January 10, 1983.

Publishers Weekly, January 14, 1983.

Spectator, December 15, 1990, p. 35.

Voice of Youth Advocates, April, 1993, p. 33.

Washington Post, July 23, 1987; March 16, 1989.

Washington Post Book World, December 27, 1981.*

*　　　*　　　*

AGEE, Jon 1960-

Personal

Born in 1960, in Nyack, NY; son of a teacher and an artist. *Education:* Received B.F.A. from Cooper Union School of Art.

Addresses

Agent—c/o Farrar, Straus, Giroux, 19 Union Sq. West, New York, NY 10022.

Jon Agee

Career

Author and illustrator of children's books, c. 1982—.

Awards, Honors

Notable Book designation, *New York Times* and American Library Association, both for *The Incredible Painting of Felix Clousseau;* best illustrated children's book designation, *New York Times,* 1998, for *Dmitri the Astronaut.*

Writings

SELF-ILLUSTRATED

If Snow Falls: A Story for December, Pantheon (New York City), 1982.
Ellsworth, Pantheon, 1983.
Ludlow Laughs, Farrar, Straus, Giroux (New York City), 1985.
The Incredible Painting of Felix Clousseau, Farrar, Straus, Giroux, 1988.
Go Hang a Salami! I'm a Lasagna Hog! and Other Palindromes, Farrar, Straus & Giroux, 1991.
The Return of Freddy Legrand, Farrar, Straus, Giroux, 1992.
Flapstick: Ten Ridiculous Rhymes with Flaps, Dutton (New York City), 1993.

So Many Dynamos! and Other Palindromes, Farrar, Straus, Giroux 1994.
Dmitri the Astronaut, HarperCollins (New York City), 1996.
Who Ordered the Jumbo Shrimp? and Other Oxymorons, HarperCollins, 1998.
Sit on a Potato Pan, Otis!: More Palindromes, Farrar, Straus, Giroux, 1999.

ILLUSTRATOR

Lucia Monfried, *Dishes All Done,* Dutton, 1989.
Dee Lillegard, *Sitting in My Box,* Dutton, 1989.
Mary H. Heyward, *The Toy Box,* Dutton, 1989.
(With others) *The Big Book for Peace,* Dutton, 1990.
Jennifer Jacobson, *Mr. Lee,* Open Court (Chicago), 1995.
Erica Silverman, *The Halloween House,* Farrar, Straus, Giroux, 1997.
Tor Seidler, *Mean Margaret,* HarperCollins, 1998.

Sidelights

Jon Agee grew up along the Hudson River in Nyack, New York. As a kid he created picture books, detective comics, and flip books made out of train ticket stubs. In high school he spent an inordinate amount of time in the art room. In college, at the Cooper Union School of Art in New York City, he studied painting, dabbled in animation, and made an "art" film. Soon after graduating, in 1982, he began publishing his first books.

In addition to creating stories of mysterious painters, canine professors, and forgotten astronauts, Agee's fascination with language has inspired a series of books of wordplay, and the books and lyrics for two off-off Broadway musicals. Occasionally he gets a cartoon published in the *New Yorker.*

Agee's *If Snow Falls* is about a young boy who dreams of his grandfather, who gradually evolves into Santa Claus. A reviewer for *Publishers Weekly* found *If Snow Falls* to be "an extraordinary visual treat" that "unfolds like a lullaby."

Ellsworth relates the story of a dog who is a university professor. He loses the respect of his colleagues and students when he is observed chasing cats, burying bones, and marking trees. Ellsworth worries about his career until he meets a poodle who is quite comfortable just being a dog. *Horn Book* reviewer Karen Jameyson commented particularly on Agee's "textured, shadowy illustrations," which she maintained produce "a slightly comical, pleasing effect." A "lighthearted gem," was Debra Hewitt's summation of *Ellsworth* in *School Library Journal.* A *Publishers Weekly* reviewer concluded that Agee "scores a hit again" and noted that his "big, lusty, full-color pictures illustrate this frolic perfectly."

Ludlow Laughs tells the tale of a grumpy man with an enormous frown and a perpetually sour demeanor. His tedious daily routine is shaken up when he has an amusing dream. Ludlow begins to laugh, and his laughter becomes contagious as it spreads throughout his neighborhood and then throughout the world. *Ludlow*

Laughs was a featured selection narrated by Phyllis Diller on the PBS children's show *Reading Rainbow*.

Agee spent more than two years completing *The Incredible Painting of Felix Clousseau*. A contributor to *Publishers Weekly* found the resulting volume "an unusual picture book that works on several levels: as a work of art, as an inventive fantasy, and as a satirical comment on the academic art world." The artist Clousseau wins a grand prize when his entry, a painting of a duck, quacks. His other paintings, including a waking snake, an erupting volcano, a firing cannon, and a flowing river and waterfall also come to life. Clousseau is jailed because of the chaos his paintings cause, but is released when a dog jumps from one of his canvasses to stop a thief attempting to steal the king's crown from the royal palace. The artist returns to his studio and enters one of his own pictures. Raymond Briggs wrote in the *Times Educational Supplement* that Agee's style "is a bizarre mixture of Peter Arno and Magritte." "Mr. Agee's pictures make even the most ordinary objects appear just strange enough to be worth our most wide-eyed attention," opined Leonard Marcus in the *New York Times Book Review*. "In their intensely quirky way, the author's paintings are every bit as lifelike as Clousseau's." In reviewing the book for the *Times Literary Supplement*, Jan Dalley wrote that Agee's "monochro-

The paintings of an unknown artist come to life and create chaos in Agee's self-illustrated The Incredible Painting of Felix Clousseau.

matic, block-like figures" provide "a counterweight to its whimsy."

Go Hang a Salami! I'm a Lasagna Hog! and Other Palindromes was called "delightful visual and verbal fun" by a *Kirkus Reviews* commentator. The approximately sixty entries are a collection of palindromes, phrases, and words that, when read left to right or right to left, say the same thing. Illustrating one such phrase, Agee paints a parking lot filled with animals, called the "Llama Mall." In another, a cook yells: "Stop pots!" "Hilarious," was Michael Steinberg's description in the *New York Times Book Review*. "It all adds up to plenty of fun," concluded a *Publishers Weekly* contributor.

The Return of Freddy Legrand is Agee's tale of an early twentieth-century pilot who crosses the Atlantic in his biplane, the *Golden Gull*, only to crash in the French countryside. Unhurt, Freddy stays at the farm of Sophie and Albert, who put the broken plane in their barn and begin working to repair it. Freddy bicycles to Paris and is declared a hero. He embarks on another trip in the *Silver Swan* and flies over the Great Wall of China, the pyramids, the Golden Gate Bridge, and the Panama Canal. Freddy again crashes, this time in the Alps. With survival skills he learned from the French couple, he builds a shelter. Once again Sophie and Albert are his rescuers as they fly the repaired *Golden Gull* to the peak where Freddy is marooned. "Delightful entertainment," was Linda Phillips Ashour's description of *The Return of Freddy Legrand* in her *New York Times Book Review* appraisal. *Horn Book* reviewer Mary M. Burns wrote that Agee "knows how to woo the comic spirit so that various elements are exaggerated but stop short of heavy-handed caricature." "High-flying text and art convey the effervescent spirits of this simpler era," wrote a *Publishers Weekly* reviewer.

According to a *Publishers Weekly* contributor, the four-line rhymes in Agee's *Flapstick: Ten Ridiculous Rhymes with Flaps* "range from the sublimely slapstick to the mundanely silly.... Both children and adults ... will giggle at the sight gags." In this interactive lift-the-flap book, Agee hides the last word of each rhyme under a flap. An example: "'There's something wrong,' said Mrs. Goode,/ 'My motor barks and squeals.'/ The man looked underneath the hood./ He said, 'Miss, it's your—.'" When the flap is lifted, a picture of barking seals is revealed. Edward Sorel wrote in the *New York Times Book Review* that Agee's illustrations "are loose as a goose.... Drawn with a brush, they have a spontaneous, unlabored look." Sorel felt they are "child-like enough to inspire children to try their own hand with brush and paint." *School Library Journal* reviewer Kathleen Whalin called *Flapstick* "a genuine delight.... This book is a salute to the zaniness in all of us."

Susan Sullivan of the *Los Angeles Times Book Review* called Agee's second collection of palindromes, *So Many Dynamos! and Other Palindromes*, "even better" than his first. Sullivan noted the example of two owls sitting on a tree limb in the sun. Because of the heat, one

A French farm couple aid an adventurous biplane pilot in **The Return of Freddy Legrand,** *written and illustrated by Agee.*

falls, unable to even flap its wings. Sullivan called the caption, "Too hot to hoot," "pure whimsy." She said the more than sixty entries are "a truly inspired marriage of cartooning and wordplay." A *Publishers Weekly* reviewer noted that some entries were slightly off-color, "but likely to please kids." An example is a dog lifting his leg by a tree as he says to a man painting the Tower of Pisa, "As I pee, sir, I see Pisa!"

Dmitri the Astronaut is the story of a space explorer who has returned from the moon after an absence of more than two years. He soon realizes that the world has forgotten him and that his moon rocks are insignificant. Rejected, Dmitri throws his rocks into a trash can. Unknown to Dmitri, his friend Lulu, a pink polka-dotted alien, is hiding in the bag. She is a sensation, bringing Dmitri back into the limelight. "The wry humor of Agee's clever book springs in equal measure from the minimal, tongue-in-cheek text and adroitly exaggerated cartoon illustrations," wrote a *Publishers Weekly* reviewer. Writing in the *New York Times Book Review*, Christopher Lehmann-Haupt called the pictures "exuberant" and the story "deliciously nonsensical." "Agee scores again," wrote a *Kirkus Reviews* critic, who called *Dmitri the Astronaut* "a charmer."

Abbott Combes said in the *New York Times Book Review* that *Who Ordered the Jumbo Shrimp? and Other Oxymorons* is an "almost perfect collection." A *Publishers Weekly* reviewer said Agee's sixty sayings and illustrations demonstrate that "his pleasure from oxymo-

rons depends on observational humor, a la George Carlin or Jerry Seinfeld." *School Library Journal* reviewer Pamela K. Bomboy noted that some of the themes are sophisticated, for example, "stiff drink," and "Great Depression." Bomboy called the book "highly amusing."

Agee returned to the palindrome for a third offering titled *Sit on a Potato Pan, Otis!: More Palindromes.* As Deborah Stevenson of *Bulletin of the Center for Children's Books* commented, "this is more of the same, but when the same is fine entertainment it is hard to quibble." As before, each palindrome appears as either a caption or the punch line to a pen-and-ink cartoon, such as two cowpokes pondering the wanted poster of a big cat who kidnaped the deputy sheriff. One cowboy says to the other: "Darn ocelots stole Conrad." "The book hits some hilarious heights," enthused Stevenson, and a critic for *Kirkus Reviews* stated that "readers will enjoy [this book] backwards and forwards."

In addition to creating artwork to accompany his own stories, Agee illustrates work by other authors. *The Toy Box,* by Mary H. Heyward, and *Dishes All Done,* by Lucia Monfried, are both flap books. A *Publishers Weekly* reviewer said Agee's "sophisticated use of color and light ... gives each book a daring, distinctive look." In *Sitting in My Box,* by Dee Lillegard, a young boy shares a box with an assortment of jungle animals. "Agee's distinctive pictures are full of lush vegetation and lively detail," noted a *Publishers Weekly* reviewer. *Booklist* reviewer Susan Dove Lempke called Agee's illustrations for *The Halloween House,* by Erica Silverman, "hilarious ... reminiscent of *New Yorker* cartoons." Agee illustrated *Mean Margaret,* by Tor Seidler, a story of a woodchuck couple, Fred and Phoebe, who adopt a human child. *Booklist* reviewer Michael Cart said Agee's drawings "match the text in wit and boundless good humor." M. P. Dunleavey wrote in the *New York Times Book Review* that Agee "infuses his black-and-white drawings with great comic energy. He nails poor Fred's hapless expression, and his Bunyan-esque depiction of Margaret, who dwarfs her woodchuck caretakers, is hilarious."

Works Cited

Agee, Jon, *Flapstick: Ten Ridiculous Rhymes with Flaps,* Dutton, 1993.

Ashour, Linda Phillips, review of *The Return of Freddy Legrand, New York Times Book Review,* January 10, 1993, p. 18.

Bomboy, Pamela K., review of *Who Ordered the Jumbo Shrimp? and Other Oxymorons, School Library Journal,* November, 1998, p. 133.

Briggs, Raymond, "The Logic of Nonsense," *Times Educational Supplement,* September 6, 1989.

Burns, Mary M., review of *The Return of Freddy Legrand, Horn Book,* January-February, 1993, p. 71.

Cart, Michael, review of *Mean Margaret, Booklist,* December 1, 1997, p. 619.

Combes, Abbott, review of *Who Ordered the Jumbo Shrimp? and Other Oxymorons, New York Times Book Review,* November 15, 1998, p. 48.

From Agee's second self-illustrated collection of palindromes, **So Many Dynamos! and Other Palindromes.**

Dalley, Jan, "Adult Assumptions," *Times Literary Supplement,* April 7, 1989, p. 380.

Review of *Dmitri the Astronaut, Kirkus Reviews,* July 15, 1996, p. 1044.

Review of *Dmitri the Astronaut, Publishers Weekly,* July 29, 1996, p. 87.

Dunleavey, M. P., "Woodchuck Nation," *New York Times Book Review,* November 16, 1997, p. 34.

Review of *Ellsworth, Publishers Weekly,* December 2, 1983, p. 89.

Review of *Flapstick: Ten Ridiculous Rhymes with Flaps, Publishers Weekly,* August 23, 1993, p. 68.

Review of *Go Hang a Salami! I'm a Lasagna Hog!, Kirkus Reviews,* August 1, 1992, p. 996.

Review of *Go Hang a Salami! I'm a Lasagna Hog!, Publishers Weekly,* July 20, 1992, p. 247.

Hewitt, Debra, review of *Ellsworth, School Library Journal,* April, 1994, p. 97.

Review of *If Snow Falls: A Story for December, Publishers Weekly,* July 23, 1982, p. 132.

Review of *The Incredible Painting of Felix Clousseau, Publishers Weekly,* July 29, 1988, pp. 133-136.

Jameyson, Karen, review of *Ellsworth, Horn Book,* April, 1984, pp. 179-180.

Lehmann-Haupt, Christopher, "Turning Pages to Children's Pleasure," *New York Times Book Review,* December 9, 1996, p. C18.

Lempke, Susan Dove, review of *The Halloween House, Booklist,* September 1, 1997, p. 141.

Marcus, Leonard, review of *The Incredible Painting of Felix Clousseau, New York Times Book Review,* November 27, 1988, p. 37.

Review of *The Return of Freddy Legrand, Publishers Weekly,* September 14, 1992, p. 123.

Review of *Sit on a Potato Pan, Otis!, Kirkus Reviews,* January 15, 1999, p. 142.

Review of *Sitting in My Box, Publishers Weekly,* September 29, 1989, p. 66.

Review of *So Many Dynamos! and Other Palindromes, Publishers Weekly,* November 14, 1994, p. 65.

Sorel, Edward, "What's Under the Hood?," *New York Times Book Review,* November 14, 1993, p. 22.

Steinberg, Michael, review of *Go Hang a Salami! I'm a Lasagna Hog!, New York Times Book Review,* June 21, 1992.

Stevenson, Deborah, review of *Sit on a Potato Pan, Otis!, Bulletin of the Center for Children's Books,* February, 1999, p. 194.

Sullivan, Susan, review of *So Many Dynamos! and Other Palindromes, Los Angeles Times Book Review,* June 4, 1995, p. 6.

Review of *The Toy Box* and *Dishes All Done, Publishers Weekly,* March 24, 1989, p. 66.

Whalin, Kathleen, review of *Flapstick: Ten Ridiculous Rhymes with Flaps, School Library Journal,* March, 1994, p. 224.
Review of *Who Ordered the Jumbo Shrimp? and Other Oxymorons, Publishers Weekly,* August 17, 1998, pp. 72-73.

For More Information See

PERIODICALS

Booklist, December 15, 1990, p. 836; November 1, 1992, p. 517; February 1, 1993, p. 978; December 15, 1994, p. 747; April 1, 1995, p. 1412; October 15, 1996, p. 429.
Bulletin of the Center for Children's Books, October, 1992, p. 34; January, 1995, p. 156.
Horn Book, spring, 1993, pp. 18, 101; January, 1994, p. 59; spring, 1994, p. 24; spring, 1995, p. 112; spring, 1997, p. 17; September, 1997, p. 564; January, 1998, p. 80.
Kirkus Reviews, October 1, 1992, p. 1251; October 1, 1993, p. 1268.
New York Times Book Review, March 2, 1997, p. 25.
Publishers Weekly, October 26, 1990, p. 71; April 18, 1994, p. 65; August 8, 1994, p. 450; February 24, 1997, p. 93; August 18, 1997, p. 93; October 6, 1997, p. 49; March 23, 1998, p. 102.
School Library Journal, January, 1990, p. 83; November, 1992, p. 65, p. 125; December, 1992, p. 19; November, 1996, p. 76; November, 1997, pp. 40, 99-100; March, 1998, p. 119; March, 1999, p. 216.

*   *   *

ANDREW, Ian (Peter) 1962-

Personal

Born August 8, 1962, in Beckenham, Kent, England; son of Frederick James Henry (an electrical engineer) and Eileen Christine (a nurse; maiden name, O'Connor) Andrew. *Education:* Attended Croydon College of Art; Camberwell, B.A. (with honors); Croydon Intermedia, Certificate in Animation; Royal College of Art, M.A. *Hobbies and other interests:* Collecting rubber stamps, exhibitions, live music concerts, comedy, cinema, theater, cycling, human rights activities, writing letters, "mysteries and the unknown."

Addresses

Office—24 Brookside Way, Shirley, Croydon, Surrey CR0 7RR, England. *Agent*—Rosemary Sandberg, Rosemary Sandberg Ltd. Agency for Writers and Illustrators, 6 Bayley St., London WC1B 3HB, England.

Career

Freelance animator, London, England, 1989-94; Len Lewis-Shootsey Animation, London, illustrator of backgrounds and renderer of models; worked as animator for TVC, Grand Slamm, Stuart Books, Alison de Vere, and Cinexa. *Member:* Society of Authors, Association of Illustrators, Institute of Contemporary Arts.

Ian Andrew with Virginia McKenna

Awards, Honors

First Bite Award, Bristol Festival, for the film *Dolphins;* short-listed for Mother Goose Award, 1996, for *The Lion and the Mouse,* and Carnegie Medal, 1999, for *The Kin.*

Illustrator

Amanda Jane Wood, *The Lion and the Mouse: An Aesop's Fable,* Millbrook Press (Brookfield, CT), 1995.
Julia Derek Parker, *The Complete Book of Dreams,* Dorling Kindersley, 1995.
Rumer Godden, *Premlata and the Festival of Lights,* Greenwillow (New York City), 1996.
Caroline Repchuk, *The Forgotten Garden,* based on an idea by Mike Jolley, Millbrook Press, 1997.
Robert Louis Stevenson, *The Strange Case of Dr. Jekyll and Mr. Hyde,* adapted by Michael Lawrence, DK Publishing, 1997.
Virginia McKenna, *Back to the Blue,* Millbrook Press, 1998.
Berlie Doherty, *The Midnight Man,* Candlewick Press (Cambridge, MA), 1998.
Peter Dickinson, *The Kin,* Macmillan, 1998.
Charles Dickens, *Oliver Twist,* adapted by Naia Bray-Moffatt, DK Publishing (New York City), 1999.
Michael Morpurgo, *Colly's Barn,* Mammoth, 1999.

Contributor of illustration to the *Greenpeace Book of Dolphins,* 1990.

Work in Progress

Illustrating *The Aeneid,* for publisher Frances Lincoln; *Jim's Lion,* by Russell Hoban, for Candlewick Press; and *The Aeneid in Search of a Homeland.*

Sidelights

Ian Andrew told *SATA:* "When Templar and Millbrook Press approached me to work on *Back to the Blue,* it was a subject I have been passionate about for some time. It has been a strange journey to the point where I find myself now.

"I now realize it's important to grab opportunities with both hands, which is probably why I was at college for much longer than I intended. I was originally trained as an illustrator, but I found my obsession with animation growing, as I had a desire to work with sound and had always been inspired by film. This transition has always seemed to be a natural one. It was a move that proved invaluable, allowing experimentation and thinking on a completely different scale, with total awareness of time, producing hundreds and hundreds of drawings for just a few seconds of screen time. Your drawing becomes looser, and the process opens you to use media you wouldn't have considered before just to save time.

"When I finished at the Royal College of Art, I had completed a short animation called *Dolphins.* It was inspired by a lone dolphin off the west coast of Ireland in Dingle Bay, where I spent many of my summers during that time. Even though the film is really a study of dolphins in motion, it makes reference to the use of drift nets, which, sadly, cause many to drown when they become entangled. To my delight, Greenpeace saw the film on an animation program and asked to use it as part of a campaign in response to concerns over the status of small cetaceans around the coasts of Britain and Ireland. The Greenpeace vessel *Moby Dick* visited Cardigan Bay in Wales and Moray Firth in Scotland; these two habitats are home to virtually the entire British semi-resident coastal population of bottlenose dolphins. The tour was used to make people aware, locally and nationally, that there were dolphins in these particular areas and that they were under threat. My liaison with Greenpeace culminated in frames of the film and commissioned illustrations appearing in the *Greenpeace Book of Dolphins* in 1990.

"In the same year I ventured to Berlin to try to get work on a production of *The Little Prince,* but it turned out to be a fruitless venture. So I turned my attention to the National Film Board of Canada in Montreal. I went to see the 'pinscreen' housed there. Created by Alexandre Alexieff and Claire Parker, it enables you to animate with light, using hundreds of retractable pins. The quality is just beautiful, and some moments in their films *Night on Bare Mountain* and *The Nose* greatly influenced me. I became very aware of the drama achieved in

Back to the Blue

Andrew employed the same techniques he used in his acclaimed animated film on dolphins when he provided pencil-and-pastel illustrations for Virginia McKenna's story of three dolphins released from captivity in the United Kingdom. (From Back to the Blue.*)*

the use of black and white. Someone at Candlewick Press asked me where I found the inspiration for the illustrations in *The Midnight Man.* I replied that the book grew out of 'my love of black and white films of the 1930s with their use of dramatic lights and shadows.' I try to capture on paper the luminous feel of those films.

"Seeing the pinscreen was a defining moment, and it inspired my black and white drawings for *The Lion and the Mouse,* which were intended for an animated film. I did manage to get them onto film for the Annecy animation festival, but the project was later shelved. That is why I owe so much to Templar and Millbrook Press, who saw the box of black and white drawings, chose the ones they liked, and added a text by Amanda Jane Wood. It was a real gamble for them, and it was my first published picture book.

"So, in full circle in 1996, they came back to me with *Back to the Blue.* I used the same techniques used in the animated film on dolphins—pencil and pastel. I knew the story well, having followed the jubilation at the closure of the last 'dolphinariums.' It was incredible to be able to work with Virginia McKenna, whose work with Bill Travers through the Born Free Foundation showed unparalleled conviction to saving animals in appalling situations. It was one of the most rewarding projects to be involved with. The publicity was like nothing I'd seen before—celebrities lending their support, attending signings with Virginia, a poster produced with my drawing on it, and quite wonderful feedback, from children especially, but also from readers of all ages—a joyous experience.

"I hope at some point I am destined to renew my acquaintance with such incredible subject matter as the dolphins, with their musicality, their easy sensuality and evident intelligence, but most of all their ability to call our assumed dominion over nature into question."

For More Information See

PERIODICALS

Booklist, February 1, 1996, p. 936; August, 1998, p. 2007; February 15, 1999, p. 1074.
Horn Book, May-June, 1997, p. 320.
Publishers Weekly, November 13, 1995, p. 60; January 27, 1997, p. 107; December 14, 1998, p. 75.
School Library Journal, September, 1997, p. 191; March, 1998, p. 184.

*   *   *

ARNOLD, Tedd 1949-

Personal

Born January 20, 1949, in Elmira, NY; son of Theodore Arnold (a machinist) and Gabriela (Rosno) Arnold; married Carol Clark (a teacher), August 15, 1970; children: Walter, William. *Education:* University of Florida, B.F.A.

Addresses

Agent—Peter Elek Associates, P.O. Box 223, Canal St. Station, New York, NY 10013.

Career

Author and illustrator. Tallahassee, FL, textbook illustrator, 1973-78, creative director and owner of a graphic design studio, 1978-81; Cycles USA, Tallahassee, advertising art director, 1981-84; Workman Publishing, New York City, book designer, 1984-86; freelance author and illustrator, Elmira, NY, 1986—. *Military service:* U.S. Army Reserve, medic, 1969-75.

Awards, Honors

Children's Choice Award, International Reading Association-Children's Book Council (IRA-CBC), 1988, Georgia Children's Picture Storybook Award, 1990, North Dakota Children's Choice Picture Book Award, 1991, and Volunteer State Book Award, 1992, all for *No Jumping on the Bed!;* North Dakota Flicker Tale Award, 1993, for *The Signmaker's Assistant;* PBS Storytime Featured Selection: Parent's Choice, 1993, and Children's Choice Award, IRA-CBC, 1994, both for *Green Wilma;* Children's Choice Award, IRA-CBC, 1995, for *My Working Mom;* Children's Choice Award IRA-CBC, 1996, for *No More Water in the Tub!;* National Association of Parenting Publications Award, 1996, for *Bialosky's Bedtime;* "Tellable" Stories for Ages 4-7 Award, Storytelling World, and Books Mean Business selection, American Booksellers Association-Children's Book Council, both 1998, and Colorado Children's

Tedd Arnold

Book Award, 1999, all for *Parts;* Notable Books for Children citation, *Smithsonian,* 1999, for *Axle Annie.*

Writings

FOR CHILDREN; AUTHOR AND ILLUSTRATOR UNLESS OTHERWISE NOTED

Sounds, Little Simon, 1985.
Opposites, Little Simon, 1985.
Actions, Little Simon, 1985.
Colors, Little Simon, 1985.
My First Drawing Book, Workman Publishing, 1986.
No Jumping on the Bed!, Dial, 1987.
My First Play House, Workman Publishing, 1987.
My First Play Town, Workman Publishing, 1987.
Ollie Forgot, Dial, 1988.
Mother Goose's Words of Wit and Wisdom: A Book of Months, Dial, 1990.
(And designer of samplers) *Cross-Stitch Patterns for Mother Goose's Words of Wit and Wisdom: Samplers to Stitch,* New American Library/Dutton, 1990.
The Signmaker's Assistant, Dial, 1992.
The Simple People, illustrated by Andrew Shachat, Dial, 1992.
Green Wilma, Dial, 1993.
No More Water in the Tub!, Dial, 1995.
Five Ugly Monsters, Scholastic, Inc., 1995.
Bialosky's Bedtime: An Opposites Book, Workman Publishing, 1996.

Bialosky's Big Mess: An Alphabet Book, Workman Publishing, 1996.

Bialosky's Bumblebees: A Counting Book, Workman Publishing, 1996.

Bialosky's House: A Color Book, Workman Publishing, 1996.

Parts, Dial, 1997.

Huggly Gets Dressed, Scholastic, Inc., 1997.

Huggly Takes a Bath, Scholastic, Inc., 1998.

Huggly and the Toy Monster, Scholastic, Inc., 1998.

Huggly's Pizza, Scholastic, Inc., 2000.

Huggly Goes to School, Scholastic, Inc., 2000.

No Jumping on the Bed! has been translated into Spanish.

FOR CHILDREN; ILLUSTRATOR

Helen Witty, *Mrs. Witty's Monster Cookies,* Workman Publishing, 1983.

Ron Atlas, *Looking for Zebra: Hotel Zoo: Happy Hunting from A to Z,* Little Simon, 1986.

R. Atlas, *A Room for Benny,* Little Simon, 1987.

Rena Coyle, *My First Baking Book,* Workman Publishing, 1988.

Anne Kostick, *My First Camera Book,* Workman Publishing, 1989.

Laurie Abel, *Bisnipian Blast-off: An Action Counting Book,* Discovery Toys, 1991.

David Schiller and David Rosenbloom, *My First Computer Book,* Workman Publishing, 1991.

Peter Glassman, *My Working Mom,* Morrow, 1994.

Jim Sargena, *The Roly-Poly Spider,* Scholastic, Inc., 1994.

Alyssa Satin Capucilli, *Inside a Barn in the Country: A Rebus Read-along Story,* Scholastic, Inc., 1995.

David Galef, *Tracks,* Morrow, 1996.

Suzanne Williams, *My Dog Never Says Please,* Dial, 1997.

Capucilli, *Inside a House That Is Haunted: A Rebus Read-along Story,* Scholastic, Inc., 1998.

Robin Pulver, *Axle Annie,* Dial, 1999.

Capucilli, *Inside a Zoo in the City: A Rebus Read-along Story,* Scholastic, Inc., 2000.

Sidelights

Whimsy has become artist Tedd Arnold's stock in trade. A successful author and illustrator of children's picture books, Arnold fills the tales he writes, and those by other authors, with lovable but quirky characters who have a sense of fun. His breakthrough book, *No Jumping on the Bed!,* won numerous awards, including the International Reading Association-Children's Book Council "Children's Choice" for 1988. "Arnold's soft pencil and watercolor illustrations are full of amusing details," commented *School Library Journal* contributor Anne Connor in reviewing the 1995 sequel, *No More Water in the Tub!,* adding that such details "will keep young readers coming back again and again." Other tales written by Arnold include characters like his fly-eating girl, *Green Wilma,* the nervous boy convinced that he is falling apart in the 1997 book, *Parts,* and the quickly growing series of adventures with Huggly, the loveable monster under the bed.

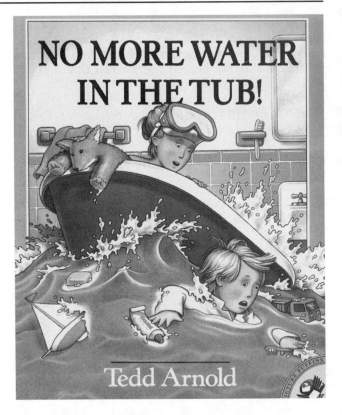

In Arnold's self-illustrated tale, young William sails through his apartment building in his bathtub, collecting neighbors who are described in humorous rhymes. (Cover illustration by Arnold.)

Born in 1949, Arnold attended the University of Florida where he earned a bachelor of fine arts degree. Although he originally specialized in text book illustration and graphic design for advertising, he became interested in picture book illustration thanks to the books his wife, Carol, was collecting for her kindergarten classroom. He approached several publishers with samples of his work, eventually receiving as his first illustration project Helen Witty's *Mrs. Witty's Monster Cookies,* published in 1983. Since then, Arnold has contributed his humorous drawings to books by Robin Pulver, Alyssa Satin Capucilli, and Peter Glassman, among others. Of Capucilli's *Inside a Barn in the Country: A Rebus Read-along Story, Booklist* contributor Stephanie Zvirin said that Arnold's "lively pictures, filled with exaggerated, bug-eyed, cartoon-like characters and melodrama, should make this a childhood favorite." His illustrations for *Axle Annie,* by author and friend Robin Pulver, helped win that book a place on *Smithsonian's* 1999 list of Notable Books for Children. *Booklist* contributor, Ilene Cooper, wrote that *Axle Annie's* "pictures shiver with energy and fun."

No Jumping on the Bed!, published in 1987 inspired by his first son Walter, a notorious four-year-old bed-jumper. Arnold was, at the time, living with his family in an old apartment building in Yonkers, New York, and became intrigued by the possibility of Walter's bed falling through the floor into the neighbor's apartment below. The success of that book with children and parents confirmed Arnold's decision to specialize in illustrating children's books. *Ollie Forgot* and *The Signmaker's Assistant* soon followed. But what Arnold says he needed was a book for his younger son, William. *No More Water in the Tub!,* a sequel to his first book, was published in 1995. It is a warmhearted take on bath time, featuring young William who looks forward to snorkeling in the tub. Arnold's rhyming prose and illustrations found favor with Ann A. Flowers in her *Horn Book* review: "Young readers will love the ridiculous incidents and cumulative rhymes, and the illustrations ... are hilarious."

Arnold has continued to focus on appealing to young children in the many volumes of children's books he has written and illustrated since beginning his career. In a series including *Huggly Gets Dressed, Huggly Takes a Bath,* and *Huggly's Pizza,* the author-illustrator introduces his audience to a likable monster from under the bed whose forays into the world of humans uncover many curiosities. In *Huggly's Pizza,* the monster, together with his non-human friends, Booter and Grubble, leaves the safe place under the bed to search for some delicious human food. In *Huggly Takes a Bath,* the green-skinned monster sets forth from his home under a little boy's bed and discovers a small room nearby. It is full of porcelain objects that swish or spray water, a slippery cube that makes suds, bottles of sudsy, pretty-smelling lotions just perfect for mixing together to make a monster slime pit, and a row of tiny long-handled brushes for which he finds a funny use. Calling Arnold's illustrations "cartoon-like" and "colorfully appealing," *Booklist* contributor Shelley Townsend-Hudson praised *Huggly Takes a Bath* as a "simple, efficient text [that] is sure to elicit many laughs."

Equally fanciful, Arnold's *Green Wilma* recounts a child's dream that she has turned green and developed a talent for catching flies with her tongue. "Fast, funny, and froggy, *Green Wilma* is guaranteed to be a hit with the story hour silly set," enthused Annie Ayres of *Booklist* in a review of the author-illustrator's 1993 effort. For this book, Arnold's style of illustration is particularly appropriate, featuring rounded lines and exaggerated, saucer-like, "goggle" eyes that give characters in many of his books a frog-like appeal. Characterizing *Green Wilma* and *No More Water in the Tub!* as "wacky action romps" in a 1996 review, a *Publishers Weekly* contributor praised illustrator Arnold for his use of both color and humor in making stories come alive for youngsters.

Arnold once told *SATA:* "It still comes as a great surprise to me that I'm now an author. I've always drawn pictures, taken art classes, and thought of myself as an artist. In school, my cartoons graced many a desktop, chalkboard, and math paper. (The teachers and the girls always noticed.) In the army, extra duty could be avoided by letting the sergeants know how nice the barracks would look with 'inspirational' murals painted on the walls. After college, I quickly learned that art-related jobs were more comfortable than construction-related jobs. And even today I find that drawing pictures for books is a great way to avoid doing real work.

"Back in college, I began writing titles across the bottoms of my drawings. The titles became lengthy, growing into sentences and paragraphs. The drawings and writings were like fragments of stories, pages torn from books. My interest in the words developed into a renewed interest in an old love—comics. It was in the form of comics that I first explored storytelling.

"However, the writing was always for the pictures. The pictures were the real thing, the reason for being, the fun. Which is why the label of 'author' still feels like brand-new dress shoes, while 'artist' feels like well-worn, street-running, tree-climbing, can-kicking, ball-park sneakers. But don't we all just love a new pair of shoes!"

Works Cited

Ayres, Annie, review of *Green Wilma, Booklist,* March 1, 1993, p. 1234.

Connor, Anne, review of *No More Water in the Tub!, School Library Journal,* October, 1995, p. 96.

Cooper, Ilene, review of *Axle Annie, Booklist,* February 15, 2000, p. 1120.

Flowers, Ann A., review of *No More Water in the Tub!, Horn Book,* January-February, 1996, p. 59.

Townsend-Hudson, Shelley, review of *Huggly Takes a Bath, Booklist,* February 1, 1999, p. 978.

Review of *Tracks, Publishers Weekly,* January 29, 1996, p. 99.

Zvirin, Stephanie, review of *Inside a Barn in the Country, Booklist,* January 15, 1995, p. 935.

For More Information See

PERIODICALS

Booklist, August, 1997, p. 1904.

Growing Point, July, 1989, p. 5196.

Language Arts, April, 1988, p. 415.

The Mailbox Bookbag, November-December, 1996.

The Mailbox Bookbag Kindergarten, April-May, 1998.

New Yorker, November 30, 1987, pp. 140-141.

Publishers Weekly, November 21, 1994, p. 75; December 7, 1998, p. 58; August 23, 1999, p. 58.

School Library Journal, October, 1987, p. 110; December, 1988, p. 79; November, 1990, p. 76; May, 1993, p. 80; August, 1994, p. 130; April, 1995, p. 98; June, 1997, p. 103; September, 1998, p. 165.

Smithsonian, November, 1999, pp. 42-46.

Times Literary Supplement, April 7, 1989, p. 380.

ON-LINE

Author's website located at http://www.teddarnold.com.

*   *   *

AYRES, Becky
See HICKOX, Rebecca (Ayres)

B

BELL, Jadrien
See GOLDEN, Christie

* * *

BIAL, Raymond 1948-

Personal

Born November 5, 1948, in Danville, IL; son of Marion (a U.S. Air Force officer) and Catherine (a medical secretary) Bial; married Linda LaPuma (a librarian), August 25, 1979; children: Anna, Sarah, Luke. *Education:* University of Illinois, B.S. (with honors), 1970, M.S., 1979. *Politics:* Independent. *Religion:* Catholic. *Hobbies and other interests:* Gardening, fishing, hiking, travel.

Addresses

Home—208 West Iowa St., Urbana, IL 61801. *Office*—Parkland College Library, 2400 West Bradley Ave., Champaign, IL 61821.

Career

Parkland College Library, Champaign, IL, librarian, 1980—. *Member:* Children's Reading Roundtable, Society of Children's Book Writers and Illustrators.

Awards, Honors

Best Publicity of 1984, Library Public Relations Council, 1984, for "In All My Years" exhibit poster; Historian of the Year, Champaign County, Illinois, 1984; Award of Superior Achievement, Illinois State Historical Society, 1985; First Annual Staff Development Award, Parkland College, 1985, for presentation on print media and computer resources in academic libraries; Certificate of Commendation, American Association for State and Local History, 1986; Writer's Choice selection, National Endowment for the Arts and the Pushcart Foundation,

Raymond Bial

1986, for *First Frost;* Best Publicity of 1986, Library Public Relations Council, 1987, for poster advertising "Changing Image of Rural and Small Town Life" panel discussion; Staff Development Award, Parkland College, 1990, for presentation entitled "The Language of Photography"; Outstanding Science Trade Book for Children, 1991, for *Corn Belt Harvest.*

Writings

FICTION FOR CHILDREN

The Fresh Grave and Other Ghostly Stories, illustrated by Anna Bial, Face to Face Books, 1997.
The Ghost of Honeymoon Creek, illustrated by Anna Bial, Face to Face Books, 1999.
Shadow Island (novel), Face to Face Books, 2000.

NONFICTION FOR CHILDREN; AND PHOTOGRAPHER

Corn Belt Harvest, Houghton, 1991.
County Fair, Houghton, 1992.
Amish Home, Houghton, 1993.
Frontier Home, Houghton, 1993.
Shaker Home, Houghton, 1994.
Portrait of a Farm Family, Houghton, 1995.
The Underground Railroad, Houghton, 1995.
With Needle and Thread: A Book about Quilts, Houghton, 1996.
Mist over the Mountains: Appalachia and Its People, Houghton, 1997.
The Strength of These Arms: Life in the Slave Quarters, Houghton, 1997.
Where Lincoln Walked, Walker, 1997.
Cajun Home, Houghton, 1998.
One-Room School, Houghton, 1999.
A Handful of Dirt, Walker, 2000.

"LIFEWAYS" SERIES; PUBLISHED BY BENCHMARK BOOKS

The Navajo, 1999.
The Cherokee, 1999.
The Iroquois, 1999.
The Sioux, 1999.
The Ojibwe, 2000.
The Pueblo, 2000.
The Seminole, 2000.
The Comanche, 2000.
The Apache, 2001.
The Huron, 2001.
The Haida, 2001.
The Cheyenne, 2001.

OTHER

Ivesdale: A Photographic Essay, Champaign County Historical Archives, 1982.
In All My Years: Portraits of Older Blacks in Champaign-Urbana, Champaign County Historical Museum, 1983, revised edition, 1985.
Upon a Quiet Landscape: The Photographs of Frank Sadorus, Champaign County Historical Museum, 1983.
There Is a Season, Champaign County Nursing Home, 1984.
(With Kathryn Kerr) *First Frost,* Stormline Press, 1985.
Common Ground: Photographs of Rural and Small Town Life, Stormline Press, 1986.
Stopping By: Portraits from Small Towns, University of Illinois Press, 1988.
(With wife, Linda LaPuma Bial) *The Carnegie Library in Illinois,* University of Illinois Press, 1988.
From the Heart of the Country: Photographs of the Midwestern Sky, Sagamore Publishing, 1991.
Looking Good: A Guide to Photographing Your Library, American Library Association, 1991.
Champaign: A Pictorial History, Bradley Publishing, 1993.
Visit to Amish Country, Phoenix Publishing, 1995.
Zoom Lens Photography, Amherst Media, 1996.

Also author of introduction to *Beneath an Open Sky,* by Gary Irving, University of Illinois Press, 1990. Contributor of photo-essay to *Townships,* University of Iowa Press, 1992.

In Corn Belt Harvest, *Bial blends his photographs and straightforward, sometimes lyrical text to tell the story of the Corn Belt region of the United States and to describe the planting, harvesting, storage, and marketing methods of its farmers.*

Sidelights

Raymond Bial has blended a love of photography and writing with a special feeling for rural and small-town America to create numerous illustrated books looking at subjects from harvesting corn to one-room schools. His books on various lesser-known cultures of America—from Cajun to Appalachian—also introduce young readers to a type of living history that makes dry facts come alive. In addition, he has penned a series of books about individual Native American tribes for Benchmark Books that blend photography with cultural and social history, and several books of history dealing with slavery and with the life of Lincoln.

Born in Illinois, Bial grew up in the sort of small-town and rural America that he portrays in many of his books. Bial once told *Something about the Author* (SATA): "When I was growing up in the 1950s I spent several of the most joyous years of my young life in a small town in Indiana. With my friends, I bicycled around the neighborhood, went swimming at the municipal pool,

Through direct photographs and text in **Portrait of a Farm Family,** *Bial outlines the sacrifices and rewards of family life on a farm through the experiences of the Steidingers, owners of a dairy farm in Illinois.*

stopped for ice cream at the local hotspot, and frequently visited our Carnegie public library. Some people might think that such memories are simply nostalgic, but I know that our little town was pleasant, comfortable, and safe—and I will always cherish those years.

"Later, our family moved to a farm in southern Michigan. Although I missed my old friends, as well as the charming atmosphere of my old 'hometown,' I enjoyed taking care of our livestock and running free through the woods, marsh, and fields around our new home. The moment I walked out of the house, I was truly outside. The marsh, in particular, was bursting forth with wildlife—turtles, frogs, muskrats, ducks—and I delighted in my explorations and discoveries.

"Not all my childhood was wonderful. At times there were financial difficulties, family arguments, and other painful experiences. Yet for the most part I was simply thrilled to be alive, directly experiencing the world

around me, especially when I could be out of doors in the light and weather."

Educated as a librarian, Bial has been a librarian at Parkland College Library in Champaign, Illinois, since 1980. He is also married to a librarian, and working together the two have produced several books of local history. But it was not until 1991 that Bial began producing books for juvenile readers. As he told *SATA,* this was the culmination of a long-time dream. "Ever since I was in fourth grade, I wanted to be a writer, but only as an adult in my early twenties did photography happen to me. I say 'happen to me,' because I never consciously decided to become a photographer. I simply loved the experience of making photographs. I've never received any formal training or education in the art form. Rather, I have relied upon my own instincts in making photographs which matter to me personally."

Bial had no difficulty in thinking of a theme or content for his work. Growing up in middle America, in the heart of the country, he developed a life-long devotion to the outdoors and the values of a non-urbanized country. That was the America he experienced directly as a child. "My work as a writer and photographer first drew upon these early moments of delight," Bial told *SATA.* "For most of my books, I have returned to rural and small town subjects. Just as when I was a child, I still love to be outside, absolutely free, making photographs. With every photograph I try to recapture that heightened sense of feeling for people, places, and things which meant so much to me as a child. I believe that adults as well as children should live not only in their minds, but through their senses."

Bial's first nonfiction, self-illustrated title, *Corn Belt Harvest,* paved the way for things to come. Blending photographs and straightforward (and sometimes lyrical) text, Bial tells the story of the Corn Belt region of the United States and describes the planting, harvesting, storage, and marketing methods of its farmers. This first title was well-received by critics and also garnered an Outstanding Science Trade Book for Children citation. Reviewing the title in *Booklist,* Hazel Rochman called the book an "informative photo-essay" which focused on "clear color photographs" to explain the corn growing and harvesting process. "Midwesterner Bial communicates a sense of process and connection in machines and nature," concluded Rochman. A *Kirkus Reviews* critic noted that both text and photos were "commendably clear and informative," and went on to observe that the book was "[u]nusually handsome and useful." Writing in *School Library Journal,* Joyce Adams Burner noted Bial's "big, beautiful color photographs," and further remarked that "Bial writes in a smooth, precise manner, yet conveys his love for the region." Burner concluded, "Overall, this is a jewel of a book, well suited for reports."

Bial continued in this same vein with his *County Fair,* a photo-essay that traces a fair from set-up to opening day to break-down of the tents. "Bial captures the sense of anticipation that swirls around a fair, as well as offering an insightful look at what goes on behind the scenes," noted *Booklist* contributor Ilene Cooper. Bial examines each aspect of the fair, including livestock barns, homemade pies, and the rides. "Attractive color photos ... stand out on the pages," Cooper concluded. Dairy farming was the subject of his 1995 book *Portrait of a Farm Family* in which he profiled the Steidinger family to portray how milk gets into cartons. Mary Harris Veeder, writing in *Booklist,* thought "Bial brings the Steidinger's everyday world to life, fitting it neatly into an excellent discussion of family-farm based agriculture in the U.S. economy." *Horn Book* contributor Elizabeth S. Watson wrote, "[T]his fine photo-essay radiates the warmth of a close ten-member family engaged in hard work toward a common goal—the survival of the family farm."

With *Amish Home,* Bial struck on a winning formula: introducing some of the cultures of America through

their domestic artifacts. The home was, of necessity, a metaphor for the Amish in this first title, for the Amish themselves do not wish to be photographed. But in succeeding books such as *Frontier Home, Shaker Home,* and *Cajun Home* these artifacts take on almost totemic values, introducing readers to the language, culture, food, and even history of the groups described. Writing of Bial's *Amish Home,* a *Kirkus Reviews* writer said, "The absence of the Amish themselves, in honor of their beliefs, is a powerful statement, reflected in Bial's concise but admirably detailed descriptions of Amish ways." Kay Weisman called *Amish Home* a "haunting photo-essay" in a *Booklist* review, and went to note how Bial details the lives of these people who live simply and plainly. Weisman felt Bial's title "will be welcomed by libraries everywhere." Alexandra Marris, reviewing the book in *School Library Journal,* felt the book was an "attractive and compelling photo-essay of the Amish" and that "Bial clearly demonstrates his deep respect for these people and their complex system of values."

In **Cajun** Home, *Bial employs domestic images in describing the culture of this ethnic group, which originated in France and emigrated to Canada and, later, Louisiana.*

Bial has continued to use this format in several more titles that specifically look at the homes of various cultural and ethnic groups. *Frontier Home* conjures up a bygone life through photos taken at pioneer villages and sites and through the letters of pioneers. *Booklist* critic Carolyn Phelan commented of this book, "Bial's photography gives the book a look of integrity as well as a window into the lives of the pioneers." Of his 1994 *Shaker Home* Ellen Fader commented in *Horn Book,* "Readers finish the book with a clear understanding of how the Shakers, or Believers, as they often referred to themselves, and their idealistic belief in utopian society have enriched our lives." And in his *Cajun Home,* Bial does the same for this ethnic group, which originally came from France, settled in Canada, and later moved on to Louisiana. "As he has done in previous photo-essays, Bial combines an interesting, well-written text with simple yet compelling color photographs that give insight into a community," observed *Booklist* writer Cooper. Judith Constantinides, reviewing *Cajun Home* in *School Library Journal,* remarked on Bial's "stunning full-color pictures of little things" by means of which he "meticulously builds a portrait of a fascinating people." Constantinides concluded, "The book provides an excellent look at this unique culture and is by far the most informative and accurate children's title on this subject.... All together, a quality production."

The people of Appalachia received the Bial treatment in *Mist over the Mountains: Appalachia and Its People.* As much a culture as a place, this region of small farms and folk arts is rich in culture and history, both of which Bial illuminates in text and photos. A *Kirkus Reviews* contributor called Bial's book a "superb photo-essay," while *Booklist*'s Phelan concluded that "this handsome book casts its beam of light with care and respect." Quilts formed the focus of a further Bial title, *With Needle and Thread,* a survey of such stitchery from pioneer days through the era of the AIDS quilt. "With quiet prose and clear, lovely full-color photographs, Bial has stitched together a 'sampler' about people and the quilts they sew," commented *Booklist*'s Hazel Rochman of this title.

Bial has also tried to capture history in the format of the photo-essay, even though some of the events he hopes to chronicle occurred before photography was widely used. He captures the days of slavery in two related titles, *The Underground Railroad* and *The Strength of These Arms: Life in the Slave Quarters,* and he also illuminates the life of the man who finally stopped slavery in the United States, Abraham Lincoln, in his *Where Lincoln Walked.* For *The Underground Railroad,* Bial photographed places and objects related to the underground escape route for slaves. "Like a museum exhibit, the stirring photographs help us imagine what it must have been like for those who found the courage to run and to help others," concluded *Booklist*'s Rochman. Of that same book, a *Publishers Weekly* critic observed, "Advantageously reproducing first-hand accounts and his own arresting photographs, Bial ... effectively evokes the era of slavery and its divisive effects on the United States."

Bial presents a brief portrait of Abraham Lincoln in *Where Lincoln Walked,* tracing the career of the great president from his humble log-cabin beginnings to Washington and the presidency. Interspersed with the text are photos of places associated with Lincoln, his homes and offices. Eunice Weech, writing in *School Library Journal,* called this book "Another of Bial's beautifully executed photo-essays," while a *Kirkus Reviews* writer dubbed it an "extraordinarily honest, if brief, pictorial portrayal." The versatile Bial has also penned two story collections, as well as a series of photo-essays profiling the world of Native American tribes such as the Sioux, Cherokee, and Navajo.

"I now live in an old house in a middle-sized town in the Midwest with my wife and three children," Bial told *SATA.* "Above all else I love being a husband and a father. For me, the only thing better than being a child oneself is to grow up and have children of one's own. In writing and making photographs, I now draw upon my experiences with my family as well as upon the memories of my childhood. I am often able to write my books at home in the midst of my family, which is just wonderful. As far as possible, I also coordinate photography assignments with family vacations so that I can make photographs and have a great time with my wife and children."

Works Cited

Review of *Amish Home, Kirkus Reviews,* February 1, 1993, p. 142.

Burner, Joyce Adams, review of *Corn Belt Harvest, School Library Journal,* February, 1992, p. 92.

Constantinides, Judith, review of *Cajun Home, School Library Journal,* May, 1998, p. 150.

Cooper, Ilene, review of *Cajun Home, Booklist,* March 15, 1998, p. 1236.

Cooper, Ilene, review of *County Fair, Booklist,* February 1, 1992, p. 1023.

Review of *Corn Belt Harvest, Kirkus Reviews,* December 1, 1991, p. 1529.

Fader, Ellen, review of *Shaker Home, Horn Book,* May-June, 1994, p. 332.

Marris, Alexandra, review of *Amish Home, School Library Journal,* May, 1993, p. 112.

Review of *Mist over the Mountains, Kirkus Reviews,* February 15, 1997, p. 297.

Phelan, Carolyn, review of *Frontier Home, Booklist,* November 1, 1993, p. 516.

Phelan, Carolyn, review of *Mist over the Mountains, Booklist,* March 1, 1997, p. 1156.

Rochman, Hazel, review of *Corn Belt Harvest, Booklist,* December 15, 1991, p. 761.

Rochman, Hazel, review of *With Needle and Thread, Booklist,* March 1, 1996, p. 1175.

Rochman, Hazel, review of *The Underground Railroad, Booklist,* April 1, 1995, p. 1390.

Review of *The Underground Railroad, Publishers Weekly,* January 16, 1995, p. 455.

Veeder, Mary Harris, review of *Portrait of a Farm Family, Booklist,* September 1, 1995, p. 73.

Watson, Elizabeth S., review of *Portrait of a Farm Family, Horn Book,* November-December, 1995, pp. 759-60.

Weech, Eunice, review of *Where Lincoln Walked, School Library Journal,* February, 1998, p. 94.

Weisman, Kay, review of *Amish Home, Booklist,* February 15, 1993, p. 1055.

Review of *Where Lincoln Walked, Kirkus Reviews,* November 15, 1997, p. 1704.

For More Information See

PERIODICALS

Booklist, September 15, 1997, p. 224; March 1, 1998, p. 1125.

Horn Book, July-August, 1995, p. 474; May-June, 1998, p. 355.

Kirkus Reviews, July 15, 1993, p. 930; July 15, 1995, p. 1021; January 1, 1996, p. 64; February 15, 1998, p. 264.

Publishers Weekly, March 22, 1993, p. 80; December 15, 1997, p. 59.

School Library Journal, March, 1994, pp. 225-26; April, 1995, p. 140; December, 1995, p. 112; June, 1996, p. 134; May, 1997, p. 142; November, 1997, p. 125; December, 1997, p. 120; February, 1999, p. 39.

—*Sketch by J. Sydney Jones*

*   *   *

Francesca Lia Block

BLOCK, Francesca Lia 1962-

Personal

Born December 3, 1962, in Hollywood, CA; daughter of Irving Alexander (a painter) and Gilda (a poet; maiden name, Klein) Block; married Chris Schuette (an actor). *Education:* University of California, Berkeley, B.A., 1986. *Politics:* Democrat. *Hobbies and other interests:* Dance, film, vegetarian cooking.

Addresses

Home—Los Angeles, CA. *Agent*—Lydia Wills Artists Agency, 230 West 55 Street, Suite 29 D, New York, NY 10019.

Career

Writer. *Member:* Authors Guild, Authors League of America, Writers Guild of America, Phi Beta Kappa.

Awards, Honors

Shrout Fiction Award, University of California, Berkeley, 1986; Emily Chamberlain Cook Poetry Award, 1986; Best Books of the Year citation from the American Library Association (ALA), Best of the 1980s list from *Booklist,* YASD Best Book Award, and Recommended Books for Reluctant Young Adult Readers citation, all 1989, all for *Weetzie Bat;* Recommended Books for Reluctant Young Adult Readers citation, 1990, for *Witch Baby;* Best Books of the Year citation from the ALA, Recommended Books for Reluctant Young Adult Readers citation, Best Books citation from the *New York Times,* and Best Fifty Books citation from *Publishers Weekly,* all 1991, all for *Cherokee Bat and the Goat Guys;* Best Books of the Year citations from *School Library Journal* and the ALA, and Recommended Books for Reluctant Young Adult Readers, all 1993, all for *Missing Angel Juan;* and numerous others.

Writings

NOVELS; PUBLISHED BY HARPERCOLLINS

Weetzie Bat, 1989.
Witch Baby, 1990.
Cherokee Bat and the Goat Guys, 1991.
Missing Angel Juan, 1993.
The Hanged Man, 1994.
Baby Be-Bop, 1995.
Girl Goddess #9: Nine Stories, 1996.
Dangerous Angels: The Weetzie Bat Books, 1998.
I Was a Teenage Fairy, 1998.
Violet and Claire, 1999.
The Rose and the Beast, 2000.

POETRY

Moon Harvest, illustrated by Irving Block, Santa Susanna Press, 1978.
Season of Green, illustrated by Irving Block, Santa Susanna Press, 1979.

OTHER

Ecstasia, New American Library, 1993.
Primavera, New American Library, 1994.

(With Hillary Carlip) *Zine Scene,* Girl Press, 1998.
Nymph, Circlet Press, 2000.

Contributor of short stories to anthologies, including *Am I Blue?,* edited by Marion Dane Bauer, 1994; *When I Was Your Age,* edited by Amy Ehrlich, 1994; and *Soft Tar,* a benefit for a global children's organization, 1994. Block has also developed soap operas for the USA and MTV networks. Her books have been translated into seven languages, including French, Italian, German, and Japanese.

Sidelights

Only a few years after her first publication, Francesca Lia Block has already carved out a unique piece of literary turf for herself and the characters she has created. With the publication, in 1989, of *Weetzie Bat,* she set the agenda for a new direction in young adult novels for the nineties: stories of Los Angeles subculture replete with sex, drugs, and rock 'n' roll—stories for adults and young adults alike. With a cast of characters ranging from Weetzie Bat, a punk princess in pink, to her lover, My Secret Agent Lover Man, and her best friend Dirk and *his* boyfriend, to their common off-spring, Witch Baby and Cherokee, Block's novels create postmodernist fairy tales where love and art are the only cures in a world devoid of adult direction. Praised and criticized for her edgy tales of urban adventure, Block is still somewhat in awe of her instant success and of the stir her books are creating. "I wrote *Weetzie Bat* as a sort of valentine to Los Angeles at a time when I was in school in Berkeley and homesick for where I grew up," the author once stated in a *Something about the Author* (*SATA*) interview with J. Sydney Jones. "It was a very personal story. A love letter. I never expected people to respond to it the way they have. I never imagined I could reach other people from such a very personal place in me."

But reach people the stories have. Block's "technicolor lovesong to Los Angeles," as *Publishers Weekly* writer Diane Roback described *Weetzie Bat,* sold steadily through several printings and have been translated into seven languages, including French, Italian, German, and Japanese. There have been three sequels to that original novel and a fourth is in the works, each one focusing on a different character and exploring new variations on the theme of the curative power of love and art. "The whole experience is magical," Block said of the success of her series. And there is something a little magical about Block's life as well. Born in Hollywood, the center of the modern fairy tale industry, she was exposed to the power of art and creativity from an early age. Her parents were both artists: her father, who died in 1986, was a well-known painter and teacher and one-time special effects technician and writer for Hollywood studios; her mother is a poet who once wrote a children's poetry book. "My parents taught me that you could be creative in this world. That it was possible," Block remarked. Books were always part of her life. "I can't remember not having books. There were trips to the library for books and there were books all around our

home. It feels like I was always able to read." In addition to traditional childhood favorites such as Charlotte Zolotow's *Mr. Rabbit and the Lovely Present,* Randall Jarrell's *Animal Family,* and Maurice Sendak's *Where the Wild Things Are,* Block was also greatly influenced by Greek mythology and legend. "My father used to tell me bits of the *Odyssey* for my nighttime story," she recalled. "It was an incredibly rich upbringing."

Creating stories is something that has been with Block from an early age. "I remember walking around the house," she once said, "telling stories to myself. Or sometimes like-minded friends would get together with me and we would make up stories together." This knack for telling stories soon grew into a passion. "I always wanted to be a writer," Block recalled. "Even when I was really small. My mom would write down things I said before I could write them, and that somehow validated my thoughts and expression. Made them worth recording. Soon I was writing short poems." Growing up in the Hollywood area was also an enriching experience for Block, who came into daily contact with the world of art and creative talent. Her family lived in the San Fernando Valley and she attended North Hollywood High, but her fondest memories of the time are after-school activities. "I really pushed myself hard in school, so I didn't enjoy it," she said. "My parents didn't expect or demand it of me; it was just something I felt I had to do. I liked the creative side of school, but largely the experience was unsatisfying."

A teenager in the late 1970s, Block and her friends were fond of going into Hollywood after school. "When I was seventeen years old, my friends and I used to drive through Laurel Canyon after school in a shiny blue vintage Mustang convertible," Block wrote in an article for the *Los Angeles Times Book Review.* "The short distance of the canyon separating us from Hollywood made that city a little enchanted." Once in Hollywood they would hang out at Schwab's soda fountain, check out the street scene with all the punk costumes, cruise Sunset Strip, or frolic at the Farmer's Market. It was on one such trip that Block first saw the prototype of Weetzie: "A punk princess with spiky bleached hair, a very pink '50s prom dress and cowboy boots," as she described her. It was a momentary glimpse of a hitchhiker that stayed with her over the years, and later a name came with the apparition, for she saw a pink Pinto on the freeway with a driver who looked like that hitchhiker and with a license plate spelling "WEETZIE." The character of this punk princess would ferment for another six years before coming to full bloom in Block's first novel. She continually made up stories about Weetzie and drew her innumerable times: Block came to know Weetzie long before she first wrote about her in a novel.

"I lived a little bit of the Weetzie lifestyle in those years," Block once said in an interview. "Being around creative people, a little bit on the edge, listening to bands like X, being a part of the punk scene because it was something different and expressive." But soon the punk scene took on a violent edge with beatings at concerts and punks wearing swastikas, and the specter of AIDS had appeared. Block left Los Angeles to attend college in Berkeley, California, where she fell in love with the modernist poetry of H. D. (Hilda Doolittle) and the magic realism of Colombian novelist Gabriel Garcia Marquez. "College was a very intense time. I took a course with Jayne Walker in modernist poetry my first year and loved its mix of concrete images and classical references." She also took a poetry workshop with Ron Loewinsohn, developing her poetry into short-short stories and then longer short stories, all with a minimalist influence to them. "And then came my father's illness, and I got increasingly homesick for L.A. and stressed out at school," Block remembered. "I started to write *Weetzie* at that time. It's a nostalgic look at that time and place. A sort of therapy for me."

The therapy worked. Block graduated from the University of California and weathered her father's death. She returned to Los Angeles, took a job in a gallery, lived alone, and wrote. It was a very productive time for Block, during which she completed the manuscripts of two novels, as well as several pieces of short fiction. Of course, Block did not think about the "young adult" genre at the time. "I just wrote," she once explained. "I wanted to tell a story and let it find its readers."

In 1989, a friend at the gallery where Block worked, children's illustrator Kathryn Jacobi, read the manuscript of *Weetzie Bat,* was impressed, and sent it off to the writer and editor Charlotte Zolotow at HarperCollins. Zolotow—continuing the magic—liked the book and told Block that she wanted to bring it out as a young adult title. She also encouraged Block to go further with the characters, that there seemed to be more stories there. "I was incredibly lucky that the manuscript went to Charlotte," Block said. "I loved her work as a child and here *she* was responding to mine in return."

Weetzie Bat tells the story of Weetzie and her gay friend Dirk—the only person who seems to understand her—who set up house together in a cottage Dirk's grandmother has left him in Los Angeles. Soon they fill it with a loving extended family (Weetzie Bat's divorced, booze-ridden parents have left a vacuum in this regard). Dirk finds the surfer Duck, Weetzie finds My Secret Agent Lover Man, and even their dog finds a mate. Together they make underground movies and much more. Soon a baby they name Cherokee is born, and the extended family take it as natural that it should belong to all of them. Even the abandoned Witch Baby, reminder of a dalliance My Secret Agent Lover Man has had, is taken in as one of the family. Love is the connecting rod here, the one thing that makes life possible. "I hear that rats shrivel up and die if they aren't like, able to hang out with other rats," Duck says at one point. And this band of punk, hip youth learn that lesson well. "I don't know about happily ever after," Weetzie muses at the end of the book, "but I know about happily."

A modern fairy tale, *Weetzie Bat* blends Block's love of modernist poetry with magical realism—there's a genie granting three wishes and an evil witch—to come up with a potent narrative of love and loyalty in an age of pessimism and AIDS. Using a mixture of L.A. slang and inventive personal hip talk, Block created an "off-beat tale that has great charm, poignancy, and touches of fantasy," wrote Anne Osborn in *School Library Journal.* *New York Times Book Review* contributor Betsy Hearne also praised the author's style: "Block's far-ranging free association has been controlled and shaped into a story with sensual characters. The language is inventive California hip, but the patterns are compactly folkloristic and the theme is transcendent."

In spite of such glowing reviews, the book still caused a minor uproar among other reviewers and some librarians. Patrick Jones, writing in *Horn Book,* summed up and put such criticism into context: "It is not that the sex [in Block's books] is explicit; it is not. It is just that Block's characters *have* sex lives . . . . In the age of AIDS—whose ugly shadow appears—anything less than a 'safe sex or no sex' stance is bound to be controversial." Jones points out that the homosexual relationship between Dirk and Duck was also hard for some reviewers to deal with, as was the communal rearing of the baby, Cherokee. This alternate family lifestyle, so validating for teenager readers whose own lives seldom fit the "Father Knows Best" model, became a sore spot for some. But Block recounted the story of one such critic in her *Los Angeles Times Book Review* article. Having heard of this purportedly perverse book, Frances V. Sedney of the children's department of the Harford, Maryland, County Library read it, then wrote a letter in the novel's defense: "This short novel epitomizes the 'innocent' books where the *reader's* mind and experience make all the crucial difference." *Weetzie Bat* went on to be short-listed for the ALA Best Book of the Year as well making the Recommended Books for the Reluctant Young Adult Reader list.

Following the advice of her editor, Charlotte Zolotow, Block went on to enlarge the stories of other characters from *Weetzie Bat.* In 1990 she published *Witch Baby,* a novel "reminiscent of a music video," Maeve Visser Knoth wrote in *Horn Book.* "Scenes and sensory images flash across the page; characters speak in complicated slang and create a safe haven for themselves in the midst of a shifting, confusing world." Witch Baby stumbles and sometimes crashes through the book, searching for her own identity, trying to understand her place in the scheme of things, looking for an answer to her own poetic question: "What time are we upon and where do I belong?" Witch Baby, endowed with tilted purple eyes and a Medusa head of black hair, collects newspaper clippings of tragedies in an attempt to understand the world. Ultimately Witch Baby is able to find her real mother and then can deal with her place in the extended family of Weetzie Bat. As Ellen Ramsay noted in *School Library Journal,* Block is "a superior writer and has created a superior cast of characters," and in *Witch Baby* she "explores the danger of denying life's pain." This assessment mirrors what the author herself says about her work. "My books talk about tolerance," Block explained, "though I never consciously think of themes like that as I write. I guess my general theme is the value of love and art as healers. That you must face the darkness, acknowledge it and still have hope. I think that is what is important in life."

With the next installment of the Bat family saga, Block further pursued the theme of family loyalty and the importance of love and a balance of spiritual powers in the world. *Cherokee Bat and the Goat Guys* opens with the adults, Weetzie Bat and others, off on a filming expedition in South America. Teenage Cherokee and Witch Baby are left under their own direction and soon they team up with Raphael Chong Jah-Love and Angel Juan Perez to form a rock band, the Goat Guys. These four receive and depend on powerful gifts from a Native American family friend, Coyote, to perform. They are an instant hit, but quickly the euphoria goes to their heads and "everything begins to fly apart in wild and outrageous ways," according to Gail Richmond in *School Library Journal,* as the band loses itself in sex and drugs. "The group descends into the bacchanalian hell of the nightclub scene with tequila and cocaine, skull lamps and lingerie-clad groupies drenched in cow's blood," noted Patty Campbell in a *New York Times Book Review* article. When Angel Juan slashes himself while performing, Cherokee figures it is time to turn in their magic totem gifts to Coyote and "be cleansed of the pain and guilt," according to Campbell. "An emotionally charged story with a contemporary message," Richmond noted, and Roback and Richard Donahue, writing in *Publishers Weekly,* similarly observed: "This latest effort provides yet another delicious and deeply felt trip to Block's wonderfully idiosyncratic corner of California."

It is this very idiosyncratic nature of much of Block's work that has also prompted some criticism. Ramsay praised the quality of Block's work but wondered if she was not "just a tad too Southern California cool for broad appeal." Campbell, in an overview on Block's work in *Horn Book,* argued, however, that "many novels are set in New York, and ... no one thinks those books are strange or labels them as depicting 'an alternate lifestyle' because the characters ride to work on the subway or shop at Bloomingdale's .... Why should the second largest city in the United States be perceived so differently? It is doubly puzzling considering that America sees Los Angeles every night on television."

Puzzling or not, Block moved the action of *Missing Angel Juan* to New York when Witch Baby's boyfriend, Angel Juan, takes off on his own musical career in the Big Apple. Witch Baby misses him and soon follows Angel Juan to New York, and the book is about her search for him—aided by the ghost of Weetzie's father—through the nightmare world of Manhattan. Her search ultimately takes her into the subways of New York, with "strong echoes of Orpheus' descent into Hades," as Michael Cart noted in *School Library Journal.* But in the end Witch Baby realizes she has to leave Angel Juan to find his own way, as she must find hers. "Love will come," she muses, "because it always does, because why else would it exist, and it will make everything hurt a little less. You just have to believe in yourself." Like its predecessors, *Missing Angel Juan* is

"an engagingly eccentric mix of fantasy and reality, enhanced—this time—by mystery and suspense," Cart remarked. And Judy Sasges, writing in *Voice of Youth Advocates,* likewise called the story "imaginative, mystical, and completely engaging."

In *The Hanged Man,* Block looks at the "descent of a woman into madness of a sort," as the author stated. Set in the same L.A. club scenes as the Weetzie books, *The Hanged Man* is about the darker side of life. The story deals with a young woman named Laurel, who is struggling with her emotions in the wake of the death by cancer of her father, with whom she has had an incestuous relationship. "Block's prose moves like a heroin trip through the smog and wet heat, heavy flowers, and velvet grunge of Hollywood," reviewer Vanessa Elder wrote in *School Library Journal.* "There is lots of fairy tale imagery," Block said of the work, "but there is also an ominous side. It's about obsession and being haunted by the past. This time the cure, the healing power, is much more art than love. In that sense I feel I am in a sort of transition in my writing. So much of my earlier stuff was about searching for love, and in fact love was missing in my own life. But now that exists for me. The result is less of a yearning tone in my books."

In 1995, Block returned to the world of Weetzie Bat with the novel *Baby Be-Bop.* This book is actually a prequel to those earlier ones in that it tells the story of Weetzie's friend Dirk, and of how he deals with the realization that he is gay. "What might seem didactic from lesser writers becomes a gleaming gift from Block," a *Publishers Weekly* reviewer wrote. "Her extravagantly imaginative settings and finely honed perspectives remind the reader that there is magic everywhere."

Block's next two books *Girl Goddess #9* and *I Was a Teenage Fairy* deal with similar themes: young people fighting to come to grips with a rapidly changing world and their place in it. *Girl Goddess #9* is a collection of nine short stories about girls, which are arranged chronologically; the first tales in the book are about toddlers, while the last one concerns a young woman entering college. The stories are written in Block's "funky, richly sensual style," Dorie Freebury of *Voice of Youth Advocates* noted, and the characters "are painfully real, facing the challenges of life that can make or break one's spirit."

The novel *I Was a Teenage Fairy* is a modern-day fairy tale about a girl named Barbie who is being pushed into modeling by her mother. The appearance of an acid-tongued, finger-sized fairy named Mab changes Barbie's life and eventually helps her overcome the emotional trauma of being molested by a well-known photographer, whose crime is ignored by the girl's mother. According to a critic in *Publishers Weekly,* "The prose, less obviously lush than in previous books, sustains steady crescendos of insight. This fairy tale is too pointedly a social critique to be entirely magical, but its spell feels real."

Block's next novel, *Violet and Claire,* is the story of the friendship that develops between Violet and Claire, two teenage girls as different as night and day. Seventeen-year-old Violet is an aspiring screenwriter and filmmaker, and an outsider at her high school. Past depression and a suicide attempt have left her hard-edged and isolated; she devotes her time to studying the films she loves and to writing her own screenplay. Then she meets Claire, a poet with glittering gauze fairy wings sewn on the back of her Tinker Bell T-shirt, and the two become fast friends. As the novel unfolds, the friendship between Violet and Claire is tested as the girls are divided by personal ambition and the intrusion of the outside world. Violet is willingly seduced by a rock star, who gets her a job with a screen agent, while Claire enrolls in a poetry workshop and becomes attached to the instructor. The action reaches its peak at a wild party the girls attend after Violet sells a screenplay. Claire flees into the desert, and Violet follows in search of her. "Block excels in depicting strong and supportive friendships between teen girls," wrote Debbie Carton in *Booklist,* "and *Violet and Claire* is at its best when the two protagonists reach past their own pain to help each other." According to a *Kirkus Reviews* critic, "Fans of the author's previous works will take to this one; newcomers will be captured by the rainbow iridescence of Block's prose."

In addition to these books, Block has published two fantasy titles, *Ecstasia* and *Primavera.* "Greek myth plays in these books as well," Block once declared, "and they deal with my eternal theme of art and love as healing forces. They are a longer format, though, with more poetry and actual song lyrics in the text. They are poetic fantasies set in mythic landscapes."

Block plans to continue writing in various fields, including for television and film, but finds particular satisfaction in her HarperCollins titles, which, after the retirement of Zolotow, are now edited by Joanna Cotler and often marketed to young adults. "My books reach readers of all ages," Block told *SATA.* "There is a certain openness and receptivity in young readers. I've found a real depth of feeling from kids who have written to me. It's so hard for these kids in the time of AIDS. And they are still so full of hope, though I see a lot of despair, as well."

"I hope my work is poetic," Block once said. "I want my books to be contemporary fairy tales with edge. And I love the magical realism in my work. It's not as if you can escape the world. You're in the world. You're part of it. But there is solace and hope through the magic. There is something of another world. Hope, but in a grounded way." It is exactly this sense of hope that Block has given her readers and that has led to her success. She has validated their experience by writing about it. "One of the things about *Weetzie Bat* is that it has given readers freedom to take their own contemporary culture and write about it themselves seriously as fiction or poetry. In letters from my readers, I see that I have done something of the same service as my mother did for me writing down my early stories. I have made

this other culture real and worthy. My readers discover it's okay to write about whatever is important to them and do it in a poetic way. Writing has saved my life in a way. Being able to express myself creatively was the way I could survive at certain parts of my life. If I can give others that message, that their lives and experiences are worth writing about, I would be very happy."

Works Cited

Review of *Baby Be-Bop, Publishers Weekly,* July 31, 1995, p. 82.

Block, Francesca Lia, *Weetzie Bat,* HarperCollins, 1989.

Block, Francesca Lia, *Witch Baby,* HarperCollins, 1990.

Block, Francesca Lia, "Punk Pixies in the Canyon," *Los Angeles Times Book Review,* July 26, 1992, pp. 1, 11.

Block, Francesca Lia, *Missing Angel Juan,* HarperCollins, 1993.

Block, Francesca Lia, in a telephone interview with J. Sydney Jones for *Something about the Author,* June 9, 1994.

Campbell, Patty, review of *Cherokee Bat and the Goat Guys, New York Times Book Review,* September 20, 1992, p. 18.

Campbell, Patty, "People Are Talking about . . . Francesca Lia Block," *Horn Book,* January-February, 1993, pp. 57-63.

Cart, Michael, review of *Missing Angel Juan, School Library Journal,* October, 1993, p. 148.

Carton, Debbie, review of *Violet and Claire, Booklist,* September 1, 1999, p. 122.

Elder, Vanessa, review of *The Hanged Man, School Library Journal,* September, 1994, p. 238.

Freebury, Dorie, review of *Girl Goddess #9, Voice of Youth Advocates,* February, 1997, p. 326.

Hearne, Betsy, "Pretty in Punk," *New York Times Book Review,* May 21, 1989, p. 47.

Review of *I Was a Teenage Fairy, Publishers Weekly,* September 21, 1998, p. 86.

Jones, Patrick, "People Are Talking about . . . Francesca Lia Block," *Horn Book,* November-December, 1992, pp. 697-701.

Knoth, Maeve Visser, review of *Witch Baby, Horn Book,* January-February, 1992, pp. 78-79.

Osborn, Anne, review of *Weetzie Bat, School Library Journal,* April, 1989, pp. 116-17.

Ramsay, Ellen, review of *Witch Baby, School Library Journal,* September, 1991, p. 277.

Richmond, Gail, review of *Cherokee Bat and the Goat Guys, School Library Journal,* September, 1992, p. 274.

Roback, Diane, "Flying Starts: Francesca Lia Block," *Publishers Weekly,* December 22, 1989, p. 27.

Roback, Diane, and Richard Donahue, review of *Cherokee Bat and the Goat Guys, Publishers Weekly,* July 20, 1992, p. 251.

Sasges, Judy, review of *Missing Angel Juan, Voice of Youth Advocates,* December, 1993, p. 287.

Review of *Violet and Claire, Kirkus Reviews,* September 15, 1999, p. 1497.

For More Information See

BOOKS

Children's Literature Review, Volume 33, Gale, 1994.

PERIODICALS

Booklist, August, 1992, p. 2004; October 1, 1996, p. 340.
Bulletin of the Center for Children's Books, December, 1993, p. 115; September, 1994, p. 6; October, 1996, p. 49; September, 1999, p. 5.
English Journal, December, 1990, p. 78; October, 1991, pp. 94-95.
Five Owls, January-February, 1999, p. 66.
Horn Book, September-October, 1992, p. 587.
Los Angeles Times Book Review, November 12, 1995, p. 4.
New Yorker, November 25, 1991, p. 148.
New York Times Book Review, January 19, 1992, p. 24; February 26, 1995, p. 21.
Publishers Weekly, March 10, 1989, p. 91; July 18, 1994, pp. 246-47.
School Library Journal, December, 1993, p. 24; September, 1994, p. 238; December, 1998, p. 118; September, 1999, p. 218.
Voice of Youth Advocates, December, 1995, pp. 297-98; February, 1997, p. 326.

*   *   *

BLY, Stephen A(rthur) 1944-

Personal

Born August 17, 1944, in Visalia, CA; son of Arthur Worthington (a farmer) and Alice (a homemaker; maiden name, Wilson) Bly; married Janet Chester (a freelance writer), June 14, 1963; children: Russell, Michael, Aaron. *Education:* Fresno State University, B.A. (summa cum laude), 1971; Fuller Theological Seminary, M. Div., 1974. *Religion:* Christian.

Addresses

Home—P.O. Box 157, Winchester, ID 83555.

Career

Worked as a ranch foreman in central California, 1965-71; ordained to Presbyterian ministry, 1974; youth pastor in Orosi, CA, 1969-70, Los Angeles, CA, 1971-72, Woodlake, CA, and Fillmore, CA; pastor, Winchester, ID, 1981—. lecturer, Moody Bible Institute; member of teaching staff, Mount Hermon Christian Writer's Conference; mayor, city of Winchester, ID, 2000—.

Awards, Honors

Writer of the Year Award, Mount Hermon Writer's Conference, 1982.

Stephen A. Bly

Writings

FOR CHILDREN

The President's Stuck in the Mud and Other Wild West Escapades, illustrated by Scott Gustafson, Chariot Books, 1982.
Quality Living in a Complicated Age, Here's Life, 1984.
Trouble in Quartz Mountain Tunnel, Chariot Books, 1985.
The Land Tamers, Tyndale, 1986.

"NATHAN T. RIGGINS" SERIES; FOR YOUNG ADULTS; PUBLISHED BY CROSSWAY BOOKS

The Dog Who Would Not Smile, 1992.
Coyote True, 1992.
You Can Always Trust a Spotted Horse, 1993.
The Last Stubborn Buffalo in Nevada, 1993.
Never Dance with a Bobcat, 1994
Hawks Don't Say Goodbye, 1994.

"LEWIS AND CLARK SQUAD" SERIES; FOR YOUNG ADULTS; PUBLISHED BY CROSSWAY BOOKS

Intrigue at the Rafter B Ranch, 1997.
The Secret of the Old Rifle, 1997.
Treachery at the River Canyon, 1997.
Revenge on Eagle Island, 1998.
Danger at Deception Pass, 1998.
Hazards of the Half-Court Press, 1998.

"STUART BRANNON" SERIES; PUBLISHED BY CROSSWAY
*   BOOKS*

Hard Winter at Broken Arrow Crossing, 1991.
False Claims at the Little Stephen Mine, 1992.
Last Hanging at Paradise Meadow, 1992.
Standoff at Sunrise Creek, 1993.
Final Justice at Adobe Wells, 1993.
Son of an Arizona Legend, 1993.

"AUSTIN STONER FILES" SERIES; PUBLISHED BY
*   CROSSWAY BOOKS*

The Lost Manuscript of Martin Taylor Harrison, 1995.
The Final Chapter of Chance McCall, 1996.
The Kill Fee of Cindy Lacoste, 1997.

"CODE OF THE WEST" SERIES; PUBLISHED BY CROSSWAY
*   BOOKS*

It's Your Misfortune and None of My Own, 1994.
One Went to Denver and the Other Went Wrong, 1995.
Where the Deer and the Antelope Play, 1995.
Stay Away from That City—They Call It Cheyenne, 1996.
My Foot's in the Stirrup—My Pony Won't Stand, 1996.
I'm Off to Montana for to Throw the Hoolihan, 1997.

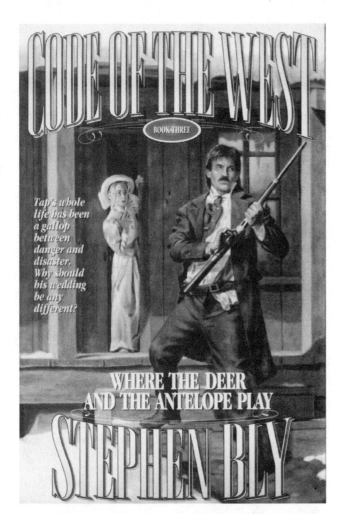

A series of misadventures and mishaps conspire to ruin
the wedding between hapless Tap Andrews and his
forbearing fiancee, Pepper Paige.

"OLD CALIFORNIA" SERIES; PUBLISHED BY CROSSWAY
*   BOOKS*

Red Dove of Monterey, 1998.
The Last Swan in Sacramento, 1999.
Proud Quail of the San Joaquin, 2000.

"HEROINES OF THE GOLDEN WEST" SERIES; PUBLISHED
*   BY CROSSWAY BOOKS*

Sweet Carolina, 1998.
The Marquesa, 1998.
Miss Fontenot, 1999.

"FORTUNES OF THE BLACK HILLS" SERIES

Beneath a Dakota Cross, Broadman & Holman, 1999.
Shadow of Legends, Broadman & Holman, 2000.

WITH WIFE, JANET BLY

Devotions with a Difference, Moody Press, 1982, revised
    edition published as *Winners and Losers: Quiet Times
    Between Teens and God,* Moody Press, 1993.
Questions I'd Like to Ask, Moody Press, 1982.

"CRYSTAL" SERIES; WITH JANET BLY; PUBLISHED BY
*   CHARIOT BOOKS*

Crystal's Perilous Ride, 1986.
Crystal's Solid Gold Discovery, 1986.
Crystal's Blizzard Trek, 1986.
Crystal's Grand Entry, 1986.
Crystal's Mill Town Mystery, 1986.
Crystal's Rodeo Debut, 1986.

"HIDDEN WEST" SERIES; WITH JANET BLY; PUBLISHED
*   BY SERVANT PUBLICATIONS*

Fox Island, 1996.
Copper Hill, 1997.
Columbia Falls, 1998.

FOR ADULTS

Radical Discipleship, Moody, 1981.
God's Angry Side, Moody, 1982, revised edition published
    as *The Surprising Side of Grace,* Discovery House,
    1994.
How to Be a Good Dad, Moody, 1986.
(With Janet Bly) *How to Be a Good Mom,* Moody Press,
    1988.
(With Janet Bly) *How to Be a Good Grandparent,* Moody
    Press, 1990.
Just Because They've Left Doesn't Mean They're Gone,
    Focus on the Family, 1993, paperback edition pub-
    lished as *Once a Parent, Always a Parent,* Tyndale,
    1998.

Work in Progress

"The Carson City Chronicles" series (historical/Western
fiction) with Janet Bly for Servant Publications, *Judith
and the Judge, Marthellen and the Major,* and *Roberta
and the Renegade,* all due in 2000; "The Goldfield
Skinners" series for Crossway Books, *Fool's Gold* and
Buried Treasure, due in 2000-2001. Also Sarah Connor's "Oregon Trail" series for elementary age readers,
and a Western history for a children's fiction series for
Crossway Books.

In Bly's first book in his series about strong female pioneers, Carolina Cantrell travels to the Montana Territory to settle the estate of her dead brother and finds herself battling gold rush fever, a cheating partner, and the emotional upheaval of a new love. (Cover illustration by Dan Brown.)

Sidelights

Stephen A. Bly is a prolific author of Christian-related books which include not only nonfiction inspirational and self-help works, but also a large collection of fiction in genres ranging from historical Westerns to contemporary detective novels. Bly, who worked as a ranch foreman before becoming ordained as a Presbyterian minister in 1974, has penned series for both juvenile and adult readers, though young adults can appreciate all his works. Written specifically for a preteen audience are his Western series "Nathan T. Riggins" and an adventure series featuring a basketball team, the "Lewis and Clark Squad" series. For readers of all ages he has created several popular Western series, including "Stuart Brannon," "Code of the West," "Heroines of the Golden West," and "Old California." His "Austin Stoner Files" is a series built around contemporary mysteries, as is the "Hidden West," written with his wife, Janet Bly, which features a fictional husband and wife writing team who also solve mysteries. With his wife, Bly has also written

a juvenile Western series featuring the plucky young heroine, Crystal. With more than sixty works to his credit, Bly has blended a Christian message with genre fiction to create popular and believable books.

"My writing career is indebted to the inspiration and guidance of seminars taught at Mount Hermon Writer's Conferences," Bly once told *Something about the Author* (*SATA*). "Much of my writing relates directly to Christian readers. I also have an interest in nineteenth-century western historical writings." Born in California, Bly was a pastor at several locations before moving to Idaho, where he is pastor at a community church and a full-time writer. Encouraged by his wife, a freelance writer, to write a magazine article in 1976, Bly now is a full-time wordsmith, writing two or more projects simultaneously, heavily researching and then rewriting each book up to six or seven times.

An early collaborative effort from Bly and his wife, the "Crystal" series includes six books featuring fourteen-year-old Crystal Blake, whose adventures in the West span the gamut from discovering a buried treasure to foiling a robbery at a rodeo. Along the way, Christian values of faith and prayer come in handy for the young girl. In *Crystal's Perilous Ride,* the heroine and her friend Megan accompany Crystal's father on a trip to Idaho, where they find themselves investigating a series of strange occurrences in a small town. The leading citizens of the town are actually a notorious gang, and Crystal and company become involved in a robbery at the rodeo. In *Crystal's Rodeo Debut,* she tries out for the high school rodeo team during her first week in her new home in Winchester, Idaho, and with new friend Betsy Jo discovers a lost treasure, a cache of gold buried in a local valley in 1902. Another treasure is uncovered in *Crystal's Solid Gold Discovery,* and its discovery helps her and her father take care of a would-be swindler.

Reviewing all three of these titles in *School Library Journal,* Gayle W. Berge noted, "Rapid plot development and action on every page quickly move readers through each of these Western mysteries. Crystal Blake is a modern Christian girl who just happens to be in the right place at the right time for adventure and excitement." Berge went on to conclude, "These are innocent romances spiked with predictable drama."

In *Crystal's Blizzard Trek,* rivals on a high school rodeo team learn to deal with each other when they are snowed in by a high mountain blizzard in Montana. Crystal's trusted horse, Caleb, is stolen just before the state high school rodeo finals in *Crystal's Grand Entry,* and when Crystal, her sister, and friends mount a search for the animal they come into contact with terrorists. With *Crystal's Mill Town Mystery,* a locked safe in a burned-out lumber mill attracts the attention not only of Crystal and her friends, but also of some other unsavory characters. Charlene Strickland, reviewing these three titles in *School Library Journal,* called the series a "[b]lend of Nancy Drew mystery with horse story" with "a dash each of Christian precepts and 'The Girls of Canby Hall'" thrown in, all transported to Idaho.

Strickland concluded, "The frequent mention of the Lord and Crystal's reliance on prayer might increase the series' appeal to some readers."

Writing on his own, Bly penned another six-book series with his "Stuart Brannon" books set in the late nineteenth century and beginning with *Hard Winter at Broken Arrow Crossing.* Brannon is wandering in the Colorado mountains during a blizzard with a horse near death. Luckily he comes on what appears to be a deserted cabin where he takes shelter only to discover a wounded miner inside. Brannon, a Christian in action, takes care of the man as well as he can, and soon these two are joined by a pregnant Indian girl who has been severely beaten and who delivers a baby just in time for Christmas. Add to this plot stew a gang of gold-hungry ruffians and some eccentric foreigners hoping to get a jump on the spring gold rush, and you have a recipe that "will keep the young reader captivated for hours," according to Pam Hurley in *Voice of Youth Advocates.* Hurley also noted that the "reader can experience the harsh environment through the excellent writing of Bly."

More of Brannon's adventures can be found in *Standoff at Sunrise Creek,* where the morally upright Brannon finds himself in an actual historical incident, the Yavapai County War in Arizona, which started when settlers tried to steal Apache land by using forged Spanish land grants. "There's a lot of shooting," remarked John Mort in *Booklist,* "but the bad guys are *very* bad, and Brannon often prays for a more peaceful world." Mort went on to note that Bly, a rancher and minister, "does a lot of things right for the traditional Western," and that his telling details in everything from weather to guns convinces the reader that he "clearly knows the country he writes about."

Bly's "Code of the West" series features gunfighter Tap Andrews and his fiancee (who later becomes his wife), Pepper Paige. With *Where the Deer and the Antelope Play,* the third book, a series of misadventures conspire to ruin the young couple's wedding plans. There are outlaws and cattle rustlers, a fire at a brothel, and a dispute over the ownership of the Andrews ranch. "Believing that God will provide for them and direct their paths, Andrews and Paige endure these interruptions with faith, hope, and love," commented Henry Carrigan, Jr., in *Library Journal.* Carrigan went on to comment, "Despite the stock characters found in any Western ... the novel carries the reader through the simple plot with great good humor."

With *My Foot's in the Stirrup—My Pony Won't Stand,* Tap and Pepper are newlyweds and the new groom has had enough of being a shooting target. However, his gunslinger reputation won't allow him to simply hang up his guns. A new job escorting a man to Texas turns out to be a gun-for-hire position, and Tap must wrestle with his conscience "to do God's will and provide for his growing family," according to Melissa Hudak in *Library Journal.* Hudak also noted, "Fans of former gunslinger Tap Andrews and his new wife, Pepper, won't be disappointed with this fifth entry in the popular ...

series.... [T]his is a fast-moving Western adventure with touches of romance and humor."

Another Western series from Bly features strong female protagonists who helped settle the country. Bly's "Heroines of the Golden West" series begins with *Sweet Carolina* in which Carolina Cantrell travels to Montana Territory to settle the estate of her dead brother only to discover that his partner is trying to cheat her. She determines to stick it out and fight for what is hers, and when the handsome Ranahan Parks comes to town, she is happy she stayed on. Carolina's faith in God helps her to weather the storms of her life, including the changes wrought to her small town by the gold rush. Hudak, writing in *Library Journal,* had positive words for this new series: "Romantic and action elements mingle well in this oldie that inaugurates a series." The series continues with *The Marquesa* and *Miss Fontenot.* The latter deals with a woman's dreams of becoming a photographer in the Montana of the late 1800s. Oliole Fontenot pursues this dream despite the cultural climate of the times, but when she meets a charming fellow it

Oliole Fontenot dreams of becoming a photographer in late 1800s Montana and trusts that her faith in God will help in the agonizing choice she has to make between a husband and a career. (Cover illustration by Dan Brown.)

seems she must choose between her career and him. "Of special interest is the unusual portrayal of a highly independent yet deeply religious woman who knows her own mind and isn't afraid to express her thoughts and feelings," commented *Library Journal* critic Hudak in her review of this third title in the series.

More contemporary in tone and content is Bly's "Austin Stoner Files" series, featuring the adventures of editor Lynda Dawn Austin and the trail guide, Brady Stoner. In the three books of this series, the unlikely duo, in pursuit of a missing manuscript, encounter all sorts of rogues and villains. Reviewing *The Final Chapter of Chance McCall*, the second title in the three-part series, *Library Journal* contributor Carrigan concluded that "Bly deftly fashions a comic tale of human greed and human potential."

Bly combines a busy literary life with involvement in his community and love of things Western. He actively pursues the three R's of the West—riding, roping, and rodeo—and is also working on a false-front Western village, Broken Arrow Crossing, that he is constructing at his home in Idaho. A frequent speaker at schools, Bly advises young writers on the most important elements in a good novel: "Good descriptions, good characters, good intensity, good focus, good plot, and great dialogue. The only unimportant part," Bly told *SATA*, "is the author's bio blurb."

Works Cited

Berge, Gayle W., review of *Crystal's Perilous Ride, School Library Journal,* fall, 1987, p. 76.
Carrigan, Henry, Jr., review of *The Final Chapter of Chance McCall,* June 1, 1996, p. 90.
Carrigan, Henry, Jr., review of *Where the Deer and the Antelope Play, Library Journal,* September 1, 1995, p. 156.
Hudak, Melissa, review of *Miss Fontenot, Library Journal,* April 1, 1999, p. 79.
Hudak, Melissa, review of *My Foot's in the Saddle—My Pony Won't Stand, Library Journal,* November 1, 1996, p. 52.
Hudak, Melissa, review of *Sweet Carolina, Library Journal,* April 1, 1998, p. 74.
Hurley, Pam, review of *Hard Winter at Broken Arrow Crossing, Voice of Youth Advocates,* February, 1992, pp. 368-69.
Mort, John, review of *Standoff at Sunrise Creek, Booklist,* February 1, 1993, p. 969.
Strickland, Charlene, review of *Crystal's Blizzard Trek, School Library Journal,* March, 1987, p. 153.

For More Information See

PERIODICALS

Booklist, June 1, 1998, p. 1728.
Library Journal, February 1, 1996, p. 64; June 1, 1996, p. 90; November 1, 1996, p. 52.

Voice of Youth Advocates, February, 1994, p. 364; April, 1996, p. 24; October, 1996, p. 205; August, 1998, p. 192.

—*Sketch by J. Sydney Jones*

*   *   *

BRADLEY, Marion Zimmer 1930-1999 (Elfrida Rivers, John Dexter, Lee Chapman, Miriam Gardner, Morgan Ives, Valerie Graves)

OBITUARY NOTICE—See index for *SATA* sketch: Born June 3, 1930, in Albany, NY; died of a heart attack, September 25, 1999, in Berkeley, CA. Science fiction and fantasy writer, editor. Marion Zimmer Bradley began writing science fiction in pulp magazines of the 1950s, and in 1958, her *Planet Savers,* which was the first of twenty-one books in her popular Darkover fantasy series, was published. *The Shattered Chain,* her most popular Darkover novel, was published in 1976. She won the Leigh Brackett Memorial Sense of Wonder Award in 1978 for her novel *The Forbidden Tower,* and *The Mists of Avalon,* Bradley's best-selling revision of the Arthurian legends, earned her the *Locus* Award for best fantasy novel in 1984. Under various pseudonyms, she often contributed to anthologies and periodicals such as *Magazine of Fantasy and Science Fiction* and *Amazing Stories.* In addition to editing several collections of short stories based on her Darkover series, she also served as editor of the annual anthology *Sword and Sorceress,* and was editor of her own fantasy magazine.

OBITUARIES AND OTHER SOURCES:

PERIODICALS

Los Angeles Times, September 30, 1999, p. A24.
New York Times, September 29, 1999, p. A25.
Washington Post, October 3, 1999, p. C6.*

*   *   *

BROWN, Reeve Lindbergh
See LINDBERGH, Reeve

*   *   *

BUCHANAN, Paul 1959-

Personal

Born October 4, 1959, in Belfast, Northern Ireland; son of William (a mechanical engineer) and Ruth (a homemaker; maiden name, Lowry) Buchanan; married Revelation Versoza (a university administrator), August 15, 1981; children: William Ryan, Heather, Dylan. *Education:* Biola University, B.A., 1981; University of California, Riverside, M.A., 1985; University of Southern California, M.P.W., 1997. *Politics:* Democrat. *Religion:* Presbyterian.

Paul Buchanan

Addresses

Home—24191 Adonis St., Mission Viejo, CA 92691.
Office—Department of English, Biola University, 13800
Biola Ave., La Mirada, CA 90639. *Agent*—Mary Jack
Wald, 111 East 14th St., New York, NY 10003. *E-mail*—paul_buchanan@peter.biola.edu.

Career

Biola University, La Mirada, CA, assistant professor of
English, 1996—. *Member:* International PEN, Society of
Children's Book Writers and Illustrators.

Writings

Uncle from Another Planet (based on an idea by Buchanan
    and Rod Randall), Broadman & Holman (Nashville,
    TN), 1999.
Wild Ride on Bigfoot Mountain (based on an idea by
    Buchanan and Randall), Broadman & Holman, 1999.

Dances with Werewolves, Broadman & Holman, 2000.

"THE MISADVENTURES OF WILLIE PLUMMET" SERIES;
    WITH ROD RANDALL

Invasion from Planet X, Concordia (St. Louis, MO), 1998.
Anything You Can Do I Can Do Better, Concordia, 1998.
Battle of the Bands, Concordia, 1998.
The Rat That Ate Poodles, Broadman & Holman, 1998.
Hail to the Chump, Concordia, 1998.
The Monopoly, Concordia, 1998.
Ballistic Bugs, Concordia, 1998.
Gold Flakes for Breakfast, Concordia, 1998.
Shooting Stars, Concordia, 1998.
Submarine Sandwiched, Concordia, 1998.
Tidal Wave, Concordia, 1998.
Ask Willie, Concordia, 1999.
Dog Days, Concordia, 1999.
Heads I Win, Tails You Lose, Concordia, 1999.
Stuck on You, Concordia, 1999.
Friend or Foe?, Concordia, 2000.
Brain Freeze, Concordia, 2000.

Adaptations

The books *Welcome to Camp Creeps* and *The Mysterious Treasure of the Slimy Sea Cave,* written by Rod
Randall and published by Broadman & Holman in 1998
and 1999 respectively, were based on ideas by Randall
and Buchanan.

Work in Progress

If Roses Never Faded, a novel based on the life of Emily
Dickinson.

Sidelights

Paul Buchanan told *SATA:* "While a student in the
graduate writing program at the University of Southern
California, I met Ben Masselink, who became my good
friend and mentor. Masselink, who also wrote extensively
for television, published several young adult novels.
Under his influence I began experimenting with children's literature. I sold my first children's novels while I
was a student in that program.

"While publishing children's novels, I also studied
children's literature as an academic specialty and now
teach that subject (and creative writing) at Biola
University.

"In my work, and in my reading, I am especially
interested in how matters of faith and moral reasoning
influence the lives of characters. Adele Griffin, author of
Sons of Liberty and *Split Just Right,* is my hero."

C–D

CAPES, Bernard (Edward Joseph) 1854-1918

Personal

Born August 30, 1854, in London, England; died November 2, 1918; son of Fredrick Capes (proctor of Doctor's Commons); married; children: three. *Education:* Attended Slade School, London, England, 1870s. *Religion:* Catholic.

Career

Worked in a tea broker's office during the 1870s; worked for publishers Eglington and Company, 1888; *Theatre* magazine, co-editor, 1890, editor, 1891-92; journalist and novelist, 1892-1918.

Awards, Honors

Second place in *Chicago Record* contest, 1896.

Writings

The Mill of Silence, Rand, McNally (Chicago, IL), 1896.
Adventures of the Comte de la Muette during the Reign of Terror, Dodd, Mead (New York City), 1898.
The Lake of Wine, Appleton (New York City), 1898.
The Mysterious Singer, Arrowsmith (Bristol, England), 1898.
At a Winter's Fire, Doubleday & McClure (New York City), 1899.
Our Lady of Darkness, Dodd, Mead, 1899.
From Door to Door: A Book of Romances, Fantasies, Whimsies, and Levities, Stokes (New York City), 1900.
Joan Brotherhood, Pearson (Edinburgh, Scotland), 1900.
Love Like a Gipsy: A Romance, Constable (Edinburgh, Scotland), 1901.
Plots, Methuen (London, England), 1902.
A Castle in Spain: Certain Memoirs of Robin Lois, Ex-Major of His Majesty's 109th Regiment of Foot, Smith, Elder (London, England), 1903.
The Secret in the Hill, Smith, Elder, 1903.

The Extraordinary Confession of Diana Please, Methuen, 1904.
A Jay of Italy, Methuen, 1905.
The Romance of Lohengrin, Founded on Wagner's Opera, Page (Boston, MA), 1905.
Loaves and Fishes, Methuen, 1906.
A Rogue's Tragedy, Methuen, 1906.
Bembo: A Tale of Italy, Dutton (New York City), 1906.
The Great Skene Mystery, Methuen, 1907.
The Green Parrot, Smith, Elder, 1908.
Amaranthus: A Book of Little Songs, Unwin (London, England), 1908.
The Love Story of St. Bel, Methuen, 1909.
Historical Vignettes, Stokes, 1910.
Jemmy Abercraw, Brentano's (New York City), 1910.
Why Did He Do It?, Brentano's, 1910.
The Will and the Way, John Murray (London, England), 1910.
Gilead Balm, Knight Errant: His Adventures in Search of the Truth, Baker & Taylor (New York City), 1911.
The House of Many Voices, Unwin, 1911.
Jessie Bazley, Nelson (Edinburgh, Scotland), 1913.
Bag and Baggage, Constable (London, England), 1913.
The Pot of Basil, Constable, 1913.
The Story of Fifine, Constable, 1914.
The Fabulists, Mills & Boon (London, England), 1915.
If Age Could, Duckworth (London, England), 1916.
Moll Davis: A Comedy, Allen & Unwin, 1916.
Where England Sets Her Feet: A Romance, Collins (London, England), 1918.
The Skeleton Key, Doran (New York City), 1920.

Contributor to periodical publications, including *Blackwood's Magazine, Cornhill Magazine, Current Literature,* and *Living Age.*

Sidelights

British-born Bernard Capes was a prolific, popular writer of the late nineteenth century. Though Capes cranked out stories for a living, he also added unusual touches to his fiction that placed him somewhat above the level of other penny dreadful writers. As G. K.

Chesterton noted in his introduction to Capes' *The Skeleton Key* (1920): "It may seem a paradox to say that [Capes] was insufficiently appreciated because he did popular things well. But it is true to say that he always gave a touch of distinction to a detective story or a tale of adventure; and so gave it where it was not valued, because it was not expected." Capes is still best remembered as a diligent producer of spicy reading material for the public. He was also prolific, as Carolyn Mathews noted in an essay for *Dictionary of Literary Biography:* "[I]n the course of a writing career that spanned little more than twenty years, Capes published twenty-nine novels, six collections of short fiction, a book of children's poetry, and more than fifty stories and essays."

Bernard Edward Joseph Capes was born on August 30, 1854, in London, England. His father, Fredrick Capes, was a proctor of Doctor's Commons, as was his father before him. But the family had an artistic streak as well. Fredrick Capes often published articles about artwork, and Fredrick's brother, John Moore Capes, wrote both fiction and opera. Capes attended Beaumont College, where he excelled in literary studies, but after school his career wandered aimlessly. A job as a clerk led nowhere, and other businesses left little impression. Eventually, he decided to study art at the recently founded Slade School in London.

The Slade School contributed to Capes's aesthetic, though it trained his visual skills rather than his writing abilities. In both his visual artwork and his books, however, he followed the school's reverence for originality and imagination. As Mathews explained, "the role of imagination and the development of individual style were to be [Capes'] main concerns as a writer. While much of his short fiction implicitly explores imagination as a component of the ghastly or fantastic in experience, stories such as 'A Danse—Macabre,' collected in *From Door to Door: A Book of Romances, Fantasies, Whimsies, and Levities,* explicitly draw on philosophical discussions of the imagination." Indeed, some of the most attractive aspects of Capes' work were precisely these reflections on the nature of creativity and style. After his studies at Slade, Capes worked briefly for a publishing company—even editing *Theatre* magazine for its last year—but eventually settled into the profession of a popular writer.

As Brian Stableford commented in the *St. James Guide to Horror, Ghost & Gothic Writers,* "Capes turned to writing in middle age, having already tried his hand at several very various careers. He regarded it as one more trade to be tried and was unashamedly professional in his approach." Capes published rapidly: serialized mystery stories, historical romances, and some fairly creepy ghost stories. Stableford shrugged, "Many of his short stories are mundane thrillers and romances, but he did take advantage of the relative acceptability of supernatural elements in short fiction. Perhaps he did so simply because such devices allowed him a convenient extra turn of the melodramatic screw, but it is probably that—as with many late Victorian and Edwardian writers of ghost stories—these seemingly arbitrary elements gave his private sentiments their freest expression."

Capes' job, however, was to produce pages upon pages of genre fiction, and he did so thoroughly. In 1898, two years after his first published book, Capes published three books: *Adventures of the Comte de la Muette during the Reign of Terror, The Lake of Wine,* and *The Mysterious Singer.* In 1899, he produced two more volumes: *At a Winter's Fire* and *Our Lady of Darkness.* On average, Capes produced two or three books per year, though in 1910 he published four: *Historical Vignettes, Jemmy Abercraw, Why Did He Do It?,* and *The Will and the Way.* Because of this hectic pace, critics suggest the overall quality of his work often suffered. Capes' flashes of brilliance among largely mundane prose is seen by many as a result of his prolific output. As Stableford suggested, "Capes's fiction is often careless and sometimes crude, but this was a failure—or perhaps a refusal—to exercise a capacity for stylishness that he undoubtedly possessed. It seems likely that he was a one-draft writer who thought it unprofitable to waste time in careful revision. His fertile imagination worked on its own to produce memorable imagery and curiously touching resolutions."

But Capes consistently produced novels marked by his own style. That style often led him into difficulties with readers, though he insisted upon writing in his own voice anyway. In *The Green Parrot,* for example, his hero John Wisdom, a brilliant writer who is terribly misunderstood by readers and critics, remarks: "The public ... wanted neither art nor stories. They were both out of date .... The critics, for the most part, did not want them either .... One thing there was which they seldom regarded, and that was style; or if they did mention it, it was with some impatient disparagement, as a thing bothering and unnecessary."

Capes' insistence on his own style led him to include creepy, even uncanny moments in which artwork becomes a sort of phantom presence that haunts the living. In "The Marble Hands," for example, a young woman dies after paying a sculptor to craft a model of her hands; the narrator of the story puts his own hand on this model after the girl's death, only to experience "a period of horror and blankness—of crawling, worm-threaded immurements and heaving bones—and then at last the blessed daylight." In "The Cursing Bell," too, a woman is made wretched by the tolling of a bell nearby. "The Queer Picture" involves a murder that can only be discovered by looking at the murdered artist's work. "The Operation" tells the horrible story of a brilliant, blind artist whose work is ruined by the restoration of her sight. At times, Capes seems to be commenting on theories of art for art's sake by showing the detrimental consequences of separating art from any other human values. Mathews declared that "Capes departs from the philosophy of aesthetes such as Walter Pater, who declared the supreme value of beauty .... Capes ... pulls in passages of realism to depict the horror of war. This atypical realism, as well as Capes's creation of a most unsympathetic character in the artist, undercuts the philosophy of art for art's sake central to aestheticism."

Toward the end of his life, Capes' resolute insistence on writing in his own style won him the critics' regard. Writing in *Dial*, William M. Payne applauded Capes' 1906 *Bembo: A Tale of Italy,* saying that "Mr. Capes has produced in this moving and opulent work something that comes near to being a masterpiece." An *Atheneum* critic, too, praised the work, saying: "Not even Mr. Hewlett has so successfully reproduced the mediaeval atmosphere. The whole characterization is of a piece with the swing and virility of the style. It is a fine work, and reaches the high-water marks of living romance."

Capes wrote his own style of unique genre fiction until the end of his life in 1918. Though he may have been snubbed for his "distinctive touches" at first, he eventually won over his readership. His own original style, which Chesterton predicted would be lost to time, nonetheless raised the quality of genre fiction in the earliest years of the twentieth century.

Works Cited

Review of *Bembo: A Tale of Italy, Atheneum,* August 19, 1905.

Capes, Bernard, *The Green Parrot,* Smith, Elder, 1908.

Chesterton, G. K., author of introduction, *The Skeleton Key,* Doran, 1920.

Mathews, Carolyn, *Dictionary of Literary Biography, Volume 156: British Short-Fiction Writers, 1880-1914: The Romantic Tradition,* Gale, 1992.

Payne, William M., review of *Bembo: A Tale of Italy,* Dial, September 1, 1906.

Stableford, Brian, "Bernard Capes," *St. James Guide to Horror, Ghost & Gothic Writers,* St. James, 1998.

For More Information See

BOOKS

Cox, Michael, and R. A. Gilbert, editors, *Victorian Ghost Stories: An Oxford Anthology,* Oxford University Press, 1991.

Harris, Wendell V., *British Short Fiction in the Nineteenth Century,* Wayne State University Press, 1991.

Reginald, Robert, *Science Fiction & Fantasy Literature, 1975-1991,* Gale, 1992.

PERIODICALS

Chicago Record, April 24, 1896, p. 8.*

*   *   *

CHAPMAN, Lee
See BRADLEY, Marion Zimmer

COOKSON, Catherine (McMullen) 1906-1998 (Catherine Marchant)

OBITUARY NOTICE—See index for *SATA* sketch: Born June 20, 1906, in Tyne Dock, South Shields, England; died June 11, 1998, in Jesmond Dene, England. Novelist. Cookson's hardscrabble life began in the northeast part of England where she was the illegitimate daughter of a drunken mother and father she never knew. She believed her father was a gentleman and thought she should act accordingly as a lady. This led to her reading voraciously and taking elocution lessons to improve herself, all the while fetching beer for her mother from the local pub or taking items to hock at a pawnshop. When she was old enough to leave home she headed for the seaside town of Hastings, where she bought a home with her meager salary as a laundress and opened a rooming house for men. One of her boarders, teacher Tom Cookson, caught her eye and they married in 1940. Three miscarriages and a stillborn resulted in a nearly crippling depression for Cookson, and her husband suggested she start writing to work through her grief. Her first book, *Kate Hannigan,* was published in 1950 and after that she averaged two books a year. Most of her stories are set in the area where she grew up, and feature salty characters one might find near the docks and beach where she spent her youth. Two of Cookson's best-known books are *Our Kate: An Autobiography* and *Katie Mulholland,* both published in the late 1960s. Other popular books include *The Glass Virgin, The Dwelling Place* and the *Mallen* novels trilogy. In addition to her adult novels, she wrote several books for young people, including *Matty Doolin* (1965), *Joe and the Gladiator* (1968), *The Nipper* (1970), *Blue Baccy* (1972), and *Our John Willie* (1974). She also wrote several books under the pseudonym Catherine Marchant. Two of her works were made into movies for television and by the time of her death she was one of England's most-read authors. Her books made up one-third of the most-borrowed from English libraries and by 1997 she had written nine out of ten books on the most-circulated list. Her last book is expected to be published in 2000. Her more than 90 titles have sold over 100 million copies.

OBITUARIES AND OTHER SOURCES:

PERIODICALS

Chicago Tribune, June 12, 1998, sec. 1, p. 12.
Los Angeles Times, June 12, 1998, p. A22.
New York Times, June 12, 1998, p. A19.
Times (London; electronic), June 12, 1998.
Washington Post, June 12, 1998, p. C9.*

*   *   *

CRAIG, Kit
See REED, Kit

DALE, Gary
See REECE, Colleen L.

*   *   *

DEXTER, John
See BRADLEY, Marion Zimmer

*   *   *

DRAGISIC, Patricia

Personal

Born in Chicago, IL; daughter of Nick P. (a machinist) and Georgiana (a retail sales manager; maiden name, Eckstein) Dragisic. *Education:* Northwestern University, B.S. *Hobbies and other interests:* Reading, viewing and studying films, travel (especially Honolulu, London, and New York City).

Addresses

Home—860 North Dewitt, No. 908, Chicago, IL 60611. *Office*—American Medical Association, 515 North State St., Chicago, IL 60610. *E-mail*—Pat_Dragisic@ama-assn.org.

Career

Encyclopaedia Britannica, Chicago, IL, yearbook editor, 1966-73; *World Book* (encyclopedia), Chicago, senior editor, 1977-81; freelance editor and writer, 1981-90; American Medical Association, Chicago, managing editor of consumer books, 1990—. Mayor's Committee on New Residents, tutor in reading, 1967-68; *Come for to Sing,* member of board of directors, 1973-81; Chicago Public Library, Chicago, docent, 1992-98.

Writings

How to Write a Letter, F. Watts (Danbury, CT), 1998.

Work in Progress

Research on Jane Austen and today's students and on film and communication.

Sidelights

Patricia Dragisic told *SATA:* "When my idea for the book *How to Write a Letter* was accepted for the Franklin Watts series 'Speak Out, Write On,' one of my main goals was to help students love writing, if possible. For this reason, I used humor and a light touch in the sample phrases and sentences, and also in the sample letters. Having edited a number of English textbooks as a freelancer, I noticed that many, or most, are still very dry and dull-sounding; I wanted to write something livelier, long having admired the writing of Karen Elizabeth Gordon in *The Transitive Vampire.*

Patricia Dragisic

"In the same vein, I provided a chapter on letters by famous people and letters in literature to give students some samples of great writing. Diversity being an essential component in teaching every subject, I included letters from writers including Frederick Douglass, African-American abolitionist and writer; Jose Maria Morelos, the first president of Mexico; and several women, including my favorite writer, Jane Austen. Many students read and love science fiction, so I also included two quotations from an epistolary novel by Gordon R. Dickson.

"On a practical level, the major goal was to give students the skills they need to write business letters and personal letters of all kinds, including e-mails. When a student wants to apply for a job or write to a college for information, he or she can use *How to Write a Letter* for guidance on the format of cover letters and resumes. I also included sample letters that might be useful in adult literacy classes—for example, complaint letters or letters to the editor. This book also contains tips on how to research topics in the library—for example, companies where you might like to work. The information on research reflects not only my own experiences as a writer and editor, but also the ideas I have gleaned from volunteering at the Chicago Public Library, where I helped to point students and adults toward the information they needed or wanted. Most people love to pick up a telephone to communicate, but letter-writing skills will always be useful and necessary."

For More Information See

PERIODICALS

Booklist, November 15, 1998, p. 578.
School Library Journal, January, 1999, p. 138.

G

GADD, Jeremy 1949-

Personal

Born November 25, 1949, in Dartford, England; son of David Henry Edgar (a university administrator) and Elsie Mary (a homemaker; maiden name, Lomas) Gadd; married Sarah Grant, August 6, 1974 (marriage ended March 7, 1999); children: (from previous relationship) Linda Fagan. *Education:* Attended Sydney Technical College, 1969; National Institute of Dramatic Art, 1970-71, B.D.A., 1996; University of New England, M.A. (Honors), 1998. *Politics:* "Apolitical leaning conserva-

Jeremy Gadd

tive." *Religion:* Church of England. *Hobbies and other interests:* Camping, reading.

Addresses

Home—New South Wales, Australia. *Office*—P.O. Box 1437, Bondi Junction, New South Wales 2022, Australia. *E-mail*—jgadd@one.net.au.

Career

Theatrical practitioner in England and Australia, including work as touring stage manager for Bunraku Japanese National Puppet Theatre, company manager for West Australian Ballet, lighting operator for the original production of *The Rocky Horror Show* at Royal Court Theatre Upstairs, London, production manager for Marian Street Theatre, Sydney, Australia, stage manager at Shakespearean Globe Theatre project, London, stage manager of National Theatre of Great Britain, assistant director of Yvonne Arnaud Theatre in Surrey, England, founding director of Off Broadway Theatre in Sydney, and affiliate of Australian Elizabethan Theatre Trust, all during 1972-87; writer, 1987—. J & S Gadd Pty. Ltd., director, 1980-98; researcher and compiler of national database of Australian Physical Theater groups, 1985-1999; Australian Research Council, 1999—. *Member:* Fellowship of Australian Writers.

Awards, Honors

Ian Mudie Literary Award, Fellowship of Australian Writers, 1989; second prize, International Science Fiction and Fantasy Poetry Competition, Maplecon 12, 1991; winner of short story competition, Austcare and Refugee Council of Australia, 1996; award from John Clemenger Advertising/*Billy Blue* Magazine Short Story Competition.

Writings

A Tale of Tai Ringal and Other Poems, engravings by P. John Burden, Bournehall Press (London, England), 1974.

(With Brian Moses and Val Segal) *Molls to Maidens: Tales of Suspense and Suspenders, from Seedy, Sepia, Bedsitdom through the Cold Light of Day to James Bond,* Excello & Bollard (Corby, England), 1977.

More Champagne (play), produced in Sydney, Australia, at Living Room Theatre, 1979.

Realities (play), produced in Sydney at Off Broadway Theatre, 1985.

Camera Capers (stage piece), produced in Sydney at Clontarf Cottage Theatre, 1995.

Escaping the Triad (novel), Holy Angels Publishing (North Fitzroy, Australia), 1998.

Twenty-six Poems, Write Off Publications (Sydney, Australia), 2000.

Author of the play *Ironman,* 1996; creator of the dance *LM 514,* performed in Sydney by Sydney Dance Company, Opera House, 1982. Work represented in anthologies, including *A Moment in Time,* edited by Andrew Head, Arrival Press (England), 1996; *Two Hundred Years of Australian Writing: An Anthology from the First Settlement to Today,* edited by James F. H. Moore, VDL Publications (Australia), 1997; and *Eternal Words,* edited by Head, Poetry Now (England), 1997. Contributor of articles, stories, and poems to periodicals in Australia, England, India, Germany, and the United States, including *Art Times, Aboriginal Science Fiction, Performing Arts Review, Prophetic Voices, Conservative Review,* and *Poetry Break.*

Work in Progress

Research on Australian physical theater groups, 1985-1999.

* * *

GARDNER, Miriam
See BRADLEY, Marion Zimmer

* * *

GOLDEN, Christie 1963-
(Jadrien Bell)

Personal

Born November 21, 1963, in Atlanta, GA; married an artist. *Education:* University of Virginia, B.A. (English), 1985. *Hobbies and other interests:* Herbalism, making soap.

Addresses

Home—Colorado. *Agent*—c/o Ace Books, Putnam Berkley Group, Inc., 200 Madison Ave., New York, NY 10016.

Christie Golden

Career

Author. *Member:* Science Fiction Writers of America, Horror Writers of America, Society for Creative Anachronism.

Writings

Instrument of Fate, Ace, 1996.
Star Trek Voyager: The Murdered Sun, Pocket, 1996.
Star Trek Voyager: Marooned, Pocket, 1997.
King's Man and Thief, Ace, 1997.
Star Trek Voyager: Seven of Nine, Pocket, 1998.
Invasion America (based on the animated series "Invasion America"), ROC, 1998.
Invasion America: On the Run (based on the animated series "Invasion America"), ROC, 1998.
(With Michael Jan Friedman) *Star Trek the Next Generation: Double Helix: The First Virtue* (sixth book in a series), Pocket, 1999.
(Under pseudonym Jadrien Bell) *A.D. 999,* Ace, 1999.

"RAVENLOFT" SERIES

Ravenloft: Vampire of the Mists, TSR (Geneva, WI), 1991.
Dance of the Dead, TSR, 1992.
The Enemy Within, TSR, 1994.

OTHER:

Also contributor to anthologies, including *Realms of Valor,* TSR, 1993; *Realms of Infamy,* TSR, 1994;

Realms of Magic, TSR, 1995; *Blood Muse,* Fine, 1995; *Lammas Night,* Baen, 1996; *OtherWere,* Ace, 1996; *Urban Nightmares,* Baen, 1997; and *Highwaymen: Robbers and Rogues,* DAW, 1997.

Sidelights

Christie Golden combines elements of Gothic horror, fantasy, and science fiction in her work. Her first published novel, *Vampire of the Mists,* follows the horror-laden realm of Ravenloft, a land packed with ghosts and werewolves and ruled by the Count Strahd Von Zarovich. The plot revolves around a vampire elf who is forced out of the Forgotten Realm and into Ravenwolf, where he must confront the Count.

Golden continues the saga of Ravenloft in *Dance of the Dead,* the story of a young dancer named Larisa Snowmane who travels by ship through Ravenloft

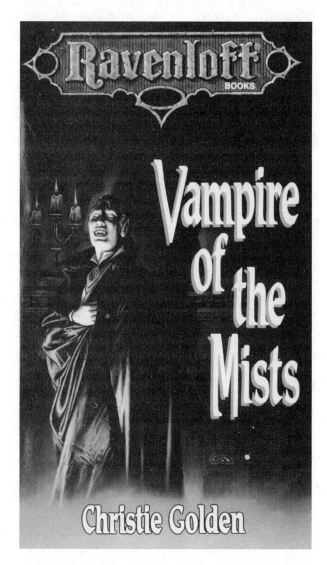

In the first of a series of tales intended to complement the "Ravenloft" game, a vampire elf, exiled from the Forgotten Realm, must fight ghosts, werewolves, and the evil count who rules the horrific world of Ravenloft. (Cover illustration by Clyde Caldwell.)

seemingly unaffected by all the potentially sinister possibilities there. Unknown to her, an evil captain with a chilling secret directs the ship Larisa boards. When the ship arrives at a Ravenloft island full of zombies, Larisa must enlist the help of its residents and perform the magic Dance of the Dead in order to save herself from the evil that the Captain represents. Praising the "exciting, well-developed story with excellent character development," *Kliatt* reviewer Amos C. Patterson claimed *Dance of the Dead* will keep readers attention "to the completion of the story."

Golden mixes aspects of romantic literature, fantasy, and history in *King's Man and Thief.* The main character, Deveran, has two disparate identities. Publicly he is a man of wealth and great benefactor of the arts. However, after his wife's brutal murder eight years earlier, he also rules the city's thieves in secret. While attempting to lead the thieves away from a life of crime and into a more honorable line of work, Deveran must fight factions within his group who oppose him. Led by Marrika, the evil forces launch a plan to make every inhabitant of the city capable of new levels of evil and darkness. In a romantic twist, Deveran encounters the goddess Health, who holds for him the key to saving the city. Calling *King's Man and Thief*'s intricate seven-layered religion "the novels most distinctive feature," *Voice of Youth Advocate* critic Margaret Miles suggested readers of fantasy, horror, and romance continue to look for Golden's work in the future.

Works Cited

Miles, Margaret, review of *King's Man and Thief, Voice of Youth Advocates,* August, 1997, pp. 192-3.
Patterson, Amos C., review of *Dance of the Dead, Kliatt,* November, 1992, p. 14.

For More Information See

BOOKS

Reginald, Robert, *Science Fiction and Fantasy Literature, 1975-1991,* Gale, 1992.

PERIODICALS

Locus, October, 1991, p. 46; November, 1991, p. 35.
Rapport, April, 1992, p. 21.*

*   *   *

GRAVES, Valerie
See BRADLEY, Marion Zimmer

*   *   *

GRIESSMAN, Annette 1962-

Personal

Born January 29, 1962, in Princeton, NJ; daughter of John (an electrical engineer) and Phyllis (a secretary) Schumacher; married Detlef Griessman (an electrical

Annette Griessman

engineer), December 22, 1984; children: Alex, Kayla. *Education:* Purdue University, B.S., 1984. *Hobbies and other interests:* Reading, gardening, astronomy, "watching good movies, and spending time with my kids."

Addresses

Home—Kokomo, IN. *E-mail*—dgriessm@holli.com.

Career

Delco Electronics, Kokomo, IN, test engineer, 1984-88; writer. *Member:* Society of Children's Book Writers and Illustrators.

Awards, Honors

Polly Bond Award, for *Jenny's Prayer.*

Writings

Jenny's Prayer, Morehouse Publishing (Harrisburg, PA), 1998.
Gabriel, God, and the Fuzzy Blanket (Christian children's picture book), Morehouse Publishing, 2000.

Work represented in anthologies, including *No Limits: Developing Scientific Literacy Using Science Fiction,* edited by Julie Czerneda, in press. Contributor of short stories to periodicals, including *Spider* and *Nature Friend.*

Work in Progress

The Quiet Witness, a Christian children's picture book, for New Hope Publishers (Lahaska, PA), completion expected in 2001.

Sidelights

Annette Griessman told *SATA:* "When I was young, I developed a strange habit—I would read anything. I read books, newspapers, magazines, and when those were in short supply, I turned to receipts, cereal boxes, and soup cans. My collection of books grew to enormous proportions, and I learned to read even faster to get through new ones. My favorite authors couldn't write fast enough to keep me in books. To fill my time I tried a variety of hobbies, but inevitably I found myself bored to tears. It finally occurred to me that maybe I should try writing. By writing, I could not only stay busy, but also tell the kinds of stories I loved to read. It was a wonderful and fateful day. Now I write as obsessively as I read. In another few years, I may even be good at it.

"I am very happy with my success in the children's market so far, as I think children have a great need for good stories. If a child learns to love books when he is young, the habit will stay with him for life, enriching that life with bits of wisdom, humor, joy, and just plain fun."

*   *   *

GROENING, Matt 1954-

Personal

Surname is pronounced "*gray*-ning" (rhymes with "raining"); born February 15, 1954, in Portland, OR; son of Homer (a filmmaker) and Margaret (a teacher) Groening; married Deborah Caplan (his manager and business partner), October 29, 1986; children: two. *Education:* Evergreen State College, B.A., 1977. *Hobbies and other interests:* Watching badly translated foreign films; nurturing ducks.

Addresses

Home—Los Angeles, CA. *Office*—Twentieth Century-Fox, 10201 West Pico Blvd., Los Angeles, CA 90035. *Agent*—c/o Susan A. Grode, 1999 Avenue of the Stars, Suite 1600, Los Angeles, CA 90067.

Career

Writer, cartoonist, and business executive. Held numerous odd jobs in Los Angeles, CA, including cemetery landscaper, dishwasher in a nursing home, clerk in recording and copy shops, and ghostwriter/chauffeur for an elderly filmmaker, 1977-79; *Los Angeles Reader,* Los Angeles, worked variously as circulation manager, editor, writer, cartoonist, and author of "Sound Mix" music column, 1979-84; cofounder and partner with Deborah Caplan, Life in Hell Cartoon Co. and Acme

Matt Groening

Features Syndicate, beginning in 1980s; Twentieth Century-Fox Television, Los Angeles, creator, developer, animator, director, and producer of "The Simpsons" episodes for *The Tracy Ullman Show,* 1987-89; Twentieth Century-Fox Television, Los Angeles, creator, developer, animator, and executive producer with James L. Brooks and Sam Simon, *The Simpsons* television series, 1989—, director of voice recording sessions, 1990—, and creator and executive producer of *Futurama,* 1999—; publisher, Bongo Comics Group, 1993—, and Zongo Comics, 1994—.

Awards, Honors

Won short story contest, *Jack and Jill,* 1962; Emmy Award nominations, Academy of Television Arts and Sciences, for outstanding writing in a variety program, 1987, 1988, and 1989, for *The Tracey Ullman Show,* and for outstanding animated program, 1990, for Christmas program *The Simpsons Roasting on an Open Fire; The Simpsons* television program has won ten Emmy Awards, including Outstanding Animated Program in 1990, 1991, and 1995, a Peabody Award in 1997, seven Annie Awards, three Genesis Awards, three International Monitor Awards, and three Environmental Media Awards, among others.

Writings

"LIFE IN HELL"

Love Is Hell, privately printed, 1984, revised edition, Pantheon, 1985.
Work Is Hell, Pantheon, 1986.

School Is Hell, Pantheon, 1987.
Childhood Is Hell, Pantheon, 1988.
Akbar and Jeff's Guide to Life, Pantheon, 1989.
Greetings from Hell, Pantheon, 1989.
The Big Book of Hell, Pantheon, 1990.
With Love from Hell: A Postcard Book, HarperCollins, 1991.
How to Go to Hell, HarperCollins, 1991.
The Road to Hell, HarperCollins, 1992.
Binky's Guide to Love, HarperCollins, 1994.
Love Is Still Hell: Special Ultra-Jumbo 10th Anniversary Edition, Random House, 1994.
The Huge Book of Hell, Penguin, 1997.

The *Life in Hell* comic strip was privately printed, beginning in late 1970s, appeared in *Wet,* 1978, *Los Angeles Reader,* 1980-86, and *L.A. Weekly,* 1984—, and has been syndicated by Groening and Caplan to over two hundred periodicals worldwide through Acme Features Syndicate, 1980—. Also creator of "The Life in Hell Fun Calendars."

"THE SIMPSONS"

The Simpsons Xmas Book (adapted from a screenplay by Mimi Pond), HarperCollins, 1990.
Greetings from the Simpsons, HarperCollins, 1990.
The Simpsons Rainy Day Fun Book, HarperCollins, 1991.
(With sister, Maggie Groening) *Maggie Simpson's Alphabet Book,* HarperCollins, 1991.
(With Maggie Groening) *Maggie Simpson's Book of Animals,* HarperCollins, 1991.
(With Maggie Groening) *Maggie Simpson's Book of Colors and Shapes,* HarperCollins, 1991.
(With Maggie Groening) *Maggie Simpson's Counting Book,* HarperCollins, 1991.
The Simpsons Uncensored Family Album, HarperCollins, 1991.
The Simpsons Fun in the Sun Book, HarperCollins, 1992.
Making Faces with the Simpsons: A Book of Ready-to-Wear Masks, HarperCollins, 1992.
The Simpsons Ultra-Jumbo Rain-or-Shine Fun Book, HarperCollins, 1993.
Cartooning with the Simpsons, HarperCollins, 1993.
Bart Simpson's Guide to Life, HarperCollins, 1993.
Simpsons Comics Extravaganza, HarperCollins, 1994.
Simpson's Comics Spectacular, HarperPerennial, 1995.
Bartman: The Best of the Best!, HarperPerennial, 1995.
Simpsons Comics Simps-O-Rama, HarperCollins, 1996.
Simpsons Comics Stike Back, HarperPerennial, 1996.
The Simpsons: A Complete Guide to Our Favorite Family, edited by Ray Richmond and Anonia Coffman, HarperPerennial, 1997.
Simpsons Comics Wingding, HarperCollins, 1997.
Simpsons Comics Big Bonanza, HarperPerennial, 1998.
Simpsons Comics on Parade, Bongo Comics Group, 1998.
The Simpsons Guide to Springfield, HarperCollins, 1998.
Bart Simpson's Treehouse of Horror: Heebie-Jeebie Hullabaloo, HarperPerennial, 1999.
Homer's Guide to Being a Man, HarperCollins, 2000.

Creator of Simpsons calendars published by Random House and HarperCollins; creator, *Simpsons Illustrated*

Magazine, 1991-93; creator, "Simpsons Trading Cards," SkyBox, Series I, spring, 1994, Series II, fall, 1994.

TELEVISION SCRIPTS

(Contributor of fifty "Simpsons" segments) *The Tracy Ullman Show,* broadcast on Fox-TV, 1987-89.
(With others) *The Simpsons,* broadcast on Fox-TV, 1990—.
(Contributor of animated character dialogue) *The Ice Capades Fiftieth Anniversary Special,* broadcast on ABC-TV, 1990.
(With others) *Futurama,* broadcast on Fox-TV, 1999—.

OTHER

(With Steve Vance) *Postcards That Ate My Brain,* Pantheon, 1990.

Also creator, with Steve Vance, of "Postcards That Ate My Brain" calendars, Portal, 1990, and *Futurama Y2Kalender,* HarperCollins, 1999.

Sidelights

"I had a very typical childhood," said Matt Groening in a *San Jose Mercury News* article by Michael Oricchio. "The only difference was that I took notes and vowed never to forget what it was like." Groening's vow helped drive him into cartooning, where he has been taking revenge on his childhood tormentors and a lot of other pretentious people for most of his adult life. In his *Life in Hell* comic strip and *The Simpsons* animated television series, Groening lampoons authority figures from playground bullies to classroom and office tyrants, viewing life through the eyes of children and adults who feel doomed, overpowered, or defiantly obnoxious. His best-known creation is Bart Simpson, who has his adventures chronicled on the most successful prime-time animated series since *The Flintstones. The Simpsons* went on to win ten Emmy and a slew of other awards, earn $500 million in merchandising, air in over 70 countries, become America's longest-running sitcom, and is set to be a feature film, *The Simpsons Movie,* in 2000. For a time, students across America shocked their teachers by wearing T-shirts that displayed the Bart attitude: "'Underachiever'—And proud of it, man!" *Futurama,* Groening's futuristic series that debuted on Fox in 1999, was a gauge of the cartoonist's success—he was allowed to indulge his long-time dream of creating a science-fiction show and air it on Fox television, part of one of the most known entertainment networks in the world, Twentieth Century Fox.

Groening was born and raised in Portland, Oregon. Strangely, the names of his family resemble those of the Simpson clan, including father Homer, mother Margaret, and sisters Lisa and Maggie. Groening now suggests that the coincidence was an inside joke that got out of hand. "My whole family was smart and funny," he told Jim Sullivan in the *Boston Globe,* "where the Simpsons are stupid and funny." Unlike Bart Simpson's condescending attitude towards Homer, Groening considered his father the "hippest" dad in the neighborhood: a man who, during the conformist 1950s, sought out such unusual jobs as cartoonist and creator of short films.

Because of his work, Homer Groening subscribed to a huge range of general-interest magazines; accordingly, Matt was gazing at the cartoons in the *New Yorker* and *Punch* even before he could read. Soon he was doodling like his dad.

The closest resemblance between the Simpsons and the Groenings lies in the bickering between siblings. As the third child of five, Matt was picked on by an older brother and sister, and he, in turn, picked on his two younger sisters. For Groening such childhood memories are amazingly vivid—even intense. "I really do remember being in my crib and being bathed in the sink," he declared in the *Los Angeles Times.* "I remember being that small. At the time, I thought everything was dramatic.... Adults have forgotten how scary it is."

Scariest of all for Groening was elementary school. He found it a rigid, humorless, uncreative place that had no use for a child whose talent was doodling. "I could understand getting sent to the principal's office for dropping an encyclopedia out the window, but I couldn't understand them ripping my cartoons up," he continued. To console himself Groening started keeping a diary in the fifth grade. That way, in years to come, he could examine the record and decide if he'd been right to rebel.

Resisting all threats and pleas, Groening remained a nonconformist. He became a fan of satirical comics like Walt Kelly's *Pogo* and the notorious *Mad* magazine. When *Jack and Jill* magazine invited readers to submit their own ending to a Halloween story, Groening won a prize for his morbid finale: a boy dies from a bump on the head and swoops down from the attic once a year to join his family for dinner. By high school Groening began to hit his stride. He wrote and cartooned for the school newspaper, hung out with antiwar students from a nearby college, and, with fellow misfits from his high school, formed a sarcastic political party called Teens for Decency and got himself elected student body president. "You are what you are," he said in the *Los Angeles Times,* "basically despite school."

When it came time for college, Groening applied to only two: far-off Harvard University (he didn't make it) and nearby Evergreen State in Olympia, Washington. Founded in the late 1960s, Evergreen was a classic hippie school with no tests, no grades, and no classes (they were called seminars). Groening, who was really too conservative to be a hippie, responded to the freedom of Evergreen with a burst of self-discipline. Since he didn't see cartooning as a viable career, he decided to be a writer and soon became editor of the student newspaper. There he met Lynda Barry, an aspiring artist who cartooned on the side and who later created the best-selling strip *Ernie Pook's Comeek.* "I had been trying to make other people laugh and I found out by looking at Lynda's cartoons that if you make yourself laugh, it's generally good for other people as well," Groening told Richard Harrington in the *Washington Post.* He decided to publish some of Barry's cartoons in the paper and, inspired by her example, published some of his own as well. This didn't change Groening's plans, however: "I didn't expect there to be an audience for what I was drawing because I didn't see anything drawn that crummy. There was nothing else as crude."

Eager for a writing job after graduation, Groening moved to an apartment in Los Angeles, but nothing went right for him. The only writing job that materialized was as ghostwriter/chauffeur to a forgotten, eighty-eight-year-old Hollywood filmmaker who was trying to compose his memoirs. Other memorable jobs included record-store clerk, copy-shop clerk, graveyard landscaper, and dishwasher in a convalescent home. Faced with the prospect of explaining his lack of success to folks back home, Groening decided to entertain them with his cartoons instead. His life in Los Angeles was thus reborn as *Life in Hell,* the chronicle of a frustrated, harassed-looking rabbit named Binky. The first *Life in Hell* comic strips were run off on photocopiers, stapled into booklets, and mailed by Groening to old friends. Soon he tried selling some of the booklets to punk patrons of the record store where he worked. "The punks' reactions were pretty much either they liked it or they tore it up," he told *Newsweek* contributor Jennifer Foote, "which could have meant they liked it too."

Wet magazine, a pioneer of off-the-wall New Wave graphics, liked the strip enough to run several installments in 1978. Groening also tried to interest both of Los Angeles's alternative weeklies in his work, and in 1979 he landed a job with the *Los Angeles Reader.* Within a year *Life in Hell* was a weekly feature of the *Reader,* and Groening's job soon expanded into editor and rock music columnist. As originally seen in the *Reader, Life in Hell* was different from the comic strip now popularized in books and calendars; Binky the rabbit "was really hostile, ranting and raving, the way I felt," Groening explained in a *Rolling Stone* article by Tish Hamilton. "After a year of doing the comic strip and not getting much response, I decided to make the rabbit a victim instead of an aggressor. And the second I made the rabbit a victim, people started liking the comic strip. The more tragedies that befell this poor little rodent, the more positive response I got."

Binky took his present-day form: a lonely, beleaguered office worker with a nightmarish love life that results in his having an illegitimate son. The son, Bongo, is a troubled school-aged rabbit with only one ear. With the addition of Sheba, Binky's girlfriend (and not Bongo's mother), Groening had a cast of characters on whom he could inflict the humiliations of everyday life, including love, work, and childhood. When a girlfriend dumped Groening, for instance, he responded with "Love Is Hell," a thirteen-part comic-strip miniseries that told readers about the nine types of boyfriends (such as Old Man Grumpus), nine types of girlfriends (Ms. Vaguely Dissatisfied), and nine types of relationships (Sourballs vs. The World). He also wrote about a more pressing frustration: having an office job. "Isn't It About Time You Quit Your Lousy Job?" asked one of Groening's favorite strips. "Wake up, chumply. You're not getting

any younger. The clock is ticking. You can't just sit there in your cubbyhole while life passes you by."

Groening might still be writing for the *Reader* if not for Deborah Caplan, who worked in the advertising department and was quick to see his potential. "It didn't take many sales calls before I realized that Groening's comic strip was the major drawing card of the newspaper," she told Joanne Kaufman in *People* magazine. Caplan fell in love with Groening, and, as an added bonus, she helped organize his life. In the mid-1980s Groening and Caplan quit their jobs and formed the Life in Hell Cartoon Company and Acme Features Syndicate, which syndicated the comic strip and sold all kinds of hell-related products, from posters to T-shirts to coffee mugs. Even before *The Simpsons* became a mass-market phenomenon, the Life in Hell Cartoon Company was pulling down a six-figure income. "Everyone I know goes, 'Well, if I had a Deborah, I could be a success, too,'" he said in the *Los Angeles Times.* "And they're right." The pair was married in 1986, and figurines of Binky and Sheba topped the wedding cake.

The company's success made Groening more ambitious, leading to a string of comic miniseries and cartoon books. The first book, *Love Is Hell,* was privately published by Caplan in 1984 and sold more than twenty thousand copies; subsequent books are titled *Work Is Hell, School Is Hell,* and *Childhood Is Hell.* To gear up for the *School Is Hell* series, Groening ransacked high school dumpsters for the notebooks and papers that students toss out at the end of the year. The final product surveyed such topics as "Trouble: Getting In and Weaseling Your Way Out" and "How to Drive a Deserving Teacher Crazy." *Childhood Is Hell,* based in part on Groening's fifth-grade diary, included a "Childhood Trauma Checklist" and a tribute to "Your Pal the TV Set." For variety Groening gave an increasing role in *Life in Hell* to gay entrepreneurs Akbar and Jeff, whose empty grins were somehow as creepy as Binky and Bongo's frowns. *Los Angeles Times Book Review* critic Charles Solomon noted that while Groening's artwork is not great in the traditional sense, it serves as a vehicle for good writing and sharp wit. "Groening," Solomon declared, "is one of the funniest and most original cartoonists working in the comics today."

The increasing popularity of Groening's "Hell" cartoon led to inquiries from the television industry, which found him a tough bargainer. When asked about potential projects, he told Sullivan, "I'd talk about how bad TV cartoons were and that I'd like to do something with the same standards as [the 1960s cult favorite] 'Rocky and Bullwinkle'—great writing, great voices, great music. They got all cold and distant after that and claimed that 'Rocky and Bullwinkle' was a failure because it only appealed to smart kids." Groening, who felt that TV viewers were ready again for something like smart animation, held tight. Finally he got an offer from James L. Brooks, the noted producer and writer for such television programs as *The Mary Tyler Moore Show* and *Taxi* and movies like *Terms of Endearment* who was now at the adventurous new Fox television network. At first the pair planned to do an animated version of the comic strip, but then Fox laid down its terms: Groening must surrender all legal rights to the characters. Instead Groening sold Fox the concept for a whole new animated show, with human characters who were nearly as frazzled as his rabbits—"a messed-up American family," as he put it. The Simpsons were born.

The Simpsons are a blue-collar clan who live in the mythical town of Springfield—the same hometown as the Andersons, the well-adjusted television family of the 1950s comedy *Father Knows Best.* The Simpsons, however, look like somebody's parody of a happy television family. Ten-year-old Bart is irreverent, irrepressible, and usually in trouble. He cheats on tests, sneaks into movies, and never misses a chance to one-up his father. Homer is fat, bald, stupid, and often grumpy—just a regular guy. He works at a nuclear power plant, where his blunders often put Springfield on the edge of annihilation. Marge Simpson, wife and mother, is crowned by an enormous blue beehive hairdo. She holds the family together with kindhearted wisdom, although sometimes her advice is a little off target. Lisa is an eight-year-old genius who's full of common sense, but vaguely smug. And Baby Maggie "isn't TV-baby-cute; she's just there, all wide eyes and sucking noises," wrote Ken Tucker in *Entertainment Weekly.* "At its heart this is guerrilla TV," said Tucker's colleague Joe Rhodes—"a wicked satire masquerading as a prime-time cartoon."

As a television series, *The Simpsons* started small: it was a supplement to another prime-time series, *The Tracey Ullman Show.* At first the animation spots—written, directed, and produced by Groening—were used as fifteen-second lead-ins to commercial breaks; finally it got its own ninety-second segment. There was just enough time for a joke, but the Simpsons characters were clearly established. In one segment, for instance, Marge blithely sings "Rock-a-Bye Baby" to little Maggie, who takes the words literally and imagines herself cradled in a treetop and crashing to the ground. Going to a full-length series, however, was by no means a foregone conclusion. Because animation is generally drawn by hand, it requires a lot of time and money. But an advance screening of the show impressed Fox chairman Barry Diller, and a commitment for a series was approved. After the full-length program debuted on Fox in January of 1990, it was soon one of the fifteen most-watched shows on American television—an amazing feat for a fledgling network that had yet to reach one-fifth of the country. "*The Simpsons* kept Fox in business in the early years," *Futurama* animation director Claudia Katz told writer Alex Needham for *Face.* Needham also commented about the effect *The Simpson* had on American TV culture. "In America, TV used to be so diffuse: There was no country-unifying soap, no one who was watched by the whole family. *The Simpsons* had become this show." *The Simpsons* became America's longest-running sitcom.

Named one of three executive producers of *The Simpsons,* Groening aimed for quality. He wanted animation

with enough depth to appeal to grown-ups, animation with characters so vivid that people would forget it was animation, and a situation comedy that would transcend the old sitcom formula of one-liners and easy sentiment. But beyond production values—as everyone from TV critics to sociologists agreed—*The Simpsons* clicked because the audience was ready for it. The show was seen as a revolt against decades of happy family sitcoms, from *Father Knows Best* to *The Cosby Show,* which projected a world that was too good to be real. As America faced a long list of stubborn social and economic woes, many of which took a toll on family life, the "messed-up" Simpsons looked surprisingly realistic.

Like many people in the audience, the Simpsons weren't fulfilled in life; they were lucky to survive it. In one episode Homer is treated like a hero for preventing a nuclear explosion, then has to admit that he pushed the right button by accident. In another plotline when

Groening's enormously successful and long-lived animated television show, centering on the inimitable Simpson family, has won ten Emmy awards and airs in over seventy countries.

playground bullies menace Bart, he does not win by taking the high road, instead, he teams up with a local gun nut and fights dirty. When he's threatened with flunking out of fourth grade, he studies pathetically hard, and he is delighted to scrape by with a "D." And when Lisa suffers from childhood depression, an old musician teaches her how to survive by playing the blues: "The blues isn't about feeling better," he confides, "it's about making other people feel worse." Yet despite all their flaws, bickering, and money troubles, the Simpsons still manage—just barely—to love each other. "Part of the Simpson appeal," Groening said in a *Chicago Sun-Times* article by Earnest Tucker, "is the acknowledgment that you can still love the people who drive you crazy."

The popularity of *The Simpsons* created a marketing tidal wave as fans scooped up as many as one million Simpsons products a day, including T-shirts, caps, bubble gum, boxer shorts, and a talking Bart doll. Not surprisingly, some authority figures did not find the Simpsons funny at all. Across America various principals, teachers, and child psychologists warned that Bart was providing a bad example to the young. Bart's foes included United States drug enforcement chief William Bennett, who backed off on his attack when he was forced to admit that he had never watched the show. Many blasted the notorious "Underachiever" T-shirt, which was banned from some classrooms. "If you read the T-shirt, it says, 'Bart Simpson, quote, underachiever, unquote,'" Groening commented to Dave Rhein in the *Des Moines Register.* "[Bart] has been labeled an underachiever and his response to that is that he's proud of it. He didn't call himself an underachiever. He does not aspire to be an underachiever." Besides, as the author told *Mother Jones* contributor Sean Elder, "Kids are smarter than a lot of adults give them credit for. I feel sorry for authority figures who are troubled by kids having fun."

Continued success for Groening came in 1993 with the founding of the comic book company Bongo Comics Group, for which he serves as publisher. The company's first titles were *Simpsons Comics, Radioactive Man, Itchy & Scratchy, Bartman,* and *Krusty Comics.* During Bongo Comics' first year of publication, the company was honored with a Diamond Gem Award for best new publisher of the year and the Will Eisner Award for best short story for "The Amazing Colossal Homer." The success of Bongo Comics ultimately led to the creation of Zongo Comics in 1994.

By the late 1990s, with the success of *The Simpsons,* the door was opened to many other animated shows not necessarily made for kids. The raucous *South Park* debuted on Comedy Central and was wildly received, spinning off into a full-length film. MTV had a hit with *Beavis and Butthead,* two animated teenage losers who made rude and lewd comments over music videos, and who also starred in a feature film. Fox produced *King of the Hill,* yet another animated dysfunctional family somehow keeping it together while audiences laughed at their expense. So, based on his success with *The Simpsons,* Groening decided to indulge a long-time

fantasy—he wanted to produce a science-fiction show. In 1997, he teamed up with David X. Cohen, a fellow sci-fi buff and a scriptwriter for *The Simpsons* who'd worked on *Beavis and Butthead.* The two conspired over sci-fi movies, sci-fi books by writers like Isaac Asimov and Phillip K. Dick, 1980s computer games, vintage sci-fi magazines, and old TV shows like *Lost in Space* and *Doctor Who.* What they came up with was *Futurama.*

"Matt Groening has seen the future, and, quite frankly," wrote Dan Snierson in *Entertainment Weekly,* "it looks ridiculous." Fry, a 25-year-old pizza delivery boy, accidentally gets cryogenically frozen on December 31, 1999 and wakes up 1,000 years later. He meets Leela, a tough, beautiful, one-eyed female alien, and Bender, a lazy, lying, thieving, beer-drinking robot. Eventually Fry is taken in by his only surviving relative, Professor Hubert Farnsworth, a senile old scientist and inventor, and owner of the Planet Express Delivery Service. The Professor hires Fry and the others to make interplanetary deliveries for him, thus setting the stage for all manner of outrageous adventures. In addition to a cast of characters that includes a bureaucratic Jamaican limbo champion, a lobster-clawed surgeon, and an ego-maniacal warship captain and his long-suffering alien first officer, Groening's future is populated with jet-powered scooters, evil mega-corporations, all manner of robots and spaceships, mobile phones implanted directly into thumbs, and the robot mafia.

While Groening and Cohen were inspired by sci-fi classics, *Futurama* also pokes fun at them. The *Futurama* world features Stop'n'Drop (25¢ suicide booths), coin-operated prostitutes, and a state motto of, "You gotta do what you gotta do," which means working a state-assigned job. Like *The Simpsons, Futurama* features a host of celebrity cameo appearances, only in *Futurama,* stars like Pamela Anderson, Dennis Rodman, Leonard Nimoy and the Beastie Boys gave voices to animated versions of their own heads, kept in jars in the "Head Museum."

"The way I sold them the show," Groening said in *Face,* "was by saying, 'This is *The Simpsons* in the future,' and the dollar signs danced in front of their eyes." When Fox executives saw the first episode of *Futurama,* the dollar signs stopped dancing. *Futurama,* they complained, was nothing like *The Simpsons.* "Yes it is," Groening replied. "It's new and original." There was no way Groening could outdo *The Simpsons,* Groening told Snierson. "I won't. I can't. Nothing can. I just hope every review isn't '*Futurama* is no *Simpsons.*' It's not a horse race." Despite executive worries, 19 million people watched the first episode.

More than anyone Groening was having fun. "Everybody's got a fantasy of watching television and getting annoyed with it and saying, 'Boy, if I had my own TV show, this is what I would do.' And in an extremely easy way, I have arrived at that," he told *Philadelphia Inquirer* writer Rip Rense. "We lucked out. I'm real comfortable now. I'm real lucky." He even has plans for a theme park, his answer to Disneyland. "It'd be great!"

he told *Face,* "You'd have Simpsons island with a 600ft statue of Homer. They'd sell donuts and beer in his head." As happy as anyone who lives in hell can expect to be, Groening and Caplan remodeled their house near the ocean and began raising their children. He remains friends with Lynda Barry, and in many papers their comic strips run side by side. And, most of all, he has learned the true meaning of success. "It means," he told Earnest Tucker, "that people who used to beat me up in high school call me up and want to be friends."

Works Cited

Elder, Sean, "The Rehabilitation of Bart Simpson," *Mother Jones,* January, 1991, p. 13.

Foote, Jennifer, "A Doodle God Makes Good," *Newsweek,* September 28, 1987, pp. 70-71.

Groening, Matt, *The Big Book of Hell,* Pantheon, 1990.

Hamilton, Tish, "Rabbit Punch," *Rolling Stone,* September 22, 1988, p. 81.

Harrington, Richard, "Drawing on the Humor in Life's Little Horrors," *Washington Post,* December 18, 1988.

Kaufman, Joanne, *"Life in Hell*'s Matt Groening Goes Overboard to Make *The Simpsons* the First Family of TV 'Toons," *People,* December 18, 1989, p. 108.

Krier, Beth Ann, "An Alternative Cartoonist Who Draws the Line," *Los Angeles Times,* August 23, 1987.

Morgenstern, Joe, "Bart Simpson's Real Father," *Los Angeles Times,* April 29, 1990.

Needham, Alex, "Nice Planet ... We'll Take It!", *Face,* October, 1999, pp. 70-78, 209.

Oricchio, Michael, "Hell Ain't So Bad," *San Jose Mercury News,* November 8, 1988.

Rense, Rip, "The American Family (Cartoon-Style)," *Philadelphia Inquirer,* February 11, 1990.

Rhein, Dave, "Bart's Philosophy Concerns Some Teachers," *Des Moines Register,* August 26, 1990.

Rhodes, Joe, "The Making of 'The Simpsons,'" *Entertainment Weekly,* May 18, 1990, p. 36.

Snierson, Dan, "Space Case," *Entertainment Weekly,* March 26, 1999, p. 46.

Solomon, Charles, review of *Love Is Hell, Los Angeles Times Book Review,* June 29, 1986, p. 2.

Sullivan, Jim, "Animation's Answer to the Bundys," *Boston Globe,* January 14, 1990.

Tucker, Ernest, "Success of 'Simpsons' Overwhelms Creator," *Chicago Sun-Times,* April 15, 1990.

Tucker, Ken, review of *The Simpsons, Entertainment Weekly,* May 18, 1990, p. 43.

For More Information See

PERIODICALS

American Film, October, 1989, p. 112.

Animation, fall, 1989, p. 22.

Booklist, March 15, 1994.

Detroit Free Press, July 16, 1990.

Entertainment Weekly, May 18, 1990, p. 36; February 21, 1992, p. 9; August 7, 1992, p. 70; March 12, 1993, p. 48; May 28, 1993, p. 73; December 9, 1994, p. 68; April 2, 1999, p.73.

Esquire, July 1999, p. 32.

Los Angeles Times, February 23, 1990.

Los Angeles Times Book Review, December 1, 1991; June 6, 1993, p. 15.

Mother Jones, December, 1989, p. 28; March, 1999, p. 34.

Newsweek, December 25, 1989, p. 70; April 23, 1990, pp. 58, 64; March 29, 1999, pp. 70-71.

New York Times, February 21, 1990; July 14, 1991, p. H1.

Parenting, September, 1992, p. 19.

People, October 30, 1995, p. 17.

Publishers Weekly, August 10, 1992, p. 72; September 14, 1992, p. 127.

Rolling Stone, June 28, 1990, p. 40.

San Francisco Examiner, November 16, 1988; January 21, 1990.

Saturday Review, March, 1985, p. 50.

School Library Journal, September, 1991, p. 298.

Village Voice, February 2, 1988.

Voice of Youth Advocates, April, 1988, pp. 15-16.

Washington Post Book World, September 22, 1991, p. 12.

ON-LINE

Futurama Web site, located at http://www.fox.com/futurama/index.html.

The Simpsons Web site, located at http://www.foxworld.com/simpsons/simpsons.htm.*

H–I

HALL, Melanie 1949-

Personal

Born November 20, 1949, in Gloucester, MA; daughter of Edward A. (a doctor) and Doris (a housewife; maiden name, Goldfield) Winsten; married Ronald Hall (an artist and musician), 1982. *Education:* Attended Rhode Island School of Design, 1967-70; Pratt Institute, B.F.A., 1978; Marywood College, M.A., 1993. *Hobbies and other interests:* Archery, reading, meditation.

Addresses

Home and office—Cat's Paw Studio, 22 Krom Rd., Olivebridge, NY 12461.

Melanie Hall

Career

Worked variously as a painter, museum curator, printer's assistant, editorial illustrator, graphic designer, and fashion illustrator. Children's book illustrator, 1991—. *Member:* Society of Children's Book Writers and Illustrators.

Awards, Honors

Received an award for work exhibited at the Original Art Show, Society of Illustrators, 1992; Don Freeman Grant, Society of Children's Book Writers, 1993.

Illustrator

Charles Temple, *On the Riverbank,* Houghton, 1992.
Washington Irving, *The Legend of Sleepy Hollow,* adapted by Freya Littledale, Scholastic, 1992.
Weather, edited by Lee Bennett Hopkins, HarperCollins, 1994.
Patrick Lewis, *July Is a Mad Mosquito,* Atheneum, 1994.
Charles Temple, *Shanty Boat,* Houghton, 1994.
Cathy Goldberg Fishman, *On Passover,* Atheneum, 1997.
Cathy Goldberg Fishman, *On Rosh Hashanah and Yom Kippur,* Atheneum, 1997.
Cathy Goldberg Fishman, *On Hanukkah,* Atheneum, 1998.
Nancy Sohn Swartz, *In Our Image: God's First Creatures,* Jewish Lights, 1998.
Cathy Goldberg Fishman, *On Purim,* Atheneum, 2000.

Also contributor to *The Very Best of Children's Book Illustration,* compiled by the Society of Illustrators, Northlight Books, 1993.

Sidelights

Melanie Hall is an illustrator of children's books noted for employing a variety of mixed media, from watercolors to crayons. Hall's artwork can be both folksy and flashy-vibrant, depending on the theme of the material she is illustrating. Working with authors such as Charles Temple and Cathy Goldberg Fishman, she has illustrated

Hall's evocative mixed-media illustrations highlight Cathy Goldberg Fishman's story of Passover, narrated by a young girl who asks a series of questions of her family as they prepare for the holiday. (From On Passover.*)*

books dealing with topics from a day on the river to the months of the year and weather to the Jewish holidays.

"Illustrating children's books is a dream come true for me," Hall once told *Something about the Author (SATA).* "When I was a little girl I made a series of books called 'The Fun Book,' which came out seasonally and were filled with illustrations, rebuses, puzzles, and stories. I laugh to myself remembering how I sat on the beach with colored pencils and paper finishing up the latest fun book so I wouldn't be late for the deadline. I didn't know that was a taste of what was to come."

Attending the prestigious Rhode Island School of Design from 1967 to 1970, Hall thereafter worked in a variety of careers allied to the visual and studio arts. "I've had a checkered career as a painter, museum curator, printer's assistant, editorial illustrator, graphic designer, and fashion illustrator," Hall recalled for *SATA.* Hall returned to earn her B.F.A. at the Pratt Institute, but still had not found her niche. "I wasn't very happy. One day, while sitting at my drawing table doing my umpteenth fashion illustration, I wondered, 'Will I be doing this boring stuff when I'm sixty?' I complained to my girlfriend, 'I want to do children's books!' She replied, 'Well, why don't you?' At that moment, lights flashed and bells rang. I said to myself, 'Yeah, why don't I? What's stopping me?' Everything fell into place. I went back to school and learned how to do children's books.

"The day I got my first book contract changed my life forever. After my editor, Matilda Welter of Houghton Mifflin, offered me *On the Riverbank,* I jumped up and down and whooped for joy. I tried to sound calm, cool, and collected but failed miserably. Matilda chuckled appreciatively at my delight. I told her, 'This is the day all my dreams come true,' quoting Bob Dylan's song 'New Morning.' Afterwards, I called up every member of my family and every friend to crow about the news."

That first title, authored by Temple, was a story of a family of three out for a fishing trip on the shores of a river lit by moonlight. Daddy and Mama bring along a picnic basket and all the assorted gear necessary for an evening of catfishing. Together the young narrator and his father bait the lines and eagerly await the first bites. Told in pulsing, rhythmic stanzas, the book details the simple joys of catching fish and swapping tall tales around a campfire. Hall added to the down-home feel with her debut illustration effort. "Hall's rustic-looking, mixed-media paintings call to mind colored woodblock prints," noted a reviewer for *Publishers Weekly.* "Her cool palette of blues, purples and shimmering whites winningly matches the story's setting of a June night steeped in moonglow." *Booklist* contributor Denia Hester called attention to Hall's heavy application of paint in her illustrations. "The several applications of paint give the art a textured look," commented Hester. "This effect sometimes roughens the art, occasionally obscuring a facial detail, but it also gives the book a unique look." And Anne Connor, reviewing *On the Riverbank* in *School Library Journal,* felt that the "soft, mixed media illustrations have a verve that echoes the text and adds a romanticized dimension of a fond reminiscence to this story of an African-American family that has spent a winter anticipating such an outing."

Hall again collaborated with Temple on *Shanty Boat,* a 1994 picture book about the life of Uncle Sheb, a boatman who plies his trade on the Mississippi River. Sheb has spent his whole life on the river, never settling down or having a family. Sheb's home was the river, and after his death, people say you can still see him and his ramshackle little boat when the moon shines brightly. Again Hall paced her paintings to Temple's hard-driving textual rhythms. "Hall's mixed-media illustrations … portray the bucolic existence of this solitary oarsman," observed *Booklist* critic Kay Weisman. A *Publishers Weekly* reviewer called Hall and Temple's picture book "part ballad, part ghost story and part tall tale," noting that "Hall's collagraphs bustle with a tone of joyous confusion." Reviewing the same title in *School Library Journal,* Lisa S. Murphy commented, "The art is luminous with light ranging from the warmth of the morning sun to the mysterious glow of the moon."

Hall has also provided artwork for an adaptation of the classic *The Legend of Sleepy Hollow,* as well as for an anthology of art work from children's book illustrators, *The Very Best of Children's Book Illustration,* compiled by the Society of Illustrators. This latter was a heady compliment paid to an illustrator with—at the time of publication—only two books to her credit. In 1994 Hall teamed up on two poetry book projects: *Weather,* a book of verses edited by Lee Bennett Hopkins, and Patrick Lewis's *July Is a Mad Mosquito.* In the former title, Hall provided artwork to accompany the poems of both famous—such as Carl Sandburg and Ogden Nash—and unknown versifiers. "The dominant colors are pink and orange—more sunny than rainy," noted Ruth K. MacDonald in *School Library Journal.* MacDonald went on to observe, "The overall impression is of brightness, lightheartedness, and fun." *Horn Book* critic Margaret A. Bush noted that "Melanie Hall's illustrations are pastel sketches, warmly energetic views of children and simple nature scenes."

For Lewis's twelve poems about the months of the year in *July Is a Mad Mosquito,* Hall contributed "zippy collagraphs," according to a critic for *Publishers Weekly.* And if the text falters, "Hall's literal interpretations should clear up any confusion," this same reviewer decided. Judy Greenfield, writing in *School Library Journal,* called attention to Hall's "full-color, double-spread impressionistic painting" which interprets the central motif of each poem, while *Booklist*'s Carolyn Phelan noted "Hall's lively illustrations, fanciful scenes in popsicle-bright pastels and muted blues and browns."

Hall has also worked with author Cathy Goldberg Fishman on several books dealing with Jewish holidays. Passover is the subject for their first collaborative effort, 1997's *On Passover,* which *Booklist* critic Ilene Cooper called "[m]ore attractive and lyrical than many other Passover books." Here the story is told by a young girl who asks a series of questions of her family as they prepare for the holiday. There is the ritual dinner, the Seder plate, and the Passover service, among other parts of the ceremonial aspects of the holiday. A *Publishers Weekly* reviewer concluded, "Hall's rich mixed-media

creations bustle with energy, and her warm portraits of a contemporary family are also amply decorated with religious symbols and snippets of biblical scenes." Further collaborative efforts have produced *On Rosh Hashanah and Yom Kippur* and *On Hanukkah,* as well as *On Purim.* In the first-named book, the High Holidays are explored, with particular focus on Rosh Hashanah, again employing a little girl's voice to get to the heart of the celebration. Once more, Fishman's text explores both the meaning of the holiday as well as the common holiday practices and food. "Hall's beautiful, rosy, expressionistic pictures are a fine complement to Fishman's text," according to Stephanie Zvirin in *Booklist.* Reviewing *On Hanukkah* in *Booklist,* Julie Corsaro felt the "fanciful, mixed-media paintings feature strong texturing and glowing, gilt-edged colors."

Hall turned to biblical stories for her illustrations of Nancy Sohn Swartz's picture book *In Our Image: God's First Creatures.* This "nondenominational, nonsectarian retelling of the creation story ... focuses on the period before man and woman were created," as Yapha Nussbaum Mason described the book in a *School Library Journal* review. A group of animals informs God of the gifts they would like to present to humans, including the chimps who think curiosity would be a fine thing, and the ostriches who opt for humans minding their own business. Worried when God tells them that humans will have dominion over them, the animals are finally reassured when God further informs them that the humans will not abuse this sacred trust. "The vibrantly colored illustrations nearly leap off the page in this delightful interpretation," concluded Mason. *Booklist*'s Cooper felt Hall's "particularly nice" illustrations both extend and elaborate Swartz's text. "Inventive watercolors, dappled with sunlight and cloistered by moonlight,

Hall produced the vibrant pictures for Nancy Sohn Swartz's story of the period shortly before God's creation of man and woman, focusing on the interconnectedness between humans and animals. (From In Our Image.*)*

capture the feeling of life that is the essence of the story," Cooper went on to observe. A reviewer for *Publishers Weekly* concluded, "Hall combines soft watercolors with black-and-neon toned scratchboard work to depict animals cavorting in the lush, new earth; the effect is both complex and magical."

Both magical and earthy, Hall's illustrations have graced the pages of highly praised picture books and assure her a continued place in children's book illustration. She has come a long way from her fashion designing days, and there is no indication she will seek yet another career change. As she concluded to *SATA:* "I am completely happy now and love what I do!"

Works Cited

Bush, Margaret A., review of *Weather, Horn Book,* July-August, 1994, p. 468.

Connor, Anne, review of *On the Riverbank, School Library Journal,* November, 1992, p. 79.

Cooper, Ilene, review of *In Our Image, Booklist,* October 1, 1998, p. 345.

Cooper, Ilene, review of *On Passover, Booklist,* March 1, 1997, p. 1165.

Corsaro, Julie, review of *On Hanukkah, Booklist,* September 1, 1998, p. 132.

Greenfield, Judy, review of *July Is a Mad Mosquito, School Library Journal,* April 1994, p. 120.

Hester, Denia, review of *On the Riverbank, Booklist,* November 15, 1992, p. 64.

Review of *In Our Image, Publishers Weekly,* September 28, 1998, p. 95.

Review of *July Is a Mad Mosquito, Publishers Weekly,* February 14, 1994, p. 89.

MacDonald, Ruth K., review of *Weather, School Library Journal,* March, 1994, p. 216.

Mason, Yapha Nussbaum, review of *In Our Image, School Library Journal,* March, 1999, p. 202.

Murphy, Lisa S., review of *Shanty Boat, School Library Journal,* July, 1994, p. 98.

Review of *On Passover, Publishers Weekly,* February 24, 1997, p. 83.

Review of *On the Riverbank, Publishers Weekly,* October 5, 1992, p. 70.

Phelan, Carolyn, review of *July Is a Mad Mosquito, Booklist,* July, 1994, p. 1950.

Review of *Shanty Boat, Publishers Weekly,* February 14, 1994, p. 87.

Weisman, Kay, review of *Shanty Boat, Booklist,* June 1, 1994, p. 1846.

Zvirin, Stephanie, review of *On Rosh Hashanah and Yom Kippur, Booklist,* October 1, 1997, p. 322.

For More Information See

PERIODICALS

Artist's Magazine, May, 1992; January, 1994.*

—*Sketch by J. Sydney Jones*

HAMMOND, Ralph
See HAMMOND INNES, Ralph

*　　*　　*

HAMMOND INNES, Ralph 1913-1998
(Ralph Hammond, Hammond Innes)

Personal

Indexed in some sources under Innes; born July 15, 1913, in Horsham, England; died June 10, 1998; son of William and Dora Beatrice (Crisford) Hammond Innes; married Dorothy Mary Lang (an actress, playwright, and author; deceased, 1989), 1937. *Education:* Educated in England. *Avocational interests:* Traveling, forestry, ocean racing and cruising.

Career

Member of staff, *Financial News,* 1934-40; freelance writer, 1946-98. *Military service:* British Army, Royal Artillery, 1940-46; served with Eighth Army in Sicily landings and as war correspondent for the British Army Newspaper Unit during the invasion of southern France; became major.

Awards, Honors

Decorated Commander of the British Empire, 1978; Bouchercon Lifetime Achievement award; received honorary degree from Bristol University.

Writings

NOVELS; UNDER HAMMOND INNES

The Doppelganger, Jenkins (Lancaster, England), 1937.

Air Disaster, Jenkins, 1937.

Sabotage Broadcast, Jenkins, 1938.

All Roads Lead to Friday, Jenkins, 1939.

Wreckers Must Breathe, Collins (London, England), 1940, published in the United States as *Trapped,* Putnam, 1940.

The Trojan Horse, Collins, 1940

Attack Alarm, Collins, 1941, Macmillan, 1942.

Dead and Alive, Collins, 1946, reprinted, Fontana, 1970.

The Killer Mine, Collins, Harper, 1947, published as *Run by Night,* Bantam, 1951.

The Lonely Skier, Collins, 1947, published in the United States as *Fire in the Snow,* Harper, 1947.

Maddon's Rock, Collins, 1948, published in the United States as *Gale Warning,* Harper, 1948.

The Blue Ice, Harper, 1948.

The White South, Collins, 1949, published as *The Survivors,* Harper, 1950.

The Angry Mountain, Collins, 1950, Harper, 1951.

Air Bridge, Collins, 1951, Knopf, 1952.

Campbell's Kingdom (also see below), Collins, Knopf, 1952.

The Strange Land, Collins, 1954, published in the United States as *The Naked Land,* Knopf, 1954.

The Mary Deare, Collins, 1956, published in the United
   States as *The Wreck of the Mary Deare,* Knopf, 1956.
The Land God Gave to Cain, Collins, Knopf, 1958.
The Doomed Oasis, Collins, Knopf, 1960.
Atlantic Fury, Collins, Knopf, 1962.
The Strode Venturer, Collins, Knopf, 1965.
Levkas Man, Collins, Knopf, 1971.
Golden Soak, Collins, Knopf, 1973.
North Star, Collins, 1974, Knopf, 1975.
The Big Footprints, Collins, Knopf, 1977.
Solomon's Seal, Collins, Knopf, 1980.
The Black Tide, Collins, 1982, Doubleday, 1983.
High Stand, Collins, 1985, Atheneum, 1986.
Medusa, Collins, Atheneum, 1988.
Isvik, Chapmans (London, England), St. Martin's, 1991.
Target Antarctica, Chapmans, 1993.
The Delta Connection, Macmillan, 1996.

OTHER; UNDER HAMMOND INNES

(Editor) Richard Keverne, *Tales of Old Inns,* second
   edition, Collins, 1947.
(With Robin Estridge) *Campbell's Kingdom* (screenplay;
   based on the novel of same title), Rank (Leicester,
   England), 1957.
Harvest of Journeys (travel), Collins, 1959, Knopf, 1960.
(With the editors of *Life*) *Scandinavia* (travel), Time-Life
   (London, England), 1963.
Sea and Islands (travel), Knopf, 1967.
The Conquistadors (history), Knopf, 1969.
Hammond Innes Introduces Australia, edited by Clive
   Turnbull, McGraw, 1971.
The Last Voyage: Captain Cook's Lost Diary, Collins,
   1978, Knopf, 1979.
Hammond Innes' East Anglia, Hodder & Stoughton (Lon-
   don, England), 1986.

Also author of television play, *The Story of Captain
James Cook,* 1975. Contributor to *Saturday Evening
Post* and *Holiday.*

FOR CHILDREN; UNDER RALPH HAMMOND

Cocos Gold, Collins, Harper, 1950.
Isle of Strangers, Collins, 1951, published in the United
   States as *Island of Peril,* Westminster (Philadelphia,
   PA), 1953.
Saracen's Tower, Collins, 1952, published in the United
   States as *Cruise of Danger,* Westminster, 1952.
Black Gold on the Double Diamond, Collins, 1953.

Adaptations

Fire in the Snow was filmed as *Snowbound,* RKO, 1948;
The White South was filmed by Columbia, 1953;
Campbell's Kingdom was filmed by Rank, 1957; *The
Wreck of the Mary Deare* was filmed by Metro-
Goldwyn-Mayer, 1959; *Golden Soak* and *Levkas Man*
were adapted for television; *The Doomed Oasis* was
adapted by the British Broadcast Corporation (BBC).

Sidelights

Ralph Hammond Innes drew upon his many years as a
seafaring yachtsman and world traveler to write highly-
acclaimed adventure novels set on the high seas or in
exotic foreign locales. When his wife was alive, he
would normally spend six months each year traveling
with her and six months writing at his fourteenth-century
home in the Suffolk countryside. His adventure novels
were set in East Africa, the Antarctic, the Canadian
Northwest, Morocco, and the South Pacific—all places
Hammond Innes himself visited. "I seldom make notes
on these trips," he once told Alan Bestic of the *Radio
Times.* "I'm like a sponge, absorbing people, atmo-
spheres." The resulting novels were as often praised for
their vividly recreated settings as for their exciting plots.
Hammond Innes was one of the most popular adventure
writers in the world; some forty million copies of his
books have been sold in over fifty different languages.

Hammond Innes's success as a writer came after a
grueling apprenticeship. His first four novels, published
in the 1930s, earned him a total of one hundred twenty
English pounds and are now out of print. He was obliged
to work on the staff of the *Financial News,* a daily
newspaper for the banking industry, to support himself.
But with *Attack Alarm,* published in 1941, Hammond
Innes began to receive critical recognition for his work.
Set in London during the early years of the Second
World War, the novel was written while Hammond
Innes was serving as a gunner during the Battle of
Britain, a period when the Nazis made nightly bombing
raids over England. His description of those harrowing
nights has been critically praised. For example, *Books*
reviewer David Tilden claimed that *Attack Alarm*
"contains pages of some of the most convincing and
graphic descriptions of air raids, air fighting and
bombing, especially of the work of anti-aircraft, yet to
come out of the war, and all in human and story terms."
"The description of daily life at the station," a reviewer
for the *Times Literary Supplement* believed, "and the
almost terrifyingly graphic picture of a dive-bombing
attack on the aerodome bear the imprint of truth."

After his service in the British Army, Hammond Innes
embarked on a freelance writing career in 1946. With
this career, he turned out an average of one book per
year, "all of them bestsellers in the most extravagant
sense of the term," as William Green maintained in the
Telegraph Sunday Magazine. Although the novels do
not follow a predictable formula, there are qualities they
all share. Roger Baker of *Books and Bookmen* found that
all of Hammond Innes's work was characterized by "a
narrative that possesses ... pace, excitement, theatrical
set-pieces and open-air drama." Green reported that
"familiar elements recur in every story—the first person
narrator and the lone girl he falls for; the half-legendary
father-figure; the sense of quest. But they are only a kind
of jumping-off point." Hammond Innes once explained
to Green: "If I wrote to a formula, I would have got
bored long ago, and so would the reader."

Among Hammond Innes's most successful novels is *The
Blue Ice,* an adventure story set in the rugged Norwegian
mountains. It tells of the hunt for an escaped criminal
who knows the location of a valuable mine. But "the
plot," wrote Anthony Boucher of the *New York Times,*

"is merely a just-strong-enough thread to hold together a series of descriptions ... as breathtaking as anything you'll find in contemporary adventure literature, fact or fiction." R. W. Henderson of *Library Journal* described *The Blue Ice* as "a typical Innes thriller, packed with suspense, mystery, horror, murder and surprises."

Another critically-acclaimed novel, *The Doomed Oasis,* is set in Arabia where a young Englishman has gone to work in the oil fields. There he meets his long-lost father and gets entangled in the dangerous machinations of Arab chieftains and British oil tycoons. According to Rex Stout, in his appraisal for the *New York Times Book Review, The Doomed Oasis* "is the best tale of adventure I have read in many desert moons, and I thank Mr. Innes warmly, and salute him." Taliaferro Boatwright of the *New York Herald Tribune Book Review* called the novel "bloody, exotic, colorful, and completely plausible.... [It] is an adult adventure story complex and involute, solidly anchored to today's headlines and yet adequately escapist, entertaining but nonetheless engaging to the mind. This is the way adventure stories ought to be written."

Perhaps Hammond Innes's most popular novel is *The Mary Deare,* published in the United States as *The Wreck of the Mary Deare.* The story of a sea captain who struggles to save his ship when it runs aground on a treacherous reef in the English Channel, the adventure novel became a bestseller in several countries and was adapted into a successful film. *The Mary Deare* has also garnered critical acclaim as one of the finest sea adventures of recent times. "I have been reading sea stories for more than half a century," Gene Markey maintained in the *Chicago Sunday Tribune,* "and this is the most exciting one I've read." Although she had some reservations about the quality of the prose, Isabel Quigley, a reviewer for *Spectator* called *The Mary Deare* "first-rate and the climax one of the most thrilling, in the old danger-and-endurance tradition, that I remember meeting." Several critics especially praised the portrait of the ship's captain in his struggle with the sea. A *New Yorker* critic claimed that "the characterization of Patch, master of the *Mary Deare,* is expertly done." G. H. Favre, contributing to *Christian Science Monitor,* believed that the novel is "dominated by the bold figures of a man and a ship, both equally scarred by the vicissitudes of a hard life and seafaring."

The novel was so popular that Hammond Innes named his own boat, a forty-two-foot ocean racer, the *Mary Deare.* For over ten years he and his wife used it to explore the European coastline from Scandinavia to Turkey. His travels made him sensitive to the ecological damage that man has caused in all parts of the world. Several of his books focus on environmental issues: *The Big Footprints* concerns the dwindling herds of African elephants; *The Black Tide* tells about the damaging spills from huge oil tankers; and *High Stand* reflects upon the destruction of forest land.

Hammond Innes was involved with reforesting projects for over twenty-five years. During that time he, Bestic

reported, "planted a million trees." He also owned four forest areas in England and Wales, and devoted so much of his time to forestry that he was obliged in the late 1970s to give up sailing the *Mary Deare.* Speaking of his reforesting projects to Bestic, Hammond Innes once explained: "I'm replacing some of the timber used up by my books." In *High Stand,* "an old-fashioned tale of intrigue and treachery," as a reviewer for *Maclean's* described it, Hammond Innes built his plot around efforts to preserve a forest of red cedars from some unscrupulous loggers. But the plot is almost incidental to the novel. Hammond Innes was more concerned with the forest setting of the story than with its characters and their actions. There are "lovely descriptive passages" of the forest, Jack Sullivan wrote in the *New York Times Book Review.* But ultimately, *High Stand* is "a book where the nonhuman world is depicted," Sullivan wrote, "as more admirable and more alive, than the human."

Hammond Innes also tried his hand at several novels of interest to young readers. Writing under the name Ralph Hammond, the author penned the 1950 children's book *Cocos Gold.* The work follows the adventures of Johnny Keverne, a fifteen-year-old boy in possession of a treasure map to the buried gold on Cocos Island. Unscrupulous treasure hunters nearly kill Johnny while trying to get their hands on the map. In the end, Johnny perseveres against the bandits though readers must discover for themselves if the untold riches are ever reclaimed. "Well-written and absorbing," claimed *New York Times Book Review* critic Howard Pease, "a perfect addition to that special shelf of books reserved ... for boys who think they don't care for reading." A contributor to *Kirkus Reviews* called *Cocos Gold* "one of the most high-powered examples of juvenile suspense fiction we've seen."

Hammond Innes was usually described as a master storyteller whose novels were invariably exciting, entertaining, and believable. "There is no one in our time," D. B. Hughes wrote in *Bookweek,* "who can compare with him in creating the saga of man against the elements." William Hogan of the *San Francisco Chronicle* called him "a born story-teller." Edwin Fadiman, Jr., believes that Hammond Innes is part of an important literary tradition. "Hammond Innes," Fadiman explained in the *Saturday Review,* "belongs to a group of British writers whose artistic heritage derives from such craftsmen as Somerset Maugham. To these men, novel writing represents an opportunity to serve the reader, to entertain, to amuse and, occasionally, to educate him— unobtrusively." Hammond Innes's own evaluation of his work was modest. "I write by the seat of my pants," he once told Green. "I don't know where the story comes from, and I never know quite how it will turn out.... I rely on what I know I can do well—tell a story." Speaking to Green of his life as a freelance writer, Innes once remarked: "I am a novelist. I am one of the self-employed. I have to rely on myself."

Works Cited

Review of *Attack Alarm, Times Literary Supplement,* October 25, 1941.

Baker, Roger, review of *Levkas Man, Books and Bookmen,* March, 1971.

Bestic, Alan, interview with Ralph Hammond Innes, *Radio Times,* August 18-24, 1984.

Boatwright, Taliaferro, review of *The Doomed Oasis, New York Herald Tribune Book Review,* November 13, 1960.

Boucher, Anthony, review of *Blue Ice, New York Times,* August 14, 1949.

Review of *Cocos Gold, Kirkus Reviews,* April 15, 1950, p. 239.

Fadiman, Edwin, Jr., review of *Levkas Man, Saturday Review,* July 3, 1971, pp. 28-29.

Favre, G. H., review of *The Wreck of the Mary Deare, Christian Science Monitor,* October 8, 1956.

Green, William, review of *Solomon's Seal, Telegraph Sunday Magazine,* August 10, 1980.

Henderson, R. W., review of *Blue Ice, Library Journal,* July, 1949.

Review of *High Stand, Maclean's,* October 21, 1985.

Hogan, William, review of *The Wreck of the Mary Deare, San Francisco Chronicle,* October 21, 1956.

Hughes, D. B., review of *The Strode Venturer, Bookweek,* November 21, 1965.

Markey, Gene, review of *The Wreck of the Mary Deare, Chicago Sunday Tribune,* October 21, 1956.

Pease, Howard, review of *Cocos Gold, New York Times Book Review,* May 7, 1950, p. 30.

Quigley, Isabel, review of *The Wreck of the Mary Deare, Spectator,* July 13, 1956.

Stout, Rex, review of *The Doomed Oasis, New York Times Book Review,* November 13, 1960, p. 4.

Sullivan, Jack, review of *High Stand, New York Times Books Review,* June 21, 1985.

Tilden, David, review of *Attack Alarm, Books,* April 12, 1942.

Review of *The Wreck of the Mary Deare, New Yorker,* October 27, 1956.

For More Information See

BOOKS

Contemporary Novelists, Sixth Edition, St. James, 1996.

PERIODICALS

Atlantic, June, 1971; April, 1979.

Best Sellers, November 15, 1967.

Books, May, 1994, p. 15.

Christian Science Monitor, April 22, 1968.

Globe and Mail (Toronto), November 15, 1985.

Harper's, May, 1971.

Library Journal, December, 1988, p. 132; March 15, 1989, p. 98; October 15, 1989, p. 118; May 15, 1990, p. 118.

Los Angeles Times Book Review, September 15, 1981; March 27, 1983.

National Observer, December 15, 1969.

New York Herald Tribune Book Review, October 21, 1956; November 25, 1956.

New York Times, March 8, 1942; October 21, 1956; May 26, 1977.

New York Times Book Review, November 25, 1956; December 24, 1967; December 7, 1969; April 14, 1974; February 8, 1981; December 21, 1986.

Observer, August 6, 1967.

Saturday Review, April 28, 1979.

Spectator, February 19, 1977.

Times (London), September 26, 1985.

Times Literary Supplement, May 28, 1970; March 4, 1977.

Village Voice, August 6, 1979.

Washington Post Book World, January 21, 1968; June 29, 1971; July 22, 1979; December 27, 1980; April 3, 1983; October 20, 1985.

World Literature Today, winter, 1979.

Writer, March, 1970.

Obituaries

PERIODICALS

Times, June 12, 1998, p. 27(1).*

—Sketch by J. Sydney Jones

Autobiography Feature

Christie Harris

1907-

Looking back a long, long way, I can see my delight in secretly shaping any and all events into a story line. I can see that I was always picking up what I needed to become a storyteller.

What I cannot see is that that possibility ever entered my mind. Born in New Jersey, U.S.A., I came to Canada as an infant. We took the train west from Ontario to Fernie, a mining camp in the Rockies a little north of the border, just in time to be caught up in the drama of the 1908 Fernie Fire. A forest fire had been raging out there in the mountains for days when, one morning, the strange color of the sky alarmed my young Irish mother; she thought the end of the world had come. She was clutching me and my brother and sister when my father raced in to say, "Get you down to the railroad! The town is on fire."

The Fernie Fire was always one of our family stories: how my mother had rushed her small brood down to the Canadian Pacific Railway tracks, astounded at women who were clinging to fur coats and jewelry and other such trivia, amazed at "a pigtailed Chinaman" who was trying to save a bundle of oranges that would keep dropping off and rolling away from him.

We were piled into a boxcar. And there were men on the roof with wet sacks, slapping at sparks and blazing bits as we chugged across the trestle over a wild mountain river. We spent the night on a sandbar out in the river, with flaming debris floating by and a minister leading groups in prayers for delivery from the inferno. Apparently my mother was too involved with breast-feeding more babies than her own to join in such organized supplications. When the night was over, we were taken to the nearby town of Cranbrook—refugees in a strange land. From there we were routed on to the pioneer city of Vancouver on the west coast to live in a tent—with bears snuffling around—until my father and his helpers could build a house for us to live in. Arriving there at the end of August, we were still tenting at Christmas. I know because a family story has my brother, seeing the moon's shine through the canvas, asking if it was Santa Claus. I don't imagine "Father Christmas" left many sugar plums at our tent; the stovepipe chimney was not all that big for the jolly old fellow to get down.

I vaguely remember pioneer life in Vancouver—just enough, in fact, to give me the feeling and a head start on research when I'm writing Western historical novels. I remember that the whole family went out there when land was being cleared; we roasted potatoes black in the coals of burning stumps and brush piles. The whole family went out with lard pails and a big copper boiler to pick the small vine-blackberries that provided us with preserves and jam of a flavor no berries since ever seem to have equalled. The whole family went to the homes of other people recently out from the British Isles for evenings of songs and stories; and my father was the prime storyteller. Though his stories always started with "I mind the time . . . ," it was obvious that they could not all be true. But what did that matter? They were hilariously entertaining, or scary; and true to oral tradition, they were as right for the children as they were for the grown-ups. A story was a story, full of happenings and strange characters, including the wee folk who were sometimes glimpsed around the "gentle bush" where they lived.

I started school when I was five because, if I didn't start, there would not be enough children to have a school. There, the "curly-headed Irwin girl" was always called up to read for visitors. And no doubt that had something to do with the pleasure I still take in public readings and talks. It was not confidence I lacked for my first performance at a school Christmas concert; it was a doll. I needed a doll for my recitation; and I had no doll . . . until my father took some potatoes and my mother took some scraps of cloth to make what I have since heard has long been popular with Ulster country people—a Spud Doll.

I know now that old country folkways have a lot to do with pioneer ways in a new country. When I cut my forehead through being knocked down by a dog while I was making doll's clothes, cobwebs were placed over the cut and held on by the lining of a raw eggshell. And when we went home from school for lunch, we got "champ"—well-whipped potatoes greened with peas or new onions and formed into a well on the plate. We took a forkful of champ from the outside of the well and dipped it into the butter melting inside. And we never "made a poor mouth" about a shortage of anything. Family pride was at stake here.

Both parents had been brought up on good farms in the north of Ireland, then called "Ireland" just like the south. Both yearned for the land. So my school days were briefly interrupted by a move to a homestead several hundred miles north in the Shuswap country. This time our shelter was made of lodgepole pines (because they were not too heavy for my brother to help carry), with a dirt floor until we could take over a good log cabin abandoned by another homesteading family. Evidently we had a hay barn; old-timers have told me they lived in it until they could raise their log cabin. Pioneers were good neighbors.

And as far as I was concerned, so were native Indians. I can still remember those Shuswap families driving by in their democrats, with children sitting in the back and dogs walking in the shade under the wagons. The grown-ups

Christie Harris, between brother, Willie (far left) and father, Edward Irwin, with mother, Tillie Irwin, and three younger sisters, Norah, Helen, and Myrtle, Vancouver, 1914.

always smiled at me and called out, "Hello, little papoose!" I liked the Indians; and that early rapport probably contributed to the easiness of relations I have always enjoyed with our First Nations while doing research for my retellings of their marvellous myths and legends. Storytellers have always been my kind of people.

My redheaded brother had a pony and the glory of riding out with the cowboys when a neighboring rancher rounded up his stock. I remember being at the ranch (because my mother was helping the Chinese cook) the day Willie, as we did not dare call our brother later on, rode in with the mail and a newspaper with a big, black headline: WAR DECLARED. In that August of 1914, Britain had declared war on Germany; and Canada, like the rest of the British Empire, was soon at war, too.

My father immediately joined up. I suspect that he was not altogether reluctant to end his brief foray into homesteading. That homestead was a far cry from the green fields and the well-clipped hedges of Farlough, the County Tyrone farm where the Irwins had lived for centuries. The

rest of us followed by train as far as Vancouver, where we spent the war years. When my father returned from the trenches in the spring of 1919, he moved us out to a farm in the Lower Fraser Valley—a good farm acquired under Soldier Settlement arrangements. He moved the furniture in a big wagon drawn by our new team of heavy horses. Willie and I drove the new saddle horse in a light buggy; while Mother and my three sisters caught the electric tram that rattled through the valley.

Now we had horses and cows and pigs and chickens. We had carrots to thin, potatoes to hill, hay to winnow, and grain to thresh with a leather-hinged flail; we had a lot of leather hinges on our farm. And the chore I liked best was walking through the woods to bring the cows home from pasture. The trees heard a lot of poetry at those times; I could declaim with gusto out there on the trails.

Bill (the name my brother now enforced) had his beautiful little mare, Daisy, who had come from the Brighouse racing stables. Too small for the racetrack, she had been raffled off for the Red Cross. Our Sunday school

Christie at twenty: teacher, published author, and flapper.

teacher had won her; and it had taken a long, anxious time for Bill to negotiate her purchase for two goats, four rabbits, and twenty-five hard-earned dollars. Swift and nervous, called Duty Lightfoot by our father, Daisy carried us as smoothly as the proverbial swallow. But before sisters were permitted to ride out through the gate, we had to circle and circle a field until we had proved that we could post. Then we rode out with strict instructions to walk her to the next farm, trot her to the next one, and then we could gallop.

As soon as Bill acquired a two-wheeled cart, a sort of racing sulky, he, my sister Helen, and I went out exploring our world—a world of green fields and green forests with mountains always blue off there in the distance. It was a world where cows grazed in the fields while milk cans waited at the roadside for trucks that would take them to the "milk train" on roads that were gravel, never pavement. Ours was a world of coal-oil lamps and outdoor plumbing, of old-fashioned scrubbing boards and clotheslines. We churned our own butter and sold it, with crates of eggs, to pay for the tea and sugar and flour and kerosene we took home from the country store. We knew nothing of radio or television. We seldom saw a movie; and when we did, it was in soundless black and white, with only a piano breaking the silence with wild simulations of hoofbeats and train noises.

My mother had the land in her blood. She loved every cow, every chicken—even the chicken with one leg and one wing that my father had named Passchendaele after the war's worst battle. She "had the green thumb." "And sure didn't she need it, with her sending off city visitors with enough carrots, rhubarb, and lilacs to drown in?" She was pretty and easygoing. At any suggestion that she spank her children, she quoted her own mother. "Och, no! The world will beat them enough."

My father was not quite so easygoing. Every Saturday morning he had us out there until that farmyard was as tidy as "the ould home" had been; he only regretted there were no hedges for us to clip. Every year he had us out there for spring training. You ran, far and properly; you did your jumps over the beautifully crafted stand he had made for us; then you had your legs rubbed down with salt. And then—win or lose at the Sports Days—you never "made a poor mouth" about anything. In that, Mother backed him up. "The most important thing any girl wears is the look on her face," she told me fairly often.

In the books I wrote later on, my pioneer women say things like that to their daughters because my pioneer women are apt to be Irish. That's what I know—Irish families coping with a world that is long gone.

There was another thing my father was strict about. We never made fun of even the most peculiar people; and we had our share of characters dropping in at the farm for a chat and a cup of my mother's ever-ready tea. There was the gaunt woman in trollopy skirts who had been to the Klondike Gold Rush. Now she had two heavy horses she called Petey Dear and Mikey Love as she grazed them on what my father called "the long acre"—the grass along the side of the road. Then there was the old neighbor who always complained that life got "montonious"; though our parents did suggest that "he wants a turf of being a full load," we treated him like Einstein. And we never dared follow suit when our twinkling-eyed parent referred to our friends Gwyneth and Leithwold as "Granite" and "Leaf-mould." A rather elegant classical musician once crawled under our granary and stayed there for hours after she had had a fight with her husband, my piano teacher. People could and did do the weirdest things. Actually, though, characters made life interesting out there in the Fraser Valley.

So did stories. Stories could lift any old job into another dimension. Bill liked me to carry the lantern for him when he bedded down the cattle because, as I followed him around the barn and the extra cowsheds, I was always telling him what happened next to the Lady of the Lake or David Copperfield or one of King Arthur's knights. And when I was given a really boring job, like keeping the turkeys out of the garden while the fence was being fixed, I worked on my own stories. Those turkeys had to share the blame for a fourteen-verse atrocity about a Baghdad princess. What did I know about Baghdad princesses?

Yet nobody—including me!—ever seemed to notice that I had the makings of a storyteller. My sisters simply gave up on me as a participant in their pre-sleep chatter; sleepiness was all the cover I needed for my nightly plotting, for my "what-happened-next?" in a personal serial story.

I loved pouring out words on paper, too—even the words of the essay-type answers we had to give on examination papers. I loved our grammar sessions at school; it was fascinating to parse sentences, and to see how the proper placement of a phrase could make all the difference. Not that I was hoping to be a writer. I'm not sure I knew that people could be writers. But when I badly needed a source of spending money at high school, I just naturally got myself the job of sending the district news in to the weekly *Columbian* we all subscribed to; the farmers did not seem to mind about my age when I reported their meetings.

Actually, not one teacher ever suggested that I might become a writer. Although I could recite practically the entire output of the poets of the Romantic Revival, my teachers slotted me into a job in mathematics. I loved mathematics. I spent a lot of time helping boys get ready for their math finals.

But I never dated any of those boys. With farm distances and early twenties transportation plus the family habit of going en masse to the local dances, I didn't really need to. Besides, none of them ever asked me.

We were a sociable family. If a party was needed, the neighbors could always arrange a "surprise" party on the Irwins, who had a piano and also a free-and-easy attitude about having a bedroom cleared out to accommodate another set in the square dance. We never actually invited people for Sunday visits, either; they just turned up. Several young war veterans who had come out from the British Isles to try their hand at farming frequently arrived to chat with my father and sing around the piano. Two of them were Scots with good voices. One was a really young Englishman, also with a good voice.

The first time I saw him was on a Sunday afternoon when I passed him on the road. An unusually upright, brisk walker, he carried a cane and lifted his cap to me; and when I got home, there he was again, rising at my entrance and speaking with what I recognized as a "good" English accent. He was something new in my world, more of a country gentleman than a farmer. I began to hear that he was not exactly "handy" with a hammer; he could not patch a roof or fix an engine. But I also heard that he was "handy with his fists." I could see that my father held him in special regard. And as time went by, I began to notice that his eyes always brightened on me, though his manner toward me stayed as impeccable as his tweeds and his accent.

Once he turned up on a Saturday, just as I was hoping to go for a ride. Bill and my father were busy; and since I had been caught standing on Daisy's feedbox while I tried to put on her bridle, I had been forbidden to do my own saddling-up. So I asked our friend if he would catch Daisy for me and get her ready. He seemed delighted to do it; but he was so long in bringing her round I was sure that his horse catching was on a par with his roof-patching. It was only when he finally brought her round, with her coat gleaming and her leather newly polished, that I began to suspect the truth—that he was a superb horseman schooled in the English fashion.

Not long after that, on the day before my sixteenth birthday, he turned up in a raincoat and felt hat and asked to speak to me, alone. When I walked along the path with him, out by the hayfield, he told me that he would not be at my birthday party. Having enlisted with the "Mounties," he was leaving for Regina. He gave me a box of chocolates—

my first!; and his eyes still brightened on me. But that was all. He went off. And that, it seemed, was that.

That was the autumn of 1923 and my final year at high school, where I always won the proficiency prize, a book. Yet I was enrolled in Normal Entrance, not in University Entrance. Oh, I dreamed of going to university; I begged to be allowed to swim in both academic streams; but that was not permitted. So I took the examinations that would qualify me for the teachers' college, and then spent the summer studying for the two extra exams that would let me into the university if a miracle should happen. I spent July on European history only to be informed that all I would actually need was physics. I had never taken physics. But I had the textbook, the month of August, a lot of faith in four-leaf clovers, and a lingering dream of higher education. I studied physics there on the farm, entirely without instruction, and made a 99 percent grade. But I still did not manage to enrol at the University of British Columbia in Vancouver.

Instead, with some contributions from Helen's nursing paycheck and with a lot of tutoring effort on my part, mainly for children having trouble with arithmetic, I trained as a teacher. And I loved teaching. Especially I loved teaching primary classes where I could tell stories and read stories and observe children's responses to the different stories.

I was twenty years old, teaching in Vancouver, when it came like a dazzling revelation: I could tell my own stories. For two weeks I could scarcely wait for recess and noon and after school and the weekend to get on with those ideas that were keeping me awake at night; I could scarcely wait to read them to my pupils, who seemed to love them. So I

"At the typewriter as scriptwriter, broadcaster, and mother of four."

took my sheaf of handwritten tales downtown to the only market I knew of—the weekend "Tillicum Page" in the Vancouver *Daily Province.*

Then I waited ... and waited ... and waited.

When I could stand the suspense no longer, I went back to the *Province.* And as soon as I walked into the Children's Department, someone jumped up from a desk and said: "We didn't know how to get in touch with you." I had not left an address or a phone number. And they were buying all nine stories; in fact, two were already set up in type.

I had sold my very first stories! And I became a regular contributor to the "Tillicum Page." When I ran into an old farm neighbor, he said: "So you tell stories, too, like your father." I just hoped mine would be as entertaining.

So. Now I was a teacher, a writer, and a flapper with bobbed hair, short skirts, long beads, and fancy garters—a flapper doing the Charleston at dances I no longer attended with the family. Dates were now an important part of my life. Dates and tennis.

One day when I had walked the mile home from school, I found a young man waiting on the porch. Well-dressed and upright as a lodgepole pine, he lifted his hat.

"Tommy Harris!" He had ridden his Mountie patrols on the Canadian prairies, had gone home to Argentina to visit an ailing father, and had stayed on there for a time to ride the pampas as assistant majordomo on a big estancia where they raised polo ponies. Now he was back, reenlisted in the Royal Canadian Mounted Police, and waiting to move into their Vancouver barracks.

"I always intended to see what you were like when you grew up," he told me in that impeccable English accent.

Daughter Sheilagh, the toe-hanger in **Confessions of a Toe-Hanger,** *1954.*

And one glance seemed to do it. He was even a trifle cavalier about the news that I was unofficially engaged to somebody else.

Away back then, in the twenties, "nice girls" did not have "relationships"; long engagements were the rule rather than the exception, while marriage was apt to be a "till death us do part" commitment to battling through any differences that threatened the strength of family ties. And it all gave me an emotionally charged summer, having two genuinely nice, very attractive men in their twenties determined to be the one and only man in my life. The fact that a Mountie could not marry without permission, and then only after he had served for seven years, seemed to be beside the point. I celebrated my twenty-first birthday at a ball where the walls glinted with pennanted lances and where my partners all wore scarlet tunics and did not dance the Charleston. Carefree footwork did not go all that well with spurred heels.

Neither did romance. Mounties were highly mobile. In no time at all, it seemed, mine was posted to Prince George, five hundred miles north of Vancouver, leaving me lots of time to notice an exciting new field for writers—RADIO!

Radio was so new that the father of one of my friends spent happy evenings draping wires around the kitchen and turning knobs until he achieved a squawk. Small radio stations were springing up around town. People were getting excited about "newscasts" and "Fibber McGee and Molly." But who knew how to write a script? I undoubtedly would have found out then and there if I had not decided to teach school in Prince George, where I arrived in time for the fall term, shortly before my fiance was posted west to Vanderhoof and then even farther west, to Hazelton. You could not win with the Mounties.

But I have never regretted that move north. Even the drive to Prince George expanded my world into a new dimension. I discovered a fascination with frontier life in the Canadian West, a world vastly different from the frontier times in the American West that were featured in all those movies. Quite without realizing it, I was picking up what I needed for the historical novels I would someday write.

I had bought a Model-T Ford "bug," a tiny convertible complete with rumble seat, no gear shift, and a braking system that made it advisable to carry a rock; when the radiator started to boil, going uphill, someone could jump out and put it under a back wheel; when going downhill, it was sometimes even more advisable to be dragging a tree.

Helen's husband, who was teaching me to drive, got me safely to Prince George. The road north was a dirt/gravel road with wooden platforms hanging out over some awesome spots in the Fraser Canyon. Then there were marvellous snake fences through the ranching country north of the Canyon, and reminders of the ox teams and the Barnard Express (BX) stagecoaches that had taken prospectors north to the Cariboo Gold Rush of the 1860s. The old stopping places were still there and derelict log cabins and traces of the even older Hudson's Bay Company's palisaded fur-trading post at Fort Alexandria. I could see the old fur brigades: beribboned boatmen bringing the furs out of the north; red-shirted packers taking those furs east and south to the Columbia District by long, long trains of horses led by a frock-coated, beaver-hatted chief trader who was treated like royalty along the trail.

Christie and T. A. Harris with their four oldest children: (clockwise, from left) Moira, Michael, Sheilagh, and Brian, about 1945.

Fort George had been an important HBC post; and by the time I got to Prince George, the town that had grown up nearby, I was breathless from more than placing and removing that rock behind the back wheel. For me, this was a storied world. I was eager for every story: the fur brigades, the paddle wheelers, the Hanging Judge, the Royal Engineers, the 1858 invasion of the forty-niners from California's worked-out prospects into the new, law-abiding British Colony where the Royal Navy was standing offshore and the Royal Marines had landed, ready for trouble. This I would write about.

Though not at the moment. First, there was the Royal Canadian Mounted Police world actually seen for the first time at close hand—a world of horses and court and Indian reserves and backwoods settlers and renegades and taking the census out in the wilderness. This was the Silent Force, quietly strong, the world's most famous police force, quietly incorruptible. Maintiens le Droit "without fear, favour, or affection," its motto had nothing about always getting its man. Keeping the Peace was its mandate; federal laws its jurisdiction.

Then there was the new school, the new friends, the tennis club, then the badminton club and the teachers' basketball team. There was my Girl Guide (Girl Scout) company, captained with considerable help from the local

scoutmaster. And there was the COLD of a northern winter: fifty below, or ten below with a gale blowing for weeks. There was the Trappers' Ball, the dances, the parties. There were letters to write to my westering Mountie. I was too busy to think of writing stories. Yet that year and a half north of the canyon was invaluable to me as a writer.

I was back in Vancouver, teaching and writing, when Tommy finally dismounted and went into the Immigration Service, where a man did not have to wait and wait for permission to marry.

Now the Depression was the problem, and the rule against married women on school staffs. Since we were married in mid-February 1932, I was out of a job on March 1, 1932. Still, that gave me time to really get back to writing—a time rather cut into by the arrival of three babies within four years: Michael, Moira, and Sheilagh. Beautiful children! I found myself writing humor pieces for the women's page of the Vancouver *Daily Province*.

And coming up with marvellous ideas for a radio program for children. I had met a writer who had actually sold a radio script, for two dollars; I had borrowed a copy to see how you laid out a script. Obviously, there was nothing to it: narrator, characters, dialogue, sound effects, and a lot of fading in and fading out with music. It was still just a story. Anybody could do it.

Son Michael, the original "high flyer" of **Let X Be Excitement,** *1957.*

I dreamed up a series of fifteen-minute programs of stories and songs; for the songs I put new words to old melodies. And since I clearly intended to fly high on those airwaves, I handed my pilot script in to the Vancouver station of the new national network. Obviously they were not impressed. All I got was Silence. But I soon had another idea for another such series. Again I got Silence. Actually I had handed in three pilots by the morning my telephone rang. Someone from that station, now rather elegantly housed in the Vancouver Hotel, asked if I could be there at noon that day.

"Right now?" I rounded up a baby-sitter. I caught a bus. And then, there I was, sitting at a boardroom table with the station's executive staff. The topic in hand was the coronation of the next king, King George VI. Coronation Day would be in May of 1937, not all that many months ahead. The national network was planning a coast-to-coast official Coronation Day Programme. Vancouver had been assigned a half-hour juvenile musical fantasy that was to be a Canadian child's dream of the coronation, dedicated to the two princesses: Elizabeth and Margaret Rose. But the Vancouver station had no children's programs, no children's writers ... until someone unearthed my three pilot scripts.

Obviously, they hadn't much choice, or much time. So did I think I could hand in a fairly well worked-out script, complete with sample lyrics, by noon the next day? Toronto was understandably anxious.

So was Christie Harris. I swallowed and said, "Yes, of course I can." I kept the baby-sitter, worked all night, and was back at noon the next day with my child's dream of the

coronation, complete with at least a verse or two of the lyrics.

They liked it! Rushed it to Toronto. And Toronto liked it. In fact, Toronto said it was to be expanded into a full hour. And the sky was the limit! Singers, actors, orchestra, choirs, fanfares, sound effects, whatever it took!

For starters, it took Harry Biener, a gifted local composer with a Strauss touch and a flair for rousing marches. It took John Avison's orchestra, the Elgar Junior Choir, Vancouver's top singers and actors, and Frank Vivyyan's sound effects. We had no canned sounds then. Even the horses pulling the royal coach were just coconut shells, skilfully manipulated. And it was wonderful, working on a live show!

That was the first of seven juvenile musical fantasies Harry Biener and I wrote for the Canadian Broadcasting Corporation. It was the start of a quarter century of writing adult plays and humor sketches, women's talks, school broadcasts, and a children's adventure serial, all for CBC production. And in those early, experimental days in radio, even the school broadcasts could be exciting. For a series called "Living in Other Times," I created Charlie Chickinick, a nice little fellow with the soul of a nightingale and the courage of a mouse. In that series of half-hour dramatizations, Charlie was searching for one valiant ancestor. He kept finding ancestors "Living in Other Times" only to discover that each was—again!—just a nice little fellow with the soul of a nightingale and the courage of a mouse. Alan Young played Charlie in that and later series; and before he went to Hollywood to star in "Mr. Ed" with a Talking Horse, Alan, who wrote his own comedy show for the CBC, was a marvellous radio comic. And with

Daughter Moira, life model for Linsey of **You Have to Draw the Line Somewhere,** *1951.*

an actor of that caliber to spur me on, I wrote some good lines, some good scenes for those old school broadcasts. Eventually someone from Columbia University wrote about Charlie Chickinick, as pioneering humor in school broadcasts.

Even before my Coronation Day fantasy went on the air, we had moved out to the Fraser Valley, to Huntingdon on the Canada-U.S. border. And there two more beautiful children—Brian and Gerald—joined the Harris family. And there my children were very involved in my radio writing. They also provided me with a lot of characters and scenes for my as-yet-unplanned children's books. Finding them fascinating, if exasperating at times, I made notes on their patterns of behaviour, their patterns of speech. I tried out everything on them and took them along on research outings, like the interviewing of valley "old timers," both native and immigrant. Often that was easier than finding a baby-sitter.

We lived in a big, inconvenient old brick house with a clothesline that kept breaking. We had an orchard, bantam chickens, and a dog who could never quite decide whether he was a doormat or just part of an obstacle course for a woman who was always rushing around with baskets of wet wash, a woman with a steady stream of radio deadlines to meet, a woman with one spot she could call her own—a swivel chair and a rolltop desk in the dining room.

A friend remembers coming upon me in the back garden one summer afternoon—me with my typewriter on an apple box, a child in the playpen, another up an apple tree, and two more playing in the sandbox. (The fifth had not yet arrived.)

Son Gerald, life model for the small brother in six of the novels, 1964.

A woman like that just naturally spawns domestic disasters.

Still, even disasters are grist for a writer's mill. And the CBC had a weekly humor program called "Miscellany," fifteen-minute scripts read by professional actors. That program did nothing for the Harris family's public image, but it did let me get rid of a lot of frustration in a profitable way. Laughter was Survival in my situation; and twenty-five dollars meant gumboots all round or maybe a holiday outing. Or nearly two months of "mother's help."

There was, for instance, "Dyeing the Carpet." It was our budding artist who yearned to have "that awful carpet" replaced by something "hand-crafted" in an "earth color." But it was my idea to make do with what we had; dyeing was sort of "hand-crafting," wasn't it? And moss green was an "earth color." We waited until Dad was away for a weekend on Reserve Army maneuvers before the children rolled up the carpet and, after undulating it around the backyard like a carnival dragon, helped scrub the moss green dye into it. By the time we had it back on the floor, they all looked like leafing trees. But we were sure it was dry enough to play on by the time a rather humorless girl turned up with a child she was baby-sitting—a child in frilly pink dress and panties. When the pair departed looking like fugitives from the army's camouflage course, our artist was horribly embarrassed.

Not that embarrassment was a new sensation to the Harris children. There were my disaster birthday cakes—the one that went on fire and the one with icing that stretched out like super-elastic. There was my moaning and groaning around the house to develop my "deeper registers" for the broadcast talks I was doing; the girls found it

Son Brian, the original Anthony in the "family" novels, 1954.

Investiture into the Order of Canada: being decorated by Governor General Edward Shreyer at Rideau Hall, Ottawa, 1981.

hard to explain to astonished friends why their mother was acting like that; and then it was on "Miscellany." Not until they were grown up and helped put those disasters into my trilogy of family novels did they find them as funny as I had found them after I had dried my tears back there in the old brick house. Laughter had indeed been Survival.

Yet my children were staunchly supportive of my literary efforts. They read everything I wrote. And they would go to any trouble to be sure there was nothing "phoney" in my scripts. Their father was even more concerned to see that I got my horses right, and my boats, dogs, and guns. Even now, all married and with families of their own, my children are my willing technical advisors, my most loyal fans. You can juggle Family and Career and survive to write about it. But it takes a bit of doing.

Radio led me directly into books. In the mid-fifties, I had a juvenile adventure serial running Monday evenings on CBC; and it was not mere coincidence that my heroine, Maeve, was remarkably like my adventurous daughter Sheilagh, while Maeve's small brother had a distinct resemblance to Sheilagh's small brother, Gerald. I had life

models right there in my backyard. When the series was over, Longmans Green of Toronto asked me to turn it into an historical novel. It came out in 1957 as *Cariboo Trail.*

A book was something solid, permanent, not gone with the airwaves like a radio program. And I was ready to turn my energy to writing books now that all but one of my children had trotted out of the home corral.

Coincidence was with me. My husband was posted to Prince Rupert as Officer-in-Charge of Immigration for the area encompassing the Queen Charlotte Islands and the mainland from Alaska south to Kitimat and eastward along those northern rivers—an area that was to add yet another dimension to my writing, though I was unaware of it at the time.

I was particularly enthusiastic about leaving school broadcasts with their endless research and their tendency to spoil a story line to cram in more information. A new teachers' script committee seemed to threaten my artistic integrity. So I went happily into "Schools" to announce, "No more scripts!" I was leaving for the north coast.

The director actually jumped up in excitement. "YOU'RE going up there? We've always wanted to do a series on those great old Indian cultures."

Well. I had always been interested in our native people. And a commission to write something that would be aired on the Canadian Broadcasting Corporation would give me an excuse to be as nosey as I would want to be up there in the land of the totem pole. "Okay," I agreed, "ONE more series."

Tommy, Gerald, and I went north by coastal steamer; Brian saw us off at the Vancouver dock. And in glorious May weather that mountainous, island-fringed coast was magnificent. Then, my first day in Prince Rupert, I was standing in front of the museum admiring the totem poles when a woman said to me, "I just love these old Chinese things, don't you?" Obviously it was time somebody did something about "those great old Indian cultures."

Although I had been on the west coast for half a century, this was a new world to me, the world of the people who had produced a stunning art and a wonderful mythology. I found their myths and legends in museum collections like the one Franz Boas made for the Smithsonian at the turn the century. But the stories, like the art, were understandable only to someone who knew the code these people had lived by, someone who knew the mind-set of a people whose culture had been uniquely right for an area where the seas and the rivers were wild, the mountains and the forests impenetrable, a people truly at one with nature in a fabulously rich environment. A people with the vigor of northern peoples.

I had been warned. The director had shown me a letter about a recent national school broadcast. A Toronto scriptwriter who may have known a lot about the Iroquois and the Sioux had adapted a Haida legend from the Queen Charlotte Islands. And an angry Haida man had listed thirty-nine basic errors, thirty-nine things that could not have happened to those people at that time at that place. So!

Although I easily managed an informational series for "Schools," I had over three years of almost total immersion in books and in the field before I dared to retell even one story. I was fortunate in having a friend, Chief Kenneth Harris (Hagbegwatku), to advise me. An artist friend's car or Tommy's sailing sloop took me wherever I needed to go to get the feel of the setting.

My first five retold legends, titled *Once upon a Totem,* were sent off to Longmans Green as specified by my first contract. When they were rejected, without comment, Moira, now a fashion artist in New York, gave them to a Manhattan agent who handed them on to Jean Karl, the superb editor who had just launched the new children's book department at Atheneum. Jean loved the stories, but said they seemed to have been written for the EAR. Of course! For nearly a quarter of a century I had been writing for radio. Of course I wrote for the ear, with fragmentary sentences and a careful avoidance of much direct narration. She also said that if I were willing to work on my style, she would like to publish those stories.

I was more than willing. And since Tommy had taken early retirement and we were going to Europe for a year, via New York, I was able to discuss with Jean what I should do: study classics of children's literature and work through a book on style. I did that while I rewrote and rewrote those stories, mainly in Spain. Michael and Gerald

were there with us when we celebrated the contract. And *Once upon a Totem* was singled out by the anthropology staff of the Museum of Natural History for giving an accurate picture of North West Coast native culture by slipping in information so unobtrusively that it never slowed down a story. The Vancouver Public Library presented me with a leather-bound copy of the book, as a Canadian book since McClelland and Stewart of Toronto brought it and my subsequent Atheneum books out in simultaneous publication. Like me, my books have dual nationality.

Long before it was out, though, we were back in New York, where Moira was now sketching children's fashions for Bergdorf Goodman ads. Intrigued by a sweltering young model's strangled "How do you get to be the artist?" I thought that many children might like to know that. Moira agreed; in fact, so many funny things had happened to her while she was getting to be the artist, she had considered writing a book. But she was too busy to think about it. So I thought about it. If she would tape the incidents we thought relevant to her story of getting to be the artist, I would man the typewriter. As it turned out, I also studied her art books, haunted the Metropolitan Museum of Art, followed young fashion artists around Seventh Avenue with a notebook, and went to artists' parties in Greenwich Village, where we were staying. Somewhere, deep down inside, I became a fashion artist, remembering how it had been getting to be the artist.

When we had two chapters ready, we took them to the agent, who promptly said, "This won't sell. It's a career book, and you have to write a career book to formula."

"No way!" We were going for the "awful truth" or nothing. Finally she said, "Well, the only editor I know who might look at such an offbeat career book is the one who liked your offbeat Indian legends." Jean Karl! So we went off to Atheneum. And there, in front of us, Jean started to read, and to laugh. "This is wonderful!" she said. "We'll do it." *You Have to Draw the Line Somewhere,* illustrated by Moira Johnston, was in the running for the *New York Herald Tribune*'s Spring Book Festival Award. A reviewer called it "funny as Cheaper by the Dozen."

By the time it came out, in 1964, I was back in Vancouver, wrapping up another historical novel: *West with the White Chiefs.* Tommy had helped me get my horses over the Rockies back in the wilderness of 1863. And since my main characters—apart from an Assiniboine boy—were Viscount Milton and Dr. W. B. Cheadle, two adventurous young Englishmen who left a lively journal of their travels, I had no trouble with my dialogue; I knew how adventurous young Englishmen spoke and how they treated their horses. Their unwelcome Irish hanger-on was no problem to me, either; Mr. Felix O'Byrne was born to be comic relief in a children's adventure story.

Now the North West Coast was calling me back. When I had been doing my research in Prince Rupert, I had discovered Charles Edenshaw, a great Haida Eagle Chief, Edinsa, who had also been one of Canada's finest artists. Though his carvings and his jewelry were treasured in the world's great museums, he had died in obscure poverty. I couldn't find enough information about him to do a school broadcast on him.

I had to find out about Charles Edenshaw and write his biography, something I could do only by going back to the

Queen Charlotte Islands to talk with his descendants. Too, I knew I could not write about a Haida artist without knowing about Haida art. Fortunately, I knew Bill Reid, the superb modern Haida artist whose latest sculpture, Spirit of Haida Gwai, will have place of honor in the new Canadian Embassy in Washington, D.C. Bill was willing to be my art consultant only if he could get on with his own work while we talked, in his studio; so it was there that he told me about the tragedy of the Lords of the Coast after the coming of the white man.

He did not say what others were telling me: that the proud Edenshaw family would never talk freely to a white woman. Still, I took the precaution of not telling them I was coming; when they saw me, perhaps they would talk to me.

When Tommy and I arrived at Haida (Masset), Charles Edenshaw's daughter Florence Davidson (Jadal q'eganga) was pointed out to me on the street. When I introduced myself, she said, "We have been expecting you." In fact, they had planned a reception for me that very evening so that all the family could meet me (and decide whether or not to talk to me?).

Fortunately for my project, it was agreed that Florence would tell me all the treasured old family stories. And it was wonderful that summer, listening to this gentle, high-ranking woman there by the northern sea at the edge of the forest, looking across the waters, north to Alaska. Her eyes twinkled when there was humor; but there was little humor in the story of a great culture slowly but surely dying of shame during three generations of culture contact.

And how could I tell the story of a valiant chief driving himself to record his culture in wood, argillite, and silver for the museums without first showing how truly great that culture had been? This could not be the biography of an Indian chief. It had to be a three-generation saga, the tragedy of culture contact.

To put the Edenshaw family stories into historical context for my saga, I needed to be in Victoria for ready access to the Provincial Archives, the Provincial Museum, and to Wilson Duff, Provincial Anthropologist and the scholar most knowledgeable about the Haida. So we rented a beach house on Cordova Bay for a year.

Illustrated by Bill Reid, *Raven's Cry* won the Canadian Association of Children's Librarians' Book of the Year for Children medal, my first major award. Considered a moving and accurate account of what happened to native people along the west coast after the coming of the white man, it has been required reading for some University of British Columbia anthropology courses. But it is the Haida people's enthusiasm for it, their use of it in their remarkable Rediscovery Program for youth, that "makes my heart sing."

Before it was out on the shelves, I had finished my year's work on another "family" novel: *Confessions of a Toe-Hanger.* Readers of *You Have to Draw the Line Somewhere* had kept telling me that they loved the sister, Feeny; what happened to her? So I asked her life model; and Sheilagh's answer was a shocker. I had never realized she had been growing up feeling that her talents weren't important, like her sister's. The proverbial "middle child," she had always been a bit of a rebel; but a mother does not worry overly about a daughter who is bright, pretty, athletic, popular—a daughter who can hide her insecurities in some breath-stopping expertise on an exercise bar in an upstairs sun porch. Her grandfather had made it for her, as he had made an easel for her sister, a wearable toolkit for her older brother, and satin-smooth building blocks for her younger brother's projects in the sandbox. My father never mentioned talent; he just supported it; and Sheilagh had not realized that her beloved exercise bar was a tribute to hers.

I was dismayed to discover that she had been losing her self-confidence year by year. Fortunately, now the mother of four on Prince Edward Island—Anne of Green Gables country—she agreed to help me tell her story. So we rented an old farmhouse near her home. And there, with mingled wit and tears and determination, she revealed the loss of her confidence and the valiant struggle to go beyond loss of confidence to a realization of how talented she actually was. *Confessions of a Toe-Hanger* was an instant success, getting marvellous reviews and going into four printings its first year. Though now out of print, it is still treasured by women who found fun and hope in it when they desperately needed those things. And children of the Computer Age, taking it out on their library cards, have no trouble identifying with the girl growing up in the forties and fifties. I would love to write a sequel about the accomplished woman who can backpack and paddle with any of the young "protectors" dedicated, as she is, to Saving the Wilderness and writing about it.

It took years of persuasion to get one of my sons to add a boy's growing-up story to make this a family trilogy.

On her 85th birthday, Christie signs books and celebrates a new edition of **Raven's Cry,** *her classic work on the Haida.*

When he agreed, reluctantly, Michael was a research engineer and test pilot at the Cornell Aeronautical Laboratory near Buffalo. And after giving me a brief course in aeronautics generally, he turned out forty hours of tape for *Let X Be Excitement,* which Jean Karl frequently called a "cliffhanger" during the writing. Listening to my son's accounts of doing test runs on his inventions, rafting a wild river, working down in a mine, rowing in world-class competition, skiing in scary situations, and flying in even scarier ones, made me thankful that I had not known what he was doing most of the time. Michael edited the manuscript, chapter by chapter; he scrutinized every word in the final draft. So that book is authentic, scientifically accurate, and more than a little hair-raising. It has the Harris Family Guarantee of authenticity. For, as Sheilagh commented when it was her turn to confess, "Might as well tell the truth. The kids'll know if it's phoney."

Friends commented that I still had two confessors to go: Brian and Gerald. Both declined the dubious pleasure of telling Mother what they had been doing all those years. At the moment, though, Gerald is revealing some of his past in a young adult novel we are coauthoring. (Brian has still to be worked on.)

Moira worked with me again, as coauthor and illustrator for *Figleafing through History: The Dynamics of Dress.* My husband coauthored *Mule Lib,* a true tale of a sixteen-year-old soldier and an incredible mule in World War I. He also helped me sail a sloop through some stormy northern waters in *Mystery at the Edge of Two Worlds.* And he looked after my horses in *Forbidden Frontier,* a novel about the outrage of two teenaged children-of-the-fur-trade over humiliations inflicted on them during the influx of white settlers at the time of the Cariboo Gold Rush in the 1860s.

In *Secret in the Stlalakum Wild,* a Junior Literary Guild selection and winner of a British Columbia Library Commission award, grandchildren were the models for characters caught up in a fantasy-adventure in the mountains where my own children had loved to hike. A native friend, Cornelius Kelleher, had told me about stlalakums, the unnatural beings in the natural world of the Lower Fraser Valley.

Family was with me on both occasions when I know I sighted UFOs. But they were not involved in my relating those sightings to the old native myth of "The Man Who Came from the Sky." A mixture of mythology and science fiction, *Sky Man on the Totem Pole?* was another Junior Literary Guild selection.

My books were going on special lists on both sides of the border; they were winning awards, mainly in Canada. The Canadian Authors Association gave me two—one, the Vicky Metcalf Award for a body of significant work for young people. And awards are gratifying.

But it was those old North West Coast stories that had the continuing magic for me. I wrote *Once More upon a Totem.* And then I found Mouse Woman; that is, I suddenly realized her potential as a story character.

Mouse Woman was and still is dear to the hearts of the Tsimshian, Nisgha, Haida, and Tlingit peoples. A supernatural being who can appear as a mouse or as the tiniest and most imperious of grandmothers, she is always scampering in and out of their stories, especially when young people have stumbled into trouble or have been tricked into trouble

by monsters of one kind or another. She took a lot of research and some discussions with Wilson Duff and with native people before she could be built up into the main character in my "Mouse Woman" collections: *Mouse Woman and the Vanished Princesses; Mouse Woman and the Mischief-Makers, Mouse Woman and the Muddle-heads,* the first of which brought me my second CACL medal. Even more gratifying, native people tell me that my Mouse Woman is exactly right.

Because theirs was an extremely rank-conscious, matrilineal society, princesses were very important; only their sons could become the great chiefs; and only they seemed to be desired as human wives by the Myth People—the supernatural human/animal shape-shifters. Princesses were important characters in the North West Coast's stories.

So an idea struck me. Why not put these native story-tale princesses into context of the world's fairy-tale princesses? By the time I had spent a summer tracking down the Old World's princesses, I had decided that princesses were trouble, trouble, trouble. The trouble with princesses was that they vanished, or they fell into dire straits, or they were very hard on adventurous young men out to win their hand in marriage.... When I had settled on the seven main troubles, I searched the old museum collections for native examples of identical troubles.

The Trouble with Princesses won the Canada Council Children's Literature Prize, now designated the Governor-General's Award, to set children's books on the same level as adult books in being worthy of Canada's top literary honor.

Naturally *The Trouble with Princesses* set me researching *The Trouble with Adventurers,* and I found animals as well as humans among the adventurers.

Now, I am finding it an easy step from the native sensitivity to Nature-and-the-Spirit-World to the new general awareness of the plight of our planet; and, as always, my family is providing helpful criticism and technical advice for books-in-the-works.

It was this family participation, this unflagging support and enthusiasm for my storytelling, that put a special shine on my Great Occasion: Investiture into the ORDER OF CANADA in 1981.

One of my grandchildren, in Ottawa for the event, although not allowed to attend the ceremony, asked about the decoration that was to be pinned on me by the Queen's representative, the governor-general. "Is this like the medals Granny gets for her books?"

When her mother explained that no, it was more like the insignia of one of the old orders of knights, with the Queen as Sovereign Lady, my granddaughter squealed, "Oh! Sir Granny!"

Well, since the old knights, encumbered as they were by heavy armor, always stood a good chance of falling off their horse and/or running into a dragon, that may be a suitable way to end the story of a woman whose storytelling was not altogether unencumbered.

Still, she chose it. She loved it. And she always thought it was worth the doing.

UPDATE

I ended my autobiography, more or less, with receiving my Order of Canada in 1981, and with my 1982 book, *The Trouble with Adventurers,* published when I was 75. But so much has happened since then. The high honor of being made a member of the Order of Canada may have seemed, to some, like the marking of the autumn of a long career. Perhaps I did qualify as a golden oldie, in terms of years. But I was still writing every day, with more books in my mind than I could ever finish. I was flying all over Canada, to schools and libraries often in remote communities, delivering lectures to children who'd never met an author before. Flown in by a bush pilot, I had found myself celebrating my 70th birthday in a village on Hudson Bay, blowing out candles on not one, but four birthday cakes!

But the early '80s were a time of dramatic changes in my life that would keep me from publishing another book until 1994, twelve years later—when I was 87. Tommy Harris, the stalwart gentleman I had met when I was fifteen, died in 1983, a year after our Golden Wedding. After his death, I continued the lecture tours. And kept writing every day. I had two books underway. The first, a book about a lonely child and an imaginary playmate, was set in Vancouver. As always, I drew from the life around me. Part of Tommy's and my weekly routine for the years we lived in Vancouver's West End was the trip by tiny ferry to the farmers market at Granville Island, with its lively marine activity and backdrop of steep blue mountains that are so basic to the compelling power of the Northwest Coast. As he had for previous books, Tommy helped with the sailing scene, making sure my storm was just right. Another book I had in mind was based on my youngest son Gerald's years in the fisheries as a junior biologist, working with the salmon in the creeks of the Queen Charlotte Islands (known to the Haida as Haida Gwaii) where *Raven's Cry* was set. Gerald began as consultant, but his own enthusiasm for writing emerged as we worked, and he became my collaborator. The story of a young man whose salmon studies on a wilderness island lead to his discovering his life passion, defending an urban stream in his home city, the book gradually became more his book than mine, with me still working over the drafts with him. I'd collaborated with a daughter on *Figleafing,* and relished collaboration with another of my children.

But the familiar patterns of life—the reliable routine that had freed me for flights of fantasy at my typewriter—had been broken. Gone was the companion who had helped me with every adventuresome scene, joined me on daily walks along the seawall, cheerfully cleaned up as a writer wife rushed to meet yet another deadline. I stayed in the West End, near the sea, but moved next door to a highrise that looked out over English Bay and south towards Granville Island, scene of the new book. This invigorating view of the sea was becoming increasingly important to me. For, suddenly, I was less able to, physically, walk the seawall.

Hip surgeries had begun; I would have a total of four hip replacements during these years. It was more difficult for me to knock out books with the physical ease and energy I'd always had. There were several minor strokes which impaired my memory somewhat. I could still recite all the romantic poets by heart, but the complex thought it requires to structure a book and to do intense research was becoming more difficult. There were other losses. Jean Karl, the Atheneum editor I had been blessed to work with on most of my books, went into semi-retirement. And Atheneum fell prey to the corporate takeover wars, being devoured, and then devoured again. I had lost the safe and welcoming harbor that had been my publishing home since 1963. I began to see how lucky I had been to have had this stability for so long.

It was also a time of cultural tumult for native peoples, and for writers using their myths and ethic, the stories in which I had found such riches and learned such respect for these great, wounded cultures. As a mark of their growing confidence and vitality, the Northwest Coast tribes, too, were taking possession of their past, finding their own voice, repatriating their artifacts, and their stories. I cheered this strengthening, and was honored, in 1991, to attend, with my two daughters, an extraordinary pole raising at the abandoned village of Yan. Settled into the shade of huge driftlog, I witnessed today's Haida bringing Yan back to life, with a great carved cedar pole, seagoing canoes, ceremonial regalia, and children again filling the beach with laughter. Raised on the fantasy and epic of Celtic tales as I had been, I had always felt at home with native ideas of transformation between the human, animal, and spirit worlds. I felt at home here now, surrounded by the same

On her 90th birthday, Christie was surrounded by four of her five children: (from left) Brian, Moira, Gerald, Michael. Sheilagh was in the Amazonian rain forest!

Christie was toasted at this millennium family gathering of all her children, and some of her grand- and great-grandchildren. "Toehanger" Sheilagh is left center, with pendant.

gracious, gentle friendliness the Haida had always shown me.

But, on the beach, the girls were picking up hostile vibrations—an expression, perhaps, of this cultural assertiveness, this belief that they must become strong through their own efforts, not with the help of a pink-cheeked Irish-Canadian writer. It was therefore doubly gratifying when, the following year, Bill Reid's artistic heir, Robert Davidson—who'd been a teen-ager at the Edenshaw family meeting those years ago in Masset when Florence had given me her stories—wrote (with anthropologist Margaret Blackman) a foreward for a new edition of *Raven's Cry,* setting my books in context to the renaissance of the Haida culture. How proud I was to read Robert's tribute to *Raven's Cry:* "It filled a gap in my life as a Haida person ... I didn't realize that I was Haida, that we had our own culture and our own heroes.... There was no information anywhere so that I could relate to them.... It helped give me an idea of why we were such a devastated people, spiritually and culturally."

I began to see my legacy reflected in other ways that gave me particular joy. I could see the legacy of my writing in my childrens' work—and lives. Moira had become a writer of nonfiction books and magazine articles. Sheilagh had become first a teacher, like me, then an editor and

magazine writer, and—to my delight—worked with Moira as her assistant on all her books. It thrills me that they work together so well. Gerald has completed the salmon book we began together more than a decade ago, and I hope this will be his first published book—the next generation of Harrises writing books for young people. Brian responded to the sight of the French battlefields where his father had fought in World War I by writing an empassioned and very good poem. Even my eldest son, Michael, an aeronautical engineer, got the book writing bug and spent two years working with Sheilagh on a book about overpopulation and its impending impacts on the environment and social stability. It may not yet have found a publisher.

But its emphasis on the environment is an example of another legacy the children tell me my writing has given them: an active concern for protecting the earth and nature's balances—the same nature ethic I found embedded in the myths of the Northwest Coast as I retold them in the early 1960s, when environmental awareness had barely been born. In an article in the *National Geographic,* Moira argued for saving the vanishing forests of the Queen Charlotte Islands as a national wilderness park. If my five have translated ecological sensitivity into their lives by reading their mother's books, I hope my young readers have, too.

I saw this legacy in action when I drove in with my family to two wilderness forests in British Columbia, rattling over washboard roads to the site of major battles to save the ancient trees from clearcut logging. At Stein Valley, with my children and grandchildren camping out in a pine forest while I, admittedly, took refuge in a comfortable motel, I spoke, along with the music of Gordon Lightfoot, to the huge crowd that had gathered with the native people to try to save the forest. And then, on Vancouver Island, as an exhausted, rain-soaked group gathered round a fire at the end of a day on the barricades, fighting to save the great cedars of Clayquot Sound, I spurred them on by telling them the worth of what they were doing. They listened, as I had listened to the stories that taught me about the native ethic of the land. It was remarkable, here in these wild, wet forest settings—me in my late-eighties stumbling through rough trails on my walker—to find that the stories I had so loved telling had made me something of an elder statesman for the environmental movement. I can think of no better legacy.

Legacies are fine. But, at 92, I am still a writer. All my life, I've awakened with ideas I just had to get down. I'm still eager to write the stories of several of British Columbia's amazing native women, like Amelia Connolly, who became Lady Douglas and the first lady in the crown colonies of Vancouver Island and British Columbia. In recent years, I've increasingly wanted to tell my own story, a memoir, and I still scribble down ideas. The difficulty now, though, is getting on with it and getting the book done. And yet a number of wonderful things have happened to me in the last decade of this century that make me feel, still, very much a writer, and very much alive.

A great event for me was to have a handsome new edition of *Raven's Cry* published by distinguished Vancouver publishers, Douglas & McIntyre, on my 85th birthday, November 21, 1992. At the big book party, Bill Reid's wife, Martinne, turned up with flowers from Bill, whose illustrations still graced the book and who was now severely weakened by his many years of Parkinson's disease. Just a year earlier, my daughters, Moira and Sheilagh, had flown to Washington, D.C. to represent me at the unveiling of that great artist's masterwork, Spirit of Haida Gwaii—known as the Black Canoe—at the Canadian Embassy. The girls took off their shoes and waded into the reflecting pool at the base of the canoe to touch Mouse Woman, the little busybody my books had helped lift from obscurity. I would outlive my old friend; Bill's death was a terrible blow to me, the breaking of a link of friendship and a renaissance shared that were among the great treasures of my life.

Then, at last, in 1994, the Granville Island book that had been hatched from all the shopping-and-tea trips Tommy and I had made there was published. Titled *Something Weird Is Going On*, it was my twentieth book. The dedication was "To T. A. H. who helped me, this one last time, to handle a wild sea." It is very exciting, at 87, to be signing your latest book!

Inescapably a golden oldie, the time came for me to move into the caring environment of a very comfortable seniors home in West Vancouver. I often look with the fondest of memories at my rogue's gallery—photographs of Tommy and my children, their families, and a copy of each of my books. Having my children turn up in person, though—Brian from Calgary, Michael from California—is my greatest pleasure, reinforcing for me the value of family that I had written about in many of my books. But I can't pretend it didn't delight me to find myself still honored for the writing I'd so loved doing. In 1998, I received the B. C. Gas Lifetime Achievement Award, with a $5000 prize, and a Christie Harris plaque embedded in the Walk of Fame, in the arcade of Vancouver's main library. As always, several of my children were there, as they were for my 90th birthday party, held, appropriately, in an historic old building right on the beach. They'd gathered a huge crowd of family and old friends, a crowd that spanned most of my life, from earliest school years to the young writers (well, to me they're young!) who've been such pals and colleagues in the Writers' Union of Canada over the years.

The only one of my five children missing at that party was Sheilagh, but her absence fit wonderfully with the adventursome spirit of her life, the spirit I'd captured in *Confessions of a Toe-Hanger* those decades earlier: as we toasted my 90th, Sheilagh was swinging on rope bridges in the canopy of the Amazonian rain forest and tramping the ruins of Machu Picchu!

Confessions was one of three books my children let me write about their lives. Now, at 92, with my memory not quite what it was, I'm grateful that my children are helping me tell the rest of my story in these pages. Looking back over 65 years as a professional writer, I suspect that my Irish father, who always started his tales with "I mind the time . . . ," would be proud that he'd hatched several more generations of storytellers.

Writings

FOR YOUNG READERS; FICTION

Cariboo Trail, Longmans, Green, 1957.
Once upon a Totem, illustrated by John Frazer Mills, Atheneum, 1963.
You Have to Draw the Line Somewhere, illustrated by Moira Johnston, Atheneum, 1964.
West with the White Chiefs, illustrated by Walter Ferro, Atheneum, 1965.
Raven's Cry, illustrated by Bill Reid, Atheneum, 1966.
Confessions of a Toe-Hanger, illustrated by Moira Johnston, Atheneum, 1967.
Forbidden Frontier, illustrated by E. Carey Kenney, Atheneum, 1968.
Let X Be Excitement, Atheneum, 1969.
Secret in the Stlalakum Wild, illustrated by Douglas Tait, Atheneum, 1972.
(With husband, Thomas Arthur Harris) *Mule Lib,* McClelland & Stewart, 1972.
Once More upon a Totem, illustrated by Douglas Tait, Atheneum, 1973.
Sky Man on the Totem Pole?, illustrated by Douglas Tait, Atheneum, 1975.
Mystery at the Edge of Two Worlds, illustrated by Lou Crockett, Atheneum, 1978.

The Trouble with Princesses, illustrated by Douglas Tait, Atheneum, 1980.

The Trouble with Adventurers, illustrated by Douglas Tait, Atheneum, 1982.

Something Weird Is Going On, Orca Book Publishers, 1994.

"MOUSE WOMAN" SERIES

Mouse Woman and the Vanished Princesses, illustrated by Douglas Tait, Atheneum, 1976.

Mouse Woman and the Mischief-Makers, illustrated by Douglas Tait, Atheneum, 1977.

Mouse Woman and the Muddleheads, illustrated by Douglas Tait, Atheneum, 1979.

NONFICTION

(With Moira Johnston) *Figleafing through History: The Dynamics of Dress,* illustrated by M. Johnston, Atheneum, 1971.

OTHER

Radio scripts include several hundred school programs, adult plays, juvenile stories, women's talks. Women's editor, A S & M News. Literary papers housed at the University of Calgary, Calgary, Alberta.

HICKOX, Rebecca (Ayres)
(Becky Ayres)

Personal

Female.

Addresses

Home—Salem, OR. *Agent*—c/o Holiday House, Inc., 425 Madison Ave., New York, NY 10017.

Career

High-school librarian; children's book author.

Awards, Honors

Oregon Book Award for young readers, 1993, for *Matreshka.*

Writings

FOR CHILDREN

(As Becky Ayres) *Victoria Flies High,* Cobblehill, 1990.

Matreshka, illustrated by Alexi Natchev, Doubleday, 1992.

Per and the Dala Horse, illustrated by Yvonne Gilbert, Doubleday, 1995.

Zorro and Quwi: Tales of a Trickster Guinea Pig, illustrated by Kim Howard, Doubleday, 1997.

The Golden Sandal: A Middle Eastern Cinderella Story, illustrated by Will Hillenbrand, Holiday House, 1998.

OTHER

Salt Lake City, Dillon Press (Minneapolis, MN), 1990.

Sidelights

Rebecca Hickox has made a niche for herself retelling folktales and creating her own folktale-like stories in such picture books as *Matreshka, Per and the Dala Horse, Zorro and Quwi: Tales of a Trickster Guinea Pig,* and *The Golden Sandal: A Middle Eastern Cinderella Story.* Employing the colorfully painted, nesting Russian dolls called "Matreshka" as her first picture-book subject, Hickox tells the story of Kata, who takes refuge from a snowstorm in the house of Baba Yaga, a Russian witch. When the witch is out of sight, the magical dolls come alive and help Kata escape before Baba Yaga can turn her into a goose and cook her for dinner. A *Kirkus Reviews* critic, noting the colloquial tone and use of rhyming chants, called *Matreshka* a "lively retelling" and a "winning" tale.

Hickox was inspired to write about a Dala horse after buying one of the Swedish children's toys. When she could find no existing tales about this toy, she set out to write *Per and the Dala Horse,* which *Quill and Quire* book reviewer Joanne Schott judged to be "solidly in the folktale spirit." Using a "vigorous" text, according to Cynthia K. Rickey in *School Library Journal,* Hickox tells the story of three brothers who, upon their father's death, are each given a different kind of horse. The eldest son gets a strong workhorse, while the second son receives a fine riding horse, and the third son takes a wooden Dala horse. Although the two older brothers poke fun at their youngest sibling, Per recognizes that the Dala horse may someday prove its usefulness, and, indeed, it does. An "appealing adventure story," asserted *Booklist* contributor Carolyn Phelan.

Hickox turned to the common figure of the trickster for her next picture book, *Zorro and Quwi: Tales of a Trickster Guinea Pig.* Adapting material from the Peruvian Andes, Hickox recounted four episodes about Quwi, a guinea pig who continually out thinks Zorro, the red fox. Reviewers found much to like about *Zorro and Quwi.* In *Kirkus Reviews,* a critic called the episodes "delightful," while in *Publishers Weekly,* a reviewer judged Hickox to be a "master of comic timing."

In Rebecca Hickox's original folk story, a family's youngest son is bequeathed a toy Dala horse instead of a real horse like those left to his older brothers, but he fiercely believes in the usefulness and value of his wooden horse. (Cover illustration by Yvonne Gilbert.)

Although the Cinderella story has been retold many times, Hickox decided to tell an Iraqi version in the picture book *The Golden Sandal: A Middle Eastern Cinderella Story*. This time the heroine is Maha, the daughter of a widowed Iraqi fisherman, while the fairy godmother is a little red fish whose life Maha has spared. Maha desperately wishes to see her father remarry despite his protests that stepmothers do not always treat stepchildren kindly. When the fisherman father gives in and finds a new wife, she ends up treating Maha like a servant and favors her own daughter. When a large celebration arises for a new bride in the village, Maha fears she will not be allowed to go. However, with the help of the little red fish, Maha attends the gala party. Rushing home from the festivities, she loses her golden sandal. Fortunately, the bride's brother Tariq recovers the sandal and declares that its owner will be his wife. Despite the efforts of Maha's stepmother, Tariq eventually finds Maha and the couple enjoy a lavish wedding together. According to a writer for *Kirkus Reviews,* the "unusual setting, comic characters," and universal emotions give the story its appeal, an opinion echoed by a *Publishers Weekly* critic, who deemed the work an "able retelling" of the Cinderella fable. Writing in *Horn Book,* Susan P. Bloom called *The Golden Sandal* a "new and appealing version" of the tale. "Charmingly told," added a critic for the *New York Times Book Review.*

Works Cited

Bloom, Susan P., review of *The Golden Sandal: A Middle Eastern Cinderella Story, Horn Book,* March-April, 1998, p. 227.

Review of *The Golden Sandal: A Middle Eastern Cinderella Story, Kirkus Reviews,* February 15, 1998, p. 267.

Review of *The Golden Sandal: A Middle Eastern Cinderella Story, New York Times Book Review,* September 20, 1998, p. 32.

Review of *The Golden Sandal: A Middle Eastern Cinderella Story, Publishers Weekly,* January 26, 1998, p. 91.

Review of *Matreshka, Kirkus Reviews,* October 15, 1992, p. 1306.

Phelan, Carolyn, review of *Per and the Dala Horse, Booklist,* December 15, 1996, p. 730.

Rickey, Cynthia K., review of *Per and the Dala Horse, School Library Journal,* January, 1996, pp. 84-85.

Adapting material from the Peruvian Andes, Hickox recounts four episodes about the trickster Quwi, a guinea pig who continually outwits Zorro, the voracious red fox. (Cover illustration by Kim Howard.)

Schott, Joanne, review of *Per and the Dala Horse, Quill and Quire,* January, 1996, p. 45.
Review of *Zorro and Quwi: Tales of a Trickster Guinea Pig, Kirkus Reviews,* December 1, 1996.

Review of *Zorro and Quwi: Tales of a Trickster Guinea Pig, Publishers Weekly,* December 9, 1996, p. 68.

For More Information See

PERIODICALS

Booklist, January 15, 1993, p. 910.
Horn Book, spring, 1996, pp. 30-31.
Kirkus Reviews, December 1, 1996, p. 1738.
Publishers Weekly, November 9, 1992, p. 84; November 18, 1996, p. 78.
School Library Journal, February, 1997, pp. 92-93; April, 1998, pp. 117-18.*

*   *   *

HYDE, Shelley
  See REED, Kit

*   *   *

INNES, Hammond
  See HAMMOND INNES, Ralph

*   *   *

IVERSON, Eric G.
  See TURTLEDOVE, Harry

*   *   *

IVES, Morgan
  See BRADLEY, Marion Zimmer

K

KERNS, Thelma 1929-

Personal

Born May 2, 1929, in Chester, WV; daughter of Roscoe (a potter) and Loretta (a homemaker; maiden name, Edwards) Chandler; married Robert E. Kerns (an insurance agent), December 23, 1946; children: Bob II, Laura Kerns Henderson, Ross, Betsann Kerns Henderson. *Education:* Attended East Tennessee State College (now University), 1950-53. *Politics:* Republican. *Religion:* Baptist. *Hobbies and other interests:* Collecting antiques, writing poetry and anecdotes, golf.

Thelma Kerns

Addresses

Home—2236 Bruce St., Kingsport, TN 37664. *E-mail*—kernsbob+th@intermediaTn.net.

Career

Writer. State of Tennessee, member of Malpractice Review Board, 1981; District Bureau of the Census, assistant manager of office operations, 1990. *Member:* Appalachian Writers Association, Tennessee Writers Alliance, Kingsport Writers Guild.

Awards, Honors

World of Poetry Award, 1990.

Writings

Flea Market Fleas from A to Z, illustrated by Bryant Owens, Overmountain Press (Johnson City, TN), 1998.
A Ducky Wedding, illustrated by Owens, Overmountain Press, 1999.

Contributor of articles and poems to magazines and newspapers, including *Mature Living.*

Work in Progress

The Boardwalk Kitty; You Don't Pat a Bee, publication expected in summer, 2000.

*   *   *

KEYES, Greg
See KEYES, J. Gregory

KEYES, J. Gregory 1963-
(Greg Keyes)

Personal

Born in 1963; married; wife's name, Nell (a jewelry maker). *Education:* University of Georgia, Athens, M.A. (anthropology).

Addresses

Agent—c/o Ballantine Publishing Group, 201 East 50th St., New York, NY 10022. *E-mail*—gkeyes@uga. cc.uga.edu.

Career

Author, 1996—. University of Georgia, Athens, instructor.

Writings

"CHOSEN OF THE CHANGELING" SERIES

The Waterborn, Ballantine, 1996.
The Blackgod, Ballantine, 1997.

"THE AGE OF UNREASON" SERIES

Newton's Cannon, Ballantine, 1998.
A Calculus of Angels, Ballantine, 1999.

OTHER

Babylon 5 Final Reckoning: The Fate of Bester, Del Rey, 1999.

Sidelights

J. Gregory Keyes is an author of fantasy fiction as well as an instructor at the University of Georgia, in Athens. When Keyes was a child, his father's job took the family to an Arizona Navajo reservation. On the reservation he was exposed to the storytelling that led to his first writings, the retelling of Southeastern Indian legends and myths. While in college, Keyes continued his investigation of other cultures and languages, studying Russian, French, Mandarin, Japanese, and old Norse. After receiving an M.A. in anthropology, he began teaching and researching folklore and mythology in addition to subjects relevant to his class.

Keyes was inspired to write his first fantasy, *The Waterborn,* after taking a world history class which discussed ancient civilizations, such as Mesopotamia and Egypt, that were organized around the control of water. In the novel, two young people make their way in separate plots that interweave in a tale of mythical beasts, gods, and fantasy. Hezhi is a young princess, the daughter of the emperor of Nhol. Her blood carries the seed of the River, a powerful god who controls Nhol. Hezhi is on a journey to find her cousin who was taken away by priests. In the distant land of the Forest Lord, Perkar, son of a chieftain, falls in love with a Stream Goddess who is threatened by the River. Perkar vows to

J. Gregory Keyes

kill the River and is drawn toward Nhol, where Hezhi lives, after dreaming of a girl calling to him. In his quest, he encounters monsters and magic and engages in sword fights. A contributor to *Publishers Weekly* declared *The Waterborn* "a satisfying, robust, impressive debut that offers some genuine surprises," while *Booklist* reviewer Sally Estes claimed that "Keyes has created a memorable world." Estes went on to call the fantasy novel a "richly detailed tapestry, steeped in American Indian myth and lore." *Voice of Youth Advocates* reviewer Sandra M. Lee wrote that Keyes "provides engaging battles, strong characterization, and solid relationships to tie blood and quest into final confrontation and maturation."

The Blackgod is Keyes's 1997 sequel to *The Waterborn,* and both works are from the "Chosen of the Changeling" series. Hezhi flees from the River, who sends a ghoul to find her. She and her bodyguard take refuge with the horse-worshiping Mangs, where Brother Horse teaches her how to bring forth her own powers. Blackgod the Raven reveals to Hezhi how she can defeat the River at its source. The River sends the ghoul Ghe into the mountains to kill Hezhi. During a dramatic clash at She'ling, all parties engage in a fierce battle over the young princess. A *Publishers Weekly* reviewer called Ghe "a wonderful, Dostoyevskian character, at once repelling and touching," and noted Keyes's "mastery of the internal lives of his characters and his artful, theatrical shifts of point of view." *Library Journal* reviewer Susan Hamburger said the book is "enriched by spiritualism, mystery, and cultural detail." *Booklist* reviewer Sally Estes called *The Blackgod* "a richly developed page-turner for the fantasy cognoscenti."

Newton's Cannon is the first book of Keyes's alternate history series "The Age of Unreason." The series details

In the first volume of Keyes's imaginative alternate history series, Ben Franklin and Isaac Newton are drawn into the rivalry between King Louis XIV of France and King George I of England as they vie for control of one of Newton's devices which is being used as a powerful weapon. (Cover illustration by Terese Neilsen.)

events during the Enlightenment, a time where scientific knowledge flourished throughout Europe. However in this alternate world, alchemy and science exist harmoniously. The book begins in 1715 when the young Boston printer's apprentice Ben Franklin studies alchemic devices invented by Isaac Newton and decides to try to meet the famous scientist. Across the Atlantic, an immortal King Louis XIV of France uses a disgruntled student of Newton's to devise a way to send a comet on a crash course with London. With the English city's demise imminent, young Franklin desperately tries to warn Newton in time to save the city. Jackie Cassada said in a *Library Journal* review that *Newton's Cannon* is "intricately crafted, elegantly delivered." A critic in *Kirkus Reviews* noted the book "is colorful, intriguing, and well handled, if somewhat difficult to swallow." "Eminently worthwhile reading for both fantasy and alternate-history lovers," wrote Roland Green in *Booklist.*

In the next book in the alternate world series, *A Calculus of Angels,* cold has shrouded Earth after its collision with a comet. Franklin and Newton are in Prague, looking for the secrets of the beings whose science and powers have nearly destroyed the world. Peter the Great, affected by the same malakus or demon that Louis XIV was in the first novel, desires to conquer Europe. As the Tzar sets his sights on Venice, Charles XII of Sweden enlists the help of Franklin in a clash of military, alchemical, and political forces. Describing the work as "lavish and thoughtful," a *Publishers Weekly* reviewer applauded Keyes's adept handling of plot elements from the first novel as well as preserving the "masterful integrations.... It's a bravura performance."

Works Cited

Review of *The Blackgod, Publishers Weekly,* March 24, 1997, p. 63.

Review of *A Calculus of Angels, Publishers Weekly,* March 22, 1999, p. 74.

Cassada, Jackie, review of *Newton's Cannon, Library Journal,* May 15, 1998, p. 118.

Estes, Sally, review of *The Blackgod, Booklist,* March 1, 1997, p. 1068.

Estes, Sally, review of *The Waterborn, Booklist,* April 1, 1996, p. 1324.

Green, Roland, review of *Newton's Cannon, Booklist,* May 15, 1998, p. 1601.

Hamburger, Susan, review of *The Blackgod, Library Journal,* April 15, 1997, p. 123.

Lee, Sandra M., review of *The Waterborn, Voice of Youth Advocates,* October, 1997, p. 252.

Review of *Newton's Cannon, Kirkus Reviews,* April 15, 1998, p. 537.

Review of *The Waterborn, Publishers Weekly,* June 10, 1996, p. 90.

For More Information See

PERIODICALS

Library Journal, June 15, 1996, p. 96.
Magazine of Fantasy and Science Fiction, April, 1997, p. 130; March, 1999, p. 35.
Publishers Weekly, April 13, 1998, p. 57.*

*　　　*　　　*

KINSEY-WARNOCK, Natalie 1956-

Personal

Born November 2, 1956, in Newport, VT; daughter of Frederick (a farmer) and Louise (a day-care provider; maiden name, Rowell) Kinsey; married Tom Warnock (a teacher), May 8, 1976. *Education:* Johnson State College, B.A. (art and athletic training), 1978. *Religion:* Presbyterian.

Addresses

Home—3590 Country Rd., Barton, VT 05822. *Agent*—Gina Maccoby, New York, NY 10010.

Career

Writer. University of Vermont Extension Service, Newport, VT, energy auditor, 1980-85; Craftsbury Sports Center, Craftsbury, VT, elderhostel director and cross-country ski instructor, 1987-91. Albany Library trustee, 1988-90; leader of East Craftsbury Recreation Program, 1983-2000; elder of East Craftsbury Presbyterian Church, 1989—.

Awards, Honors

American Library Association Notable Book citation, 1989, New York Library's 100 Best Books citation, 1989, and Joan Fassler Memorial Book Award, Association for Children's Health, 1991, all for *The Canada Geese Quilt;* American Booksellers Pick of the List citation, 1991, for *The Night the Bells Rang; The Wild Horses of Sweetbriar* and *The Night the Bells Rang* were both chosen as "Children's Books of the Year" by Bank Street College; Children's Choice Award, International Reading Association-Children's Book Council, 1993, for *The Bear that Heard Crying;* Smithsonian Notable Books for Children Award, 1996, for *The Fiddler of the Northern Lights,* and 1997, for *The Summer of Stanley.*

Writings

FOR CHILDREN

The Canada Geese Quilt (chapter book), illustrated by Leslie W. Bowman, Cobblehill Books, 1989.
The Wild Horses of Sweetbriar (picture book), illustrated by Ted Rand, Cobblehill Books, 1990.
The Night the Bells Rang (chapter book), illustrated by Leslie W. Bowman, Cobblehill Books, 1991.
Wilderness Cat (picture book), illustrated by Mark Graham, Cobblehill Books, 1992.
When Spring Comes (picture book), illustrated by Stacey Schuett, Dutton, 1993.
The Bear that Heard Crying (picture book), illustrated by Ted Rand, Cobblehill Books, 1993.
On a Starry Night, illustrated by David McPhail, Orchard Books, 1994.
The Fiddler of the Northern Lights, illustrated by Leslie W. Bowman, Cobblehill Books, 1996.
The Summer of Stanley (picture book), illustrated by Donald Gates, Cobblehill Books, 1997.
Sweet Memories Still (chapter book), illustrated by Laurie Harden, Cobblehill Books, 1997.
As Long as There Are Mountains (chapter book), Cobblehill Books, 1997.
In the Language of Loons, Cobblehill Books, 1998.
If Wishes Were Horses, Dutton, 2000.

Adaptations

The Canada Geese Quilt was adapted for audio cassette, Recorded Books, 1998.

Work in Progress

What Emma Remembers, illustrated by Kathleen Kolb, Cobblehill Books, 2001.

Sidelights

Natalie Kinsey-Warnock was born, raised, and still lives in Vermont—a fact that is felt directly in almost all of her picture books and juvenile novels. Kinsey-Warnock tells warm stories of rural families and country home truths, coming-of-age tales, and epiphanies that involve the natural world and the close and loving sphere of families and best friends. In novels such as *The Canada Geese Quilt, The Night the Bells Rang, Sweet Memories Still,* and the heavily autobiographical *As Long as There Are Mountains,* the Vermont writer places stories in history and near-history, recreating the flavor of bygone times and scenes. Her picture books, such as *The Wild Horses of Sweetbriar, Wilderness Cat, When Spring Comes, The Bear That Heard Crying,* and *The Summer of Stanley,* often feature animals in realistic ways, another favorite Kinsey-Warnock motif.

"My Scottish ancestors settled here in the Northeast Kingdom of Vermont almost two hundred years ago," Kinsey-Warnock once told *Something about the Author* (*SATA*). "It is this land that they settled—where I grew up and still live—that means so much to me and provides the setting for almost all of my stories. I feel a part of this hill country and I'm grateful to the legacy these ancestors passed down. I grew up on a dairy farm in the Northeast Kingdom, along with a sister and three brothers. This fostered a strong connection to the land, a sense of nurturing and caring for the earth. My father was a baseball and track star before he became a farmer and passed on both his love of sports and of history to us, while my mother, a former teacher, instilled in us her insatiable appetite for books and words. It is because of her that my brother Leland and I are writers."

Kinsey-Warnock married while still in college and then went on to graduate from Johnson State College with a B.A. in both art and athletic training, twin passions. She held various jobs, including a position as a cross-country ski instructor, until the time she penned her first children's book and decided that she had finally found her career. "My first children's book, *The Canada Geese Quilt,* grew out of my love and admiration for my grandmother and a special quilt we made together. My grandmother began quilting when she was in her sixties, and over the next fifteen years she made 250 quilts. I designed about twenty of the quilts, most of them of birds, wildflowers, and starry skies, including one of Canada geese which inspired the book. My grandmother died in February, 1991, at age eighty-nine."

The Canada Geese Quilt tells the story of ten-year-old Ariel, who loves the Vermont farm where she lives with her parents and grandmother. But Ariel is fearful that her life will change for the worse when a new baby is born and when her grandmother suffers a stroke and seemingly cannot recover. Finally, Ariel combines her grandmother's skill at quilt-making and her artistic abilities to make a very special quilt, one for the new baby that also makes her grandmother want to join the living once again. Critical response to Kinsey-Warnock's first book was very positive. A *Publishers Weekly* reviewer wrote, "In one gorgeous, slim volume, Kinsey-Warnock tells a story of a particular time, from spring to fall, in a 10-year-old's life . . . . Kinsey-Warnock's language is simple and direct as it conveys both the loving relationship between the old woman and the girl, and the girl's love of the land." Reviewing the 1998 audio version of the novel, Stephanie Bange remarked in *School Library Journal,* "The novel remains timeless and fresh." An American Library Association Notable Book, *The Canada Geese Quilt* set Kinsey-Warnock's career off on the right foot.

For her next children's novel, Kinsey-Warnock went back in time to the First World War. "I guess anything to do with history appeals to me," Kinsey-Warnock told *SATA.* "History teaches us who we are, and in all my talks with school groups I encourage every person to record their family histories and stories before they are lost forever. The stories about our Scottish ancestors instilled in all of us a sense of our heritage and an interest in Scotland. In 1999 I fulfilled a lifelong dream when I took thirteen members of my family to Scotland. Since returning home from that trip, I have been taking bagpipe lessons and hope to play them on a return trip to Scotland in May, 2000.

"Many of my books come from family stories. My sister Helen is the family genealogist, and I have often joined her in reading town histories and walking old cemeteries. Most of my stories take place before I was born; I enjoy putting my characters into time periods I'm interested in. I guess I feel that in some small way I get to live in that time period, at least while I'm writing the story."

With *The Night the Bells Rang,* Kinsey-Warnock pushes the clocks back to 1918 and the nation is still talking about the war in Europe. But for young Mason, who lives on a farm in rural Vermont, the war is closer to home in the shape of an older bully, Aden Cutler. Mason wishes for Aden's death, and gets his wish when Aden enlists and goes to war never to return. Thereafter, Mason must deal with his guilt feelings over this incident, as well as come to terms with his younger brother. *Horn Book* critic Ellen Fader, in her review of *The Night the Bells Rang,* called attention to details of farm life, such as maple sugaring and birthing a foal, which "realistically evoke life in another time and place." Fader concluded, "This quiet, affecting coming-of-age story, marked by its fluid, graceful prose, is a natural for reading aloud in classrooms."

Kinsey-Warnock returned to the intergenerational theme with a grandmother who figures prominently in *Sweet Memories Still.* In this chapter book, Shelby is initially put off by having to spend time with her ailing grandmother, then gradually understands that this older woman has much to teach her. Her grandmother's

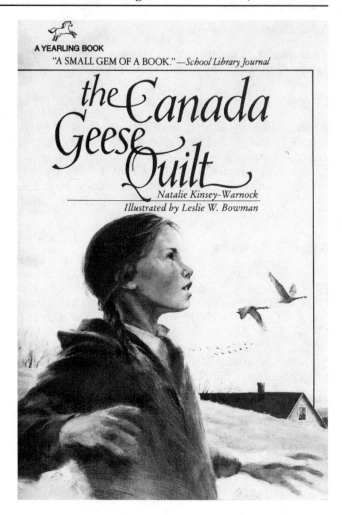

In Natalie Kinsey-Warnock's tender story, ten-year-old Ariel is upset by the upcoming birth of a new sibling and her grandmother's ill health, but creating a special quilt helps the young girl find solace. (Cover illustration by Leslie W. Bowman.)

present to her on her birthday, an old box camera, does little to cement Shelby's love for the woman, but ultimately the camera becomes a metaphor for the stories of her childhood that the grandmother shares with Shelby. *Booklist*'s Carolyn Phelan felt that while it tried to take on too much for a chapter book format, the story was "written with skill and sensitivity" and "the narrative is more vivid than many longer novels written for children." A *Publishers Weekly* critic noted, "Kinsey-Warnock . . . continues to show a gentle touch in peeling back the small layers of life to reveal simple epiphanies."

"*As Long as There Are Mountains* is my longest and most autobiographical book," Kinsey-Warnock reported to *SATA.* "It centers on twelve-year-old Iris Anderson and her family on their northern Vermont farm in 1956. Her father wants to pass on the farm to Iris's brother, who wants to be a writer instead. Then her father loses his leg, and the farm must be sold unless her brother can be persuaded to give up his dream and come home." Reviewing this novel in *Booklist,* Hazel Rochman concluded, "Most moving is Iris' quiet, lyrical, first-person narrative, which expresses her closeness to the land and her sense of freedom in taking care of a farm." Writing in *School Library Journal,* Carol Schene remarked, "This is a powerful and beautifully written story of love and determination set during the 1950s." Schene went on to note, "The author masterfully captures the gamut of Iris's feelings from passion for the land and compassion for a classmate whose family is homeless." A *Kirkus Reviews* contributor commented, "The profound pleasure of living on a farm ... pervades this story of a Vermont farm family."

The summer of 1969 is the setting for 1998's *In the Language of Loons,* the story of young Arlis, who spends the months with his grandparents in Vermont and learns some home truths about responsibility that he takes back home with him in the fall. Arlis's grandfather teaches the boy about nature and also encourages his participation in cross-country running. "This is a touching and poignant story of a boy starting on his journey to manhood," reflected Arwen Marshall in a *School Library Journal* review. "The emotions and relationships are the true driving force of this story, and they are timeless."

"My interests are varied—athletics, nature, art and writing—but all of them are rooted to this area where I live," Kinsey-Warnock told *SATA.* "Sports are an integral part of my life: I run five to ten miles each morning, cross-country ski, mountain bike, roller blade, swim, play tennis, and I played field hockey all across the country for thirteen years. I love the outdoors, and study and sketch birds and wildflowers, which are most often the subjects of my watercolor paintings.... My husband, Tom, and I have been building a timber-frame house on this land; both of us enjoy working with wood. Tom shares my love of the land, sports and animals; we have three horses, seven dogs and seven cats. I always wished I could open a shelter for animals—and I guess I have!"

Many of Kinsey-Warnock's picture books for children display this love for animals. *The Wild Horses of Sweetbriar* recounts the severe winter of 1903 during which a young girl lives on a small island with her father, who works for the Coast Guard. They share the island with ten wild horses, and the young girl feeds these horses when the cold becomes such that the animals cannot find feed. "Kinsey-Warnock's appealing, poetic text is a stirring account of the struggle between people and the forces of nature," declared a reviewer for *Publishers Weekly.*

A heroic cat follows the family that left it from Vermont to Canada in *Wilderness Cat,* a true family story set in the late 1700s. "A fine book for cat lovers," wrote *Horn Book*'s Ann A. Flowers. In *When Spring Comes,* a little girl and her dog gaze out the window at early spring in Vermont, imagining the many activities of the season— maple sugaring, planting, the return of the Canada Geese. This picture book is a "convincing portrait of a

close-knit farm family living decades ago," as *Booklist* contributor Deborah Abbott described it.

"Another book, *The Bear that Heard Crying,* is a collaboration between my sister and me and is the true story of our great-great-great-great-aunt Sarah Whitcher," Kinsey-Warnock explained to *SATA.* "In 1783, when she was three years old, she was lost in the woods for four days and was found and protected by a bear." This tale was dubbed "an unusually appealing slice of Americana" by a *Kirkus Reviews* critic. "Plainly told, this sturdy tale exudes comfort," concluded a reviewer for *Publishers Weekly.* Another animal figures in *The Summer of Stanley:* a troublesome goat that comes to the rescue.

Overcoming a child's fear of the dark and fanciful stories inform the storylines of *On a Starry Night* and *The Fiddler of the Northern Lights* respectively. Of the former title, Shirley Wilton wrote in *School Library Journal* that the book is "a gentle story that celebrates a family's enveloping warmth." Quebec is the setting for *The Fiddler of the Northern Lights* in which a grandfather's stories of the mythical fiddler entertain eight-year-old Henry in this tale of the Aurora Borealis that "delivers the anticipated magic," according to a *Publishers Weekly* reviewer.

While Kinsey-Warnock takes inspiration from her native Vermont and from the world of nature surrounding us all, she blends these elements with small and touching stories that tell individual human truths. Kinsey-Warnock concluded for *SATA:* "I've had such strong role models in my life—especially strong, enduring women have influenced me: women like my grandmother, Helen Urie Rowell, my great-aunt Ada Urie (who was featured in a book titled *Enduring Women* by Diane Koos Gentry), and down to my mother. I want my books to portray strong female characters, and I hope they honor these women."

Works Cited

Abbott, Deborah, review of *When Spring Comes, Booklist,* March 1, 1993, p. 1236.

Review of *As Long as There Are Mountains, Kirkus Reviews,* June 1, 1997, p. 875.

Bange, Stephanie, review of *The Canada Geese Quilt, School Library Journal,* November, 1998, p. 69.

Review of *The Bear that Heard Crying, Kirkus Reviews,* August 1, 1993, p. 1003.

Review of *The Bear that Heard Crying, Publishers Weekly,* September 6, 1993, p. 95.

Review of *The Canada Geese Quilt, Publishers Weekly,* July 28, 1989, p. 222.

Fader, Ellen, review of *The Night the Bells Rang, Horn Book,* January-February, 1992, pp. 71-72.

Review of *The Fiddler of the Northern Lights, Publishers Weekly,* November 11, 1996, p. 74.

Flowers, Ann A., review of *Wilderness Cat, Horn Book,* March-April, 1993, p. 197.

Marshall, Arwen, review of *In the Language of Loons, School Library Journal,* March, 1998, p. 214.

Phelan, Carolyn, review of *Sweet Memories Still, Booklist,* February 15, 1997, p. 1023.

Rochman, Hazel, review of *As Long as There Are Mountains, Booklist,* August, 1997, p. 1901.

Schene, Carol, review of *As Long as There Are Mountains, School Library Journal,* August, 1997, p. 157.

Review of *Sweet Memories Still, Publishers Weekly,* December 30, 1996, p. 67.

Review of *The Wild Horses of Sweetbriar, Publishers Weekly,* October 26, 1990, p. 67.

Wilton, Shirley, review of *On a Starry Night, School Library Journal,* May, 1994, p. 96.

For More Information See

PERIODICALS

Booklist, August, 1992, p. 2018; August, 1993, p. 2070; November 15, 1996, p. 594.

Horn Book, July-August, 1994, p. 441; November-December, 1998, p. 766.

Kirkus Reviews, November 15, 1996, pp. 1670-71; May 1, 1997, p. 723; December 1, 1997, pp. 1776-77.

Publishers Weekly, October 12, 1992, p. 78; February 1, 1993, p. 95; February 21, 1994, p. 252; April 21, 1997, p. 71.

School Library Journal, February, 1992, p. 86; October, 1992, p. 90; April, 1993, p. 98; November, 1996, p. 87; June, 1997, p. 94.

—Sketch by J. Sydney Jones

L

LANSDALE, Joe R(ichard) 1951-
(Ray Slater)

Personal

Born October 28, 1951, in Gladewater, TX; son of Alcee Bee (a mechanic) and Reta (in sales; maiden name, Wood) Lansdale; married Cassie Ellis, June 25, 1970 (divorced, 1972); married Karen Ann Morton, August 25, 1973; children: (second marriage) Keith Jordan, Kasey JoAnn. *Education:* Attended Tyler Junior College, 1970-71, University of Texas at Austin, 1971-72, and Stephen F. Austin State University, 1973, 1975, 1976.

Addresses

Home and Office—113 Timber Ridge, Nacogdoches, TX 75961. *Agent*—Jimmy Uines, The Uines Agency, Inc., 648 Broadway, Suite 901, New York, NY 10012.

Career

Transportation manager, Goodwill Industries, 1973-75; custodian, Stephen F. Austin State University, Nacogdoches, TX, 1976-80; foreman, LaBorde Custodial Services, Nacogdoches, 1980-81; writer, 1981—. Also worked variously as a bouncer, bodyguard, factory worker, carpenter, ditch digger, plumber's assistant, and martial arts instructor. Founder and Grand Master of the Shen Chuan martial science.

Awards, Honors

Bram Stoker Award, Horror Writers of America, 1988, 1989, twice in 1993, 1997, and 1999; American Horror Award, 1989; British Fantasy Award, 1989; notable book, *New York Times,* 1994.

Writings

YOUNG ADULT NOVELS

Terror on the High Skies, illustrated by Edward Hannigan and Dick Giordano, Little, Brown, 1992.
The Boar, Subterranean Press, 1999.
Something Lumber This Way Comes, illustrated by Doug Potter, Subterranean Press, 1999.

MYSTERY NOVELS

Act of Love, Zebra (New York City), 1981, CD Publications (Edgewood, MD), 1993.
The Nightrunners, Dark Harvest (Arlington Heights, IL), 1987.
Cold in July (also see below), Bantam, 1989.
Lansdale's Limited Edition: Cold in July & Savage Season, (as boxed set), Ziesing (Shingletown, CA), 1990.
Freezer Burn, Mysterious Press, 1999.
The Bottoms, Mysterious Press, 2000.

"HAP AND LEONDARD" SERIES

Savage Season (also see above), Bantam, 1990.
Mucho Mojo, Mysterious Press (New York City), 1994.
Two Bear Mambo, Mysterious Press, 1995.
Bad Chili, Mysterious Press, 1997.
Rumble Tumble, Mysterious Press, 1998.

FANTASY NOVELS

The Drive In: A B-Movie with Blood and Popcorn, Made in Texas, Bantam, 1988.
The Drive In 2: Not Just One of Them Sequels, Bantam, 1989.
Batman: Captured by the Engines, Warner, 1991.
On the Far Side of the Cadillac Desert with Dead Folks (chapbook), Roadkill (Denver, CO), 1991.

WESTERN NOVELS

(Under pseudonym Ray Slater) *Texas Night Riders,* Leisure Press (Champaign, IL), 1983.
Dead in the West, Space & Time Books (New York City), 1986.
The Magic Wagon, Doubleday, 1986.
Jonah Hex: Two-Gun Mojo (graphic novel), DC Comics, 1994.

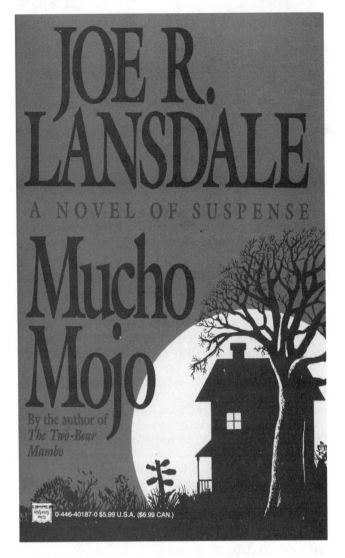

After Leonard Pine inherits a house from his uncle, he and his friend Hap Collins discover the skeleton of a murdered child under the floorboards and vow to find the killer in Joe R. Lansdale's suspense novel. (Cover illustration by Matt Tepper.)

Lone Ranger (graphic novel), Topps, 1994.
Blood Dance, Subterranean, 2000.

SHORT STORY COLLECTIONS

By Bizarre Hands, Ziesing, 1989.
Stories by Mama Lansdale's Youngest Boy, Pulphouse (Eugene, OR), 1991.
Best Sellers Guaranteed, Ace, 1993.
A Fist Full of Stories (and Articles), Cemetery Dance Publications, 1996.
Atomic Chili: The Illustrated Joe R. Lansdale, Mojo, 1997.
Writer of the Purple Rage, Carrol & Graf, 1997.
The Good, the Bad, and the Indifferent: Early Stories and Commentary, Subterranean, 1998.
High Cotton: Selected Stories, Golden Gryphon, 2000.

Also author of *The Steel Valentine,* 1991; *Tight Little Stitches in a Dead Man's Back,* 1992; *The Lone Ranger*

and Tonto, 1996; and more than 200 other short stories, articles, essays, and reviews.

EDITOR

Best of the West, Doubleday, 1986.
The New Frontier: Best of Today's Western Fiction, Doubleday, 1989.
(With Pat LoBrutto) *Razored Saddles,* Dark Harvest, 1989.
(With wife, Karen Lansdale) *Dark at Heart,* Dark Harvest, 1992.
(With Thomas W. Knowles) *The West That Was,* Wings (Avenel, NJ), 1994.
(With Thomas W. Knowles) *Wild West Show,* Wings, 1994.

Co-editor with Rick Klan of *Weird Business,* an anthology of horror comics from Mojo Press.

OTHER

(Co-author and adapter) *Edgar Rice Burroughs' Tarzan: The Lost Adventure,* Dark Horse Comics (Milwaukie, OR), 1995.

Also contributor to several anthologies, including *Fears,* 1984, and *Book of the Dead,* Bantam, 1989, among others. Contributor of articles, stories, and reviews to magazines, including *Horror Show, Modern Stories, Espionage, Mike Shayne,* and many more.

Sidelights

Joe R. Lansdale once commented: "The Martian series by Edgar Rice Burroughs got me started, and I've been writing my own stories ever since. My work ranges from popular to literary. I believe the purpose of fiction is to entertain. Enlightening the reader is nice, but secondary. If you don't have a good tale to tell, no one is listening anyway.

"My preferred genre is the fantastic, but suspense runs a close second, followed by mystery, westerns, and the mainstream. Actually, much of my work and intended work is a combination of these things. I am also interested in screenplays, and hope to work in that medium on occasion.

"I like all kinds of horror and fantasy writing, especially the contemporary horror tale. I am not too fond, though, of the vague ending that seems so popular in many publications today. Much of what I write, although it is called horror, is really just oddball or weird fantasy, perhaps never becoming scary, but certainly striking a note of the unusual."

Horror, fantasy, science fiction, mystery, suspense, Western: Lansdale's fiction encompasses all of the above, frequently combining several genres in the same story or novel while at the same time defining a distinctive voice of its own. Writing in *New York Times Book Review,* Daniel Woodrell characterized Lansdale's work as "country noir," likening him to such authors as James M. Cain and Erskine Caldwell. Lansdale, himself, has listed Cain as a major influence. The "country" in this case is East Texas, where Lansdale was born, raised, and continues to reside. The "noir" refers to the dark vision of human nature and contemporary life that pervades nearly all of his work. Other writers that Lansdale mentions as influential include Ray Bradbury, Robert Bloch, Flannery O'Connor, Dashiell Hammett, Raymond Chandler, and Richard Matheson. Lansdale departs from these literary icons, however, on at least two counts, each of which reflects one of his stated non-literary influences: B-movies and comic books. No matter the genre in which he is writing, graphic horror and violence are usually present. No matter how dark the vision he is rendering, satirical and humorous elements often abound.

Author of over one hundred stories, Lansdale first made his mark in short fiction. "I prefer the short-story medium," he told Stanley Wiater in *Dark Dreamers: Conversations with the Masters of Horror.* "I think if I could make a living as a short-story writer, I would do that primarily." Lansdale's stories began appearing widely in both commercial and alternative publications by the late 1970s. Some of this work is collected in *By Bizarre Hands* and *Stories by Mama Lansdale's Youngest Boy,* and *Best Sellers Guaranteed.* Writing in *Locus,* Edward Bryant described *Best Sellers Guaranteed* as "a first-rate retrospective, particularly of Lansdale's earlier career." He went on to characterize "Lansdale's strong suit" as "whacked-out humorous melodrama with a distinctive voice (East Texas) and a keen sense of place (ditto)."

Lansdale's novels began appearing in the early 1980s. Although marketed within particular genres, they transcend traditional genre definitions. Typical of a Lansdale Western is *Dead in the West.* Set in the pioneer days of Mud Creek, Texas (a fictionalized version of Lansdale's own Gladewater), the story relates a series of events involving animated corpses that would seem more at home in a contemporary horror tale than in a Western. The more recent *Magic Wagon,* set in East Texas in 1909, tells of a traveling medicine show that includes a wrestling chimpanzee and the corpse of Wild Bill Hickok. Writing on *The Magic Wagon* for *New York Times Book Review,* Anne Roston offered another example of how Lansdale's work defies simple categorization: "Behind this entertaining and seemingly innocent Western ... lies a subtle discussion of racism and the myths people create for themselves."

Prime examples of Lansdale's science fiction and fantasy/horror fiction can be found in *The Drive In: A B-Movie with Blood and Popcorn, Made in Texas* and *The Drive In 2: Not Just One of Them Sequels.* In the first novel, the patrons of a Texas drive-in movie are whisked into another universe where the horror films they have been watching and the drive-in itself become the sum of their reality. In the sequel, the patrons leave the drive-in to enter the strange world surrounding it, where they encounter both dinosaurs and vampires. Richard Gehr in *Village Voice* saw these two books as "semiparodistic novels" that "turn the horror spectacle upon itself."

Lansdale's mystery and suspense novels tend to adhere more closely to genre conventions. *Savage Season,* set in the nineties, relates the story of Hap Collins, a sixties draft-dodger who is lured by his ex-wife Trudy into a scheme to locate stolen money at the bottom of the Sabine River in East Texas. Accompanied by his friend Leonard, a gay Vietnam veteran, Hap must eventually confront the nefarious gang with whom Trudy has become involved. Liz Currie in *Armchair Detective* wrote: "When 1960s idealism meets 1990s cynicism, the stage is set for a violent confrontation between good intentions and evil results." Hap Collins and Leonard return in *Mucho Mojo.* After Leonard inherits a house from his uncle, the skeleton of a murdered child is discovered under the floorboards. Hap and Leonard proceed to track down the killer. Daniel Woodrow in *Village Voice* stated: "Mr. Lansdale sets his story in motion and carries through with great, sneaky skill. The individual scenes are sometimes not only funny, but also

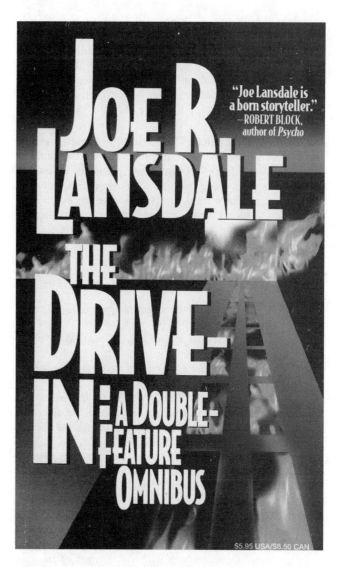

Lansdale's compilation of **The Drive-In** *and* **The Drive-In 2** *features the fantastic plots of the two novels, in which patrons of a Texas drive-in movie are whisked into alternate worlds of horror and astonishing phenomenon.*

slyly offer acute commentary on matters of race, friendship and love in small-town America."

Lansdale's fiction has often been praised and blamed for the same reasons. The extreme, graphic violence he depicts can be viewed as gratuitous or as a pointed exaggeration of the violence in America. Depending on one's perspective and sensibilities, his humor on the darkest subjects can be perceived as poor taste or as satire on American popular culture. Many critics suggest that there is far more to his work than run-of-the-mill genre fiction written for the sake of entertainment. In summing up *Mucho Mojo* for *Locus,* Bryant wrote that what "Lansdale proceeds to spin is not only a top-drawer thriller, but a social portrait of a society in painful evolution. His East Texas is a place of entrenched tradition in painful conflict with new ideas about race relations, gender politics, and more open choices in sexual preference."

Lansdale told Kevin E. Proulx in *Fear to the World: Eleven Voices in a Chorus of Horror:* "Good fiction can actually tell you how people relate to one another. How they really feel about things. What life is all about. What makes it worth living, or, for some people, not worth living. I find a lot more truth in fiction than nonfiction, and that's why I prefer to write it."

Lansdale once admitted: "My writing is done to entertain and to please me. And to put bread on the table. I like to think my work has something going for it besides momentum. That there is some thematic depth that will ring in the reader's head afterwards like an echo. I'm attempting to blend the pacing and color of genre fiction with the character and style of the mainstream. And maybe doing a ... bad job of it. But I'm trying."

Works Cited

Bryant, Edward, review of *Best Sellers Guaranteed, Locus,* July, 1993, p. 23.
Bryant, Edward, review of *Mucho Mojo, Locus,* May, 1994, p. 25.
Currie, Liz, review of *Savage Season, Armchair Detective,* spring, 1991, p. 227.
Gehr, Richard, review of *The Drive In: A B-Movie with Blood and Popcorn, Made in Texas,* and *The Drive In 2: Not Just One of Them Sequels, Village Voice,* February 6, 1990, pp. 57-58.
Proulx, Kevin E., interview with Joe R. Lansdale, *Fear to the World: Eleven Voices in a Chorus of Horror,* Starmont House (Mercer Island, WA), 1992, pp. 43-58.
Roston, Anne, review of *The Magic Wagon, New York Times Book Review,* December 14, 1986, p. 24.
Wiater, Stanley, interview with Joe R. Lansdale, *Dark Dreamers: Conversations with the Masters of Horror,* Avon, 1990, pp. 111-18.
Woodrell, Daniel, review of *Mucho Mojo, New York Times Book Review,* October 2, 1994, p. 37.
Woodrow, Daniel, review of *Mucho Mojo, Village Voice,* c. 1994.

For More Information See

BOOKS

Twentieth-Century Science-Fiction Writers, 3rd edition, St. James, 1991.
Twentieth-Century Western Writers, 2nd edition, St. James, 1991.

PERIODICALS

Antioch Review, winter, 1987, p. 117.
Armchair Detective, fall, 1989, p. 435; winter, 1996, p. 107.
Bloomsbury Review, December, 1991, p. 27; June, 1992, p. 17.
Deathrealm, fall-winter, 1988, pp. 42-44.
Horror Show, January, 1987.
Locus, April, 1993, p. 21; May, 1993, p. 23; January, 1995, p. 31.
Mystery Scene, August, 1987.
People Weekly, November 10, 1997, p. 44.
Small Press Review, April, 1990, p. 27.

*   *   *

LINDBERGH, Reeve 1945-
(Reeve Lindbergh Brown)

Personal

Born in 1945; daughter of Charles (an aviator) and Anne (an author; maiden name, Morrow) Lindbergh; married Richard Brown (a photographer and teacher; divorced); married Nat Tripp (a writer); children: (first marriage) Elizabeth, Susannah, John (died 1985); (second marriage) Benjamin. *Education:* Radcliffe College, Cambridge, M.A.

Addresses

Agent—c/o Simon & Schuster, 1230 Avenue of the Americas, New York, NY 10020.

Career

Author. Taught in Vermont.

Awards, Honors

Redbook magazine award, 1987, for *The Midnight Farm,* and 1990, for *Benjamin's Barn.*

Writings

FOR CHILDREN

The Midnight Farm, illustrated by Susan Jeffers, Dial, 1987.
Benjamin's Barn, illustrated by Susan Jeffers, Dial, 1990.
The Day the Goose Got Loose, illustrated by Steven Kellogg, Dial, 1990.
Johnny Appleseed: A Poem, illustrated by Kathy Jakobsen, Joy Street (Boston, MA), 1990.
A View from the Air: Charles Lindbergh's Earth and Sky, photographs by Richard Brown, Viking, 1992.

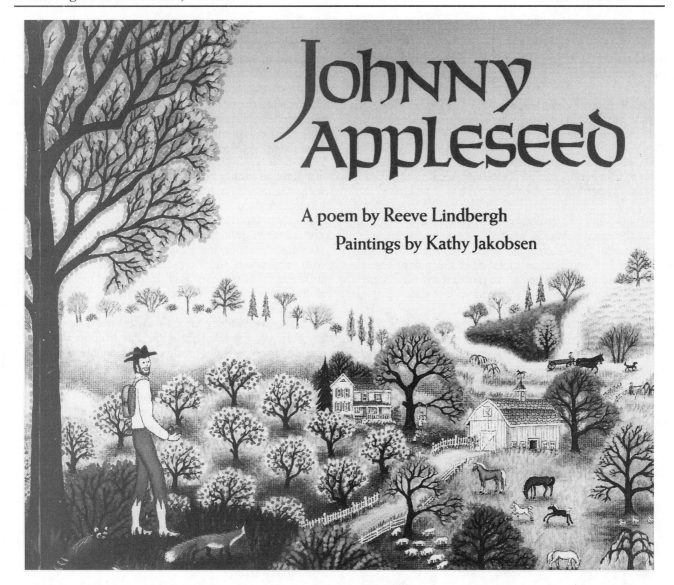

Reeve Lindbergh's verse portrays the American folk hero who traveled across the country planting apple seeds during the first half of the nineteenth century. (Cover illustration by Kathy Jakobsen.)

Grandfather's Lovesong, illustrated by Rachel Isadora, Viking, 1993.

There's a Cow in the Road!, illustrated by Tracey Campbell Pearson, Dial, 1993.

If I'd Known Then What I Know Now, illustrated by Kimberly Bulcken Root, Viking, 1994.

What Is the Sun?, illustrated by Stephen Lambert, Candlewick, 1994.

Nobody Owns the Sky: The Story of "Brave Bessie" Coleman, illustrated by Pamela Paparone, Candlewick, 1996.

The Awful Aardvarks Go to School, illustrated by Tracey Campbell Pearson, Viking, 1997.

The Circle of Days, illustrated by Cathie Felstead, Candlewick, 1997.

North Country Spring, illustrated by Liz Sivertson, Houghton Mifflin, 1997.

(Compiler) *In Every Tiny Grain of Sand: A Child's Book of Prayers and Praise,* illustrated by Christine Davenier, Candlewick, 2000.

The Awful Aardvarks Shop for School, illustrated by Tracey Campbell Pearson, Viking, 2000.

OTHER

(Under name Reeve Lindbergh Brown) *Moving to the Country* (novel), Doubleday, 1983.

The View From the Kingdom: A New England Album (essays), photographs by Richard Brown, introduction by Noel Perrin, Harcourt Brace Jovanovich, 1987.

The Names of the Mountains: A Novel, Simon & Schuster, 1992.

John's Apples (poems), illustrated by John Wilde, Perishable Press (Mt. Horeb, WI), 1995.

Under a Wing: A Memoir, Simon & Schuster, 1998.

Some of Lindbergh's works have been translated into Spanish.

Sidelights

Children's author, novelist, and poet Reeve Lindbergh is the daughter of the world-renown aviator Charles Lindbergh and his wife, the talented writer Anne Morrow. In 1927, Charles flew the first solo transatlantic flight, traveling from New York to Paris. Growing up with famous parents subjected the children to much media attention, though the elder Lindberghs protected their family from public scrutiny as best they could. Reeve Lindbergh and her siblings went on to lead private lives.

Lindbergh and her first husband, Richard Brown, moved from Cambridge, Massachusetts to Vermont, where they both taught school and had three children. Their son John died of encephalitis in 1985, at the young age of twenty months. Lindbergh began writing children's books soon after John's death. Prior to that time, she had published her autobiographical novel *Moving to the Country.* The book follows the story of Nancy and Tom King, who move with their two daughters from a Massachusetts suburb to rural Vermont. Tom teaches high school English to students lacking basic skills. Meanwhile, Nancy deals with an unplanned pregnancy. The couple's marriage is strained as they adapt to a much different life in the country and seemingly indifferent neighbors. While Nancy loses the baby, Tom worries about the security of his job. They eventually overcome their internal and external obstacles and gain the favor of the townspeople. A *Publishers Weekly*

Lindbergh uses rhyming couplets to describe how spring unfolds in New England. (Cover illustration by Liz Sivertson.)

reviewer called *Moving to the Country* "comforting, hopeful, sensitively written, an honest and believable portrayal of marriage, change, and putting down roots." Critic Diane Cole described the novel as "an old-fashioned ode to country pleasure and domestic love" in the *New York Times Book Review.*

In her second autobiographical novel *The Names of the Mountains: A Novel,* Lindbergh reveals what life as a Lindbergh was like after the death of her father through her fictional family headed by aviator Cal Linley and his wife Alicia. Paula Chin wrote in *People Weekly* that Lindbergh used the book "to dispel previous notions about their family and the tragedies that have beset it." The story is told through the eyes of Cress Linley, youngest daughter of the couple, who spends a weekend with her siblings and their elderly mother Alicia, who is suffering from memory loss. In real life, the Lindbergh children were caring for their own mother, eighty-six at the time of the book's publication, who was suffering from similar memory lapses and strokes. *Library Journal* reviewer Jan Blodgett wrote that Lindbergh "gently and perceptively unfolds this complex family history."

Under a Wing: A Memoir reveals Lindbergh's life as a child growing up in Darien, Connecticut. "This gentle memoir shows a unique and uniquely poignant family life," wrote a *Publishers Weekly* reviewer. Charles was a loving but stern father. He would not allow his children to drink soda or eat candy, marshmallow fluff, or grape jelly. He favored discussion over television and protected his family with his rules. Lindbergh said "There were only two ways of doing things—Father's way and the wrong way." Geoffrey C. Ward wrote in the *New York Times Book Review* that Lindbergh's *Under a Wing* "beautifully recaptures the determinedly ordered life her father insisted his family lead in their Connecticut home after the war."

Lindbergh has written many children's books as well. Her first, *The Midnight Farm,* is a counting book. Unable to sleep, a young child is led by his mother on a walk around their farm where they observe the activities of the animals as night descends. Eventually the child grows tired and peacefully slips into slumber. *Times Literary Supplement* reviewer Jane Doonan called *The Midnight Farm* "a gentle progression from disturbed waking to sleeping worlds." "This warm, loving story will comfort any child afraid of the dark," wrote noted children's author Eve Bunting in the *Los Angeles Times Book Review.* Lindbergh continued her animal theme in *Benjamin's Barn.* A young boy carries his teddy bear into a big, red barn, to find not only the usual farm animals, but also jungle and prehistoric creatures, pirate ships, a princess, and a brass band. "The rhyming text has a comforting circular flow, well-suited to Benjamin's flight of fancy and ... return to reality," wrote Anna DeWind in *School Library Journal.*

The Day the Goose Got Loose features a farmer's goose who, seeing the wild geese flying overhead, creates an uproar in the barnyard. The boy who knows the reason for the goose's behavior later dreams of geese and

The Circle of Days *is a verse adaptation of a portion of the* **Canticle of the Sun,** *Saint Francis of Assisi's tribute to the beauty of all creation. (Illustrated by Cathie Felstead.)*

magical lands. A *Publishers Weekly* reviewer claimed the "soothing, exquisitely illustrated dream sequence ... offsets the frenzy of the rest of the tale." "The satisfying rhyme and rhythm of this book make it a good choice for reading aloud," advised Anne Price in *School Library Journal.*

Lindbergh turns to the American folk hero John Chapman in her 1990 work *Johnny Appleseed: A Poem.* The author retells how Chapman traveled from the East Coast to the Midwest, planting apple seeds for future generations to enjoy. "This work shows him as a gentle, religious man on a mission, a lover of the land," wrote a *Publishers Weekly* reviewer. *Horn Book* reviewer Mary M. Burns called *Johnny Appleseed* "a splendid production." The book also features a map tracing Chapman's journey from Massachusetts to Indiana.

Lindbergh expresses her father's love of the natural world in *A View from the Air: Charles Lindbergh's Earth and Sky.* Her long poem is accompanied by photographs taken by Richard Brown, when he flew with Charles Lindbergh over northern New England in the early 1970s. *Booklist* reviewer Deborah Abbott wrote that the verses "capture the pilot's awe and respect for the natural beauty of our land."

Lindbergh uses relationships between grandfathers and their grandchildren as inspiration for her 1993 poem *Grandfather's Lovesong.* In the book, seasonal scenes of rural Maine are depicted, each accompanied by a quatrain. A *Publishers Weekly* reviewer said Lindbergh's *Grandfather's Lovesong* "tenderly expresses a man's love for his grandchild." "Fall and winter scenes are especially captivating," wrote Leda Schubert in *School Library Journal.*

In *There's a Cow in the Road,* a little girl rushes to get ready for school. Looking through her Vermont farmhouse window, she spots a cow who is then joined by other barnyard animals until there's a "crowd in the road." By the time the girl and the other children board the school bus, a goat, sheep, horse, pig, and goose have gathered to see them off. "The story has warmth and vitality and a sense of community," wrote Hazel Rochman in *Booklist.* A *Publishers Weekly* reviewer noticed that the details and action are not always described in the text, resulting in "a great deal of kid-pleasing, between-the-lines action." A contributor to *Kirkus Reviews* called *There's a Cow in the Road* "a joyous, comical pacesetter for a busy morning."

A man's inept do-it-yourself projects in building and maintaining a farm are the focus of *If I'd Known Then What I Know Now.* Sally R. Dow wrote in *School Library Journal* that the book's "tall-tale humor ... will appeal to all those 'just learning how.'" In *What Is the Sun* a young boy questions his grandmother, and each answer leads to another question. Patricia Crawford noted in *Language Arts* that the text demonstrates the "comfort" provided to young children "through their interactions with a caring, older adult."

Nobody Owns the Sky: The Story of "Brave Bessie" Coleman is a 1996 account of how Bessie Coleman became the first African-American aviator in the world. Coleman was denied entrance to flying schools in the United States and instead obtained her pilot's license in France. She then worked as a stunt pilot in the United States and Europe during the 1920s before dying in a plane accident in Jacksonville, Florida, in 1926. A critic for *Kirkus Reviews* called the work a "homage to a brave and dedicated aviation pioneer," while a *Publishers Weekly* reviewer said Lindbergh "chooses the elements likeliest to inspire a young audience." *Washington Post Book World* reviewer John Cech called *Nobody Owns the Sky* "an important book for the little ones who might think they can't and for those who are learning that they can."

A *Publishers Weekly* reviewer called Lindbergh's next children's book, *The Awful Aardvarks Go to School,* a "witty, giddy alphabet book." The aardvarks terrorize the animals that attend the school, angering anteaters, eating ants, bullying a bunny, and tossing turtles. A contributor to *Kirkus Reviews* noted that the aardvarks "are more gleeful than rude" and "come across as much ado about nothing." A *School Library Journal* reviewer called *The Awful Aardvarks Go to School* "a flying success."

The Circle of Days is Lindbergh's 1997 adaptation of Francis of Assisi's *Canticle of the Sun,* written in 1225. *School Library Journal* reviewer Patricia Lothrop-Green called it a book "for the eye, if not the ear." "The gentle, rhyming text follows the form of a prayer in praise of brother sun, sister moon, and mother earth and in gratitude to the Lord for providing such wondrous gifts," observed a *Publishers Weekly* reviewer. Janice M. Del Negro wrote in *Bulletin of the Center for Children's Books* that in *The Circle of Days,* "Francis of Assisi's hymn of thanks to the Creator is granted glowing life."

Lindbergh uses rhyming couplets in describing how spring unfolds in New England in *North Country Spring.* The book features a glossary of the fourteen animals included in the text. Kay Weisman wrote in *Booklist* that junior high students will find *North Country Spring* to be "a springboard for writing seasonal poetry." "Lindbergh's ebullient verse is a triumph song of spring's melting, sensory flush," wrote a *Publishers Weekly* reviewer.

Works Cited

Abbott, Deborah, review of *A View from the Air: Charles Lindbergh's Earth and Sky, Booklist,* August, 1992, p. 2015.

Review of *The Awful Aardvarks Go to School, Kirkus Reviews,* September 15, 1997.

Review of *The Awful Aardvarks Go to School, Publishers Weekly,* August 25, 1997.

Review of *The Awful Aardvarks Go to School, School Library Journal,* December, 1997.

Blodgett, Jan, review of *The Names of Mountains: A Novel, Library Journal,* November 15, 1992, p. 102.

Bunting, Eve, review of *The Midnight Farm, Los Angeles Times Book Review,* November 22, 1987, p. 6.

Burns, Mary M., review of *Johnny Appleseed: A Poem, Horn Book,* September-October, 1990, p. 593.

Cech, John, review of *Nobody Owns the Sky: The Story of "Brave Bessie" Coleman, Washington Post Book World,* December 8, 1996, p. 23.

Chin, Paula, review of *The Names of Mountains: A Novel, People Weekly,* January 25, 1993, p. 63.

Review of *The Circle of Days, Publishers Weekly,* March 23, 1998, p. 95.

Cole, Diane, review of *Moving to the Country, New York Times Book Review,* January 1, 1984, pp. 20-22.

Crawford, Patricia, review of *What Is the Sun, Language Arts,* September, 1996, p. 354.

Review of *The Day the Goose Got Loose, Publishers Weekly,* July 13, 1990, p. 53.

Del Negro, Janice M., review of *The Circle of Days, Bulletin of the Center for Children's Books,* April, 1998, p. 286.

DeWind, Anna, review of *Benjamin's Barn, School Library Journal,* June, 1990, p. 103.

Doonan, Jane, review of *The Midnight Farm, Times Literary Supplement,* November 20, 1987, p. 1284.

Dow, Sally R., review of *If I'd Known Then What I Know Now, School Library Journal,* July, 1994, p. 79.

Review of *Grandfather's Lovesong, Publishers Weekly,* April 19, 1993, p. 59.

Review of *Johnny Appleseed: A Poem, Publishers Weekly,* July 13, 1990, p. 54.

Lindbergh, Reeve, *There's a Cow in the Road,* Dial, 1993.

Lindbergh, Reeve, *Under a Wing: A Memoir,* Simon & Schuster, 1998.

Lothrop-Green, Patricia, review of *The Circle of Days, School Library Journal,* April, 1998, p. 119.

Review of *Moving to the Country, Publishers Weekly,* July 22, 1983, p. 118

Review of *Nobody Owns the Sky: The Story of "Brave Bessie" Coleman, Kirkus Reviews,* November 1, 1996.

Review of *Nobody Owns the Sky: The Story of "Brave Bessie" Coleman, Publishers Weekly,* November 18, 1996, p. 74.

Review of *North Country Spring, Publishers Weekly,* March 24, 1997, p. 82.

Price, Anne, review of *The Day the Goose Got Loose, School Library Journal,* September, 1990, p. 206.

Rochman, Hazel, review of *There's a Cow in the Road, Booklist,* July, 1993, p. 1975.

Schubert, Leda, review of *Grandfather's Lovesong, School Library Journal,* April, 1993, p. 100.

Review of *There's a Cow in the Road, Kirkus Reviews,* July 1, 1993.

Review of *There's a Cow in the Road, Publishers Weekly,* June 21, 1993, p. 103.

Review of *Under a Wing: A Memoir, Publishers Weekly,* August 24, 1998, p. 38.

Ward, Geoffrey C., review of *Under a Wing: A Memoir, New York Times Book Review,* September 27, 1998, pp. 14-15.

Weisman, Kay, review of *North Country Spring, Booklist,* May 15, 1997, p. 1580.

For More Information See

PERIODICALS

Booklist, September 1, 1987, p. 65; March 1, 1989, p. 1200; April 15, 1990, p. 1634; September 1, 1990, p. 58; September 15, 1990, p. 171; November 15, 1991, p. 633; November 15, 1992, p. 579; January 15, 1993, p. 915; January, 1997, p. 869; October 15, 1997, p. 402; April, 1998, p. 1325.

Books, December, 1987, p. 24.

Children's Book Review Service, November, 1987, p. 26; August, 1990, p. 160; October, 1990, p. 20; November, 1990, p. 26; October, 1992, p. 20; February, 1997, p. 76; May, 1997, p. 111.

Children's Book Watch, April, 1991, p. 1; May, 1993, p. 3; January, 1997, p. 5.

Christian Science Monitor, November 6, 1987, p. B6; January 4, 1993, p. 12.

Horn Book, November, 1990, p. 729, pp. 774-75.

Junior Bookshelf, April, 1988, p. 84; June, 1991, p. 95; August, 1993, p. 129.

Kirkus Reviews, September 1, 1987, p. 1323; July 1, 1990, p. 933; September 1, 1992, p. 1140; October 1, 1992, p. 1208; February 15, 1997, p. 302.

Kliatt, September, 1996, p. 24.

Library Journal, November 15, 1992, p. 102; October 1, 1998, p. 104.

Maclean's, November 9, 1998, p. 86.

Magpies, September, 1991, p. 28; March, 1997, p. 23.

Minneapolis-St. Paul Magazine, November, 1987, p. 156.

New York Times Book Review, December 13, 1987, p. 29; April 3, 1988, p. 16; December 2, 1988, p. 38; December 2, 1990, p. 38; March 7, 1993, p. 12; May 16, 1993, p. 31; November 14, 1993, p. 58; May 11, 1997, p. 24.

People Weekly, September 28, 1998, p. 157.

Publishers Weekly, July 10, 1987, p. 66; June 8, 1990, p. 52; July 13, 1992, p. 53; October 12, 1992, p. 65; May 9, 1994, p. 71; January 29, 1996, p. 101; June 17, 1996, p. 67; January 19, 1998, p. 380.

School Library Journal, October, 1987, p. 115; August, 1990, p. 122; September, 1992, p. 222; August, 1994, p. 140; November, 1996, p. 98; February, 1997, p. 113; April, 1997, p. 113.

Skipping Stones, March, 1997, p. 8.*

*   *   *

LITCHFIELD, Jo 1973-

Personal

Born January 21, 1973, in Liecestershire, England; daughter of Marcus Henry and Jane Erica (Lee) Litchfield. *Education:* Derby University, B.A. (with honors), 1995.

Jo Litchfield

Addresses

Home—1 Barn Close, Quarndon, Derby, DE22 5JE, England. *E-mail*—jolitchfield@quarndon01.fsnet.co.uk.

Career

Freelance artist. Also worked as a designer and model maker for Usborne Publishing Ltd., London, England.

Illustrator

Everyday Words, Usborne Publishing (London, England), 1999.

Everyday Words in Spanish, Usborne Publishing, 1999.

Everyday Words in German, Usborne Publishing, 1999.

Everyday Words in French, Usborne Publishing, 1999.

The Missing Cat, Usborne Publishing, 1999.

Birthday Surprise, Usborne Publishing, 1999.

Runaway Orange, Usborne Publishing, 1999.

Very First Words, Usborne Publishing, 2000.

First Words Animals, Usborne Publishing, 2000.

First Words at Home, Usborne Publishing, 2000.

First Words Things that Move, Usborne Publishing, 2000.

Work in Progress

Illustrating a book of numbers and a picture dictionary; research on animation.

Sidelights

Jo Litchfield told *SATA:* "*Everyday Words* is my first published work, and I have been working on it for three years, from planning and design to getting it to production. I was hired by Usborne Publishing fresh out of university, and *Everyday Words* was the first project I was handed.

"I didn't study model-making at university, but I have always been interested and have made models since an early age. I created a three-dimensional piece for an advertising campaign at college—and, against the advice of my tutors, I kept it in my portfolio. This was spotted by my managing designer, Mary Cartwright, at my interview with Usborne, and it went some way toward my getting the job.

"My style developed itself somewhat during the first few months of working on the book. I had never tackled anything of this scale and hadn't envisaged my model-making leading to a career. I enjoy the work—although it can be repetitive—and hope to continue to illustrate in this way. Further published works have only just been released. These are a range of easy-reading storybooks of which I am quite proud. All future projects are aimed at the very young. I am currently designing a book of numbers and a picture dictionary, both to be illustrated with models. I would like to work on more challenging pieces. My own personal work is more sophisticated and refined, involving themes of legends and fairy tales.

"It is an exciting time for me. My career is only just beginning, and I'm very pleased that *Everyday Words* has received such a warm reception. It means most to me when friends have given the book to children they know. A seal of approval from a child means the book has reached its intended audience. Hopefully I will have the opportunity to continue to work on projects which are both challenging and fun."

*   *   *

LORAINE, Connie
See REECE, Colleen L.

*   *   *

LOVEJOY, Jack 1937-

Personal

Born November 25, 1937, in Chicago, IL; son of Christian P. (a dental ceramist) and Amy (a homemaker; maiden name, Closs) Lovejoy. *Education:* University of Illinois at Chicago Circle, B.A., 1971, M.A., 1973;

Jack Lovejoy

Northeastern Illinois University, M.A., 1972; attended University of Chicago, 1973-74.

Addresses

Home—2203 Eastwood, Chicago, IL 60625.

Career

Bankers Life and Casualty Co., Chicago, IL, insurance underwriter, 1964-69; freelance writer, 1974—. Also worked as postal clerk, bartender, schoolteacher, and factory worker. *Military service:* U.S. Navy, electronics technician, 1959-63.

Writings

FOR CHILDREN

The Rebel Witch, Lothrop, 1978.

SCIENCE FICTION NOVELS

Star Gods, Major (Canoga Park, CA), 1979.
The Hunters, Pinnacle, 1982.
A Vision of Beasts (trilogy; contains Book 1: *Creation Descending,* Book 2: *The Second Kingdom,* and Book 3: *The Brotherhood of Diablo*), Pinnacle, 1984.
Outworld Cats, DAW Books, 1994.

FANTASY NOVELS

Magus Rex, Pinnacle, 1983.
The Defenders of Ar, Bantam, 1990.

OTHER

A Ring of Keys (lyric poetry), Winston-Derek (Nashville, TN), 1989.

Also author of *Pictures of Truth.* Contributor to periodicals, including *Argos, South Dakota Review, Texas Quarterly, Lyric, Illinois Quarterly,* and *Limnos.*

The Hunters was translated into Italian, and *The Defenders of Ar* was translated into Japanese.

Work in Progress

A novel, *The Salem Bequest.*

Sidelights

Jack Lovejoy once commented: "I came to fiction writing by chance. My original program was a scholarly elucidation of Roman history through a better understanding of the Roman environment. I earned master's degrees in Roman history and geography but was forced to abandon my doctoral work when I exhausted all financial hopes. Then I began writing novels. I still hope to resume my work on ancient history and environment, but now as a writer rather than an academician.

"I believe that writing is more than a career, even more than art and craftsmanship—it is a way of life. There is a kind of wonder in discovering new means for expressing the old truths and values, or in making some original premise logical and believable, that forgives all the doubt and drudgery and alarming bank balances that a freelance writer must endure. I thoroughly enjoy writing, and I generally do it every day—fiction during the week and, on weekends, poetry and translations of Goethe.

"It seems to me that there are always fresh ways of looking at our world and its conventions, which may lead to a finer understanding of both. One means is by delineating alternate worlds and societies. My science fiction novels project current social and environmental trends into the future. My fantasy *Magus Rex,* for example, moves through a series of decadent or totalitarian societies, and my [unpublished] novel *Catiline* is set in the late Roman Republic, an age of violence, terrorism, and the breakdown of traditional values, much like our own."

Lovejoy's *The Rebel Witch* stars a bright young apprentice who must rescue her teacher, Madame Mengo, from the evil pursuit of Professor Sinistrari. Stealing a magic wand, Suzie disappears into the Veneficon, or witch world, embarking on a terrifying adventure filled with sorcerers, circus people, and an amphibian creature named Wumpo. Writing in *Publishers Weekly,* a critic claimed the "comic and fearful events that follow are edge-of-the-chair reading adventures." Despite noticing that the books length might be a bit long for some readers, *School Library Journal* reviewer Cynthia Percak Infantino predicted that "fanciers of occult stories will enjoy the descriptions of Veneficon and its residents." Combining "magical situations" and "a contemporary heroine" lead *Booklist* contributor Barbara Elleman to observe that *The Rebel Witch* "will appeal to children looking for witchy stories."

Lovejoy concluded, "Above all, I want to tell good stories about interesting and believable characters. Even in science fiction there is room for humor."

Works Cited

Elleman, Barbara, review of *The Rebel Witch, Booklist,* September 1, 1978, pp. 50-51.

Infantino, Cynthia Percak, review of *The Rebel Witch, School Library Journal,* December, 1978, p. 54.

Review of *The Rebel Witch, Publishers Weekly,* October 23, 1978, p. 61.

For More Information See

Kliatt, fall, 1984, p. 29; July, 1994, p. 16.

* * *

LOWENSTEIN, Sallie 1949-

Personal

Born July 20, 1949, in Washington, DC; daughter of Frank (an agricultural economist) and Mindel (a teacher and mathematician; maiden name, Wolberg) Lowenstein; married Robert E. Kenney (an attorney), August 24, 1974; children: John Kenney, Rachel Kenney. *Education:* Attended Carnegie-Mellon University, 1967-68; Tulane University, B.F.A., 1971; American University, M.F.A., 1973; University of Arizona at Guadalajara, Mexico, summer, 1972.

Addresses

Home—4921 Aurora Drive, Kensington, MD 20895. *E-mail*—lionstone@juno.com.

Career

Studio artist, 1966—; freelance illustrator and book illustrator, 1970—; writer, 1991—. Teacher, Arlington County Division of Recreation, Arlington, VA, 1973-80; Glen Echo National Park, Glen Echo, MD, 1973-76; BCC-JCG, Inc., 1988-93; administrator, 1991-93; also, senior adult arts specialist, 1974-84. Visual arts director, Glen Echo Park Art Gallery, 1974-75; consulting director, Arlington Arts Center, 1976; Round House Theatre Arts Camp, 1989.

Program planning and presentation in arts enrichment to public and private schools, 1985—. *Member:* Society of Children's Book Writers and Illustrators.

Awards, Honors

Max Beckman Memorial Award, Brooklyn Museum of Fine Arts, 1971; Honorarium, National Collection of Fine Arts, Smithsonian Institution, Children's Day, 1974-76; Service Award, Drew School, Arlington, VA, 1984; Artists in Education award, Maryland State Council of the Arts, 1988-89; Council of Governments' Summer Quest Artist for the Public Libraries, DC metropolitan area, 1992; Excellence in Print Award, Printing and Graphic Communication Association, 1997, for design and production of *The Mt. Olympus Zoo;* Women in the Arts Recognition Award, Montgomery County Commission for Women and Montgomery County Public Schools, 1998; Best Books for Young Adults nomination, American Library Association, 2000, for *Evan's Voice.*

Writings

SELF-ILLUSTRATED

The Frame-It-Alphabet Book, self-published, 1977.

Daniel the Medusa Hunter, Lion Stone Books (Kensington, MD), 1996.

(With John Kenney) *The Mt. Olympus Zoo,* Lion Stone Books, 1997.

Evan's Voice, Lion Stone Books, 1999.

The Festival of Lights: A Family Hanukkah Service, Lion Stone Books, 1999.

Also author of "Writing Science Fiction: A Ticket to Distant Travels," *Children's Book Insider,* 1999. Illus-

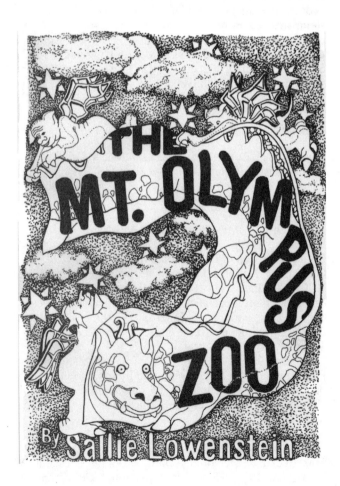

A trip to a zoo becomes an adventure when the Powers family encounters a menagerie of living mythological creatures in Sallie Lowenstein's self-illustrated fantasy. (Cover illustration by Lowenstein.)

trator of posters and informational brochures for Bartleby Books, Arlington Arts Center, Books Unlimited, Glen Echo Park, DC Advisory Neighborhood Commission, Tulane University, and American University.

Work in Progress

Paintings and sculptures and works with paper; screens and handmade books; *Lou Emma Montana Hills,* a young adult historical/romance/mystery; *Focus,* a young adult science fiction novel; *Things Outgrown,* young adult fantasy/science fiction; and *Shadows of the Schwedagon,* young adult science fiction.

Sidelights

"I love kids," Sallie Lowenstein told *SATA.* "They are funny, endearing, imaginative, creative, and usually happy. So as an artist, author, and illustrator I try to have a lot of contact with them. When my kids were little that was easy. Now I find as many opportunities as I can to work with them in schools, book groups, libraries, and bookstores. And there is one question they ask me that always makes me pause: if I had to choose one thing that I would be, what is it? And I can't answer. From the time I was ten I knew I was going to be an artist. My family had traveled around the world to seventeen countries on a trip that took us to and from Rangoon, Burma, where we lived for a little over a year. On that trip I saw most of the great art galleries and architectural monuments that those countries we visited in Asia and Europe had to offer. I was going to be an artist. By the time I was fifteen, I was selling my paintings. I went to art school, earned an M.F.A., won awards, exhibited, had one-person shows, and created. Years later, when my husband and I bought our house, he happily pointed out that we had bought a studio with a house attached. While in college, I began illustrating professionally for universities and businesses. And while pregnant with my first child, I began stone carving. I come from a family that loves to tell stories and I had always loved writing, but as a younger person I found it hard to both write and paint, and so put off the inevitable. When my second child was eight I began writing seriously and because I loved kids and was so involved with them, I chose to write for children. I discovered that as I wrote, I saw how the books would look. I could see the illustrations. They were an integral part of the writing process, even when I wrote novels. It was a natural outgrowth of both my lifelong involvement in art, and of a developing interest in screens and books formatted like screens, that the art and writing would be so entangled. So now I was a painter, sculptor, illustrator, and writer. And I could no more choose one of these art forms over another than I could stop breathing.

"So when kids ask me which part of my creativity I would choose over another, I pause, I stutter, and finally I shrug. True creativity cannot be separated out of one's life like a piece of clothing. It is not a choice any more than being born is. It has taken me a while to stop thinking of myself solely as an artist and accept that I am also a writer, and it was probably this very question that the children asked me that made me realize how integral all aspects of creativity are to my life.

"The other question that kids and adults frequently ask me is, "Where do you get your ideas?" I have a rampant imagination and always have had. I am not afraid to pretend, which is really what is at the core of all good fiction writing. I hope my books will take readers where they cannot go without my words and art, but what I always hope for with kids is that once they have traveled there, they will find how to take themselves to these wonderful new places on their own and grow up to use their own rampant imaginations."

Lowenstein's first children's book, *Daniel the Medusa Hunter,* is the tale of Daniel, a modern-day hero who seeks out the ugly in order to transform it into something beautiful. Daniel saves Amy from her Aunt and Uncle's tacky house, which offends the little girl's aesthetics during an extended stay while her parents are away. The slender story is wrapped around twenty-seven illustrations, described by Sunil Freeman in the *Montgomery Gazette* as "luscious, with a subtle play of colors and a fine line throughout." The illustrations are actually silk-screened prints hand-bound in the traditional Japanese fashion in an edition of three hundred; each print can be removed from the binding for framing and hanging and instructions for reinserting the print back into the book are included. "[The artwork] can stand on its own," Freeman observed, "but it also has a light, almost dreamy charm that is quite in tune with the narrative."

Lowenstein took her inspiration from mythology in *The Mt. Olympus Zoo,* a children's novel that follows a family visiting various unusual zoos on their vacation. At the Mt. Olympus Zoo, mythological creatures originating in cultures all over the world live and breathe and talk to the Powers family during their visit. The Powers are so sympathetic to the creatures they meet that they intervene between them and the worried townspeople, who are agitating to close the zoo after seeing one of the animals disguised as a vampire. A reviewer for *Library Talk* contended that *The Mt. Olympus Zoo* "combines good story with a lot of information about mythology." The book concludes with factual information on the mythological creatures featured in the story, written and compiled by John Kenney, the author's son. "Kenney's compilation is so rich in references ... it could inspire adults as well as children to further study of these strange creatures so deeply rooted in our collective memory," averred Freeman.

For her next book, Lowenstein stepped out of the realm of fantasy and into the realm of science fiction. In *Evan's Voice,* the author imagines a future world staggering under the aftereffects of a plague that has decimated the world population, with the remaining people divided strictly into the haves and have-nots. The book stars Jake, an adolescent boy who cares for his plague-sickened little brother Evan in the absence of their mother. Jake and his friend Mellie travel into the Dead Zone to interview a mysterious storyteller whose tales hint at the possibility of a better future. *Indepen-*

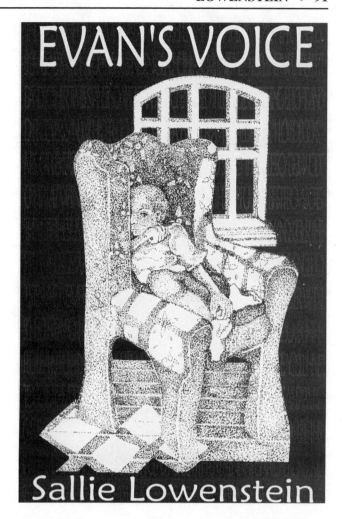

In Lowenstein's futuristic novel, a storyteller with promising tales of future survival gives teenage Jake hope in his attempt to move his little brother Evan from their plague-stricken environment. (Cover illustration by Lowenstein.)

dent Publisher reviewer Paula Frosch praised the realism with which Lowenstein depicts her teenage characters: "The characters in the story combine the raucous teasing qualities of their ages with the sensitivity and needs common to us all." Lowenstein's illustrations contrast scenes of Jake's world and the scenes of the storyteller's tales shown on television and the combination makes for a highly illustrated story. "Young adults will savor this unique marriage of story with image in a classy form of almost-graphic novel," predicted Anne Raymer and Cathi Dunn MacRae in *Voice of Youth Advocates.* For Roger Leslie in *Booklist,* the highlight of *Evan's Voice* lies in the scenes in which the need for literature and education is argued "with such conviction the reader is sure to recall that message long after the book is shut."

Works Cited

Freeman, Sunil, "Mythological Figures Inspire Children's Literature," *Montgomery Gazette,* June 6, 1997.

Frosch, Paula, review of *Evan's Voice, Independent Publisher,* January-February, 1999.

Leslie, Roger, review of *Evan's Voice, Booklist,* March 1, 1999, p. 1214.

Review of *Mt. Olympus Zoo, Library Talk,* March-April, 1998.

Raymer, Anne, and Cathi Dunn MacRae, review of *Evan's Voice, Voice of Youth Advocates,* June, 1999.

M

MARCHANT, Catherine
    See COOKSON, Catherine
    (McMullen)

*   *   *

MARSHALL, Felicity 1950-

Personal

Born February 13, 1950, in Perth, Western Australia; daughter of Lloyd (a journalist) and Dorothy Elizabeth (an equestrienne) Marshall; married Ian Baker (a director of photography), 1982 (divorced); children: Leo Marshall, Kate Imogen. *Education:* Western Australian Institute of Technology (now Curtin University of Technology), Associate in Fine Art (with honors), 1969; Hawthorn State College, Diploma of Education, 1973; studied ballet in Australia. *Religion:* Anglican.

Addresses

Home and office—20 Balmoral Cres., Surrey Hills, Victoria 3127, Australia.

Career

Western Australian Ballet Company, member of *corps de ballet,* 1969; Claremont Technical College, Claremont, Australia, lecturer in painting, drawing, and illustration, 1970; Film House Pty. Ltd., Melbourne, Australia, began as production assistant, became post-production manager, 1971-73; teacher, 1973-74; Fresh Flicks Pty. Ltd. (film production company), cofounder, 1974, operator, 1975-88; Geelong Grammar School, Glamorgan, Australia, library assistant and relieving teacher of art and history, 1990-94; illustrator and writer of children's books, 1994—. Artist, with group and solo exhibitions throughout Australia; work represented in private collections in Australia, New Zealand, England, and the United States. *Member:* Australian Society of Authors, Australian Society of Book Illustrators, Society

Felicity Marshall

of Children's Book Writers and Illustrators (United States).

Awards, Honors

Commonwealth scholar; Certificate of Encouragement from Children's Book Council of Australia.

Writings

(Illustrator) Kerri Hashmi, *You and Me, Murrawee,* Viking (Ringwood, Australia), 1998.
(Author and illustrator) *Sage's Ark,* Fremantle Arts Centre Press, 2000.

Work represented in anthologies, including *Saddle Up Again,* HarperCollins, 1994.

Sidelights

Felicity Marshall told *SATA:* "I grew up in the country outside Perth in Western Australia. Throughout my childhood reading, painting, and dancing were my sanctuaries during times of boredom, heat waves, and family friction. Later, working in the film industry for many years helped me visualize my stories, and consequently I think about them in 'filmic' terms—scene by scene. I am a romantic. I do believe that children learn the most profound things by traveling through the imaginary world of storybooks, myths, fairy tales—often learning more by what is implied rather than by what is instructed."

*   *   *

MATTHEWS, John (Kentigern) 1948-

Personal

Born January 14, 1948, in Kendal, Westmorland, England; married Caitlin Stillwell, January 2, 1952; children: one son.

Career

Writer, lecturer, storyteller, and workshop teacher of Celtic Shamanism in Europe and the United States. Consultant and contributor to media projects, including an animated series on King Arthur produced by Hit Productions. Co-organizer of the Merlin Conference, 1989-92. Editor at *Labrys,* 1979-86.

Writings

The Grail, Crossroad (New York City), 1981.
(Editor) *At the Table of the Grail,* Routledge & Kegan Paul (London, England and Boston, MA), 1984.
The Grail Seeker's Companion, Thorsons (London), 1987.
(With Bob Stuart) *Warriors of Arthur,* Blandford (London, England), 1987.
An Arthurian Reader, Aquarian (Wellingborough, England), 1988.
Boadicea, Firebird (Poole, England), 1988.
El Cid, Champion of Spain, Firebird, 1988.
Fionn Mac Cumhail, Firebird, 1988.
Richard Lionheart, the Crusader King, Firebird, 1988.
Tales of Arthur, Javelin (New York City), 1988.
Warriors of Christendom, Firebird, 1988.
Taliesin, Thorsons, 1990.
The Celtic Reader, Aquarian, 1991.
The Song of Taliesin, Aquarian, 1991.

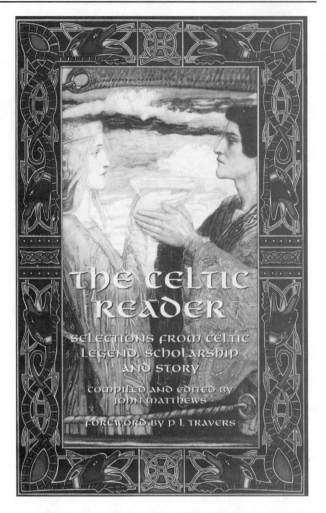

In his comprehensive collection of materials dating from the earliest days of Celtic civilization to the twentieth century, Matthews has created a history of Celtic society and the attitudes and prejudices that continue to shape subsequent notions of it. (Cover illustration by John Duncan.)

The Celtic Shaman, Element (Rockport, ME), 1992.
(Editor) *The World Atlas of Divination,* Little, Brown (Boston, MA), 1992.
Celtic Warrior Chiefs, Firebird, 1993.
From the Isles of Dream, Lindisfarne (Hudson, NY), 1993.
The Little Book of Celtic Wisdom, Element (Shaftesbury, England), 1993.
Warriors of Medieval Times, Firebird, 1993.
King Arthur and the Grail Quest, Blandford, 1994.
The Little Book of Arthurian Wisdom, Element, 1994.
Within the Hollow Hills, Floris (Edinburgh, Scotland), 1994.
The Celtic Shaman's Pack, Element, 1995.
King Arthur's Britain, Blandford, 1995.
Merlin through the Ages, Blandford, 1995.
The Unknown Arthur, Blandford, 1995.
The Druid Source Book, Blandford, 1996.
The Elements of the Arthurian Tradition, Element, 1996.
Mystic Grail: The Challenge of the Arthurian Quest, Sterling, 1997.
Classic Celtic Fairy Tales, Blandford, 1997.

Healing the Wounded King, Element, 1997.

Landscapes of Legend, Blandford, 1997.

Secret Camelot, Blandford, 1997.

Sources of the Grail, Lindisfarne, 1997.

The Bardic Source Book, Blandford, 1998.

(With wife, Caitlin Matthews) *Hallowquest: The Arthurian Tarot Course: A Tarot Journey through the Arthurian World,* Harper (San Francisco, CA), 1998.

The Winter Solstice, Quest (Wheaton, IL), 1998.

The Little Book of Celtic Lore, Element, 1998.

(With Caitlin Matthews) *The Wizard King,* Barefoot Collections (New York City), 1998.

Drinking from the Sacred Well, Harper, 1998.

(Compiler) *Tales of the Celtic Otherworld,* illustrated by Ian Daniels, Blandford, 1998.

(Editor) *The Celtic Seers' Source Book: Vision and Magic in the Druid Tradition,* Blandford, 1999.

Contributor to books, including *Arthurian Tarot Deck and Book Set,* by Caitlin Matthews and Miranda Gray, Thorsons, 1990; and *Ladies of the Lake,* by Caitlin Matthews, Thorsons, 1992. Consultant and contributor to the film *Shaman,* directed by Sean Greoghegan.

Sidelights

John Matthews is a well-known and highly prolific expert in Celtic and early-English history. He has endeavored through his books to educate a wider public, adults and children, about the historical and literary sources for common contemporary legends surrounding King Arthur, Merlin, and the Holy Grail. Combining a scrupulous concern for historical accuracy with a concern for religious matters, Matthews has, through his work, attempted to keep the spirit of the pre- to early-Medieval era alive.

Matthews' first book, *The Grail,* appeared as part of a ten-part series, *The Illustrated Library of Sacred Imagination.* In it, he presents a thorough survey of both the legends and the limited historical information about the Grail, speculating on its possible location and ruminating on its symbolic and religious significance. Beginning with Celtic myths involving a magical cauldron capable of feeding an unlimited number of people as well as bringing the dead back to life, Matthews traces the gradual merger of these myths with the legend of Christ's cup from the Last Supper, the Holy Grail. According to Matthews, around the year 1200, Grail stories became increasingly popular and both Christian and Celtic mystics further embroidered and expanded the stories. Unlike many other experts in folklore who are content to leave the development of the Grail story at that, Matthews goes further, attributing certain specific elements of later Grail myths to the influence of secret societies, heretics, and other, unrelated popular folktales.

Returning to the Grail, Matthews probes deeper into its function as a symbol in works of the imagination. In *At the Table of the Grail,* Matthews gathers eleven meditative essays about the contemporary spiritual significance of the Grail. Various authors interpret the Grail legend in terms of diverse esoteric traditions. Matthews followed

up this volume with a number of books detailing the lives of legendary heroes and heroines, including King Arthur, El Cid, and Boadicea. He has edited several anthologies of related material, including a comprehensive collection of Celtic stories and secondary studies sampled from the earliest days of Celtic civilization to the twentieth century, creating an extremely rich and wide-ranging sourcebook. The result, *The Celtic Reader,* is a history not only of Celtic society but of the attitudes and prejudices that continue to shape subsequent notions of it.

At the heart of ancient English Celtic life were the mysterious Druids, about whom very little is known, owing to the fact that they had no written language. The only firsthand accounts of Druid practices were provided by Roman invaders who witnessed them and regarded the rituals as little better than barbaric. A more objective historical source is wanting, and as a result, speculation about the Druids is a common pastime among Celtic historians. Matthews turned his attention to them in *The Druid Source Book,* which, much like his *Celtic Reader,* studies not only the ancient sources but also their latter-day interpretation and the contemporary Druidic revival as well.

Turning from pagan Druids to Celtic Christians, Matthews provided a similar survey of the lives of twelve Celtic saints in *Drinking from the Sacred Well.* Starting

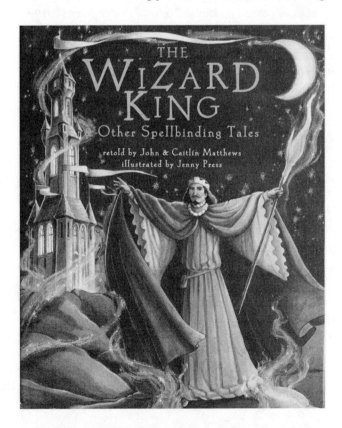

Matthews and his wife collected nine stories about magical people from Algonquin, Hopi, French, Greek, English, Russian, Armenian, Italian, and Welsh folklore in their compilation of tales about enchantment. (Cover illustration by Jenny Press.)

with his own namesake, Kentigern, Matthews combines both historical and folkloric information in great detail in each study. In addition to Kentigern, Matthews provides in depth analysis of Maedoc, Brighid, Berach, David, Senan, Patrick, Brendan, Kevin, Columba, Mochuda, and Ciaran. Matthews' most recent work, *The Wizard King,* written in collaboration with his wife Caitlin, shows his synthesizing style at work over a much broader range of material. Here he collects nine stories about magical people from Algonquin, Hopi, French, Greek, English, Russian, Armenian, Italian, and Welsh folklore.

For More Information See

PERIODICALS

American Historical Review, October, 1991, p. 1177.
Booklist, May 1, 1988, pp. 1463-1464; February 15, 1989, p. 973.
Books, May-June, 1991, p. 22.
British Book News, March, 1982, p. 163; August, 1987, p. 503.
Choice, December, 1994, p. 570.
Library Journal, April 1, 1982, p. 737; October 15, 1982, p. 1986; April 15, 1996, p. 89; October 15, 1996, p. 64; January 1, 1998, p. 109; October 1, 1998, p. 98; January, 1999, p. 108; July, 1999, p. 99.
Los Angeles Times Book Review, August 26, 1984, p. 8.
Parabola, winter, 1992, pp. 95-100.
Publishers Weekly, October 26, 1998, p. 60; May 31, 1999, p. 84.
Religious Studies Review, July, 1983, pp. 239-240.
School Librarian, February, 1989, p. 34.
School Library Journal, October, 1989, p. 148; December, 1998, p. 110.

ON-LINE

Author's website at http://www.hallowquest.org.uk.

* * *

McCAFFREY, Anne (Inez) 1926-

Personal

Born April 1, 1926, in Cambridge, MA; daughter of George Herbert (a city administrator and U.S. Army colonel) and Anne D. (maiden name, McElroy) McCaffrey; married H. Wright Johnson, January 14, 1950 (divorced, 1970); children: Alec Anthony, Todd, Georgeanne. *Education:* Radcliffe College, B.A. (cum laude), 1947; graduate study in meteorology, University of City of Dublin; also studied voice for nine years. *Politics:* Democrat. *Religion:* Presbyterian. *Hobbies and other interests:* Singing, opera directing, riding and horse care.

Addresses

Home—Dragonhold-Underhill, Timmore Lane, Newcastle, County Wicklow, Ireland. *Agent*—Virginia Kidd, Box 278, Milford, PA 18337.

Anne McCaffrey

Career

Liberty Music Shops, New York City, copywriter and layout designer, 1948-50; Helena Rubinstein, New York City, copywriter and secretary, 1950-52; author. Director of Fin Film Productions, 1979—, and Dragonhold, Ltd. Former professional stage director for several groups in Wilmington, DE. *Member:* Science Fiction Writers of America (secretary-treasurer, 1968-70), Mystery Writers of America, Authors Guild, Novelists' Ink.

Awards, Honors

Hugo Award for best novella, World Science Fiction Society, 1968, for "Weyr Search"; Nebula Award for best novella, Science Fiction Writers of America, 1969, for "Dragonrider"; E. E. Smith Award for fantasy, 1975; American Library Association notable book citations, 1976, for *Dragonsong,* and 1977, for *Dragonsinger; Horn Book* Fanfare Citation, 1977, for *Dragonsong;* Ditmar Award (Australia), Gandalf Award, and Eurocon/Streso Award, all 1979, all for *The White Dragon;* Balrog citation, 1980, for *Dragondrums;* Golden Pen Award, 1981; Science Fiction Book Club Awards, 1986, for *Killashandra,* 1989, for *Dragonsdawn,* and 1990, for *The Renegades of Pern* (first place) and *The Rowan* (third place); Margaret A. Edwards Lifetime Achievement Award for Outstanding Literature for Young Adults, American Library Association's Young Adult Library Services and *School Library Journal,* 1999; "Juli" Award for Services to Fantasy Art and Literature, 1999.

Writings

SCIENCE FICTION/FANTASY

Restoree, Ballantine, 1967.
(Editor) *Alchemy and Academe,* Doubleday, 1970.
To Ride Pegasus, Ballantine, 1973.
Get Off the Unicorn (short stories), Del Rey, 1977.
The Worlds of Anne McCaffrey (stories), Deutsch, 1981.
The Coelura, Underwood-Miller, 1983.
Stitch in Snow, Del Rey, 1984.
Pegasus in Flight, Del Rey, 1990.
Three Women, Tor Books, 1992.
(With Elizabeth A. Scarborough) *Powers That Be,* Del Rey, 1993.
Lyon's Pride (limited edition), Putnam, 1993.
(With Scarborough) *Power Lines* (sequel to *Powers That Be*), Del Rey, 1994.
The Girl Who Heard Dragons (story collection; includes *The Girl Who Heard Dragons;* also see below), Tor Books, 1994.
An Exchange of Gifts, illustrated by Pat Morrissey, ROC, 1995.
Freedom's Landing, Putnam, 1995.
(With Scarborough) *Power Play,* Del Rey, 1995.
No One Noticed the Cat, ROC, 1996.
(Editor with Scarborough) *Space Opera,* DAW Books, 1996.
(With Margaret Ball) *Acorna: The Unicorn Girl,* Harper-Prism, 1997.
(With Ball) *Acorna's Quest,* HarperPrism, 1998.
If Wishes Were Horses, ROC, 1998.
Nimisha's Ship, Ballantine, 1999.
(With Scarborough) *Acorna's People,* HarperPrism, 1999.

"DRAGONRIDERS OF PERN" SERIES; SCIENCE FICTION

Dragonflight, Ballantine, 1968, hardcover edition, Walker & Co., 1969.
Dragonquest: Being the Further Adventures of the Dragonriders of Pern, Ballantine, 1971.
A Time When, Being a Tale of Young Lord Jaxom, His White Dragon, Ruth, and Various Fire-Lizards (short story), NESFA Press, 1975.
The White Dragon, Del Rey, 1978.
The Dragonriders of Pern (contains *Dragonflight, Dragonquest,* and *The White Dragon*), Doubleday, 1978.
Moreta: Dragonlady of Pern, Del Rey, 1983.
The Girl Who Heard Dragons (for children), Cheap Street, 1985.
Nerilka's Story, Del Rey, 1986.
Dragonsdawn, Del Rey, 1988.
The Renegades of Pern, Del Rey, 1989.
All the Weyrs of Pern, Del Rey, 1991.
The Chronicles of Pern: First Fall, Del Rey, 1992.
The Dolphins of Pern, Del Rey, 1994.
Dragonseye, Del Rey, 1997.
The Masterharper of Pern, Del Rey, 1998.
Pern, Del Rey, 2001.

"PEGASUS" SERIES; SCIENCE FICTION

To Ride Pegasus, Del Rey, 1973.
Pegasus in Flight, Del Rey, 1990.
Pegasus in Space, Del Rey, 2000.

"HARPER HALL" SERIES; SCIENCE FICTION

Dragonsong, Atheneum, 1976.
Dragonsinger, Atheneum, 1977.
Dragondrums, Atheneum, 1979.
The Harper Hall of Pern (contains *Dragonsong, Dragonsinger,* and *Dragondrums*), Doubleday, 1979.

"FREEDOM" SERIES; SCIENCE FICTION

Freedom's Landing, Putnam, 1995.
Freedom's Choice, Putnam, 1997.
Freedom's Challenge, Putnam, 1998.

"DOONA" SERIES; SCIENCE FICTION

Decision at Doona, Ballantine, 1969.
(With Jody Lynn Nye) *Crisis on Doona,* Ace, 1992.
(With Nye) *Treaty at Doona,* Ace, 1994.

"SHIP WHO SANG" SERIES; SCIENCE FICTION

The Ship Who Sang, Walker & Co., 1969.
(With Mercedes Lackey) *The Ship Who Searched,* Baen Books, 1992.
(With Margaret Ball) *PartnerShip,* Baen Books, 1992.
(With S. M. Stirling) *The City Who Fought,* Baen Books, 1993.
(With Nye) *The Ship Who Won,* Baen Books, 1994.
(With Stirling) *The Ship Avenged,* Baen Books, 1997.

"DINOSAUR PLANET" SERIES; SCIENCE FICTION

Dinosaur Planet, Futura, 1977, Del Rey, 1978.
The Dinosaur Planet Survivors, Del Rey, 1984.
The Ireta Adventure (contains *Dinosaur Planet* and *The Dinosaur Planet Survivors*), Doubleday, 1985.

"CRYSTAL SINGER" SERIES; SCIENCE FICTION

Crystal Singer, Del Rey, 1981.
Killashandra, Del Rey, 1985.
Crystal Line, Del Rey, 1992.
Crystal Singer Trilogy (contains *Crystal Singer, Killashandra,* and *Crystal Line*), Del Rey, 1996.

"PLANET PIRATE" SERIES; SCIENCE FICTION

(With Elizabeth Moon) *Sassinak,* Baen Books, 1990.
(With Nye) *The Death of Sleep,* Baen Books, 1990.
Generation Warriors, Baen Books, 1991.
(With Moon and Nye) *The Planet Pirates,* Baen Books, 1993.

"ROWAN" SERIES; SCIENCE FICTION

The Rowan, Berkley Publishing, 1990.
Damia, Ace, 1993.
Damia's Children, Putnam, 1993.
Lyon's Pride, Putnam, 1994.
The Tower and the Hive, Putnam, 1999.

OTHER

The Mark of Merlin, Dell, 1971.
The Ring of Fear, Dell, 1971.
(Editor) *Cooking Out of This World,* Ballantine, 1973.
The Kilternan Legacy, Dell, 1975.
Habit Is an Old Horse, Dryad Press, 1986.
The Year of the Lucy (novel), Tor Books, 1986.
The Lady (novel), Ballantine, 1987, published in England as *The Carradyne Touch,* Futura/Macdonald, 1988.

(Author of text) Robin Wood, *The People of Pern,* Donning, 1988.

(With Nye) *The Dragonlover's Guide to Pern,* Del Rey, 1989.

Three Gothic Novels: The Ring of Fear, The Mark of Merlin, The Kilternan Legacy, Underwood-Miller, 1990.

Dragonflight Graphic Novel, HarperCollins, 1993.

Black Horses for the King (juvenile historical fiction), Harcourt, 1996.

(Editor with John Betancourt) *Serve It Forth: Cooking with Anne McCaffrey,* Warner Books, 1996.

Dragon, HarperCollins Juvenile, 1996.

(With Richard Woods) *A Diversity of Dragons,* illustrated by John Howe, HarperPrism, 1997.

Contributor to anthologies, including *Infinity One,* 1970, *Future Love,* 1977, and *Once Upon a Time,* 1991, and to magazines, including *Analog, Galaxy,* and *Magazine of Fantasy and Science Fiction.*

Collections of McCaffrey's manuscripts are housed at Syracuse University, Syracuse, NY, and in the Kerlan Collection, University of Minnesota, Minneapolis, MN.

Adaptations

Dragonsong and *Dragonsinger* have been adapted as children's stage plays by Irene Elliott and produced in Baltimore, MD; the "Pern" books have also inspired a cassette of music, *Dragonsongs,* a board game, and two computer games. *The White Dragon, Moreta: Dragonlady of Pern, Nerilka's Story,* and *The Rowan* are all available on cassette, as is the 1999 *Nimisha's Ship;* a television series, *The Dragonriders of Pern,* to be announced.

Sidelights

Anne McCaffrey is a writer of many firsts: the first woman to win science fiction's coveted Hugo and Nebula Awards; the first sci-fi writer to break into the *New York Times* bestseller lists; and the first sci-fi writer to be awarded the prestigious Margaret A. Edwards Award for lifetime achievement in young adult literature. Her award-winning "Dragonriders of Pern" series, fifteen strong and growing, rank, as James and Eugene Sloan noted in the *Chicago Tribune Book World,* as "the most enduring serial in the history of science fantasy." The series has proved so popular, with each new volume hitting the bestseller lists, "that it has almost transcended genre categorization," Gary K. Reynolds asserted in the *Science Fiction and Fantasy Book Review.* There are fan clubs galore, several websites, reference books that delineate the geography of McCaffrey's fanciful planet, Pern, other reference works that deal with all the characters in the richly textured series, board games, computer games, and television shows. McCaffrey's dragons are very busy critters.

The prolific American writer who makes her home in Ireland is far from being a one-trick pony, however. She has written over sixty books, both in series and stand-alones, translated into twenty-one languages in a career spanning over three decades. In addition to the "Dragonriders," McCaffrey has penned multi-volume adventures such as the "Ship Who Sang" series, "Crystal Singer" series, "Planet Pirate" series, "Rowan" series, and "Freedom" series, among others.

Noted for her well-developed characters and emphasis on emotion over science in her fictions, McCaffrey is often labeled a fantasy writer rather than a sci-fi novelist. Michael Cart put the question to her in a *School Library Journal* interview in celebration of the Margaret A. Edwards Award. Science fiction or fantasy author? "We keep having to settle that question," McCaffrey replied. "*I write science fiction.* It may seem fantasy because I use dragons, but mine were biogenetically engineered; ergo the story is science fiction." McCaffrey's character-driven and emotion-filled approach to sci fi allows her to weave serious social commentary into her work, according to Edra C. Bogle in the *Dictionary of Literary Biography.* "Most of McCaffrey's protagonists are women or children, whom she treats with understanding and sympathy," Bogle commented. The injustices these characters suffer, brought about by a sometimes-stifling social system, "are at the heart of most of McCaffrey's books." In fact, the majority of McCaffrey's novels feature strong heroines: the ruling Weyrwomen of the "Dragonrider" books; the determined young musician of *Crystal Singer* and *Killashandra;* the talented psychics of *To Ride Pegasus;* and Helva, the independent starship "brain" of *The Ship Who Sang.* Through these works, Bogle indicated, "McCaffrey has brought delineations of active women into prominence in science fiction." Such considerations have won her a wide readership across gender and generations, making McCaffrey one of the most popular and prolific sci fi writers of her generation.

McCaffrey was born on April Fools' Day, 1926, in Cambridge, Massachusetts. "I've tried hard to live up to being an April-firster," McCaffrey told Cart, but in fact there was not much room for levity in her early years. The daughter of a U.S. Army colonel father and a successful real estate agent mother, McCaffrey had a lot to live up to. Her father was "a grand figure—not very approachable, though," she told Cart. His children called him "The Colonel," and though he appeared more interested in his garden than offspring, he instilled in McCaffrey a desire to excel. He also gave her the gift of a love for riding, something the author has kept with her all her life. McCaffrey's mother, unlike other women of her generation, was not only a homemaker but a successful career woman, and she shared a secret with her daughter: as expected of her, she would probably grow up, go to college, marry, and have children. But then what would she do with the rest of her life? "My parents gave me ambition and motivation to go do it," McCaffrey commented to Cart.

"It" in this case was to become a writer, something she knew she wanted to be from an early age. "When I was a very young girl, I promised myself fervently (usually after I'd lost another battle with one of my brothers) that

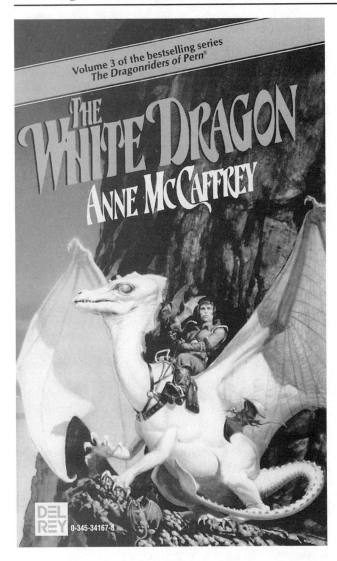

With the Pern series, McCaffrey created a colony named P.E.R.N., or Parallel Earth Resources Negligible, and her novels revolve around the conflict between the landowners and the dragonriders, who enjoy a unique telepathic relationship with the creatures they ride. (Cover illustration by Michael Whelan.)

I would become a famous author and I'd own my own horse," McCaffrey commented in her *Something about the Author Autobiography Series* (*SAAS*) essay. "Few women during my adolescence were encouraged to think of having independent careers, or careers at all: marriage was considered quite enough to occupy most women's lives. That's where I . . . lucked out: being subtly conditioned to have marriage, motherhood, AND self-fulfillment."

Books became, in addition to horses, early friends to McCaffrey. "I was not a popular child—being domineering, opinionated, disruptive, hyper," McCaffrey noted in her Edwards Award acceptance speech published in *JOYS* magazine. "Reading so much while other girls played with dolls reinforced the notion that I was 'different' . . . . I pretended to glory in being 'different.' But, Gawd, I was a brat!" Her reading was wide and all-

encompassing, but she especially loved utopian and dystopian literature. Tarzan's adventures were early favorites, as were the tales of Kipling. "When I was fourteen, I read *Islandia* by Austin Tappan Wright, and it blew my mind, absolutely blew my mind," McCaffrey noted in a *Booklist* interview with Pat Monaghan. She began writing short stories by the age of eight, yet she did not have many best friends in those years. McCaffrey's self-esteem was given a boost, if one was needed, by attending Radcliffe, the sister college to Harvard at the time. "We were enjoined when I graduated to be first in whatever field of endeavor we chose to enter," McCaffrey remarked to Cart. "No one thought science fiction would be a proper venue. So, typically, I did what no one expected me to do."

Out of college, McCaffrey took several copywriting jobs, and then, as prophesied by her mother, married. During one of her occasional bouts of bronchitis, she was stuck in her apartment and the only thing left to read was a pulp publication, *Amazing Stories.* Quickly she saw that she could produce such stories, and from there it was not a long jump to writing for science fiction magazines, a field not over-populated with women writers. Andre Norton was perhaps the one pre-eminent female writer in the genre when McCaffrey started out, and she was a great influence on McCaffrey. Since that time, women have become a strong presence in both science fiction and fantasy, but at the outset of McCaffrey's career, she was something of an anomaly, a pioneer.

McCaffrey's first novel, the 1967 work *Restoree,* announced some of her major themes: the use of a strong female protagonist and a blend of science and fiction in which the latter takes prominence. Sara is snatched from Central Park by a low flying space ship in what a reviewer for *Publishers Weekly* termed a "well-written and carefully plotted story," and is spirited away to "a fascinating world that is technologically sophisticated, but culturally quaint and archaic," as the same reviewer noted. There Sara comes out of a sort of amnesia and discovers she is encased in a new body; she has become a "restoree."

In May 1967, with her children expected home from school any moment, McCaffrey came up with the idea of a land called Pern populated by symbiotic, biogenetically engineered, fire-breathing, telepathic dragons. Remembering what Andre Norton once said about dragons—that they had bad press—McCaffrey decided to make them a major character in what was intended as a short story. She created a major cottage industry with that one afternoon's thoughts.

McCaffrey's short story ultimately turned into the 1968 novel *Dragonflight,* the work that introduces the Terran-populated planet of Pern and its knight-like Dragonmen and Weyrwomen who fly telepathic dragons in defense of their planet against the scourge of life-destroying Thread. Thread infests Pern every two hundred years when the planet passes close to the Red Star which attempts to colonize Pern. Now, however, the ranks of the defenders have been thinned and they must battle a new onslaught of Thread.

Reviews of this first book in the Pern cycle often pointed out the fantasy elements in the book. A reviewer for the *Junior Bookshelf,* for example, noted that Pern and its Weyr satellite "is Tolkien-land rather than futuristic space-world," and *Publishers Weekly,* in its review of *Dragonflight,* felt that "readers surfeited with gadget-ridden supermodernistic space epics will welcome" this "science-fantasy." In the other two books of the initial Pern trilogy, *Dragonquest* and *The White Dragon,* McCaffrey continued the saga of Pern, a former colony of Earth which has lost much of its scientific and historical knowledge. Hundreds of years after its founding, Pern is divided into a near-feudal society of landholders who often work against the less rigid

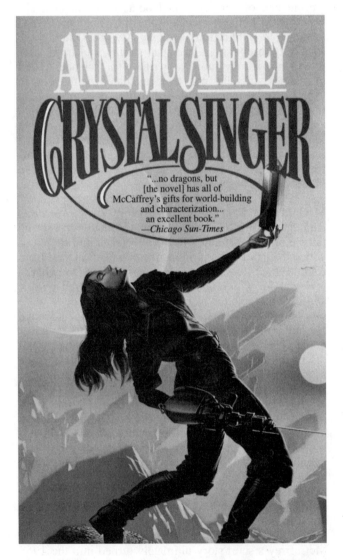

Using music as a metaphor for individual growth and personal freedom, McCaffrey relates the tale of Killashandra Ree, whose overwhelming desire to be a singer leads her, despite the risk, to join a band whose members use voice to mine precious crystal on the mysterious planet Ballybran. (Cover illustration by Michael Whelan.)

communities of dragonriders, called Weyrs. McCaffrey's emphasis on the conflicts between individuals, the fight against Thread, and the unique telepathic relationship between dragon and rider made these early works popular with readers of all ages, and led to *The White Dragon* becoming, in 1978, the first hardcover sci-fi novel to reach the *New York Times* bestseller list.

To entice young female readers to the pages of science fiction, McCaffrey's editor prompted her to write a trilogy of Pern novels directed at young adults and featuring a female protagonist. Thus was born the "Harper Hall" series, which follows a teenage girl who comes from a very different situation than the robust dragonriders. In *Dragonsong,* the first book, Menolly has been forbidden to play or sing her music solely because she is a girl and "girls aren't harpers." After her hand is accidentally injured and then deliberately mistreated to prevent proper healing that would allow her to play again, Menolly runs away. Outside of the Hold, she faces the dangers of Thread and the challenges of survival by herself—but she is not alone, as she befriends and cares for a set of young fire lizards, small cousins to Pern's mighty dragons. The book concludes as Menolly is rescued from Threadfall and her talent is discovered by the Harper Guild. Reviewing this first title in the YA trilogy, Joan Barbour concluded in *School Library Journal,* "The author explores the ideas of alienation, rebellion, love of beauty, the role of women and the role of the individual in society with some sensitivity in a generally well-structured plot with sound characterizations."

Menolly encounters a new set of problems in *Dragonsinger,* the second book in the trilogy. Although she has arrived at Harper Hall and has started training to be a harper, she still must face the prejudice of some teachers and the resentment of students jealous of her talent and her fire lizards. With her usual determination, and the aid of new friends such as the apprentice Piemur, Menolly overcomes these troubles to achieve happiness. Piemur takes center stage in the third "Harper Hall" book, *Dragondrums.* The trilogy contains "strong characters" as well as "a nice balance between problems that are present in any civilized society and a sense of humor that lightens both exposition and dialogue," Zena Sutherland wrote in the *Bulletin of the Center for Children's Books.*

Although Pern is inhabited by flying dragons and dominated by a near-feudal society—elements typical of fantasy worlds—McCaffrey's creation is based on solid scientific principles. The author frequently consults with scientific experts in order to make her ideas fully-fleshed and believable; 1988's *Dragonsdawn,* in fact, reveals the story of how the original colonists of Pern used genetic manipulation to develop Pern's dragons. The book features two of Pern's first dragonriders, young lovers Sean and Sorka, as they participate in the grand experiment and take up the battle against Threadfall. "Pernophiles, rejoice!" announced *Booklist*'s Sally Estes in a review of this addition to the Pern series. "At last McCaffrey unfolds her early vision of the colonizing of

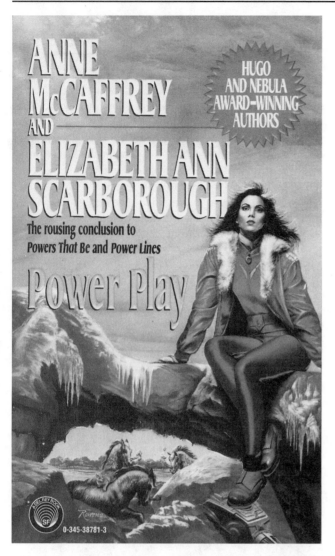

McCaffrey and coauthor Elizabeth Ann Scarborough penned a trilogy featuring strong female protagonist Yanaba Maddock, who in the final title of the series finds herself being held captive in an attack on her beloved, sentient planet Petaybee. (Cover illustration by Rowena.)

the beautiful, Earthlike, uninhabited planet of Pern ... [T]his will delight Pern fans while satisfying their curiosity about how it all began."

McCaffrey has continued her saga with books published throughout the 1990s, building the entire series to fifteen books in all. With her 1994 *The Dolphins of Pern,* McCaffrey emphasized dolphins over dragons—the third most intelligent species on Pern. *Kirkus Reviews* commented of this title, "McCaffrey's solid characterizations and lush descriptions counterbalance the feathery plot, making this latest trip to Pern a pleasant, sentimental respite among old and familiar friends." With the 1998 novel *The Masterharper of Pern,* McCaffrey brings front and center the harpist Robinton, who had walk-on roles in many of the earlier books. "McCaffrey is amazing," remarked *Booklist*'s Estes in a review of the book. "She is so steeped in the lore, history, and environment of her

brilliantly created planet Pern and its people that she doesn't have to write her tales about it in sequence." Estes went on to describe *The Masterharper of Pern* as "[t]autly plotted and featuring good characterization." McCaffrey's most popular series, originally planned as one short story, shows no signs of faltering or ending, after over three decades of life.

As has been noted, the emotional focus of the Dragonrider series—and other McCaffrey works such as the "Crystal Singer" novels—puts the technology in the background, unlike many science fiction novels. This emphasis on people and feelings has led some critics to christen the Pern books "science fantasy." McCaffrey, however, believes the use of emotion is appropriate to science fiction. As she related in her *SAAS* entry, one of her first (and most popular) stories, "The Ship Who Sang," was born of her grief over her father's death: "'Ship' taught me to use emotion as a writing tool. And I do, with neither apology nor shame, even though I am writing science fiction, a *genre* not often noted, in those days, for any emotions, only intellectual exercise and scientific curiosities."

This moving short story spawned another popular McCaffrey series, all of which—except for the first in the series—are co-written with various other authors. The books in this series follow the lives of men and women who have been physically crippled and use their brains to operate various spaceships. Often such tales end in a quirky resolution of love between brain and brawn. Reviewing the first in the series, *The Ship Who Sang,* a reviewer for *Publishers Weekly* noted that the book was "a sure-fire love story for man or machine." Helva has been separated from her malformed body since the time of her birth. Now her physical being is manifested in a spaceship which has intelligence and emotions. She manages to find love with human "brawn," such as Jennan, who help operate the ship, eventually coming so in tune with his musical talents that she becomes known throughout the galaxies as the Singing Ship. Reviewing another book in the series, *The Ship Who Searched,* co-written with Mercedes Lackey, *Kliatt*'s Linda Tashbook concluded, "A perfect combination of SF, adventure, and romance, this is sure to please a wide variety of readers."

Other popular McCaffrey series include the "Rowan" books that deal with an advanced society which uses telepathy and telekinetics to support its technology. The books also tell the story of a mother and daughter's search for love, a typical McCaffrey motif. In her "Crystal Singer" series, McCaffrey once again uses music as a metaphor for individual growth and personal freedom. Music is in fact a passion of McCaffrey's—she studied voice for nine years. In the lead title in the series, *Crystal Singer,* Killashandra Ree is rejected as vocal soloist, but then joins a band of Crystal Singers, who use voice to mine precious crystal on the planet Ballybran. Gerald Jonas, reviewing the novel in the *New York Times Book Review,* noted the "exotic and meticulously detailed" locale, and the "young, beautiful, intelligent, sexy, and courageous" heroine. But for Jonas, the real heart of the book was McCaffrey's "preoccupation with obsession. Obsession on a Melvillean scale is Miss McCaffrey's subject, and her method as well." Jonas concluded that "Killashandra's obsession [for crystal singing] comes alive, and readers who get past the first fifty pages will find themselves sharing it."

Independence and survival are the subjects of McCaffrey's "Freedom" series, launched in 1995 with *Freedom's Landing*. The Catteni conquerors of Earth take human slaves with them to a potentially habitable new planet they have just discovered. These humans become pawns in this new universe in a war between galactic powers after they are abandoned on the planet Botany. Here the former slaves initiate a Robinson Crusoe style adventure of survival. There is also a love story thrown in, between a human and one of the former Catteni masters, as well as the discovery of a mysterious civilization which is using the planet in bizarre ways. Reviewing this first title in the series, *Publishers Weekly* remarked, "McCaffrey has created another set of winning protagonists and a carefully detailed, exotic background on which to develop a new series." With the 1998 work *Freedom's Challenge,* the third and perhaps final installment in the story, the planet Botany is now under attack by the Eosi and the original human colonists must repulse this new onslaught, using technology they have stolen from their former masters. *Booklist*'s Estes called the book a "very satisfying tale," and also remarked that "McCaffrey continues to amaze with her ability to create disparate, well-realized worlds and to portray believable humans, convincing aliens of varied sorts, and credible interactions between them all."

A further group of related novels deals with the infant Acorna who has amazing powers of intellect, curing, and analysis. Written with Margaret Ball, *Acorna: The Unicorn Girl* introduces the precocious infant with a unicorn-like strange protuberance growing out of her forehead. Another collaborative effort are the books in the "Power" series written with Elizabeth Ann Scarborough, *Powers That Be, Power Lines,* and the 1995 *Power Play,* all of which feature the strong female protagonist, Yanaba Maddock, and her adventures on the icy planet Petaybee.

The multi-faceted McCaffrey has also tried her hand at historical fiction for young readers, with her Arthurian tale *Black Horses for the King.* Another stand-alone title is the 1999 *Nimisha's Ship,* in which the title character shows an early proclivity for things mechanical. Nimisha becomes heir to her father's starship factory and develops into a starship designer of no meager talents herself. When her father dies, she is beset with enemies who want her out of the way; on a test flight of one of her ships, Nimisha is sucked into a wormhole and lands on a distant planet. According to Estes in *Booklist,* "this is a page-turner all the way."

McCaffrey, who moved to Ireland in 1970 following her divorce, maintains a rigorous work schedule. In addition to her writing, she also owns a livery stable and equitation center at her home in County Wicklow, an outgrowth of her long-held love of horses and riding. McCaffrey denies that horses were her inspiration for dragons of Pern, however. "Horses are stupid," she told *Booklist*'s Monaghan. "Dragons are smart. But cats are fire lizards. So they're derived from cats." McCaffrey is pragmatic when it comes to describing her work. "Do not ascribe to me any deep philosophical messages," she wrote in her *SAAS* entry. "I don't have any, merely examples of what people can do when pushed to perform at their limits. Most of my books are love stories, too.... Generally I write for a purely commercial reason: I've signed a contract and received an advance. I find 'inspiration' when working with the elements of the story I'm already writing: I don't wait around for Inspiration to strike me.... I shall continue to write—I can't NOT write anyhow—until I am too frail to touch the keys of my wordprocessor."

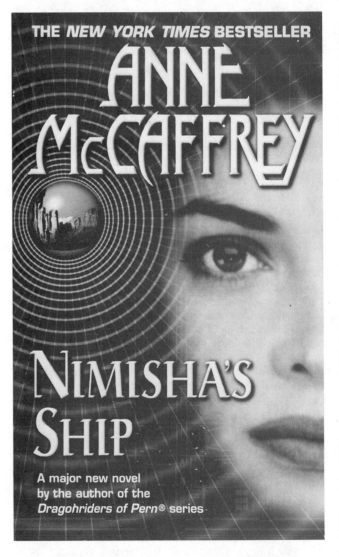

THE *NEW YORK TIMES* BESTSELLER

ANNE McCAFFREY

NIMISHA'S SHIP

A major new novel by the author of the *Dragohriders of Pern®* series

Talented starship builder Nimisha is stranded on a distant, menacing planet while ruthless relatives try to harm her child and steal the business Nimisha has inherited from her father in McCaffrey's suspenseful futuristic novel.

Works Cited

Barbour, Joan, review of *Dragonsong, School Library Journal,* April 1, 1976, p. 91.

Bogle, Edra C., "Anne McCaffrey," *Dictionary of Literary Biography,* Volume 8: *Twentieth-Century American Science Fiction Writers,* Gale, 1981.

Cart, Michael, "Miss M the Divine," *School Library Journal,* June, 1999, pp. 23-26.

Review of *The Dolphins of Pern, Kirkus Reviews,* August 14, 1994, p. 1031.

Review of *Dragonflight, Junior Bookshelf,* August, 1969, p. 259.

Review of *Dragonflight, Publishers Weekly,* July 8, 1968, p. 166.

Estes, Sally, review of *Dragonsdawn, Booklist,* September 1, 1988, p. 4.

Estes, Sally, review of *Freedom's Challenge, Booklist,* March 1, 1998, p. 1044.

Estes, Sally, review of *The Masterharper of Pern, Booklist,* October 15, 1997, p. 363.

Estes, Sally, review of *Nimisha's Ship, Booklist,* January 1, 1999.

Review of *Freedom's Landing, Publishers Weekly,* April 24, 1995, p. 64.

Jonas, Gerald, "Imaginary People," *New York Times Book Review,* August, 29, 1982, pp. 10-11.

McCaffrey, Anne, "The 1999 Margaret A. Edwards Award Acceptance Speech," *JOYS,* Summer, 1999, pp. 19-21.

McCaffrey, Anne, entry in *Something about the Author Autobiography Series,* Volume 11, Gale, 1991, pp. 241-56.

Monaghan, Pat, "The Booklist Interview: Anne McCaffrey," *Booklist,* March 15, 1994, pp. 1300-1.

Review of *Restoree, Publishers Weekly,* August 21, 1967, p. 76.

Reynolds, Gary K., *Science Fiction and Fantasy Book Review,* July, 1979.

Review of *The Ship Who Sang, Publishers Weekly,* September 15, 1969, p. 61.

Sloan, James, and Eugene Sloan, *Chicago Tribune Book World,* July 13, 1986.

Sutherland, Zena, review of *Dragondrums, Bulletin of the Center for Children's Books,* July-August, 1979, p. 195.

Tashbook, Linda, review of *The Ship Who Searched, Kliatt,* November, 1992, p. 16.

For More Information See

BOOKS

Authors in the News, Gale, 1976.

Bestsellers 89, Issue 2, Gale, 1989.

Children's Books and Their Creators, edited by Anita Silvey, Houghton Mifflin, 1995.

Children's Literature Review, Volume 49, Gale, 1997.

Contemporary Literary Criticism, Volume 17, Gale, 1981.

St. James Guide to Young Adult Writers, St. James Press, 1999.

Walker, Paul, *Speaking of Science Fiction: The Paul Walker Interviews,* Luna, 1978.

PERIODICALS

Booklist, May 15, 1995, p. 1611; December 15, 1996, p. 692; March 15, 1999, p. 1260.

Library Journal, June 15, 1995, p. 98; May 15, 1997, pp. 106, 165; June 15, 1997, p. 101; May 15, 1998, p. 119; February 15, 1999, p. 187.

New York Times Book Review, August 29, 1982; January 8, 1984; January 8, 1989; June 22, 1997, pp. 22, 24.

Publishers Weekly, January 20, 1997, p. 398; May 26, 1997, p. 71; November 24, 1997, p. 363; April 26, 1999, p. 60.

School Library Journal, July, 1997, p. 116; April, 1998, p. 161; August, 1998, p. 196.

Wilson Library Bulletin, February, 1989; November 1993, pp. 90-91; May, 1995.

* * *

McGINLEY, Jerry 1948-

Personal

Born March 3, 1948, in Boscobel, WI; son of John C. and Marguerite (maiden name, McCormick) McGinley; married Gail Hefty, August 1, 1970; children: Shannon, Megan. *Education:* University of Wisconsin-Stevens Point, B.S., M.S. in English.

Addresses

Home—500 Linde St., DeForest, WI 53532. *E-mail*—jmcginley@mail.deforest.k12.wi.us.

Career

Clintonville High School, Clintonville, WI, English teacher, 1972-78; DeForest High School, DeForest, WI, English teacher and department chair, 1978-99; University of Wisconsin, Madison, Summer Institute teacher, 1993-2000.

Awards, Honors

Kohl Outstanding Educator Fellowship; Newsweek/Sallie Mae Inspiring Teacher; Jarvis Bush Teaching Award from the Wisconsin Council of Teachers of English.

Writings

Waupaca County: 7 A.M. (poetry), Apollo, 1986.

Joaquin Strikes Back (novel), Tudor (Greensboro, NC), 1998.

A Goal for Joaquin (audio drama), The Fiction Works (Lake Tahoe, NV), 1998.

Miles to Go Before I Sleep (e-book novel), The Fiction Works, 1998.

Work in Progress

Recently completed a novel, *Cyclops: Seeing without Seeing.*

Jerry McGinley

Sidelights

"As a writer, I am a very sporadic worker," Jerry McGinley told *SATA*. "I will write hundreds of pages during a two- or three-month period, revise and rewrite for three or four weeks, and then when I'm almost satisfied, I'll set the project aside for several months and not write or revise a single page. I envy those disciplined writers who can force themselves to write regularly every day. I am either too lazy to write that way or am just unwilling to turn my back on distractions.

"I hate the process of getting work published. It's too slow. After publishing nearly a hundred poems in magazines and anthologies, I just quit mailing them out. I haven't published a poem in about five years. I'm happy that I found a couple of publishers who like my novels. So far I've had a chance to publish a hardcover novel, an audio drama (complete with actors, music, and sound effects), and an e-book novel that can be either purchased on disk or downloaded directly from the publisher. Now I'd like to see my work in paperback and, of course, on the movie screen.

"My advice to young writers is to start today! Don't wait until you are forty years old like I did. Get a project going right now."

Jerry McGinley is an award-winning high school teacher and a writer. His young adult novel, *Joaquin Strikes Back*, tells the story of a sixteen-year-old boy named Joaquin Lopez. The title character moves with his family from California to Wisconsin. Although Joaquin intends

to be a star soccer player at his new school, just as he was at his old one, his new coach taunts him with racial slurs and refuses to allow him to play. Joaquin is determined to stick it out on the team, but eventually quits in frustration. Then his parents buy a farm in a rural district, and at his new school several girls are seeking permission to start a co-ed soccer team. Joaquin joins, with the expectation of taking a starring role in the new team, but finds his new coach insistent that he be a team player. Eventually, Joaquin's new team meets up with his old team in the regional finals and wins through the efforts of the whole team.

"There is some good soccer action, especially in the culminating games of the season, and a bit of romance as well," observed Sylvia V. Meisner in *School Library Journal*. *Booklist* reviewer Roger Leslie commended the "variety of likable characters and a few subplots that weave together nicely by the final competition." Both reviewers remarked favorably on McGinley's messages about what it feels like to be the object of racial prejudice and how to be a team player in sports and in life. These themes are portrayed in the action and discussed in the narrative of *Joaquin Strikes Back*, making them easily accessible to young adult readers.

The story of *Joaquin Strikes Back* was also published as a drama on audiotape under the title *A Goal for Joaquin*. Betty D. Ammon reviewed the audio version of McGinley's story for *Kliatt* and concluded: "This lively story with a positive message and agreeable characters will attract listeners in the middle- and junior-high-school range."

Works Cited

Ammon, Betty D., review of *A Goal for Joaquin, Kliatt*, November, 1998, p. 46.

Leslie, Roger, review of *Joaquin Strikes Back, Booklist*, March 15, 1998, p. 1236.

Meisner, Sylvia V., review of *Joaquin Strikes Back, School Library Journal*, March, 1999, pp. 211-212.

*   *   *

McKINNEY, Barbara Shaw 1951-

Personal

Born July 12, 1951, in Norwalk, CT; daughter of Robert B. (a utilities manager) and Lillian (a homemaker; maiden name, Swenson) Shaw; children: Robin Leigh McKinney, Reed Burton McKinney. *Education:* Central Connecticut State University, B.S. in elementary education, plus graduate work in elementary education. *Hobbies and other interests:* Pet black cocker spaniel, Barnaby; playing classical piano, tennis, reading, directing school drama club musicals.

Addresses

Home—51 Finley St., Manchester, CT 06040.

Barbara Shaw McKinney

Career

Industrial resource teacher, building curriculum coordinator, and staff developer in East Hartford, CT, 1973-99. Educational consultant for various school districts; member of the Manchester Arts Council; BEST Program, seminar leader, Connecticut State Dept. of Education. Writer. *Member:* Society of Children's Book Writers and Illustrators, Wit and Wisdom Poetry Club, Connecticut Poetry Society.

Awards, Honors

Silver finalist in Science/Nature category for Publishers Marketing Association Ben Franklin Award, 1999, for *A Drop around the World.*

Writings

A Drop around the World, illustrated by Michael S. Maydak, Dawn (Nevada City, CA), 1998.
Pass the Energy, Please!, illustrated by Chad Wallace, Dawn, 2000.

Work in Progress

The Dawning, a fictional rhyming text incorporating nature awareness and character education; *Rock Cycles,* designed for elementary science curriculum.

Sidelights

Barbara Shaw McKinney told *SATA:* "My personal literary journey has taken me on a whirlwind course of reading, researching, writing, and speaking. Along the way I have met editors, authors, illustrators, librarians, scientists, radio and TV personalities, bookstore owners, museum curators, educators, parents, and most importantly ... children! My three careers as teacher, educational consultant, and children's author have enhanced each other. As a teacher, I work to help children become active, independent learners and lifelong readers and writers. As a consultant, I am called upon to share exciting and effective learning strategies with elementary teachers. As a writer, I craft the vehicles that children and teachers can use to implement the reading comprehension processes that I promote as a consultant. In an effort to dovetail my professional goals, my children's books have taken on a unique style. Their nonfiction rhyming texts take readers on a scientifically literate journey that integrates language arts across the curriculum. I hope that children will not only be inspired by the topics, but be entertained by the words that deliver the 'big ideas' about nature. My editor, Glenn Hovemann, gave me a most helpful hint. He said, 'Don't be afraid to touch the hem of the divine.' I find that poetry allows me to do just that—joining the head and heart of the reader. Somehow, its beauty and musical quality reaches the heart, allowing children to *feel* the importance of the message. I am challenged to give children an understanding of Mother Nature's 'grand plans' by addressing natural cycles in a thoughtful, heartfelt way. I believe in the power of words, and I'm always trying to put them together in just the right way to evoke the ultimate kid response ... 'Awesome!' Such a response just might prompt action—to read more—to learn more—to do more to protect our 'Awesome' Earth!"

*   *   *

MICHAELS, Joanne Louis
See TEITELBAUM, Michael

*   *   *

MICHAELS, Neal
See TEITELBAUM, Michael

*   *   *

MILLER, William R. 1959-

Personal

Born February 8, 1959, in Anniston, AL; son of William R. Sr. (an insurance executive) and Joyce Summerlin (Bartley) Miller; married Jill Anderson, 1984 (divorced, 1998); children: Julian Wilson. *Education:* Eckerd College, B.A., 1982; Hollins College, M.A., 1983; Binghamton University, Ph.D., 1989. *Politics:* Independent. *Religion:* Episcopalian.

Addresses

Home—182-G Dew Drop Rd., York, PA 17402. *Office*—English Department, York College, York, PA 17405.

Career

Jacksonville State University, Jacksonville, AL, instructor in English, 1984-87; York College, York, PA, associate professor of literature. Visiting associate professor in master's program in writing for children at Hollins College.

Awards, Honors

Patterson Prize for Poetry, 1997; "Reading Rainbow" (children's television program) selection, Public Broadcasting System, for *Zora Hurston and the Chinaberry Tree.*

Writings

FOR CHILDREN

Zora Hurston and the Chinaberry Tree, illustrated by Cornelius Van Wright and Ying-Hwa Hu, Lee & Low, 1994.

William R. Miller

Frederick Douglass: The Last Day of Slavery, illustrated by Cedric Lucas, Lee & Low, 1995.
The Knee-high Man, illustrated by Roberta Glidden, Gibbs Smith, 1996.
The Conjure Woman, illustrated by Terea D. Shaffer, Atheneum, 1996.
A House by the River, illustrated by Cornelius Van Wright and Ying-Hwa Hu, Lee & Low, 1997.
Richard Wright and the Library Card, illustrated by Gregory Christie, Lee & Low, 1997.
The Bus Ride, illustrated by John Ward, Lee & Low, 1998.
Jenny and the Peddler, illustrated by Rod Brown, Dial, 1998.
Night Golf, illustrated by Cedric Lucas, Lee & Low, 1999.

POETRY

Old Faith, Mellen Press, 1992.
Breathed on Glass, Druid Press, 1993.

Sidelights

William R. Miller has written a number of books for children that feature stories of African Americans. In addition, he has also authored two volumes of poetry. His first published children's story, *Zora Hurston and the Chinaberry Tree,* depicts a period in the life of celebrated author and folklorist Zora Neale Hurston, a respected African-American author. *Zora Hurston and the Chinaberry Tree* offers an inspirational story intended to show children they can be whatever they want to be no matter their circumstances in life. As a child, Zora had an overbearing father, but also a mother from whom she gained great strength. Tragically, Zora suffered the loss of her mother when the author was only nine years old. Miller portrays the tension between Zora and her father, as well as the independent, resilient nature Zora developed under her mother's influence. The tale ends following the death of Zora's mother. Readers see the young girl climbing a chinaberry tree, one Zora's mother taught her to climb, and she vows to "never stop climbing" in life. "Readers will embrace this book . . . for its lyrical affirmation of life's unlimited potential," concluded Ellen Fader in a review for *Horn Book.*

Miller followed *Zora Hurston and the Chinaberry Tree* with 1995's *Frederick Douglass: The Last Day of Slavery.* In another biographical portrait of a famous African American, Miller describes the early life of abolitionist Frederick Douglass and his rebellion against a slave holder. *School Library Journal* contributor Carol Jones Collins proclaimed, "Miller's narrative is movingly rendered," while *Horn Book* writer Margaret A. Bush deemed the work a "thought-provoking biographical tale."

In 1996, Miller published *The Knee-high Man.* The story features a very small African-American man who is so short that he must look up to a rabbit. Tormented by his small stature, the man seeks various ways—all unsuccessful—to grow bigger until an owl shows him the importance of accepting who he really is. A *Publishers Weekly* writer judged the book as a "well-paced, amiable retelling of [a] folktale."

When author and folklorist Zora Neale Hurston was nine years old, she suffered the death of her mother, a tragedy depicted in Miller's picture book along with the resiliency with which the young Zora faces her sorrow and vows to strive for the best. (From Zora Hurston and the Chinaberry Tree, *illustrated by Cornelius Van Wright and Ying-Hwa Hu.)*

Miller also produced *The Conjure Woman* in 1996. In this tale, a young boy named Toby, stricken with fever, is taken to a conjure woman, Madame Zina, in the hopes that she can heal his illness. During his treatment, Toby and Madame Zina travel to their homeland of Africa, where his ancestors—the Nakani people of Ghana—cure the boy of his illness. After he is healed, Toby returns to his relieved parents. Hazel Rochman, a contributor to *Booklist,* wrote, "this picture book makes dramatic use of magic realism." *School Library Journal* reviewer Martha Rosen believed that "young readers and listeners will make the leap between illusion and reality, and the happy ending will please and satisfy them."

Another children's story by Miller, 1997's *A House by the River,* portrays a young girl who is disappointed by her home that is far from town and is threatened by a river. It is not until a storm rages that the young girl, with the help of her mother, gains an appreciation for the protection that her home provides. Carolyn Phelan observed in a *Booklist* review, "words and pictures alike depict this ... household with warmth and dignity."

Miller's *Richard Wright and the Library Card* also appeared in 1997. The book recounts the true tale of another African-American writer, Richard Wright, who wanted access to the whites-only library in Memphis

before segregation laws were repealed. The story, which is based on Wright's account in his autobiography *Black Boy,* relates how Wright had to find a Caucasian to write him a note stating Wright was checking books out for a white person and not for himself. Even with the note, Wright experienced resistance from the librarian. However, he was able to check out books, and Miller's story goes on to illustrate the positive influence books can have on readers. Hazel Rochman wrote in *Booklist,* "words and pictures express ... the power [Wright] found in books," while a *Kirkus Reviews* critic praised it as "a challenging endeavor, and an accomplished one."

In 1998 Miller introduced *The Bus Ride* to his young readers. This story is inspired by the real life experience of civil rights activist Rosa Parks, whose landmark decision to not give up her seat on the bus to a white man changed the course of history. In the tale, a young African-American girl, Sara, wants to know what it is like to sit at the front of the bus during a time when black people can only ride in the back. One day she decides to defy the law and sits in the front seat. While her action gets her removed from the bus by a police officer, it also eventually results in the reversal of the law. *Booklist* writer Kathleen Squires determined *The Bus Ride* to be "a fine example of a child taking a stand and making a difference."

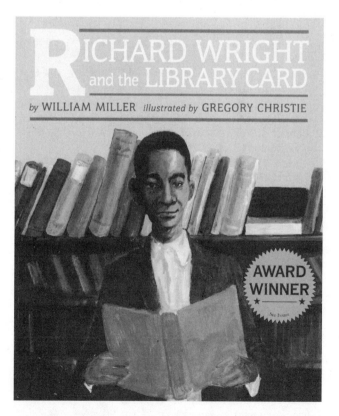

Miller recounts the true tale of African-American writer Richard Wright, who gained access to the whites-only library in segregated Memphis of the 1920s and found inspiration through reading. (Cover illustration by Gregory Christie.)

Night Golf, a 1999 title, features a young African-American boy, James, who enjoys the game of golf and wishes he could play. However, the golf course near him is only open to white golfers. In order to gain access to the golf course, James becomes a caddy, and he is soon able to play golf on the course, but only after it is closed at night. The story also provides James with the opportunity to show the white men his talent as a golfer when he is faced with a challenge from one of them. A reviewer for *Publishers Weekly* called the story a "hefty but well-paced text."

For his young readers, Miller has developed a group of strong, independent, and intelligent characters who have dealt with and survived adversity. Many critics resoundingly applaud his accomplishments, especially his ability to write convincing and inspirational stories.

Works Cited

Bush, Margaret A., review of *Frederick Douglass: The Last Day of Slavery, Horn Book,* September-October, 1995, p. 622.

Collins, Carol Jones, review of *Frederick Douglass: The Last Day of Slavery, School Library Journal,* June, 1995, p. 103.

Fader, Ellen, review of *Zora Hurston and the Chinaberry Tree, Horn Book,* January-February, 1995, p. 69.

Review of *The Knee-high Man, Publishers Weekly,* January 22, 1996, p. 72.

Miller, William R., *Zora Hurston and the Chinaberry Tree,* Lee & Low, 1994.

Review of *Night Golf, Publishers Weekly,* May 24, 1999, p. 79.

Phelan, Carolyn, review of *A House by the River, Booklist,* May 15, 1997, p. 93.

Review of *Richard Wright and the Library Card, Kirkus Reviews,* November 15, 1997.

Rochman, Hazel, review of *The Conjure Woman, Booklist,* February 15, 1996, p. 92.

Rochman, Hazel, review of *Richard Wright and the Library Card, Booklist,* December 1, 1997, p. 642.

Rosen, Martha, review of *The Conjure Woman, School Library Journal,* March, 1996, p. 179.

Squires, Kathleen, review of *The Bus Ride, Booklist,* August, 1998, p. 2016.

For More Information See

PERIODICALS

Booklist, October 15, 1994; March 15, 1995.

Bulletin of the Center for Children's Books, July-August, 1995, p. 392.

Horn Book, July-August, 1997.

Kirkus Reviews, January 1, 1996; May 15, 1997; July 15, 1998, p. 1039.

Library Journal, November 1, 1991.

Library Quarterly, January, 1999, p. 90.

Nation, September 11, 1982.

National Review, September 17, 1982.

New York Times Book Review, February 12, 1995.

Publishers Weekly, August 29, 1994; March 20, 1995; April 28, 1997; November 17, 1997; July 6, 1998.

School Library Journal, December, 1994, pp. 100-101; July, 1997, p. 71; February, 1998; October, 1998, p. 108.*

*　　*　　*

MOON, Lily
See WARNES, Tim(othy)

*　　*　　*

MORTIMER, Anne 1958-

Personal

Born March 28, 1958, in England; married August 30, 1980, husband's name Buscombe. *Education:* South Wales College of Art, Natural History diploma in illustration. *Religion:* Church of England.

Addresses

Home and office—Parklands, Dulverton, Somerset, England TA22 0EJ. *Member:* Royal Society of Miniature Painters, Society of Botanical Artists.

Career

Illustrator for greeting cards and stationary for clients Images & Editions, W. H. Smith, and Marks & Spencer (all in England); illustrations have been licensed to appear on woven tapestry pillows, tableware, coffee mugs, plates, tins, prints, puzzles, needlecraft kits, and fabrics. Children's book illustrator.

Awards, Honors

Honourable Mention, Miniature Society, 1986.

Writings

ILLUSTRATOR

Matthew Sturgis, *Tosca's Christmas,* Dial, 1989.

Matthew Sturgis, *Tosca's Surprise,* Dial, 1991.

Margaret Wise Brown, *A Pussycat's Christmas,* HarperCollins, 1994.

Eleanor Farjeon, *Cats Sleep Anywhere,* HarperCollins, 1996.

Carol Greene, *Cat and Bear,* Hyperion, 1998.

Nancy Raines Day, *A Kitten's Year,* HarperCollins, 2000.

Kittycat Lullabye, Hyperion, 2000.

Owl and Pussycat, HarperCollins, in press.

Work in Progress

Zodiac Cats, due from HarperCollins in 2001; *The Snow Cat,* due from Hyperion in 2002.

Sidelights

Anne Mortimer has made a career of illustrating picture books about cats, in which, reviewers note, her realistic

Anne Mortimer

miniature paintings evoke the essence of a cat's rippling, soft fur. Her first book, *Tosca's Christmas,* written by Matthew Sturgis, tells the story of the holiday from the disgruntled, woebegone cat's perspective, as she is chased out of the kitchen, shooed away from the room where presents are being wrapped, and finally deposited out of doors after accidentally pulling down the Christmas tree. "Both Sturgis and Mortimer have succeeded in capturing the warmth of the holidays from a delightfully different viewpoint," remarked Diane Roback in *Publishers Weekly.* A sequel, *Tosca's Surprise,* tells the story of Tosca's search for a quiet place to have her kittens. In a statement that other reviewers would echo, *School Library Journal* contributor Caroline Ward averred that Mortimer's paintings of Tosca and her mate "are so precise and finely textured that the fur appears real enough to stroke."

Among Mortimer's other illustration projects is Eleanor Farjeon's poem *Cats Sleep Anywhere,* in which the feline propensity to climb into any small place and curl up for a nap is celebrated. *Booklist* reviewer Laura Tillotson remarked that Mortimer's painted cats "look so cozily realistic ... that they almost purr." Mortimer's skill as a miniaturist was again remarked upon, as her paintings were praised for their detailed precision of small, homey scenes. In that sense, they seemed an apt complement to Farjeon's poem. "The easy rhythm of the spare text and the attractive paintings will appeal to cat lovers of all ages," predicted Margaret Bush in *School Library Journal.*

Works Cited

Bush, Margaret, review of *Cats Sleep Anywhere, School Library Journal,* December, 1996, p. 112.

Roback, Diane, review of *Tosca's Christmas, Publishers Weekly,* October 13, 1989, p. 53.

Tillotson, Laura, review of *Cats Sleep Anywhere, Booklist,* September 1, 1996, p. 133.

Ward, Caroline, review of *Tosca's Surprise, School Library Journal,* August, 1991, p. 156.

For More Information See

PERIODICALS

Publishers Weekly, September 16, 1996, p. 81.

N

Autobiography Feature

Lensey Namioka

1929-

OUTSIDER

My fiction for young people falls into two distinct types: One set of stories consists of mystery-adventure stories set in feudal Japan or Song dynasty China. The other set consists of contemporary stories about Chinese immigrants adjusting to a new life in America. Both types of stories share one theme in common, however. The protagonists are usually outsiders.

In the series of adventure stories set in feudal Japan, the main characters are two *ronin,* or unemployed samurai. They wander around the country looking for work, and in almost every case they arrive as newcomers at some locality. The Song dynasty China adventure story is about a band of outlaws, and of course nobody can be more of an outsider than an outlaw.

The stories about immigrants describe outsiders trying to fit into a new country and a new society. In one book, *Yang the Youngest and His Terrible Ear,* the hero is an outsider even in his own family. Everybody in his family is a talented musician, except for Yang the Youngest, who can't play the violin to save his life.

My preoccupation with outsiders may have originated from my parents' families. Both my father and mother came from the families of officials in China (called mandarins by Westerners). It was the policy of the government to move their officials around constantly. For if they were too closely connected with any one region, they might accept favors from some local faction and lose their impartiality.

My father said his memories of his childhood were filled with packing up and traveling to a new home. He became really efficient at packing his little bag of toys and favorite books. All his life he remained an expert at packing.

On one occasion Father's family started to cross a river by ferry. After the boat pushed off, they heard a pitiful yowling from the bank. It was the family cat, who had been left behind because cats were supposed to be more attached to a place than to people. But this cat was exceptionally loyal, and it started to swim after the boat! They managed to rescue the cat and took it with them. My father's love for cats dated from that incident. Wherever our family lived, we always kept a cat. Years later, I wrote a book titled *The Loyal Cat,* and cats appear in several other of my books (one of them a vampire cat, however).

When my father was old enough to go to college, he went to America and attended Cornell University, which is situated in a small, upstate New York city. There was no Chinese community there, and no Chinese groceries for sale. For four whole years he ate solid meat-and-potatoes American food. He was truly an outsider, although he made good friends from those days and never lost touch with them.

My mother's family also traveled. They went all over China by riverboat, sedan chair, and train. They also went abroad by ocean liner. My maternal grandfather went to Europe, spending three years in London at the Chinese legation. He visited the Paris Exposition in 1889 and saw the newly erected Eiffel Tower.

My mother studied medicine in Japan for seven years. Again, she was an outsider in a foreign country. At least she could eat rice, not meat and potatoes. In China it's not safe to eat anything raw, even salads, but in Japan Mother finally got used to raw fish.

I still remember how she tried to serve Japanese food to us at home. I hated it at first, but finally learned to like it.

Namioka's family, the Chaos, at home in Beijing. (From left) Namioka on rocking horse, her mother, Buwei, holding younger sister, Bella, older sister, Xinna, oldest sister, Rulan, and father, Yuen Ren.

This was fortunate because I later married a Japanese and spent time living in Japan. Now I love raw fish.

My parents continued their roving lives after they got married. They traveled to America in the 1920s, and my two older sisters were born in Boston. My parents even took their children to Europe with them. They soon found that it was hard work carrying two infants around, and they stashed the two girls with a French family. That was why my sisters spoke French as their first language. They were outsiders in France, and when they returned to China they were still outsiders because none of our family friends could speak French.

I was born in Beijing after my parents returned to China. But they didn't stay long in Beijing. They went back to America in 1933 and spent a year in Washington, D.C. My sisters were speaking Chinese by then, and they found themselves outsiders again in America. Returning to China, my parents moved to Nanjing, which was the national capital at that time.

In our family we grew up speaking the northern dialect (called Mandarin by Americans). In Nanjing, which means "Southern Capital," people spoke a different dialect, although not so different that we couldn't understand. But when Japan started invading China in 1937, we had to move out of Nanjing and go inland. My father, who worked for a research institute, followed the institute to the interior away from the invaders.

The farther we moved away from the coastal cities, the harder it was for us to understand the people we met. In Changsha I went to a local school, where I couldn't understand the teacher at all. Soon enemy planes began bombing the city, and there were scary times when we had to scatter and look for air-raid shelters. Strangely enough, my more vivid memories were of struggling to understand my teacher and of trying to eat the school lunch, which was very, very HOT. (Changsha was the capital of Hunan, a province notorious for its spicy hot food.)

My father was a linguist, and his work involved traveling up and down China studying various dialects.

Because of the war, it became impossible for him to travel around. When he was offered a teaching job at an American university, he decided to go to America with his family. His idea was to stay there until the war ended. He didn't expect at first that our family would settle in this country and become immigrants.

Naturally we were outsiders when we arrived in America. My sisters and I went to school speaking hardly any English at all. But like baby ducks thrown into the water, we had to keep our heads above water by learning English as fast as we could. In fact my father was more worried about our forgetting Chinese. He made a rule that we should speak only Chinese at home and not mix English words into our conversation. He fined us a penny for every English word that slipped in. After a while he gave up the rule because my mother refused to pay the fine. Besides, there were words that just had no Chinese translation. How do you say "cheeseburger" in Chinese, for instance?

Eventually we all learned English pretty well, and we also made friends in school. But I never felt that I really belonged. At first it made me unhappy always to be an outsider. Gradually I began to accept the fact. We enjoyed our social lives, and what did it matter if we looked or sounded differently from our friends and neighbors? Several of my books, in particular *Who's Hu?* and *Yang the Third and Her Impossible Family,* discuss this gradual acceptance of one's differences and becoming resigned to being an outsider.

In some ways my husband, Isaac, is just as much of an outsider as I am. We met when we were graduate students at the University of California in Berkeley. I noticed that he looked a bit different from most Asian boys, and later he told me about his family.

He came from Japan, and his grandparents grew up at a time of great changes in the country. After centuries of being closed off, Japan finally opened its doors to the outside world. Some Japanese were excited at the prospect of going abroad and investigating foreign countries. Among them was Isaac's maternal grandfather, who managed to get on a ship to America. After many adventures, he wound up in Brooklyn, New York. There, he met a girl whose family had just immigrated from France. They fell in love and got married. Several children were born to them in Brooklyn, one of them being Isaac's mother, my future mother-in-law. Eventually the family moved back to Japan.

Japan was—and still is—a country of great homogeneity, where the people came from pretty much the same racial stock. Being half French, Isaac's mother and her siblings all looked different from other children. They were immediately marked as outsiders.

Isaac's mother grew up to marry another outsider: Saburo Namioka, who was a Christian. In Japan, Christians formed a small minority of less than one percent. In the 1930s and 1940s they were systematically persecuted by the militaristic government then governing the country. My future father-in-law was a suspect in the eyes of the authorities for another reason: He was opposed to Japan's war of aggression, and he spoke out about it. As a result he was arrested and sent to prison, and his health never completely recovered from the harsh conditions there. The rest of the family became outsiders, and for them the last years of the war were grim.

After the war, Isaac received a fellowship to study at a Christian college in America. He did graduate work at the University of Kansas, and later went to Berkeley, where we two outsiders found each other.

We moved around quite a bit after we got married. Even after we moved to Seattle in 1963 and bought a house, we still traveled whenever we could. Isaac teaches at the University of Washington, and, during his sabbaticals, we manage to live abroad. Like my parents, we feel that traveling is not only enjoyable, but the normal way to live.

On Isaac's first sabbatical, we spent a year in Kyoto, Japan. Our daughters went to the local public school, and they found out what it was like to be outsiders. They started school without speaking any Japanese, and, like me, they had to swim hard to keep their heads above water. Aki, our elder daughter, initially suffered bullying from some of the boys in her class. Bullying is common in Japanese schools where there is little tolerance for diversity, and anyone who seems different gets picked on. The teacher finally took a hand and told the class they should be more hospitable toward their guest from America. Things improved, and our daughters began making friends in school.

During our stay I found that in Japan you got better treatment as an outright foreigner than as a Japanese who was somehow different. Although my face could pass for that of a Japanese, I found it paid to let people know right away that I was a Chinese who was only visiting their country.

Once I was traveling alone on my way back to America from China, and I had to change planes in Tokyo. Because of bad weather, the flight was canceled, and I had to spend the night in Tokyo. I hadn't planned for this extra stay in one of the world's most expensive cities. It was long past midnight, and I stood forlornly in front of the air terminal, holding an untidy shopping bag printed with the characters for "China." Immediately a policeman and a taxi driver came over. When they heard my story, they kindly called up an inexpensive hotel nearby and arranged for me to stay. That was one time when it paid to be an outsider.

In Seattle there is a large Asian community, and we have friends among both the Chinese Americans and the Japanese Americans. We enjoy the firecrackers during Chinese New Year celebrations, and we go to the local Cherry Blossom Festival. Yet, because we are a mixed couple, we don't belong completely to either the Chinese or the Japanese ethnic groups. In a sense, we are still outsiders. And, like Mary Yang in *Yang the Third and Her Impossible Family,* we have learned to be content.

Mathematics

When I started going to school in America, one of the things I learned was that girls weren't supposed to do well in mathematics. In China, as well as in Japan and many other Asian countries, women are expected to be good at figures and regularly keep the household accounts and manage the budget. A husband hands over his wages to his wife. She pays the bills and gives him an allowance for going out with the boys.

My mother made the financial decisions in our family. Once when my parents were living in Berkeley, California, Mother attended a land auction with a friend. She went more out of curiosity than from any real desire to buy land.

A plot of land near our house was up for sale, and just for fun Mother made a bid on it. She was sure somebody would top her bid.

She was stunned when nobody else said a word, and she found herself the owner of a large plot of land.

As she and her friend started to leave, a man rushed up to them. He was a realtor who was supposed to make a bid, but had arrived too late for the auction. Right on the spot, he offered Mother whatever she had paid, plus an extra $1,000.

"No, thank you," Mother replied. By then she was rather tickled by her purchase.

The realtor raised his offer to $2,000, but Mother still turned him down. He managed to get our address and phone number and called up our house. When Father answered the phone, the realtor shouted, "Your wife just threw away $2,000!" "I'm sure she had her reasons," Father answered calmly, confident that Mother knew what she was doing.

As it turned out, the land increased in value, and my parents had a comfortable nest egg in their old age.

I didn't know at first that in America girls weren't supposed to be good in math. When I got good grades in math, I found out the other kids thought I was weird. My first book with a contemporary setting was *Who's Hu?* which dealt with the subject of an immigrant Chinese girl who was good at math and discovered that this made her a freak in the eyes of her classmates. Later, I wrote an article for an anthology about my own experiences with mathematics, titled "Math and After Math."

There were reasons why math was my best subject. My English was still pretty shaky at first, but in math we used the same Arabic numbers as my Chinese schools did. Moreover, Chinese schools were (and still are) way ahead of American schools in math. But even in China, I had been ahead of other students in arithmetic because I sang the multiplication table.

"You can remember a tune more easily than a string of numbers," Father would tell us. "To remember the multiplication table, it's better to sing it." To teach musical notation in Chinese schools, numbers were given to the notes of the diatonic scale: do was one, re was two, mi was three, and so on. Therefore to remember that two times seven was fourteen, all I had to do was hum the tune re-ti-do-fa. It wasn't a very pretty tune, but it stuck in my mind a lot better than a bunch of numbers. Even today, I multiply in Chinese. I hum when I try to figure out how much two candy bars cost, for instance.

I maintained my reputation as a freak in high school when we started algebra. The reason was that I loved story problems, something most of the other kids loathed. To this day, I don't understand why students hate story problems. When I taught calculus in college, it was the same. Kids moaned and groaned if they were assigned story problems.

As for me, multiplying (even with music) or dividing long columns of figures was terminally boring. Differentiating or integrating formulas in a calculus class was equally boring. In story problems, however, I found color, excitement, even romance.

I remember problems involving an army column marching toward the enemy. A messenger was sent to the rear with a message warning of an imminent ambush. Given the length of the column, the speed of the messenger's horse, etc., would the warning arrive on time? Some of the ambushers might even be outlaws wearing baggy pants, or a princess with a bamboo sword.

Although I received good grades in math throughout my school and college years, I came to the conclusion finally that I was not cut out to be a mathematician. It took more than simply doing all the homework assignments.

My parents reproached me when I told them I was giving up mathematics and going into writing. "You spent so many years studying math!" they said. "How can you give up such a beautiful subject?"

"Enjoying beauty is not the same thing as being able to produce it," I told them.

They were still disappointed, however, especially my father. He had a double major in mathematics and physics when he was a student, although he ultimately became a linguist.

My mother was afraid that by giving up a teaching job with a regular salary and becoming a freelance writer, I would lose my independence, for she knew that very few writers were self-supporting. Mother was a strong believer in women having independent careers. My parents had four daughters and no sons, but they saw no reason why their daughters couldn't be just as successful as any son.

In her autobiography (*Autobiography of a Chinese Woman* published by John Day), Mother described how her parents, with strong support from her remarkable grandfather, had broken with Chinese tradition by allowing her to obtain a medical degree and to start a hospital in Beijing.

Lensey, around age two.

She gave up her career when she got married, and she said she regretted it for the rest of her life.

At least my parents should be glad to see that my sisters became a musician, a chemist, and an astrophysicist respectively. My husband and I have two daughters, no sons, and my daughters are in computers and engineering respectively. None of them gave up a career upon getting married.

The attitude toward women in math and science seems to be gradually changing in America, and my daughters say that it's possible to be a scientist, engineer, or mathematician without being considered weird—atypical, maybe—but not outright freakish.

There are times, though, when I think over my parents' words and wonder if all my years of studying and teaching mathematics have been wasted.

Maybe not. I married a mathematician, and my social life revolves largely around mathematicians and their spouses. In some respects this shows.

Mathematicians never lose a sense of fun, and even at a ripe old age they still play games. A less flattering description is that they never reach maturity. So far, I have never lost my juvenile capacity to enjoy myself.

Another trait that most mathematicians share is that of thrift. They are not actually mean with money, and they give generously to causes they believe in. But they *hate* unnecessary spending. I think this attitude first develops when they learn to prove theorems. A theorem is strong if you spend very little on the hypothesis and get a lot as a conclusion: In other words, you want the best bargain possible. Mathematicians, in their quest for a strong theorem, are avid bargain hunters.

I've gone dutch to lots of restaurants with mathematicians. After the waiter presents the bill, there is a prolonged discussion of how much each person pays.

"You had the chef's salad with cheese, so you pay a dollar more than I do," or "I had the house wine, not French merlot," and so on.

The waiter stands there, looking very patient. If you're not used to this, you might curdle with embarrassment and want to crawl under the table. Nobody objects to paying his proper share, but nobody wants to pay a *penny* more than he has to.

A related characteristic is the mathematician's attitude toward elegance. An elegant proof is a short one, and when two mathematicians obtain the same result, the one with the shorter proof is declared the winner. The aim of mathematicians when improving their papers is to get rid of all unnecessary baggage.

Maybe these traits show in my writing. I don't throw in something just for color or to jazz up my writing. A character, an incident, a locality—these are used to advance the plot or to make a point. In reading other people's work, or—especially—listening to public speeches, I dislike long-windedness more than anything else, even more than pretentious terminology.

This makes my writing sound rather plain and bleak. Perhaps it is. But I truly believe that suspense, pathos, or humor can be conveyed economically. It takes skill to accomplish this, and I'm still working at it. In every book, there are places where my editors tell me, "This passage is slow. Can't we tighten it?" Then I know that there is more

Lensey with her sisters. (Clockwise from upper left) Rulan, Zinna, Lensey, and Bella.

work to do and, like my husband and his colleagues, I have to get rid of the extra baggage.

Music

Music figures in a number of my books. This is not because I'm musically gifted; on the contrary, I have the worst ear in my family. *Yang the Youngest and His Terrible Ear* describes the problems of a boy from a family where everyone else is gifted musically. My ear is not quite as bad as his, but I know just how he feels.

My father composed songs at one time, and some of them became famous, especially a love song for solo voice and piano. One of my sisters said she heard this, song at a Hong Kong Karaoke bar.

My eldest sister was picking out tunes on the piano at the age of two, and she eventually became a professor of musicology at Harvard. My other two sisters also play instruments and regularly make music.

A great deal of our family leisure time was spent in some form of musical activity, usually playing the piano or singing. The family practice of unaccompanied singing developed during the war years when we moved around a lot and had no instruments with us. We sang the multiplication table, as I mentioned before. We also sang more pleasant music, mostly part songs. Father had to write or arrange music to accommodate the voices available. In our case, we four daughters provided two sopranos and two altos, while Father provided the lone male voice.

I continued to sing when I grew up. In college I sang in choirs, and I also belonged to smaller groups singing madrigals and other unaccompanied songs. You might ask why these groups accepted me when I had a poor ear. The fact was that I was a whiz at sight-reading: I might be a bit too high or too low, but I was always *there* at the right time. Maybe the other singers regarded me as sort of a conductor, giving them cues for their entrances.

Mother was the only person in our family who didn't sing. She had a lovely baritone voice, but her ear was even worse than mine. She could read musical notation for the piano, and in fact she was the one who gave me my start on the piano by telling me which note on the staff corresponded to which black or white key. But she couldn't keep a tune. The only piece of music she recognized was the slow movement of Haydn's *Surprise* Symphony.

Mother became involved with Haydn when she was attending a missionary school in Shanghai. The school decided to hold a concert in which some of the students played musical solos, and Mother had been chosen to play in the program, not because she was musical, but because she never experienced stage fright. Her piece was a piano arrangement of the slow movement of Haydn's *Surprise* Symphony. This was her first and last public performance of music, and the tune made a deep impression on her.

Mother's solo caused a terrible ruckus in her family. Some of the relatives had opposed sending her to the missionary school in the first place. It was bad enough that a girl of good family should sit in a room with strangers and learn all sorts of foreign subjects. But to go on stage and make music for the public, that was taking the first step toward becoming a singsong girl! The storm eventually

blew over because the piano was considered a relatively harmless instrument. Traditionally, opera was considered a vulgar art, and instruments connected with the opera were vulgar. These included a kind of violin, drums, and various percussion instruments. The genteel instruments, those that could be played by gentlemen and ladies, included the *pipa,* or lute, the bamboo flute, and a zitherlike instrument called a *qin.* When the piano was introduced into China from the West, it was called *gang-qin,* or steel *qin* because it also had many parallel strings. Therefore the piano looked respectable to Chinese eyes. By the time my parents were growing up, the piano was the most popular Western instrument in China.

The piano, then, was our family instrument. Father liked to play the music of the Classical and early Romantic composers. His taste was influenced by his music teachers while he was in college, and what he liked best was the music of Haydn, Beethoven, Schumann, Schubert, and Mendelssohn. If his early musical training had been different, he might have grown to like Bach because he had the kind of mathematical mind often attracted to Bach. When our family moved to America, we had very little money, but Father immediately bought a piano. Mother insisted that a dining table and chairs came first, but the piano came before things like box springs and bed frames. For years we slept on thin mattresses and steel-linked springs balanced on orange crates. But we had the piano.

This didn't mean we could play the piano anytime we wanted, for it was understood that Father always had priority. Even when he wasn't playing, we were nervous about sitting down to play if he was within earshot because he would rush over to correct our mistakes. And he was within earshot almost everywhere in the house, since his ear was unusually acute. Even in his old age, he could hear better than people thirty or forty years younger.

Mistakes in rhythm bothered Father the most. It's because of his stern attitude that we all became very good at counting time. I have trouble with pitch because my ear isn't keen, but I can count time like nobody's business. I never get lost when playing with other people (though sometimes they wish I *would* get lost).

In *Who's Hu?* the mother is a piano teacher. Emma, my protagonist, doesn't have a very good ear but she never gets lost while playing duets with her mother. She is also glad that her mother is too busy playing her own part to notice all of Emma's mistakes.

You'd think that having a father ready to pounce on our every mistake would discourage us from music altogether. Like Emma Hu, we found we could play duets with Father. He would be so busy with his own part that some of our mistakes would escape his notice.

Over the years Father bought an enormous quantity of piano duet music. Some of the pieces were original compositions written for four hands, but most were orchestral music arranged as piano duets. We played overtures by Beethoven, von Weber, Mozart, and Rossini. We played most of the better-known symphonies of Mozart, Haydn, Schubert, and Mendelssohn.

Because I lived at home the longest, I played more duets with Father than any of my sisters. In the weeks before I left home to get married, Father and I went through a marathon of symphonies of Beethoven. When we came to

Graduation from Cambridge High and Latin School.

In Berkeley with husband, Isaac, shortly after their marriage.

the choral movement of the Ninth, Father sang the bass solo.

While playing duets with Father, it was necessary to obey his rules. Rule Number One was that we didn't play any of the repeats indicated by the composer. We wanted to finish a whole symphony, and doing all the repeats would take too long. There was one exception: we did all the repeats in the slow movement of Haydn's *Surprise* Symphony because that was the one piece of music Mother recognized. She always came over to listen, and we wanted to prolong her pleasure.

Rule Number Two was that we never stopped for mistakes. If I missed a note, if I reduced a passage to complete chaos, still we ploughed on. I remember a terrifying session playing Beethoven's *Eroica* Symphony with Father. In the development section of the first movement, there is a passage that consists almost entirely of crashing chords. To my dull ear, every measure sounds like every other measure. My attention must have wandered. From the kitchen I heard Mother's voice saying, "We'll have to set the table soon. There are fourteen people for dinner tonight."

Suddenly I realized that something was wrong. From the sound of things, I must have skipped a line. We were still playing crashing chords, and I tried to compensate by jumping back to the previous line. But it didn't work, and I could feel the sweat trickling down my back.

Father must have noticed that I was floundering in a morass. Would he stop for me? Never! I continued to play crashing chords, but my crashes were getting feeble. At long last, Father played a recognizable melody, an oboe solo with the principal theme. I finally knew where we

were and found my way back into the music. To this day, I can't listen to an orchestra play the *Eroica* Symphony without suffering an anxiety attack.

Besides the piano, a couple of Chinese flutes, and Father's cello, we also owned a number of other instruments. When guests opened the coat closet of our house in Cambridge, they had to be careful not to bring down on them two violins, a clarinet, and a trumpet.

In the late 1940s, Father made a series of recordings of spoken Mandarin for Folkway Records in New York. Upon receiving his first royalty check, he went on a splurge. The size of the check limited his splurging to a pawn shop on Seventh Avenue, where his eye was caught by some musical instruments in the window. He probably thought, "It's time the family branched out and took up something besides singing and piano playing."

He bought four instruments because he had four children, and he saw himself accompanying us on the piano while we played. Why did he choose this particular combination? They were probably what were available in the pawn shop that day. When he came home and distributed the instruments, I wound up with one of the violins.

My eldest sister took the trumpet, but I don't remember which sisters had the other two instruments. Up to now, our family had practiced togetherness whenever possible. If we couldn't find ready-made music, Father would arrange pieces to suit us. But the violin-violin-clarinet-trumpet combination was just too unwieldy, and we had to go our separate ways.

My eldest sister tooted her trumpet for a while, but gave up when the neighbors complained. I was the only one to take lessons. This was not because I was the most musical one of the family—rather the opposite. As soon as I drew my bow across the violin strings, the family decided that I needed help—outside help. Money was tight then, but this was an emergency! We managed to find a music teacher willing to give me lessons at fifty cents a shot. At least it got me and my fiddle out of the house once a week. For some reason my music teacher got sick a lot; my exercise book mysteriously disappeared, and when I declared that I'd rather play the piano than the violin, nobody objected strenuously.

In addition to this assortment of Western instruments, we also had a few Chinese instruments. The one that fascinated me most was a Chinese oboe, called a *suona*, and it was used in religious ceremonies and processions. I found its nasal, plaintive voice strangely moving. Years later the *suona* appeared in a comic scene from my book about Chinese outlaws, *Phantom of Tiger Mountain*.

My craving to play the *suona* was partially satisfied when my eldest sister Rulan (who had married and was living a safe distance away) gave me an oboe for my birthday. I still remember my excitement at putting the oboe reed to my lips for the first time. I huffed and I puffed, but nothing happened. After repeated tries, I finally blew a great big *blaat*. Our cat jumped under the bed, and it was a long time before I could coax it out again.

Playing the oboe was harder than I had thought. The difficulty isn't in blowing hard, but in not being able to release the air as fast as you want. I began to get migraine headaches. Strangely enough, Father also got migraine headaches when he heard my oboe. But he never tried to talk me out of playing, since he believed in encouraging musical activity, even if it hurt.

I gave up the oboe after a while. Some years later, when my daughters were both playing instruments, I took up the cello in order to play music together with them and their friends. Although my cello didn't inflict as much pain as my violin, I noticed that other players began to sidle away when I approached wistfully with my instrument. I gave up the cello and faced the bitter truth that a person with a poor ear should not play a string instrument. A piano is better because it can be tuned by somebody else.

My musical activities continued even when I left home to get married. My husband and I play piano duets almost daily, the same arrangements of classical symphonies that I used to play with my father. We also play four-hand arrangements of string quartets by Mozart and Beethoven.

Only now I have the upper hand: namely the primo part, which used to be my father's. The rules are different, too. We now do all the repeats, and when my husband gets lost, he insists on stopping. He refuses to grope around on the keys until he finds his place again, the way I did with my father.

Isaac Namioka's family. (From left) Isaac's younger brother, Shigeo, father, Saburo, and mother, Evelyn. Himeji Castle, the inspiration for Namioka's **White Serpent Castle,** *is in the background.*

Another difference is that we always draw the drapes when we play. Our piano can be seen from the street, and we don't want our neighbors to know who is making that awful racket.

My musical life isn't always an awful racket, since my husband and I go regularly to concerts. In my series of books about the musical Chinese immigrant family, the Yangs play string quartets. I feel safest writing about string quartets because that's what I hear most often in concerts, and I also play arrangements of them on the piano with my husband.

The scenes describing music lessons and recitals in the Yang books, however, actually come from my daughters' experiences. They took lessons in the flute and violin respectively and went through the usual torments of children forced to play in recitals. Their love for music managed to survive, however, and today they still play chamber music with their friends. Both of them are very good at sight-reading. One of them told me that when she was auditioning for the orchestra at her university, the conductor said to her, "You sight-read better than you play." Maybe she's a chip off the old block.

Writing

I wrote my first book when I was eight, and it was a swashbuckler titled *Princess with a Bamboo Sword.* I illustrated the book, drawing pictures of the heroine wearing a long, flowing traditional Chinese gown held together by a flapping sash. Maybe the book should be described as a "swashsash" or a "sashbuckler." Anyway, it was full of derring-do and sword fights, interspersed with acrobatic kung fu.

You might think that an eight-year-old girl would write about dolls having tea parties with cuddly teddy bears. The fact is, we write what we read, and action stories formed the bulk of my childhood reading. Our house was filled with piles of paperback novels, and their covers always featured a leaping swordsman wearing the traditional Chinese costume of baggy pants and cloth boots. Almost as often, they featured a woman warrior wearing the sort of gown and sash that were in my illustrations.

Who read these books in our family? Chiefly my mother and my elder sisters. My father held to the traditional belief that a gentleman and a scholar wasn't supposed to read fiction. In the old days, an educated man read history, philosophy, and maybe some poetry—of the Tang dynasty. Fiction was written by people who had failed the state examinations and were ineligible to get a job as an official. To make a living with their hard-earned education, many took up the sordid occupation of writing novels. Novels were called *xiao sh uo,* or "small talk," and they were considered a low form of literature read only by womenfolk and servants. If a man was caught buying a novel at a bookstore, he would claim he was buying it for one of his wives or daughters. Today, some of these novels have finally been recognized as masterpieces of Chinese literature, but in the old days men had to read fiction in secret.

One great novel, written in the Ming dynasty, was *Shui Hu,* sometimes translated as "Outlaws of the Marsh." It has delighted readers to this day with its action-packed pages and gave rise to a whole genre of action novels. In the

Isaac Namioka (left) with his uncle (lower right) and family at Cat Temple. Isaac's uncle was head priest at the temple and teller of the story that led to Namioka's book **The Loyal Cat.**

twentieth century, many men finally came out of the closet and began to read novels openly. Among people of my parents' generation, men and women both enjoyed action stories, especially those filled with sword fights and kung fu. My mother and her friends often exchanged piles of these paperback novels, the way kids today exchange comic books.

I grew up surrounded by action novels. In addition to my mother's paperback books, I started to read translations of Western adventure stories, such as *The Three Muske-teers* and *Treasure Island.*

Predictably enough, when I started writing fiction my first work was an action novel. *The Princess with the Bamboo Sword* had no sequels, however, and many years passed before I tried to write fiction again. I started seriously writing for children in the early 1970s. My first thought was to write about a band of Chinese outlaws. But the Cultural Revolution was still sweeping through China, and books such as *Outlaws of the Marsh* were banned. I was afraid that if word got out that I had written an action novel about outlaws, my relatives in China could get into real trouble.

I decided to write about a couple of unemployed Japanese samurai instead. Those of you who have seen Japanese television or the movies of directors like Kurosa-

wa know that there is a genre of stories, called *chambara,* about the wandering samurai (the term *chambara* comes from the sound of clashing swords). Our family spent a year in Japan from 1968 to 1969, and during that time I saw my fill of samurai movies and TV programs, with enough sword fights to fill buckets of blood and to send hundreds of severed limbs flying off into space.

My father-in-law encouraged my interest in feudal Japan. My husband's hometown was Himeji, noted for its White Heron Castle, the most beautiful castle in the country still in its original state. I made repeated visits to the castle, learned about its construction, and heard stories about the ghosts that haunted the place. When I eventually started writing novels, my first work was *White Serpent Castle,* and the castle scenes were based on what I had seen at Himeji.

Altogether I've written seven books in the samurai series. When the Cultural Revolution ended in China, I finally decided to write an action story about a band of outlaws in China. *Phantom of Tiger Mountain* incorporated all the things I loved most in my childhood reading: kung fu, sword fights, humor, pathos, suspense, and horror. Among all my books, it was the easiest to write. It almost wrote itself.

But this book and my samurai series are different in one respect from the Chinese paperback novels and the Japanese *chambara.* My books are mysteries as well. The reason is that in addition to action stories, my youthful reading included a lot of mystery stories. One of my sisters always had her nose in a book about a detective called "Fuermosi." He was an odd looking man who wore a funny wool hat and smoked a pipe. But he was very clever at solving mysteries and was always miles ahead of his bumbling doctor friend.

I became addicted to these stories, too. Years later, I discovered that "Fuermosi" was the way Fujian people pronounced "Holmes." The first Chinese translator of the Sherlock Holmes stories was a man from Fujian!

Today I'm still a fan of mystery stories, and I belong to the Mystery Writers of America. It's hard to decide which is more fun: reading or writing mysteries.

Actually I hadn't seriously considered writing as a career until rather late in life. It was something that started creeping up on me when I was nearly forty years old. True, I had written *Princess with a Bamboo Sword,* but that was something half-forgotten from my childhood.

Things changed when my daughters were born and I had to find day care for them if I was to continue teaching. We were living in Ithaca, a small town in upstate New York at the time, and in those days there weren't many reliable day-care centers. For a while we hired nannies for the girls. One was not very good, and a second one was

Namioka and husband at Himeji Castle.

well intentioned, but absolute putty in the hands of the children.

When the children kept getting sick, I decided to give up teaching and stay home. For a while I worked at translating papers by Chinese mathematicians into English. Then during the Cultural Revolution, mathematical research ceased in China, and the only papers I received were written by academicians beating their breasts and confessing their political sins. Translating these papers was not a rewarding occupation.

About this time, my mother was writing a book about Chinese restaurants. She had written a successful Chinese cookbook, and her publisher, Random House, asked her to write a short work on how to order a good meal in a Chinese restaurant. My eldest sister had translated the cookbook, but she was too busy to work on the present one. Mother asked if I would like to do the translation. It was enjoyable work, and it whetted my appetite for writing.

My next attempts at writing were short articles for a Seattle newspaper on local Asian activities. One of my articles was about Japanese toilets and how to use them. It created a stir, and for a while I achieved some local notoriety and became known as the "Toilet Lady." I wasn't paid much for these articles, but they were fun to write.

The first real money I received was for a humorous article I sent to one of the two major Seattle newspapers. It was about squirrels. We had a peach tree in our yard that produced luscious peaches every summer. But before they could ripen, pesky squirrels would come and take bites from the green peaches. Finding the peaches bitter, the squirrels would fling them on the ground. Our lawn would be covered with green peaches, each with a bite taken out of it.

There is a recipe for squirrel stew in our edition of *The Joy of Cooking,* together with an illustration of how to skin the animal. At that time, however, it was illegal in Seattle to kill squirrels. The only thing we could do was to trap them and release them somewhere else. Accordingly we bought a trap, placed a couple of peanuts in it, and set it under our peach tree. It worked! In no time we had an angry, spitting, foulmouthed squirrel inside. We drove the squirrel across the canal and released it on the campus of the university. It was a humane procedure, since hundreds of students would be feeding the little beast.

But the number of squirrels did not decrease and green peaches with bites in them continued to litter our lawn. Finally we found out why. People on the other side of the canal were trapping squirrels and releasing them on our side. All we did by our trapping was to exchange squirrels.

I wrote up the squirrel article, and it was accepted for the tabloid section of the newspaper. I've kept the yellowing pages of the article ever since.

I continued to write articles and started to aim at the magazine market. My next big sale was an article about Japanese castles, which I sold to the magazine *Travel.* It began to seem that a career in writing might be possible after all.

Isaac heartily encouraged me. He said it was through my April Fools' jokes that he first became convinced I had real creativity. When we were graduate students together, I had printed a fake notice that circulated around the math department on April 1, telling everybody that an eminent mathematician was coming to give a talk. The title of the

Daughters Michi (left) and Aki (right).

talk was so absurd that I was sure nobody would be fooled for long. I was a little scared when many people took it seriously and made elaborate plans to welcome the famous man.

This didn't prevent me from continuing my April Fools' activities. When Isaac was a visiting scholar at the Institute of Advanced Studies at Princeton, we all received an invitation to the annual banquet from the director, Robert Oppenheimer. The invitation stipulated black tie. Since very few visiting scholars owned a tuxedo, I circulated a fake notice about an EZ Fit Tuxedo Rental Company. Again, more people than I expected fell for the hoax. I was badly frightened by a letter from Dr. Oppenheimer, asking Isaac to go to the director's office and explain the fake notice. The letter was, of course, another hoax!

Still, I continued my nefarious activities. But gradually, Isaac became my only victim because I was spending most of my time at home. That was why he was so eager for me to exercise my creativity on writing fiction.

As I mentioned earlier, the story about the White Serpent Castle was my first juvenile novel (not counting the one about the princess with the bamboo sword). It was not the first one to be published, however. All the characters in it are Japanese, and I was told that I couldn't hope to sell a book with Asian characters. This was before the interest in multicultural literature.

After falling off a horse, one should get right back on again, and failing to sell a book, one should start another one right away. Therefore I wrote another book about my two Japanese samurai, but this time I was careful to include a Portuguese soldier of fortune called Pedro as one of the main characters. The book was titled *The Samurai and the Long-Nosed Devils.* Pedro was called a long-nosed-devil because when the Japanese saw their first Europeans, what struck them the most were the amazingly long noses of the Caucasians.

It's ironical that I had to add a Caucasian character, Pedro, to get my first novel published. Years later, I wrote a

science-fiction story, "LAFFF," which featured a girl called Angela. My editor suggested making her Asian American, although there was nothing whatever in the story to require that she should belong to an ethnic minority. After some soul-searching, I finally decided to make the girl Chinese American and added some ethnic touches such as egg rolls and bean sprouts.

There is no question that my writing career received a big boost because of the growing interest in multicultural literature. More and more publishers asked for books about ethnic minority groups, including Asians. I was certainly standing in the right place at the right time.

Before cultural diversity became fashionable, marketing my books was hard. Selling a few newspaper and magazine articles was one thing, selling a full-length book was a different matter altogether. It hadn't occurred to me at first that writing was a craft that had to be learned, like playing a musical instrument. Unless you have a hopelessly bad ear, like Yang the Youngest, you can improve your writing by hard work, namely study and practice.

I learned this vital fact in Seattle through a writing teacher who read my manuscript for *White Serpent Castle.* Very tactfully, she suggested that I attend writing classes. I had taken freshman English in college, but the course was more concerned with great literature than with the nitty-gritty aspects of writing.

By attending my first adult writing course, I found out that, as a writer, I was a beginner. I also had the good fortune to join a support group of writers who read their current work to each other and gave frank but constructive criticism. I owe an immense debt to this group, and I still go to meetings regularly. We call ourselves the Rejects because we get many rejections from editors and from agents, although we are all published writers.

Getting published, in my case, would not have been possible without the help of a literary agent. If you're a

Granddaughter Leila (Michi's daughter) with her father, Jim.

beginning writer, it's not easy to find an agent willing to take you as a client. On the advice of my friends, I submitted sample chapters of *The Samurai and the Long-Nosed Devils* to a contest sponsored by the Pacific Northwest Writers Conference. It won a prize in the juvenile division, and on this basis I was able to interest an agent from New York, Patricia Lewis. Within a couple of months, she sold the book to David McKay.

After David McKay bought the book about the long-nosed devils, my agent asked whether I had another book with the same setting and characters. I was able to hand her *White Serpent Castle,* already typed up. Therefore the first novel I wrote was the second one to be published.

I confess that when I wrote *White Serpent Castle,* I had intended it to be a mystery novel for adults. After all, those Chinese books about outlaws and flying swordsmen were enjoyed by young and old alike. Moreover, people of all ages loved mysteries.

But everybody who read my manuscript—family, friends, writing teacher, literary agent—immediately saw it as a book for young people. At first I was a little offended. "You mean my book isn't good enough for grown-ups?" I asked.

The answer is even more unflattering. It took some years for me to accept the fact that my writing is suited to young people because in some ways I have never grown up. I had more fun when I visited Disneyland and Disney World than the children who were there!

Two of my books were written for adults, however. One is *Japan: A Traveler's Companion,* a guide for the foreign tourist in Japan. It took a lot of nerve to write about Japan when I barely mumble enough of the language to get around. Actually, the book developed out of my earlier newspaper article about Japanese toilets. The whole book is from the point of view of a foreigner who faces daunting and embarrassing situations while struggling to get around Japan. There are chapters about inns, trains, food, museums, and, of course, castles. But readers and reviewers still like the toilet chapter best.

My agent sold the book to Vanguard Press, a small independent house which was later bought by Random House. Vanguard wanted me to do another travel book, and I wrote one about traveling in China. This time, it was not from the point of view of a foreigner, but of a native returning after many years. Yes, there is a section on toilets in this book, too.

So far, my writing has been either mystery-adventure stories set in feudal Japan or adult nonfiction. Again, it was Vanguard Press that suggested a juvenile book with a contemporary setting. I wasn't enthusiastic about the idea at first. I preferred flashing swords and eerie castles.

But it was around this time that my daughters were taking advanced math courses, and I began to remember my own experiences in school. I wrote *Who's Hu?* which, as I said earlier, is about a girl being thought a freak when she likes mathematics. It is also the first of my contemporary books about the experiences of Chinese immigrant families in America.

Over the years, a number of people have helped me to develop as a writer. The Rejects, of course, have had the greatest influence. So did my literary agents. After Pat Lewis died, I tried to manage on my own for a couple of years, but without success. Through a friend, I found another agent, Ruth Cohen. She was the one who suggested more books about Asian Americans, and that led to the series about the Yang family. A couple of my editors worked very hard on transforming me from a storyteller to a novelist.

Many people ask me whether my books are autobiographical. Is Emma Hu, the math whiz, my alter ego? The answer is no, unfortunately. Emma is a much better mathematician than I am, and the book contains some wishful thinking. True, some of the characters in that book are taken from life. Friends of the family immediately recognized Emma's father as my father, but most of the other characters are made up from an arm here and a leg there. Nor do I usually write about real incidents. My books are fictional, and so are the characters. Many of them are outsiders, like myself, but they are not real people.

Some of the books contain themes that are important to me, such as women in mathematics and science. But I don't write books primarily because I have a crusade or a wish to right a social wrong.

I write books because it's fun. There's nothing else I enjoy more.

Writings

YOUNG ADULT FICTION

The Samurai and the Long-Nosed Devils, McKay (New York), 1976.

White Serpent Castle, McKay, 1976.

Valley of Broken Cherry Trees, Delacorte, 1980.

Village of the Vampire Cat, Delacorte, 1981.

Who's Hu? Vanguard, 1981.

Phantom of Tiger Mountain, Vanguard, 1986.

Island of Ogres, Harper, 1989.

The Coming of the Bear, HarperCollins, 1992.

Yang the Youngest and His Terrible Ear, illustrated by Kees de Kiefte, Joy Street Books (Boston), 1992.

April and the Dragon Lady, Boston, Joy Street Books, 1994.

The Loyal Cat, illustrated by Aki Sogabe, Harcourt Brace, 1995.

Yang the Third and Her Impossible Family, illustrated by Kees de Kiefte, Little, Brown, 1995.

Den of the White Fox, Harcourt Brace, 1997.

The Laziest Boy in the World, Holiday House, 1997.

Yang the Second and Her Secret Admirers, illustrated by Kees de Kiefte, Little, Brown, 1998.

Ties that Bind, Ties that Break: A Novel, Delacorte, 1999.

Yang the Eldest and His Odd Jobs, illustrated by Kees de Kiefte, Little, Brown, 2000.

The Hungriest Boy in the World, illustrated by Aki Soyabe, Holiday House, 2001.

NONFICTION FOR ADULTS

(Translator) Buwei Y. Chaos, *How to Order and Eat in Chinese,* Vintage, 1974.

Japan: A Traveler's Companion, Vanguard, 1979.

China: A Traveler's Companion, Vanguard, 1985.

Contributor of plays to *Center Stage,* edited by Donald
Gallo.

NEAL, Michael
See TEITELBAUM, Michael

O

OTFINOSKI, Steven 1949-

Personal

Surname is pronounced ott-fin-*a*-ske; born January 11, 1949, in Queens, NY; son of Anthony (an insurance salesman) and Helen (a homemaker; maiden name, Zaspel) Otfinoski; married Beverly Larson (a freelance writer, editor, and harpist), April 18, 1981; children: Daniel, Martha. *Education:* Attended Boston University, 1967-69; Antioch College, B.A., 1972.

Addresses

Home and office—1559 North Peters Lane, Stratford, CT 06614.

Career

Hartford Times, Hartford, CT, news reporter, 1972-73; Field Publications, Middletown, CT, assistant editor for *Read* magazine, 1974-75; freelance author, 1975—. *Member:* Dramatists' Guild.

Awards, Honors

One-Act Play Award from Quaigh Theatre, 1983, and Westchester County Playwriting Competition runner-up, 1985, both for *The Bookworm;* Playwriting Award from the Community Children's Theatre of Kansas City, MO, 1985, for musical play *The Princess and the Pea;* winner of Summer Festival of New Plays Competition, Rhode Island Playwrights Theatre, 1989, for historical drama *Still Life with Dead Grizzly; Triumph and Terror: The French Revolution* and *Poland* selected as Books for the Teen Age by the New York Public Library; winner of Connecticut Playwrights One-Act Festival, Warner Studio Theatre, 2000, for one-person play *A Pirate's Life.*

Writings

FOR YOUNG READERS

The Monster That Wouldn't Die and Other Strange But True Stories, Field Publications, 1976.

(With Diane Carlson) *The Blood Suckers and Other True Animal Stories,* Field Publications, 1976.

The Rubber-Soled Kid and Other Funny Superstars, Field Publications, 1976.

Plays about Strange Happenings, Field Publications, 1976.

The World's Darkest Days: Stories of Great Tragedies of the Past, Field Publications, 1977.

The Red Ghost and Other True Animal Stories, Field Publications, 1977.

(Compiler) *Fun for All: Jokes and Cartoons to Make You Laugh,* Field Publications, 1977.

High Flier and Other Fast Action Stories, Field Publications, 1977.

The Third Arm and Other Strange Tales of the Supernatural, Field Publications, 1977.

Monsters to Know and Love: Stories of Chills and Fun, Field Publications, 1977.

Sky Ride and Other Exciting Stories, Field Publications, 1977.

The Verlaine Crossing, illustrated by Stanley Fleming, Pitman, 1977.

Tony, the Night Custodian, Janus Books, 1977.

Plays for Group Reading, Field Publications, 1977.

Space Trucker and Other Science Fiction Stories, Field Publications, 1978.

The Zombie Maker: Stories of Amazing Adventures, Field Publications, 1978.

Village of Vampires, illustrated by Chris Kenyon, Pitman, 1979.

Fun to Read Funny Stories, Playmore, 1979.

(With Annie Mueser) *Cobra in the Tub and Eight More Stories of Mystery and Suspense,* Field Publications, 1980.

(Editor and contributor) *Face at the Window and Other Stories of Suspense and Adventure,* Field Publications, 1980.

(Contributor) *My Giant Story Book,* Playmore, 1981.

(Contributor) *Christmas Fun World,* Playmore, 1981.

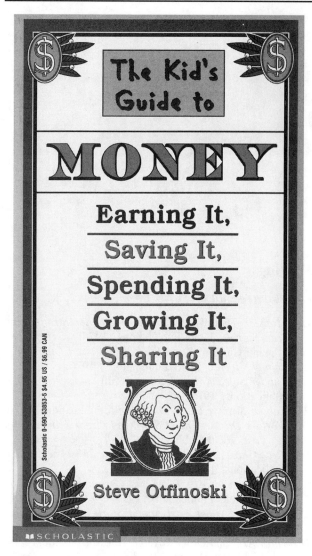

Directed at an audience of young people from upper-elementary grades through high school, Steven Otfinoski's instructional book covers all facets of earning money and managing finances.

(Compiler and contributor) *Know Power: Everything to Know about Everything,* Playmore, 1981.

The Screaming Grave, Weekly Reader Books, 1982.

History Alive! (plays), Educational Insights, 1982.

Midnight at Monster Mansion (multiple adventure novel), illustrated by Michael Racz, Scholastic, 1984.

TV Superstars Scrapbook 1, Weekly Reader Books, 1984.

TV Superstars Scrapbook 4, Weekly Reader Books, 1985.

Superworld (adventure), Scholastic, 1985.

James Bond in Barracuda Run (multiple adventure novel), Ballantine, 1985.

TV Superstars '86, Weekly Reader Books, 1986.

Wild on Wheels, Weekly Reader Books, 1986.

Carnival of Terror (multiple adventure novel), Weekly Reader Books, 1986.

Cosby, Punky, Kate, and Allie, Weekly Reader Books, 1986.

The Secret of Pirate Island, Weekly Reader Books, 1986.

Master of the Past (multiple adventure novel), Weekly Reader Books, 1987.

The Shrieking Skull, Weekly Reader Books, 1988.

(Contributor) *Hispanic American Biographies,* Globe Books, 1988.

Hispanics in American History, Volume 2: *1865 to the Present,* Globe Books, 1989.

Jesse Jackson: A Voice for Change, Fawcett, 1989.

Mikhail Gorbachev, the Soviet Innovator, Fawcett, 1989.

Marian Wright Edelman: Defender of Children's Rights, Blackbirch Press, 1991.

Nineteenth-Century Writers, Facts on File, 1991.

Alexander Fleming: Conquering Disease with Penicillin, Facts on File, 1992.

Lewis and Clark: Leading America West, Fawcett, 1992.

The Stolen Signs: A Southside Sluggers Baseball Mystery, illustrated by Bert Dodson, Simon & Schuster, 1992.

Who Stole Home Plate?: A Southside Sluggers Baseball Mystery, illustrated by Bert Dodson, Simon & Schuster, 1992.

Nelson Mandela: The Fight against Apartheid, Millbrook Press, 1992.

Gun Control: Is It a Right or a Danger to Bear Arms?, Twenty-First Century, 1993.

Oprah Winfrey: Television Star, Blackbirch Press, 1993.

William Gaines: MAD Man, Rourke, 1993.

Triumph and Terror: The French Revolution, Facts on File, 1993.

Igor Sikorsky: Father of the Helicopter, Rourke, 1993.

Joseph Stalin: Russia's Last Czar, Millbrook Press, 1993.

Putting It in Writing ("Scholastic Guides" series), Scholastic, 1993.

Blizzards, Twenty-first Century, 1994.

Great Black Writers, Facts on File, 1994.

The Truth about Three Billy Goats Gruff, illustrated by Rowan Barnes-Murphy, Whistlestop, 1994.

Poland, Facts on File, 1995.

Whodunit?: Science Solves the Crime, illustrated by Betsy Scheld, Scientific American, 1995.

Boris Yeltsin and the Rebirth of Russia, Millbrook Press, 1995.

Scott Joplin: A Life in Ragtime, F. Watts, 1995.

The Czech Republic, Facts on File, 1996.

Speaking Up, Speaking Out: A Kid's Guide to Making Speeches, Oral Reports, and Conversation, Millbrook Press, 1996.

The Kid's Guide to Money: Earning It, Saving It, Spending It, Growing It, Sharing It, Scholastic, 1996.

Bulgaria, Facts on File, 1999.

New Hampshire, Benchmark, 1999.

Ukraine, Facts on File, 1999.

John Wilkes Booth and the Civil War, Blackbirch Press, 1999.

Bugsy Siegel and the Post-War Boom, Blackbirch Press, 2000.

Hammerheads and Other Sharks, World Book, 2000.

Hedgehogs and Other Insectivores, World Book, 2000.

Ladybugs and Other Beetles, World Book, 2000.

Time to Share: The Wild Thornberrys, Simon Spotlight, 2000.

Georgia, Benchmark, 2001.

"HERE WE GO" SERIES; FOR CHILDREN

Into the Wind: Sailboats Then and Now, Benchmark, 1997.

Riding the Rails: Trains Then and Now, Benchmark, 1997.

Pedaling Along: Bikes Then and Now, Benchmark, 1997.
Behind the Wheel: Cars Then and Now, Benchmark, 1997.
Taking Off: Planes Then and Now, Benchmark, 1997.
To the Rescue: Fire Trucks Then and Now, Benchmark, 1997.
Around the Track: Race Cars Then and Now, Benchmark, 1998.
On the High Seas: Ships Then and Now, Benchmark, 1998.
Wild on Wheels: Motorcycles Then and Now, Benchmark, 1998.
On the Road: Trucks Then and Now, Benchmark, 1998.
Blasting Off: Rockets Then and Now, Benchmark, 1999.
Whirling Around: Helicopters Then and Now, Benchmark, 1999.

FOR ADULTS

Idea to Manuscript: Writing Books and Stories for Children and Young Adults, Calco Publishing, 1993.
The Golden Age of Rock Instrumentals: A Loving Tribute to the Pioneers of the Instrumental Era, Billboard, 1997.
The Golden Age of Novelty Songs, Billboard, 2000.

PLAYS

A Revolution Relieved: In Word and Song, toured schools and churches in CT, 1976.
At Crazy Jayne's (one-act comedy), produced at Stagelights Theatrical Club, New York City, 1978.
Love of Frankenstein (comedy), produced at Actor's Playhouse, New York City, 1978.
Great Moments from the Good Book (comedy sketches), produced at Arts Café, Hartford, CT, 1982.
The Bookworm (one-act comedy), produced at Quaigh Theatre, New York City, 1983.
The Ventriloquist (musical comedy), produced at Quaigh Theatre, New York City, 1983.
Stooge Night (drama), produced at Quaigh Theatre, New York City, 1985.
Wedding Bell Blues (one-act comedy), produced at American Theater of Actors, New York City, 1986.
Cutting Edge (one-act adaption of a short story), produced at American Theater of Actors, 1987, and Theatre Artists' Workshop Playwrights' Lab, Westport, CT, 1992.
Conscience (one-act adaption of a short story), produced at American Theatre of Actors, 1987.
We the People (musical), music by Richard Amend and Mary Lang, produced in Stratford, CT, 1987.
Still Life with Dead Grizzly (historical drama), produced by the Rhode Island Playwrights' Theatre, Providence, RI, 1989.
Remember Then (comedy-drama), produced by the Theatre Artists' Workshop, Westport, CT, 1990, and Lincoln Center New Playwrights' Series, New York, 1991.
Stratford Characters (historical drama), produced in Stratford, CT, and Festival of the Arts, Stratford-on-Avon, England, 1991.
Two for Freedom, New England Woman, Phillis Wheatley: Black Poet of Boston, and *Braggarts, Bulldoggers, and Desperadoes: The Black Cowboys* (one-person shows based on American history), produced by History Alive!, 1992—.
Direct from Hell: An Evening with Ambrose Bierce (one-man show), produced by the Oronoque Reader's Theater, 1998, and Stratford Library's Readers' Theater, 1999.
A Pirate's Life (one-man show), produced by Warner Studio Theater, Torrington, CT, 2000.

CHILDREN'S MUSICALS

The Birdfeeder, produced at Quaigh Theatre, New York City, 1982.
The Ghosts of Gloomy Manor, music by Karl Blumenkranz, produced at Quaigh Theatre, 1982.
The Christmas Santa Lost His Ho! Ho! Ho!, music by Mary Lang, produced at Quaigh Theatre, 1983.
Snow White, music by M. Lang, produced at Calliope Storybook Theatre, Eatontown, NJ, 1984.
Mrs. Claus to the Rescue!, music by K. Blumenkranz, produced at Quaigh Theatre, 1984.
Sleeping Beauty, music by Richard Amend, produced at Club Bene Theatre, Sayerville, NJ, 1985.

Containing numerous photographs and maps, as well as a pronunciation guide, Otfinoski's volume clarifies the history of a nation that has gone through many changes before and since the rise of communism, including modernization and the struggle to establish a working democracy.

The Princess and the Pea, music by R. Amend, produced at Club Bene Dinner Theatre, 1985.

Rumpelstiltskin Is My Name!, music by M. Lang, produced at Club Bene Dinner Theatre, 1985.

Adaptations

Cobra in the Tub and Eight More Stories of Mystery and Suspense (cassette for the blind), Field Publications, 1980.

Sidelights

A professional writer for children, Steven Otfinoski is the author of plays, mystery novels, and numerous works of nonfiction that allow young readers to pursue their interests in people, places, and historic events. From profiles of both nations and states to biographies of such notable individuals as helicopter inventor Igor Sikorsky and children's rights advocate Marian Wright Edelman, Otfinoski's books have been praised for their clear prose and unbiased presentation. Reviewing 1995's *Boris Yeltsin and the Rebirth of Russia, School Library Journal* contributor Pat Katka described Otfinoski's writing style as embodying "clarity and verve."

Born in Queens, New York, in 1949, Otfinoski was raised in Farmingdale, Long Island, the oldest of three boys. "When I was ten, our family moved to my father's hometown of Middletown, Connecticut," he told *SATA.* "I was an introspective boy and spent much of my time reading books, watching television, and daydreaming. I fell in love with horror and suspense movies at an early age." This early love of the mysterious would inspire much of Otfinoski's later fiction for children, including *The Third Arm and Other Strange Tales of the Supernatural* and *The Screaming Grave.*

"Although I wrote comics, stories, and poems throughout my childhood, it wasn't until studying a year abroad in London while in college that I truly discovered the joys of writing," Otfinoski explained. "I kept a journal and wrote down descriptions of places and people and my thoughts and feelings of the life around me. After graduation back in the states, I quickly got my first writing job, as a reporter for the now-defunct *Hartford Times.* Newspaper writing with its tight deadlines and emphasis on clear, precise writing was excellent training for me, as it is for most writers. However, I soon grew tired of writing about town meetings and car accidents, and quit after only a year."

After leaving the *Times,* Otfinoski spent a summer traveling, then returned home to Middletown, "determined to start a spectacular career as a freelance writer." However, he quickly realized that such a goal was going to take more than ambition. "My efforts at writing witty greeting cards and spine-tingling short stories for mystery magazines were doomed to failure," he admitted. "As the rejection slips piled up on my writing desk, I decided I'd better get a full-time job doing anything to earn money before I tried my dear parents' patience beyond endurance." Luckily, Otfinoski's hometown was also the home of Xerox Educational Publications, publishers of the *My Weekly Reader* school newspaper and other educational periodicals. Although Xerox had no openings in their editorial department, Otfinoski took a job in the company's mail room. After getting to know several editors, he was offered the job of assistant editor on *Read* magazine, a periodical for secondary students. "I enjoyed the mixture of editing and creative writing and might be there still," Otfinoski noted, "if I wasn't laid off in one of several notorious staff cutbacks after only a year on the job. My boss cried openly at the suddenness of my 'termination,' but I was actually quite happy. I knew working in an office wasn't for me and I was already looking forward to once again trying my hand at being an independent freelancer."

Because of his experience in writing to deadlines, and with the help of the contacts made at Xerox, Otfinoski's second attempt to strike out on his own as a professional writer was successful. Surprisingly, he never deliberately decided to channel his efforts into books for young people, the avenue that has been his greatest success. "It just sort of happened by accident," he admitted, "and I've never regretted it. [Kids'] interests in adventure, the mysterious, and the supernatural, are my interests as well. And when I sit down to write I don't ask whether my readers will like what I'm writing. I try to please myself first. If I'm interested in what I'm writing, I take it for granted that they'll be interested too. And nine times out of ten I'm right."

Following his personal interests in the area of nonfiction has resulted in a wide-ranging list of titles to Otfinoski's credit. From politics to personalities, he has written on many topics relevant to top-of-the-news issues, enabling young readers to grasp the political and social changes occurring throughout the world. In the early 1990s, after the fall of communism in Russia, Otfinoski published books on Soviet leaders Boris Yeltsin and Mikhail Gorbachev, as well as books profiling Eastern Europe. In *Boris Yeltsin and the Rebirth of Russia,* he examines the rise of a democratic Russia against Yeltsin's long political career as an advocate of change in a formerly oppressive state. Commenting on the book in *Booklist,* Frances Bradburn noted that "Otfinoski captures [Yeltsin's career] with an easy writing style that belies the complexity of both the man and his country."

Otfinoski's *Bulgaria* is one of several books profiling modern nations in a timely manner. Part of Facts on File's "Nations in Transition" series, the book focuses on the past, present, and future in this Eastern European country. Containing numerous photographs and maps, as well as a pronunciation guide, Otfinoski's volume clarifies the history of a nation that has gone through many changes before and since the rise of communism. Praising the volume as of value to both teachers and students, *Booklist* contributor Shelle Rosenfeld commented that *Bulgaria* aids in "learning about a variety of governments, . . . political transitions, and the intriguing history of a country still trying to find its identity."

In addition to writing on political, geographical, and biographical topics, Otfinoski has also put together several books to help young people in the day-to-day navigation of their lives. The subtitle of his *Kid's Guide to Money: Earning It, Saving It, Spending It, Growing It, Sharing It* covers the gamut of money management for the modern teen. And in *Speaking Up, Speaking Out: A Kid's Guide to Making Speeches, Oral Reports, and Conversation,* he helps teens deal with the hurdle of their first public speaking experiences: everything from small talk at parties to introductions between friends to classroom presentations. Calling the text "brisk [and] fluent," Stephanie Zvirin praised *Kid's Guide to Money* in her *Booklist* review, noting "It's about time to see [the discussion of charitable contributions] given some due." And in *School Library Journal,* Jonathan Betz-Zall maintained that "Otfinoski's friendly, low-key approach" made his book particularly effective in "encourag[ing kids] to behave responsibly."

Besides writing books for young people, Otfinoski is also a popular playwright, and since 1992, has produced and written for his own traveling theater company for young audiences, History Alive! The company performs one-person shows about people from American history at schools and libraries throughout Connecticut and New York. Recently, Otfinoski has begun writing books for adults on popular music. *The Golden Age of Novelty Songs,* published in 2000, traces the humorous history of novelty music in the rock era.

Asked where he gets his story ideas, Otfinoski explained to *SATA* that a major source for his fiction and plays has been the "vast treasure chest of literature, movies, and theatre that is our cultural heritage. I enjoy adapting famous works and sometimes spoofing them. In other cases I draw on my own childhood and experiences as a student. If there's a germ of truth and real experience in the story, it's always easier to write and make believable to others." In many cases, it is the publisher that determines the story. "A good instance of this is one of my favorite books, *The Screaming Grave.* The publisher called, gave me the title, a one-sentence description about a boy walking through a graveyard at night and hearing a scream, and asked me to write the book in about four weeks. From this meager beginning, I came up with a plot and characters and wrote the thing. My 'inspiration' was that if I didn't meet the deadline I might not get paid!"

Describing his life as a freelance writer for young people, Otfinoski told *SATA:* "Being a professional writer means being able to write well, quickly, and sometimes, on demand. Sometimes it's frustrating, but, all in all, I wouldn't want to be doing anything else."

Works Cited

Betz-Zall, Jonathan, review of *Kid's Guide to Money,* *School Library Journal,* June, 1996, pp. 145-50.
Bradburn, Frances, review of *Boris Yeltsin and the Rebirth of Russia, Booklist,* April 1, 1995, p. 1385.
Katka, Pat, review of *Boris Yeltsin and the Rebirth of Russia, School Library Journal,* March, 1995, p. 233.
Rosenfeld, Shelle, review of *Bulgaria, Booklist,* March 1, 1999, p. 1201.
Zvirin, Stephanie, review of *Kid's Guide to Money, Booklist,* April 1, 1996, p. 1360.

For More Information See

PERIODICALS

Booklist, January 1, 1997, p. 852.
School Library Journal, September, 1994, p. 228.

*   *   *

OWENS, Bryant 1968-

Personal

Born July 20, 1968, in Kingsport, TN; son of Keith (a quality control specialist for a chemical manufacturer) and Linda (a secretary for an insurance agency; maiden name, Conkin) Owens; married Karen Griffith (an educator), September 21, 1990; children: Logan. *Education:* East Tennessee State University, B.F.A., 1993. *Religion:* "Independent Christian." *Hobbies and other*

Bryant Owens and son, Logan

interests: Outdoor activities, including hiking, camping, and fishing.

Addresses

Home—3708 Bartlett Dr., Cookeville, TN 38506. *E-mail*—bkowens@multipro.com.

Career

McCloud Marketing Associates, Cookeville, TN, creative director, 1998-99. *Military service:* U.S. Army, 1986-88; served in Germany. U.S. Army Reserve, 1988-91; served in Saudi Arabia during the Persian Gulf conflict.

Illustrator

Julie Voudrie, *The Prayer of a Righteous Man,* Shepherd's Tales, 1995.

Voudrie, *Mighty Man vs. Almighty God,* Shepherd's Tales, 1995.

Voudrie, *Spying Out the Land,* Shepherd's Tales, 1995.

Voudrie, *Taking the Land,* Shepherd's Tales, 1995.

Thelma Kerns, *Flea Market Fleas from A to Z,* Overmountain Press (Johnson City, TN), 1998.

Kerns, *A Ducky Wedding,* Overmountain Press, 1999.

Kerns, *Don't Pat a Bee,* Overmountain Press, 2000.

P

PACKER, Kenneth L. 1946-

Personal

Born July 2, 1946, in Long Island City, NY; son of George (a civil engineer) and Annette (a social worker) Packer; married Carol J. Packer (a professional beauty consultant), December 19, 1971; children: Jason Packer, Ryan Packer. *Education:* State University College at Oneonta, B.S. in biology, 1968; New York State Emergency Medical Technician, 1970; Adelphi University, M.A. in Health Education, 1971; New York University, post graduate work in health education, 1971-80. *Politics:* Democrat. *Religion:* Jewish. *Hobbies and other interests:* Family genealogy, bird watching.

Addresses

Home—41 Cardinal Dr., Washingtonville, NY 10992. *E-mail*—Packer18@flash.net.

Career

Teacher, consultant, writer. Teacher, Rye High School, Rye, NY, 1968-70; White Plains High School, White Plains, NY, 1970-71; North Salem Public Schools, North Salem, NY, district health coordinator, 1971-73; Putnam/North Westchester Board of Cooperative Educational Services, Yorktown Heights, NY, regional health coordinator, 1973-76; Hudson Valley Health Systems Agency, Tuxedo, NY, director of public relations and health education planner, 1977-80; American Heart Association, Goshen, NY, executive director of Orange, Rockland, Sullivan chapter, 1980-82; self-employed health education consultant, 1982—; Scarsdale Public Schools, district health coordinator, 1984-87; Regional Health Education Center, Yorktown Heights, NY, regional AIDS education coordinator, 1987-96; The Golden Skate, Washingtonville, NY, general manager, 1993—; FlashNet Internet Service, independent distributor, 1999—. Russell Sage College and State University College at Brockport, adjunct assistant professor, 1975; Westchester Community College, adjunct assistant professor, 1976; Lehman College, program administrator, 1991-96.

Volunteer for American Heart Association, March of Dimes, Port Chester/Rye and North Salem Ambulance Corps, American Red Cross, New York State Education Dept. Health Syllabus Advisory Committee and Drug Education Curriculum Writing Committee, American Lung Association, Newburgh Health Advisory Council, HIV/AIDS Advisory Councils, and others. *Member:* American Public Health Association, American School Health Association, American Alliance for Health, Physical Education, Recreation, and Dance, New York State Federation of Professional Health Educators (state treasurer, 1975-77, 1986-95), Alpha Phi Omega (past president of State University College at Oneonta chapter and life member).

Awards, Honors

Richard Silverman Award, New York State Federation of Professional Health Educators, 1993.

Writings

(With J. Bower) *Let's Talk about Drugs, Alcohol, and Tobacco,* Allyn & Bacon, 1980.
(With J. Bower) *Let's Talk about Family Living,* Allyn & Bacon, 1980.
(With J. Bower) *Let's Talk about Mental Health,* Allyn & Bacon, 1980.
(With J. Bower) *Let's Talk about Health,* Allyn & Bacon, 1980.
Puberty: The Story of Growth and Change, illustrated by Anne Canevari Green, Franklin Watts, 1989.
HIV Infection: The Facts You Need to Know, Franklin Watts, 1998.

Editor of *Pulse Beats,* monthly newsletter, 1973-96; editor of *Hudson Valley Health,* a monthly newsletter, 1977-78; editor of *Packer Family Newsletter,* quarterly, 1997—. Articles have appeared in *Health Values: Achieving High Level Wellness, Health Education,* and *Journal of School Health.*

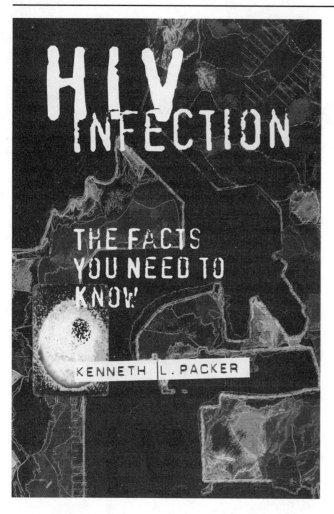

Kenneth L. Packer's in-depth discussion of human immunodeficiency virus opens with several chapters describing the virus, what it does to the body, and how it is passed from person to person, and then focuses on strategies for preventing the spread of HIV.

Sidelights

"Professionally, I have had an exciting career," Kenneth L. Packer told *SATA*. "I have taught health education in every grade level from kindergarten to graduate school. I have done health education planning, administration, and on the public health level, was an Executive Director of an American Heart Association Chapter. I have traveled and lectured on a variety of health topics in the U.S. and other countries. I have written three books and countless curriculum guides and government documents and reports.

"My goal has always been to help people grow and remain healthy. When AIDS became such a devastating disease, I knew that was where I had to direct my attention. My goal was to help prevent its spread through prevention. My book and workshops were designed to get individuals to practice the lowest level of risk-taking behavior that was acceptable to them.

"On a personal level, I believe that nothing is more important than family. I try to spend as much time as

possible with my children, supporting them whenever possible in anything they decide to do. One of my hobbies is family genealogy. I write a newsletter to family members all over the world, and keep records and charts of the family history.

"The rules I try to live by are: be proud of who you are, your heritage and religion; be true to your values; reach out to others, and do what is right and healthy."

Kenneth Packer has written two books on health topics for young people. In his first, *Puberty: The Story of Growth and Change,* the author offers a comprehensive examination of the changes in both boys' and girls' bodies as they mature into adults. "Unlike other books on the topic, Packer's goes into depth about the bodily changes during this time of life, chapter by chapter," remarked Mary Stucker in *Voice of Youth Advocates*. Stucker suggested the most likely use for the book would be as a resource for answering children's questions about their bodies. In *HIV Infection: The Facts You Need to Know,* "Packer succeeds in [his] mission to dispel myths and to communicate, honestly and intensely, the truth about the HIV virus," averred Jennifer A. Fakolt in *School Library Journal*. The book opens with several chapters describing the virus, what it does to the body, and how it is spread from person to person. This part of the book garnered praise for the depth of the author's knowledge, his use of up-to-date and even controversial research, and his clear explanation of complicated scientific terms. The second half of the book focuses on strategies for preventing the spread of HIV. Packer was praised for explicitly discussing how to avoid sexual situations rather than merely exhorting teens to abstain from sexual intercourse, and for providing information on condom use and cleaning and disinfecting needles for those teens who don't choose abstinence or who are drug addicted. *HIV Infection* concludes with a chapter each on surviving with HIV and on the AIDS quilt, lending "a final, human face to this deceptively complex, information-rich book," Frances Bradburn remarked in *Booklist*. "Readers will find vital information appropriate both for reports and personal elucidation," concluded Fakolt.

Works Cited

Bradburn, Frances, review of *HIV Infection, Booklist,* April 15, 1998, p. 1434.

Fakolt, Jennifer A., review of *HIV Infection, School Library Journal,* April, 1998, pp. 151-52.

Stucker, Mary, review of *Puberty, Voice of Youth Advocates,* February, 1990, p. 361.

For More Information See

PERIODICALS

School Library Journal, May, 1990, p. 133.*

PARSONS, Martin (Leslie) 1951-

Personal

Born November 12, 1951, in Reading, England; son of Donald Leslie and Doreen Lillian Olive (maiden name, Brown) Parsons; married Josephine Marina Redgrave (a schoolteacher), July 19, 1975; children: Kimiko Marina Parsons, Hannah Doreen Yamamura Parsons. *Education:* Borough Rd. College, University of London, Certificate of Education, 1973; University of Reading, Diploma of Youth Leadership, 1976; Open University, B.A., 1978; D.E.S., Certificate in Pastoral Management, 1979; University of Reading, Ph.D. in History, 1997. *Religion:* Church of England.

Addresses

Home—Oak Cottage, Southend Rd., Southend Bradfield, W. Berks. RG7 6E5. *Office*—School of Education, University of Reading, Woodlands Ave., Reading RG6 1HY. *Agent*—Paul Holness, DSM Publishing, The Studio, Denton, Peterborough. *E-mail*—m.1.parsons@reading.ac.uk.

Career

Educator, writer. Theale Green School, assistant history and geography teacher, 1973-75, head of lower school Humanities, 1975-83, deputy-head of lower school, 1977-83, head of house, 1983-89, head of lower school, 1989-90; Institute of Education, London, England, teacher-fellow (part-time), 1985-86; College of Preceptors, Theydon Bois, Norfolk, fellow, 1986—; University of Reading, lecturer in History method, 1990—; Royal Historical Society, fellow, 1999—; University of Reading, Deputy Head of the School of Education; 1999—. Consultant to Blakeway Productions, 1999, Imagine Productions, 1999 and Wayland Publishers, 1995; also consultant to the Isles of Scilly Oral History Project; has established an Evacuation Archive in Bulmershe Library. Has lectured extensively on oral history methods and the history of civilian evacuation, including public lectures at the Imperial War Museum and Cabinet War Rooms in London, and in New York City, Kansas, San Francisco, and Poland. *Member:* UCET Secondary National Committee, Executive Committee of the Evacuee Reunion Association (Chairman).

Writings

History GSCE Coursework Companion, Charles Letts & Co., 1989.

The Life and Times of St. Andrew's Church, Bradfield, Bradfield Publishing, 1994.

The Victorian Village, Wayland, 1995.

Insight into History: Second World War: Evacuation, Historical Association, 1996.

Essential History Dates, illustrated by Patrice Aggs, Hodder and Stoughton, 1996.

Victorian Society, Wayland, 1998.

Martin Parsons

The British Home Front: World War Two, Volumes 1 and 2, Wayland, 1998.

I'll Take That One!: Dispelling the Myths of Civilian Evacuation in the UK During World War Two, Beckett Karlson, 1998.

Waiting to Go Home!: A Collection of Evacuee Letters, Beckett Karlson, 1999.

(With P. Starns) *The Evacuation: The True Story,* DSM and BBC, 1999.

"HISTORY DETECTIVE" SERIES

History Detective Investigates Local History, Wayland, 1997.

History Detective Investigates Evacuation, illustrated by Richard Hook, Wayland, 1999.

History Detective Investigates Air Raids, Wayland, 1999.

History Detective Investigates Rationing, Wayland, 1999.

History Detective Investigates Women at War, Wayland, 1999.

JUVENILE NONFICTION

Foundation Skills History Book 1, Charles Letts & Co., 1986.

Foundation Skills History Book 2, Charles Letts & Co., 1986.

Foundation Skills History Book 3, Charles Letts & Co., 1987.

Articles have appeared in *The Living Earth,* edited by Niall Marriott and Roger Hammong, Hodder & Stoughton, 1994, and in the journals *Teaching History, Times Educational Supplement,* and *Working Paper* (University of Reading). Also author of a series of five programs broadcast on BBC Radio 4 on Civilian Evacuation in 1999. Editor, *Berkshire Old and New* (local history journal), 1995-97. Author of an interactive CD-ROM based on evacuation research; with J. Newitt and G. Walker, two multi-media packs including video and IT material, *The Victorians,* Volumes I and II, published in 1996 and 1998. A copy of a conference paper on oral history is on deposit in the Vietnam War Oral Archive. Producer of the historical videos *From Peckham to Publovaugh: The Journey of Two Ex-evacuee Brothers* and *A Handful of Miracles: The Memories of a Holocaust Survivor.*

Work in Progress

The Letters of Leo Schnitter: The Experience of a German POW, 1944-51, The Effect of Evacuation on the Infrastructure of War-Time Dorset, and with P. Starns, *Evacuation and Education: The Effect of Evacuation of Post-War Teaching,* all for Beckett Karlson. Also working on a video with Salisbury Cathedral, entitled *The Day in the Life of a Victorian Chorister.*

Sidelights

Martin Parsons is a well-regarded educator and historian whose writings are often intended for use as classroom guides. An example of this is his "History Detective" series, in which the methods and resources available to historians are clearly explained for young adults. In *History Detective Investigates Local History,* Parsons is "unfailingly practical," according to Clive Barnes in *Books for Keeps.* To that end, Parsons outlines how to select a topic of study in local history, what sources are available, and how to interpret the data gleaned from them. Reviewers praised Parsons's emphasis on selecting a well-defined topic of investigation (and his suggested examples of such), his thorough explanation of the types of resources and what information they offer, and how to record and present clearly the historian's findings. Throughout, "Martin Parsons's enthusiasm for his subject is well communicated," observed Peter Andrews in the *School Librarian.* Barnes concurred: "This is a lively and knowledgeable book that will be useful to secondary school children and to teachers."

Works Cited

Andrews, Peter, review of *History Detective Investigates Local History, School Librarian,* August, 1997, p. 153.
Barnes, Clive, review of *History Detective Investigates Local History, Books for Keeps,* July, 1997, p. 26.

PEGUERO, Leone

Personal

Born in Grafton, Australia; married Gerard Michael Pegeuro; children: Adrian Michael. *Education:* University of New South Wales, B.A., Dip.Ed., 1968. *Hobbies and other interests:* Reading, gardening, walking.

Addresses

Home and office—26 Allison Crescent, Elthan, 3095 Victoria, Australia. *E-mail*—peguero@bigpond.net.au.

Career

Has taught primary and secondary school for ten years; has taught part-time at a professional state institution in the diploma course, professional writing and editing. Owner, Peguero Enterprises Pty. Ltd., manuscript assessment service, 1989—.

Awards, Honors

Honour Book Award (Junior Readers), Children's Book Council of Australia, 1991, for *Mervyn's Revenge;* Notable Book (Picture Story Book Text), Children's Book Council of Australia, 1998, for *What a Goose!*

Leone Peguero

Writings

FOR YOUNG ADULTS

Poetry Speaks, (nonfiction), Heinemann (Melbourne), 1982, 1993.

The Rainbow Umbrella, illustrated by Gerard Peguero and Jan Neil, Greenhouse (Melbourne), 1987.

Stop, Look & Listen, (nonfiction), illustrated by Graham Base, Greenhouse, 1987.

I Made It Myself, (nonfiction), Greenhouse, 1987.

Names for Your Pet, (nonfiction), illustrated by Gerard Peguero, Snowball Educational & Peguero Publications (Melbourne), 1989.

Lionel and Amelia, illustrated by Gerard Peguero and Adrian Peguero, Martin Educational (Sydney), 1989, Mondo (New York), 1996.

Laurence's Water Wings, illustrated by David Pearson, Octopus (Melbourne), 1990.

Mervyn's Revenge, illustrated by Shirley Peters, Margaret Hamilton Books/Scholastic (Sydney), 1990.

Mervyn's Christmas, illustrated by Shirley Peters, Margaret Hamilton Books/Scholastic, 1992.

The Ragged Old Bear, illustrated by Donna Gynell, Era (Adelaide), 1992.

The Mystery of the Missing Garden Gnome, Margaret Hamilton Books/Scholastic, 1994.

Mervyn's Nightmare, illustrated by Shirley Peters, Margaret Hamilton Books/Scholastic, 1994.

Mystery of the Silver Animals, illustrated by Amanda Graham, Era, 1996.

What a Goose!, illustrated by Simone Kennedy, Era, 1997.

Beat Street Mysteries, Books 1 & 2, illustrated by Shirley Peters, Margaret Hamilton Books/Scholastic, 1997.

Beach Dog, Barrie Publishing, 1998.

Beat Street Mysteries, Books 3 & 4, illustrated by Shirley Peters, Margaret Hamilton Books/Scholastic, 1998.

Mrs. Wilkinson's Chooks, illustrated by Mike Spoor, Random House (Sydney), 1999.

Sails & Snails, Macmillan Education (Melbourne), 1999.

The Great Family Talent, Barrie Education (Melbourne), 1999.

Bad Boy Bud, Barrie Education, 1999.

TEXTBOOKS

Basic English Skills, Longman Cheshire (Melbourne), 1978.

Word Works: Building Spelling and Word Skills, Books 1-4, Lloyd O'Neil (Melbourne), 1979, Macmillan Educational (Melbourne), 1995.

Language Link-Up, Books 1 & 2, Heinemann, 1986.

Work in Progress: *Crafting and Redrafting Your Writing,* Oxford University Press (Melbourne), 1994.

GENERAL NONFICTION

Victorian Rider, Melbourne Road Traffic Authority, 1983.

Victorian Traffic Handbook, Melbourne Road Traffic Authority, 1985.

Locker Hooking: An Introduction to the Craft, Edward Arnold (Melbourne), 1986, new edition titled *Creative Locker Hooking,* illustrated by Gerard Peguero, Kangaroo Press/Simon & Schuster Australia (Sydney), 1990, Lacis Publication (Berkeley, CA), 1998.

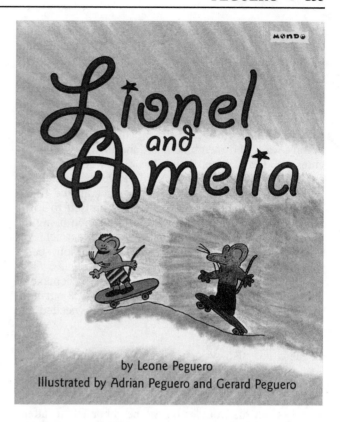

In Peguero's whimsical picture book, two mice of very different temperaments find friendship while maintaining their own opinions and personalities. (Cover illustration by Adrian and Gerard Peguero.)

Wheels New Drivers Guide, Australian Consolidate Press (Sydney), 1988.

Victorian New Drivers Guide, Five Mile Press (Melbourne), 1992.

Mervyn's Revenge and *The Ragged Old Bear* are available as audio books. Also author of newspaper and magazine articles.

Work in Progress

Numerous children's books, also working on a novel for adults.

Sidelights

Leone Peguero told *SATA:* "I never at any time set out to 'become' a writer, so I'm not entirely sure how it happened. Storytelling is simply a vital part of how I think and communicating those thoughts is an important part of who I am. An equally important part is telling those stories with humour. I don't see that aspect as an embellishment, rather as an essential and healing part of dealing with who we are."

Leone Peguero is a prolific Australian author of children's picture books. Only a few of her stories have been made available to audiences outside her homeland, however. Among these are one of her first, *Lionel and Amelia,* which tells the story of a friendship that blossoms between two mice, one tidy, the other unkempt and disorganized, who eventually learn to take on some of the best aspects of each other's personality while remaining true to him or herself. One of Peguero's most successful efforts, *The Ragged Old Bear,* won an award in Australia. In this story, a little girl visiting her grandmother adopts the worn-out old teddy bear of the title, which she finds in a spare bedroom. Josi and her granny wash and mend the bear, and then Josi lovingly cares for it, and takes it with her everywhere she goes, for she finds it much more comfortable than her fancy new toys. The story also takes into account the bear's feelings of inadequacy as he compares himself to Josi's other toys, and pride and joy the bear takes in being the chosen one. "Leone Peguero's economical text achieves the right balance of emotional feeling without being maudlin," observed Mandy Cheetham in *Magpies.* "This is not just a story about resurrection and acceptance," continued Cheetham, "rather Bear's doubts about himself personify that desire we all have to be needed and loved."

Peguero has also written a series of humorous stories featuring a self-satisfied cat named Mervyn. In *Mervyn's Revenge,* Peguero imagines a feline who feels left out when his family takes off on vacation without him, and so takes out his troubles on the neighbor left to attend him. Then, when the family returns, he strives for his ultimate revenge by running away, but when he overhears the family deciding to adopt two kittens to replace him, he shows his face again. Intended for first readers, the book contains numerous black-and-white illustrations. "There is a good balance of text and illustrations, and both provide humour and gentle irony," observed Margot Tyrrell in *Magpies.*

In *What a Goose!,* another award-winning effort, Peguero's narrative was praised for its simple language dotted with the kind of intriguing vocabulary especially appealing to the read-aloud audience, according to reviewers, a compliment extended to several of the author's earlier stories. In *What a Goose!,* Gwendolyne the goose is given the job of guarding Hilltop Farm from a local fox, and with some difficulties, succeeds. "Above all," wrote Margaret Mallett concluding her laudatory review in *School Librarian,* "children will find this story satisfying because it is a powerful tale of how a young creature achieves competence after some false starts."

Works Cited

Cheetham, Mandy, review of *The Ragged Old Bear, Magpies,* September, 1992, p. 4.
Mallett, Margaret, review of *What a Goose!, School Librarian,* August, 1997, p. 132.
Tyrrell, Margot, review of *Mervyn's Revenge, Magpies,* May, 1991, p. 21.

For More Information See

PERIODICALS

Booklist, January 1, 1997, p. 870.
Junior Bookshelf, August, 1991, p. 163; April, 1993, p. 60.*

*   *   *

PITA
See RENDON, Maria

R

REECE, Colleen L. 1935-
(Connie Loraine, Gary Dale)

Personal

Born October 1, 1935, in Darrington, WA; daughter of William E. (a woodsman) and Pearl (a teacher; maiden name, Towne) Reece. *Education:* Attended Everett College, Washington Business College, Everett Community College, and Vancouver (Washington) Community College, and took a medical receptionist course. *Religion:* Christian. *Hobbies and other interests:* Reading, walking, growing roses.

Addresses

E-mail—colleenreece@juno.com.

Career

Secretary in Washington state schools in Darrington and Vancouver, WA, 1952-71, for the Veterans Administration Hospital in Vancouver, 1971-73, for Bonneville Power, in Vancouver, 1973-78; self-employed author, teacher, and speaker, 1978—. Creative writing instructor, for Writer's Digest School for 15 years, for Green River Community College, Auburn, WA, for 15 years, and for Auburn Senior Center. Spent more than twenty years as a camp counselor, and taught church and Bible school.

Awards, Honors

Favorite Author, *Heartsong Presents* Christian Book Club, 1993, 1994; first author inducted into *Heartsong* Hall of Fame; Employee of the Year, Bonneville Power Administration.

Writings

FOR YOUNG ADULTS

It's Okay, Mom, McCormick-Mathers, 1979.
Long Way Home, Scholastic, 1981.
The Outsider, illustrated by Furan Illustrators, Crestwood House (Mankato, MN), 1981.
The Summer of Peter and Pam, Baker Books, 1982.
Mark of Our Moccasins, Council for Indian Education, 1982.
Thank You, illustrated by Gwen Connelly, Child's World (Elgin, IL), 1982.
Saying Thank You, Child's World, 1982.
What?, illustrated by Lois Axeman, Children's Press (Chicago, IL), 1983.
My First Halloween Book, illustrated by Pam Peltier, Children's Press, 1984.
My First Christmas Book, illustrated by Linda Hohag, Children's Press, 1984.
(With Jane Buerger) *What Was It Before It Was Ice Cream?,* illustrated by Lois Axeman, Child's World, 1985.
Last Page in the Diary, Review and Herald (Washington, DC), 1986.
Comrades of the Trail, Review and Herald, 1986.
Summer of Fear, Pacific Press (Boise, ID), 1986.
More than Confetti, Pacific Press, 1987.
Julie's Three Special Letters, Pacific Press, 1987.
Give Me a Break, Review and Herald, 1988.
Escape from Fear, Review and Herald, 1988.
A Gold Star for Eric, illustrated by Darrel Tank, Pacific Press, 1989.
Plain, Plain Melissa Jane, Review and Herald (Washington, DC), 1990.
P.K. the Great, Review and Herald, 1990.
JumpStart!, Review and Herald, 1990.
The Mysterious Treadle Machine, Autumn House, 1991.
Interrupted Flight and Delayed Dream, Barbour (Uhrichsville, OH), 1992.
Prudence of Plymouth Plantation, Barbour, 1994.
Mike, Review and Herald, 1995.
Heidi, a Retelling, Barbour, 1995.
Pollyanna, a Retelling, Barbour, 1995.
Pollyanna Comes Home, Barbour, 1995.
Pollyanna Plays the Game, Barbour, 1995.
Pocahontas, Barbour, 1995.
Nature Trilogy 1: Secrets of the Forest, Review and Herald, 1997.

Juli Scott Super Sleuth Book 1

Mysterious Monday

Colleen L. Reece

Sophomore Juli Scott is overwhelmed by the death of her policeman father and finds herself and a friend at her new school involved in a surprising adventure in the first installment of Colleen L. Reece's "Juli Scott Super Sleuth" series.

Plymouth Pioneers, Chelsea (Philadelphia, PA), 1998.
The Mayflower Adventure, Chelsea, 1998.
Little Women, a Retelling, Barbour, 1998.
Nature Trilogy 2: Secrets of the Canyon, Review and Herald, 1999.
Nature Trilogy 3: Secrets of the Sea, Review and Herald, 2000.

"JULI SCOTT SUPER SLEUTH" SERIES

Mysterious Monday, Barbour, 1997.
Trouble on Tuesday, Barbour, 1997.
Wednesday Witness, Barbour, 1998.
Thursday Trials, Barbour, 1998.
Friday Flight, Barbour, 1998.
Saturday Scare, Barbour, 1998.

OTHER

The Unknown Witnesses, Herald (Independence, MO), 1974.
In Search of Twilight, Thorndike, 1977.
A Girl Called Cricket, Kearny, 1979.
Dream Stories I, Dreams Unlimited, 1981.

The Other Nine, Herald, 1981.
The Calling of Elizabeth Courtland, Moody, 1982.
Honor Bound, Moody (Chicago, IL), 1983.
Sanctuary, Herald, 1983.
Cherish: A Love Story, Moody, 1983.
The Ninety and Nine, Herald, 1984.
Above the Winds of Change, Herald, 1987.
The Torchbearer, Herald, 1988.
(With Albert B. Towns) *Crows' Nests and Mirrors,* Barbour, 1994.
Writing Smarter, Not Harder: The Workbook Way, Kaleidoscope (Puyallup, WA), 1995.
(With Anita Corrine Donihue) *Apples for a Teacher,* Barbour, 1996.
Women of the Bible, Barbour, 1996.
Everlasting Melody, Macmillan, 1996.
Belated Follower, Barbour, 1996.
(With Anica C. Donihue) *Joy to the World,* Barbour, 1996.
Alpine Meadows Nurse, Thorndike, 1997.
Life 101, Barbour, 1997.
Bible Promise Book for Couples, Barbour, 1997.
(With Anita Corrine Donihue) *A Teacher's Heart,* Barbour, 1998.
Nurse Julie's Sacrifice, Thorndike (Thorndike, ME), 1998.
Heritage of Nurse O'Hara, Thorndike, 1999.
(With Julie Reece-DeMarco) *Finding Your Way: Words of Wisdom for the Graduate,* Barbour, 1999.

Books and stories have been published in Australia, Brazil, Denmark, England, Finland, Italy, Indonesia, and Sweden. Contributor to *Historical Collection,* Barbour, 1996, *Christmas Treasures,* Barbour, 1996, *An Old-Fashioned Christmas,* Barbour, 1997, *A Nostalgic Noel,* Barbour, 1998, and *Winter Wishes,* Barbour, 1999. Articles and stories have appeared in *National Research Bureau, Writer's Digest, Pen Woman, ByLine, Christian Communicator, Mature, Living, Ideals, Catholic Digest, 40+, Youth Leader, Cornerstone Connections, Advance, Freeway, Focus on the Family, Guideposts, R-A-D-A-R,* and *Reader's Digest.*

Work in Progress

A Christmas gift book, a weekly devotional book, an inspirational novel.

Sidelights

Colleen L. Reece told *SATA* that her reason for writing is "to provide books that hold attention from the first through the last paragraph with well-crafted plots, characters, and settings; not sex, violence or profanity. Authors need not rely on such to sell, just work harder!" Reece describes her age as "presently sixty-three years old on the outside, any age I choose to be on the inside, which is why I can write books for pre-school through senior adult." Reece was taught to read by her school-teacher mother, by the light of a kerosene lamp. Her mother taught all eight grades in a one-room school where Reece later lived for thirty-four years. Reece learned many "curious nature facts" at the knee of her father, a woodsman, and this information formed the basis for her nature trilogy, *Secrets of the Forest, Secrets of the Canyon,* and *Secrets of the Sea.*

Reece "always dreamed of writing books," though this was "not a valid dream for Darrington," where she was raised, in Washington state. At age eleven, the future author won a bicycle by writing to a radio giveaway, and graduated from high school at age sixteen as class valedictorian. Reece completed her first book-length project, a young adult mystery, when she was seventeen. It was "not publishable, but taught me I could complete a long project. This whetted my desire to one day write an inspirational mystery series, which I later did," citing her "Juli Scott Super Sleuth" series published by Barbour.

Since leaving government service in 1977, where she had worked as a secretary for twenty-five years, Reece has supported herself with her writing and speaking engagements. "The ability to be prolific without sacrificing quality comes from my unique, innovative 'prewrite,' don't rewrite method shared in *Writing Smarter, Not Harder: The Workbook Way.* It helped me sell over one hundred books in twenty years," Reece told *SATA.**

*   *   *

REED, Kit
(Kit Craig, Shelley Hyde)

Personal

Daughter of John Rich (a lieutenant commander in the United States Navy) and Lillian (Hyde) Craig; married Joseph Wayne Reed, Jr. (a writer, painter, printmaker, and professor), December 10, 1955; children: Joseph McKean, John Craig, Katherine Hyde. *Education:* College of Notre Dame of Maryland, B.A., 1954.

Addresses

Home—45 Lawn Ave., Middletown, CT 06457. *Agent*—Richard Pine, Arthur Pine Associates, Suite 417, 250 West 57th St., New York, NY 10019.

Career

St. Petersburg Times, St. Petersburg, FL, reporter and television editor, 1954-55; *Hamden Chronicle,* Hamden, CT, reporter, 1956; *New Haven Register,* New Haven, CT, reporter, 1956-59. Book reviewer for *New Haven Register* and *St. Petersburg Times;* freelance author of fiction. Visiting writer in India, 1974; Wesleyan University, Middletown, CT, visiting professor of English, then adjunct professor of English, 1974—. American Coordinator, Indo-U.S. writers exchange, 1990-92. *Member:* Writers Guild, PEN, National Book Critics Circle (board member, 1991-95).

Awards, Honors

Named New England Newspaper Woman of the Year, New England Women's Press Association, 1958 and

Kit Reed

1959; Abraham Woursell Foundation literary grant, 1965-70; Guggenheim fellowships, 1964-65 and 1968; Rockefeller fellow, Aspen Institute, 1976; "Best Books for Young Adults" list, American Library Association, 1979, for *The Ballad of T. Rantula;* Best Catholic Short Story of the Year Award, Catholic Press Association; short-listed for the James Tiptree, Jr. Award, James Tiptree, Jr. Literary Award Council, 1995, for *Little Sisters of the Apocalypse,* and 1998, for "Bridge of Bigfoot."

Writings

FOR YOUNG ADULTS

Mother Isn't Dead, She's Only Sleeping, Houghton, 1961.
The Better Part, Farrar, Straus, 1967.
The Killer Mice (science fiction), Gollancz (London, England), 1976.
The Ballad of T. Rantula: A Novel, Little, Brown, 1979.

FOR ADULTS

At War as Children, Farrar, Straus, 1964.
Armed Camps (science fiction), Faber & Faber (London, England), 1969, Dutton, 1970.
Cry of the Daughter: A Novel, Dutton, 1971.
Tiger Rag, Dutton, 1973.
Captain Grownup: A Novel, Dutton, 1976.
Magic Time (science fiction), Berkley, 1980.
(Under pseudonym Shelley Hyde) *Blood Fever* (science fiction), Pocket, 1982.
Fort Privilege (science fiction), Doubleday, 1985.
Catholic Girls: A Novel, Donald I. Fine, 1987.
(As Kit Craig) *Gone,* Little, Brown, 1992.

(As Kit Craig) *Twice Burned: A Novel,* Little, Brown, 1993.

Little Sister of the Apocalypse (science fiction), Fiction Collective Two (Boulder, CO), 1994.

J. Eden: A Novel, University Press of New England (Hannover, NH), 1996.

At Expectations: A Novel, Forge Books (New York, NY), 2000.

SHORT STORIES

Mister Da V. and Other Stories (science fiction), Faber & Faber, 1967, Berkley, 1973.

Other Stories and ... The Attack of the Giant Baby (science fiction), Berkley, 1981.

The Revenge of the Senior Citizens Plus a Short Story Collection (science fiction novella and sixteen stories), Doubleday, 1986.

Thief of Lives: Stories, University of Missouri Press (Colombia), 1992.

Weird Women, Wired Women, University Press of New England, 1998.

Seven for the Apocalypse, University Press of New England, 1999.

OTHER

When We Dream (for children), illustrated by Yutaka Sugita, first published in 1965, first English language edition, Hawthorne (New York City), 1966.

(Compiler) *Fat* (anthology), Bobbs-Merrill, 1974.

The Bathyscaphe (radio play), National Public Radio, 1979.

(Under pseudonym Shelley Hyde) *The Savage Stain,* Pocket, 1982.

Story First: The Writer as Insider (textbook; contains exercises by husband, Joseph W. Reed), Prentice-Hall, NJ), 1982, revised edition published as *Mastering Fiction Writing,* Writer's Digest, 1991.

Revision, Writer's Digest, 1989.

Contributor of short stories to more than sixty anthologies in the United States, Great Britain, Italy, and France, including *Winter's Tales,* Macmillan. Contributor of short stories and articles to periodicals, including *Transatlantic Review, Cosmopolitan, Ladies' Home Journal, Magazine of Fantasy and Science Fiction, Argosy, Fiction, Town, Seventeen* and *Voice Literary Supplement.* Manuscript collection held at Beinecke Library, Yale University, New Haven, CT.

Sidelights

Kit Reed's publications are of interest to both juveniles and older readers. As the author told *SATA,* "Although I write primarily for adult readers, a great many teens seem to wander into my novels, perhaps because I do not believe there is an enormous difference between adults and young people." Reed's writing falls into a variety of categories. "Some of her stories are realistic, some impressionistic, some fantasy, some science fiction," indicated C. W. Sullivan III in the *St. James Guide to Science Fiction Writers.* "Reed does not write hard, or technologically oriented, science fiction," explained Sullivan. Instead, "Reed seems to deal primarily with the people and to use the science fiction elements as another

writer might use a car or truck—as a detail necessary to the story .... The two main themes of her work [are] the impact of technology on people's lives and the plight of senior citizens." Sullivan, who noted that "one of [Reed's] strongest pieces of social criticism is 'Golden Acres,' about a home for the elderly," commented that in "the final analysis, it is Reed's characters that carry her fiction—science fiction, fantasy, or mainstream. To be sure, the other aspects of her writing are not found wanting, but her characters—especially the women struggling to find themselves in an indifferent or hostile society, or struggling against various institutions—remain in the reader's mind."

Reed described her genre-crossing writing this way: "Most people write what they want to read. In my case this mean a lot of early science fiction because, starting with the Oz books, I loved stories that departed from reality. Now I am more interested in what seems real.

Four families from New York share a summer at a New England farmhouse, scrutinizing and reassessing their personal histories and goals and trying to reconnect their tenuous relationships. (Cover illustration by Judith Lerner.)

Sometimes I go for reality in a completely everyday way, as in *Captain Grownup* and *The Ballad of T. Rantula,* and at other times as in *Magic Time,* from a position halfway up the wall. The work that pleases me most combines both elements."

The Ballad of T. Rantula: A Novel, which was named to the "Best Books for Young Adults" list by the American Library Association, deals with a thirteen-year-old hero's attempts to come to terms with the fact of his parents' divorce. Making matters worse, Futch's best friend dies of anorexia nervosa, a condition brought on by the young man's feelings of neglect by his parents. Futch perseveres, however, and though his future is uncertain at the end of the novel, readers understand that he will endure. According to Anne Tyler in the *New York Times Book Review,* the character is "a stable, honest, earnest human being, the living center of a richly satisfying book." In "an era rampant with novels on marital bust-ups, Kit Reed's comes as refreshingly different, bringing with it a new point of view," claimed a *West Coast Review of Books* critic. "Told through the eyes of young Fred (Futch) during his last year at elementary school, the narrative avoids the cute and the obvious, rather it is brilliantly, uncannily accurate."

Reed also wrote a second novel about a teen coming of age, but this time from a female perspective. *The Better Part* features Mart Ewald, a young girl who lives with her father, the superintendent of a state correctional facility for girls. Taking his job personally, Mr. Ewald devotes all of his time trying to reform the young women assigned to him, all the while alienating his own daughter. Wishing to attract his attention, Mart escapes the institution with one of the most troubled inmates. Once on the mean streets, however, Mart finally understands what her father's work is all about. Writing in *Kirkus Reviews,* a critic called the novel "spunky, touching, and marvelously alive," while a contributor to *Publishers Weekly* deemed the book "on the whole quite successful, most notably so in its portrayal of Mart and her frustrations."

Captain Grownup: A Novel is an adult novel about a newspaper reporter experiencing a mid-life crisis. After his wife kicks him out of their house, he gives up his job to become an English teacher in a small town high school. Perceiving himself as a person who can help bring out young talent, he becomes platonically involved with a female student. A reviewer for *Booklist* noted that the characters' unsuccessful attempts at changing the course of their lives make "a convincing, often wildly amusing narrative."

During the 1990s Reed released a number of works, including her 1996 *J. Eden: A Novel,* a title that "shows us the extent to which people can hurt one another and still be loved and go on," related Molly E. Rauch in the *Nation.* The "cleverly assembled and often insightful" story portrays "four New York families shar[ing] a milestone summer in a New England country farmhouse," related a *Publishers Weekly* critic who complimented Reed's dialogue but noted that "some readers

WEIRD WOMEN, WIRED WOMEN

K I T   R E E D

FOREWORD BY CONNIE WILLIS

Reed's collection of nineteen short stories focuses on women, particularly their mother-daughter relationships and their roles in an American male-dominated society. (Cover illustration by Joseph Reed.)

may find that the bulk of the novel meanders too slowly through predictable lives." Calling *J. Eden* the "most ambitious ... [and] slowest" novel by Reed, a *Kirkus Reviews* writer stated that the tale's "suspense hangs on the question of who's sleeping with whom and what everyone is thinking about aging, parenthood, mortality, etc." Telling the story from ten different viewpoints "gets us through in one piece," determined Rauch, who believed that "the sustained hatred and doubt would be devastating otherwise." *Entertainment Weekly* critic Suzanne Ruta similarly praised Reed for getting her readers to empathize with the story's "self-absorbed boomers and their desperately precocious offspring."

In 1998, Reed published *Weird Women, Wired Women,* a gathering of nineteen short stories focusing on women—particularly their mother-daughter relationships and their roles in an American male-dominated society. "Covering more than thirty years of her darkly speculative fiction," in the collection, *Weird Women, Wired Women* "offers a definitive, indispensable sampling of Reed in top form," reported a *Kirkus Reviews* contributor. "Anger, resentment, love, and obligation blur in tales that blend pathos and irony with the downright weird," summarized *Library Journal* contributor Eleanor J. Bader. Crediting the "unique blend of humor" of this "versatile" and "prolific" author, *Booklist* reviewer Ted Leventhal believed the collection of "humorous, ironic prose ... [in] surreal short stories" was undoubtedly "a worthwhile read." The "crisp and to the point" text in the "impressive ... [but] somewhat cold" collection contains "unrelenting obsessiveness," determined a *Publishers Weekly* reviewer who concluded that the "lack of contrast to offset the prevailing darkness becomes unnerving." In contrast, Bader judged the perspectives Reed presents to be "refreshing."

Reed once told *SATA:* "Adults are bigger, sometimes smarter, but all the old curiosities and passions that propelled us as children propel us now, and if we seem more *suave,* it's because we've gotten better at hiding those feelings."

Works Cited

Bader, Eleanor J., review of *Weird Women, Wired Women, Library Journal,* February 1, 1998, p. 115.
Review of *The Ballad of T. Rantula: A Novel, West Coast Review of Books,* September, 1979.
Review of *The Better Part, Kirkus Reviews,* February 15, 1967, p. 224.
Review of *The Better Part, Publishers Weekly,* February 27, 1967, p. 100.
Review of *Captain Grownup: A Novel, Booklist,* June 15, 1976, p. 1452.
Review of *J. Eden: A Novel, Kirkus Reviews,* January 15, 1996, p. 94.
Review of *J. Eden: A Novel, Publishers Weekly,* December 18, 1995, p. 39.
Leventhal, Ted, review of *Weird Women, Wired Women, Booklist,* March 15, 1998, p. 1203.
Rauch, Molly E., review of *J. Eden: A Novel, Nation,* April 22, 1990, p. 36.
Ruta, Suzanne, review of *J. Eden: A Novel, Entertainment Weekly,* March 15, 1996, p. 59.
Sullivan, C. W., III, "Kit Reed," *St. James Guide to Science Fiction Writers,* 4th edition, St. James, 1996.
Tyler, Anne, review of *The Ballad of T. Rantula: A Novel, New York Times Book Review,* June 17, 1979.
Review of *Weird Women, Wired Women, Kirkus Reviews,* February 1, 1998, p. 143-44.
Review of *Weird Women, Wired Women, Publishers Weekly,* February 9, 1998, p. 75.

For More Information See

PERIODICALS

Best Sellers, July 1, 1970; April 1, 1971.
Booklist, June 1, 1986.
Books and Bookmen, March, 1968.
Book World, July 5, 1970.
Kirkus Reviews, July 15, 1987; September 1, 1992; July 1, 1994.
Library Journal, August, 1987; October 15, 1992.
Listener, September 18, 1969.
Locus, May, 1989; November, 1993.
Los Angeles Times Book Review, April 21, 1996.
New York Times, April 12, 1976.
New York Times Book Review, March 8, 1964; July 4, 1976; March 8, 1981; November 1, 1987; January 17, 1993; April 21, 1996.
Observer, October 5, 1969.
Publishers Weekly, July 24, 1987; August 17, 1992; July 25, 1994.
School Library Journal, January, 1992.
Sewanee Review, July, 1990; October, 1992.
Times Literary Supplement, October 16, 1969.
Voice of Youth Advocates, August, 1985; August, 1986.
Washington Post Book World, August 30, 1981; April 28, 1985; May 25, 1986.
Women's Review of Books, July, 1995.

*   *   *

RENDON, Maria 1965-
(Pita)

Personal

Born May 3, 1965, in Mexico City, Mexico; daughter of Enrique (an engineer) and Guadalupe Aguila (a homemaker; maiden name, Gomez) Rendon; married Dwight Harmon, May 8, 1993 (deceased). *Education:* Art Center College of Design, Pasadena, CA, B.F.A. (with honors), 1992. *Hobbies and other interests:* Music, art, nature.

Addresses

Home—1142 North Hudson Ave., Pasadena, CA 91104. *E-mail*—mariarendon@mindspring.com.

Career

Illustrator. Art Center College of Design, Pasadena, CA, instructor, 1997-99. Work represented at shows, colleges, and galleries, including Random Gallery and Riverside Community College. *Member:* Society of Illustrators of Los Angeles.

Awards, Honors

Gold, silver, and bronze awards from Society of Illustrators of Los Angeles, for work submitted to three-dimensional illustration awards show.

Illustrator

Brian Swann, *Touching the Distance: Native American Riddle-Poems* (for children), Harcourt, 1998.

Illustrator of book covers and corporate communications, such as brochures and annual reports. Contributor of illustrations to periodicals, including *Business Week, Discover, Harper's, Money, Worth,* and *Wall Street Journal.* Some work appears under the pseudonym Pita.

Using mixed-media constructions, Maria Rendon illustrated Brian Swann's **Touching the Distance,** *a collection of Native American riddles, some told in rhyme and revealed through Rendon's artistic creations.*

Sidelights

Maria Rendon told *SATA:* "I see both illustration and personal work as an opportunity to explore new ways of communicating visually. I put together all kinds of materials (wood, metals, glass, paint, found objects, crafted objects) to convey the meaning in the work. In addition, I find myself using openings of 'windows' to contain, shelter, and give importance to ideas.

"I steal from both personal work and illustration, each to feed the other. In illustration, deadlines often force me to work faster, and that results in some creative solutions that I wouldn't have thought of otherwise. That expands the language that I can use in both areas of my work. Likewise, keeping a hand in a personal body of work influences me to put more of myself into my illustrations.

"What it comes down to is—I love making objects. I love getting an idea in my head and, through many types of exploration, creating an object out of it."

For More Information See

PERIODICALS

Booklist, May 15, 1998, p. 1625.
School Library Journal, April, 1998, p. 154.

RICHARDSON, Sandy 1949-

Personal

Born December 8, 1949, in Sumter, SC; daughter of Eugene C. and Suzanne (Matthews) Funderbarke; married Phillip C. Richardson (landscape and nursery business owner), November 9, 1974; children: Christy Richardson, Jay Richardson. *Education:* University of South Carolina, B.A. in Interdisciplinary Studies (Honors), 1996.

Addresses

Home and office—19 Courtney Ct., Sumter, SC 29154. *E-mail*—phrichardson@infoave.net.

Career

Central Carolina Technical College, Sumter, SC, English instructor, 1997—; University of South Carolina-Sumter, assistant to gallery director. Chair and co-chair of the Writer's Forum sponsored by Sumter Arts Commission. Former teacher of kindergarten and middle grades. Lecturer and speaker at various colleges and libraries in South Carolina, Georgia, Alabama, and Tennessee. *Member:* Society of Children's Book Writers and Illustrators, South Carolina Artists-in-Residence (juried member).

Sandy Richardson

Awards, Honors

Short story "The Girl Who Ate Chicken Feet" won first prize in a contest sponsored by Sandhill at the University of South Carolina in 1995; Bank Street College Best of Children's Books List, 1999, for *The Girl Who Ate Chicken Feet.*

Writings

The Girl Who Ate Chicken Feet, Dial, 1998.
(Fiction editor and contributor) *Literature, Reading, Reacting, Writing, 4th Edition Instructors' Manual,* Harcourt/Brace, 1999.

Short story has appeared in the *Story Telling Magazine,* and articles have been published in *The Bottom Line* (newspaper for University South Carolina-Sumter).

Work in Progress

With Jayne DuBose Fort, *Hot Babes and Cool Dudes: The Turtles of Caretta Island;* a sequel to *The Girl Who Ate Chicken Feet;* a picture book, *The Children of Sandy Island.* Research into the paintings of Anne Worsham Richardson.

Sidelights

Sandy Richardson told *SATA:* "Returning to college to study creative writing was the best thing I ever did for myself. It provided me the opportunity to study with professional writers such as William Price Fox, Kwame Dawes, and Dinah Johnson—an opportunity that would not have been available to me otherwise. In fact, for students who don't believe their college assignments are of any 'true' value, please read on. It was in an Adolescent Literature class that I got my big break! I wrote five short stories as a creative project, turned them in to my professor, Dr. Dinah Johnson, and when she returned the stories, she handed me my dream—an introduction to a New York editor! Dial Books for Young Readers published those stories and four others in *The Girl Who Ate Chicken Feet!* Later, another professor, Dr. Laura M. Zaidman, offered me the opportunity to explore academic writing and editing, which led to additional publishing credits.

"College not only furnished mentors, but also it taught me the discipline I needed to pursue a writing career. It's not easy, but the trick is to keep at it! Read, read, read— write, write, write! Stay in contact with people who write. Don't pass up opportunities to meet and learn from others. Follow your passions; immerse yourself in your craft. The doors will open."

Sandy Richardson's first short stories are collected in *The Girl Who Ate Chicken Feet,* a novel for the middle grades that reviewers praised for its likeable heroine and its genuine feel of a small Southern town in the early 1960s. Sissy is ten years old when the book begins. She becomes older as the chapters progress, turning twelve and fourteen. As she ages, the nature of her problems changes from sibling rivalry and a cousin who constantly gets her into trouble to a growing recognition of issues of race and class that the adults in her small Southern town would prefer not to discuss. Richardson's sensitive treatment of the episode in which Sissy's beloved black housekeeper leaves to join the burgeoning civil rights movement in Alabama inspired some reviewers to recommend *The Girl Who Ate Chicken Feet* as additional reading in classrooms studying the history of the civil rights movement in the United States. And while not all readers will be familiar with Richardson's historical or geographical setting, observed Gerry Larson in *School Library Journal,* "they will find familiarity, humor, and insight in Sissy's early adolescent anxieties, desires, decisions, and discoveries."

"The many charming moments in Richardson's inaugural novel read more like a collection of southern tall tales, with 10-year-old Sissy at the center," observed a reviewer in *Publishers Weekly.* Similarly, Jean Westmoore, a reviewer for the *Buffalo News,* compared Sissy to Scout in Harper Lee's classic *To Kill a Mockingbird* for her innate ability to raise grown-up hackles and get into trouble. For these reasons, *Booklist* reviewer Lauren Peterson predicted that "Richardson's debut novel should find a huge audience with middle-grade girls, who will strongly identify with budding teen Sissy." For others, it is the strongly Southern flavor of the setting and characters that makes *The Girl Who Ate Chicken Feet* a worthwhile addition to the literature.

Works Cited

Review of *The Girl Who Ate Chicken Feet, Publishers Weekly,* May 4, 1998, p. 214.
Larson, Gerry, review of *The Girl Who Ate Chicken Feet, School Library Journal,* March, 1998, p. 218.
Peterson, Lauren, review of *The Girl Who Ate Chicken Feet, Booklist,* March 1, 1998, p. 1134.
Westmoore, Jean, review of *The Girl Who Ate Chicken Feet, Buffalo News,* May 10, 1998, p. 5F.

For More Information See

PERIODICALS

Kirkus Reviews, January 1, 1998, p. 61.
New Advocate, Fall, 1998.*

*   *   *

RIVERS, Elfrida
See BRADLEY, Marion Zimmer

ROOP, Connie
See ROOP, Constance (Betzer)

*　　　*　　　*

ROOP, Constance (Betzer) 1951- (Connie Roop)

Personal

Born June 18, 1951, in Elkhorn, WI; daughter of Robert Sterling (a funeral director) and Marjorie (a homemaker; maiden name, Gary) Betzer; married Peter G. Roop (an educator and author), August 4, 1973; children: Sterling Gray, Heidi Anne. *Education:* Lawrence University, B.A., 1973; attended University of Wisconsin-Madison and Colorado School of Mines, 1974; Boston College, M.S.T., 1980. *Politics:* Independent. *Religion:* Unitarian-Universalist. *Hobbies and other interests:* Reading, traveling, camping, sewing, skiing, and activities with her husband and children.

Addresses

Home and office—2601 North Union St., Appleton, WI 54911.

Career

Appleton Area School District, Appleton, WI, science teacher, 1973—. Fulbright exchange teacher at Lady Hawkins School, Kingston, England, 1976-77. Consultant, D.C. Heath Company, 1986-87; workshop coordinator, Duquesne University, 1986—; "Belize Bound" participant, 1997, 1998. *Member:* American Association of University Women (chairperson of international relations, 1984-87; issue chairman, 1987-88), National Education Association, Society of Children's Book Writers and Illustrators, Wisconsin Society of Science Teachers, Wisconsin Society of Earth Science Teachers (treasurer, 1987—), Wisconsin Regional Writers, American Field Service, Friends of the Appleton Library (board of directors for community nursery school, 1986-87), Wild Ones.

Awards, Honors

Children's Choice Award, International Reading Association/Children's Book Council, 1984, for *Out to Lunch!* and *Space Out!;* Children's Book of the Year designation, Child Study Association, 1985, for *Keep the Lights Burning, Abbie,* and 1986, for *Button for General Washington;* Irma Simonton Black Award Honor Book, and Children's Book of the Year Award, both from Bank Street College of Education, and Outstanding Trade Book in the Language Arts, National Council of Teachers of English, all 1986, all for *Keep the Lights Burning, Abbie;* Outstanding Trade Book in the Field of Social Studies designation, National Council for Social Studies/Children's Book Council, 1986, for *Buttons for General Washington;* Florida Sunshine Award, 1992, for *Ahyoka and the Talking Leaves;* Wisconsin Library Association Award, and Outstanding Trade Book in the Field of Social Studies designation, National Council for Social Studies/Children's Book Council, both 1993, both for *Off the Map: The Journals of Lewis and Clark;* Kansas Reading Circle Book award, 1999, for *Girl of the Shining Mountains: Sacagawea's Story.*

Writings

UNDER NAME CONNIE ROOP; WITH HUSBAND, PETER ROOP

Keep the Lights Burning, Abbie, illustrated by Peter E. Hanson, Carolrhoda, 1985.
Buttons for General Washington, illustrated by P. E. Hanson, Carolrhoda, 1986.
Snips the Tinker, Milliken, 1988.
Seasons of the Cranes, Walker, 1989.
(Editor) *I, Columbus: My Journal, 1492-93,* illustrated by P. Hanson, Walker, 1990.
Ahyoka and the Talking Leaves, illustrated by Yoshi Miyake, Lothrop, 1992.
One Earth, a Multitude of Creatures, illustrated by Valerie A. Kells, Walker, 1992.
(Editor) *Off the Map: The Journals of Lewis and Clark,* illustrated by Tim Tanner, Walker, 1993.
(Editor) *Capturing Nature: The Writings and Art of John James Audubon,* illustrated by Rick Farley, Walker, 1993.
Pilgrim Voices: Our First Year in the New World, illustrated by Shelley Pritchett, Walker, 1995.
Westward, Ho, Ho, Ho!, illustrated by Anne Canevari Green, Millbrook Press, 1996.
Walk on the Wild Side!, illustrated by A. Green, Millbrook Press, 1997.
Let's Celebrate Christmas, illustrated by Katy Keck Arnsteen, Millbrook Press, 1997.
Let's Celebrate Halloween, illustrated by K. Arnsteen, Millbrook Press, 1997.
Grace's Letter to Lincoln, illustrated by Stacey Schuett, Hyperion, 1998.
If You Lived with the Cherokee, illustrated by Kevin Smith, Scholastic, 1998.
Martin Luther King Jr., Heinemann, 1998.
Susan B. Anthony, Heinemann, 1998.
Brazil, Heinemann, 1998.
China, Heinemann, 1998.
Egypt, Heinemann, 1998.
India, Heinemann, 1998.
Israel, Heinemann, 1998.
Japan, Heinemann, 1998.
Vietnam, Heinemann, 1998.
A Home Album, Heinemann, 1998.
A City Album, Heinemann, 1998.
A Farm Album, Heinemann, 1999.
A School Album, Heinemann, 1999.
A City, Heinemann, 1999.
A Suburb, Heinemann, 1999.
A Town, Heinemann, 1999.
A Farming Town, Heinemann, 1999.
Let's Celebrate Thanksgiving, illustrated by Gwen Connelly, Millbrook Press, 1999.

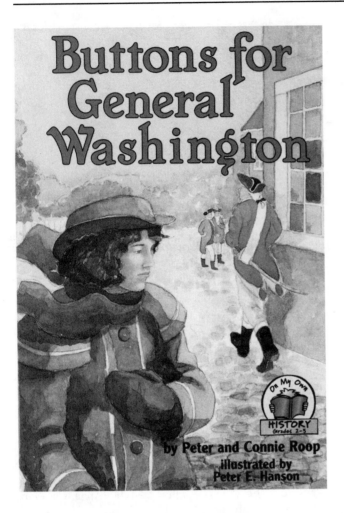

In Constance Roop's work, cowritten with her husband Peter, fourteen-year-old John Darragh carries messages in the buttons of his coat to George Washington during the Revolutionary War. (Cover illustration by Peter E. Hanson.)

Let's Celebrate Valentine's Day, illustrated by Arnsteen, Millbrook Press, 1999.
Girl of the Shining Mountains: Sacagawea's Story, Hyperion, 1999.
Goodbye for Today: A Girl's Whaling Journal, illustrated by Thomas Allen, Atheneum, 2000.
Whales and Dolphins, illustrated by Carol Schwartz, Scholastic, 2000.
Christopher Columbus: A Biography, Scholastic, 2000.
An Eye for an Eye, Jamestown, 2000.

"MAKE ME LAUGH" SERIES; UNDER NAME CONNIE ROOP; WITH P. ROOP

Space Out! Jokes about Outer Space, illustrated by Joan Hanson, Lerner, 1984.
Go Hog Wild! Jokes from down on the Farm, illustrated by J. Hanson, Lerner, 1984.
Out to Lunch! Jokes about Food, illustrated by J. Hanson, Lerner, 1984.
Stick out Your Tongue! Jokes about Doctors and Patients, illustrated by J. Hanson, Lerner, 1986.

Going Buggy! Jokes about Insects, illustrated by J. Hanson, Lerner, 1986.
Let's Celebrate! Jokes about Holidays, illustrated by J. Hanson, Lerner, 1986.

"GREAT MYSTERIES" SERIES; UNDER NAME CONNIE ROOP; WITH P. ROOP

Dinosaurs: Opposing Viewpoints, Greenhaven, 1988.
Poltergeists: Opposing Viewpoints, Greenhaven, 1988.
The Solar System: Opposing Viewpoints, Greenhaven, 1988.
Stonehenge: Opposing Viewpoints, Greenhaven, 1989.

OTHER

Contributor to Harcourt Brace Jovanovich's reading texts. Also contributor of stories, articles, and reviews to periodicals, including *Learning, Appraisal, Cricket, Cobblestone,* and *Curriculum Review.*

Work in Progress

Take Command, Mr. Farragut, illustrated by Michael McCarey, Atheneum, due in 2001; *Benjamin Franklin: A Biography,* Scholastic, due in 2001; *Ernest Shakleton,* Scholastic, due in 2001; *Octopus,* Scholastic, due in 2001; *Joseph Martin: The Diary of a Revolutionary War Soldier,* Marshall Cavedish, due in 2001; *Mary Jemison: The Diary of a Captive,* Marshall Cavendish, due in 2001; *Down the Colorado: John Wesley Powell's Diary,* Marshall Cavendish, due in 2001; *The Gold Rush Diary of David Leeper,* Marshall Cavendish, due in 2001; and two titles for Millbrook Press, *Let's Celebrate Earth Day!* and *Let's Celebrate President's Day!,* both due in 2001.

Sidelights

Together with her husband, Peter Roop, Constance (Connie) Roop makes a point of featuring actual young people in the many books they write for children. Drawing from actual journals, traveling to the locations they write about in their books, and drawing on their combined skills as educators, the Roops have contributed substantially to the growing number of nonfiction titles designed to capture the imagination of young readers. Among their books are biographies of David Farragut, Sacagawea, Martin Luther King, Jr., and Susan B. Anthony; their other nonfiction books are as diverse as the lighthearted "Let's Celebrate" series describing holiday traditions and the far more serious *One Earth, a Multitude of Creatures.*

Born in 1951 in Elkhorn, Wisconsin, Roop was raised in a family where reading was encouraged. "I loved school and was an avid reader," she once explained to *SATA.* "I [also] actively participated in everything from bassoon and forensics to scouting where I gained a love for the outdoors." Although her writing skills brought Roop recognition during her middle school years, she never thought them significant enough to consider a career as an author. Instead, she fed her natural curiosity; during the summer of her junior year in high school, she traveled to Italy and lived with a family there as an

American Field Service student. "This experience confirmed my desire to learn," Roop recalled, "and to discover the uniqueness of different cultures."

Roop enrolled at Lawrence University in 1969, with the intention of becoming a physician. But a field camp experience in geology changed all that; instead, she decided to study geology. "The vastness of geologic time still humbles me," she noted. Combining her fascination with nature with her empathy for people, she decided to go into teaching, and became a junior high science teacher. She also married "an equally adventurous and curious person, Peter," she admitted. Together, the Roops took advantage of travel and study opportunities, among them a year's stint teaching in England as part of the Fulbright Exchange Program.

Content with her choice of career, Roop did not branch out into her second career as a children's book author until the late 1970s, while pursuing a master's degree in science teaching at Boston College. "I began to read many of the books assigned to my husband in his master's of children's literature program as a welcome change from [the] science journals [I was required to read for my own degree]. Based on this reading, I developed a fiction booklist to supplement the science curriculum in my junior high school science classes. These scientifically accurate and exciting books provided my entry into the world of writing for children and young adults."

With this grounding in the juvenile nonfiction market, Roop wrote several articles for educational journals and worked as a reviewer and science specialist for *Appraisal* magazine. From there, she and her husband began their first book-length project, a series of six joke and riddle books that include the titles *Space Out! Jokes about Outer Space* and *Going Buggy! Jokes about Insects.*

While researching a travel article off the coast of Maine, the Roops learned the story of a young heroine named Abbie Burgess, who, according to local legend, in 1856 singlehandedly kept two lighthouses lit during weeks of stormy weather. The resulting book, *Keep the Lights Burning, Abbie,* was published in 1985, beginning a long and prolific writing collaboration between the Roops. Whereas *Buttons for General Washington* was a work of fiction, the other books stemming from the Roops' fascination with exceptional men and women from the past have been nonfiction efforts, such as *Pilgrim Voices: Our First Year in the New World,* a series of books profiling nations around the world, and editorship of the journals of explorers Lewis and Clark, ornithologist John James Audubon, and Christopher Columbus. In *Pilgrim Voices,* too, the Roops used actual writings from the period they profiled, "contribut[ing] authenticity and vitality to the text," in the opinion of *Booklist* contributor Karen Hutt. While basing their book on the works of William Bradford and other pilgrims, the Roops modernized the language but retained the journal format. *Pilgrim Voices* "is successful at creating a human sense

of history beyond facts and timelines," noted Heide Piehler in *School Library Journal.*

Off the Map: The Journals of Lewis and Clark are based on the explorers' original eight volumes of diaries recounting their explorations between 1804 and 1806. Entries, which begin with Thomas Jefferson's letter to Lewis setting forth guidelines and objectives for the trip, follows the duo's impressions of the natural world they encountered, their interactions with native people, and the joys and dangers of their historic trek to the Pacific Ocean. Calling the Roop's editing of those journals "judicious," a *Publishers Weekly* contributor added that the editors, through their creative approach and organization of the material, "impart ... a feel for the challenges and dangers of the 8,000-mile trip through the Louisiana Purchase." In *Booklist,* Carolyn Phelan added that *Off the Map* was a "vivid source ... [that] would be a welcome part of any classroom study of the subject." On a similar topic but in a more lighthearted vein, the Roops' *Westward, Ho, Ho, Ho!* contains jokes and riddles about the history of the American West.

With Roop's background in science, it is not surprising that many of the books she has coauthored with her husband have been science-related. Several titles written for Greenhaven Press's "Great Mysteries" series explore quandaries that have yet to be solved by scientific methods. "Scientific debate, key to the scientific process, is a critical element of these books," Roop once noted to *SATA.* "I believe young people need to realize that there are many unanswered questions in science and that they can be part of solving these questions." Among

The Roops present information about the origins of Halloween celebrations and offer suggestions for related crafts and activities. (Cover illustration by Katy Keck Arnsteen.)

the "Great Mysteries" included in the series are dinosaurs, poltergeists, and Stonehenge.

In another science-related text, the Roops' *One Earth, a Multitude of Creatures,* they profile a dozen creatures that live in the Pacific Northwest: black bears, rainbow trout, foxes, humpback whales, owls, and others. Illustrated with detailed drawings by Valerie A. Kells, the volume shows, visually, the survival chain existing within a contained ecosystem, and provides "a gentle, nonpreachy introduction to the interdependence and diversity of animals in an environment," according to *Booklist* contributor Leone McDermott.

Many other books have been published as a result of the Roops' interests and energy: from studies of the way people live in such titles as *A City, A Suburb, A Town,* and *A Farming Town,* to a series of books describing holiday traditions in the United States. In *Let's Celebrate Valentine's Day,* for example, the origins of the holiday are discussed, and riddles, little-known facts, and trivia about the day are presented. In addition, heart-shaped cookie recipes, poetry, and holiday activities allow readers to create a special day for those they love. Other holidays included in the series are Halloween, Christmas, and Thanksgiving; praising one series installment, *School Library Journal* reviewer Patricia Mahoney Brown commented that the "book offers facts and fun from beginning to end.... This is no trick; it's a treat!"

"I look forward to writing projects on a variety of topics as my involvement with science, literature, history, and reading continues," Roop once wrote. "Peter and I are committed to children. I hope to always be able to look at the world with the eyes of a young person—full of fresh wonder, awe, and surprise. I am hopeful that through our books we can help young people discover the joy of learning. This is a precious gift that Peter and I possess and treasure and hope to share with others."

Works Cited

Brown, Patricia Mahoney, review of *Let's Celebrate Valentine's Day, School Library Journal,* August, 1997, p. 150.

Hutt, Karen, review of *Pilgrim Voices, Booklist,* February 1, 1996, p. 929.

McDermott, Leone, review of *One Earth, a Multitude of Creatures, Booklist,* November 15, 1992, p. 603.

Review of *Off the Map: The Journals of Lewis and Clark, Publishers Weekly,* May 17, 1993, p. 82.

Phelan, Carolyn, review of *Off the Map: The Journals of Lewis and Clark, Booklist,* September 1, 1993, pp. 54-55.

Piehler, Heide, review of *Pilgrim Voices, School Library Journal,* January, 1996, p. 125.

For More Information See

PERIODICALS

Booklist, December 15, 1996, p. 723; September 1, 1997, p. 137; February 14, 1999, p. 1073.

Publishers Weekly, September 18, 1995, p. 92; October 6, 1997, p. 52.

School Library Journal, December, 1992, p. 107; June, 1993, p. 122; April, 1999, p. 122.

*　　*　　*

ROOP, Peter (G.) 1951-

Personal

Born March 8, 1951, in Winchester, MA; son of Daniel Morehead (an engineer) and Dorothy (a homemaker; maiden name, Danenhower) Roop; married Constance Betzer (an educator and author), August 4, 1973; children: Sterling Gray, Heidi Anne. *Education:* Lawrence University, B.A., 1973; Simmons College, M.A., 1980; also attended University of Wisconsin-Madison. *Politics:* Democrat. *Religion:* Unitarian-Universalist. *Hobbies and other interests:* Reading, traveling, speaking to educators, librarians and writers, playing with his children.

Addresses

Home and office—2601 North Union St., Appleton, WI 54911.

Career

Appleton Area School District, Appleton, WI, teacher, 1973-99; writer, 1977—. Fulbright exchange teacher at Kingston County Primary School, Kingston, England, 1976-77; University of Wisconsin-Fox Valley, Menasha, instructor, 1983-84; University of Wisconsin, School of the Arts, Rhinelander, instructor, 1986-87. Workshop coordinator, Duquesne University, 1986-99; consultant, D.C. Heath Company, 1986-87; teacher consultant for *Learning* Magazine, 1988-99. Member of board directors of Friends of the Appleton Public Library, 1974-84, and board of trustees of Appleton Public Library, 1983-89. *Member:* Society of Children's Book Writers and Illustrators, National Education Association, Wisconsin Regional Writers (president, 1983-86), Authors and Illustrators Who Visit Schools, Council for Wisconsin Writers, Chicago Reading Roundtable.

Awards, Honors

Jade Ring Award, Wisconsin Regional Writers Association, 1979, for play *Who Buries the Funeral Director?,* and 1982, for *The Cry of the Conch;* Reading Teacher of the Year award, Mideast Wisconsin Reading Council, 1983; Children's Choice Award, International Reading Association/Children's Book Council, 1985, for *Out to Lunch!* and *Space Out!;* Child Study Association's Children's Books of the Year selection, 1985, for *Keep the Lights Burning, Abbie,* and 1986, for *Buttons for General Washington;* Teacher of the Year, and Outstanding Elementary Educator for Wisconsin, both from the Wisconsin Department of Public Instruction, both 1986; named Outstanding Elementary Educator in Appleton, Mielke Foundation, 1986; Children's Book of the

In his tale about a youth from the Blackfeet Indian Nation, Peter Roop blends the universal theme of jealousy among siblings with the exciting and unique custom of the Native American buffalo jump. (Cover illustration by Bill Farnsworth.)

Year Award, and Irma Simonton Black Award Honor Book, Bank Street College, and Outstanding Trade Book in the Language Arts, National Council of Teachers of English, all 1986, all for *Keep the Lights Burning, Abbie;* Outstanding Trade Book in the Field of Social Studies, National Council for Social Studies/Children's Book Council, 1986, for *Buttons for General Washington;* In Honor of Excellence Award, Burger King Corp., 1987, for excellence in education; Florida Sunshine Award, 1992, for *Ahyoka and the Talking Leaves;* Wisconsin Library Association Award, and Outstanding Trade Book in the Field of Social Studies, National Council for Social Studies/Childrens Book Council, both 1993, both for *Off the Map: The Journals of Lewis and Clark;* Finalist for Storyteller Award, Western Writers of America, 1996, for *The Buffalo Jump;* Kansas Reading Circle Book award, 1999, for *Girl of the Shining Mountains: Sacagawea's Story.*

Writings

FOR CHILDREN

The Cry of the Conch, illustrated by Patric, Press Pacifica, 1984.

Little Blaze and the Buffalo Jump, illustrated by Jesse Wells, Montana Council for Indian Education, 1984, published as *The Buffalo Jump,* Northland Press, 1996.

Sik-Ki-Mi, illustrated by Shawn Running Crane, Montana Council for Indian Education, 1984.

Natosi: Strong Medicine, illustrated by S. Running Crane, Montana Council for Indian Education, 1984.

WITH WIFE, CONNIE ROOP

Keep the Lights Burning, Abbie, illustrated by Peter E. Hanson, Carolrhoda, 1985.

Buttons for General Washington, illustrated by P. E. Hanson, Carolrhoda, 1986.

Snips the Tinker, Milliken, 1988.

Seasons of the Cranes, Walker, 1989.

(Editor) *I, Columbus: My Journal, 1492-93,* illustrated by P. E. Hanson, Walker, 1990.

Ahyoka and the Talking Leaves, illustrated by Yoshi Miyake, Lothrop, 1992.

One Earth, a Multitude of Creatures, illustrated by Valerie A. Kells, Walker, 1992.

(Editor) *Off the Map: The Journals of Lewis and Clark,* illustrated by Tim Tanner, Walker, 1993.

(Editor) *Capturing Nature: The Writings and Art of John James Audubon,* illustrated by Rick Farley, Walker, 1993.

Pilgrim Voices: Our First Year in the New World, illustrated by Shelley Pritchett, Walker, 1995.

Take Command, Mr. Farragut, illustrated by Henri Sorensen, Lothrop, 1996.

Westward, Ho, Ho, Ho!, illustrated by Anne Canevari Green, Millbrook Press, 1996.

Walk on the Wild Side!, illustrated by A. Green, Millbrook Press, 1997.

Let's Celebrate Christmas, illustrated by Katy Keck Arnsteen, Millbrook Press, 1997.

Let's Celebrate Halloween, illustrated by K. Arnsteen, Millbrook Press, 1997.

Grace's Letter to Lincoln, illustrated by Stacey Schuett, Hyperion, 1998.

If You Lived with the Cherokee, illustrated by Kevin Smith, Scholastic, 1998.

Martin Luther King Jr., Heinemann, 1998.

Susan B. Anthony, Heinemann, 1998.

Brazil, Heinemann, 1998.

China, Heinemann, 1998.

Egypt, Heinemann, 1998.

India, Heinemann, 1998.

Israel, Heinemann, 1998.

Japan, Heinemann, 1998.

Vietnam, Heinemann, 1998.

A Home Album, Heinemann, 1998.

A City Album, Heinemann, 1998.

A Farm Album, Heinemann, 1999.

A School Album, Heinemann, 1999.

A City, Heinemann, 1999.

A Suburb, Heinemann, 1999.

A Town, Heinemann, 1999.

A Farming Town, Heinemann, 1999.

Let's Celebrate Thanksgiving, illustrated by Gwen Connelly, Millbrook Press, 1999.

Let's Celebrate Valentine's Day, illustrated by Arnsteen, Millbrook Press, 1999.

Girl of the Shining Mountains: Sacagawea's Story, Hyperion, 1999.

Goodbye for Today, illustrated by Thomas Allen, Atheneum, 2000.

Whales and Dolphins, illustrated by Carol Schwartz, Scholastic, 2000.

"MAKE ME LAUGH" SERIES; WITH C. ROOP

Space Out! Jokes about Outer Space, illustrated by Joan Hanson, Lerner, 1984.

Go Hog Wild! Jokes from down on the Farm, illustrated by J. Hanson, Lerner, 1984.

Out to Lunch! Jokes about Food, illustrated by J. Hanson, Lerner, 1984.

Stick out Your Tongue! Jokes about Doctors and Patients, illustrated by J. Hanson, Lerner, 1986.

Going Buggy! Jokes about Insects, illustrated by J. Hanson, Lerner, 1986.

Let's Celebrate! Jokes about Holidays, illustrated by J. Hanson, Lerner, 1986.

"GREAT MYSTERIES" SERIES; WITH C. ROOP

Dinosaurs: Opposing Viewpoints, Greenhaven, 1988.

Poltergeists: Opposing Viewpoints, Greenhaven, 1988.

The Solar System: Opposing Viewpoints, Greenhaven, 1988.

Stonehenge: Opposing Viewpoints, Greenhaven, 1989.

Work in Progress

Take Command, Mr. Farragut, illustrated by Michael McCarey, Atheneum, due in 2001; *Benjamin Franklin: A Biography,* Scholastic, due in 2001; *Ernest Shakleton,* Scholastic, due in 2001; *Octopus,* Scholastic, due in 2001; *Joseph Martin: The Diary of a Revolutionary War Soldier,* Marshall Cavedish, due in 2001; *Mary Jemison: The Diary of a Captive,* Marshall Cavendish, due in 2001; *Down the Colorado: John Wesley Powell's Diary,* Marshall Cavendish, due in 2001; *The Gold Rush Diary of David Leeper,* Marshall Cavendish, due in 2001; and two titles for Millbrook Press, *Let's Celebrate Earth Day!* and *Let's Celebrate President's Day!,* both due in 2001.

Sidelights

Peter Roop credits his many years spent working in elementary school classrooms as "one of the prime motivations for my writing for children. When I began my career in education, teaching grades one through four, I was reading numerous children's books," he explained to *SATA.* "I said to myself, 'I can write these stories.' Little then did I realize the scope of children's literature and the skills it would take to write quality stories for children. The 'easy' appearance of many children's books hides the hours of hard work involved in creating a worthwhile book for young readers." Fortunately for young people, together with his wife, Connie, Roop determined to put in those hours, with such highly praised books as *Grace's Letter to Lincoln* and *Buttons for General Washington.* In addition, the Roops have edited actual journals of such individuals as Christopher Columbus and members of the Pilgrims who founded the Plymouth Colony, even travelling to the locations featured in their books to bring past lives to life in a way that would captivate young minds. Other works by Roop and his wife include biographies of

Sacagawea, Martin Luther King, Jr. and Susan B. Anthony, as well as a collection of lighthearted joke and riddle books.

Born in Winchester, Massachusetts, in 1951, Roop attended Lawrence University. After graduating in 1973, he married fellow Lawrence University student Connie Betzer and began a teaching career. Although he had talked about doing some writing for children his student's age, he didn't set pen to paper until he was inspired to do so while teaching in England as a Fulbright exchange teacher in 1976. "I decided to stop talking and start writing," Roop once noted. "That year I wrote four children's stories and articles, two of which were eventually published in magazines. My route to writing children's books was focused first on writing for the many children's magazines. By taking this approach I hoped to gain the necessary background in the profession, to hone my writing skills, and to establish a name in preparation for writing my books."

In 1980 Roop earned his master's degree at Simmons College's Center for the Study of Children's Literature. "The work at Simmons was pivotal in my understanding

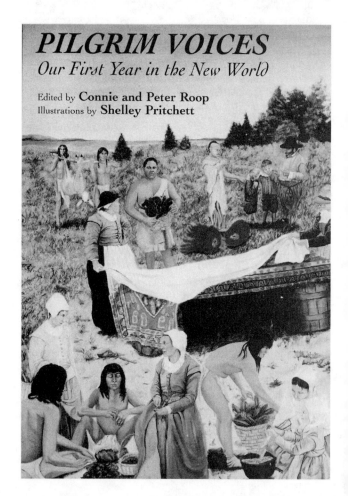

As editors of a collection of writings from the seventeenth-century journals of American Pilgrims, the Roops modernized the language but captured the timelessness and personal quality of the accounts. (Cover illustration by Shelley Pritchett.)

of children's literature and in writing for children," Roop explained, counting among his favorite teachers fellow children's authors Nancy Bond and Scott O'Dell. In fact, O'Dell's work—especially *Island of the Blue Dolphins*—Roop counts as "the mainstay of my perspective on writing for children. O'Dell's style, sensitivity, and adept mixing of history and fiction are models for my own writing efforts."

After Roop had been writing for magazines for several years, he published his first book, *The Cry of the Conch,* in 1984. This story about ancient Hawaii was followed by three books for the Blackfeet Indian Nation: *Little Blaze and the Buffalo Jump, Sik-Ki-Mi,* and *Natosi: Strong Medicine.* In 1985 he was finally joined by his wife, Connie, who also worked as a teacher of elementary-age children. "Inspired by a walk along the coast of Maine, we wrote a joke and riddle book about the seashore," Roop recalls of their first collaboration. This book, while not published, developed into a six-book series that includes such wacky titles as *Space Out! Jokes about Outer Space* and *Going Buggy! Jokes about Insects.*

While playing with words has long been a Roop "family tradition," a shared fascination for the past has also focused the couple's writing efforts. "Our abiding interest in Maine led us to write *Keep the Lights Burning, Abbie,* an historical story about Abbie Burgess, a brave young woman who singlehandedly kept two lighthouses going during a month-long siege of bad weather in 1856," Roop once explained. *Keep the Lights Burning Abbie* was featured on Public Broadcasting System's popular *Reading Rainbow,* and helped publicize the work of the Roops.

One of the reasons the Roops' books are so popular with young readers is that they feature young people of history, "children who, like Abbie, are 'footnotes in history,'" according to Roop. "By researching and writing these heroic stories, we hope to provide children with an exciting glimpse into the past." In fact, it has been Roop's personal interest in history—an interest he shares with his wife—that has inspired most of his writing, even from the start of his career. "As a writer on assignment for *Cobblestone,* a history magazine, I researched and wrote about topics ranging from the origins of Native Americans to the creation of video games," Roop noted. These *Cobblestone* assignments have inspired several books, including 1999's *Girl of the Shining Mountains: Sacagawea's Story* and *Goodbye for Today,* the story of a nine-year-old girl who leaves her home to sail with her father aboard his whaling ship in the Arctic Ocean. Roop's *Little Blaze and the Buffalo Jump,* originally published by the Montana Council for Indian Education in 1984, was republished as *The Buffalo Jump* in 1996. Focusing on a young runner of the Blackfeet Indian tribe, Roop's story describes the manner in which Montana's Native American tribes hunted buffalo by using a decoy to lead them over a steep cliff to their death. In *School Library Journal,* contributor Celia A. Huffman called Roop's story "well-researched" and "compelling," praised its "engaging

main character," and noted that *The Buffalo Jump* "recreates and important part of Native American history and livelihood." While less enthusiastic about Roop's "romanticizing" of his Native American characters, a reviewer for *Publishers Weekly* also had praise for the work, noting that it "keeps alive the memory of a traditional Native American practice."

Other books inspired by the Roops' fascination with history have included several edited journals, among them *Pilgrim Voices: Our First Year in the New World,* and the diaries of explorers Lewis and Clark, ornithologist John James Audubon, and Christopher Columbus. In *Pilgrim Voices,* the Roops use of actual writings from the period they profiled, "contributes authenticity and vitality to the text," according to *Booklist* reviewer Karen Hutt. Based on the seventeenth-century writings of William Bradford and his fellow colonists, the text in *Pilgrim Voices* has been modernized for twenty-first-century readers while retaining the flavor of the original writing. This technique by the Roops has resulted in a book that *School Library Journal* contributor Heide Piehler deemed "successful at creating a human sense of history beyond facts and timelines."

The Roops' *Off the Map: The Journals of Lewis and Clark* are based on the explorers' eight-volume work recounting their explorations in the western territories during the years 1804-1806. Beginning with Thomas Jefferson's letter to Lewis wherein the president sets forth guidelines and objectives for the trip, *Off the Map* follows Lewis and Clark's impressions of the natural world they encountered, their encounters with Native Americans, and the other aspects of their historic trek to the Pacific Ocean. Deeming the book's editing "judicious," a *Publishers Weekly* contributor added that the Roops' creative approach and organization of the material, "impart[s] ... a feel for the challenges and dangers of the 8,000-mile trip through the Louisiana Purchase." And in *Booklist,* Carolyn Phelan called *Off the Map* a "vivid source ... [that] would be a welcome part of any classroom study of the subject."

Another interest the Roops share is science; in fact, Connie Roop began her teaching career as a junior high school science teacher. This interest resulted in several books, including a three-volume series published by Greenhaven Press that explores such great mysteries as the extinction of the dinosaurs, the existence of poltergeists, and the marvels of the solar system. Another science-related book is their *One Earth, a Multitude of Creatures,* which includes descriptions of twelve creatures that call the Pacific Northwest region home. Illustrated with detailed drawings of black bears, rainbow trout, foxes, humpback whales, and owls by artist Valerie A. Kells, *One Earth, a Multitude of Creatures* depicts the links between creatures in an ecosystem, and serves as what *Booklist* contributor Leone McDermott called "a gentle, nonpreachy introduction to the interdependence and diversity of animals in an environment."

Roop's interest in travel has allowed him to effectively bring to life many of the topics he presents to young readers. "As a writer I believe that getting the right sense of setting is critical to the impact of a story," he once explained to *SATA.* "Experiencing the sacredness of a *pu'unhonua* in Hawaii was essential to *The Cry of the Conch.* Feeling the chilling blasts of a nor'easter was vital in creating the atmosphere of *Keep the Lights Burning, Abbie.* Walking the cobbled streets of Philadelphia established the feeling of place in *Buttons for George Washington.* Taking his responsibility as an author of books for children seriously has also contributed to Roop's success. "Writing the best books possible for young readers is my goal," he maintained. "By providing the best for children, I can open more vistas and distant horizons to their wondering eyes and minds. What better role for a writer?"

Works Cited

Review of *The Buffalo Jump, Publishers Weekly,* August 19, 1996, p. 67.

Huffman, Celia A., review of *The Buffalo Jump, School Library Journal,* February, 1997, p. 84.

Hutt, Karen, review of *Pilgrim Voices, Booklist,* February 1, 1996, p. 929.

McDermott, Leone, review of *One Earth, a Multitude of Creatures, Booklist,* November 15, 1992, p. 603.

Review of *Off the Map: The Journals of Lewis and Clark, Publishers Weekly,* May 17, 1993, p. 82.

Phelan, Carolyn, review of *Off the Map: The Journals of Lewis and Clark, Booklist,* September 1, 1993, pp. 54-55.

Piehler, Heide, review of *Pilgrim Voices, School Library Journal,* January, 1996, p. 125.

For More Information See

PERIODICALS

Booklist, December 15, 1996, p. 723; September 1, 1997, p. 137; February 14, 1999, p. 1073.

Publishers Weekly, September 18, 1995, p. 92; October 6, 1997, p. 52.

School Library Journal, December, 1992, p. 107; June, 1993, p. 122; April, 1999, p. 122.

*   *   *

ROSSI, Joyce 1943-

Personal

Born July 11, 1943, in Marin County, CA; daughter of Harold (an insurance agent) and Hazel (a homemaker) Muller; married Louis Rossi (a chemist), January, 1966; children: Vincent, Michael. *Education:* University of Nevada, Reno, B.S. *Politics:* Republican. *Religion:* Lutheran.

Addresses

Home—3915 Falling Water Dr., Reno, NV 89509.

Career

Teacher of third grade in Reno, NV, 1965-68; graphic designer, Reno, 1983-85; freelance illustrator, 1985—. Children's Literary Interest Group, member. *Member:* Society of Children's Book Writers and Illustrators (regional adviser to Sierra Nevada chapter, 1995-98), Sierra Nevada Watercolor Society.

Awards, Honors

Grant from Sierra Arts Foundation, 1996; Arizona Author/Illustrator Award, Judy Goddard Libraries Ltd., 1999. *The Gullywasher* was a Consortium of Latin American Studies Programs (CLASP) Commended Book and has been featured on Public Television's *Storytime.*

Writings

(Author and illustrator) *The Gullywasher,* Northland Publishing (Flagstaff, AZ), 1995, published as *The Gullywasher (El Chaparron Torrencial),* 1998.

Work in Progress

Research on the Basque sheep herders of Nevada.

Sidelights

Joyce Rossi told *SATA:* "Following the publication of my first book, *The Gullywasher,* a woman came to me at a book festival and said, 'You are living my dream. I want to write and illustrate children's books, too.'

"'I'm living my own dream,' I confessed, reflecting on the years of acquiring skills, not just as an illustrator, but as a writer. There had been many obstacles in getting a

Joyce Rossi

book published. Endurance, patience, and the encouragement of family and friends finally paid off, and it felt wonderful to finally hold *The Gullywasher* in my hands.

"The rewards have been many, the greatest being letters from readers. Some letters made me laugh, others made me cry, but the one I cherish most came from my son, Mike. 'I am so proud you are my mom,' he wrote. In the life of an author/artist/mom, it doesn't get much better than that.

"My life has been filled with experiences that have ultimately helped me in my career. As an elementary schoolteacher, I had the great advantage of being in constant contact with kids. As an artist, I painted murals and portraits and also sold my work at festivals and in galleries. As a graphic designer, I learned how books are made and how to prepare art for the printer. As a writer, I continue to work on new books. And as a lecturer and instructor, I hope to help others make their dreams of becoming an artist or writer possible."

For More Information See

PERIODICALS

Booklist, December 15, 1995, p. 705.
Horn Book Guide, spring, 1996, p. 43.
Publishers Weekly, October 16, 1995, p. 61.
School Library Journal, January, 1996, p. 95.

Autobiography Feature

Gillian Rubinstein

1942-

I'm sitting writing this essay on my life in a little hundred-year-old stone cottage, in a small coastal town in South Australia called Goolwa, an aboriginal word meaning elbow. The elbow is that of the River Murray, which ends its long journey here, in a series of lakes and lagoons which give out onto the Southern Ocean. It's always been a dream of mine to have a country cottage by the sea, and I was able to buy this cottage a few weeks ago, with money I earned from writing. Here I spend my time cycling, swimming, and walking on the beach with my husband, Philip, still, after twenty-five years, my best friend, and our two dogs, Jon and Libby. In the afternoons, when the sun is too hot to go out, and in the evenings I read and read, novel after novel.

We used to go away to the seaside every summer when I was a child growing up in England. These holidays stand out in my memory. I loved the sense of freedom, the smell of the sea, and the coastal plants, thrift, pine, lavender, rosemary. I loved swimming, no matter what the weather, and one of my earliest memories is of my mother teaching me to ride waves in Cornwall on an old-fashioned wooden surfboard. The water was always freezing, but we stayed in until our fingers and toes went white with cold. Our parents lit huge fires of driftwood on the sand, and we would stand around them to warm up, eating biscuits and pieces of chocolate that we called "shivering bites." I still love catching waves, but now I do it on a modern, light, body board, and the water in South Australia is a lot warmer than in Cornwall.

Like many writers I have a strong sensual awareness and can be instantly transported by the beauty of nature, evocative smells, sounds, and music. As a child I was always in some dramatic state or other, either deliriously happy or desperately miserable. I cried easily and fell into terrible rages. My parents described me as exasperating or, more kindly, as highly strung. I suffered terribly from night fears and nightmares. I dreaded going to bed, even more going to sleep, so I would try to keep myself awake by making up stories. The nightmares were always worse away from home, so the excitement and joy of summer holidays were somewhat tempered by the knowledge that sooner or later I would have to go to bed in the strange room which I was convinced was haunted.

From the vantage point of fifty years on, I can see that all these characteristics were part of growing up to be a writer. I still use ideas and imaginings that I remember so clearly from when I was a child. When I was writing *At Ardilla,* for example, I drew on my memories of childhood summer holidays, blending them with holidays I had spent in South Australia with my own children and updating both to the 1990s. But while I was still that child, my troublesome sensitive nature was a great burden to me. I seemed to have fewer skins than my sister and our friends. I was ashamed of feeling everything so deeply. Now I know that this sensitivity is an essential part of being a writer, and I'm thankful for it. But there's no doubt it made growing up hard.

I was born in 1942 in the middle of the Second World War. My husband says that after I was born things started

Gillian Rubinstein (with Jon), 1994.

looking up for the Allies. But it must have been an anxious time for my parents starting a family. My father, as a research chemist, was considered to be on essential war work, so he stayed at home throughout the war. The only major excitement was when his laboratory was bombed by mistake by a German plane dropping its bombs too late and missing London. We lived in a small English village called Potten End. Most of the signposts for miles around had been altered to read Rotten End. I remember my sister pointing this out to me and thinking how clever she was to be able to read.

My sister, Jocelyn, was nineteen months older than me. She had a fearless, confident nature and was sometimes called Tigger because she bounced a lot. I admired her and looked up to her, and much to her annoyance wanted to do everything with her. She tried to discourage me in various sibling ways. She let go of my pram at the top of a hill when I was a baby, and later with one of her school friends tied me up with a rope and dropped a rock on my head. It made no difference. I still adored her.

During the war my mother made friends with another young woman, who had two children the same age as Jocelyn and me. Lavender Helen Hatt-Cook was living in a big house with her father and her two children, Pippa and Mark, while her husband John was away with the army. When the war ended and we started going away on summer

holidays, we always went with the Hatt-Cooks, to Devon, Cornwall, or Guernsey in the Channel Islands. Later when my mother and my stepfather went to live in Nigeria, my sister and I made our home with the Hatt-Cooks, and they became like a foster family to us. I drew on this situation for some of the feelings Victoria has in *Beyond the Labyrinth.* Lavender, as we always called her, though she much preferred Helen, could have been a considerable artist, but diverted her talent into being a wonderful cook, dressmaker, and craftswoman. For Christmas presents she always made us soft toys and glove puppets. My sister had one tiny rabbit called Dinky, because it came inside one of Mark's Dinky car boxes.

We usually spent Christmas as well as summer holidays with the Hatt-Cooks, amazingly traditional affairs with twenty-two for the dinner, enormous turkeys stuffed with chestnuts, mince pies, and puddings with brandy butter. I didn't like plum pudding, so a fruit salad was always made especially for me. There was always a big party on Christmas eve. It had become a tradition that the children did terrible things to the parents' beds while the adults were downstairs drinking. We made apple-pie beds and put holly under the sheets. We still got our Christmas stockings though.

My parents were changed people when we were at the Hatt-Cooks. At home they did not get on well. Their backgrounds and characters were very different. My father, Thomas Kenneth Hanson, was from Halifax in the West Riding of Yorkshire. He was the younger son of kind but rather strict Nonconformist parents. He had won scholarships to Oxford, where he got a double first, and London and had just completed his Ph.D. when he met my mother. His older brother, always called Lars after the film star Lars Hanson, had also obtained a first from Oxford and later became Keeper of Printed Books at the Bodleian Library. He used to take us into the underground storage department of the Bodleian and once showed me Caxton's Bible there. He handled it as if it were the Holy Grail, and that's what it seemed like to me.

My grandfather, also a Thomas, was a book collector, in particular the books of John Edwardes, an eighteenth-century bookbinder. When you fanned the pages of an Edwardes edition, a beautiful scene appeared on the edges. I loved these books and longed to own them, but on his death his collection was donated, more fittingly, to the British Museum. He was also a local historian and had published a book called *The Story of Old Halifax.* So on my father's side I came from a family who revered and treasured books.

My father himself loved poetry and often quoted it. He seemed to have an appropriate line for any situation. It wasn't until I was much older that I found out where most of his snippets came from. I loved him very much, but my mother's attitude to him was scornful and dismissive. Even as a child I was aware he drank too much. But he hid his drinking from his teetotal parents most of his life. Sadly he died in a car accident when I was fourteen, before I had a chance to get to know him as a person.

My mother, Margaret Jocelyn Wigg, was the oldest child of Oscar and Amy, another profoundly mismatched couple. My grandfather Oscar was a civil servant of great moral rectitude and rather difficult nature. Amy was a beauty, with a wonderful singing voice, and a musical talent which she put aside to marry Oscar. They were very unhappy together, but did not believe in divorce. My parents' divorce was a terrible shock to them. As a child my mother developed osteomyelitis in her hip, a very dangerous disease before antibiotics. She had to undergo many painful operations and spend long periods in hospital, and had to wear a leg brace. She was left with a deep scar and ongoing arthritis. But her spirits were undamaged. She was a very attractive woman, who loved company and parties. She was also strong-willed and sharp-tongued. With her abilities and drive, she would have been happier in this generation, probably heading a multinational company. With only bridge and charity work for outlets, she had too much energy to be a comfortable person to live with. I spent a lot of time as a child studying her to find out what sort of mood she was in. Perhaps this is the source of my understanding of character. When she was in a good mood, no one was more fun to be with. She took us on many outings—to the theatre, to musicals, and to ballet. She was also musical and played the piano beautifully. Her father had given her a baby grand piano as a twenty-first birthday present, and one of my happiest memories of childhood is of lying in bed listening to my mother playing Chopin on a summer evening.

When I was seven my family moved from Potten End to a small village called Drayton in the Thames Valley, near Abingdon in Berkshire. My father had a new job with Standard Oil, working at Esso House, an old mansion that had been owned by the Singer family, at Milton on the Newbury road on the edge of the Berkshire Downs. My parents bought a small house called Forge Cottage, which, as you might expect from the name, had been the old blacksmith's. We were always digging up horseshoes in the garden. My sister and I went to a girls' school in Abingdon called St. Helen's and St. Catherine's. It was run by Anglican nuns and was very high church. We celebrated Saints' Days and all the religious holidays, and had daily prayers and bible readings. I loved the drama and the theatricality of the religious side of school, but my mother had a strong distrust of Anglo-Catholicism and dreaded us becoming too religious.

But religion and history seemed to be tied up together in Berkshire. The place was full of echoes of both. Forge Cottage backed onto the churchyard of a Norman church with carvings and other relics from the thirteenth century, and down the road was Drayton Manor which had been a priory up till the time of Henry VIII. It was known locally as "Bassett's"—the name of the misanthropic and reclusive present owner. By a stroke of luck my mother met Mr. Bassett at bridge. She must have charmed him as she did most men. After that my sister and I were allowed the run of the place.

It was paradise for children. On one side of the manor was a string of old hay barns and stables. The horses had gone, but the traps and buggies still stood moldering away there. Behind the house lay a huge fruit orchard, and a walnut orchard, said to be the oldest and largest in England, as well as the usual English hazelnut coppices and water meadows. Occasionally we met Mr. Bassett and he would give us a basket of walnuts or apples for our mother or invite us in for a glass of lemonade, but most often we saw no one else there, just the wild animals, foxes, rabbits, stoats, moles, squirrels, hedgehogs, and dormice. Most of them were almost tame, having been untroubled in their wilderness for years.

Our main source of entertainment was in the fantasy games we made up and played out far from adult eyes. These were often based on books we'd been reading or on the occasional film we saw—often on cowboy and Indian films. Most of our games involved animals—we either were them or befriended them, and we had strings of imaginary horses, dogs, and other animal friends.

When the Manor was sold after Mr. Bassett's death, the walnut orchard was cut down and the wild gardens tamed. We children were no longer allowed to play there. Perhaps my sorrow at this event partly inspired my picture book, *Mr. Plunkett's Pool.*

Our closest friends in the village were Jill and Celia Haddon, who lived on a farm up the road from us. We spent most of our time together playing in their barn, making dens and tunnels through the bales and being animals from *The Jungle Book.* Jill was a Kipling fan, and I still have a copy of *Thy Servant a Dog, Told by Boots,* which we all cried our eyes out over, with her name in it. Obviously I borrowed it and never gave it back. I spent a lot of my time then pretending to be some animal or other, usually a horse or pony. For years I didn't walk anywhere. I cantered.

A love of animals was a major part of my childhood and is a strong part of my writing now. And I owe a great debt to the authors of animal books that I read when I was young: Kipling, Ernest Thompson Seton, Mary O'Hara, the Pullein-Thompson sisters. When we moved to Drayton we took our first dog, Remus, with us, and shortly after acquired another puppy, Sparky. Sadly they were both run over on the road outside our house. Remus was the first great loss of my life. I wanted to go to church to pray for him, but my mother said it was better to carry on as normal and sent us off to school.

The next dog we had was Libby, a brown-and-white terrier that my father brought home after my sister had gone away to boarding school. Libby became my companion and confidante. She slept on my bed and was my best friend. She was rather a naughty dog—she snapped at strangers and chased anything: sheep, cows, rabbits, cats, which was a terrible liability, living as we did in the middle of farming country—but I adored her. When my parents finally separated and we left Drayton, my mother gave Libby away. It was the worst part of the whole trauma for me, and for years after I dreamt about finding her again. When we bought a Labrador puppy for our children ten years ago, we named her Libby after the dog I lost.

I wanted to have a kitten but my mother disliked cats. (Now I have three of them, Snerkle, Bobadoo, and Little Orange Cat.) My sister had a black-and-white rabbit called Skippy, and I had a series of stick insects, magical creatures that could reproduce without sexual partners. We also had a pet tortoise who escaped every summer but who somehow kept being brought back to us. After Libby, however, the main love of my life was horses. I longed to have my own pony, but even without this dream ever coming true, there were plenty of horses around to ride. I spent all my pocket money on riding lessons and had several friends who had ponies that they would let me ride for sixpence an hour. I had any number of imaginary horses Sorrel, Magic, Jayette, Night Sky, Wildfire—and I would take them all out for a ride in turn. Magic was also my bicycle's name, and every time I went out on it I pretended I was riding, like Lizzie does in my pony story *Pure Chance.*

After animals my other passion was for reading. I can't remember a time when I couldn't read. I was certainly reading fluently before I went to school. At the age of seven or eight, I suddenly started reading at enormous speed and could get through a novel in an afternoon. My mother finally let me join the local public library, and here I discovered a kingdom of unbelievable richness. My favourite authors were Geoffrey Trease and Violet Needham, as well as Enid Blyton, of course, who was everybody's favourite author. But when I went to the library on Saturday morning, I made a point of getting out the thickest and longest books I could find to last me through the weekend and so discovered books like *The Three Musketeers, Robbery under Arms, Gone with the Wind,* and *War and Peace.* Then as now I was a very eclectic reader.

I loved poetry as well, and as we had to learn a lot of it by heart at school, I usually had verses going through my head. I was fascinated by songs and ballads that told a fragment of a story. Trelawney, Sir Patrick Spens, Lord Randall, Barbara Allen ... who had they been, these mysterious people who now lived on in the pages of our school anthologies?

Because I had a good memory and was a good reader, I was often called on at school to recite poetry or read the lesson. I became very fond of acting. My mother made a point of taking us to the theatre, and the New Theatre at Oxford, which was only ten miles or so away, often had excellent productions of plays, operettas, ballets, and musicals, and a pantomime every Christmas. After the pantomime we would put on our own version with the Hatt-Cooks. Mark always played the Dame, and I would be the Principal Boy. The high point of my acting career was when I played the part of Queen Elizabeth I in a school play in 1953, the year of the present queen's coronation. I had a splendid costume made out of a maroon velvet dressing gown of my mother's, and later won a prize in a fancy dress competition for it.

So my childhood up to the age of eleven was reasonably happy, and as far as I was concerned would go along like this until I grew up. I liked school and did well at it, in all subjects. I knew my mother wanted me to go away to Queen Anne's, the boarding school, where my sister had been for a year already. But Jocelyn seemed to be enjoying the new school and, though I wasn't looking forward to leaving my friends, particularly my best friend, Jenny Whitehead, Jenny herself had already had a year away in Saudi Arabia, and we were still good friends when she came back. There would still be the holidays when we would be together to ride ponies, go roller skating or to the cinema, and talk endlessly about every subject under the sun.

But at around about that age two things happened that changed my life lastingly. The first was my parents' separation. Their relationship had deteriorated beyond saving, and the fights and arguments had escalated. Now I lay awake at night and listened to shouting instead of Chopin. My father slept in the spare room. One day all his things disappeared out of the house. My mother said he had

Infant Gillian with big sister Jocelyn, 1943.

gone away for a short holiday. Finally she told me he had left for good. Even though the atmosphere in the house was better and my mother did all she could to soften the shock, I was devastated. No one else in my school, no one else I knew, had divorced parents. My strongest feeling was one of terrible shame. I couldn't bear to tell anyone. I tried to hide it from people.

Apart from the shame, the worst thing about the divorce was the loss of a home and a life that I had been very attached to and that had suited me. Forge Cottage was sold and we moved to an outer London suburb, Northwood, near where my mother's parents lived. Libby had to be given away. We had no friends, and the only horses were in smart riding stables where it cost the earth to ride, and you had to have all the right clothes.

The second thing was equally a surprise and possibly even more devastating. I began to stammer. I remember clearly the first time it happened. I was in the village shop asking for a brand of sweet I was particularly fond of, Exhibition Candy. I opened my mouth to say "Exhibition" and no sound would come out. It was as if something had tightened my throat and would not let me speak. I pointed to the candy instead, and went home puzzled, wondering what had happened to me.

My uncle Lars had stammered as a child, and my parents assumed my stammer was hereditary. Even though it started when I was still at primary school, it did not become completely disabling until I was thirteen or fourteen. At Queen Anne's it was suggested I should take elocution lessons as a way of helping me overcome it. I think the lessons had rather the reverse effect as I took half an hour to stumble through a poem to my agonised embarrassment and that of everyone else in the class. At one stage a speech therapist came to the school to help me. I found the treatment helpful, but it was not continued, I can't remember why.

I don't know whether the stammer caused my subsequent extreme shyness or if it was the other way round, but for the next few years I was terribly unhappy. I felt like a freak every time I tried to open my mouth. I hated going out and meeting people because I couldn't talk to them. Even going into a shop to buy something was major trauma for me. It was before the wonderful days of self-service in supermarkets, and every item had to be requested. I thought my family were ashamed of me, and my self-esteem disappeared altogether. I suppose only another stammerer knows how it feels when the faculty of speech which for most people is free and unself-conscious suddenly becomes a hurdle to be faced every day in every relationship. Nothing I said was spontaneous. Every sentence was a fearful struggle, and a compromise between what I wanted to say and what I could actually articulate. Stammering is physically exhausting, compounded by the constant and paralysing fear of being suddenly called on to speak. I was also well aware that my facial contortions were extremely ugly to watch, and I thought that I repelled listeners.

I stammered least with my close friends at school, and they were wonderfully supportive and protective. My family life meanwhile had become even more complicated. One afternoon at Queen Anne's when I came back from sport, my friend Eileen, who had been inside with a cold, told me my father had been to the school and had had a blazing row with our house mistress, Miss Faull. He had

"With my father, Thomas Hanson, and my sister," 1948.

wanted to see Jocelyn and me, but she had refused to let him. A few days later a letter arrived from him, telling us of his remarriage. I'd often read in books of people fainting from shock, but this was the first time I'd realised it could actually happen. I didn't faint, but I started shivering and shivered for the next twelve hours. It seemed to be more of a shock than the divorce. I suppose it made everything final. Also my father had married someone for whom my sister and I had formed a strong dislike, and who had a daughter we also thought we didn't like. Looking back I can see that this probably sprang from my mother's reaction to the woman who had been part of the cause of the marriage's breakdown. When I got to know my stepmother better, I came to appreciate her strength of character, her kindness, and her patience. I wish we had had more time together.

A few months later my mother also remarried. She and my stepfather lived in Northwood; my father and my stepmother in Woodbridge in Suffolk. My sister and I went from one place to the other in school holidays, but made our base with our mother. Early in 1957 my stepfather, who also worked for Standard Oil, was offered a job in Kano in Northern Nigeria. I don't know what his reasons were for accepting—a chance of a new start, a sense of adventure, the lure of a semi-colonial lifestyle, and maybe, as I've often suspected, the opportunity for a man who was still young to enjoy married life away from two hostile teenage step-daughters! We were to go out for the long summer holidays and spend the other holidays between the Hatt-Cooks, who were now living in a small village in Wiltshire near Salisbury, and with our father in Woodbridge.

We spent one Easter holiday in Woodbridge. In the last few days I've been reminded often of that time, nearly forty years ago and on the other side of the world. Like Goolwa, Woodbridge is an estuary town. It has the same wide stretches of water, the same huge skies, the same sounds of wind, seagulls' cries, the lap of water, and the tinkling of moored yachts. The holiday was fraught with arguments, despite my stepmother's efforts to provide a loving home. My father did not want us to go to Nigeria. He wanted us to live with him and go to the local school. He would refuse to give consent for our passports.

We returned to school in April with the dilemma still unsolved. My stepmother sent me a dress she had made for me. I liked it enormously and felt very warm towards her. I was sure things were going to work out somehow. One evening I had gone out onto the sports field to practice cricket. Eileen came running up the field and told me Miss Faull wanted to see me immediately. I knew instantly that something terrible had happened to one or other of my parents. When I went into the house-mistress's room, my sister was sitting on the sofa sobbing. Miss Faull told me very briefly that there had been a car accident. My father was dead. She then left Jocelyn and me together. I was crying, but I remember thinking how foolish I felt crying in my red shirt and grey shorts which were my sports uniform. I couldn't believe death happened on an ordinary summer evening with no warning. I felt as if I should have been prepared for it in some way, and at least have been wearing something more appropriate.

Many years later I was going through some old papers and letters of my mother's that she had kept from our boarding school days, and I found letters written by Miss Faull at the time of my father's death, telegrams from my godfather, newspaper clippings and two letters from my grandfather who had attended the inquest. There was even a road map with the exact location of the crash. All of this helped me to come to terms with my father's death, which I had never done before. My mother had strongly recommended we should not go to the funeral, and for a long time I simply did not believe my father was dead. I suspected him of running away to South America, and I often dreamed of suddenly meeting him in the most unlikely of places.

My memory is very good, but I can't remember anything about the rest of that school term. I have no idea how I survived it. Once again my mother's philosophy was to carry on as normal, as if nothing had happened. So apart from a weekend with my aunt and uncle, we stayed on at school. I don't remember how we got ready for the first trip to Nigeria, who took us to the airport, or even getting on the plane. But I do remember arriving there, early in the morning. My stepfather drove us around Kano, as we gazed in amazement at the African streetscape, which was quite unlike anything two English girls who had never even been abroad had ever seen before in their life. My parents' house was still being built and they were staying in a chalet in the Central Hotel. When we arrived back there, two dogs came racing to the door to welcome us. My parents were looking after them while their owners were on leave. I was really happy that we had dogs again.

It was 1957 and I was about to turn fifteen. Kano was then a cheerful, prosperous city, proud of its history as an ancient trading post and home to people of dozens of different nationalities. I fell completely in love with the place and the way of life. I loved the brightness of the colours, the exotic flowers and fruits, the hot sun, the tropical nights with marvellous stars. I had never seen a night sky like that in England. I suppose we led a privileged life there, swimming in the club pool, playing tennis and riding polo ponies, lent to us by one of my parents' friends, Rex Raccah, but after the sadness and grief of the previous years it was like balm to the soul.

My parents spent eight years in Nigeria, and the pattern of my life became one of spending the long summer holidays with them in Kano, and later Lagos, the school terms at Queen Anne's, until I went to Oxford in 1961, and the holidays at Whiteparish with the Hatt-Cooks. It was rather an unsettled life, and I felt as if none of these places was a real home, but it had many compensations. Because of my stammer and because I was still very shy, I was usually somewhat on the outside of life, observing it, and observing people, storing up all sorts of ideas and images that I would later use in my books for children and young people. I was making some attempts to write—apart from poems in the school magazine, I wrote a verse play on the life of Vercingetorix, a leader of the Gauls, and after my first trip to Spain I wrote a short novel. It was called "Malaguena," after a Spanish song I loved, and was a romantic story about two French boys I had met in Spain— and me.

I was studying languages and history at school and for the final exams in the English school system, A Levels, did French, Spanish, Latin, and history. I was offered a place at Lady Margaret Hall to read Modern Languages. I probably would have been more sensible to have stuck with history, as my stammer meant I would never be truly fluent in speaking French and Spanish, no matter how well I could read and write them, but I was influenced by all the fascinating French-speaking people we knew in Kano, and I had a passionate love for Spanish history and culture. I visited Spain for the first time in 1960, spending four weeks at a language school in San Sebastian. The following year I spent three months at the University of Madrid before going to Oxford. I decided I would make Spanish my main subject, French my secondary one. There were only nine people in our year taking Spanish, and we formed a close group. One of these was a half-Chilean girl, Joan Shenton, who became a great friend of mine. She persuaded me to come along with her to an audition for a play. She got the leading role and I signed on to do props. The play was a bittersweet romance called *A Penny for a Song,* and the company was the Worcester College Players.

We took the play to the Minack Theatre in Porthcurno in Cornwall. It was an idyllic summer. I remembered how much I loved theatre and the following year threw myself into stage management for the university theatre companies. In the Lent term I was the stage manager on the Oxford University Dramatic Society (OUDS) production of *Othello* (the future film star Michael York played Cassio), and in the summer vacation again travelled with a play, this time with the Experimental Theatre Company (ETC)'s production of *The Scarecrow* to the Edinburgh Festival. In those days membership of OUDS was still strictly male, but I was co-opted as a member of the technical subcommittee, and so became one of the first ever female members of this famous university company. I enjoyed stage management for its own sake, but I was also fired with ambition to write for the theatre, and did in fact write a one-act play for an OUDS competition.

Schools (final exams) came all too soon, and then exams were over and so was my time at Oxford. I did one more student production, *The Taming of the Shrew,* which we took to Stratford on Avon, and then had to think seriously about finding work. Like all the other Arts graduates I wanted to work for the British Broadcasting Corporation (BBC), or in some other artistic field, but none of my interviews came to anything. Eventually I found part-time work on a student survey for the London School of Economics. The survey was being coded to be put on computers. It was my first introduction to these mythic machines which were then still in their massive mainframe stage. I worked with punch cards on sorters and verifiers. It was not the most enthralling of jobs, but it paid the rent and it meant I could move out of home (my parents had returned from Nigeria and were living in Northwood again) and find a bedsit in central London. And possibly my introduction to computers at this time started my fascination with modern technology and the way it is changing our lives and society, a theme which is always turning up in my writing.

A year or so later I was living in a tiny flat in South Lambeth. I had a black cat called Tiffany and a job at the Greater London Council in the Treasurer's Department. I'd thought I might end up in Arts funding (the GLC ran the Festival Theatre and the National Film Theatre), but I found myself dealing with compensation claims after compulsory purchase orders. It was a strange job and entailed making field trips to areas of London that I didn't know existed, usually in the path of some future motorway or comprehensive school or shopping centre. I was still trying to write, but it was hard to find the time while I was working full-time, and just staying alive in London without very much money took up all my energy.

During this time I met up again with an old friend from Oxford, Ion Will. He had been working in Europe for a few years and wanted me to return there with him. The temptation was just too great: we got married and I spent the next two and a half years travelling around Europe. We were based in Switzerland in Ticino and travelled from Portugal to Turkey and back again. We spent six months in Milan, and three in Madrid. It was fascinating, exciting, and often lonely and frustrating. When we came back to England, we realised we were not really suited to each other and parted more or less amicably. I found work as a picture researcher, and eventually got a job with a publishing company in London, Tom Stacey Ltd. Here I did all sorts of editing work, ending up as the Arts and Entertainment Editor on *Chambers's Encyclopaedia Year Book.* London in the mid-sixties was an exciting place to be. I was at last working in the field of the Arts and was receiving some recognition and encouragement for my writing.

I went on to try freelance journalism and film criticism. I visited Australia in 1970 for the first time with Philip Rubinstein, who would become my second husband, and worked for the *Sunday Australian* and the *Bulletin* among other publications. On returning to England we both became very involved in the encounter group movement and in a search for some spiritual meaning to our lives. Philip went to a Buddhist monastery, Kham Tibetan House, while I decided a worthwhile form of employment would be teaching. While I was doing a postgraduate certificate of education at Stockwell College in London, I worked as a part-time cook in a "stately home," Oxenhoath in Kent, in return for a flat in the old servants' quarters. It was an extraordinary experience which I've always wanted to write about. My novel *Under the Cat's Eye* is based on this house.

Philip and I were married in 1973, and we returned to Australia to live. We bought a house in Sydney and our son, Matthew, was born there in 1974. Our daughter, Tessa, was born in Sydney in 1977, and our second daughter, Susannah, in Byron Bay in 1979. We were rather old parents when Matthew was born—Philip was nearly forty and I was thirty-one—but one of the advantages of this was that we were prepared to lead a very child-centred life. I had wanted to have children for a long time. My family

School play, 1953 (Gillian is sitting in the front row, third from the right).

became the centre of my existence. My main ambition was to provide a stable and loving environment for my children to grow up in. I made a vow to myself that I would never put them down, and I would always put their needs before my own.

While the children were growing up, we lived first in Sydney, then in Byron Bay, and moved to Adelaide in 1981. In all three places we tried to "live simply so others may simply live," still one of the principles I try to live by. Until 1986 we did not have a car, which meant we stayed close to home or used public transport, walked and cycled a lot. For many of those years we did not have television either, but made our own entertainment, and read masses of books together. We grew our own vegetables, kept chickens, and tried to eat only healthy food. The children rarely had sweets or chocolate. Fairly early on, both my daughters became vegetarians through their own choice, and still are today. We were a little bit like Caspian's family in *Answers to Brut*. In fact Brut was based on a dog we owned when we lived in Byron Bay. He was called Pepper, and sadly we had to find another home for him when we moved to Adelaide.

I suspect it was the move to South Australia that finally forced me to become a writer. It's a more reserved and private place than New South Wales. When we came to live here the children and I missed our friends very much, and took a long time to make new ones. I began making up stories for them when we walked to the bus stop or to school. We had two cats then called Bobby and Sandy, and I made up a whole series of exciting adventures about these two cats. Every time we walked out the gate the kids would beg, "Tell us a Bobby-Sandy story!" I didn't write any of them down, and I've forgotten most of them now, but one of my most recent books, *Jake and Pete*, is about two stray kittens, and in it I can hear echoes of those Bobby-Sandy stories.

In Byron Bay we had become quite involved in the local church. When we moved to Adelaide, I joined the Christian Dance Fellowship and for several years was part of a group dancing in churches and at conferences and seminars as a form of praise and healing. It was a very important part of my life, and both healed me of past hurts and grief and opened up my creativity. I began to write poems and prose pieces that could be used in dance, and once I had begun writing again, it seemed as if I couldn't stop! Suddenly I had a flood of ideas, characters, images, and stories whirling around inside my head.

My youngest child was at school and I needed to find some sort of work. I was cleaning the children's school on a part-time basis, but I thought I should look for something a little more fulfilling. I decided it was "Now or Never." I had to see if I could write a novel. I told my husband I would spend three months writing and see if I could have a novel finished by the end of that time. If I couldn't, I would go out and get a job. I had in my head two characters, a boy and a girl, and I knew I wanted to write a fantasy adventure with a school setting. My main role model was Diana Wynne Jones. I'd discovered her books by accident in the Byron Bay library and was completely captivated by how she made the impossible totally believable. I read her novel *Charmed Life* over and over again to work out how she did it. Together with the authors I loved as a child—Masefield, Stevenson, Kipling, Needham among many others—I owe

her an enormous debt. My novel *Nexhoath Nine* is dedicated to her.

So I sat down one morning in February, 1985, and working three days a week from nine to three, wrote out longhand 120 pages of the novel that was to become *Space Demons*. It was originally going to be called "Waking/ Dreaming," but halfway through the second chapter a computer game suddenly made its way into the story. I decided to call the game "Space Demons." From then on it became an integral part of the plot. When I'd finished my first draft, I gave it to a friend to read to tell me if I was wasting my time or not. She thought the story had a few things wrong with it, but encouraged me to persevere. I typed out the manuscript and started sending it off to publishers. The second publisher liked it enough to encourage me to rewrite it, sending me the readers' reports. One was from Eleanor Nilsson, whom I did not know at the time, but has since become a great friend and colleague. Eighteen months and many drafts later, my novel *Space Demons* was published.

As with all my books, it wasn't until I actually started writing that I found out what I wanted to write about. I rarely have an outline of my story, and usually I do not know what the ending is going to be. I write to find out what is going to happen, and it is through writing that I explain the world to myself. Often my books take ideas and themes from the interests and lives of my children. When I started writing *Space Demons,* Matthew was eleven years old and mad about computer games. But I try not to use my children, or anyone I know, directly as characters, or to steal important stories from their lives. I think the art of fiction is to tell stories that are yours alone; I suppose the art of teaching creative writing is to enable other people to tell their own stories.

By the time *Space Demons* was published, I had already finished my second novel, *Beyond the Labyrinth*. Whereas *Space Demons* had been a conscious effort to write a "children's" book, *Beyond the Labyrinth* was written entirely for myself. I wrote it in a sort of trance, not thinking about the reader at all, but following the dictates of the story that demanded to be written. Often with a novel, the genesis of the book will be almost like a vision. I see the whole finished book inside my head at one swoop. It's a strange process which is very hard to explain, but most creative people will understand what I am saying. I don't know the plot or even all the characters, but I know exactly what the book is like. Writing it is the long hard slog of getting the vision out of my mind and down on paper, and trying to stay as faithful to it as possible.

This process usually takes me about two years. I don't like talking about the book when I am writing it, and I don't show it in its early stages to anyone. Sometimes I bounce ideas off Philip on our daily walks, and he has often been the first reader of the manuscript. I try to persuade my children to read and vet the books for me, but as they grow up and lead their own lives it's getting harder for them to find the time. Now it's more likely to be my agent, Jenny Darling, who will be the first person to read a new story. Her reaction is always very important to me.

Sometimes the book will have a distinctive "colour." *Beyond the Labyrinth* was blue and gold. It is one of the most personal of my books, and still one of my favourites. It is a strange book, full of unexpected twists. People either

"My mother, Margaret Jocelyn Wigg, in Kano, Nigeria," 1958.

love it or hate it. The publishers who had done *Space Demons* did not want to publish it, unless it was rewritten considerably. I tried very hard to rewrite it, but it was impossible. The book was in the right shape and form for what it was, it was very close to the original vision I had had of it, and I was unable to alter it. I sent it to another publisher, Hyland House, a small independent Melbourne company who had a reputation for doing unusual teenage fiction. To my delight they accepted it unchanged.

This began my relationship with Anne Godden, who has now edited three of my novels, *Beyond the Labyrinth, Galax-Arena,* and *Foxspell.* She has always been able to grasp what I am trying to do in a novel, even when I haven't quite grasped it myself. When I've worked with her on these three books I've always felt that they have ended up the best it was possible to make them. I trust her totally.

While *Beyond the Labyrinth* was looking for a publisher, I wrote two shorter books—the first I had written on the computer, an Amstrad, that I'd finally bought, with the advance for *Space Demons.* Both these books were in a way experiments with different types of "children's" books. One was a family story, *Melanie and the Night Animal,* the other an adventure story, *Answers to Brut.*

We had by now moved into the house where we still live, 29 Seaview Road, Lynton. Lynton is a suburb on the edge of the Adelaide Hills, on the railway line to Melbourne. At the end of our street is a wild area, where the hills used to be quarried for stone. There are old

quarries, creeks and cliffs, gum trees and kangaroo thorn, magpies, kookaburras, rabbits and foxes. It became a special place for my children. They roamed the area and played games there. My son set part of his verse novel, *Solstice,* there. I found it an equally inspiring place to set stories. *Skymaze* uses the quarry, *Melanie and the Night Animal* uses the street and the local school, and *Foxspell* is inspired by the whole place. It's a hybrid area, where the city encroaches on the bush, and where many exotic invaders struggle with the native plants. Generations of local gangs of kids have made it their territory, like the Breakers do in *Foxspell.* After ten years I feel as if this is my landscape, a place that speaks to me and inspires me.

Melanie was a relatively easy and straight-forward book to write. *Brut* was more complex. I intended it to be an adventure story of the sort I had loved reading when I was young but from what I read in the newspapers and saw on television (we had finally given in and bought one!) society had become a lot more dangerous and criminals a lot more ruthless and intelligent than in Enid Blyton's day. Caspian's parents, like many of the parents in my books, spend all their time and energy worrying about the wrong things. They can control what their children eat, but they can't control the world beyond, and they are unable to stand up to intimidation. I often find when I am writing that I am led by the implications of the characters and plot that I have set up, into areas where I would probably rather not venture, but I am forced to by the power of the story I am creating, and by my desire to stay truthful to this story.

In 1989 *Space Demons,* which had been a huge success, won many awards in Australia, and was selling in large numbers, was adapted as a thrilling stage play. It was a strange experience to see my characters on stage. I felt as if they had escaped from me and now belonged to everyone. I watched the play about ten times to work out how the writer, Richard Tulloch, had done the adaptation. I had been asked to be writer-in-residence with one of the local youth theatre groups, Magpie, and was renewing my old love affair with theatre. My three books published the previous year had all been short-listed for the Children's Book Council Book of the Year Award. My fifth novel, *Skymaze,* had just been published, and I had written my first short stories. But in many ways 1989 was also a year of difficulty and stress. My closest friend committed suicide, and *Beyond the Labyrinth,* which won the Book of the Year Award in August, came in for a great deal of criticism for its use of swearing. For a couple of weeks it was a cause celebre with editorials in the newspapers and even a television program on the subject. I found the publicity painful and embarrassing. It showed me all too clearly that there were boundaries in children's literature and I had crossed them. I have never written again with the same freedom and unself-consciousness.

My next two books were lower-key and less controversial. I think I was withdrawing a little to recover and rethink. And I had other distractions. In 1989 my older daughter had acquired her first pony, a twelve-year-old chestnut mare called Summer Wine. Little did I know when I agreed she could lease this horse just down the road from us that it would lead my daughters and me into an all-absorbing passion for the next seven years. (My son and my husband steadfastly refused to get involved.) I had promised myself I would buy a horse for myself if I won the Book of the Year, but the horse I chose turned out to be too inexperienced for me and I had to sell her again. For a year Tessa and Suzy and I took it in turns to ride Summer. Then Tessa wanted to go to pony club. She started having proper instruction. We bought a horse float and a big car to tow it. Tessa wanted to do eventing, and Larrikin, a 16.2 chestnut thoroughbred, entered our lives. Suzy took over Summer and I leased a quarter horse, Chisholm. Weekends became totally taken up with pony club rallies, events, and shows. And our lives became taken up with the joys and thrills, the disappointments and despair that owning horses brings.

I wrote a short book about a horse, *Flashback, the Amazing Adventures of a Film Horse,* which was a comedy adventure, drawing heavily on the conventions of "children's" books. I have recently written another short pony book, *Pure Chance,* which is based on a horse Suzy leased for three years after she outgrew Summer. Pure Chance, or Gumpy as he was nicknamed, turned out to be a marvellous dressage horse, and Suzy won heaps of classes on him, including a first at the Royal Adelaide Show. And I am planning a long novel, "South Road," which will be based on the lives of several families involved with horses in the southern part of Adelaide.

Flashback was published in 1990 and in 1991 I had three books published. One was the novel I mentioned earlier, *At Ardilla,* a story about three families at a holiday house. I had also started branching out into other forms of writing. One of the things that I love about working in this field is that there is always something different to experiment with. A lot of my books come about because I want to see if I can do it! With *Flashback* I wanted to see if I could write a comedy, and next I wanted to see if I could write picture books. *Dog In, Cat Out* was an experiment in writing a picture book with very few words (the four words of the title in all their different combinations!). *Keep Me Company* was published by Penguin in 1991 and *Mr. Plunkett's Pool* by Mark Macleod in 1992. I also wrote two short books of the type called junior novels or "chapter books." This is a form I particularly enjoy writing in. One of these was *The Giant's Tooth* and the other *Squawk and Screech.*

We had acquired even more pets, and Squawk was a musk lorikeet who stayed with us for a while after he had been hit by a car. I've written a story about my daughter's pet rat (*Peanut the Pony Rat*), but so far I haven't used the hermit crabs or the axolotls. But many of my stories are inspired by the pets we have had and by my children's love of animals and concern for the environment.

As well as picture books I was also learning how to write for the stage. While I was writer-in-residence with Magpie Theatre, I adapted *Alice in Wonderland* for that company. I thought the main problem for a modern audience was the fact that many of the wonderful jokes and wordplay are lost because we no longer have the same points of reference. So I wrote two short scenes at the start of each act set in the Victorian household of the Liddell family. (Alice Liddell was a child friend of Lewis Carroll and the original Alice.) Each of the characters in the family, the cook and the governess, Charles Dodgson (Lewis Carroll) and his friend Duckworth, then double as the Wonderland and Looking Glass characters that they inspired.

Next I adapted my own novel, *Melanie and the Night Animal,* for Patch Theatre, another Adelaide children's theatre group. In 1992 I wrote an original play for Patch called *Paula,* about a little girl in hospital after a bicycle accident. I think writing for theatre is the most difficult form of writing, and each of these plays had flaws in them. But I had the marvellous opportunity of seeing my work performed and learning from my mistakes. My next play was to be an adaptation of my novel *Galax-Arena,* presented at the Youth Arts Festival, Come Out, in 1995.

In 1992 *Galax-Arena* had just been published. It was a novel I had been working on, on and off, for about five years. As with *Beyond the Labyrinth,* I had had a snap vision of it—its colours were red and black. I kept thinking it was too hard for me to write and putting it away. But the story would not be put away. I have always been fascinated by circus work, especially trapeze, acrobatics, and gymnastics, and this theme appears frequently in my books. Australia has a strong tradition in circus and physical theatre, from Circus Oz onwards, and I had been to many performances with my children. Suzy had been going to circus skills classes with the South Australian circus school, Cirkidz. I was intrigued by the dedication she and the other children gave to learning tumbling skills and how their self-esteem increased when they had mastered them. I think if circus school were compulsory, there would be far less vandalism and teenage crime.

Apart from writing about the acrobatics the greatest challenge in *Galax-Arena* was the language of the Peb, the children kidnapped to perform the life and death stunts for aliens. I wanted to use a sort of pidgin to demonstrate to English-speaking Australians what it means to lose your language through slavery, or even through immigration. The patois is based on West Indian creole languages, but simplified so as not to be completely unintelligible to the average young Australian reader. I was anxious that my language would not appear to be patronising or demeaning

Daughter Tessa with Summer Wine, 1991.

Daughter Suzy on Pure Chance, 1994.

to the children speaking it. George Turner, a South Australian linguist and expert on contact languages, checked the manuscript for me and to my relief gave my language his approval.

When children in schools ask me which is my favourite book, I usually answer "*Galax-Arena*." Partly because it was so hard to write, and partly because I love the characters, especially Joella and Leeward. I've written and rewritten it many times, adapted it as a play and written several drafts of a screenplay, and I'm still not bored with the themes and the story. But, like *Beyond the Labyrinth,* it is a book that divides readers. They either love it or hate it. In a way I feel some adult readers misunderstand the underlying themes of the story. They miss the point that this story is an allegory about power and exploitation, which is how I feel children are treated all over the world. The book is also about animal rights. The treatment of the Peb shocks us, but this is how animals are treated daily and as a matter of course. Perhaps I did not spell out these themes clearly enough, but I prefer to treat matters obliquely and in an understated way. However, I am about to start writing a sequel, which will take on from where the first novel ends (and begins). And this time I'll try to make sure everyone understands what I'm writing about.

In 1989 I had been awarded a three-year Senior Fellowship from the Australia Council. Part of my submission had been to write a play for teenagers. Patch Theatre was interested in working with me again, and we decided to see if we could present a stage version of *Galax-Arena.* The Adelaide Festival Centre Trust came in as coproducers and the play was directed by Nigel Jamieson, who has astonishing skills in directing physical theatre. Our cast was made up of young acrobats and gymnasts, some of whom

had never acted before. Our circus trainer, who also played Leeward, was Scott Grayland, formerly of Circus Oz. The show was spectacular and thrilling, but sadly marred by an accident, when Scott broke his ankle during a performance. We were able to recast, and continue the season, but this injury to Australia's greatest acrobat cast a pall over the whole production.

However, while Scott was out of action as an acrobat, he and I worked on another idea for a play which became *Wake Baby,* first presented at the Queensland Festival of Early Childhood, Out of the Box, in 1996. *Wake Baby* is a combination of acrobatics and puppetry, using ropes as a theatrical medium, and was produced by the Canberra puppet company, Company Skylark, and directed by Nigel Jamieson. It's a magical view of childhood and has been invited to tour in 1997 to Toronto, Brussels, and Lyons. I'm very proud of it, perhaps strangely for a writer, because it has no words at all. I find this type of theatre particularly rewarding to write for and my next two plays are both going to be in this form. One is an adaptation of *Jake and Pete,* for Theatre of Image, and the other is an original play, again with Patch Theatre, called *Each Beach.* Both of these will have more text than *Wake Baby* but will still be primarily a combination of visual and physical theatre, using images, puppets, and acrobats.

In 1992 I started writing *Foxspell,* the novel about Lynton, my "place." After *Galax-Arena* it seemed like an easy book to write. The problem that occupied me most was how foxes would talk if they had the power of speech. In the end while my characters are in their fox form, they communicate through images, without words. In his human form Dan Russell, the fox spirit, uses certain aspects of fox sounds—the snarl, the yap and the howl—in his speech. *Foxspell* takes as one of its main themes the problems faced by migrants, animal and human. Are they migrants or are they invaders? When is an animal "wild" and when is it "feral"? The Australian landscape is being devastated by European animals, rabbits, foxes, cattle, wild donkeys, wild buffalo, yet in all cases the animals were introduced deliberately by humans. South Australia in particular has a very fragile landscape, and it's easy to see the deadly effects of thoughtless use of the land. The human invader is by far the most destructive, yet people prefer to mount campaigns against rabbits and cats rather than change their own lifestyle.

Another theme in *Foxspell* is one that underlies all my work. When you move from one culture to another you leave behind, as well as your landscape, the myths and legends of your childhood. This is particularly hard for a writer, and for a children's writer it means giving up the rich pool of imagery that you would otherwise be able to draw on. I feel I can use the myths and symbols of my Anglo-Celtic Christian past in my stories. I have a right to them. They belong to me. But I don't have the right to use the Aboriginal legends and beliefs of my new country in the same way. These have become a taboo ground for non-Aboriginal writers. I've always loved Kipling's stories about what happens to the old gods when people stop believing in them, and in *Foxspell* I ask the question "What happens to the spirit beings that people transport unknowingly to new worlds?"

Playing around with language is another constant theme in my work. Perhaps it comes from my love of

"With my son, Matt," 1993.

poetry and words as a child, and from the study of languages which has been a consuming interest all my life. At the moment I'm studying my first non-Indo-European language—Japanese. It's also my first language with a different writing system, though I did learn the Russian alphabet a long time ago. I'm hoping it's exercising all the neurons in my brain so they can keep working till I'm a hundred. When I planned to write the sequel to *Space Demons* and *Skymaze,* I wanted to set it in Japan. Despite the closeness of Australia and Japan economically and politically, there are very few children's books which look at modern Japan. I visited Japan for the first time in 1994 as part of an exchange trip with my daughter's school, and was completely enthralled by the country and its society and culture. *Shinkei* was published in 1996. I have been back to Japan for a second trip and have been studying Japanese for four years. I plan to go back for a longer stay in the next couple of years as I want to write a fantasy that uses Japanese history and mythology as its source, rather than the Anglo-Celtic sources of most fantasy. The title is going to be "Across the Nightingale Floor."

In *Jake and Pete* I play around with "cat language" and in its sequel, *Jake and Pete and the Stray Dogs,* I do the same with "dog language." I've also written some rhyming texts, *Sharon Keep Your Hair On,* and *Hurray for the Kafe Karaoke.* These were extraordinarily hard to write, but lots of fun to read aloud. Despite the fact that I am better known for my rather serious older novels, I love to make people laugh. I've been very lucky with the illustrators to my picture books, all of whom have been great humorists as well as skilled artists. Terry Denton illustrated *Mr. Plunkett's Pool* and *Jake and Pete.* Craig Smith did *Squawk and Screech* and *The Giant's Tooth,* and David Mackintosh drew the fantastic pictures for *Sharon Keep Your Hair On* and *Hurray for the Kafe Karaoke.*

As the children leave home I've got much more time for writing. Tessa went back to London in August, 1996, to

continue her career as a singer-songwriter. She is studying singing and dance and playing guitar and folk violin. She has just got a band together to perform her material. Matthew has just finished his law degree but wants to be a writer. His first novel, *Solstice,* was published in 1995, and was adapted for the stage and presented at the Adelaide Festival early this year. His second novel, *Nomad,* was published in August, 1997, and he is at work on his third, while travelling in Europe and America for the next four months. Suzy has just finished school and is waiting to go to university. She wants to study history and Japanese and is very keen to return to Japan and complete her tertiary studies there in some way. During the holidays she and her friend are writing a book about what it's really like to be a teenager. I'm glad all my children are so independent and so creative and that they are starting young, rather than leaving it until they are over forty, like their mother.

When I was in my early twenties and had dreams of becoming a writer, I didn't intend to write for children. One of the pieces I started then and never finished was a novel about a character called Hythe, who adopted street kids and treated them with a mixture of love and abuse. Though it was about children, it was to be an adult book. Twenty-five years later I resurrected this character and his name to use in *Galax-Arena.* I often wonder, if I had stayed in England, would I have ever written children's books? I think it was the move to Australia as an adult migrant that led me to write a children's book as my first novel. I didn't know anything about Australian adult culture, but my children were growing up as young Australians and I knew their world. I wanted to write books that they would enjoy reading, that spoke to them about their concerns and their

Husband of the author, Philip Rubinstein, with Jon, *1993.*

Gillian Rubinstein as the Duchess (back row, fourth from left) in "The Mad Hatter's Tea Party," 1996.

problems, that didn't shy away from describing the world they lived in with all its cruelties and dangers but that gave them hope and confidence in the abiding human virtues of courage, compassion, and unselfishness. Most of all when I write I want to spin the spell of words that enthralls the reader and takes them into the magic world of the imagination that inspired and consoled me when I was young. When I look back over my life I can see that everything I've ever felt, whether it's been good or bad at the time, has all contributed to the emotion that goes into my writing. I still have nightmares sometimes, but I don't stammer any more.

Writings

FOR CHILDREN; FICTION

Space Demons (novel), Omnibus/Penguin (Adelaide), 1986, Dial Books (New York City), 1988.

Melanie and the Night Animal, Omnibus/Penguin, 1988.

Answers to Brut, Omnibus/Penguin, 1988.

Beyond the Labyrinth (novel), Hyland House (Melbourne), 1988, Orchard (New York), 1990.

Skymaze, Omnibus/Penguin (Adelaide), 1989, Orchard (New York City), 1991.

Flashback, the Amazing Adventures of a Film Horse, Penguin, 1990.

At Ardilla, Omnibus, 1991.

Squawk and Screech, (chapter book), illustrated by Craig Smith, Omnibus, 1991.

Dog In, Cat Out (picture book), illustrated by Ann James, Omnibus, 1991, Ticknor and Fields (New York City), 1993.

Keep Me Company (picture book), illustrated by Lorraine Hannay, Penguin, 1991.

Mr. Plunkett's Pool (picture book), illustrated by Terry Denton, Mark Macleod/Random House (Milson's Point), 1992.

Galax-Arena, Hyland House (Melbourne), 1992, Simon & Schuster (New York City), 1995.

The Giant's Tooth (chapter book), Viking, 1993.

Foxspell, Hyland House, 1994, Simon & Schuster, 1996.

Jake and Pete (chapter book), illustrated by Terry Denton, Random House (Milson's Point), 1995.

Peanut the Pony Rat, (chapter book) Heinemann (London), 1995.

Shinkei, Omnibus, 1995.

Sharon Keep Your Hair On, illustrated by David Mackintosh, Random House (Milson's Point), 1996.

Witch Music, (collected short stories) Hyland House, 1996.

Annie's Brother's Suit, (collected short stories) Hyland House, 1996.

Jake and Pete and the Stray Dogs (chapter book), Random House, 1997.

Under the Cat's Eye, Hodder Headline (Sydney), 1997, Simon & Schuster (New York), 1998.

Pure Chance (junior novel), Walker Books (London), 1998.

Hurray for the Kafe Karaoke, illustrated by David Mackintosh, Random House, 1998.

The Pirate's Ship, illustrated by Craig Smith, Viking, forthcoming.

The Fairy's Wings, forthcoming.

PLAYS

New Baby, for Magpie Theatre, 1989.

Alice in Wonderland (adaptation), for Magpie Theatre, 1989.

Melanie and the Night Animal (adaptation), for Patch Theatre, 1990.

Paula, for Patch Theatre, 1992.

Galax-Arena (adaptation), for Come Out 95, Patch Theatre, and Adelaide Festival Centre Trust (AFCT), 1995.

Wake Baby, for Out of the Box and Company Skylark, first presented at the Queensland Festival of Early Childhood, 1996.

Jake and Pete (adaptation), for Theatre of Image, first presented at the Sydney Theatre Company, 1997.

Each Beach (original play), for Patch Theatre, first presented at the Adelaide Festival Centre, 1997.

OTHER

(Compiler) *After Dark,* Omnibus/Penguin, 1988.
(Compiler) *Before Dawn,* Omnibus/Penguin, 1988.

Has also contributed numerous short stories to anthologies including *After Dark, State of the Heart, Dream Time, Bizarre, Landmarks, The Pattern Maker,* and *Celebrate,* and several articles for periodicals including *Magpies, Literacy for the New Millenium, Island Magazine,* and *Australian Magazine.*

RUMFORD, James 1948-
(Lin Chien-min)

Personal

Born August 13, 1948, in California; son of Sydney (a salesman) and Audrey (a store clerk; maiden name, Nafzgar) Rumford; married Carol Drollinger (an office manager), 1969; children: Jonathan Rumford. *Education:* University of California-Irvine, B.A. in French literature, 1970; University of Hawaii, M.A. in English as a Second Language, 1976. *Hobbies and other interests:* Foreign languages, travel.

Addresses

Home—2702 Manoa Road, Honolulu, HI 96822. *E-mail*—Kauhau@lava.net.

Career

Peace Corps, 1971-75; Fulbright Lecturer, 1977-81; Manoa Press (publisher), owner, 1986—; writer/illustrator, 1996—. *Member:* Honolulu Printmakers, Society of Children's Book Writers and Illustrators.

Writings

SELF-ILLUSTRATED

The Cloudmakers, Houghton Mifflin, 1996.
The Island-below-the-Star, Houghton Mifflin, 1998.

When Silver Needles Swam: A Story of Tutu's Quilt, Manoa (Honolulu), 1998.

Seeker of Knowledge: The Man Who Deciphered Egyptian Hieroglyphs, Houghton Mifflin, 2000.

OTHER

(Translator and commentator) Tsung-mu Wang, *An Essay on Paper: Observations Made by Wan Zongmu at the Imperial Paper Mill at Jade Mountain,* Manoa, 1993.

(Under pseudonym Lin Chien-min) *Wu Wei-yun, Cloudmaker: A Translation of a Page from the T'ang ch'I shuo, Strange Stories from the T'ang Dynasty,* Manoa, 1996.

Has published numerous handmade books from Manoa Press, 1986—.

Work in Progress

"Too many to list."

Sidelights

James Rumford told *SATA:* "I began writing and illustrating children's books only four years ago. Since then I have had four books published. Each book has been a new and rewarding experience. Writing and illustrating children's books—I can't think of a better way to spend the rest of my life."

In his picture books, James Rumford brings to life and intermingles history and folklore. In his first book, *The Cloudmakers,* a Chinese grandfather and his grandson

James Rumford

are captured in Turkestan during a battle with the Arab troops of the Sultan of Samarkand. In a bid to win their freedom, the young man brags that his grandfather can make clouds, and when challenged to do so, they produce a billowing piece of paper. Adding poetry and drama to the process, Young Wu describes each step "as if the end product will actually be a cloud," observed Margaret A. Chang in *School Library Journal*. This explains how the secret of papermaking traveled from the Chinese world to the Arab one in the eighth century A.D., according to Arab legend. "Lyrical watercolor paintings perfectly complement the spare, engaging

text," remarked a reviewer for *Kirkus Reviews*. Considered appropriate material for early elementary school-age children, reviewers were quick to note the usefulness of the book in a classroom studying Asian history or the art and science of papermaking. Furthermore, averred Julie Corsaro in *Booklist,* the "smoothly written text and the soft, atmospheric watercolors ... encourage children to use their imaginations."

In *The Island-below-the-Star,* Rumford imagines the discovery of the Hawaiian Islands by Polynesian explorers before the era of recorded history. Five brothers, each with his own special talent, leave home in search of a certain star, and the island that lies beneath it. The youngest is a stowaway; when his brothers' skill with the wind, currents, stars, and waves can't save them after a storm blows them far off course, the youngest brother's skill with birds leads them to the island of their quest. "Told with the spare formulaic structure of a folktale ... the tale has the appeal of a youthful adventure while it uses the five brothers to tell the story of the migration of a whole people," observed Sally Margolis in *School Library Journal*. A *Kirkus Reviews* contributor compared *The Island-below-the-Star* favorably with Rumford's earlier *The Cloudmakers,* casting each as a "well-paced, engrossing story that is freighted with all sorts of fascinating nuggets of information from times long past."

Works Cited

Chang, Margaret A., review of *The Cloudmakers, School Library Journal,* September, 1996, p. 189.

Review of *The Cloudmakers, Kirkus Reviews,* June 15, 1996, p. 904.

Corsaro, Julie, review of *The Cloudmakers, Booklist,* September 15, 1996, p. 250.

Review of *The Island-below-the-Star, Kirkus Reviews,* March 1, 1998, p. 343.

Margolis, Sally, review of *The Island-below-the-Star, School Library Journal,* June, 1998, p. 121.

For More Information See

PERIODICALS

Booklist, March 15, 1998, p. 1252.*

S

SASSO, Sandy Eisenberg 1947-

Personal

Born January 29, 1947; daughter of Israel (an insurance agent) and Freda (a homemaker; maiden name, Plotnick) Eisenberg; married Dennis C. Sasso (a rabbi), June 25, 1970; children: David, Debora. *Education:* Temple University, B.A., 1969, M.A., 1972; Reconstructionist

Sandy Eisenberg Sasso

Rabbinical College, Rabbi, 1974; Christian Theological Seminary, Doctor of Ministry, 1996. *Religion:* Jewish.

Addresses

Office—Congregation Beth-El Zedeck, 600 West 70th St., Indianapolis, IN 46260. *E-Mail*—ssasso@ bez613.org.

Career

Manhattan Reconstructionist Havurah, New York City, rabbi, 1974-77; Congregation Beth-El Zedeck, Indianapolis, IN, rabbi, 1977—; Gleanders Food Bank, president, 1992-93; Butler University, Indianapolis, adjunct professor 1996—; Christian Theological Seminary, Indianapolis, lecturer, 1995—; director of POLIS project "Urban Tapestry," 1998—. Member, board of advisors of Indiana University Purdue University at Indianapolis (IUPUI), Indianapolis Children's Choir board, and Mayor's Task Force on Human Relations, 1987-88; president, Indianapolis Board of Rabbis, 1986-88; member, Rabbinic advisory committee, Jewish Fund for Justice, 1995; member, Women's Fund of Indiana Advisory Board, 2000—. *Member:* IUPUI Friends of Women's Studies.

Awards, Honors

Honorary Doctor of Humanities, DePauw University, 1986; Special Merit award, Vermont Book Publishers, 1992, for *God's Paintbrush;* Children's Books of Distinction Award finalist, 1994, for *In God's Name;* "best books of the year" honor, *Publishers Weekly,* 1995, for *But God Remembered: Stories of Women from Creation to the Promised Land;* "best books of the year" honor, *Publishers Weekly,* 1996, for *A Prayer for the Earth;* Sagamore of the Wabash award, Governor of the State of Indiana, 1995; named among Influential Women in Indiana, *Indianapolis Business Journal,* 1997; honorary D.H.L., Butler University, Indianapolis, and Doctor of Divinity, Reconstructionist Rabbinical College, both

1999; honorary degree, Christian Theological Seminary, 2000.

Writings

Call Them Builders: A Resource Booklet about Jewish Attitudes and Practices on Birth and Family Life, Reconstructionist Federation of Congregations and Havurot (New York), 1977.

(Author of foreword) *Putting God on the Guest List: How to Reclaim the Spiritual Meaning of Your Child's Bar or Bat Mitzvah,* Jewish Lights Publishing, 1992.

God's Paintbrush, illustrated by Annette C. Compton, Jewish Lights Publishing, 1992.

In God's Name, illustrated by Phoebe Stone, Jewish Lights Publishing, 1994.

But God Remembered: Stories of Women from Creation to the Promised Land, Jewish Lights Publishing, 1995.

A Prayer for the Earth: The Story of Naamah, Noah's Wife, illustrated by Bethanne Andersen, Jewish Lights Publishing, 1996.

God in Between, illustrated by Sally Sweetland, Jewish Lights Publishing, 1998.

For Heaven's Sake, illustrated by Kathryn Kunz Finney, Jewish Lights Publishing, 1999.

God's Paintbrush Celebration Kit, Jewish Lights Publishing, 1999.

What is God's Name, Jewish Lights Publishing, 1999.

God Said Amen, Jewish Lights Publishing, 2000.

Author of the article "Vayetze: Struggling on the Other Side of the River," published in *Women's Torah Commentary,* edited by Elyce Goldstein, Jewish Lights Publishing, 2000. Contributor to books, including *Women and Religious Ritual: An Interdisciplinary Investigation,* edited by Dr. Lesley A. Northup, Pastoral Press, 1993; *Life Cycles: Jewish Women on Life Passages and Personal Milestones,* edited by Rabbi Debra Orenstein, Jewish Lights Publishing, 1994; *Bar/Bat Mitzvah Basics: A Practical Family Guide to Coming of Age Together,* edited by Helen Leneman, Jewish Lights Publishing, 1996; and *Falling from Grace,* edited by Kent Calder and Susan Neville, Indiana University Press, 1998.

Contributor of articles to periodicals, including *Reconstructionist;* contributor of monthly columns to *Indianapolis Star,* 1998—, and the website beliefnet.com, 1999—.

Work in Progress

A new children's book.

Sidelights

Rabbi Sandy Eisenberg Sasso has written a number of religion-based books that celebrate young people's natural curiosity and show the benefits of accepting differences among people in their conception of God. In her first book for children, *God's Paintbrush,* Sasso explores the nature of God in words that are "well within a child's frame of reference," according to a reviewer for

Publishers Weekly. Sasso asks readers to reflect on such things as whether God can cry and how to be a friend to God. Although some reviewers find Sasso's books inappropriately anthropomorphic in their descriptions of God, others praise the uplifting quality of her prose. Sasso, who was the second woman to be ordained as a rabbi, has also received praise for the multicultural focus and poetic rhythms of her prose. In addition, her woman-centered focus in works such as *A Prayer for the Earth: The Story of Naamah,* have resulted in works that "add ... nuance and depth" to the traditional stories of the Old Testament, according to a *Publishers Weekly* critic.

Sasso's first book for children, *God's Paintbrush,* presents short essays on a variety of experiences common to children, following each with related questions for adults and children to discuss together. Some critics have found the amount of text and the great variety of issues raised in the book overwhelming, and the verdict on the book's usefulness has been mixed. Reacting to the "sheer number of situations described, feelings explored, and questions posed," *School Library Journal* contributor Susan Kaminow remarked that "perhaps [the book] would be useful in religious classes." Noting that books on spirituality are sometimes a "dicey proposition," a *Publishers Weekly* reviewer

Sasso's collection of stories elaborates on the Old Testament references to four fascinating, courageous women of biblical times. (Cover illustration by Bethanne Andersen.)

concluded that "[c]ommendably, Sasso doesn't presume to answer the questions but instead allows readers to ponder and formulate their own answers."

Sasso's 1994 effort, *In God's Name,* presents a story that explains why there are many different names for God by showing that each person finds in God a reflection of what he or she most values in the world. Hence, some call God "healer," others "giver of light," and others "protector." Although the people in Sasso's story are first puzzled and then angry when they learn of others' names for their God, they eventually come to understand that each name points to a different aspect of the same God. "This book glories in the thought that there is one true nondenominational God who fulfills each description offered," remarked P. Finn McManamy in the *Vermont Times.*

In God's Name received generally favorable reviews, some of which highlighted the book's multicultural focus and universal applicability. Mary Wade Atteberry singled out Sasso's prose for special praise in her review in the *Indianapolis Star:* "The spare and poetic text, rich in metaphor, is impressive in its simplicity.... Sasso has taken a concept and deftly developed a story children can absorb." Although a contributor in *Kirkus Reviews* found *In God's Name* "a little too earnest," Atteberry commented: "It is always pleasant to find a story that suggests the possibility of peace and unity among people—even when it is a children's book."

Another work of fiction, *God in Between,* takes place in a town where each household is isolated within its own windowless house, with yards and public spaces desolate and unused because of a lack of roadways on which to travel. Finally, the residents of this strange town, isolated from one another, decide to send emissaries out to seek God, who is said to solve all problems. The searchers return, having realized that God is between all people, and accept that His presence will allow them to inhabit the spaces outside their own homes. Describing *God in Between* as "a puzzling picture book," a reviewer for *Publishers Weekly* noted that the work would do little to help explain the concept of an ever-present spirit to small children. Perceiving *God in Between* as "didactic," *Booklist* contributor Ellen Mandel noted that Sasso's "nonsectarian urging to look beyond oneself, to look to help others and thereby find God will be welcomed" by those seeking books promoting diversity in spiritual matters.

Inspired by her own feminism, Sasso's nonfiction works include *But God Remembered: Stories of Women from Creation to the Promised Land.* The 1995 work comprises a collection of four midrashim—stories built on the few remaining Old Testament references in existence—that refer to certain characters: Lilith, the first woman in the Garden of Eden; Serach, a singer of psalms; Bityah, who scooped the infant Moses from the Nile; and the five strong-willed daughters of Zelophehad who take their property claims argument directly to God. A *Booklist* critic commended the author's choice of tales, writing, "Although part of the pleasure of the book lies in its strong feminist voice, Sasso also tells good stories." Equally enthusiastic, *School Library Journal* contributor Jane Gardner Connor noted that the four tales "are competently told and fit well with the Biblical tradition." Calling the collection "engaging," a *Kirkus Reviews* critic praised Sasso's use of "lively dialogue and occasionally modern phrasing" in telling her ancient tales.

Sasso once told *SATA,* "I have always admired the art of storytelling, marveling how a good story holds of an audience in a way no lecture or sermon can. As a rabbi I became the storyteller at family worship in my congregation and began to write my own stories. I fell in love with the sound of letters, the rhythm of words, and their power to invoke laughter, tears, hope. The beliefs about which I theorized in sermons, I began to write as stories.

"I write stories that honor our children's religious imagination. We do not give children enough credit for thinking about God and thinking profoundly. I wanted to give children a language to speak about what they care most deeply, a story about God in which they all see themselves reflected. So much of children's religious literature teaches how people are different in their beliefs. I wanted a book that celebrated those differences but also recognized that difference doesn't mean superiority and inferiority. If good words can inspire, so they can teach great tolerance and respect."

Through her focus in particular on the stories of women such as Noah's wife in her 1997 work *A Prayer for the Earth: The Story of Naamah,* Sasso attempts "to reclaim the names and stories of women, to help children and adults hear another voice," as she once explained. "So many words, so many visions have been lost. Beneath the ruins of layers of civilizations lie the oral traditions that never found their way between the hard covers of a book. Research wedded to imagination can reconstruct them for a new generation." Writing in the *Women's League Outlook for Conservative Judaism,* reviewer Ethel Zager called *A Prayer for the Earth* "refreshingly different" and described it as "a powerful plea for environmental concern."

"I write to teach and for joy," Sasso told *SATA.* "It is a great privilege, awesome responsibility, and pure delight."

Works Cited

Atteberry, Mary Wade, review of *In God's Name, Indianapolis Star,* December 1, 1994, p. E8.

Review of *But God Remembered: Stories of Women from Creation to the Promised Land, Booklist,* September 1, 1995, p. 54.

Review of *But God Remembered: Stories of Women from Creation to the Promised Land, Kirkus Reviews,* September 1, 1995, p. 1287.

Connor, Jane Gardner, review of *But God Remembered: Stories of Women from Creation to the Promised Land, School Library Journal,* December, 1995, p. 100.

Review of *God in Between, Publishers Weekly,* May 25, 1998, p. 83.

Review of *God's Paintbrush, Publishers Weekly,* December 14, 1992, p. 56.

Review of *In God's Name, Kirkus Reviews,* December 15, 1994.

Kaminow, Susan, review of *God's Paintbrush, School Library Journal,* June, 1993, pp. 100-01.

Mandel, Ellen, review of *God in Between, Booklist,* October 15, 1998, p. 425.

McManamy, P. Finn, review of *In God's Name, Vermont Times,* November 23, 1994.

Review of *A Prayer for the Earth: The Story of Naamah, Noah's Wife, Publishers Weekly,* February 24, 1997, p. 83.

Zager, Ethel, review of *A Prayer for the Earth: The Story of Naamah, Noah's Wife, Women's League Outlook for Conservative Judaism,* winter, 1997.

For More Information See

PERIODICALS

Booklist, February 15, 1997, p. 1029.
Kirkus Reviews, January 15, 1997, p. 146.
New York Times Book Review, November 20, 1994, p. 30.
Publishers Weekly, November 6, 1995, p. 67.

ON-LINE

Author's monthly online columns published at http://www.beliefnet.com.

*   *   *

SCHAEDLER, Sally

Personal

Born in St. Louis, MO; daughter of A. F. (an oil company manager) and Hertha (a teacher) Martindale; married Robert Schaedler; children: Robert, Jr., Nancy, Douglas. *Education:* Washington University, St. Louis, MO, B.F.A. *Religion:* Lutheran.

Addresses

Home—North Salem, NY. *E-mail*—schadler@bestweb.net.

Career

Amscan, Inc. (designers of gift items), Elmsford, NY, senior designer, 1990—. Book illustrator; illustrator for advertising agencies, including projects for General Foods, Nabisco, and Proctor & Gamble. Portrait artist, with work represented in collections. *Member:* Alpha Lambda Delta (past president of Delta Gamma chapter).

Awards, Honors

Awards for portraiture.

Illustrator

Cheryl Saban, *Griffin's Busy Day,* Modern Publishing (New York City), 1995.

Saban, *Griffin's Day at the Zoo,* Modern Publishing, 1995.

Saban, *Griffin's Play Group,* Modern Publishing, 1995.

Saban, *Griffin's Shopping Trip,* Modern Publishing, 1995.

Carolyn Ford, *Nothing in the Mailbox,* Richard C. Owen (Katonah, NY), 1996.

Andrew Gutelle, *I Can Do That! A Book about Confidence,* Time-Life (Alexandria, VA), 1996.

Gutelle, *Who Made This Big Mess?,* Time-Life, 1996.

Susan Striker, *Nature's Wonders for the Young at Art: Creative Activities for Ages Six and Up Using the Please Touch Philosophy,* Holt (New York City), 1998.

Lois Podoshen, *The Birthday Bird,* Richard C. Owen, 1998.

Jennifer Maze Brown, *Hooray! It's a Duck Day,* Concordia (St. Louis, MO), 1999.

Other books include *Artists at Work,* Holt; *The Wrong Hat,* Scott, Foresman (Glenview, IL); *Grandpa Retired Today, Blue Bikes, Mortimer the Frog, An Alphabet for Children, The Shoeshine Stand,* and the French textbook *Portes Ouvertes,* all Harcourt (San Francisco, CA); *Have You Met My Pet?, A Very Bad Day, Hugs and Hot Chocolate, Best Pizza Place, The Sitter, Make My Day, When Will the Sun Come Out?, The Dinosaur Trip,* and *A Fire Can Be Dangerous,* all Heritage Publishing; five Elizabeth Brian mysteries, Concordia; and *The Rooster Who Spoke Japanese* and *What Joy Found,* both Silver Burdett (Morristown, NJ).

Sidelights

Sally Schaedler told *SATA:* "I can't remember 'not drawing'—ever. I always knew that was what I wanted to do. I especially loved drawing people. I love to develop interaction between characters and make them become real people. I work in mixed media, mostly watercolor, acrylic, and pencil."

*   *   *

SCHORIES, Pat 1952-

Personal

Born July 30, 1952, in Batavia, NY; daughter of Alfred (a mechanical engineer) and Beatrice (a nurse; maiden name, Flood) Schories; married Harry Bolick (an artist and musician), July 11, 1998; children: Elizabeth Bolick (stepdaughter). *Education:* Kent State University, B.F.A., 1974. *Politics:* Democrat.

Addresses

Home—118 Lefurgy Avenue, Hastings-on-Hudson, NY, 10706. *E-mail*—pat@bolick.net.

Pat Schories

Career

Children's book author and illustrator. Also has worked as a freelance graphic designer and botanical illustrator, 1976—. *Member:* Society of Children's Book Writers and Illustrators, Authors Guild, Guild of Natural Science Illustrators.

Awards, Honors

Parents Magazine Best Children's Book of the Year and a New York Public Library Title for Reading and Sharing, both 1991, both for *Mouse Around;* Outstanding Science Trade Book for Children designation, Children's Book Council/National Science Teachers Association, 1997, for *Over under in the Garden.*

Writings

AUTHOR AND ILLUSTRATOR

Mouse Around, Farrar, Straus, 1991.
He's Your Dog!, Farrar, Straus, 1993.
Over under in the Garden: An Alphabet Book, Farrar, Straus, 1996.

ILLUSTRATOR

Louis Ross, *Puddle Duck,* Dutton, 1979.
Kit Schorsch, reteller, *The Town Mouse and the Country Mouse,* Checkerboard Press, 1989.
K. Schorsch, reteller, *Stone Soup,* Checkerboard Press, 1989.
Alyssa Satin Capucilli, *Biscuit,* HarperCollins, 1996.
Capucilli, *Biscuit Finds a Friend,* HarperCollins, 1997.

Linda Leuck, *Teeny, Tiny Mouse,* Bridgewater Books, 1998.
Capucilli, *Bathtime for Biscuit,* HarperCollins, 1998.
Capucilli, *Biscuit's Picnic,* HarperCollins, 1999.
Capucilli, *Hello, Biscuit,* HarperCollins, 1999.
Capucilli, *Happy Birthday, Biscuit,* HarperCollins, 1999.
Capucilli, *Biscuit's New Trick,* HarperCollins, 2000.

Sidelights

Trained as a graphic artist, Pat Schories has gone on to expand her talents within the field of children's books. Although Schories has indulged in a lifelong love affair with books and bookbinding—as she admitted to *SATA,* "I started writing and illustrating my own books early on [and] still have one from second grade, complete with cloth binding and endpapers"—her first efforts at writing a book of her own did not come until 1991 with *Mouse Around.* Since then, Schories has continued to write her own books and illustrate the texts of others. Among her most popular works are the illustrations she did for Alyssa Satin Capucilli's "Biscuit the Puppy" books, which have become an ever-growing series.

Born in 1952, Schories attended Kent State University after graduating from high school. There she majored in graphic design and illustration, and realized that she "wanted to make books," as she remembered. Following college, she moved from Ohio to New York City, intending to "live in a loft, create books, live a bohemian lifestyle." In New York, Schories's dreams confronted reality: "I had no idea lofts were expensive or hard to come by, and ended up in a shoe-box apartment, far from midtown." Undaunted by her less-than-ideal surroundings, Schories began freelancing for a small book design studio in the city, and began searching for illustration assignments from book publishers. Schories's efforts were rewarded with her first job: a baby's cloth book, published in 1979. "Not the highbrow children's literature I had planned for myself, but a step in the door, and I was thrilled with the opportunity to illustrate anything!" Schories later recalled.

In 1989, Schories got her first book contract: a wordless picture book titled *Mouse Around.* "I was overjoyed!" she recalled. "It took me two years to complete, working full-time days as a graphic designer, and working on the book nights and weekends. I had been used to working hard, but no one had prepared me for the minuscule advances first-time authors receive for a picture book! My obsessive love of this project kept me going, and I continued to do two more books in this manner, until finally I was able to quit my day job and work on my own books full time. Glorious!"

Published in 1991, *Mouse Around* depicts a young mouse and his foray into the world outside his quiet mouse hole in the basement. Calling Schories's effort "an engaging, wordless" story, a *Publishers Weekly* reviewer described *Mouse Around* as a story told "effectively and with great charm, . . . offering [readers] the fun and challenge of hunting for the mouse on each page."

Schories followed *Mouse Around* with several other original stories, among them *Over under in the Garden: An Alphabet Book,* which draws on her expertise as a botanical illustrator. Featuring a text that consists of the names of twenty-six different plants and animals, each one beginning with a different letter of the alphabet, *Over under in the Garden* also serves as an introduction to nature. Praising the detail used by Schories in her drawings, *Horn Book* reviewer Elizabeth Watson noted that through the author/illustrator's "carefully drawn and faithfully colored" pictures, youngsters will "have their first encounter with kohlrabi and mandrake,... [and] will be able to recognize both if they ever meet them again." *School Library Journal* contributor Carolyn Noah praised Schories's "striking artwork" and "handsome design."

Married at age forty-five to a fellow artist she met at the book design studio where she began her career several decades earlier, Schories is now a wife and a stepmother, in addition to her role as author and illustrator. "I make time to cook dinner, garden, exercise, play a little fiddle," she remarked. "But books continue to occupy the largest space in my life, and I imagine they always will. I keep a notebook with ideas, and have a lifetime of picture book making ahead of me!"

Works Cited

Review of *Mouse Around, Publishers Weekly,* May 24, 1991, p. 56.

Noah, Carolyn, review of *Over under in the Garden, School Library Journal,* June, 1996, p. 118.

Watson, Elizabeth, review of *Over under in the Garden, Horn Book,* July/August, 1996, pp. 455-456.

For More Information See

PERIODICALS

Booklist, January 1, 1994, p. 833.

School Library Journal, August, 1991, p. 154; August 30, 1993, p. 94; January, 1994, p. 98; May, 1998, p. 120.

ON-LINE

Author's website located at www.bolick.net/Childrens-Books.

*   *   *

SENISI, Ellen B(abinec) 1951-

Personal

Born May 18, 1951, in Little Falls, NY; daughter of William Martin (an electrical troubleshooter) and Elizabeth Anne Bowen (a teacher) Babinec; married John P. Senisi (an architect) August 25, 1973; children: Kate, Will, Steven. *Education:* State University of New York at Oswego, B.S. (Education), 1974; State University of New York at Cortland, M.S. (Curriculum and Instruction), 1979; Boston University, C.A.G.S. (Educational Media and Technology), 1987. *Politics:* Democrat.

Religion: Roman Catholic. *Hobbies and other interests:* Music.

Addresses

Home-1834 Lenox Road, Schenectady, NY 12308. *E-mail*—senisi@earthlink.net.

Career

Author and photo-illustrator, Schenectady, NY, 1992—. Taught in public and private elementary schools at the primary level, 1974-79; developer of educational materials for publishing company, 1980-82. *Member:* Society of Children's Book Writers and Illustrators; Albany/Schenectady League of Arts.

Awards, Honors

Educational Press Association Distinguished Achievement Award, 1993, for photo essay "Fall Came"; *Just Kids* selected among Best Children's Books of the Year in Special Interest Category, Children's Book Committee at Bank Street College, and named a Notable Children's Trade Book in the Field of Social Studies, National Council of Social Studies/Children's Book Council, both 1998.

Writings

AUTHOR AND PHOTOGRAPHER

Brothers and Sisters, Scholastic, Inc., 1993.

Kindergarten Kids, Scholastic, Inc., 1994.

Secrets, Dutton, 1995.

For My Family, Love, Allie, Albert Whitman, 1998.

Just Kids: Visiting a Class for Children with Special Needs, Dutton, 1998.

Reading Grows, Albert Whitman, 1999.

Hurray for Pre-K!, HarperCollins, 2000.

Work in Progress

Colors from Nature, Dutton, due in 2001; *Fall Changes,* Scholastic, Inc., due in 2001.

Sidelights

Photographer and writer Ellen B. Senisi has combined her several talents to create a number of inspiring and well-received works of both fiction and nonfiction for young readers. In her stories, which feature photographs rather than drawn illustrations, readers are introduced to young people who encounter a variety of experiences that allow them to grow as people. In *Just Kids: Visiting a Class for Children with Special Needs,* for example, a second grader named Cindy spends part of each school day in her school's special needs classroom, and learns that each student, although struggling with a unique disability, is just a kid like her.

Senisi was born in Little Falls, New York, a small town on the Mohawk River. "I lived in that town until I was eighteen," she told *SATA,* "and by then was sufficiently

Ellen B. Senisi

and technology, which is where I got my only formal training in photography."

Senisi's first published work, *Brothers and Sisters,* captures the relationship between siblings from a variety of families. The volume reflects the "ethnic, gender, and generational diversity" of modern families," according to *School Library Journal* contributor Jody McCoy. Presenting both the playful and conflict-riddled sides of sibling relationships, Senisi's "handsomely done" photo-essay was deemed suitable for "a parent to use with a child one-on-one, or for a story hour with a family theme," in the opinion of *Booklist* contributor Janice Del Negro.

In *Secrets,* which reached bookstore shelves in 1995, Senisi examines the many secrets that young people encounter in their day-to-day activities. The author/photographer "adds a new layer of understanding by exploring different kinds of secrets ... and the emotions associated with them," noted *Booklist* reviewer Stephanie Zvirin. Senisi "gleaned most of her information from interviews with a second-grade class," *School Library Journal* contributor Marianne Saccardi explained, "and young readers will easily identify with the various situations presented." Saccardi summed *Secrets* up as a "satisfying presentation."

In *Reading Grows,* published in 1999, Senisi introduces parents and caregivers to the stages a child goes through during the learning-to-read process. Highlighted with what *School Library Journal* contributor Lucinda Snyder Whitehurst described as "bright, cheerful photographs" of children and grown-ups reading together, *Reading Grows* illustrates the joys of books. Senisi's minimalist text augments the photographs, showing youngsters progressing from a knowledge of basic shapes and colors, through the alphabet, to vocabulary-building and realizing that, as the text exclaims, "I can read anywhere!"

Senisi explained that she is "highly allergic to the posed, self-conscious look of studio photography and most gallery photography"; she views her own work as photodocumentary in style. "When I set up my equipment on a site," she explained to *SATA,* "I strive to become invisible so I can catch faces coming alive with natural expressions in a natural environment. I also listen to what goes on while I'm photographing so I can blend natural-sounding language with the images in my books."

In addition to her works of nonfiction, Senisi has also written and illustrated several fictional works, illustrating each with photographs of real-life children in situations reflecting those in her stories. In *Just Kids,* an unfeeling remark about the "retard class" uttered by a second grader named Cindy results in a stint in the local elementary school's special-needs class, where both Cindy and the reader come to learn that autism, Down's syndrome, and epilepsy don't make kids essentially different. Praising the work—which was photographed in a New York state elementary school—in a *Booklist*

restless to be on the move for the next fourteen years. By the time I ended up at my current home in Schenectady, New York, I had attended seven colleges, earned three degrees, and lived in thirty places, including upstate New York, rural Virginia, Boston, New York, and Oxford, England. (My husband, who lived in twenty-six of them with me, kept a list of them all). I arrived in Schenectady with two children and one soon to come. Shortly after the third one arrived, in 1987, I began work on my first children's book.

"I had gotten involved in photography about ten years before that. I got started when my husband bought a camera and insisted, after all we'd paid for it, that I learn how to use it, too. I felt intimidated by the technicalities but eventually learned and became absolutely hooked. I now own a number of cameras, all of which intimidate him."

Even in elementary school, Senisi loved to write, and accumulated a vast number of stories, poems, plays, letters, and journals throughout her school years. However, once she reached college, she "decided writing would be pretty impractical work and switched from English to teaching. I quit teaching after five years when I realized how susceptible I was to photography disease and then went to graduate school for educational media review, Helen Rosenberg called *Just Kids* a "sensitive, informative book that immerses us in a world that many of us know little about." Praising the "bright, vibrant, and upbeat" color photographs, *School Library Journal* contributor Lucinda Snyder Whitehurst commented that they "project the powerful message that these children are not to be pitied; rather readers . . . are encouraged to . . . see that there are many different ways to learn."

In *For My Family, Love, Allie,* Senisi portrays a young girl from a mixed-race family as she does her share to prepare for a large family gathering. Linda Greengrass commented in her *School Library Journal* critique of Senisi's 1998 book on the naturalism of the photographs, as well as their success at "convey[ing] the powerful image of a comfortable interracial mix."

"I work full-time at the totally impractical but very fulfilling business of children's photo essay books,"

Senisi summarized. "I feel that everything I've done to this point—traveling, teaching, writing, editing, photography, and parenting—comes together in the making of the books I create. I love creating books, I love exploring the relationships between words and images, and the best part is moving on to whatever stage is next. Welding words and images with music may be next for me, or perhaps montages of photographs blended on the computer. I'll go with whatever methods work to show that illumination of expression I look for as I photograph children experiencing the world."

Works Cited

Del Negro, Janice, review of *Brothers and Sisters, Booklist,* October 1, 1993, p. 348.

Greengrass, Linda, review of *For My Family, Love, Allie, School Library Journal,* December, 1998, p. 92.

You read stories, you write your own stories,

Through minimal photographs and text, Senisi illustrates the joy of books, showing youngsters progressing from a knowledge of basic shapes and colors, through a mastering of the alphabet and a grasp of vocabulary, culminating with the acquisition of independent reading skills. (From Reading Grows.*)*

McCoy, Jody, review of *Brothers and Sisters, School Library Journal,* December 1993, p. 108.

Rosenberg, Helen, review of *Just Kids, Booklist,* May 1, 1998, p. 1517.

Saccardi, Marianne, review of *Secrets, School Library Journal,* January, 1996, p. 106.

Whitehurst, Lucinda Snyder, review of *Just Kids, School Library Journal,* April, 1998, p. 110.

Whitehurst, Lucinda Snyder, review of *Reading Grows, School Library Journal,* August, 1999, p. 150.

Zvirin, Stephanie, review of *Secrets, Booklist,* August, 1995, p. 1953.

For More Information See

PERIODICALS

Booklist, November 1, 1994, p. 504.
Kirkus Reviews, December 15, 1997, p. 1841.

*   *   *

SIDGWICK, Ethel 1877-1970

Personal

Born December 20, 1877, in Rugby, Warwick, England; died April 29, 1970; daughter of Arthur (a schoolmaster) and Charlotte S. Sidgwick. *Education:* Attended Oxford High School; private study of music and literature.

Career

Novelist and children's dramatist. Worked variously as a schoolteacher in England and France and as a translator.

Writings

Promise, Small, Maynard (Boston, MA), 1910.
Le Gentleman: An Idyll of the Quarter, Small, Maynard, 1911.
Herself, Small, Maynard, 1912.
Four Plays for Children: The Rose and the Ring, The Goody-Witch, The Goosegirl, Boots and the North Wind, Small, Maynard, 1913.
Succession: A Comedy of the Generations, Small, Maynard, 1913.
A Lady of Leisure, Small, Maynard, 1914.
Duke Jones, Small, Maynard, 1914.
The Accolade, Sidgwick & Jackson (London, England), 1915, Small, Maynard, 1916.
Hatchways, Small, Maynard, 1916.
Jamesie, Small, Maynard, 1918.
Madam, Small, Maynard, 1921.
Two Plays for Schools: The Three Golden Hairs, The Robber Bridegroom, Sidgwick & Jackson, 1922, republished as *The Three Golden Hairs (More Plays for Children),* Small, Maynard, 1922.
Restoration: The Fairy-Tale of a Farm, Small, Maynard, 1923.
Laura: A Cautionary Story, Small, Maynard, 1924.
Fairy-Tale Plays: The Elves and the Shoemaker, Ricquet and the Tuft, Sidgwick & Jackson, 1926.

When I Grow Rich, Harper (London, England and New York City), 1927.
The Bells of Shoreditch, Sidgwick & Jackson, 1928.
Dorothy's Wedding: A Tale of Two Villages, Sidgwick & Jackson, 1931, republished as *A Tale of Two Villages,* Harper, 1931.
Mrs. Henry Sidgwick: A Memoir by Her Niece, Ethel Sidgwick, Sidgwick & Jackson, 1938.

TRANSLATION

(With Kathleen E. Innes) Guy de La Batut and Georges Friedmann, *A History of the French People,* Methuen (London, England), 1923.

Sidelights

Ethel Sidgwick was born into a wealthy family in Rugby, England. Never marrying, she worked for a time as a schoolteacher and then began publishing novels when she was in her thirties. Her first novel, *Promise,* appeared in 1910. It marked the beginning of an eight-year period during which time she published approximately one novel each year. She is most remembered for her work from this early period, which earned her high praise from critics as well as comparisons to the lauded Henry James.

Promise follows the life of Antoine Edgell, a child prodigy in music, during the first fourteen years of his life. The novel explores the natural genius of this character while also examining the influence of others on his life and development. His mother, Henriette, dies when he is still a boy, and he is left in the care of his father and schoolteachers, none of whom entirely understand his talent, and so regard him strangely. Antoine's grandfather alone is the person who most understands him and becomes his biggest ally. Sidgwick was noted and praised for bringing to life this cast of supporting characters, a trait that would come to distinguish her entire body of work.

The following year, Sidgwick produced *Le Gentleman: An Idyll of the Quarter.* Set in Paris, Alexander Fergusson, a Scottish gentleman, takes a vacation to be near his fiancee, Meysie Lampeter, an English art student studying in the City of Light. While in Paris, Fergusson falls in love with a young Frenchwoman, Gilberte, who gives him a nickname after which this novel was titled. The two admit their feelings to one another, but their love is ill-fated. Fergusson decides to honor his commitment to his fiancee while Gilberte has familial obligations to keep.

Succession: A Comedy of the Generations, published in 1913, is based on Sidgwick's first novel, *Promise.* The main character from that work, Antoine Edgell, is fourteen at the opening of this story. Set in both France and England, Edgell is beginning to win some public attention for himself and his music. Edgell's relationship with his father is further explored, and at the novel's end, he comes to the aid of his despairing son. Once again Sidgwick was praised for her character development. A reviewer for the *Outlook* wrote, "It is a sincere work, is close and deep in its study of temperament and artistic 'entourage,' and is unusually true in character drawing."

Sidgwick's next three novels are all related, following the same characters through different stages of their lives. The first, *A Lady of Leisure,* introduces the setting that Sidgwick would use in the remainder of her stories, the country house. The plot revolves around Arthur Gibb, the rector at Glasswell rectory, who has just married his second wife. Both newlyweds bring their own children with them to the marriage—Arthur has two daughters and the new Mrs. Gibb has a grown son. The son moves with his mother to the English countryside where he falls in love with a local girl named Violet Ashwin. Violet is the "lady" in *A Lady of Leisure* who feels trapped in her life and tries to break free by going into business as a dressmaker.

Violet and her younger sister Marjory both appear in the next novel, *Duke Jones.* Violet is now married to Charles Shovell and the couple has befriended Marmaduke (Duke) Jones whom they met on their honeymoon. Marjory falls in love with him and the two marry. Violet appears again in *The Accolade,* published in 1915. However, the main focus of this story is on Johnny Ingestre, the heir to a grand estate. Disobeying and disappointing his father, he leaves home to try his hand at acting. In order to please his father again, he becomes engaged to Ursula, a woman who his father believes is a good match, despite being in love with Helena Faulkland. Johnny lives up to his duty, when, after marrying Ursula, he protects Helena from a sticky social situation, though he does not give into his feelings for her. In the *Dictionary of Literary Biography,* Lynn M. Alexander called *The Accolade* "the strongest of the three novels involving the Ashwins." Other critics offered similar praiseful reaction upon the novel's release. Wilson Follett wrote in the *Atlantic,* "'The accolade' gives us Miss Ethel Sidgwick at her very best: and the season that can furnish tired readers and reviewers with even one such book as this latest of hers, is already forgiven its trespasses."

The last two novels of this early period in Sidgwick's career were *Hatchways,* published in 1916, and *Jamesie,* published in 1918. Again, she followed the same family of characters, centering on Ernestine Redgate in the first novel and her niece Bess Ryeborn in the second. These were the last works of Sidgwick to be received with much praise from critics. The remainder of her work, classified as "drawing-room" stories by Alexander, was part of a genre that was no longer in fashion.

Sidgwick continued to write fiction until 1931. Her last novel, *Dorothy's Wedding: A Tale of Two Villages,* features a story about two competitive villages in the English countryside. Sidgwick records the daily activities of the people living in these two towns, one of which is much more prosperous than the other one. Reactions to this story were mixed. Some reviewers, like Iris Barry in *Books,* admired work for being "by far the best picture of English country life that current fiction

has provided." Others, such as a critic for the *Times Literary Supplement,* simply found the novel "tedious."

In addition to novels, Sidgwick also wrote children's drama and fairytales. The last book she published was a biography of her aunt, Eleanor Mildred Sidgwick, who was the principal at Newnham College in Cambridge between 1892 and 1910. *Mrs. Henry Sidgwick: A Memoir by Her Niece, Ethel Sidgwick* was released in 1938. Sidgwick stopped publishing at this time although she would live for thirty more years. Sidgwick died in 1970 at the age of ninety-two.

Works Cited

Alexander, Lynn M., "Ethel Sidgwick," *Dictionary of Literary Biography,* Volume 197: *"Late-Victorian and Edwardian British Novelists Second Series,"* Gale Group, 1999.

Barry, Iris, review of *Dorothy's Wedding: A Tale of Two Villages, Books,* October 25, 1931, p. 11.

Review of *Dorothy's Wedding: A Tale of Two Villages, Times Literary Supplement,* November 26, 1931, p. 961.

Follett, Wilson, review of *The Accolade, Atlantic,* October, 1916.

Review of *Succession: A Comedy of Generations, Outlook,* October 4, 1913.

For More Information See

BOOKS

The Feminist Companion to Literature in English, Yale University Press, 1990.

Johnson, R. Brimley, *Some Contemporary Novelists (Women),* Parsons, 1920.

World Authors, "1900-1950", H. W. Wilson Co., 1996.

PERIODICALS

Bellman, January 11, 1919.

Booklist, November, 1912; October, 1913; December, 1914; December, 1915; April, 1916; January, 1917; November, 1918; July, 1923; December, 1931.

Boston Transcript, September 24, 1913, p. 24; October 21, 1914, p. 24; October 20, 1915, p. 25; February 19, 1916, p. 6; August 14, 1918, p. 6; June 18, 1921, p. 6; July 7, 1923, p. 1; November 5, 1924, p. 6; November 7, 1928, p. 5; December 30, 1931, p. 2.

Dial, October 1, 1914; March 30, 1916; December 14, 1916; September 19, 1918.

Freeman, July 13, 1921; October 10, 1923.

Literary Review, March 26, 1921, p. 6; June 23, 1923, p. 783; December 13, 1924, p. 14.

Nation, November 28, 1912; October 2, 1913; October 21, 1915; March 2, 1916; November 30, 1916; September 7, 1918.

New Republic, December 18, 1915; August 24, 1918; June 6, 1923.

New Statesman, May 14, 1921; June 23, 1923.

New Statesman & Nation, December 12, 1931.

New York Times Review of Books, September 15, 1912; September 28, 1913; September 27, 1914; November 21, 1915; February 27, 1916; November 26, 1916;

December 3, 1916; May 8, 1921, p. 22; April 22, 1923, p. 22; October 11, 1931, p. 6.

New York Tribune, July 22, 1923, p. 23; December 14, 1924, p. 14.

New York World, May 6, 1923, p. 8E.

Outlook, November 11, 1914; October 23, 1918.

Publishers Weekly, October 15, 1916; February 19, 1916; October 21, 1916; August 17, 1918; April 16, 1921.

Saturday Review, June 8, 1912; April 4, 1914; November 7, 1914.

Saturday Review of Literature, December 13, 1924; November 17, 1928.

Speculator, April 4, 1914; December 5, 1914; March 4, 1916; April 27, 1918.

Springfield Republican, October 7, 1915, p. 5; February 20, 1916, p. 15; July 30, 1921; November 1, 1931, p. 7E.

Times Literary Supplement, December 28, 1916, p. 638; March 14, 1918, p. 128; April 28, 1921, p. 278; May 31, 1923, p. 370; December 4, 1924, p. 820.*

* * *

SILVERSTEIN, Shel(don Allan) 1930-1999
(Uncle Shelby)

Obituary Notice—See index for _SATA_ sketch: born September 25, 1930, in Chicago, IL; died on May 10, 1999, in Key West, FL. Author. Silverstein was well known for his writing for children, which usually consisted of absurd and funny verse and line drawings of the author's. Judy Zuckerman, in a _New York Times_ review, called Silverstein "that rare adult who can still think like a child." Silverstein was often compared to celebrated children's author Dr. Suess, though Silverstein's stories and poems occasionally have a darker twist. The author began drawing and writing early in life, joking later that it gave him something to do since the girls paid him no attention. He served in United States Army in the Korean War and worked as a cartoonist for the Pacific _Stars and Strips._ Later he began a long career with _Playboy_ as an artist and writer. Popular books of the author's include _The Giving Tree_ (1964), which gradually gained exposure and was used in churches and classrooms to teach children about altruism. Silverstein also published the immensely popular _Where the Sidewalk Ends,_ which sold more than 1 million hardback copies. Other works that Silverstein wrote and illustrated include _A Light in the Attic_ (1981), _The Missing Piece_ (1982), _The Missing Piece Meets the Big O_ (1982), and _Falling Up: Poems and Drawings_ (1996). He wrote plays, including _The Lady and the Tiger_ (Ensemble Studio Theater Festival, 1981) and _The Devil and Billy Markham_ (New York City at Lincoln Center, 1989), and contributed to _The Best American Short Plays 1992-1993: The Theatre Annual Since 1937_ (California, 1993). In addition, Silverstein wrote song lyrics, including the Johnny Cash hit "A Boy Named Sue" and Loretta Lynn's "One's on the Way," as well as the folk songs "Unicorn" and "25 Minutes to Go."

OBITUARIES AND OTHER SOURCES:

PERIODICALS

Chicago Tribune, May 11, 1999, Section 1, p. 16.

London Times, May 12, 1999.

New York Times, May 11, 1999, p. B10.

Washington Post, May 11, 1999, p. B5.

* * *

SLATER, Ray
See LANSDALE, Joe R(ichard)

* * *

SLOAN, Carolyn 1937-

Personal

Born April 15, 1937, in London, England; daughter of Robert Gordon (a stockbroker) and Lottie Clemmey (a housewife; maiden name, Waugh) Sloan; married David Hollis (a tea planter), May 15, 1961; children: Peter, Rupert. _Education:_ Attended schools in Newcastle, Harrogate, and Guildford, England. _Hobbies and other interests:_ "My interests are reading, theatre and films, gardening and do-it-yourself improvements to my house on the banks of the River Wey in Guildford. I also enjoy volunteer work helping children with their reading in a local primary school under the Volunteer Reading Help scheme."

Addresses

Home and office—175 Stoughton Road, Guildford, Surrey GU1 1LQ, England. _Agent_—Caroline Walsh at David Higham Associates, 5-8 Lower John Street, Golden Square, London W1R 4HA, England.

Career

Writer. _Queen_ (magazine), London, England, editorial assistant, 1956-60; freelance journalist, 1960—; co-proprietor of village shop in Send Marsh, Surrey, England, 1968-72; Unwins (printers), Old Woking, Surrey, phototypesetter, 1973-75; Yvonne Arnaud Theatre, Guildford, Surrey, press and public relations officer, 1976-80; press representative for Emlyn Williams, 1980; freelance press consultant, 1980-1986. _Member:_ Society of Authors.

Awards, Honors

The Sea Child was a Junior Literary Guild selection.

Writings

FOR CHILDREN

Carter Is a Painter's Cat (picture book), illustrated by Fritz Wegner, Simon & Schuster, 1971.

Victoria and the Crowded Pocket (picture book), illustrated by Peter Bailey, Kestrel, 1973.

Carolyn Sloan

The Penguin and the Vacuum Cleaner (picture book), illustrated by Jill McDonald, Kestrel, 1974, published in the United States as *The Penguin and the Strange Animal,* McGraw, 1975.

Sam Snake, illustrated by Barbara Swiderska, Kestrel, 1975.

Mr. Cogg and His Computer (chapter book), illustrated by Glenys Ambrus, Macmillan, 1979.

Further Inventions of Mr. Cogg (chapter book), illustrated by Glenys Ambrus, Macmillan, 1981.

Shakespeare, Theatre Cat, illustrated by Jill Bennett, Macmillan, 1982.

Skewer's Garden (novel), Chatto & Windus, 1983.

Mr. Cogg and the Exploding Easter Eggs (chapter book), illustrated by Glenys Ambrus, Macmillan, 1984.

Helen Keller (nonfiction), illustrated by Karen Heywood, Hamish Hamilton, 1984.

The Friendly Robot (picture book), illustrated by Jonathan Langley, Octopus, 1986.

An Elephant for Muthu, Bodley Head, 1986.

The Sea Child, Bodley Head, 1987, Holiday House, 1988.

Don't Go Near the Water, Scholastic, 1988.

T-Boy's Weekend (picture book), illustrated by Chris Winn, Ginn, 1988.

Working Dogs, Collins, 1991.

Working Horses, Collins, 1991.

Working Elephants, Collins, 1991.

Nine Lives, illustrated by Alice Englander, Paperbird, 1991.

(With Sally Sheringham and Pamela Oldfield) *The Marvelous Magical Storybook* (includes Sloan's *The Friendly Robot*), Dean, 1993.

Gracie, illustrated by Lisa Flather, Longmans, 1994.

An Incredible Journey (The Story of Alcock and Brown), illustrated by Simon Smith, F. Watts, 1996, published in the United States by Silver Burdett Press, 1998.

The Rat (reading series), illustrated by Michael Reid, Ginn, 1998.

Victorian Day (reading series), illustrated by Michael Reid, Ginn, 1999.

"MALL" SERIES; FOR CHILDREN

Setting Up Shop, Hippo Books, 1989.

Open for Business, Hippo Books, 1989.

Gangs, Ghosts and Gypsies, Hippo Books, 1989.

Money Matters, Hippo Books, 1989.

OTHER

Contributor to magazines and newspapers, including *Sunday Telegraph, Daily Telegraph,* and *Radio Times.* Sloan's works have been translated into German, Welsh, French, Danish, Dutch, and Japanese.

Sidelights

Carolyn Sloan is a versatile British author of picture books for young children and novels for middle-grade and juvenile readers. She often focuses on animals in her picture books, such as *Carter Is a Painter's Cat, Victoria and the Crowded Pocket,* and *The Penguin and the Strange Animal.* In her longer fiction, she demonstrates a wry sense of humor, as in her "Mr. Cogg" books, or elements of fantasy, as in *The Sea Child.* Her books are more well known in England than in America; fewer than half of them have been published or distributed in the United States.

Sloan once told *Something about the Author* (*SATA*), "I was writing one-plot girl-and-pony stories as an eight year old. Later it was poetry—light animal verses to dreadful kitsch about little dead children and lonely shepherds. I wasted my pocket money on stamps, sending the manuscript to adult literary periodicals signed 'by Carolyn Sloan, aged 12 yrs. and 4 mths.'" Sloan continued her love of writing through her school years, living in Geneva, Switzerland, for a year following school to work as an *au pair* and learn French. Returning to London she worked in a variety of office positions until she landed a job at *Queen* magazine.

"By sheer luck I became editorial secretary on *Queen* magazine at a time of total chaos. Its image and staff changed weekly. I typed, made tea, recklessly cut distinguished authors' copy, and checked proofs before anyone realized I was a complete amateur. After four years I had worked for several editors, written features and captions, put the magazine to bed during a printing strike, and was still making tea. Ever since, when I have written anything from a press release to a controversial newspaper story, a theater program to a book, I have been indebted to the writing discipline learned during those chaotic years."

Sloan married an English tea planter in 1961 and went off to live in South India for the next seven years; some of the locations and incidents of those years later found their way into Sloan's 1986 novel, _An Elephant for Muthu._ Returning to England in 1968, the couple lived in a seventeenth-century cottage and ran a village shop for several years. Sloan has also worked as a publicist for a local theater, and both that and the shopkeeping find their way into her fiction, as well.

Sloan fulfilled a long-held dream of becoming a published author with the 1971 publication of her first book for children, _Carter Is a Painter's Cat,_ the tale of a cat who exists in a new form every day, according to the whims of his artistic creator. In fact, Carter has reality only on paper, and Mr. Blob, the painter in question, might one day paint him blue or not at all. Sometimes he has three legs; sometimes no whiskers. "Sometimes he paints me so badly that I can't go out," Carter complains. Reviewing this debut effort in the _Washington Post Book World,_ Julian May called the book a "witty piece of fantasy," while a _Times Literary Supplement_ critic termed Sloan "a very welcome newcomer to the picture book scene."

Sloan followed up this initial title with a second picture book in 1973, _Victoria and the Crowded Pocket,_ in which a baby kangaroo leaves her mother's increasingly untidy pocket to find a more organized lifestyle with other families of creatures. Eventually she returns to live companionably with her mother who now has a new baby in her pocket. In _The Penguin and the Strange Animal,_ Sloan tells the story of a penguin recovering from mumps at a zookeeper's home. There he mistakes a vacuum cleaner for a strange new form of fauna. Josh the penguin is not familiar with the amenities of a household, so it is not surprising that when Mr. and Mrs. Berg take the ailing animal home he has some initial confusion. When Josh and the resident mouse uncover a strange animal and turn it on, they are amazed at how it gobbles everything up. They figure it must be very, very hungry. "The plot is based on this droll misunderstanding," noted Jean Mercier in _Publishers Weekly._ Mercier went on to call Sloan's third picture book "witty" with "brilliant, stylized pictures," remarking that "[c]hildren should love what happens afterwards, a tale of strange friendships ... nothing short of inspired." A reviewer for _Junior Bookshelf_ concluded, "[T]his will be appreciated readily by young children." Other notable picture books from Sloan include _The Friendly Robot,_ about a lonely robot who would rather be in the company of a little boy than stuck working in a factory, and _T-Boy's Weekend._

Sloan has also created a number of novels for middle-grade and older readers. One of her most popular characters, Mr. Cogg, makes appearances in _Mr. Cogg and His Computer, Further Inventions of Mr. Cogg,_ and _Mr. Cogg and the Exploding Easter Eggs._ In the second title, the zany inventor teams up with his computer, who is his best friend, to invent all manner of wacky things, from cat-care units to a compressor that creates art from flattened junk. According to a _Junior Bookshelf_ contrib-

utor, "This extravagant nonsense is told with a zest and a humour which should surely please small boys of 9 plus." Dorothy Atkinson, reviewing the book in _School Librarian,_ concluded, "If you like comic inventors, jokes about modern concerns ... and eccentric aunties with fluorescent bloomers, then this is your book." Writing in the _Times Literary Supplement_ in 1981, Nicholas Tucker felt that, in _Further Inventions of Mr. Cogg,_ "the author tried to be funny all the time, so that no firm story line ever emerges," but concluded that when Sloan "learns to balance her stories more successfully, she should be a writer worth watching out for." Tucker later reviewed Sloan's _An Elephant for Muthu_ in _Books for Your Children_ in 1986. He wrote: "The story of a young Indian elephant handler is moving and totally credible while also containing more information about elephants in 123 pages than most of us are ever going to come across in the rest of our lives. Any child who likes animal stories will enjoy this passionate tale of final victory over fear and suffering, at times inviting comparison with Kipling at his best."

A large gypsy family who were steady customers at the village shop which Sloan helped to run for a time became the inspiration for another juvenile novel, _Skewer's Garden._ The title character lives on the road with his gypsy family half of the year, selling and fixing things at fairs. But Skewer would rather stay at home, going to school and tending the garden he has carved out of the junkyard surrounding their house. One of thirteen children, he is thought to be an oddity by the others. There is tension between him and his siblings and other relatives, which is brought to a head when one of his uncles destroys Skewer's beloved garden. Skewer also threatens his traditional family pattern with his friendship with an English girl, a seemingly typical suburban kid whose own story of sadness rivals Skewer's.

This tale of family bonds versus individual development was generally well received by reviewers and readers on both sides of the Atlantic. "Strong family ties of love, loyalty and passion are well illustrated in this sensitive, often humorous story set in modern England," commented Gayle Berge in _School Library Journal._ A reviewer for _Junior Bookshelf_ noted, "There are no heroes and villains in Carolyn Sloan's lovely story, only the sensitive and sympathetic—but totally unsentimental—portrayal of real people," later commenting that "a book which we read for—and with—pleasure is also one which contributes to our education in some of the arts of living."

Other personal incidents and interests have contributed to others of Sloan's titles. "My interest in theatre developed when I shared a flat with my aunt, the late Norah Waugh," Sloan explained to _SATA._ "She was an expert on historic costume, and for over thirty years lectured and taught practical work in the theatre department of the Central School of Art and Design in London. Her three books on the subject are now standard works on both sides of the Atlantic. I wrote _Shakespeare, Theatre Cat_ after working at the Yvonne Arnaud Theatre in Guildford. It is basically a children's introduction to the theatre, told in fictionalized form by a theatre cat."

Shakespeare, the cat in question, aided by his feline and human friends, is devoted to his catlike job at the theater, but would also dearly love to be an actor. Elizabeth Porges Watson, writing in *Books and Bookmen,* felt that the "degree of fantasy involved in Shakespeare's great cleverness and the ease with which he communicates with human beings never declines into making him appear one of the latter dressed up." Reviewing the title in *School Librarian,* Chris Brown concluded, "The good, strong story-lines are so well narrated that they carve their way through potential drawbacks and hold the whole thing together, aided by a gently-pointed sense of humour and detailed little drawings."

Another popular Sloan novel, *The Sea Child,* was a Junior Literary Guild selection. This is the story of a mysterious child from the sea who comes into a nearby village and meets a lonely girl. "*The Sea Child* may have been subconsciously inspired by Matthew Arnold's poem, 'The Forsaken Merman,' which I learned at school," Sloan told *SATA.* Renee Steinberg noted in *School Library Journal* that an "aura of mystery underlies this book about The Sands, a strange land cut off from the mainland by an unusual sea storm nine years earlier." Stephen Corrin, writing in the *Guardian,* described *The Sea Child* as "an extraordinarily impressive piece of imaginative writing. Remote, other world, mysterious.... A hauntingly beautiful tale." Sloan has also created a series of novels for juvenile readers, the "Mall" series, published only in England. All the books in the series deal with children who work part-time jobs in stores in a shopping mall.

Additionally, Sloan has penned nonfiction for juvenile readers. Her biography of Helen Keller proved a real challenge. "I had to read everything she wrote," explained Sloan, "and reams that were written about her and reduce it all to 10,000 relevant words in three months. *That* took journalistic training!" Another meticulous historical re-creation is *An Incredible Journey,* Sloan's description of the first flight over the Atlantic Ocean, from Canada to England in 1919, made by John Alcock and Arthur Whitten Brown.

"I love delving for rare nuggets of fact in books and libraries, and now on the internet," Sloan concluded to *SATA.* "I have to stop myself before research becomes an excuse for not writing the book."

Works Cited

Atkinson, Dorothy, review of *Further Inventions of Mr. Cogg, School Librarian,* December, 1981, p. 329.

Berge, Gayle, review of *Skewer's Garden, School Library Journal,* March, 1984, p. 165.

Brown, Chris, review of *Shakespeare, Theatre Cat, School Librarian,* September, 1982, pp. 238-39.

Review of *Carter Is a Painter's Cat, Times Literary Supplement,* October 22, 1971, pp. 1324-25.

Corrin, Stephen, review of *The Sea Child, The Guardian,* June 26, 1987.

Review of *Further Inventions of Mr. Cogg, Junior Bookshelf,* October, 1981, pp. 202-03.

May, Julian, review of *Carter Is a Painter's Cat, Washington Post Book World,* November 7, 1971, p. 3.

Mercier, Jean, review of *The Penguin and the Strange Animal, Publishers Weekly,* June 16, 1975, p. 82.

Review of *The Penguin and the Strange Animal, Junior Bookshelf,* February, 1975, p. 27.

Review of *Skewer's Garden, Junior Bookshelf,* October, 1983, p. 214.

Sloan, Carolyn, *Carter Is a Painter's Cat,* Kestrel, 1971.

Steinberg, Renee, review of *The Sea Child, School Library Journal,* October, 1988, p. 148.

Tucker, Nicholas, review of *An Elephant for Muthu, Books for Your Children,* autumn-winter, 1986, p. 13.

Tucker, Nicholas, review of *Further Inventions of Mr. Cogg, Times Literary Supplement,* July 24, 1981, p. 839.

Watson, Elizabeth Porges, review of *Shakespeare, Theatre Cat, Books and Bookmen,* July, 1982, p. 34.

For More Information See

BOOKS

Science Fiction and Fantasy Literature, 1975-1991, Gale, 1992.

PERIODICALS

Bulletin of the Center for Children's Books, January, 1984, p. 98.

Growing Point, January, 1975, p. 2549; September, 1982, p. 3965; November, 1983, p. 4161.

Horn Book, January-February, 1989, p. 75.

Kirkus Reviews, June 1, 1975, pp. 601-02.

School Librarian, November, 1996, p. 165.

School Library Journal, September, 1975, p. 91.

—Sketch by J. Sydney Jones

* * *

SMITH, Datus C(lifford), Jr. 1907-1999

OBITUARY NOTICE—See index for *SATA* sketch: Born May 3, 1907, in Jackson, MI; died November 17, 1999, in Princeton, NJ. Executive, publisher, educator, author. Datus C. Smith, Jr. was a professor from 1943 to 1953 at Princeton University while serving as editor and finally director of the Princeton University Press. After leaving the press, he became president of Franklin Book Programs in 1952, a position he held until 1967, and of the U. S. Board on Books for Young People in the early 1980s. His writings focused on books and publishing: *American Books in the Non-Western World* was published in 1958, followed by *The Economics of Book Publishing in Developing Countries* and *A Guide to Book-Publishing,* which he wrote with others in 1966. In 1975 he was the recipient of the Association of

American University Presses' Distinguished Service Award.

OBITUARIES AND OTHER SOURCES:

BOOKS

Who's Who in America, Marquis Who's Who, 1998, p. 4167.

PERIODICALS

New York Times, December 11, 1999, p. A20.

*   *   *

STAFFORD, Paul 1966-

Personal

Born September 18, 1966, in Kurrajong, New South Wales, Australia; son of John (an accountant) and Robyn (a language teacher) Stafford. *Education:* Charles Sturt University, B.A., 1989. *Hobbies and other interests:* Land care, overseas travel, history and archaeology, bushwalking, canyoning, caving.

Addresses

Home and office—Bathampton, Bathurst, New South Wales, Australia.

Career

Charles Sturt University, Bathurst, Wales, tutor, 1996—. University of Adelaide, tutor, 1996—. *Member:* Australians for Native Title.

Writings

NOVELS FOR YOUNG PEOPLE

Ned Kelly's Helmet, Crawford House (Bathurst, Australia), 1999.

SHORT STORY COLLECTIONS FOR YOUNG PEOPLE

Blatantly Bogus, Crawford House, 1998.
Basically Bollocks, Crawford House, 1998.
Ludicrous Lies, Crawford House, 1998.
Fully Faked, Crawford House, 1998.
Chronic Crapola, Crawford House, 1999.
Heinous Humbuggery, Crawford House, 1999.
Totally Toasted, Crawford House, 1999.
Hoopy Hoaxes, Crawford House, 1999.

Work in Progress

A novel, *Matthew Flinders' Cat* (sequel to *Ned Kelly's Helmet*).

Sidelights

Paul Stafford told *SATA:* "I live outside Bathurst, New South Wales, Australia. I studied print journalism at Mitchell College of Advanced Education, Charles Sturt University, graduating in 1989, but renounced the make-

Paul Stafford

believe world of journalism for the hard and gritty reality of kids' fiction. Although a career in writing has meant abandoning my childhood dream of wealth and respectability, I now get to sleep late, dress scruffy, and gnaw on the skulls of my enemies. It's a trade-off I've learned to live with."

For More Information See

PERIODICALS

Magpies, September, 1998, p. 39.

*   *   *

STAUB, Frank (Jacob) 1949-

Personal

Born May 28, 1949, in Philadelphia, PA; son of Frank Leonard (a musician and office worker) and Virginia Anderson (a homemaker; maiden name, Ware) Staub. *Education:* Muhlenberg College, B.S. (biology), 1971; University of Rhode Island, M.S. (zoology), 1975.

Addresses

Home and office—Box 50801, Tucson, AZ 85703.

Career

Writer and photographer. Formerly worked as a high school life sciences and chemistry teacher, railroad track laborer, veterinary assistant, and white water river guide. *Member:* Nature Conservancy, Sierra Club, Wilderness Society, World Wildlife Fund, American Society for the Prevention of Cruelty to Animals, Humane Society,

People for the Ethical Treatment of Animals, National Audubon Society.

Awards, Honors

Outstanding Science Trade Book for Children designation, Children's Book Council/National Science Teachers' Association, 1993, for *America's Prairies;* Best Children's Book of the Year designation, Bank Street College, 1998, for *Moose.*

Writings

FOR CHILDREN; AUTHOR AND PHOTOGRAPHER

Let's Take a Trip to Yellowstone Park, Troll Associates, 1990.
A Day in the Life of a Ski Patroller, Troll Associates, 1991.

"EARLY BIRD NATURE BOOKS" SERIES; AUTHOR AND PHOTOGRAPHER

Mountain Goats, Lerner, 1994.
Sea Turtles, Lerner, 1995.
Alligators, Lerner, 1995.
Herons, Lerner, 1997.
Manatees, Lerner, 1998.
Prairie Dogs, Lerner, 1998.
Walruses, Lerner, 1999.
Sea Lions, Lerner, 2000.

"EARTH WATCH" SERIES; AUTHOR AND PHOTOGRAPHER

Yellowstone's Cycle of Fire, Carolrhoda, 1993.
America's Prairies, Carolrhoda, 1994.
America's Wetlands, Carolrhoda, 1995.
America's Forests, Carolrhoda, 1998.

"THE WORLD'S CHILDREN" SERIES; AUTHOR AND PHOTOGRAPHER

The Children of the Sierra Madre, Carolrhoda, 1996.
Children of Yucatan, Carolrhoda, 1996.
Children of Cuba, Carolrhoda, 1996.
Children of Belize, Carolrhoda, 1997.
Children of Dominica, Carolrhoda, 1998.
Children of Hawaii, Carolrhoda, 1999.
Children of the Tlingit, Carolrhoda, 1999.
Children of Malaysia, Carolrhoda, 2000.
Children of Thailand, Carolrhoda, 2000.
Children of Sonora, Carolrhoda, forthcoming.

PHOTOGRAPHER; FOR CHILDREN

Guy J. Spencer, *Let's Take a Trip to an Ancient Forest,* Troll Associates, 1987.
Ginger Wadsworth, *Giant Sequoia Trees,* Lerner, 1995.
Lesley A. DuTemple, *Moose,* Lerner, 1998.
Val Rapp, *Old Growth Forest,* Lerner, forthcoming.

Contributor of photographs to numerous reference books and to periodicals, including *National Geographic World, Natural History, Smithsonian, Backpacker, Fitness, Utne Reader, Woman's Day, Better Homes & Gardens, Country Life, U.S. Air,* and *Outdoor America.*

ADULT NONFICTION

(With Peter Anderson) *The Upper Arkansas River Rapids, History, and Nature, Mile by Mile,* Fulcrum, 1988.

Contributor to periodicals, including *U.S. Air, Outside, Travel and Leisure, Dodge Adventurer, Ford Times, Chevy Outdoors, Cyclist, Backpacker, Outdoor America, Bicycling, Motorland, American Forests, Tailwinds, Bicycling,* and *Colorado Monthly.* Has served as contributing editor, *Mountain Bike* and *Mountain Biking* magazines.

Staub has also scripted and photographed numerous audio-visual productions—mostly on nature-related subjects.

Sidelights

Athleticism, skill in photography, and a passion for the out-of-doors has allowed Frank Staub to channel his advanced knowledge of biology and zoology into a career as the author and photographer of a number of children's books focusing on the natural world. His experience as a schoolteacher allowed Staub to present basic facts about animal life, geography, history, culture, and ecology, enhancing young readers' growing sense of the diversity of life on earth. Among the many titles Staub has both written and illustrated are *Children of Cuba, Prairie Dogs,* and *Let's Take a Trip to Yellow-*

Frank Staub

Staub provided the text and photographs for his study of the hearty, agile mountain goat. (*From* Mountain Goats.)

stone Park. Formatted for use as a research tool, each book contains a glossary, index, and other study aids.

Born in 1949 in Philadelphia, Staub attended undergraduate and graduate school, earning his master's degree in zoology in 1975. After briefly teaching high school, Staub embarked on a career as a freelance writer and photographer. He started out writing scripts and shooting the photographs for educational slide sets and filmstrips. By the early 1980s he began to have success writing articles and taking pictures for magazines such as *Outside, Backpacker, USAir,* and *Travel and Leisure.* The first book to feature Staub's photography was Guy J. Spencer's 1987 work *Let's Take a Trip to an Ancient Forest. The Upper Arkansas River Rapids, History, and Nature, Mile by Mile* would feature Staub as both photographer and co-author when it reached bookstore shelves in 1988.

Since 1990 Staub has produced a number of books for young readers, including books in "The World's Children" series and a number of installments in the "Early Bird Nature Books" series, a group of books profiling many different plants and animals. In addition, he has written on America's geographic diversity, producing both text and photographs for such books as the award-winning *America's Prairies, America's Forests,* and *Yellowstone's Cycle of Fire.*

With straightforward titles such as *Alligators, Sea Turtles,* and *Herons,* Staub's books on animals have been formatted as part of the "Early Bird Nature Books" series published by Lerner. Each volume is designed to provide young readers in grades two through four with useful information on a single animal, providing information on habitat, a description of the animal, its eating habits, and its place in the cycle of life. Beginning each chapter with a question, Staub augments his informative texts with full-color photographs that show each animal in its natural environment. Reviewing Staub's *Mountain Goats* in *School Library Journal,* contributor Amy Nunley called the work "marvelous," and added that Staub's "spectacular full-color photographs team up with a simple, informative text to create an appealing offering." *Appraisal* critic Sarah Ayres Berma noted that "Staub is an excellent photographer and uses his skill to take readers of *Mountain Goats* as close to these interesting animals as possible." *Sea Turtles* also drew praise from critics, such as Frances E. Millhouser commenting in *School Library Journal* on its "well-organized and clearly written text" and praising the fact that "environmental dangers and attempts at protection are thoughtfully treated."

In addition to exploring the animal kingdom, Staub has also brought his attention—and his camera lens—to bear on the diversity within the human race in his "The World's Children" books. In 1996's *The Children of the Sierra Madre,* for example, he introduces readers to the young residents of Mexico's mountainous Sierra Madre region. Using photographs to show the way children live today, Staub also discusses the history of the region, its culture, and its geography. *School Library Journal* reviewer Sharon R. Pearce praised the volume as "an inviting package that shows various aspects of life" in this area of Latin America. Praising both *The Children of the Sierra Madre* and *Children of the Yucatan,* Annie Ayers noted in *Booklist:* "These photo-essays create a vital sense of immediacy. . . . Students . . . will be able to identify with these children and their lives," thus learning the lesson: "Our way is not the only way." *Children of Cuba* received particular praise from critics, both for Staub's matter-of-fact discussion of the impact of Castro's communist regime on modern life and for his photographs. As Susan Dove Lempke noted in *Booklist,* the photographs are superior to the stock photographs that are usually featured in such volumes. "Each picture is beautifully composed, crisply focused, and centered on people going about the fascinating minutiae of their daily lives," wrote the reviewer.

Several books about North American geography have also benefitted from Staub's talents as both a writer and a photo-essayist. *America's Prairies* profiles the three types of grassland environments, as well as the animals that inhabit each, in a book that a *Kirkus Reviews* critic called "an excellent presentation." In *Let's Take a Trip to Yellowstone Park,* published in 1990, Staub presents basic information via a "photo-journey" through one of America's natural wonders. In addition to describing the park's geography and geology, he discusses the ecosystem of the area, including the plant and animal life.

The Children of the Sierra Madre *focuses on the customs of the Tarahumara Indians. (Text and photos by Staub.)*

According to an *Appraisal* contributor, the author "stresses the importance of letting nature take its course" with reference to efforts to manipulate the populations of animals such as the elk. Staub revisited Yellowstone for 1993's *Yellowstone's Cycle of Fire,* which focuses on the fires that laid waste to portions of the park in 1988. By providing photos of the efforts to contain the fires, as well as of the results of the blazes that consumed thirteen million acres of wilderness, Staub "gives the experience a positive spin," according to a *Kirkus Reviews* critic. The work shows that the Natural Burn policy adhered to by the U.S. Park Service promotes a natural cycle of rebirth and new growth. Praising the work in *Booklist,* Carolyn Phelan noted that both *Yellowstone's Cycle of Fire* and *America's Prairies* "present . . . basic information in an attractive manner" and will be "valuable for classroom units or individual research."

Works Cited

Review of *America's Prairies, Kirkus Reviews,* February 1, 1994, p. 150.

Ayers, Annie, review of *The Children of the Sierra Madre, Booklist,* October 1, 1996, p. 344.

Berman, Sarah Ayres, review of *Mountain Goats, Appraisal,* fall, 1994, p. 61.

Lempke, Susan Dove, review of *Children of Cuba, Booklist,* December 1, 1996, pp. 650-51.

Review of *Let's Take a Trip to Yellowstone Park, Appraisal,* winter, 1991, pp. 76-77.

Millhouser, Frances E., review of *Sea Turtles, School Library Journal,* April, 1995, p. 146.

Nunley, Amy, review of *Mountain Goats, School Library Journal,* August, 1994, p. 152.

Pearce, Sharon R., review of *The Children of the Sierra Madre, School Library Journal,* August, 1996, p. 160.

Phelan, Carolyn, review of *America's Prairies, Booklist,* February 1, 1994, p. 1005.

Review of *Yellowstone's Cycle of Fire, Kirkus Reviews,* January 1, 1994, p. 75.

For More Information See

PERIODICALS

Appraisal, autumn, 1995, p. 67; winter-spring, 1996, p. 71.
Booklist, April 1, 1999, p. 1406.
Bulletin of the Center for Children's Books, November, 1996, p. 117.
Kirkus Reviews, June 15, 1997, p. 957.
School Library Journal, August, 1990, p. 153; June, 1994, p. 142; May, 1995, p. 116; August, 1995, p. 138; February, 1997, p. 96; August, 1997, p. 176; January, 1999, p. 116; July, 1999, p. 113.

*   *   *

STEELE, Alexander 1958-

Personal

Born August 26, 1958, in Dallas, TX; son of Joseph (an attorney) and Helen Stuhl. *Education:* Vanderbilt University, B.A. *Hobbies and other interests:* Travel, sailing, reading, films, theater, music, "meeting all kinds of people."

Addresses

Home and office—452 West 22nd St., Apt. 2-C, New York, NY 10011. *Agent*—Faith Hamlin, Sanford J. Greenburger Associates, 55 Fifth Ave., 15th Floor, New York, NY 10003. *E-mail*—xanderby@earthlink.net.

Career

Writer of books and plays. Also teaches creative writing at various institutions. *Member:* Mystery Writers of America, Dramatists Guild.

Awards, Honors

Award of Excellence, American Alliance for Theatre and Education, for the play *One Glorious Afternoon.*

Writings

"WISHBONE" SERIES

The Case of the On-Line Alien, illustrated by Genevieve Meek, Big Red Chair Books (Allen, TX), 1998.

The Case of the Unsolved Case, illustrated by Don Adair and Kathryn Yingling, Lyrick Publishing (Allen, TX), 1998.

Moby Dog, illustrated by Jane McCreary, Big Red Chair Books, 1998.

The Tale of the Missing Mascot, illustrated by Genevieve Meek, Big Red Chair Books, 1998.

The Haunting of Hathaway House, Lyrick Publishing, 1999.

Unleashed in Space (based on the story "Unleashed in Space," by Jack Williamson), Big Red Chair Books, 1999.

The Last of the Breed, illustrated by Don Punchatz, Big Red Chair Books, 1999.

The Case of the Breaking Story, Lyrick Publishing, 2000.

Huckleberry Dog, Lyrick Publishing, 2000.

OTHER

Author of seven books about a pair of brothers who are detectives, under a pseudonym. Author of several plays, including *King of Ragtime, Lightning and Frenzy,* and *One Glorious Afternoon.*

Work in Progress

A book series for young readers, dealing with the world of international espionage; an Internet storytelling site.

Sidelights

Alexander Steele told *SATA:* "I consider books the ultimate form of interactive entertainment. A good book draws the reader deeper inside the heart of a story than anything else because the author's words are interacting with the reader's imagination. Computerized effects will never be able to match that. When someone really enjoys one of my books, I'm inclined to give the reader half the credit. Since I realize that reading a book does take some effort, I try to make the journey as thrilling as possible."

Steele's books are based on the character of Wishbone, a dog created by Rick Duffield, who first appeared in a television program broadcast by the Public Broadcasting Service.

For More Information See

PERIODICALS

Astronomy, May, 1999, p. 108.

*   *   *

STREISSGUTH, Thomas 1958-

Personal

Born August 5, 1958, in Washington, DC; son of Thomas B. (a columnist/writer) and Marian I. (a computer systems analyst) Streissguth; married Marie-Christine Rouffiac (a teacher), June 10, 1988; children: Louison, Adele. *Education:* Yale University, B.A., 1981. *Hobbies and other interests:* Music, travel, languages, and history.

Addresses

Home—4020 Center Gate Blvd., Sarasota, FL 34233. *E-mail*—ninine10of@aol.com.

Career

Freelance writer and editor. Llewellyn Publications, St. Paul, MN, managing editor, 1987-90; Lerner Publications, Minneapolis, editor, 1991-95; Capstone Press, Minneapolis, MN, managing editor, 1995-96.

Awards, Honors

New York Public Library Books for the Teen Age award, 1993, for *Hoaxers and Hustlers.*

Alexander Steele

Writings

Soviet Leaders from Lenin to Gorbachev, Oliver Press, 1992.
International Terrorists, Oliver Press, 1993.
Hoaxers and Hustlers, Oliver Press, 1994.
Charismatic Cult Leaders, Oliver Press, 1994.
Say It with Music: A Story about Irving Berlin, Carolrhoda, 1994.
Hatemongers and Demagogues, Oliver Press, 1995.
Rocket Man: The Story of Robert Goddard, Carolrhoda, 1995.
Roller Coasters, Capstone Press, 1995.
Tractors, Capstone Press, 1995.
Jeeps, Capstone Press, 1995.
Convertibles, Capstone Press, 1995.
The U.S. Navy SEALS, Capstone Press, 1995.
A Career in Food Service, Capstone Press, 1995.
The Green Berets, Capstone Press, 1996.
Writer of the Plains: A Story about Willa Cather, Carolrhoda, 1996.
Innovators, Oliver Press, 1997.
Communications: Sending the Message, Oliver Press, 1997.
Legendary Labor Leaders, Oliver Press, 1998.
Utopian Visionaries, Oliver Press, 1998.
Mary Cassatt: Portrait of an American Impressionist, Carolrhoda, 1998.
Cyprus: Divided Island, Lerner, 1998.
Legends of Dracula, Lerner Publications, 1998.
Queen Cleopatra, Lerner Publications, 1998.
John Glenn, Lerner Publications, 1998.
Wounded Knee, 1890: The End of the Plains Indian Wars, Facts on File, 1998.
Lewis and Clark: Explorers of the Northwest, Enslow, 1998.
Edgar Allan Poe, Lerner Publications, 1999.
Jack London, Lerner Publications, 1999.
Jesse Owens, Lerner Publications, 1999.
John Brown, Carolrhoda, 1999.
Life among the Vikings, Lucent, 1999.
Weapons of Mass Destruction, Enslow Publishers, 1999.
Ahead of His Time: A Story about Jules Verne, Carolrhoda, 2000.
The Comanche, Lucent, 2000.
Life in Ancient Egypt, Lucent, 2000.
Nuclear Weapons: More Countries, More Threats, Enslow Publishers, 2000.
The Transcontinental Railroad, Lucent, 2000.
20th-Century Revolutionaries (two volumes), Oliver Press, 2000.

Also contributor to "One Nation" series, Capstone Press. Contributor to "Globetrotters Club" series of country books for primary grades, Carolrhoda, 1998.

Sidelights

Tom Streissguth is a professional writer who specializes in nonfiction books for young readers. His natural curiosity has found a perfect outlet in his career as a children's book author; books like *Utopian Visionaries, Legends of Dracula,* and *Wounded Knee, 1890: The End of the Plains Indian Wars* allow young readers to share the author's enthusiasm for history's small but telling details. Praising Streissguth's "less impassioned" approach to *Wounded Knee, 1890, Booklist* contributor Roger Leslie noted that the author's decision to "trace the personal motivations and historic events" leading to the "fateful standoff" between the U.S. Army and Native Americans allows the facts to bring to life "the chain of events that devastated an entire race."

Born in Washington, D.C. in 1958, Streissguth acquired a love of the past early on, and books provided the perfect vehicle to travel back in time. "I never managed to shake off a boyhood fascination with history books, detective stories, and *The Time Tunnel,* he explained to *SATA.* "I still enjoy a good story and a nice, quiet library. I enjoy discovering facts and details about the past that I didn't know—that I never suspected—and relating them to anybody with time and patience enough to read."

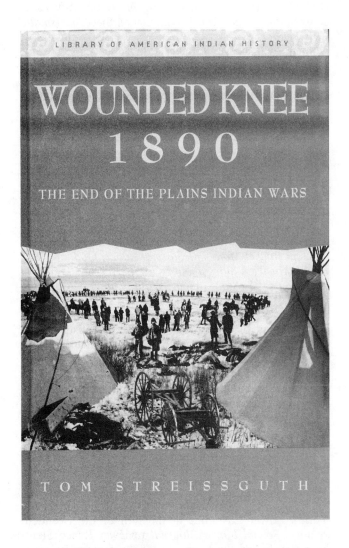

Thomas Streissguth documented the personal and historical events that culminated in the tragic massacre of Lakota men, women, and children in the Battle of Wounded Knee.

A fascination for the personalities of the people who have figured prominently in the history of the United States and elsewhere has resulted in many of Streissguth's titles. In his *Charismatic Cult Leaders,* for example, he profiles Branch Davidian leader David Koresh, Scientology advocate L. Ron Hubbard, and Mormon founder Joseph Smith. After an explanation of the Christian doctrine, Streissguth examines each cult leader individually, showing how each has been able to attract enough followers through his charismatic message to gain mass public attention—and concern. "Streissguth's conversational writing style and ability to smoothly blend the facts with [his subjects'] humanity and faith" create a book "tough ... to put down," admitted *Booklist* contributor Jeanne Triner. The author "emphasizes the events" leading to the formation of each cult, and "effectively summarizes the basic beliefs of each figure," in the opinion of *School Library Journal* reviewer Jack Forman. Triner wholeheartedly dubbed the work "fascinating," and "bound to appeal to young adults." While also praising the work as a "balanced, straightforward account," *Voice of Youth Advocates* contributor Colleen Harris commented that *Charismatic Cult Leaders* was flawed, perhaps, by its exclusion of women such as Mary Baker Eddy.

Similar books by Streissguth include *Hoaxers and Hustlers,* a 1994 work that profiles famous swindlers such as televangelists Jimmy and Tammy Faye Baker, Charles Ponzi, and Clifford Irving. Again, each figure is examined in detail within the context of the society in which they perpetrated their scheme. Each hoax described is "fascinating," noted *Booklist* critic Frances Bradburn, "in part, [because of] the author's easy style and obvious understanding of the history surrounding the event."

Many of Streissguth's books focus on a single individual, as in *Rocket Man: The Story of Robert Goddard, Say It with Music: A Story about Irving Berlin,* and *Writer of the Plains: A Story about Willa Cather.* Following Goddard's life from his childhood as a sickly boy to his success as a pioneer in astronautics, Streissguth "paints a vivid portrait of a vivid but secretive scientist," in the opinion of *Booklist* contributor Chris Sherman. Several critics noted that the book not only followed Goddard's well-known effort to break from Earth's atmosphere and his contributions to the U.S. rocket development programs undertaken during World War II, but also focused on the inventor's early research and related inventions. "Streissguth's writing is clear, objective, and interesting," added Margaret M. Hagel in her *School Library Journal* appraisal of *Rocket Man.*

Terming *Say It with Music* not only "an intriguing story" but an accurate introduction to the social milieu of New York's Lower East Side at the turn of the twentieth century, *School Library Journal* reviewer Renee Steinberg also hailed the biography of the famous Russian-born composer Irving Berlin as "one that Streissguth makes readable and enjoyable." Praising the book's description of Berlin's childhood—his family's arrival at Ellis Island in the 1890s, his upbringing in the Bowery,

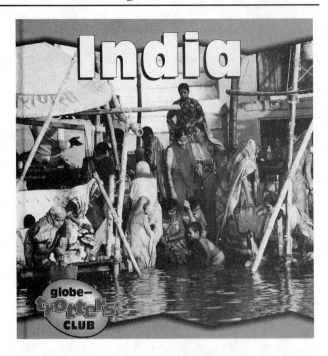

In his informational text for young readers about contemporary life in India, Streissguth offers facts about the country's geography, culture, and people.

and his reliance on his musical talent to support himself from the age of fourteen to Berlin's ultimate fame as an internationally acclaimed songwriter—*Booklist* contributor Carolyn Phelan called *Say It with Music* "a good, concise biography" and noted that Streissguth's skill as a writer makes the work "accessible to many children."

Many of Streissguth's books are part of an extended series designed to introduce young readers to various aspects of a particular topic. His "Globetrotters Club" books take young people to such faraway places as Japan, India, and Mexico, profiling history, culture, and politics. A series of books on transportation includes the titles *Roller Coasters, Tractors, Jeeps,* and *Convertibles;* each volume discusses these somewhat unique forms of conveyance, how they evolved, and their place in modern life. Although such series make up much of the author's list of writings, some titles stand on their own, reflecting a personal fascination on Streissguth's part. *Life among the Vikings, Nuclear Weapons: More Countries, More Threats,* and *The Transcontinental Railroad* each focus in depth on a particular social or historical topic, allowing the author to indulge in his love of discovering little-known facts and sharing them with his readers.

"Writing nonfiction for juvenile markets means paring down a thousand facts and details into the essence of the story, and making that story as clear and fascinating as possible," Streissguth explained of his craft. "Given the plots by research [departments of publishing companies], I have to create the plays and adapt the speeches to the audience—whatever reading level I'm assigned. It's like solving a puzzle, the format and length assigned by an editor, the deadline a slightly missed target, the audience and a few reviewers the judge, the prize a chance to do another one and make a modest living at it."

Works Cited

Bradburn, Frances, review of *Hoaxers and Hustlers, Booklist,* September 1, 1994, p. 33.

Forman, Jack, review of *Charismatic Cult Leaders, School Library Journal,* June, 1995, p. 142.

Hagel, Margaret M., review of *Rocket Man, School Library Journal,* September, 1995, p. 216.

Harris, Colleen, review of *Charismatic Cult Leaders, Voice of Youth Advocates,* December, 1995, p. 333.

Leslie, Roger, review of *Wounded Knee, 1890, Booklist,* October 1, 1998, p. 318.

Phelan, Carolyn, review of *Say It with Music, Booklist,* May 1, 1994, p. 1601.

Sherman, Chris, review of *Rocket Man, Booklist,* October 15, 1995, p. 401.

Steinberg, Renee, review of *Say It with Music, School Library Journal,* August, 1994, p. 166.

Triner, Jeanne, review of *Charismatic Cult Leaders, Booklist,* August, 1995, p. 1939.

For More Information See

PERIODICALS

Booklist, June 1, 1997, p. 1698; October 15, 1998, p. 411; May 1, 1999, p. 1593.

School Library Journal, January, 1999, p. 155; February, 1999, p. 96; July, 1999, p. 113.*

*   *   *

STUART, Ruth McEnery 1849(?)-1917

Personal

Born May 21, 1849 (some sources say 1856), in Marksville, LA; died May 6, 1917, in New York, NY; daughter of James and Mary Routh (Stirling) McEnery; married Alfred Oden Stuart (a cotton planter), 1879; children: Stirling.

Career

American short-story author.

Awards, Honors

Tulane University, honorary doctor of letters, 1915.

Writings

A Golden Wedding and Other Tales, Harper (New York City and London, England), 1893.

Carlotta's Intended and Other Tales, Harper, 1894.

The Story of Babette, a Little Creole Girl, Harper, 1894.

(With Albert Bigelow Paine) *Gobolinks, or Shadow-Pictures for Young and Old,* Century (New York City), 1896.

Sonny: A Story, Century, 1896, also published as *Sonny: Tales,* Century (London, England), 1896, also published as *Sonny: A Christmas Guest,* Century, 1897.

Solomon Crow's Christmas Pockets and Other Tales, Harper, 1896.

In Simpkinsville: Character Tales, Harper, 1897.

The Snow-Cap Sisters: A Farce, Harper, 1897.

Moriah's Mourning and Other Half-Hour Sketches, Harper, 1898.

Holly and Pizen and Other Stories, Century, 1899.

Napoleon Jackson: The Gentleman of the Plush Rocker, Century, 1902.

George Washington Jones: A Christmas Gift that Went A-Begging, H. Altemus (Philadelphia, PA), 1903.

The River's Children: An Idyl of the Mississippi, Century, 1904.

The Second Wooing of Salina Sue and Other Stories, Harper, 1905.

Aunt Amity's Silver Wedding and Other Stories, Century, 1909.

Sonny's Father in which the Father, now become Grandfather, a Kindly Observer of Life and a Genial Philosopher, in his Desultory Talks with the Family Doctor, Carries along the Story of Sonny, Century, 1910.

The Haunted Photograph, Whence and Whither, A Case in Diplomacy, The Afterglow, Century, 1911.

Daddy Do-Funny's Wisdom Jingles, Century, 1913.

The Cocoon: A Rest-Cure Comedy, Hearst's International Library (New York City), 1915.

Plantation Songs and Other Verse, Appleton (New York City and London, England), 1916.

Contributor to periodical publications, including *Ladies Home Journal, Century,* and *New York Times Review of Books.*

Sidelights

A turn-of-the-century proponent of women's rights, Ruth McEnery Stuart became known as, in the words of Mildred L. Rutherford in *The South in History and Literature,* the "laureate of the lowly." Stuart wrote of the disenfranchisement of the South: the rural residents of Arkansas, New Orleans' Italian Americans, and African Americans. She stayed on the safe side of racial politics, however, and her adherence to racial stereotypes led to a decline in her popularity among readers and critics following her death. She won the admiration of many of her literary contemporaries, though, and Edward Lewis Stevens, in *Library of Southern Literature,* commends "her own natural and unconscious optimism through which she sees her South suffused with the roseate glow of sentiment and romance." And *Harper's Bazaar* featured her as the "woman of the hour" in their December 16, 1899, issue.

Stuart was born on May 21, 1849 (some sources say 1856) in Marksville, Louisiana, to James and Mary Routh Stirling McEnery. An Irish immigrant, James McEnery established himself as a cotton merchant, planter, and slave owner. Mary Routh Stirling descended from a prominent Louisiana family. Routh McEnery (she later changed the spelling of her name to Ruth to avoid confusion) grew up in New Orleans. She gleaned her education from the diverse city, immersed in the mixture of cultures and dialects from immigrants, Creoles, and African Americans. This rich experience informed her stories, but so did her privileged perspective as an upper-class young woman. Her family's strained finances following the war obligated Ruth to teach at a local girls school and to marry her thrice-widowed cousin, Alfred Oden Stuart.

A man thirty years her senior, Alfred Stuart had eleven children (most grown), but he was wealthy and prominent in Washington, Arkansas. Here Ruth Stuart learned more about black culture and speech patterns and she is quoted in *Little Pilgrimages Among Women Who Have Written Famous Books* as saying that "most of my negro character-studies have come from my association with the negroes while [in Arkansas]. We lived right among them ... there were hundreds of negroes to one white person."

While living in Arkansas, Stuart also helped found the women's reading group, D.O.T. (Dear Old Town), sharing her first literary efforts at the group meetings. However, only after her husband died in 1880 did the thirty-one-year-old widow begin writing seriously. She indicated in interviews later on that were it not for the need to make money she might not have ever become a serious writer. In the late 1880s Stuart met Charles Dudley Warner, then an editor at *Harper's New Monthly Magazine*. Warner was instrumental in Stuart's early success by having her short story "Lamentations of Jeremiah Johnson" published in *Harper's* and "Uncle Mingo's "Speculations'" in the *Princeton Review*. Both are stories of African-American shenanigans as told by a white narrator. Stories of local color, like Stuart's, were in great demand at the time.

Toward the late 1880's to early 1890's, Stuart settled in New York, making her homes in the city and in a literary community in the Catskill Mountains. Warner ushered her work to *Harper's* and other publishers, such as *Century Illustrated Monthly Magazine*. Publishing regularly in magazines, Stuart wrote her first book, *A Golden Wedding and Other Tales,* in 1893. She brought small-town Arkansas to life in a series of stories, known as the Simpkinsville sketches. These stories feature white characters speaking in dialect about various affairs of their town. A year later she published two books, *Carlotta's Intended and Other Tales* and *The Story of Babette, a Little Creole Girl*. These more realistic stories established Stuart as a nationally popular writer. In *Carlotta's Intended,* Stuart depicts New Orleans' mafia as well as its German and Irish denizens. *The Story of Babette,* also set in New Orleans, examines the seamy side of the city and the tensions between classes there.

Although many of Stuart's stories contained racist overtones, she also wrote tales that portrayed strong, complex black characters, including such stories as "Blink" where an aspiring white writer depends on her "mammy" for literary critiquing and guidance. Based on

her advice to "Write down some *truly truth* what is *ach-chilly happened,"* the writer meets with immediate success. Discussing this work in the *Dictionary of Literary Biography,* Kathryn B. McKee states that it is difficult to generalize Stuart's ideas on race as the writer was living at a time when racial roles and relationships were in constant flux.

Sonny: A Story was Stuart's most commercially successful book. It chronicles the early life of Sonny Jones, the only child of an older white couple in an Arkansas small town. Sonny is an intractable boy who refuses both vaccination and baptism and who rules the lives of his parents with impunity. Dedicated to her own son, Stirling, Stuart no doubt drew on her experiences as the parent of a boy for the stories. The book tells the story of Sonny's father's life as well, as narrated by the family doctor. Among the comedy and reflections are commentaries on the day's social and political events.

Soon after, Stuart published *In Simpkinsville: Character Tales*. In one of the stories, "The Unlived Life of Little Mary Ellen," the deranged young woman from the title of the story is abandoned at the altar by her fiance. Following this tragedy, Mary Ellen imagines that a childhood wax doll is her child from the fiance. The other characters in the story help maintain the fantasy until Mary Ellen dies at the funeral for the doll after it has been destroyed by a family pet. McKee relates that this was one of Stuart's most "popular and striking" tales, part of a whole selection of stories in which Stuart explores female mental health and coping mechanisms.

Holly and Pizen and Other Stories, a collection of stories about unlikely heroines, was published two years later. In "Queen O'Sheba's Triumph," a young black woman named Sheba travels to New York City seeking fame and fortune. Her dreams elude her, but she paints a glamorous and completely false picture of her life in her letters home. Becoming desperate when her family decides to visit, Sheba fakes her own funeral. Like Mary Ellen in "The Unlived Life of Little Mary Ellen," she dies during the service. Extraordinary for her ingenuity and independence, Sheba is not a typical childish black caricature as many black characters were in the literature of the late nineteenth century. McKee states that "this story has attracted the attention of readers and critics, who have pointed to it when redeeming Stuart from charges of excessive sentimentality."

In addition to writing, Stuart read her stories aloud to enthusiastic audiences. She won the praises of Mark Twain and Kate Chopin, and by 1900, she was one of the highest paid writers in the United States. The tragic death of her son, who fell from a window in 1905, caused Stuart great sorrow. She never fully recovered professionally, though she produced five more books before her death. In 1915, Tulane University awarded Stuart an honorary doctor of letters degree. The accomplished writer of more than twenty books died on May 6, 1917, in New York City. Ten years earlier, the Ruth McEnery Stuart Clan, a literary society, was founded in New Orleans, an organization still in existence. Her writing eventually fell out of favor for the very reasons it had been popular: its sentimentality and its representations of blacks in the South. McKee, however, defends Stuart's place in literary history: "Raised on the ideal of an Old South, she wrote at times with an eye for the uncharted relationships possible in a New South."

Works Cited

McKee, Kathryn B., "Ruth McEnery Stuart," *Dictionary of Literary Biography, Volume 202: Nineteenth Century American Fiction Writers,* Gale, 1999, pp. 242-50.

Rutherford, Mildred L., *The South in History and Literature,* Franklin-Turner, 1907.

Stevens, Edward Lewis, *Library of Southern Literature, Compiled under the Direct Supervision of Southern Men of Letters,* edited by Edwin Anderson Alderman, Joel Chandler Harris, and Charles William Kent, Martyn and Hoyt, 1909-13.

Stuart, Ruth McEnery, "Blink," *Solomon Crow's Christmas Pockets and Other Tales,* Harper, 1896.

Stuart, Ruth McEnery, in *Little Pilgrimages Among Women Who Have Written Famous Books,* by E. F. Harkins and C. H. L. Johnston, L. C. Page (Boston, MA), 1901.

For More Information See

BOOKS

American Women Playwrights, 1900-1930, Greenwood (Westport, CT), 1992.

Nineteenth-Century American Women Writers, Greenwood, 1997.

The Oxford Companion to American Literature, sixth edition, Oxford University Press (New York City), 1995.

Simpson, Ethel C., editor, *Simpkinsville and Vicinity: Arkansas Stories of Ruth McEnery Stuart,* University of Arkansas Press (Fayetteville, AK), 1983.

Sneller, Judy E., *Gender, Race, and Identity,* Southern Humanities Press (Chattanooga, TN), 1993.

Sneller, Judy E., *Images of the Child,* Bowling Green University Popular Press (Bowling Green, OH), 1994.

Taylor, Helen, *Gender, Race, and Region in the Writings of Grace King, Ruth McEnery Stuart, and Kate Chopin,* Louisiana State University Press (Baton Rouge, LA), 1989.

PERIODICALS

Legacy, number 1, 1993.

Louisiana Literature, spring, 1987.

Xavier Review, number 2, 1987.*

*   *   *

SWANN, Brian (Stanley Frank) 1940-

Personal

Born August 14, 1940, in Wallsend upon Tyne, England; married Roberta Swann. *Education:* Queens' College, Cambridge University, B.A., M.A.; Princeton University, Ph.D.

Addresses

Office—Faculty of Humanities and Social Sciences, Cooper Union, Cooper Square, New York, NY 10003. *E-mail*—Swann@cooper.edu.

Career

Instructor at Princeton University and Rutgers University; professor of English at Cooper Union. Poetry editor of *Amicus,* 1980—; director of the Bennington Writing Workshops, 1987-91.

Awards, Honors

Proctor Fellowship, Princeton, 1964-65; Princeton National Fellowship, 1968-70; John Florio Prize for best translation from Italian published in the United Kingdom, 1976, with Ruth Feldman, for translating Primo Levi's *Shema;* National Endowment for the Arts fellowship, 1978, for creative writing; Creative Artists in the Public Service (CAPS) grant, 1981, for poetry; Premio Circe-Sabaudia, 1984, for *The Dawn is Always New;* Italo Calvino Award, Translation Center, Colombia University, 1990, for *Collected Poems of Primo Levi.*

Writings

FOR CHILDREN

The Tongue Dancing: Riddle-Poems, Rowan Tree, 1984.

The Fox and the Buffalo, Green Tiger Press, 1985.

A Basket Full of White Eggs: Riddle-Poems, illustrated by Ponder Goembel, Orchard Books, 1988.

Touching the Distance: Native American Riddle-Poems, illustrated by Maria Rendon, Harcourt, 1998.

The House with No Door: African Riddle-Poems, illustrated by Ashley Bryan, Harcourt, 1998.

FICTION; FOR ADULTS

The Runner, Carpenter Press, 1979.

Elizabeth, Penmaen Press, 1981.

Unreal Estate: Short Stories, Toothpaste Press, 1982.

Another Story: A Novella, Adler Publishing Co., 1984.

The Plot of the Mice, Capra Press, 1987.

POETRY

The Whale's Scars, New Rivers Press, 1974.

Roots, photographs by Hardie Truesdale, New Rivers Press, 1976.

Living Time, Quarterly Review of Literature Contemporary Poets Series, 1978.

Paradigms of Fire, woodcuts by Ann Khan, Corycian Press, 1980.

The Middle of the Journey, University of Alabama Press, 1982.

EDITOR

Smoothing the Ground: Essays on Native American Oral Literature, University of California Press, 1983.

Song of the Sky: Versions of Native American Song-Poems, Four Zoas Night House, 1985, University of Massachusetts Press, 1993.

Brian Swann

(With Arnold Krupat) *Recovering the Word: Essays on Native American Literature,* University of California Press, 1987.

(With Arnold Krupat) *I Tell You Now: Autobiographical Essays by Native American Writers,* University of California Press, 1987.

Essays on the Translation of Native American Literatures, Smithsonian Press, 1991.

Coming to Light: Contemporary Translations of the Native American Literatures of North America, Random House, 1995.

Wearing the Morning Star: Native American Song-Poems, Random House, 1996.

Native American Songs and Poems, Dover, 1996.

(With Arnold Krupat) *Here First: Autobiographical Essays of Native American Writers,* Modern Library, 2000.

Poetry Comes up Where it Can, University of Utah Press, 2000.

OTHER

Author of *Der Rote Schwan* (title means "The Red Swan"), published by Herder Verlag in Vienna, Austria, 1989. Swann has also translated sixteen volumes of poetry, including *Collected Poems* by Primo Levi. Contributor to hundreds of magazines and journals, including *Criticism, ELH, Nineteenth Century Fiction, Novel, American Poetry Review, American Scholar, New Republic, New Yorker, Poetry,* and *Partisan Review.*

Sidelights

Brian Swann is a poet, translator, and editor, as well as a well-respected educator. A professor of English at New York's Cooper Union, British-born Swann has published five books of poetry and five books of fiction for adults, as well as translating numerous poetry works by writers from around the world. His work in Native American studies, especially in his editing of the literature of Native Americans, has proven popular with adult and young readers alike. Swann has also published four children's books of riddle-poems that are adapted from folkloric literature from around the world: *The Tongue Dancing: Riddle-Poems, A Basket Full of White Eggs: Riddle-Poems, Touching the Distance: Native American Riddle-Poems,* and *The House with No Door: African Riddle-Poems.* "I like to try different approaches," Swann told *SATA.* "Poetry, fiction, translation, books for children. I moved from my first academic specialty, medieval literature, to nineteenth-century fiction, and then to Native American studies. Recently I've tried a non-verbal approach. I am painting—small, nothing bigger than [a] page."

Educated at Queens' College, Cambridge, and at Princeton, Swann held positions at both Princeton and Rutgers before moving on to Cooper Union in New York. He began publishing book-length fiction and poetry for adults in the 1970s, verse that was generally well received. With his turn of interest toward Native American studies came publication of a series of books on Native American literature, edited by Swann, that have attracted readers of all ages. *Smoothing the Ground: Essays on Native American Oral Literature,* published in 1983, was a compilation of essays on Native American oral literature, including stories and song. The collection of twenty essays made accessible the work of a wide range of scholars who advocated opening up the canon of American literature to include this earliest form of literature on the American continent. "Editor Brian Swann is to be commended for the gathering," noted a reviewer for *Choice.* Ben Reuven, writing in the *Los Angeles Times Book Review,* felt that the essays "are embellished with gemlike excerpts from a rich oral tradition long neglected."

Of more academic interest are the essays gathered in *Recovering the Word: Essays on Native American Literature,* edited in collaboration with Arnold Krupat, which explores the art of translation of Native American texts as well as their analysis. In *I Tell You Now: Autobiographical Essays by Native American Writers,* Swann and Krupat collected eighteen autobiographical statements from lesser-known Native American writers in what a *Choice* critic called a "notable volume." Writing in the *Times Literary Supplement,* Mark Abley called the book "a fascinating collection of autobiographical essays" that are all "written entirely in the language of enforced acculturation: English." Abley went on to comment, "*I Tell You Now* makes it abundantly clear that to be Indian in the United States today is often an act of will, a committed state of mind." Clark Blaise remarked in *Washington Post Book World,*

"I do not know of any book quite like this one. Not only does it gather 18 eloquent autobiographical essays in one place—a rarity in itself—but they are the life-stories of some very significant Native American writers. . . . *I Tell You Now* helps fill in the gaps between the celebrated and the still-obscure." Blaise concluded, "This book offers itself as a tool for culture retrieval, and becomes a major artifact of the search."

Swann moved on from anthologies of critical essays to presentations of Native American texts themselves with several volumes of myths and song-poems. *Song of the Sky: Versions of Native American Song-Poems* presents more than one hundred Native American chants and songs collected by anthropologists and revised and reworked by Swann. Frank Allen commented in *Library Journal* that these "'verbal artifacts' . . . reveal that there can be no 'conventional or single notion of the Indian.'" Allen concluded that the book was "[i]ndispensable for any library that wishes to have the most current versions of Native American verbal and musical art." Also writing in *Library Journal,* Joyce Nower called the 1985 edition of the book "an unusual collection of Indian songpoems, transcribed into freshly worded versions by Brian Swann." Sue E. Budin, reviewing the title in *Kliatt,* noted that these song-poems "are like Zen koans or Japanese haiku—posing questions with no resolution . . . . Dreamlike, mystical, the words seem to evolve from the dance or chant. This is a different way of using language." Swann provides another collection of such song-poems in *Wearing the Morning Star: Native American Song-Poems,* a "scholarly work," noted Debbie Earl in *Voice of Youth Advocates,* "although the poems are still very accessible to younger readers." In this collection Swann provides translations from poems and songs from many traditions, Aleut to Zuni. A *Publishers Weekly* critic felt that "Swann's introduction and extensive end notes add background and perspective."

More Native American literature is served up in *Coming to Light: Contemporary Translations of the Native American Literatures of North America,* "a solid entree to American Indian mythology" in a "mammoth, sweeping volume," according to one *Publishers Weekly* reviewer. In this work, Swann collected over fifty stories translated by both Native Americans and non-Indians and divided them into seven geographical regions. Here are the familiar trickster Coyote tales of the Southwest, as well as Raven and Kalapuya from the Pacific Northwest and far North, among a multitude of other tales. "Swann's knowledgeable introduction sets the translations in historical context and discusses the oral tradition," concluded the reviewer for *Publishers Weekly.* *Booklist* contributor Donna Seaman wrote, "Swann has put together a major ground breaking anthology of Native American literature." Writing in the *New York Times Book Review,* Verlyn Klinkenborg remarked, "There's a good chance that *Coming to Light . . .* will turn out to be a touchstone in the American understanding of this continent's indigenous peoples. . . . [It] offers a copious, easily accessible starting point for anyone interested in reading and learning about Native Ameri-

Song of the Sky *is a compilation of more than one hundred Native American chants and songs collected by anthropologists and revised and reworked by Swann. (Cover illustration by Joe Maktima.)*

can narratives and poetry." Klinkenborg went on to observe, "Against the pervasive stereotype of the undifferentiated red Indian—a stereotype at once romantic and revolting—this book offers historical and regional particularity." Louis Owens called Swann's anthology "an extraordinary book" in the *Los Angeles Times Book Review,* saying that it is "a work that displays almost the full range of Native American literatures and does so with responsibility, authority, and brilliance," despite what the reviewer felt was a glaring omission in tales from Southeastern tribes. L. Evers, writing in *Choice,* was more succinct: "This is by far the best anthology of translations from Native American oral traditions ever published."

Swann has also written six volumes specifically for young readers, four of them riddle-poems, a tradition he has been working in since his 1974 collection of such poems, *The Whale's Scars.* But with *A Basket Full of White Eggs, Touching the Distance,* and *The House with No Door,* he fashioned such riddles to appeal to children. In *A Basket Full of White Eggs,* Swann reworked poetically phrased riddles from various world cultures and accompanied them with watercolor illustrations by Ponder Goembel. "The book's careful matching of verbal craftsmanship with artistic beauty is perhaps epitomized in the concluding North Pontic Turkic entry about the night sky in this unusual melding of mental exercise with graphic richness," wrote *Booklist* reviewer Ellen Mandel. Included in the collection are riddle-

Swann has assembled riddles from numerous African tribes for his collection, **The House with No Door.** *(Illustrated by Ashley Bryan.)*

poems from cultures including Mayan, Alaska, Nigerian, and Saudi Arabian, to name but a few. A *Kirkus Reviews* contributor called Swann's children's book "a handsome, unusual collection," while Janet Hickman, reviewing *A Basket Full of White Eggs* in *Language Arts,* commented, "[Swann's] words sing." "These 15 riddles are poetry and puzzle rolled into one," remarked Patricia Dooley in *School Library Journal.* "They vary widely in difficulty: some are obvious enough for a four year old, while others might stump an expert of ten," Dooley added. And a *Publishers Weekly* critic called the book "thought provoking and beautiful."

With *Touching the Distance,* Swann blended his passion for Native American literature with riddle-poems, presenting fifteen such texts from the Americas. *Booklist* contributor Karen Morgan felt that children "will become engaged in both the rhyme and the mystery as they attempt to solve the riddles, which open a door on new ways of looking at the world." Teaming up with illustrator Maria Rendon, Swann created an "inspired conjoining of verbal and visual lyricism," according to a *Publishers Weekly* reviewer.

More riddle verses, from Africa this time, are presented in *The House with No Door,* a book of "original, laconic verses . . . based on Swann's collection of riddles," as a reviewer for *Publishers Weekly* described it. This same reviewer, however, felt that "too many of the riddles seem beyond the reach of the target audience." Despite such criticism, many reviewers felt Swann's riddle-

poems provide intriguing possibilities for young readers while introducing them to the cultures of different parts of the world. As a reviewer for *Kirkus Reviews* noted of *Touching the Distance,* "these pages tease the mind and jump-start the imagination."

Works Cited

Abley, Mark, review of *I Tell You Now: Autobiographical Essays by Native American Writers, Times Literary Supplement,* November 11, 1988, p. 1255.

Allen, Frank, review of *Song of the Sky: Versions of Native American Song-Poems, Library Journal,* January, 1994, p. 120.

Review of *A Basket Full of White Eggs: Riddle Poems, Kirkus Reviews,* December 15, 1987, p. 1739.

Review of *A Basket Full of White Eggs: Riddle Poems, Publishers Weekly,* January 15, 1988, p. 94.

Blaise, Clark, review of *I Tell You Now: Autobiographical Essays by Native American Writers, Washington Post Book World,* February 7, 1988.

Budin, Sue E., review of *Song of the Sky: Versions of Native American Song-Poems, Kliatt,* May, 1994, p. 24.

Review of *Coming to Light: Contemporary Translations of the Native American Literatures of North America, Publishers Weekly,* January 9, 1995, p. 58.

Dooley, Patricia, review of *A Basket Full of White Eggs: Riddle Poems, School Library Journal,* April, 1988, pp. 97-98.

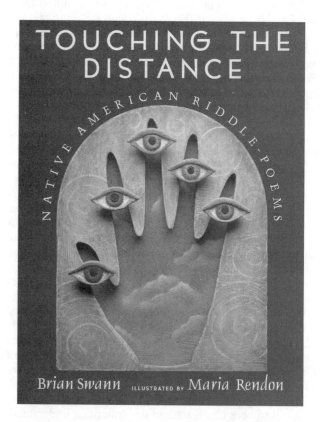

In Swann's concise text, various riddles from Native American culture are presented for young readers to decipher. (Cover illustration by Maria Rendon.)

Earl, Debbie, review of *Wearing the Morning Star: Native American Song-Poems, Voice of Youth Advocates,* June, 1997, pp. 126-27.

Evers, L., review of *Coming to Light: Contemporary Translations of the Native American Literatures of North America, Choice,* September, 1995, p. 112.

Hickman, Janet, review of *A Basket Full of White Eggs: Riddle Poems, Language Arts,* September, 1988, p. 500.

Review of *The House with No Door: African Riddle-Poems, Publishers Weekly,* November 9, 1998, p. 75.

Review of *I Tell You Now: Autobiographical Essays by Native American Writers, Choice,* April, 1988, p. 1253.

Klinkenborg, Verlyn, review of *Coming to Light: Contemporary Translations of the Native American Literatures of North America, New York Times Book Review,* March 19, 1995, p. 17.

Mandel, Ellen, review of *A Basket Full of White Eggs: Riddle Poems, Booklist,* February 15, 1988, p. 1003.

Morgan, Karen, review of *Touching the Distance: Native American Riddle-Poems, Booklist,* May 15, 1998, p. 1625.

Nower, Joyce, review of *Song of the Sky: Versions of Native American Song-Poems, Library Journal,* January, 1986, p. 89.

Owens, Louis, review of *Coming to Light: Contemporary Translations of the Native American Literatures of North America, Los Angeles Times Book Review,* April 30, 1995, p. 12.

Reuven, Ben, review of *Smoothing the Ground: Essays on Native American Oral Literature, Los Angeles Times Book Review,* April 3, 1983, p. 6.

Seaman, Donna, review of *Coming to Light: Contemporary Translations of the Native American Literatures of North America, Booklist,* February 1, 1995, p. 986.

Review of *Smoothing the Ground: Essays on Native American Oral Literature, Choice,* July-August, 1983, p. 1600.

Review of *Touching the Distance: Native American Riddle-Poems, Kirkus Reviews,* March 1, 1998, p. 345.

Review of *Touching the Distance: Native American Riddle-Poems, Publishers Weekly,* March 9, 1998, p. 70.

Review of *Wearing the Morning Star: Native American Song-Poems, Publishers Weekly,* September 30, 1996, p. 84.

For More Information See

PERIODICALS

Bulletin of the Center for Children's Books, June, 1998, p. 376.

Choice, September, 1975, p. 847; October, 1976, p. 986; July-August, 1988, p. 1700.

Horn Book Guide, fall, 1998, p. 410.

Kirkus Reviews, December 1, 1994, p. 1601.

Library Journal, March 1, 1975, p. 485; July, 1976, p. 1535; March 15, 1980, p. 746; July, 1982, p. 1329; September 1, 1982, p. 1678; June 15, 1983, p. 1260; October 1, 1984, p. 1864.

Los Angeles Times Book Review, August 3, 1986, p. 2.

New York Times Book Review, July 14, 1996, p. 28.

School Library Journal, April, 1998, pp. 154-55.

—Sketch by J. Sydney Jones

T

TALLARICO, Tony 1933-

Personal

Born September 20, 1933, in Brooklyn, NY; son of Antonio (a tailor) and Rose (a homemaker; maiden name, Pallone) Tallarico; married Elvira Gamiello (a writer), October 4, 1959; children: Nina Tallarico Reyes, Anthony J. *Education:* Attended Brooklyn Museum Art School, School of Visual Arts, and Brooklyn College. *Politics:* Independent. *Religion:* Roman Catholic.

Addresses

Home and office—26 Payan Ave., Valley Stream, NY 11580.

Career

Freelance illustrator and author. *Exhibitions:* Artwork displayed as part of the permanent collection of the International Museum of Cartoon Art, Boca Raton, FL; artwork included in "The Art of the Baseball Card," a traveling exhibit benefitting the Special Olympics. *Member:* Graphic Artists Guild.

Awards, Honors

Best Book for Reluctant Non-Readers, American Library Association, for *Drawing and Cartooning Monsters;* Life Member Award, P.T.A., and two Best Awards.

Writings

ILLUSTRATOR

Dorothy Z. Seymour, *Bill and the Fish,* Wonder Books (New York City), 1965.

Jean Bethell, *Soupy Sales,* Grosset & Dunlap (New York City), 1965.

Paul Newman, *Puff the Magic Dragon,* Grosset & Dunlap, 1965.

Dorothy Z. Seymour, *Stop Pretending,* I.T.A. (New York City), 1965.

D. J. Arneson, *The Great Society Comic Book,* Parallax (New York City), 1966.

D. J. Arneson, *Bobman and Teddy,* Parallax, 1966.

(With Water Ferguson and George J. Zaffo) Martin L. Keen, *Let's Experiment,* Grosset & Dunlap, 1968.

Martin L. Keen and Claire Cooper Cunniff, *The How and Why Wonder Book of Air and Water,* Wonder Books (New York City), 1969.

Tony Tallarico

Sara Asheron, *Funny Face at the Window,* Grosset & Dunlap, 1970.

Victor Appleton, *Tom Swift Series,* Ace Books, 1977.

Claire Boiko and Therese Angress, *Doctor Din's Disaster!: A Shadow Play,* Children's Press (Chicago), 1977.

Claire Boiko and Sandra Novick, *Who's Afraid of the Big Bad W-h-h-a-a-t?: A Play,* Children's Press, 1977.

Nancy Rockwell, *The Nancy Drew Code Activity Book,* Putnam, 1978.

Nancy Rockwell, *Hardy Boys Code Activity Book,* Putnam, 1978.

Claire Boiko and Therese Angress, *My Hero!: A Play,* Children's Press, 1979.

Oscar Weigle, *Disney's World of Riddles,* Grosset & Dunlap, 1979.

Peter Funt and Mike Shatzkin, *Gotcha!,* Putnam, 1979.

Mary Elting and Rose Wyler, *The Answer Book about You,* Grosset & Dunlap, 1980.

D. J. Arneson, *Space Creatures,* Watermill, 1981.

Marilyn M. McAuley, *What Did God Make?,* Chariot Victor Publishing, 1984.

Marilyn M. McAuley, *My Bible Says,* Chariot Victor Publishing, 1984.

Marilyn M. McAuley, *Let's Count,* Chariot Victor Publishing, 1984.

(With William Fraccio) Jerome J. Notkin and Sidney Gulkin, *The How and Why Wonder Book of Beginning Science,* J. G. Ferguson (Chicago), 1987.

Charles Perrault, *Puss in Boots,* Putnam, 1987.

Lewis Carroll, *Alice in Wonderland,* Putnam, 1987.

Chariot Family Staff, *Noah's Ark,* Chariot Victor Publishing, 1987.

Carlo Collodi, *Pinocchio,* Putnam, 1987.

J. M. Barrie, *Peter Pan,* Putnam, 1987.

The Brothers Grimm, *Little Red Riding Hood,* Putnam, 1987.

Charles Perrault, *Cinderella,* Putnam, 1987.

Maria Tropea, *Lost in the Haunted Mansion,* Kidsbooks (Chicago), 1991.

Maria Tropea, *The Missing Snowman,* Kidsbooks, 1991.

Maria Tropea, *The Silly Schoolhouse,* Kidsbooks, 1991.

Maria Tropea, *Where's Benjy Bunny?,* Kidsbooks, 1991.

Arnold Kanter and Jodi Kanter, *The Lawyer's Big Book of Fun,* Contemporary Books (Chicago), 1995.

Jane Parker Resnick, *The Kids' Fun-Filled Question and Answer Book,* Kidsbooks, 1996.

Arnold B. Kanter and Wendy Kanter, *The Teacher's Big Book of Fun,* NTC/Contemporary Publishing, 1996.

W. Hyde, *Billy McGolf,* Kidsbooks, 1999.

SELF-ILLUSTRATED

Hats, Grosset & Dunlap, 1967.

David Cassidy, Saalfield Publishing (Akron, OH), 1971.

Partrige Family, Saalfield Publishing, 1973.

Donny Osmond, Saalfield Publishing, 1973.

Great Posters, Saalfield Publishing, 1974.

Grosset Word Find Book, Putnam, 1975.

Mini Poster Book, Putnam, 1975.

Guide to Drawing Cartoons, Putnam, 1975.

Giant Apes Joke Book, Grosset & Dunlap, 1976.

Let's Draw Comics, Grosset & Dunlap, 1976.

Fonzie, Grosset & Dunlap, 1976.

Bionic Woman, Grosset & Dunlap, 1976.

1776, Charlton Publications, 1976.

Electric Company, Grosset & Dunlap, 1977.

Giant Apes Activity Book, Putnam, 1977.

Spring Activity Books, Putnam, 1977.

Nancy Drew Mystery Activity Book, Putnam, 1977.

Hardy Boys Adventure Activity Book, Putnam, 1977.

Metric Man Activity Book, Putnam, 1977.

The Great Big Busy Activity Book, Putnam, 1978.

The Bobbsey Twins Detective Activity Book, Putnam, 1978.

Santa Claus Activity Book, Putnam, 1978.

Star Jokes, Putnam, 1978.

Battlestar Galactica, Grosset & Dunlap, 1978.

Close Encounters, Grosset & Dunlap, 1978.

Tom Swift, Grosset & Dunlap, 1978.

Na-No, Na-No, the Mork & Mindy Book of Games, Puzzles and Coloring by Number, Putnam, 1979.

The Mork and Mindy Super Activity Book, Putnam, 1979.

Wacky Sports, Scholastic, 1980.

Wacky Classics, Scholastic, 1980.

Super Jokes, Putnam, 1980.

Skitter Bugs, Putnam, 1980.

Trucks and Cars, Putnam, 1980.

All through the Year, Putnam, 1980.

Colors All Around, Putnam, 1980.

I Can Draw Animals: Draw a Zooful of Animals in Easy-to-Follow Steps, Wanderer Books, 1980.

I Can Draw Monsters: Draw Madcap Monsters in Easy-to-Follow Steps, Wanderer Books, 1980.

I Can Draw Cars, Trucks, Trains, and Other Wheels, Wanderer Books, 1981.

Author-illustrator Tallarico instructs young artists in the techniques of drawing vehicles, which include assembling basic shapes, then enhancing them with detail.

Christmas Crack-Ups, Simon & Schuster, 1981.
The Alphabet Flip Book Game, Putnam, 1981.
Spooky Haunted House Puzzles, Simon & Schuster, 1981.
Search a Picture Puzzles, Simon & Schuster, 1981.
Mr. Merlin's Puzzle and Game Book, Simon & Schuster, 1981.
Gobble, Putnam, 1981.
Look Up at the Sky, Putnam, 1982.
Gobble, Gobble, Putnam, 1982.
Seasons, Putnam, 1982.
Rocket Attack, Tuffy, 1982.
Numbers, Putnam, 1982.
Colors, Putnam, 1982.
Animals, Putnam, 1982.
Monster Hunt, Tuffy, 1982.
The Giant I Can Draw Everything, Wanderer Books (New York City), 1982.
Let's Take a Trip, Putnam, 1982.
At Home, Putnam, 1983.
Who Am I?, Putnam, 1983.
What's Opposite?, Putnam, 1984.
Time To . . ., Putnam, 1984.
How Many?, Putnam, 1984.
Finger Counting, Putnam, 1984.
The Numbers Flip Book Game, Putnam, 1984.
Voltron (series), Modern Publishing Co. (New York City), 1984.
Tool Box, Putnam, 1985.
Shapes, Putnam, 1985.
School Bag, Putnam, 1985.
Lunch Box, Putnam, 1985.
I Love My Family, Putnam, 1985.
Happy Birthday, Putnam, 1985.
Doctor's Bag, Putnam, 1985.
Thank You, Putnam, 1985.
Sorry, Putnam, 1985.
Please, Putnam, 1985.
May I?, Putnam, 1985.
Simple Objects, Putnam, 1986.
Show and Tell Me, Putnam, 1986.
Easy Objects, Putnam, 1986.
Counting, Putnam, 1986.
Colors, Putnam, 1986.
Winnie the Pooh, Putnam, 1987.
The Stencil Book of Objects, Putnam, 1987.
The Stencil Book of Numbers, Putnam, 1987.
The Stencil Book of Fairy Tales, Putnam, 1987.
The Stencil Book of Dinosaurs, Putnam, 1987.
The Stencil Book of Christmas, Putnam, 1987.
Sleeping Beauty, Putnam, 1987.
Sinbad the Sailor, Putnam, 1987.
The Pied Piper of Hamlin, Putnam, 1987.
Mickey Mouse, Putnam, 1987.
Goofy, Putnam, 1987.
Donald Duck, Putnam, 1987.
The Alphabet Stencil Book, Putnam, 1987.
The Animal Stencil Book, Putnam, 1987.
Alphabet, Putnam, 1987.
Alibaba and the Forty Thieves, Putnam, 1987.
Here We Go, Putnam, 1988.
A B C, Putnam, 1988.
Time Machine, Tuffy, 1988.

Things You Always Wanted to Know about Monsters, Kidsbooks, 1988.
A Tale of Peter Rabbit, Putnam, 1988.
Peter Rabbit's Family, Putnam, 1988.
Peter Rabbit's Big Adventure, Putnam, 1988.
Opposites, Putnam, 1988.
Nursery Rhymes, Putnam, 1988.
Mickey Mouse Clock Book, Putnam, 1988.
Meet Peter Rabbit, Putnam, 1988.
Goofy Shoelace Book, Putnam, 1988.
Dinosaurs, Putnam, 1988.
Look for Lisa, Kidsbooks, 1989.
Search for Sam, Kidsbooks, 1989.
I Can Draw Spaceships Aliens, Simon & Schuster, 1989.
I Can Draw Pets, Simon & Schuster, 1989.
Find Freddie, Kidsbooks, 1989.
Spell-a-Word, Block Book, Putnam, 1989.
Drawing Things with Wings, Kidsbooks, 1989.
Drawing Cartoons, Kidsbooks, 1989.
Drawing Dogs and Cats, Kidsbooks, 1989.
Drawing Funny Faces, Kidsbooks, 1989.
Drawing Monsters, Kidsbooks, 1989.
Drawing Whales and Dolphins, Kidsbooks, 1989.
I Can Draw Sports, Simon & Schuster, 1990.
I Can Draw Christmas, Simon & Schuster, 1990.
The Little Engine that Could, Putnam, 1990.
Fire Engines, Putnam, 1990.
Animals, Putnam, 1990.
Alphabet, Putnam, 1990.
Disney's Five Board Games to Go, Putnam, 1990.
Snowboy and Snowgirl, Putnam, 1990.
Rainy Day, Putnam, 1990.
Pets, Putnam, 1990.
Let's Play, Putnam, 1990.
Let's Count, Putnam, 1990.
Haunted House, Putnam, 1990.
Happy Time, Putnam, 1990.
Going Places, Putnam, 1990.
Dot to Dot, Putnam, 1990.
Dolls, Dolls, Dolls, Putnam, 1990.
Tuffy Tiny Books, Putnam, 1991.
Preschool Can You Find Picture Book, Putnam, 1991.
My First All about Dogs Jigsaw Puzzle Book, Putnam, 1991.
My First All about Cats Jigsaw Puzzle Book, Putnam, 1991.
My First All about Dinosaurs Jigsaw Puzzle Book, Putnam, 1991.
My First All about Circus Jigsaw Puzzle Book, Putnam, 1991.
More Preschool Can You Find Picture Book, Putnam, 1991.
Where's the Bunny?, Kidsbooks, 1991.
Search for Santa's Helpers, Kidsbooks, 1991.
Five Wacky Games to Go, Putnam, 1991.
In the Haunted House, Kidsbooks, 1991.
Hector's Picture Puzzle Book, Kidsbooks, 1991.
Hunt for Hector, Kidsbooks, 1991.
At School, Kidsbooks, 1991.
At the Amusement Park, Kidsbooks, 1991.
At the Movies, Kidsbooks, 1991.
Freddie's Picture Puzzle Book, Kidsbooks, 1991.

Find Freddie and Lisa in the Haunted House, Kidsbooks, 1991.

Lisa's Picture Puzzle Book, Kidsbooks, 1991.

Sam's Picture Puzzle Book, Kidsbooks, 1991.

12 Days of Christmas, Kidsbooks, 1992.

Search for Sylvester, Kidsbooks, 1992.

Where's Columbus?, Kidsbooks, 1992.

Where's Cupid?, Kidsbooks, 1992.

Where's Wendy?, Kidsbooks, 1992.

Santa's Super Surprises, Kidsbooks, 1992.

Look for Lisa: Time Traveler, Kidsbooks, 1992.

Monster Madness, Kidsbooks, 1992.

Find Frankie and His Monster Friends, Kidsbooks, 1992.

Find Freddie around the World, Kidsbooks, 1992.

Drawing and Cartooning Monsters: A Step-by-Step Guide for the Aspiring Monster-Maker, Perigee (New York City), 1992.

Creepy Castle, Kidsbooks, 1992.

Bunny Honey's Springtime Search, Kidsbooks, 1992.

I Didn't Know That about Famous People and Places, Kidsbooks, 1992.

I Didn't Know That about How Things Work, Kidsbooks, 1992.

I Can Draw Halloween, Simon & Schuster, 1992.

What's In, Putnam, 1992.

I Didn't Know That about Sports, Kidsbooks, 1992.

Where Are They?, Kidsbooks, 1992.

I Didn't Know that about Strange but True Mysteries, Kidsbooks, 1992.

Four Books in One (contains *Find Freddie, Hunt for Hector, Look for Lisa,* and *Search for Sam*), Kidsbooks, 1992.

What Can You Find, Putnam, 1992.

Sounds, Putnam, 1992.

Preschool Can You Find Counting Picture Book, Putnam, 1992.

Preschool Can You Find ABC Picture Book, Putnam, 1992.

Search for Santa, Smithmark, 1992.

About Strange but True Mysteries; How Things Work; Sports; Famous People and Places: Four Books in One, Kidsbooks, 1993.

Four Books in One (contains *Detect Donald, Find Frankie, Look for Laura,* and *Search for Susie*), Kidsbooks, 1993.

Drawing and Cartooning Dinosaurs: A Step-by-Step Guide for the Aspiring Prehistoric Artist, Putnam, 1993.

Drawing and Cartooning Myths, Magic, and Legends: A Step-by-Step Guide for the Aspiring Myth-Maker, Berkley Publishing Group, 1994.

How to Draw Bible Pictures, Concordia Publishing, 1994.

Drawing and Cartooning Sci Fi, Berkley, 1996.

I Can Draw Star Trek, Simon & Schuster, 1996.

Halloween Search and Find, Troll Communications, 1996.

The Kids' Fun-Filled Search and Find Fascinating Fact Book, Kidsbooks, 1997.

Wishbone (series), Modern Publishing Co., 1997.

Drawing and Cartooning All-Star Sports: A Step-by-Step Guide for the Aspiring Sports Artist, Berkley Publishing Group (New York City), 1998.

A-maze-ing United States, Kidsbooks, 1998.

A-maze-ing Canada, Kidsbooks, 1998.

Celebrity Sketchbook, Kidsbooks, 1998.

I Can Draw the Bible: Old Testament, Simon & Schuster, 1998.

I Can Draw Planes and Ships, Simon & Schuster, 1998.

Wrestling Sketchbook, Kidsbooks, 1999.

Creepy Creatures, Kidsbooks, 2000.

Haunted House, Kidsbooks, 2000.

12 Days of Christmas, Kidsbooks, 2000.

Fun with Santa, Kidsbooks, 2000.

Where Are They? Over 1000 Things to Find (Blue), Kidsbooks, 2000.

Where Are They? Over 1000 Things to Find (Red), Kidsbooks, 2000.

Where Are They? Over 1000 Things to Find (Yellow), Kidsbooks, 2000.

Where Are They? Over 1000 Things to Find (Purple), Kidsbooks, 2000.

Where Are They? Over 1000 Things to Find (Green), Kidsbooks, 2000.

Where Are They? Detect Donald, Kidsbooks, 2000.

Where Are They? Find Frankie, Kidsbooks, 2000.

Where Are They? Look for Laura, Kidsbooks, 2000.

Where Are They? Search for Susie, Kidsbooks, 2000.

Kids' Fun-Filled Question and Answer Book (black), Kidsbooks, 2000.

Kids' Fun-Filled Question and Answer Book (red), Kidsbooks, 2000.

WITH SON, TONY TALLARICO JR.

Black Beauty Story Activity Book, Aerie Publishing (New York City), 1986.

War of the Worlds Story Activity Book, Aerie Publishing, 1987.

All the Presidents, Aerie Publishing, 1987.

Karate Kid (series), Modern Publishing, 1989.

Tallarico's self-illustrated fairy tale picture book also includes temporary tattoos related to the story. *(From* The Magic Forest Tattoo Book.*)*

Citco Auto Race Track, Don Jagoda Associates (New York City), 1992.
Citco Great Outdoors, Don Jagoda Associates, 1992.
Citco Amusement Park, Don Jagoda Associates, 1992.
Trailblazers (series), Modern Publishing, 1994.
Power Rangers (series), Modern Publishing, 1994.
(Co-creator, with Tony Tallarico Jr.) Tracy Christopher, *The Kids' Fun-Filled Dictionary,* Kidsbooks, 1994.
The Back Seat Fun Book, Kidsbooks, 1994.
Cars, Planes, Trains Fun Book, Kidsbooks, 1994.
Funtastic Franksters, Don Jagoda Associates, 1995.
American Airlines Flight into Fun, Diverse Promotions (New York City), 1995.
Awesome Activities (18-book series), Kidsbooks, 1996.
The Magic Forest Tattoo Book, Simon & Schuster, 1996.
Monsterous Day Tattoo Book, Simon & Schuster, 1996.
Look and Sing (music and book series), Modern Publishing, 1996.
Christmas Fun for Kids (series), Globe, 1997.
Funtastic Puzzles (18-book series), Kidsbooks, 1998.
Kids' 20th-century Question & Answer Book, Kidsbooks, 1999.
Mini-Mag (series), American Media Digest, Inc., 2000.

Also co-creator with Tony Tallarico Jr. of *Spot-a-Pix* newspaper feature, published in syndication by the Tribune Syndicate (Chicago, IL), 1993—.

WITH WIFE, ELVIRA TALLARICO

Trivia Treat School Days, Kidsbooks, 1987.
Trivia Treat Holiday, Kidsbooks, 1987.
Trivia Treat Dinosaurs, Kidsbooks, 1987.

Also co-creator with Elvira Tallarico of *Trivia Treat* newspaper feature, published in syndication by the Tribune Syndicate, 1984—.

Work in Progress

Kids' Fun-Filled Biographies, Kidsbooks, due in 2000; *Kids' Fun-Filled Encyclopedia,* Kidsbooks, due in 2000; *Kids' Fun-Filled Bible,* due in 2001; *Kids' Fun-Filled Thesaurus,* Kidsbooks, due in 2001; *Magic Rub-Offs* (under consideration).

Sidelights

Tony Tallarico told *SATA:* "I always loved to write and draw. My big break began when I was accepted as a student by the School of Industrial Arts (a New York City high school). S.I.A. specialized in the creative arts from cartooning to jewelry design. This gave me an overall view of what I wanted to do in my career. After graduation I went on to study at the Brooklyn Museum Art School, School of Visual Arts, and Brooklyn College . . . all the while freelancing in the advertising and comic book fields.

"I continued writing and illustrating in these areas, never once thinking about the book field . . . until 1966, when together with good friend and author D. J. Arneson we created a national best seller. The comic book style satire *The Great Society Comic Book* was my first book

and also the first book published by Peter Workman. Now that I was introduced to the book field, I loved it and decided that this was what I wanted to do. I began doing all sorts of books, from *The How and Why Wonder Book of Beginning Science* to *Hee Haw, The Shadow, Laugh-In* coloring books, and *Nancy Drew* and *Hardy Boys* activity books (that went on to become million sellers). My background in the 'comics' was a great help in laying out a story and picture line.

"Many other book projects followed, and in 1980 I met Philip Mann, who had a small publishing company, Tuffy Books, Inc. He needed concepts and art for a series of patented handle board books that he wanted to do for the pre-school market. I loved the idea and started working with him. . . . One hundred and fifty plus books later, he sold the company to Grossett & Dunlap (which I also was working for).

"I also started an *I Can Draw* . . . series for Simon & Schuster in the 1980s, which is still published today. The current addition to the series is *I Can Draw Planes and Ships.* At about this time an old friend of mine, Vic Cavallaro, got in contact with me. He was starting up a book company, Kidsbooks, Inc., and asked if I'd like to contribute ideas. We went on to do many books, including the 'Where Are They?' series, which sold over ten million copies worldwide, and are still being published today.

"My children have been influenced by what I do—my daughter, Nina, worked as a designer and art director for Simon & Schuster and Random House. My son, Anthony (a musician and author), has done many projects with me, including the book and musical tape series 'Look and Sing,' 'Awesome,' and 'Funtastic' activity book series and the current *Kids' 20th-century Question and Answer Book.* We have also completed a *Kids' Fun-Filled Dictionary* and are working on a *Kids' Fun-Filled Encyclopedia.*

"I am often asked: 'How do I get into the book field?' My honest answer is: 'I don't really know!' Many of my fellow authors and illustrators have taken many different roads to arrive there, but one thing is similar to all: we are 'idea-people.' We think in terms of book concepts, we do lots of concept proposals, and we occasionally sell some. I've had and hope to continue to have a successful career in the book field, and the one person I have to really thank for giving me patience and understanding through all the hills and valleys is my wonderful wife, Elvira."

For More Information See

PERIODICALS

Booklist, September 1, 1999, p. 132.
New York Times Book Review, November 11, 1984, p. 57.
Publishers Weekly, March 9, 1984, p. 113; April 25, 1986, p. 76.
School Library Journal, October, 1980, p. 151; October, 1981, p. 158.

TEITELBAUM, Michael 1953-
(Joanne Louis Michaels, joint pseudonym; Neal Michaels, Michael Neal, B. S. Watson, pseudonyms)

Personal

Born April 23, 1953, in Brooklyn, NY; son of Milton (a teacher) and Lillian (a teacher; maiden name, Klafter) Teitelbaum; married Sheleigah Grube (a vocalist), September 8, 1984. *Education:* Adelphi University, B.A. (magna cum laude), 1975. *Hobbies and other interests:* Movies (animated and otherwise), playing in the ocean, and baseball.

Addresses

Home—125 East 14th St., No. 1F, New York, NY 10009.

Career

Western Publishing Co., Inc., New York City, editor of periodicals and Golden books, 1978-84; Grossett & Dunlap, a division of Putnam Publishing Group, New York City, editor, 1984-85, creative director of PlayValue Books, 1985-87; Macmillan Publishing Co., New York City, editor-in-chief of Checkerboard Press, 1987; freelance writer and editor of juvenile books and magazines, 1987—. Writer and performer for *Family Electric Theatre* (comedy program), WBAIFM Radio; writer and puppeteer for Bond Street Theatre Coalition. *Member:* Society of Children's Book Writers and Illustrators, Editorial Freelancers Association.

Writings

JUVENILE

The Neverending Story; Picture Album, Golden Press, 1984.

Gremlins: To Catch a Gremlin, Golden Press, 1984.

(Under pseudonym Michael Neal) *A New Friend,* illustrated by Luis Dominguez, Golden Press, 1984.

Santa Claus the Movie: The Boy Who Didn't Believe in Christmas, illustrated by Barbara Stedman, Grosset, 1985.

The Cave of the Lost Fraggle, illustrated by Peter Elwell, Holt, 1985.

(With Louise Gikow and Joanne Barkan, under joint pseudonym Joanne Louise Michaels) *Baby Gonzo's Treasure Hunt,* Muppet Press, 1986.

An American Tail: Little Lost Fievel (includes cassette), Putnam, 1986.

(Adapter) *An American Tail: Escape from the Catsacks* (includes cassette), Putnam, 1986.

An American Tail: Fievel's New York Adventure, Putnam, 1986.

An American Tail: The Mott Street Maulers, Putnam, 1986.

Tony and Fievel, Putnam, 1986.

Fievel's Boat Trip, Putnam, 1986.

Fievel and Tiger, Putnam, 1986.

Fievel's Friends, Putnam, 1986.

Howard the Duck Read-Aloud Storybook, Putnam, 1986.

Meet the Blinkins, Putnam, 1986.

The Magic Light, Putnam, 1986.

The Big Show (includes cassette), illustrated by Carol Bouman and Dick Codor, Putnam, 1986.

Where Is Baby Twinkle? (includes cassette), illustrated by C. Douman and D. Codor, Putnam, 1986.

Here Come the Blinkins (coloring book), Putnam, 1986.

Holiday Fun All through the Year (coloring book), Marvel, 1987.

A Clean Sweep, Marvel, 1987.

The Haunted House, Marvel, 1987.

Ghostbusters Jokes and Riddles Coloring Book, Simon & Schuster, 1987.

Photon: The Darkness Missiles. illustrated by David Rosler, Putnam, 1987.

Photon: Prisoners of Evil, illustrated by D. Rosler, Putnam, 1987.

The Camel's Birthday: A Raggedy Ann Storybook, Macmillan, 1988.

Little Mouse in the Rocket Ship, Marvel, 1988.

Mrs. Goose and the Rock and Roll Band, Marvel, 1988.

Junior Karate (nonfiction), Kidsbooks, 1988.

The Tawny Scrawny Lion Saves the Day, Golden Books, 1989.

Journey to Magic Island, illustrated by Darrell Baker, Western Publishing, 1989.

(Adaptor) *Walt Disney Pictures Presents: The Little Mermaid,* illustrated by Ron Dias, Western Publishing, 1989, illustrated by Sue DiCicco, Western Publishing, 1992.

But You're a Duck, illustrated by Rose Mary Berlin, Western Publishing, 1990.

Alvin's Daydreams, illustrated by David Prebenna, Western Publishing, 1990.

Gremlins 2: The New Batch, Western Publishing, 1990.

(Reteller) *Jack and the Beanstalk,* illustrated by Leonard B. Lubin, Western Publishing, 1990.

(Adaptor) *Walt Disney Pictures Presents: The Rescuers Down Under,* illustrated by Franc Mateu, Western Publishing, 1990.

(Adaptor) *Walt Disney's Winnie the Pooh and the Missing Bullhorn,* illustrated by Russell Schroeder and Don Williams, Western Publishing, 1990.

(Reteller) Lily Duplaix, *Little Bunny's Magic Nose,* illustrated by Turi MacCombie, Western Publishing, 1991.

(Adaptor) *Disney's Beauty and the Beast,* illustrated by Serge Michaels, Western Publishing, 1991.

Flying Machines, illustrated by F. S. Persico, Kidsbooks, 1991.

The Solar System, illustrated by Jon Friedman, Kidsbooks, 1991.

Ghastly Giggles and Ghoulish Guffaws, Random House, 1992.

Honey, I Blew up the Kid, Disney Press, 1992.

Dracula, illustrated by Art Ruiz, Western Publishing, 1992.

Abu and the Evil Genie, illustrated by Yakovetic, Megabooks, 1993.

(Adaptor) *Welcome to Jurassic Park,* Western Publishing, 1993.

Sonic the Hedgehog, illustrated by Glen Hanson, Troll Associates, 1993.

The Jolly Jack-o-Lantern: A Yummy Book about Being Scared, illustrated by Ellen Appleby, Smithmark, 1993.

Trick-or-Treat!: A Yummy Book about Halloween, illustrated by E. Appleby, Smithmark, 1993.

Ho! Ho! Ho!: A Yummy Book about Christmas, illustrated by Appleby, Smithmark, 1993.

In the Gingerbread House: A Yummy Book about Families, illustrated by Appleby, Smithmark, 1993.

Sonic the Hedgehog: Fortress of Fear, illustrated by Hanson, Troll Associates, 1994.

Sonic the Hedgehog: Robotnik's Revenge, illustrated by Hanson, Troll Associates, 1994.

I Love You: A Yummy Book about Friends, illustrated by Appleby, Smithmark, 1994.

The Delicious Garden: A Yummy Book about Seasons, illustrated by Appleby, Smithmark, 1994.

Happy Birthday: A Yummy Book about Growing Up, illustrated by Appleby, Smithmark, 1994.

The Perfect Pizza: A Yummy Book about Feelings, illustrated by Appleby, 1994.

Disney's The Little Mermaid: Ariel's New Friend, illustrated by Cardona, Western Publishing, 1994.

Spider-Man: Dangerous Dr. Octopus, Western Publishing, 1995.

(Adapter) *Walt Disney's The Hunchback of Notre Dame,* illustrated by Aristides Ruiz and others, Western Publishing, 1996.

Meet the Amazing Spider-Man, Western Publishing, 1996.

Spider-Man: The First Adventure, Western Publishing, 1996.

Spider-Man: Caught in the Web, Golden Books, 1997.

(Adaptor) *Walt Disney's Sleeping Beauty,* illustrated by Sue DiCicco, Golden Books, 1997.

Anastasia, Rasputin, and Bartok Face Off! Harper, 1998.

Grand Slam Stars: Martina Hingis and Venus Williams, HarperActive, 1998.

The Boys against the Girls, edited by Wolfgang D. Hoelscher, Carson-Dellosa, 1999.

Scaredy Cats, illustrated by W. Hoelscher, Carson-Dellosa, 1999.

Pokomon Fire and Electric Characters, Golden Books, 2000.

Pokomon Water Characters, Golden Books, 2000.

Also author of *Danger in the Sky* and, under pseudonym Neal Michaels, *The Duke of Lorin.* Creator of comic strips "Computer Capers," "The Adventure of the MicroKids," and "The Glitch Family," under pseudonym B. S. Watson, for *MicroKids* magazine.

Contributor to magazines, including *He Man, Kirk Cameron Poster,* and *Snoopy.* Author of "Willow" coloring books, Random House, 1988, "Mighty Mouse" coloring books, Marvel, 1988, "Jetsons" coloring books, Marvel, 1988, and "Fraggle Rock" activity books, Henson Associates, 1988. Editor, *Ducktales,* 1988—, and *Ghostbusters,* 1989—.

"SLIGHTLY SPOOKY STORIES" SERIES

Did You Hear Something? illustrated by Pat Stewart, Kidsbooks, 1992.

Don't Be Afraid of the Dark! illustrated by B. Stedman, Kidsbooks, 1992.

There's No Such Thing as a Ghost ... Is There? illustrated by Stedman, Kidsbooks, 1992.

There's Something in That Cave! illustrated by Renee Grant, Kidsbooks, 1992.

"THE FACTS ABOUT DINOSAURS" SERIES

Dinosaurs and Prehistoric Creatures, Rourke, 1994.

Dinosaurs Big and Small, Rourke, 1994.

Dinosaurs of the Land, Sea, and Air, Rourke, 1994.

Dinosaurs of the Prehistoric Era, Rourke, 1994.

"SPORTS ILLUSTRATED FOR KIDS" SERIES

Play Book: Baseball: You Are the Manager, You Call the Shots, Little, Brown, 1990.

Play Book: Football: You Are the Quarterback, You Call the Shots, Little, Brown, 1990.

Sidelights

Although his name might not be that well known, Michael Teitelbaum is the prolific author of many books for children. Beginning his career as the editor of a publishing house that specialized in children's books, Teitelbaum has become adept at translating stories from film into a storybook format suitable for novice readers. Many of his books have developed into series, whereas others have been adaptations of such popular motion pictures as *Gremlins, Dracula, Santa Claus, the Movie,* Walt Disney Studios' *The Little Mermaid,* and *The Hunchback of Notre Dame,* and Don Bluth Studios' *Anastasia* and *An American Tail.* In addition, whimsical characters such as the Muppets, the Fraggles, and the Blinkins have graced the pages of comic books, picture books, and activity books, thanks to Teitelbaum's efforts.

Born in 1953, Teitelbaum grew up in Brooklyn, New York—"Who didn't?" he once quipped to *SATA*—and attended Adelphi University, graduating magna cum laude in 1975. "I'm more a product of radio and television, than of the printed word," he explained. "In college I studied radio, television, and film. My entry into the publishing world was more coincidental than planned." Teitelbaum began his career as an author of children's books by editing comic books featuring Walt Disney and Warner Bros. cartoon characters. "Cartoons remain a passion of mine: animation of all type actually, from experimental stop-motion, computer-generated, to a 1940s Bugs Bunny cartoon. My book work has dealt mostly with other people's characters."

After a decade of adapting popular cartoon characters and well-known movie plots to book form, Teitelbaum began to write original stories based on his own characters. He also began to produce nonfiction works, among these a 1994 series of books on dinosaurs that includes *Dinosaurs and Prehistoric Creatures* and *Dinosaurs of the Land, Sea, and Air.* In addition, the prolific writer teamed up with illustrator Ellen Appleby to produce a whimsical multivolume series to help young people come to terms with many aspects of their personal life: titles include *Ho! Ho! Ho!: A Yummy Book about Christmas* and *In the Gingerbread House: A Yummy Book about Families,* both published in 1993, and *Happy Birthday: A Yummy Book about Growing Up,* released in 1994.

Spine-tingling tales, which have always proved popular with the elementary-school set, have also become part of the author's stock-in-trade. In the "Slightly Spooky Stories" series, Teitelbaum presents four scary tales featuring encounters with haunted houses, legendary monsters, and the dark of night, relating them in a manner intended to attract even reluctant readers. Echoing his collection of stories designed to cause a shiver, Teitelbaum has also collected a volume of scary jokes: *Ghastly Giggles and Ghoulish Guffaws.* Calling the book's humor "more good-natured than that characterizing" more gruesome books of ghoulish humor, a *Publishers Weekly* contributor praised Teitelbaum's "whimsical tone."

Works Cited

Review of *Ghastly Giggles and Ghoulish Guffaws, Publishers Weekly,* September 7, 1992, p. 60.

For More Information See

PERIODICALS

School Library Journal, February, 1986, pp. 70-71.*

*   *   *

TRAPANI, Iza 1954-

Personal

First name is pronounced "eza"; born January 12, 1954, in Warsaw, Poland; daughter of Jozef (a salesperson) and Danuta (Wieczorek) Konopnicki; married Paul Trapani (a real estate broker), October 5, 1980 (divorced); married Robert Hare (a sculptor and fine furniture maker), May 24, 1997. *Education:* State University of New York—College at New Paltz, B.S., 1981. *Religion:* Catholic. *Hobbies and other interests:* Exhibiting work in fine art galleries, visiting elementary schools, gardening, cooking, outdoor sports—rock climbing, mountain biking, skiing, sailing.

Career

Freelance illustrator, Gardiner, NY, 1980-89; children's book author and illustrator, Wallkill, NY, 1989—. Real estate broker for husband's building and land development business, Wallkill, 1988-94. *Member:* Art Society of Kingston.

Awards, Honors

"Pick of the Lists," American Booksellers Association, 1993, for *The Itsy Bitsy Spider,* and 1996, for *I'm a Little Teapot. The Itsy Bitsy Spider* was read on PBS' *Storytime.*

Iza Trapani

Writings

AUTHOR AND ILLUSTRATOR

What Am I? An Animal Guessing Game, Whispering Coyote Press, 1992.
(Reteller) *The Itsy Bitsy Spider,* Whispering Coyote Press, 1993.
(Reteller) *Twinkle, Twinkle Little Star,* Whispering Coyote Press, 1994.
(Reteller) *Oh Where, Oh Where Has My Little Dog Gone?,* Whispering Coyote Press, 1995.
(Reteller) *I'm a Little Teapot,* Whispering Coyote Press, 1996.
(Reteller) *How Much Is That Doggie in the Window?,* Whispering Coyote Press, 1997.
(Reteller) *Mary Had a Little Lamb,* Whispering Coyote Press, 1998.
My Jack, Whispering Coyote Press, 1999.
(Reteller) *Row, Row, Row Your Boat,* Whispering Coyote Press, 1999.
Shoo Fly, Whispering Coyote Press/Charlesbridge, 2000.

ILLUSTRATOR

David Gershon and Gail Straub, *Empowerment—The Art of Creating Your Life as You Want It* (for adults), Dell, 1989.
Alice Steed, *I Am Three/I Am Four,* Whispering Coyote Press, 1993.
Carolyn Dorflinger, *Tomorrow Is Mom's Birthday,* Whispering Coyote Press, 1994.
Elise Petersen, *Tracy's Mess,* Whispering Coyote Press, 1995.

Sidelights

Iza Trapani is an artist and writer who has focused her special talents on creating picture books for young readers. In addition to writing several of her own humorous tales, Trapani has added her own twist to traditional songs and stories, providing outcomes that are different than the original work. Such well-loved songs as *"Itsy Bitsy Spider," "I'm a Little Teapot,"* and *"Twinkle, Twinkle Little Star"* take on new meaning in her words and illustrations. Trapani's version of *Mary Had a Little Lamb,* for example, finds the poor shepherdess and her flock left in the lurch when an adventurous lamb decides to explore the world on its own. In addition to illustrating her own stories and adaptations, Trapani has enhanced the work of other authors with her artwork. Her illustrations for Carolyn Dorflinger's *Tomorrow Is Mom's Birthday* brought praise from *Booklist*'s Kay Weisman, who commented, "Trapani's soft watercolor illustrations convey the warmth and humor" of Dorflinger's close-knit fictional family.

"I've always been fascinated with children's literature," Trapani once explained to *SATA*. "There is something about the pure simplicity of words matched with beautiful illustrations that makes picture books particularly intriguing to me." Born in Poland in 1954, Trapani moved to the United States as a girl. "As a child I would spend hours and hours looking through picture books," she later recalled. "It was a wonderful, magical world that I could get lost in. As I grew older, my love for children's books grew right along with me."

In addition to cultivating her growing love of picture books, Trapani worked hard to develop her talents as an artist. After graduating from the State University of New York's College at New Paltz in 1981, she embarked upon a career as a freelance illustrator. After several years of working on non-book related projects, she landed a job creating watercolor illustrations for an adult self-help book published by Dell. Three years later, her first self-illustrated children's book was released by Whispering Coyote Press. *What Am I? An Animal Guessing Game* introduces youngsters to ten animals, including an ostrich, gorilla, owl, and hippopotamus, that reveal themselves only through a series of clues. Couching her "What am I?" riddles in six rhyming lines for each animal, Trapani "effectively combines blithesome, sing-song verse and waggish watercolors" in her guessing game, according to a *Publishers Weekly* critic. Ilene Cooper added in her *Booklist* review that *What Am I?* "should ... provide enjoyment to kids, singly and during story hours."

Since beginning her career as a children's book author and illustrator, Trapani's goal has been "to be able to recreate ... magic for others to enjoy," as she once explained to *SATA*. As part of that magic, she has been careful to interject a healthy dose of humor into each of her projects. "I love to laugh," the author/illustrator explained, "and know that children also do, so there is always a humorous quality in my work. I also love animals, and even if a story is not about animals, somehow I'll always manage to put them in the illustrations."

Indeed, animals do figure prominently in the traditional songs that Trapani uses as the basis for several of her picture books. In her text and illustrations based on "Twinkle, Twinkle Little Star," she shows the star's impact on the peaceful Earth below as its gentle light caresses the planet's many sleeping creatures, as well as the ripples on the ocean's surface and other sights, all seen through the eyes of a young girl whose wish to ride in the night sky is granted. Although the title character in the original "Itsy Bitsy Spider" may have spent his time fruitlessly tackling a single water spout, in Trapani's

She slipped on some dew
And landed next to me.

Out came the sun
And when the tree was dry,
The itsy bitsy spider
Gave it one more try.

Trapani adds her own twist to the well-loved song about the Itsy Bitsy Spider in a cumulative story of the creatures the spider meets as she climbs a tree to make her web. (From The Itsy Bitsy Spider, *written and illustrated by Trapani.)*

version the ambitious arachnid is thwarted in his attempts to climb up and down walls, trees, and household furniture. Her "sing-song ... rhyme works perfectly," commented *Booklist* contributor Deborah Abbott of *Itsy Bitsy Spider*.

Animals are also central to Trapani's retellings *Mary Had a Little Lamb* and *Row, Row, Row Your Boat.* Trapani adds a dozen new verses to Sarah Josepha Hale's original poem in the former, which describes a young lamb eagerly breaking away from the flock to nose around the farmyard on its own. Calling Trapani's descriptions of the curious lamb "slapstick," Marian Drabkin praised her work in a *School Library Journal* review, asserting: "The bright and lively watercolor illustrations are sweet ... preschoolers will find [the text] both humorous and reassuring." In addition to words and pictures, the music to the traditional song is included. *Row, Row, Row Your Boat* depicts a family of bears who are joined by their pet puppy for a boat outing. To the traditional rhyme Trapani blended "clever additional verses [that] make this classic song splendidly unique," according to *School Library Journal* contributor Jackie Hechtkopk. The commentator added that children "will enjoy the rhyming, alliterative language energized by strings of gerunds," concluding: "Trapani has transformed a simple little song into a delightful adventure."

"For years when I used to blow out the candles on my birthday cakes, I had one wish—to someday illustrate a children's book," Trapani explained to *SATA*. "Now that I am enjoying a career as both author and illustrator, I believe that dreams really do come true!"

Works Cited

Abbott, Deborah, review of *The Itsy Bitsy Spider, Booklist,* March 1, 1993, p. 1239.

Cooper, Ilene, review of *What Am I?, Booklist,* December 15, 1992, p. 742.

Drabkin, Marian, review of *Mary Had a Little Lamb, School Library Journal,* December, 1998, p. 116.

Hechtkopk, Jackie, review of *Row, Row, Row Your Boat, School Library Journal,* November, 1999, p. 149.

Weisman, Kay, review of *Tomorrow Is Mom's Birthday, Booklist,* May 1, 1994, p. 1607.

Review of *What Am I? An Animal Guessing Game, Publishers Weekly,* October 12, 1992, p. 78.

For More Information See

PERIODICALS

Publishers Weekly, September 28, 1998, p. 103.

School Library Journal, January, 1993, p. 86; January, 1995, p. 94.

TURTLEDOVE, Harry (Norman) 1949-
(Eric G. Iverson, H. N. Turtletaub)

Personal

Born June 14, 1949, in Los Angeles, CA; married Laura Frankos (a writer); children: Alison, Rachel, Rebecca. *Education:* University of California at Los Angeles, Ph.D. (Byzantine history), 1997.

Addresses

Agent—Scott Meredith, 845 Third Ave., New York, NY 10022.

Career

Science fiction novelist and short story writer. Worked as a technical writer for Los Angeles County Office of Education.

Awards, Honors

HOMer Award for Short Story, 1990, for "Designated Hitter;" John Esthen Cook Award for Southern Fiction, 1993, for *The Guns of the South: A Novel of the Civil War;* Hugo Award for best novella, 1994, for *Down in the Bottomlands;* Sidewise Award honorable mention, 1995, Nebula Award and Hugo Award nominations, 1996, both for "Must and Shall;" Sidewise Award honorable mention, 1995, for *The Two Georges,* and 1996, for the "Worldwar" series; Premio Italia, 1996, for *Worldwar: In the Balance;* Sidewise Award for Long Form, 1997, for *How Few Remain; Publishers Weekly* Top Ten SF Books list, 1998, for *The Great War: American Front;* Nebula Award nomination, 1999, for *How Few Remain.*

Writings

NOVELS

A Different Flesh, Congdon & Weed (New York City), 1988.

Noninterference, Ballantine (New York City), 1988.

A World of Difference, Ballantine, 1990.

The Guns of the South: A Novel of the Civil War, Ballantine, 1992.

The Case of the Toxic Spell Dump, Ballantine, 1994.

(With Richard Dreyfuss) *The Two Georges,* Tor (New York City), 1996.

Thessalonica, Baen, 1997.

Between the Rivers, St. Martin's Press, 1998.

(With Judith Tarr) *Household Gods,* Tor, 1999.

FANTASY NOVELS; "GERIN THE FOX" SERIES

(As Eric G. Iverson) *Wereblood,* Belmont Tower, 1979.

(As Iverson) *Werenight,* Belmont Tower, 1979.

Prince of the North, Baen (New York City), 1994.

King of the North, Baen, 1996.

Fox and Empire, Baen, 1998.

FANTASY NOVELS; "VIDESSOS CYCLE" SERIES

The Misplaced Legion, Ballantine, 1987.
An Emperor for the Legion, Ballantine, 1987.
The Legion of Videssos, Ballantine, 1987.
Swords of the Legion, Ballantine, 1987.
Krispos Rising, Ballantine, 1991.
Krispos of Videssos, Ballantine, 1991.
Krispos the Emperor, Ballantine, 1994.
The Stolen Throne, Ballantine, 1995.
Hammer and Anvil, Ballantine, 1996.
The Thousand Cities, Ballantine, 1997.
Videssos Besieged, Ballantine, 1998.

SCIENCE FICTION NOVELS; "WORLDWAR" SERIES

Worldwar: In the Balance, Ballantine, 1994.
Worldwar: Tilting the Balance, Ballantine, 1995.
Worldwar: Upsetting the Balance, Ballantine, 1996.
Worldwar: Striking the Balance, Ballantine, 1996.
Colonization: Second Contact, Del Rey, 1999.
Colonization: Down to Earth, Del Rey, 2000.

SCIENCE FICTION NOVELS; "THE GREAT WAR" SERIES

How Few Remain, Del Rey, 1997.
The Great War: American Front, Del Rey, 1998.
The Great War: Walk in Hell, Del Rey, 1999.
The Great War: Breakthroughs, Del Rey, 2000.

FANTASY NOVELS; "DARKNESS" SERIES

Into the Darkness, Tor, 1999.
Darkness Descending, Tor, 2000.

SHORT STORIES

Agent of Byzantium, Congdon & Weed, 1987, revised edition, 1994.
Kaleidoscope, Ballantine, 1990.
Earthgrip, Ballantine, 1991.
Departures, Ballantine, 1993.
(Editor) *Alternate Generals,* Pocket Books, 1998.

OTHER

(Translator) *The Chronicle of Theophanes: An English Translation of Anni Mundi 6095-9305 (A.D. 602-813),* University of Pennsylvania Press (Philadelphia, PA), 1982.
(As H. N. Turtletaub) *Justinian* (historical novel), Forge, 1998, Tor, 1999.

Contributor of short stories to *Magazine of Fantasy and Science Fiction* and *Analog.* Also collaborated with Susan Schwartz, S. M. Stirling, and Judith Tar on "War World" series. Author of novella *Down in the Bottomlands.*

Work in Progress

Novels in the following series: "The Great War," *Settling Accounts;* "Worldwar," *Aftershocks;* "Darkness," *Through the Darkness,* and perhaps three or four more in the same series.

Sidelights

Harry Turtledove is "the standard-bearer for alternate history," according to Tom Squitieri writing in *USA Today.* A sub-genre of science fiction, alternate history has fast become one of the hottest new genres of the 1990s, and Turtledove is, as Russell Letson noted in *Locus,* the "best practitioner of the classic alternate-history story since L. Sprague de Camp domesticated it for American SF over a half-century ago." Letson went on to list Turtledove's virtues as an alternate history guru: "[M]eticulous research and thorough knowledge of his period, an understated but firm way with storytelling, and a sense of the exotic appeal of the past combined with a recognition of the ordinariness of ordinary life."

Turtledove has served up fantasy versions of the Roman Empire and Byzantium in his fictions, reworked the Civil War so that the South wins, allied Nazis and Jews against an unearthly power, constructed trench warfare in the United States, and rewritten the history of early man. Quite brazenly creating alternate universes, turning history on its head, and perennially making the reader ask the question, "What if?" Turtledove's alternate history takes shape not in individual novels, but in series of novels. His popular "Videssos Cycle," in which Caesar's legions are transported from ancient Gaul to a world of wizards, comprises eleven books; his "Worldwar" series began as a tetralogy and has since sprouted a further trilogy in the "Colonization" extension; his "Great War" series is planned to include five books; and "Darkness," set in a fantastical middle ages, may stretch to seven. His breakthrough, however, was not in a series, but in the stand-alone title, *The Guns of the South: A Novel of the Civil War,* his account of how the Civil War might have progressed if South African time travelers had handed over a modern arsenal to General Lee.

As Turtledove told Jeremy Bloom in the *Chicon 2000 Progress Report,* "The way I do it, I use the standard SF technique. Because one of the things SF does is postulate—if we changed this, what happens next?—most of those changes are set in the present and then you examine the future, or set in the future and then you examine the farther future. I say, all right, what if we make that change and set it in the past? With as rigorous an extrapolation as I can make." Rigor is something Turtledove can appreciate in things historical: he earned a Ph.D. in Byzantine history from the University of California at Los Angeles (UCLA) before becoming a mainstay of the alternate history book section.

Born in Los Angeles, California, on June 14, 1949, Turtledove grew up in nearby Gardena. Turtledove is descended from Romanian immigrants who first settled in Winnipeg, Canada, before moving on to California. A major turning point in his young life came when Turtledove was fourteen and discovered a copy of L. Sprague de Camp's *Lest Darkness Fall* in a second-hand bookstore. "I read it," Turtledove told Bloom, "and thought 'This is so cool,' and started trying to find out what Sprague was making up and what was real. I was hooked."

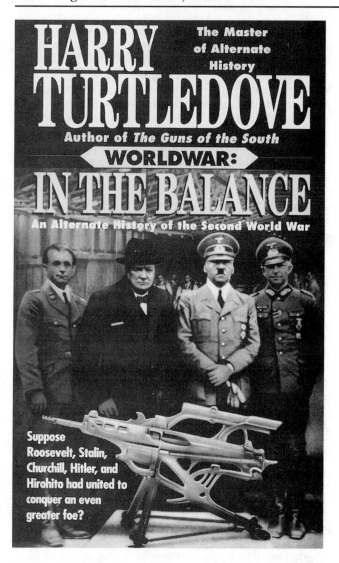

HARRY TURTLEDOVE
The Master of Alternate History
Author of *The Guns of the South*
WORLDWAR: IN THE BALANCE
An Alternate History of the Second World War

Suppose Roosevelt, Stalin, Churchill, Hitler, and Hirohito had united to conquer an even greater foe?

Set in 1942, Harry Turtledove's alternate history tale explores what might have happened if an alien menace confronted Earth at the time of the Second World War. (Cover illustration by Stan Watts.)

History also hooked him, though he was slow to realize it. He began college as an engineering major at Cal Tech, but flunked out in his freshman year. This was not simply an academic tragedy; those were the days when a college deferment kept one out of Vietnam, so Turtledove subsequently spent a year at California State in Los Angeles improving his grade point average "to the point where it was visible to the naked eye," as he told Bloom, and then entered UCLA where he ultimately—in 1977—earned a doctorate. His dissertation was on *The Immediate Successors of Justinian,* a look at late sixth-century Byzantium. "If it hadn't been for Sprague I wouldn't have the degree I have—I wouldn't have gotten interested in Byzantine history any OTHER way. I wouldn't have written a lot of what I've written, because I wouldn't know the things I happen to know." Turtledove has his own private list of what-ifs.

Turtledove's doctorate made him eminently unemployable. He quickly turned to writing, publishing his first two novels, *Wereblood* and *Werenight,* in 1979 under the pseudonym Eric G. Iverson because his editor thought that no one would believe his real name. He continued to publish as Iverson until 1985. These were lean years for Turtledove as a creative writer, and he earned his living as a technical writer for the Los Angeles County of Education. It was not until 1991 that he could leave technical writing and devote himself full time to alternate history.

Turtledove's writing has included many genres. As he noted to Bloom, he has written SF that is not alternate history—pure or hard SF—and he has written fantasy, "historically-based fantasy, high fantasy, funny fantasy," but ultimately it is Turtledove's reworking of history that influences most of his work. His first publication initiated this peculiar blending of fantasy and history. The "Gerin the Fox" novels, the first two of which were published under his Iverson pen name, deal with an empire in decline. As Peter T. Garratt noted in *St. James Guide to Fantasy Writers,* the books in the series deal with a theme and location that "resembles a cross between Rome and medieval Europe." The hero is a baron of a border province that remains aloof from central authority, paying no taxes, but when it is menaced by a powerful wizard, the province and its baron are left to themselves in a battle for survival. The first novels of this cycle were also Turtledove's first novels; since that time the series has grown to encompass five titles. Turtledove returned to the series fifteen years after the first title, to expand on Gerin's life and his attempts to make peace for his families, and to explore the concept of a universe containing multiple gods. *Prince of the North, King of the North,* and *Fox and Empire* fill out this mythical Empire of Elabon.

He began a more ambitious cycle of novels in 1987, the "Videssos Cycle." The cycle is made up of three separate series of books, as well as a few short stories. The core of the cycle includes four books published in 1987: *The Misplaced Legion, An Emperor for the Legion, The Legion of Videssos,* and *Swords of the Legion.* The hero of this quartet of books is Marcus Scaurus, a well-educated Roman officer of the late republic era who receives a mysterious sword while campaigning near Gaul. During a battle with an enemy chieftain who has an identical sword, the sword blades touch, and Scaurus, the chieftain, and all the Roman soldiers are magically transported to another world. This alternate world, the Empire of Videssos, resembles eleventh-century Byzantium, and the enemy chieftain joins forces with the Romans to make contact with the locals. Scaurus and his men become involved in palace intrigue and adventures that almost bring about the downfall of the Empire. According to Garratt, the second and third volumes of the tetralogy "are among the best things Turtledove has written." The empire is in chaos. Scaurus has married the widow of a powerful mercenary and tries valiantly to bring civil wars within Videssos to an end. Ultimately, Scaurus's wife must choose between loyalty to him or to her own kin, a long line of mercenaries.

Turtledove wrote a three-book series of prequels to the "Videssos Cycle": *Krispos Rising, Krispos of Videssos,* and *Krispos the Emperor.* Set several centuries before the main cycle, these books feature the protagonist Krispos, born a lowly farmer, but destined to become an emperor. He accomplishes this in the course of the trilogy. Turtledove returned to Videssos again in the four volume "The Time of Troubles" cycle.

Early in his career, Turtledove wrote stand-alone works, one of the most popular being the 1987 *Agent of Byzantium,* a collection of seven inter-related stories about the adventures of secret agent Basil Argyros. The tales rest upon a tweaking of history: in Turtledove's cosmology, the young Mohammed was converted to Christianity by a Nestorian priest instead of founding his own powerful religion. Turtledove then follows the historical revisions that would follow upon such a change, one of them being still powerful Byzantine and

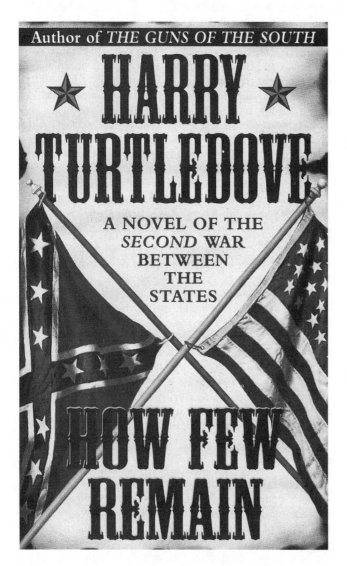

In Turtledove's alternate history, the Confederacy forms an alliance with the French and British and wins the Civil War, and decades later, war breaks out again over the Confederacy's move to purchase northern territories in Mexico.

Persian empires in the early fourteenth century. Argyros is at the center of the plots and counter-plots of the time, and helps introduce many inventions to the empire: the telescope, gunpowder, and printing among them. "The narrative carries the reader along," commented M. Hammerton in *Twentieth-Century Science-Fiction Writers,* also saying, "If we are not deeply saddened by the death from smallpox of Basil's family, we at least believe that he was." Letson reported in *Locus* that the "greatest pleasure in these stories for me . . . is the evocation of the past."

Although other stand-alone novels by Turtledove have achieved success, it was *The Guns of the South,* published in 1992, that connected his name to the genre of alternate history and brought him attention from the mainstream press as well as the SF community. The story begins in January, 1864, with General Lee's Confederate Army suffering from shortages of both arms and supplies. Lee, despondent that the war may be lost, receives an interesting visitor, Andries Rhoodie, a time traveler from South Africa, who offers the general a supply of futuristic armaments, including the AK-47. This weaponry allows the South to win the war and changes history. When the Confederacy later begins to relax its slave laws, however, the South African time travelers become nervous because their purpose in helping Lee was to create a future white supremacist culture. As Lee continues his reforms, he and his men are suddenly faced with a new threat—Rhoodie and his soldiers. Margaret Flanagan, reviewing the title in *Booklist,* called Turtledove's re-creation an "exceptionally riveting and innovative narrative that successfully straddles the gulf between fact and fantasy." Discussing his own personal fascination with the Civil War period, as well as its popularity as a theme for alternate history, Turtledove told Bloom, "There is a general fascination with that period because it's a key period in the history of the United States. We are what we are now, for better and for worse, because of what happened during those four crowded years."

Other popular individual titles include his humorous take on the environment, *The Case of the Toxic Spell Dump,* and another volume set in the same universe thirteen centuries earlier, *Thessalonica.* A similar novel is his 1998 *Between the Rivers,* related to *The Case of the Toxic Spell Dump* by the shared theme of henotheism, or the belief that many gods exist and that their strength is based on the number of adherents and worshippers they attract. Set in a fantasy world similar to ancient Mesopotamia, the gods of this universe are not only manifold, but also manifest. Their actions are all too visible as they constantly meddle in human affairs. A trio of protagonists scheme to cripple the power of some of these gods as Turtledove examines the classic SF theme of reason versus faith. *Publishers Weekly* said that Turtledove "uses all of his historiographical and narrative skills, plus his inimitable wit, to elevate his version of [this] theme to the same high level occupied by (among others) L. Sprague de Camp." Jackie Cassada, writing in *Library Journal,* said that Turtledove's "cadenced prose imparts an epic feel to this tale of humanity's attempt to forge its own destiny," and a critic for *Kirkus Reviews* called the book "[h]istorically intriguing, splendidly textured, and full of stimulating ideas."

Another popular book is *Justinian,* a straight history from Turtledove, writing under the pen name H. N. Turtletaub. The choice of pseudonym was once again an editor's choice out of the fear that a straight historical fiction would not sell well and affect the author's future sales. In the event, his portrait of Justinian II, the wily Byzantine emperor, proved quite successful and saleable. *Booklist*'s Flanagan called it an "artfully styled narrative," noting Turtledove's "painstaking attention to historical details" that combine to "vivify this mesmerizing account of one of history's most remarkable rulers." Turtledove also collaborated with the actor Richard Dreyfuss on a speculative novel, *The Two Georges,* about the American colonies, in which England never lost control of its North American relatives. Featuring King George of England and George Washington, the novel has been optioned by Britain's Granada Television.

Turtledove, for all his success with individual titles, still seems to prefer the grand sweep of cycles and series. With his "Worldwar" series he explored what might have happened had an external menace confronted Earth at the time of the Second World War. Employing an old SF theme, Turtledove creates new meanings for it. In his tale, it is late 1942, and the world is at war. Nazis are busy trying to eliminate Jews, and in America, scientists are trying to unlock the secrets of the atom, when, suddenly, the skies overhead are filled with spaceships full of alien invaders. These reptilian invaders call themselves the Race, but earthlings name them the Lizards. Earth-bound enemies form odd alliances to battle this new and devastating menace that seeks to enslave the people of this world.

Turtledove's canvas for this four-part epic is the entire planet Earth. The huge cast of characters includes real people from history, such as Generals Marshall and Patton, scientists Leo Szilard and Enrico Fermi, and the political figures of Churchill, Roosevelt, and Molotov. Settings include the United States, England, Germany, the Soviet Union, China, and Japan. Reviewing the first novel in the quartet, *Worldwar: In the Balance,* Thomas Pearson of *Voice of Youth Advocates* called the series "promising." *Booklist*'s Roland Green, in a starred review, dubbed Turtledove "one of alternate history's authentic modern masters," and called the first novel of the series an "engrossing volume." Letson, reviewing the initial title in *Locus,* commented that the novel delivers excitement "in the form of interesting characters responding to conditions both new and unchanged. . . . It is this ground-level . . . view of the world at war that I find gripping, the lives of individuals as they are affected by the macrohistorical military-economic-political forces represented by the wargames layer of the book." A reviewer for *Publishers Weekly* called Turtledove's *Worldwar: In the Balance* an "intelligent speculative novel" which "gives a surprisingly convincing flavor to

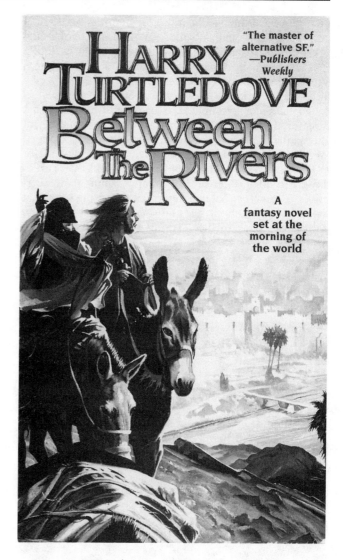

Set in a fantasy world similar to Mesopotamia, Turtledove's novel depicts three protagonists who scheme to cripple the power of the gods who rule their cities and meddle in human affairs. (Cover illustration by Gary Ruddell.)

the time-worn story of warring nations uniting to repel extraterrestrials."

Turtledove continued the story with *Worldwar: Tilting the Balance,* in which earthlings begin to fight back using ginger, addictive to the Lizards. Pearson commented in *Voice of Youth Advocates* that "[r]eal historical characters intermingle with Turtledove's fictional creatures in a wild 600 page blend of soap opera, carefully drawn character studies, and slam-bang action." *Worldwar: Upsetting the Balance* and *Worldwar: Striking the Balance* complete the tetralogy, ending with an uneasy truce declared between earthlings and the Race. Reviewing the final volume, a critic for *Kirkus Reviews* said that Turtledove had created a huge opus: "A cast of thousands with a plot to match, well-drawn if unoriginal aliens, a wealth of fascinating speculation—and scope for any number of sequels."

Turtledove's sequel was not long in coming. Set sixteen years after the end of the "Worldwar" books, the "Colonization" series begins with the arrival of a flotilla of Lizard starships carrying a cargo of forty million sleep-frozen Lizard colonists. The first of a projected three-book series, *Colonization: Second Contact* is "outstanding entertainment," according to *Booklist*'s Roberta Johnson. "In high fashion, the master of alternative SF launches a sequel series to his acclaimed 'Worldwar' tetralogy," according to a reviewer for *Publishers Weekly.* The same reviewer said that Turtledove, "[w]ith his fertile imagination running on overdrive . . . develops an exciting, often surprising story that will not only delight his fans but will probably send newcomers back to the 'Worldwar' saga to fill in the backstory."

War on a global scale also serves as the backdrop for Turtledove's "Great War" series, which had its inception

In Turtledove's historical world in which the United States and the Confederate States are separate entities, a world war which erupts in 1914 finds the two countries allied with opposing forces. (Cover illustration by George Pratt.)

in another Civil War novel, *How Few Remain.* This time, Turtledove changes history with the Confederacy winning the Battle of Antietam, and going on to win the Civil War in an alliance with the French and British. When the United States declares war on the Confederate States in 1881 over its purchase of northern territories from Mexico, the Confederacy again wins the conflict with the support of the French and British. This is the setting for the alternate history Turtledove explores in subsequent novels about the First World War. "The novel displays the compelling combination of rigorous historiography and robust storytelling that readers have come to expect from Turtledove," noted a reviewer for *Publishers Weekly,* who added, "Turtledove delivers his most gripping novel since 1992's *The Guns of the South.*"

In *The Great War: American Front,* Turtledove employs the same historical world. It is 1914 and there is a world war between Germany, an ally of the United States, and the alliance of France, England, and the Confederate States. "Turtledove sustains high interest throughout the lengthy narrative," commented a reviewer for *Publishers Weekly.* "With shocking vividness, Turtledove demonstrates the extreme fragility of our modern world. . . . This is state-of-the-art alternate history, nothing less." Turtledove extends his saga in *The Great War: Walk in Hell,* the second volume of a planned tetralogy. This book covers the year 1915 that includes a Negro rebellion in the Confederacy and a U.S. invasion of Canada where the horrors of trench warfare occur on the American continent instead of in Europe. According to *Booklist*'s Roland Green, "This is not alternate history intended to give readers the warm fuzzies; it is a remorseless working out of the consequences of greater follies producing even worse results than the ones we may read about in actual history."

Turtledove is busy working on another cycle of novels, projected to be a five or six volume series, named "Darkness." These fantasies utilize technology of the 1930s and 1940s, but set them in an imaginary world where technological advances are achieved through magic. *Into the Darkness,* the first novel in the series, opens in a fantasy world reminiscent of medieval Europe, Derlavai, where sorcery has been harnessed to create military power. This sprawling saga begins with the forces of Algarve invading the kingdom of Forthweg.

Turtledove, married to a novelist—the mystery writer Laura Frankos—spends most of his time writing. One interviewer estimated that Turtledove writes 350 days per year, hardly surprising given his prodigious output over the last two decades. In the 1990s alone he has written over two dozen action-packed and bookspine-imperiling epics. He does not simply regurgitate history; he absorbs all relevant facts about a period, throws in a what-if, and then follows the trail as it leads to a completely new history. Summing up the difference between writing history and fiction, Turtledove told Bloom, "Fiction has to be plausible. All history has to do is happen."

Works Cited

Review of *Between the Rivers, Kirkus Reviews,* January 1, 1998, p. 28.

Review of *Between the Rivers, Publishers Weekly,* January 26, 1998, p. 73.

Bloom, Jeremy, "Da Toastmaster Guest of Honor," *Chicon 2000 Progress Report 2,* http://www.sfsite.com/~silverag/toastmaster.html (June 1, 2000).

Cassada, Jackie, review of *Between the Rivers, Library Journal,* January, 1998, p. 149.

Review of *Colonization: Second Contact, Publishers Weekly,* November 30, 1998, p. 53.

Flanagan, Margaret, review of *The Guns of the South: A Novel of the Civil War, Booklist,* November 1, 1992, p. 490.

Flanagan, Margaret, review of *Justinian, Booklist,* August 19, 1998, p. 1971.

Garratt, Peter T., "Turtledove, Harry (Norman)," *St. James Guide to Fantasy Writers,* edited by David Pringle, St. James Press, 1996, pp. 562-64.

Review of *The Great War: American Front, Publishers Weekly,* April 27, 1998, p. 50.

Green, Roland, review of *Worldwar: In the Balance, Booklist,* December 1, 1993, p. 678.

Green, Roland, review of *The Great War: Walk in Hell, Booklist,* June 1, 1999.

Hammerton, M., "Turtledove, Harry," *Twentieth-Century Science-Fiction Writers,* 3rd edition, edited by Noelle Watson and Paul E. Schellinger, St. James Press, 1991, pp. 809-10.

Review of *How Few Remain, Publishers Weekly,* August 16, 1997, p. 390.

Johnston, Roberta, review of *Colonization: Second Contact, Booklist,* January 1, 1999, p. 842.

Letson, Russell, review of *Worldwar: In the Balance, Locus,* February, 1994, pp. 31-32.

Letson, Russell, review of *Agent of Byzantium, Locus,* April, 1994, pp. 23-24.

Pearson, Thomas, review of *Worldwar: In the Balance, Voice of Youth Advocates,* August, 1995, pp. 160-61.

Pearson, Thomas, review of *Worldwar: Tilting the Balance, Voice of Youth Advocates,* August, 1996, p. 172.

Squitieri, Tom, "Author Loves to Shake Up History," *USA Today,* October 13, 1998.

Review of *Worldwar: In the Balance, Publishers Weekly,* December 6, 1993, p. 60.

Review of *Worldwar: Striking the Balance, Kirkus Reviews,* October 1, 1996, p. 1434.

For More Information See

BOOKS

The Encyclopedia of Science Fiction, edited by John Clute and Peter Nicholls, St. Martin's Press, 1993.

Reginald, Robert, *Science Fiction and Fantasy Literature, 1975-1991,* Gale, 1992.

PERIODICALS

Booklist, February 15, 1987, p. 878; May 1, 1987, p. 1336; June 15, 1987, p. 1565; August, 1987, p. 1722; October 1, 1987, p. 222; May 1, 1990, p. 1688; May 15, 1990, p. 1785; January 1-15, 1996, p. 799; February 1, 1996, p. 899; March 1, 1999, p. 1104.

Kirkus Reviews, May 1, 1987, p. 682; March 15, 1988, p. 417; August 1, 1992, p. 947; January 1, 1995, p. 34; August 15, 1997, p. 1265.

Library Journal, April 15, 1988, p. 98; September 1, 1992, p. 217; November 15, 1993, p. 102; December, 1995, p. 163; June 15, 1998, p. 110; January, 1999, p. 165.

Locus, June, 1990, p. 33; March, 1991, p. 60; October, 1991, pp. 31, 56.

Publishers Weekly, January 23, 1987, p. 66; May 22, 1987, p. 69; March 18, 1988, p. 76; March 16, 1990, p. 66; January 11, 1991, p. 98; August 24, 1992, p. 63; February 20, 1995, p. 200; January 22, 1996, p. 61; February 5, 1996, p. 80; March 22, 1999, p. 74; August 23, 1999, p. 54.

Science Fiction Chronicle, October, 1987, p. 41; January, 1988, p. 49; April, 1988, p. 52.

Voice of Youth Advocates, June, 1992, p. 116; October, 1996, pp. 221-22.

Washington Post Book World, June 27, 1993, p. 12.*

—*Sketch by J. Sydney Jones*

*   *   *

TURTLETAUB, H. N.
See TURTLEDOVE, Harry

U–V

UNCLE SHELBY
See SILVERSTEIN, Shel(don Allan)

*   *   *

VanCLEAVE, Janice 1942-

Personal

Born January 27, 1942, in Houston, TX; daughter of Raymond Eugene (a truck driver) and Frankie (a beautician; maiden name, Clowers) Pratt; married Wade Russell VanCleave (a postal carrier), August 29, 1959; children: Rajene Dianne, Russell Eugene, David Wade. *Education:* University of Houston, B.S., 1962; Stephen F. Austin State University, M.S., 1978. *Religion:* Southern Baptist.

Addresses

Home—Riesel, TX. *Office*—c/o John Wiley & Sons, Inc., 605 Third Ave., New York, NY 10158-0012.

Career

Public school science teacher, 1966-91; writer, 1984—. Leader of science workshops for teachers and students. Bible study instructor.

Awards, Honors

Phi Delta Kappa Outstanding Teacher Award, 1983; Friend of Education Award, Beta Nu chapter of Delta Kappa Gamma Society International.

Writings

Teaching the Fun of Physics: 101 Activities to Make Science Education Easy and Enjoyable, Prentice-Hall, 1985.

Janice VanCleave's Guide to the Best Science Projects, Wiley, 1997.

VanCleave presents young readers with detailed instructions for over two hundred experiments which teach basic concepts in astronomy, biology, chemistry, earth science, and physics. (Cover illustration by Laurie Hamilton.)

Janice VanCleave's Science Experiment Sourcebook, Wiley, 1997.

Janice VanCleave's Science around the Year, Wiley, 2000.

Janice VanCleave's Guide to More of the Best Science Fair Projects, Wiley, 2000.

"JANICE VanCLEAVE'S SCIENCE FOR EVERY KID" SERIES, AGES 8-12

Astronomy, Wiley, 1989.

Biology, Wiley, 1990.

Janice VanCleave

Chemistry, Wiley, 1991.
Earth Science, Wiley, 1991.
Math, Wiley, 1991.
Physics, Wiley, 1991.
Geography, Wiley, 1993.
Microscopes, Wiley, 1993.
Dinosaurs, Wiley, 1994.
Geometry, Wiley, 1994.
The Human Body, Wiley, 1995.
Ecology, Wiley, 1996.
Oceans, Wiley, 1996.
Constellations, Wiley, 1997.
Food and Nutrition, Wiley, 1999.

"JANICE VanCLEAVE'S SPECTACULAR SCIENCE FAIR PROJECTS" SERIES, AGES 8-12

Animals, Wiley, 1992.
Gravity, Wiley, 1992.
Molecules, Wiley, 1992.
Magnets, Wiley, 1993.
Earthquakes, Wiley, 1993.

Machines, Wiley, 1993.
Microscopes and Magnifying Lenses, Wiley, 1993.
Volcanoes, Wiley, 1994.
Electricity, Wiley, 1995.
Weather, Wiley, 1995.
Rocks and Minerals, Wiley, 1996.
Plants, Wiley, 1997.
Insects and Spiders, Wiley, 1998.
Solar System, Wiley, 2000.

"THE BEST OF JANICE VanCLEAVE" SERIES, AGES 8-12

200 Gooey, Slippery, Slimy, Weird and Fun Experiments, Wiley, 1993.
201 Awesome, Magical, Bizarre and Incredible Experiments, Wiley, 1994.
202 Oozing, Bubbling, Dripping and Bouncing Experiments, Wiley, 1996.
203 Icy, Freezing, Frosty, Cool and Wild Experiments, Wiley, 1999.

"JANICE VanCLEAVE'S A+ PROJECT" SERIES, AGES 13 AND UP

A+ Biology, Wiley, 1993.
A+ Chemistry, Wiley, 1993.
A+ Earth Science, Wiley, 1999.

"JANICE VanCLEAVE'S PLAY AND FIND OUT: EASY EXPERIMENTS FOR YOUNG CHILDREN" SERIES, AGES 4-7

Science, Wiley, 1996.
Nature, Wiley, 1997.
Math, Wiley, 1997.
Human Body, Wiley, 1998.
Bugs, Wiley, 1999.

Work in Progress

Habitats for the "Science for Every Kid" series; *A+ Physics* for the "A+" series; *Energy* for the "Spectacular Science Project" series; *Teaching the Fun of Science* for a new series being developed for teachers; and *Science Through the Ages* and *Help! My Science Project is Due Tomorrow* for ages 8-12.

Sidelights

Janice VanCleave has authored fifty books on science for readers from kindergarten through high school. Her highly popular series, including "Janice VanCleave's Science for Every Kid," "Janice VanCleave's Spectacu-

VanCleave enhances her list of experiments with information about the display, research, and development of a creative science fair project. (Cover illustration by Ralph Butler.)

lar Science Fair Projects," "The Best of Janice Van-Cleave," "Janice VanCleave's A+ Project," and "Janice VanCleave's Play and Find Out," all introduce kids of all ages to the wonders of science through the format of easy-to-do experiments and exercises. Covering topics from chemistry to gravity and from stars to bugs, VanCleave's books are noted for their straightforward approach to information delivery. Her clear explanations, descriptions, and directions are coupled with experiments to create "user-friendly volumes that make science great fun," according to Rosie Peasley in *School Library Journal.*

VanCleave, a science teacher in public schools for over a quarter of a century, has a firm grasp on her subject matter and knows how to reach young readers. Her love of science and seeing how things work started when she herself was a kid. "I was born in Houston, Texas," VanCleave once told *SATA,* "and spent most of my childhood in the Houston area. . . . One of my fondest memories as a child was getting dressed up and riding the bus to town and shopping with my grandmother. She always let me buy one toy for myself and the one I remember the most was a wind-up car. Like most of the things I got my hands on, the car was taken apart to see what made it work, much to the chagrin of my mother.

"My curiosity did not stop at mechanical things and my insatiable appetite for reading only whetted my desire to discover things for myself. One of many memorable events in my home resulted from my usual negligence of cleaning up after completing a project. My mother, who had little curiosity about the scientific world around her, was most surprised—but not pleasantly—when she discovered some forgotten frogs in the vegetable bin of the refrigerator. I had wanted to see for myself if frogs really would hibernate when chilled. They were very quiet and immobile—until my mom screamed and threw them out. Another memorable moment resulted from my performing chemistry experiments in my bedroom. Mom did not buy the story that my bed was sitting in the middle of the room because I was trying a new decorating idea. Actually I had spilled acid on the carpet and moved the bed to cover up the problem. I learned how not to perform chemistry experiments, which was a valuable lesson since my interest in science led me to a career of teaching science."

VanCleave graduated from high school at sixteen, and after a year of college dropped out to get married and raise a family. However, at age twenty and the mother of three children, she returned to the university and majored in science education. Then began a long teaching career in schools around the country and abroad.

"My family has been very transient during my twenty-six years of teaching," VanCleave once told *SATA.* "Our frequent moves provided me with the opportunity to teach every science course offered in grades six through twelve at a multitude of schools in several states and one foreign country (Germany). I was rarely given the advanced science classes, so I have appreciation for the problems in motivating those 'just try to teach me anything' students. In retrospect, it is this group that I used as a measuring instrument to determine if an experiment was fun and interesting.

"In seeking ways to provide more laboratory experiences for my students in classroom settings that too often had little or no formal laboratory equipment and few supplies, I started writing my own activities. Learning takes place when students are involved in discovering the solution to a problem, and to provide my students with these learning experiences I designed experiments that every child could successfully perform. I had to use available supplies and these came from my home or a local store. This turned out to be a very positive factor because it allowed the children to repeat the experiments at home with parental supervision. This provided great public relations with parents and my students had fun while learning. . . . My students eagerly performed the simple, safe, fun science experiments that I designed, and with their help each hands-on activity was improved, resulting in 'sure fire' workable activities. . . . Over the years I collected hundreds of ideas which I modified and adapted for use in the different science courses I taught."

VanCleave's writing career began when she was teaching an enrichment class at a community college in Arkansas and a publishing company asked her to write a book of children's experiments using around-the-house supplies: no glass tubing, no test tubes, and only materials that could be purchased at a grocery store. The result was *Teaching the Fun of Physics: 101 Activities to Make Science Education Easy and Enjoyable.* Since that initial title, VanCleave has authored more than four dozen books.

VanCleave's initial series, "Science for Every Kid," began in 1989 with the title *Astronomy.* Over the years, that series has increased to fifteen titles and is still growing. Each book provides about twenty chapters and a wealth of experiments and activities to reinforce learning. With *Earth Science,* for example, VanCleave provides 101 experiments to reinforce the lessons. Peasley explained in a *School Library Journal* review that all the experiments contain a list of materials to be used, the purpose of the experiment, instructions to guide students through the experiments, what to expect in results, "and a scientific explanation of the results." Activities include making a peanut butter and jelly sandwich to model rock sedimentation, and Peasley felt the instructions and concepts were "so clear that students can learn just by reading and visualizing them, although it will be much more fun to actually perform the experiments."

Reviewing VanCleave's *Math* for the same series, Nancy A. Gifford, writing in *School Library Journal,* called the content "fun and inviting," with activities from get-rich-quick schemes to graphing Girl Scout cookie sales. Reviewing *Dinosaurs, Booklist* critic Denia Hester noted that VanCleave "does a fine job of explaining some complex subjects and theories." Stepha-

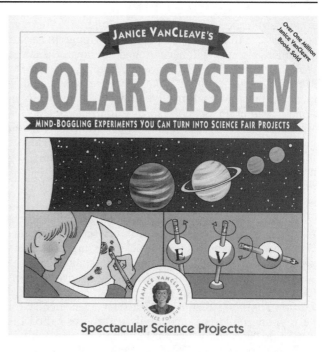

The solar system is investigated through experiments and activities along with explanations of astronomical concepts. (Cover illustration by Mona Mark.)

nie Zvirin noted in a *Booklist* review of *The Human Body* that "there's lots of good information here, and VanCleave doesn't shy away from scientific terms, which she defines with care."

Environmental matters also get the VanCleave treatment in *Ecology,* a "user-friendly approach to ecology activities, exceptionally well organized," according to Sarabeth Kalajian in *School Library Journal.* "Solid information and a generous portion of fun are combined to elevate this selection above the standard collection of experiments," Kalajian added. VanCleave has also written in the "Science for Every Kid" series about the ocean, the constellations, and food and nutrition. Reviewing her 1997 *Constellations, Booklist* contributor Helen Rosenberg concluded, "Young adults put off by the word kid in the title will be missing out on a book that will leave them both knowledgeable and excited."

Another popular VanCleave series is "Spectacular Science Fair Projects," an assortment of fourteen titles detailing projects on weather, plants, rocks and minerals, microscopes, and gravity, to name but a handful. Typically these books are under one hundred pages and employ the same well-detailed, clearly explained format as found in all of VanCleave's books, as well as emphasizing projects that can be successfully produced using commonly found ingredients and materials. *Booklist* contributor Chris Sherman, reviewing *Molecules* and *Gravity* in that series, felt that the entire series "will be popular with students at science fair time," and noted that VanCleave's clear instructions make it possible "for students simply to reproduce the activities to create an acceptable science fair project." Reviewing *Volcanoes,* Sherman noted in *Booklist* that this "takes the beloved erupting volcano to new levels of exploration." Sherman concluded, "All of the experiments use simple materials a teacher or parent will have around the house." George Gleason, reviewing *Rocks and Minerals* in *School Library Journal,* felt that "VanCleave presents stunningly clear, direct, and informative projects," while Carolyn Jenks, writing in *School Library Journal,* noted that VanCleave's 1997 book *Plants* was "inspiring without being flashy." Jenks concluded, "This is a fine example of helpful information that is neither academically dry nor ingratiatingly slangy in hopes of snagging 'today's readers'; it is just right."

VanCleave has also written for very young children, from kindergarten to grade two. In her series "Play and Find Out" she presents simple activities in science and nature that provide stimulating introductions to the scientific method. Marion F. Gallivan, reviewing Van-Cleave's *Play and Find Out About Science* in *School Library Journal,* called it an "excellent science entry for very young children," and *Booklist*'s Zvirin called the same title "especially nice for budding scientists with an adult mentor nearby." Writing about VanCleave's *Nature* in *School Library Journal,* Olga Kuharets called the title a "good choice to satisfy youngsters' curiosity and to complement curricula." And reviewing *Play and Find Out About Math* in *Booklist,* Susan Dove Lempke noted, "With these simple, straightforward, hands-on activities, even preschoolers can begin mastering the basic foundations of mathematics."

"My goal as a writer is to provide children young and old with experiments that will make them enthusiastic about learning science," VanCleave once concluded to *SATA.* "Many of my experiment ideas come from just observing my surroundings. . . . We too often are not observant enough of the world around us. You do not have to be a 'scientist' to be curious. . . . I hope never to lose my curious nature. It is my desire that through the books that I write I will encourage others to share my love and curiosity of the scientific world around us."

Works Cited

Gallivan, Marion F., review of *Science, School Library Journal,* October, 1996, p. 119.

Gifford, Nancy A., review of *Math, School Library Journal,* December, 1991, pp. 130-32.

Gleason, George, review of *Rocks and Minerals, School Library Journal,* March, 1996, p. 230.

Hester, Denia, review of *Dinosaurs, Booklist,* April 1, 1994, p. 1444.

Jenks, Carolyn, review of *Plants, School Library Journal,* March, 1997, pp. 209-10.

Kalajian, Sarabeth, review of *Ecology, School Library Journal,* April, 1996, p. 152.

Kuharets, Olga, review of *Nature, School Library Journal,* July, 1997, p. 88.

Lempke, Susan Dove, review of *Math, Booklist,* December 1, 1997, p. 633.

Peasley, Rosie, review of *Earth Science, School Library Journal,* July, 1991, p. 87.

Peasley, Rosie, review of *202 Oozing, Bubbling, Dripping and Bouncing Experiments, School Library Journal,* February, 1997, p. 126.

Rosenberg, Helen, review of *Constellations, Booklist,* December 1, 1997, p. 622.

Sherman, Chris, review of *Gravity* and *Molecules, Booklist,* January 15, 1993, p. 905.

Sherman, Chris, review of *Volcanoes, Booklist,* July, 1994, p. 1942.

Zvirin, Stephanie, review of *The Human Body, Booklist,* April 15, 1995, p. 1496.

Zvirin, Stephanie, review of *Science, Booklist,* October 15, 1996, p. 428.

For More Information See

BOOKS

Writers Directory, 14th edition, St. James Press, 1999, p. 1561.

PERIODICALS

Booklist, January 15, 1994, p. 917; December 1, 1994, p. 672; December 1, 1995, p. 633; February 15, 1997, p. 1023; March 15, 1997, p. 1241; June 1, 1997, p. 1714; December 1, 1997, p. 633; December 1, 1998, p. 675; December 1, 1998, p. 682.

Publishers Weekly, October 12, 1992, p. 81; March 13, 1995, p. 70; August 19, 1996, p. 69; July 28, 1997, p. 76; July 13, 1998, p. 79.

School Library Journal, February, 1993, p. 105; July, 1993, p. 96; April, 1997, p. 162; January, 1998, p. 106; August, 1998, pp. 156-57; April, 1999, p. 128; June, 1999, p. 154.

—*Sketch by J. Sydney Jones*

*　　*　　*

VOIGT, Cynthia 1942-

Personal

Born February 25, 1942, in Boston, MA; daughter of Frederick C. (a corporate executive) and Elise (Keeney) Irving; married first husband September, 1964 (divorced, 1972); married Walter Voigt (a teacher), August 30, 1974; children: Jessica, Peter. *Education:* Smith College, B.A., 1963. *Politics:* Independent. *Hobbies and other interests:* "Reading, eating well (especially with friends), tennis, movies, hanging around with our children, and considering the weather."

Addresses

Home—Deer Isle, ME. *Agent*—Merrilee Heifetz, Writers House, Inc., 21 West 26th St., New York, NY 10010.

Career

J. Walter Thompson Advertising Agency, secretary, 1964; high school English teacher in Glen Burnie, MD, 1965-67; The Key School, Annapolis, MD, English teacher, 1968-69, department chair, 1971-79, part-time

Cynthia Voigt

teacher and department chair, 1981-88; author of books for young readers, 1981—.

Awards, Honors

Notable Children's Trade Book in the field of social studies, National Council for Social Studies/Children's Book Council, and American Book Award nominee, both 1981, for *Homecoming;* American Library Association (ALA) Best Young Adult Books citation, 1982, for *Tell Me If the Lovers Are Losers;* ALA Best Children's Books citation, 1982, and Newbery Medal, ALA, 1983, both for *Dicey's Song;* ALA Best Young Adult Books citation, 1983, and Newbery Honor book, ALA, 1984, both for *A Solitary Blue;* Edgar Allan Poe Award for best juvenile mystery, Mystery Writers of America, 1984, for *The Callender Papers;* Silver Pencil Award (Dutch), 1988, and Deutscher Jugend Literatur Preis, 1989, both for *The Runner;* Alan Award for achievement in young adult literature, 1989; California Young Reader's Award, 1990, for *Izzy, Willy-Nilly.*

Writings

"TILLERMAN FAMILY" SERIES

Homecoming, Atheneum, 1981.
Dicey's Song, Atheneum, 1982.
A Solitary Blue, Atheneum, 1983.
The Runner, Atheneum, 1985.
Come a Stranger, Atheneum, 1986.
Sons from Afar, Macmillan, 1987.
Seventeen against the Dealer, Macmillan, 1989.

YOUNG ADULT NOVELS

Tell Me If the Lovers Are Losers, Atheneum, 1982.
The Callender Papers, Atheneum, 1983.
Building Blocks, Atheneum, 1984.
Jackaroo, Atheneum, 1985.
Izzy, Willy-Nilly, Atheneum, 1986.
Tree by Leaf, Macmillan, 1988.
On Fortune's Wheel, Macmillan, 1990.
The Vandemark Mummy, Atheneum, 1991.
David and Jonathan, Scholastic, 1992.
Orfe, Macmillan, 1993.
The Wings of a Falcon, Scholastic, 1993.
When She Hollers, Scholastic, 1994.
The Bad Girls, Scholastic, 1996.
Bad, Badder, Baddest, Scholastic, 1997.

OTHER

Stories about Rosie (picture book), Macmillan, 1986.
Glass Mountain (adult fiction), Harcourt, 1991.

Also compiler of stories and poems, with David Bergman, for *Shore Writers' Sampler II,* Friendly Harbor Press, 1988.

Sidelights

Cynthia Voigt is an accomplished storyteller noted for her well-developed characters, interesting plots, and authentic atmosphere. In her novels for children and young adults, she examines such serious topics as child abandonment, verbal abuse, racism, and coping with amputation. Reviewers have praised Voigt's fluent and skillfully executed writing style, compelling topics, and vividly detailed descriptions. Critics also have described Voigt's themes as universal and meaningful to young adults, particularly noting her expertise in fashioning convincing characters and rich relationships in which both adults and children grow in understanding. In a *Twentieth-Century Children's Writers* essay, Sylvia Patterson Iskander described the qualities that have made Voigt's writings appealing to readers: "Voigt's understanding of narrative techniques, power to create memorable characters, admirable but not goody-goody, knowledge of the problems of youth, and desire to teach by transporting readers into the characters' inner lives result in reversing unpromising, perhaps tragic, situations to positive, optimistic ones."

Voigt was born in Boston, Massachusetts, the second of her parents' five children. Most of her childhood was spent in small-town southern Connecticut. "I actually remember very little of my childhood," Voigt once stated. "I am not certain what to make of that," she also commented. "We were not neglected children." It was in this atmosphere that Voigt began to develop an interest in books. She recalled: "My grandmother lived in northern Connecticut, in a house three stories high; its corridors lined with bookcases." Voigt noted that she had already become an avid reader, with books such as "*Nancy Drew, Cherry Ames, The Black Stallion,* and the Terhune book[s]," when one day at her grandmother's house she "pulled *The Secret Garden* off one of her shelves and read it. This was the first book I found entirely for myself, and I cherished it. There weren't any so-called 'young adult' books when I was growing up. If you were a good reader, once you hit fourth grade, things got a little thin. I started to read adult books, with my mother making sure what I had chosen was not 'too adult.' I read Tolstoy, Shakespeare, Camus, and many classics, except for *Moby Dick,* which I finally read in college. It knocked me out. I came to Dickens and Trollope later in life."

By the time Voigt began high school, she had set her sights on a career as a writer. She began writing short stories and poetry, and upon entering Smith College, a women's college in Massachusetts, she enrolled in creative writing courses. Her work, however, received little encouragement from her teachers. "Clearly what I was submitting didn't catch anyone's eye," she once remarked. "I never had a bad teacher like my character, Mr. Chappelle in *A Solitary Blue.*" On the other hand, she did find that some of her teachers at Smith "resented teaching women, feeling themselves too good for the position. We had very little patience with that attitude."

Following graduation from Smith College, Voigt moved to New York City where she worked for the J. Walter Thompson Advertising Agency. "I married in 1964 and moved with my first husband to Santa Fe, New Mexico," she recalled. "I was to work as a secretary to help support us while he was in school. But even with my New York experience it was difficult to find a job. I drifted into the Department of Education one day and asked what I would have to do to qualify myself to teach school. They learned that I'd attended Smith College and signed me up for accrediting courses at a Christian Brothers college. Within six months I met the terms of certification. I vowed I would never teach when I left Smith, and yet, the minute I walked into a classroom, I loved it."

By the time of her divorce from her first husband, Voigt had settled in Annapolis, Maryland. "I had been writing throughout college, but during most of my first marriage, I didn't write much at all," Voigt once commented. Voigt had worked at the high school in Glen Burnie, Maryland. She then was hired by The Key School in Annapolis: "I was assigned to teach English in second, fifth and seventh grades. The second graders were a kick and a half. I assigned book reports to my fifth graders. I would go to the library and starting with the letter 'A' peruse books at the fifth, sixth, and seventh-grade age level. If a book looked interesting, I checked it out. I once went home with thirty books! It was then that I realized one could tell stories which had the shape of real books—novels—for kids the age of my students. I began to get ideas for young adult novels and juvenile books. That first year of teaching and *reading* really paid off in spades! I felt I had suddenly discovered and was exploring a new country."

In 1974, the author married Walter Voigt, a teacher of Latin and Greek at The Key School. "I was teaching full time, but was able to continue the writing I'd begun while I was living alone by sticking to my regime of one

hour a day," the author recalled. When Voigt became pregnant, she switched to teaching part-time and dedicated more of her time to writing. "The summer I was pregnant I wrote the first draft of *The Callender Papers.* When my son, Peter, was an infant, I took him to school and taught with him in a 'Snuggli.' When he was a year old, I wrote *Tell Me If the Lovers Are Losers,* and the next year (he was in a playpen in the faculty lounge next to my classroom), I began *Homecoming.*

"One day while I was writing *Tell Me If the Lovers Are Losers,* I went to the market and saw a car full of kids left to wait alone in the parking lot. As the electric supermarket doors whooshed open, I asked myself 'What would happen if nobody ever came back for those kids?' I made some jottings in my notebook, and let them 'stew' for a year, the way most of my ideas do. When I sat down to write the story that grew from my question (and this is typical of my process) I made a list

Newbery Medal Winner

Cynthia Voigt

FAWCETT JUNIPER
0-449-70276-6

DICEY'S SONG

Forced to grow up too soon, Dicey discovers that you can learn some things too fast....

"Voigt has plumbed and probed her character inside and out to fashion a memorable protagonist."
BOOKLIST

A Tillerman Family Novel

When four fatherless children are abandoned by their mentally ill mother, teenage Dicey, the eldest sibling, takes responsibility for the others and, after moving with them to her grandmother's house, struggles to build a relationship with the eccentric old woman.

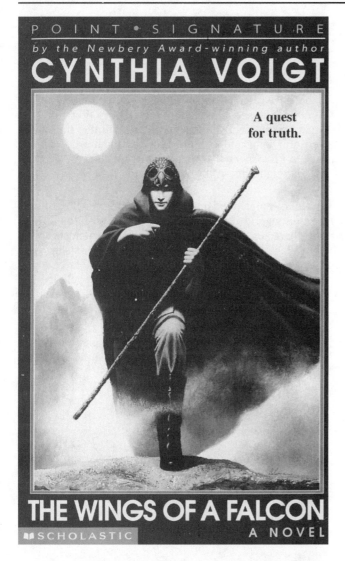

Set in a mythical land, Voigt's novel depicts two friends who escape from an island of slavery to travel across unknown territory, suffering captivity and tragedy before settling on a farm. (Cover illustration by Joe DiCesare.)

of character names. Then I tried them on to see if they fit. I knew Dicey was the main character, but was not sure precisely *who* she was. The more I wrote about her, the more real she became to me. I'd planned a book about half the size of *Homecoming.* But a few chapters into the novel, the grandmother became central and I began to see that there was a lot more going on than would fit in one book." *Homecoming* became Voigt's first published novel, appearing 1981.

With *Homecoming,* the author begins the saga of the Tillermans, four fatherless children aged six through thirteen who are abandoned in a shopping mall parking lot by their mentally ill mother. Dicey, the eldest, takes it upon herself to care for all four, and they eventually move to their grandmother's home in distant Maryland. "The plot is well developed, fast paced, with some suspense. The book deals with the pain of losses—death, separation, poverty—but also with responsibility,

friends, wisdom, happiness, survival," wrote *Christian Science Monitor* critic Joanna Shaw-Eagle. Although many critics questioned whether the length of the work and its often-negative portrayal of adults made it inappropriate for young adult readers, Kathleen Leverich of the *New York Times Book Review* took these elements into consideration when she concluded that "the accomplishments of this feisty band of complex and ... sympathetically conceived kids makes for an enthralling journey to a gratifying end."

Dicey's Song continues the Tillermans' story, concentrating on young Dicey's emerging understanding of her new life in her grandmother's house in Maryland and her relationships with her siblings and grandmother. Even better received than *Homecoming, Dicey's Song* was praised for its cohesive plot and the depth of its characterizations, particularly of Dicey and her eccentric grandmother. In her review in *Bulletin of the Center for Children's Books,* Zena Sutherland called *Dicey's Song* "a rich and perceptive book." In 1983, Voigt was awarded with the prestigious Newbery Medal for *Dicey's Song.* In *A Solitary Blue,* Voigt centers on Jeff, a friend of Dicey's introduced in the earlier Tillerman novels, whose mother abandons him to the care of his remote father while she goes off to help needy children. The story depicts the evolution of Jeff's understanding of his parents and of himself. According to Gloria P. Rohmann in her review in *School Library Journal,* the book "ultimately disappoints"; but other critics, while noting flaws, praised the depiction of the relationship between Jeff and his father. Jane Langton in her critique in the *New York Times Book Review* called *A Solitary Blue* "beautifully written," comparing it to Charles Dickens's *Bleak House.* *A Solitary Blue* was named a Newbery Honor book in 1984.

The Runner is another spin-off from the Tillerman novels, this time set a generation before the others and centered on Samuel "Bullet" Tillerman, whose obsession is long-distance running and whose torment is his autocratic father. The plot turns on Bullet's prejudice against black people, which is eventually softened by his association with Tamer Shipp, a black runner. Although some critics found the plot contrived and the writing overdone, Alice Digilio of *Washington Post Book World* concluded, "Voigt sails *The Runner* through some heavy seas, but always with a steady hand." In *Come a Stranger,* Voigt supplements the Tillerman series with another novel that takes racism as its focus. The plot centers on Mina Smiths, a character first introduced in *Dicey's Song,* whose experience of being the only black girl at ballet camp one summer impels her to try to identify with whites. Tamer Shipp appears as Mina's minister, to whom she goes for guidance. Though some critics faulted the author for stereotyping her black characters, others praised Voigt for the depth of her characterizations and smooth writing style.

Voigt completed her Tillerman series with the books *Sons from Afar* and *Seventeen against the Dealer.* She once commented on the writing process for the Tillerman books: "Bullet's story, which is what *The Runner* is, crossed my mind when I was writing *Homecoming* and put him in there. It had been in the back of my mind for that two- or three-year period. In the meantime I was writing two other Tillerman books, which had come naturally one out of the other. The ideas get in my head, and then there's a time when it's the right time to write them, I hope. And that's when I sit down to do them."

Tell Me If the Lovers Are Losers, Voigt's second published novel, focuses on three female college freshmen who become roommates, then teammates on the same volleyball team, and then friends. While some critics faulted the novel for what *New York Times Book Review* critic Kathleen Leverich called "exaggeration of character and the sacrifice of the theme to improbable theatrics," others, like Sally Estes of *Booklist,* dubbed *Tell Me If the Lovers Are Losers* "both provocative and rewarding for older, more perceptive high school age readers." Voigt's next publication was *The Callender Papers,* a Gothic mystery set in late-nineteenth-century New England. Thirteen-year-old Jean Wainwright agrees to sort through the papers of Irene Callender, who died under mysterious circumstances and whose child then disappeared. Jean eventually finds the answer to the mystery, learning some lessons about life in the process. A number of critics observed that *The Callender Papers* was lighter fare than Voigt usually offers her readers, but most also found the mystery satisfying and well written.

Voigt created another novel for slightly younger adolescents in her 1984 work, *Building Blocks.* In what Zena Sutherland of *Bulletin of the Center for Children's Books* described as "an interesting time-travel story," Voigt depicts a strengthening relationship between a father and son through understanding gained when the son is transported from 1974 to the Depression. There he becomes friends with the 10-year-old boy who will become his father. *Building Blocks* was generally well-received, even by critics who did not admire the science-fiction element in the plot. *New Directions for Women* reviewer Elizabeth Sachs wrote: "Though the transition back in time is awkward, the scenes of Brann with his young boy father are beautiful." Voigt also utilizes magical elements in *Jackaroo,* a book Karen P. Smith described in *School Library Journal* as "an intense and elegantly written historical adventure-romance." Set in a mythical place during the Middle Ages, *Jackaroo* features a strong teenage heroine who takes on the persona of the legendary Jackaroo in order to save her family and community. Mary M. Burns remarked in an article in *Horn Book:* "As in all of Cynthia Voigt's books, the style is fluid ... the setting is evoked through skillfully crafted description; the situations speak directly to the human condition."

In *Izzy, Willy-Nilly,* Voigt depicts the trauma faced by an active teenager whose leg is amputated after a car accident. Through this incident, and with the help of Roseamunde, an awkward girl who embodies all that Izzy did not before her accident, Voigt's protagonist finds resources and wisdom within herself that she might otherwise never have known. Though some critics

complained about the book's length and some unrealistic elements in the plot, Patty Campbell of *Wilson Library Bulletin* dubbed *Izzy, Willy-Nilly* the "best young adult novel of the season, and perhaps of the year." Voigt's next book, *Stories about Rosie,* is a departure from the author's earlier works. This picture book features humorous stories about the Voigt family dog from the dog's perspective. While some critics felt that the stories were too long and complex for the picture-book audience, a *Publishers Weekly* reviewer concluded: "*Rosie* is a lightweight, just-right book for dog fans everywhere."

In 1993, Voigt published *Orfe,* a novel which explores the underworld of the music business by following the title character's rock-and-roll career, her friendship with Enny, her manager, and her troubled relationship with Yuri, a recovering drug addict. Critics generally found the novel too dark, and Beverly Youree concluded her review in *Voice of Youth Advocates:* "Readers expecting a story similar to those of the Tillerman novels or her

In the 1960s, track star Samuel Tillerman finds his prejudice against blacks softened by his association with Tamer Shipp, a promising new runner on the track team.

fantasy novels will be disappointed." Voigt's *The Vandemark Mummy* was more warmly received. A mystery for younger adolescents, the plot centers on a brother and sister who go with their father when he is hired as the curator for an Egyptian collection at Vandemark College. When the collection's mummy is stolen and then found in a damaged condition, the sister disappears trying to uncover the thief. A reviewer for *Junior Bookshelf* wrote: "Serious issues are under debate, but the story is exciting and highly entertaining." In *David and Jonathan,* Voigt returns to more weighty matters for the older adolescent with a story that deals with the Holocaust, the Vietnam war, and homosexuality. A *Junior Bookshelf* contributor called *David and Jonathan* "highly serious," adding: "It is equally highly readable."

Voigt continued the story begun in *Jackaroo* with *On Fortune's Wheel*, and then resurrected the setting again in *The Wings of a Falcon*, a novel a *Kirkus Reviews* critic called "grand, thought-provoking entertainment." This work centers on Oriel and his friend Griff, who escape from an island of slavery to travel across unknown lands only to be captured by Wolfers, a destructive band of barbarians, before escaping and settling on a farm in the north. Reviewers noted the book's length and mature themes in their generally positive reviews. In her review in *School Library Journal*, Susan L. Rogers compared Voigt's fantasy trilogy to her Tillerman series: "Each volume stands on its own, but together they create a tapestry more complex, meaningful, and compelling than its individual parts."

Voigt's books have earned her acclaim from readers and critics, for both their thoughtful themes and entertaining prose. While the products of her work have achieved success in the publishing world, Voigt once commented that the actual process of writing also has an important place in her life: "Awards are external, they happen after the real work has been done. They are presents, and while they are intensely satisfying they do not give me the same kind of pleasure as being in the middle of a work that is going well.... Writing is something I need to do to keep myself on an even keel. It's kept me quiet; it's kept me off the streets." Voigt's advice to aspiring writers reflects this ethic: "Do it, not for awards, but for the pleasure of writing."

Works Cited

Burns, Mary M., review of *Jackaroo, Horn Book*, March-April, 1986, p. 210.

Campbell, Patty, review of *Izzy, Willy-Nilly, Wilson Library Bulletin*, November, 1986, p. 49.

Review of *David and Jonathan, Junior Bookshelf*, February, 1992, p. 38.

Digilio, Alice, "What Makes Bullet Run?," *Washington Post Book World*, July 14, 1985, p. 8.

Estes, Sally, review of *Tell Me If the Lovers Are Losers, Booklist*, March 15, 1982, p. 950.

Iskander, Sylvia Patterson, "Cynthia Voigt," *Twentieth-Century Children's Writers*, 3rd edition, St. James Press, 1989, pp. 1004-5.

Langton, Jane, review of *A Solitary Blue, New York Times Book Review*, November 27, 1983, pp. 34-35.

Leverich, Kathleen, review of *Homecoming, New York Times Book Review*, May 10, 1981, p. 38.

Leverich, Kathleen, review of *Tell Me If the Lovers Are Losers, New York Times Book Review*, May 16, 1982, p. 28.

Rogers, Susan L., review of *The Wings of a Falcon, School Library Journal*, October, 1993, p. 156.

Rohmann, Gloria P., review of *A Solitary Blue, School Library Journal*, September, 1983, pp. 139-40.

Sachs, Elizabeth, review of *Building Blocks, New Directions for Women*, spring, 1986, p. 13.

Shaw-Eagle, Joanna, "Cynthia Voigt: Family Comes First," *Christian Science Monitor*, May 13, 1983, p. B2.

Smith, Karen P., review of *Jackaroo, School Library Journal*, December, 1985, p. 96.

Review of *Stories about Rosie, Publishers Weekly*, September 26, 1986, p. 82.

Sutherland, Zena, review of *Dicey's Song, Bulletin of the Center for Children's Books*, October, 1982, p. 38.

Sutherland, Zena, review of *Building Blocks, Bulletin of the Center for Children's Books*, April, 1984, p. 158.

Review of *The Vandemark Mummy, Junior Bookshelf*, April, 1993, pp. 79-80.

Review of *The Wings of a Falcon, Kirkus Reviews*, August 1, 1993, p. 1009.

Youree, Beverly, review of *Orfe, Voice of Youth Advocates*, December, 1992, p. 288.

For More Information See

BOOKS

Children's Literature Review, Volume 13, Gale, 1987.

PERIODICALS

ALAN Review, spring, 1994, pp. 56-59.
Bulletin of the Center for Children's Books, September, 1993, p. 25.
Horn Book, August, 1993, pp. 410-13.
Kliatt, January, 1993, p. 13.
Publishers Weekly, July 18, 1994, pp. 225-26.
School Library Journal, December, 1992, pp. 133-34.*

—*Sketch by Mary Gillis*

WARNES, Tim(othy) 1971-
(Lily Moon, a pseudonym)

Personal

Born June 11, 1971, in Enfield, England; son of Michael (a paper conservator) and Julia (Smith) Warnes; married Jane Chapman (an illustrator), April 16, 1994; children: Noah. *Education:* Kingston Polytechnic, Diploma, 1990; Brighton University, B.A. (in illustration; with honors), 1993. *Religion:* Christian. *Hobbies and other interests:* The natural world, photography, "walking, beachcombing, and going to the cinema with my wife—and now enjoying my new role as a dad!"

Addresses

Home—Somerset, England.

Career

Freelance illustrator specializing in children's picture books, 1993—. *Member:* Royal Society for the Protection of Birds, National Trust.

Awards, Honors

Nottinghamshire Children's Book Award, Benjamin Franklin award finalist, and Dutch Libraries Association's Children's Book Prize, all 1997, all for *I Don't Want to Go to Bed!;* Nottinghamshire Children's Book Award, 1998, for *I Don't Want to Take a Bath!;* finalist, Nottingham's Experian Big Three Book Award, 2000, for *It Could Have Been Worse.*

Writings

AUTHOR AND ILLUSTRATOR

Ollie's 123, Walker, 1999.
Ollie's Colours, Walker, 1999.
Ollie's ABC, Walker, 2000.
Ollie's Opposites, Walker, 2000.

ILLUSTRATOR

Linda Jennings, *Tom's Tail,* Little, Brown, 1995.
Ragnhild Scamell, *Who Likes Wolfie?* Little, Brown, 1995.
Jane Chapman, *Peter and Pickle's Puzzling Presents,* Magi Publications, 1995.
Julie Sykes, *I Don't Want to Go to Bed!* Little Tiger Press, 1996.
A. H. Benjamin, *The Clumsy Elephant,* Golden Press, 1996.
Sykes, *Sssh!* Little Tiger Press, 1996.
Hiawyn Oram, *Counting Leopard's Spots: Animal Stories from Africa,* Orchard (London), 1996, Little Tiger Press, 1998.
Sykes, *I Don't Want to Take a Bath,* Little Tiger Press, 1997.
Christine Leeson, *Max and the Missing Mice,* Golden Press, 1997.
Leeson, *Davy's Scary Journey,* Little Tiger Press, 1997.
Oram, *Not-so-Grizzly Bear Stories,* Orchard, 1997, Little Tiger Press, 1998.
Sykes, *Hurry Santa!* Little Tiger Press, 1998.
We Love Preschool, Millbrook Press, 1998.
James Riordan, *Little Bunny Bobkin,* Little Tiger Press, 1998.
Benjamin, *It Could Have Been Worse . . .,* Little Tiger Press, 1998.
Sykes, *Little Tiger Goes to School,* Little Tiger Press, 1999.
Sykes, *Santa's Busy Day!* Little Tiger Press, 1999.
Sykes, *Little Tiger's Big Surprise!* Little Tiger Press, 1999.
Judy West, *Have You Got My Purr?* Little Tiger Press, 1999.
Dick King-Smith, *Dinosaur School,* Puffin, 1999.
Michael Coleman, *You Noisy Monkey,* Rigby, 2000.
Coleman, *George and Sylvia,* Little Tiger Press, 2000.
Sykes, *Wake up, Little Tigers,* Little Tiger Press, 2000.
Sykes, *Time for Bed, Little Tiger,* Little Tiger Press, 2000.

Books illustrated by Warnes have been translated into seventeen languages.

ILLUSTRATOR, UNDER PSEUDONYM LILY MOON

Kenneth Steven, *The Bearer of Gifts,* Dial, 1998.

Tim Warnes

Work in Progress

"In my sketchbook are ideas for a picture book about a snowman and a bird, in style of pseudonym Lily Moon."

Sidelights

Artist Tim Warnes brings to life the works of a number of children's book authors through his vibrant cartoon-like drawings and his whimsical take on life. Working with such authors as Julie Sykes, Dick King-Smith, and Hiawyn Oram, he has collaborated on several award-winning picture-book efforts, among them the humorous *I Don't Want to Go to Bed!* and *I Don't Want to Take a Bath!,* which reverberate with the adamant stance taken by children everywhere. Describing Oram's *Counting Leopard's Spots: Animal Stories from Africa* as a "handsome offering," *School Library Journal* contributor Tom S. Hurlburt noted that "the . . . paintings that grace every page are expressive, nicely capturing the characters and their environs." And praising Warnes' colorful contribution to Sykes's *Hurry Santa!, Booklist* reviewer Ilene Cooper noted that the illustrator "mixes the right amount of frenetic energy and laughs" in art work that "attracts attention with its bright colors and cute characterizations."

Born in Enfield, England, in 1971, Warnes "used to spend hours drawing, making little illustrated books and cartoon strips," as he revealed to *SATA;* consequently "my career is essentially a natural and happy progression of my main lifelong interest." Among Warnes' favorite illustrations were the cartoon characters featured in animated films, particularly those by Walt Disney, and he got much of his early training in drawing by copying those characters. "I love reading 'The Making of . . .' type books to major animated feature films; the process behind character and stylistic development is especially revealing and feeds my work probably more than any other one particular source."

For Warnes, developing well-defined characters is his favorite part of being a children's book illustrator. "When I come to a new project," he explained to *SATA,* "I really enjoy researching picture reference for it, and I'm very proud of my extensive collection of reference material gleaned over years from various magazines and newspapers, etc! Without a source of reference I feel very out of my depth; as it is, each new project is always daunting." Warnes begins each of his book projects by sketching page after page of character drawings, sometimes using photographs, "sometimes taking inspiration from people that I know, especially children, even if it is an elephant that I'm drawing!" He then reviews these drawings, picking out the ones that best fit the author's text. "At this stage I may make minor suggestions to the original text if I have a particular idea in mind, which may or may not be incorporated, and add my own incidental characters or actions."

In the book *Shhh!,* for example, which is one of several collaborations between Warnes and author Julie Sykes, the artist/illustrator wanted to provide something in each of his drawings for young readers to hunt for. So he drew a small mouse into every two-page illustration. "The publisher and [Julie Sykes] developed this idea and gave me a voice on the last spread—now Mouse is as much a part of our Santa books as Santa himself," he told *SATA.* Praising Warnes' use of "bright colors," a *School Library Journal* contributor commented of the finished product: The "lively illustrations show a round-faced, button-eyed Santa, . . . [whose] constant state of surprise and confusion . . . will delight young readers."

In his work with author Hiawyn Oram, Warnes' cartoon-like animal drawings are the perfect fit. Containing ten stories based on tales from around the world, Oram's *Not-so-Grizzly Bear Stories* reflects a wealth of tales with universal themes, such as the trickster tale. Reflecting these themes, Warnes' color-filled illustrations "represent an endearing array of animals from pandas to polar bears," commented Shelley Woods in her *School Library Journal* review of the work. Animals also feature prominently in Ragnhild Scamell's *Who Likes Wolfie?,* as a wolf tries to become more popular with the animals around him. Warnes' illustrations for Scamell's book successfully mirror Wolfie's dreams of popularity, "maintain[ing] a certain naive playfulness," according to a *Publishers Weekly* contributor. While questioning the effectiveness of Oram's text, Jacqueline Elsner praised

Warnes' illustrations in her *School Library Journal* review as "marvelous: [full of] funny, engaging, expressive animals rendered in intense winter colors." Commenting on the illustrator's technique, *Booklist* reviewer Ilene Cooper called Warnes' artwork "eye-catching . . . thick paintings with elements so well defined that at first glance the[y] . . . [seem] to be collage."

Although while in college Warnes worked primarily in black-and-white media, such as pen and ink, his more recent artwork has exhibited an increasingly more sophisticated use of color. "In my first books I used a limited palette of just one red, one yellow, one blue and white," Warnes explained to *SATA,* "but now I actively enjoy seeking out new combinations of process colors. I work in acrylic paint, with oil pastel and pencil details and Chinese ink outlines (my Dad gave me the solid ink stone when I was thirteen, and I'm still using it today)."

In addition to publishing illustrations under his own name, Warnes has also coined the pseudonym Lily Moon, under which he has released the picture book *The Bearer of Gifts,* a story written by Kenneth Steven that retells the story about Santa Claus. Using a pseudonym "gives me a new identity and the freedom to express ideas (and take on commissions) that wouldn't be possible in my usual style," Warnes explained to *SATA.* "It has also fed my other work: the technique of using oil pastel on top of acrylic that was a distinguishing feature of my Lily Moon work has now crept into some of 'my own' work." As Lily Moon, Warnes has designed a number of greeting cards and Christmas cards, as well as *The Bearer of Gifts.* "I was delighted to receive this commission," Warnes explained to *SATA* of the 1998 picture book, "since it gave me the opportunity to express my [Christian] faith in my work; I also happen to love wintry landscapes which always seem so magical to me." In the style he uses under his Lily Moon pseudonym, Warnes' inspiration for *The Bearer of Gifts* was "largely drawn from my imagination, textiles, and primitive art, and any source of color reference that grabbed me, [among them] . . . my rug and a painting by Paul Klee," he told *SATA.* Praising the folk art-style and "deep, rich hues" of Warnes' work in *Booklist,* reviewer Lauren Peterson noted that the illustrations, "in a variety of sizes and shapes and with patterned borders and intriguing compositions, add interest."

Considering his future as an illustrator, Warnes looks forward to expanding his skills as an artist. "As time goes on, I would like to get to grips with portraying light and atmosphere," he modestly admitted to *SATA.* "So far I have illustrated over twenty-five children's books with many foreign editions, but I still cannot grasp perspective!" In addition to the technical aspects of his job, he also has dreams of expanding his work beyond the printed page. "I suppose my ideal dream would be for something of mine to be properly animated as a feature, or to be involved in the character designs for such a film."

Works Cited

Cooper, Ilene, review of *Hurry Santa!, Booklist,* September 1, 1998, p. 134.

Cooper, Ilene, review of *Who Likes Wolfie?, Booklist,* April 15, 1996, p. 1447.

Elsner, Jacqueline, review of *Who Likes Wolfie?, School Library Journal,* April, 1996, p. 117.

Hurlburt, Tom S., review of *Counting Leopard's Spots: Animal Stories from Africa, School Library Journal,* December, 1998, p. 112.

Peterson, Lauren, review of *The Bearer of Gifts, Booklist,* October 15, 1998, p. 429.

Review of *Shhh!, School Library Journal,* October, 1996, p. 41.

Review of *Who Likes Wolfie?, Publishers Weekly,* April 8, 1996, p. 68.

Woods, Shelley, review of *Not-so-Grizzly Bear Stories, School Library Journal,* April, 1999, p. 106.

For More Information See

PERIODICALS

Booklist, March 15, 1995, p. 1334; December 1, 1997, p. 644; May 15, 1998, p. 1629.

Child Education, June, 1996.

Independent, March 30, 1996, p. 9.

Junior Magazine, May-June, 1999, p. 111.

Publishers Weekly, May 1, 1995, p. 58; September 30, 1996, p. 89; August 17, 1998, p. 74; October 26, 1998, p. 65; December 21, 1998, p. 66.

School Librarian, August, 1996.

School Library Journal, June, 1995, p. 88; November, 1997, p. 91.

Scotsman, November 28, 1998.

*   *   *

WATSON, B. S.
See TEITELBAUM, Michael

*   *   *

WILLIAMS, Sherley Anne 1944-1999
(Shirley Williams)

OBITUARY NOTICE—See index for *SATA* sketch: Born August 25, 1944, in Bakersfield, CA; died of cancer, July 6, 1999, in San Diego, CA. Professor and author. Williams transcended her difficult early life as a migrant worker thanks to the interest of her teachers and her own hard work. Williams' parents picked crops and cotton in Fresno and received welfare to make ends meet. By the time she was sixteen, both of her parents were dead and she found herself back in the fields picking cotton. Although her mother had discouraged her from reading too much and therefore perhaps becoming dissatisfied with her life, Williams did well in school and was encouraged to take college prep classes and then apply to a university. Williams graduated from Fresno State College (now California State University at Fresno) with a bachelor's degree and followed that with graduate study at Howard University and a master's from Brown University in 1972. She had worked at Fresno State as a lecturer in 1969 and joined the faculty there as an associate professor in English in 1972, the same year her first book, *Give Birth to Brightness: A Thematic Study in Neo-Black Literature,* was published. She later moved to the University of California system and worked at the San Diego campus. *The Peacock Poems,* published in 1975, received a Pulitzer Prize nomination and received a National Book Award. A second book of verse, *Some One Sweet Angel Chile,* also was nominated for a National Book Award and Williams received an Emmy Award for a television performance of works from that book. Other awards followed, including an American Library Association Caldecott Award and a Coretta Scott King Book Award for *Working Cotton,* a children's book. She wrote a second children's book, *Girls Together,* in 1997, but was perhaps best known for the 1986 novel *Dessa Rose.* That book told of an unlikely friendship between the wife of a white plantation owner and a pregnant black slave sentenced to die for killing a white man. The book received strong reviews from critics, who praised the work as affecting and absorbing.

OBITUARIES AND OTHER SOURCES:

PERIODICALS

Los Angeles Times, July 11, 1999, p. B5.
New York Times, July 14, 1999, p. A21.
Washington Post, July 17, 1999, p. B6.*

*   *   *

WILLIAMS, Shirley
See WILLIAMS, Sherley Anne

*   *   *

WILSON, Linda Miller 1936-

Personal

Born in Port Arthur, TX; daughter of James and Winnie Miller; married Bill D. Wilson (an accountant), 1961; children: "Two daughters, two sons-in-law, one granddaughter, and one grandchild on the way." *Education:* Lamar University, B.A., 1958; University of Oklahoma, teacher certification, 1978; University of Central Oklahoma, graduate study, 1988-90. *Religion:* Church of Christ. *Hobbies and other interests:* "Family, friends," writing, reading, gardening, painting, travel.

Addresses

Home—3804 Redbud Lane, Edmond, OK 73034. *Office*—Oakdale Elementary School, 10900 North Sooner, Edmond, OK 73013.

Linda Miller Wilson

Career

Dallas Camp Fire Girls, Dallas, TX, district director, 1958-61; instructional aide at public schools in Gorman, TX, 1974-76; teacher of the learning disabled in Purcell, OK, 1978-83; Oakdale Elementary School, Edmond, OK, teacher of the learning disabled, and special education coordinator, 1983-2000. *Member:* Association for Children with Learning Disabilities.

Writings

Summer Spy, Royal Fireworks Publishing (Unionville, NY), 1996.
A Few Days Journey, Royal Fireworks Publishing, 1998.

Work in Progress

A children's historical novel set in 1941; a preschool picture book; research on the underground railroad in Ohio and on Ohio canals in the 1800s.

Sidelights

Linda Miller Wilson told *SATA:* "Writing for children is the logical result of a life-emphasis on the education of children (camp counselor, Camp Fire Girls district director, parent, foster parent, teacher) and a love of books. Historical novels have held the greatest appeal because I truly enjoy the research.

"Writing and teaching came together in April, 1999, when I was invited to be 'author for a day' at my own school, speaking to groups of students whose teachers had already read one or both of my novels to them. In costume as a grown-up Mattie of *A Few Days Journey,* I 'reminisced' about the main events. As a result, I was profiled in our local newspaper, the *Edmond Sun.*

"Current lists of realistic children's novels seem to have become overburdened with an emphasis on society's problems. While I realize there is a place for this particular reality, I believe children still want and need to escape into a good story and just be entertained. Science fiction is not the only way to offer sheer adventure stories.

"For my own reading, I like John Grisham and Tom Clancy novels, but I also greatly enjoy children's adventure novels such as *Hatchet* by Gary Paulsen. Because I love art, I am an admirer of picture-book artists such as Kim Doner (*Buffalo on the Mall*), Gail Haley (*Dream Peddlar*), and Mike Wimmer (*Home Run*).

"Although we are living in an electronic age, nothing can take the place of getting lost in a great book."

*   *   *

Autobiography Feature

Elizabeth Winthrop

1948-

I was born and brought up in Washington, D.C., but I trace my roots back to New England on my father's side and England on my mother's.

My father grew up in Avon, Connecticut. His father was a dairy and shade tobacco farmer. I remember my grandfather had a kind face with a mischievous look about his fierce blue eyes. Once he walked me down to the barn to see his herd of prize Ayrshire cows. "Grandfather, which one gives chocolate milk?" I asked, and he led me solemnly to the end of the row and pointed to a big brown-and-white milker. "This one," he said, and we stood and admired it in reverent silence. That's my only clear memory of my grandfather. He died when I was six.

My father's mother was Theodore Roosevelt's niece. She came from a big noisy family and was brought up in the high society of New York City during the turn of the century. She married my grandfather in 1909 and moved up to his farm, which must have seemed very primitive to her in those days. But Grandmother was an energetic optimist and, like all Roosevelt women, a political activist. Soon she wormed her way into the hearts of the granite-faced New England farmers. They twice voted her into the Connecticut State Legislature, which was a remarkable thing for the time, but as she pointed out to me years later, they much rather would have voted for a woman than a Democrat.

My father was very sickly as a child. He had asthma (which I inherited) and eczema and a nurse named Agnes Guthrie who, according to the other three children in the family, spoiled Daddy terribly. The tale is told that when he was six, he spent most of his time wrapped in Vaseline and

gauze and laid out like a mummy on the tin-topped kitchen table. Aggie figured out that both the Vaseline and the company in the kitchen kept him from scratching. Years later, when my father went to England to fight in the Second World War, he wrote to Aggie almost as often as to his parents. In some ways, because Aggie spoiled him so terribly, he didn't really grow up until he went to war.

My father met my mother in England during the war. He was twenty-eight years old, and she was only sixteen. But my father noticed right away that my mother had an efficient, calm way about her and that she seemed years older than her actual age, perhaps because she had already seen a lot of war. She grew up in Gibraltar, and at the age of ten, she watched the opening battle of the Spanish Civil War from the roof of her grandparents' house. Four years later, she and her mother and her brother were evacuated from Gibraltar along with the other English women and children on two troop ships. They were told they were being sent to Southampton because the harbor there had not been mined, but to their horror, the ship in front of theirs blew up. Ever so carefully, the captain of their vessel reversed his engines and backed away. He steered a course for London up along the Cliffs of Dover. My mother remembers hanging over the side watching hundreds of boats crossing their bow. Big boats and little ones, fishing boats and trawlers, sailboats and destroyers. It wasn't until they landed in London that she found out she'd been witnessing the evacuation from Dunkirk.

So by the time my father met her, my mother had already lived through far more war than he had ever known. She was working as a code breaker for the British Admiralty, her only brother had been killed in North Africa at the age of twenty, and she had survived months of air raids in London. No wonder she seemed calm to him. With bombs dropping all around them and the sense that the world might never be the same again, theirs was a romance out of the storybooks.

They married just before he parachuted into France in June of 1944, and by December of that same year, she was crossing the Atlantic Ocean in another troop ship, pregnant with my oldest brother and headed for a new country and a new life.

I was born in Washington, D.C., when my mother was only twenty-three years old. I was the third child and the first—and as it turned out, only— girl. We lived then in a tiny house in Georgetown with one big front bedroom where my two older brothers and I slept in bunk beds. I remember the bay windows of that room and the cries of the children from the street in the summertime because my strict English mother put us to bed long before anyone else in the neighborhood. We moved from that house when I was only six because yet another brother had been born and the only place left to fit his bassinet was in the closet. My first picture book, *Bunk Beds,* came from those first and earliest memories. A child in a Texas school once asked me how I remembered everything I wanted to write about. I told him, you don't have to hold on to your memories. When you are ready to use them, they will come back.

There are many reasons that I turned out to be a writer. First of all, my father was one. He was a journalist. We lived in Washington, D.C., and he reported on the presidents and the Congress. Twice a year, he traveled abroad and reported on political situations around the world.

One afternoon, I came home from school to find John Glenn sitting in my living room. He had just completed his orbit of the earth, and my father was interviewing him for an article for the *Saturday Evening Post.* Daddy told me to come in and shake hands. Mr. Glenn was a polite man: he stood for a thirteen-year-old girl. His handshake was firm, his eyes steady, his voice low. I went to school the next day and offered my hand to various friends as the hand that had touched the hand that had been around the world three times. They were singularly unimpressed. In Washington, D.C., children are hard to impress.

My clearest memory of my father working is the distant pounding of typewriter keys, which was the first sound I heard when I opened the kitchen door after a day at school. My father used an old Underwood typewriter, and he was a "hunt and peck" typist. To the ears of a child, the unevenness of his stroke made what was actually a very sedentary job sound dangerous and indispensable through that closed study door. In my imagination, he was the classic reporter in a film noir movie, always rushing against a deadline, typing with the equivalent of a loaded gun at his temple—and if his words were good enough, they might be able to save the world.

My father and Uncle Joe, his writing partner for twelve years, mixed their entertaining with their interviewing. On party nights, one or another of my five brothers would huddle with me at the top of the stairs and peer through the banister rail as the people came through the front door, touching cheeks and shedding coats and dropping ice into glasses. Often we were called into the living room to shake hands all around, but it wasn't long before the grown-ups turned back to their conversations and we could take up our posts again on the stairs to wait for the procession into the dining room. Like the women's exotic perfume and the ever-present cloud of smoke, words like Oppenheimer, Suez, missile gap, U-2, balance of power, and Bay of Pigs hung in the air. Most of the people who came in and out of our house on a regular basis worked for the government, many of them specifically for the CIA. They were "spooks," although I didn't know that then. Because, in Washington, information represents power, the journalists and diplomats and congressmen were all spies of their own sort as well, always looking for the tip or the insight which would lift them up to the next rung on the ladder. The talk of sources and breaking stories permeated the atmosphere of our lives, and although I was too young to understand the actual facts and details of the historical events, I was drawn to the sense of urgency in the comings and goings and to the rise and fall of voices telling stories. I became a spy myself and learned the subtle art of eavesdropping, so crucial to a writer of fiction.

Our house was dripping in books. We had no television until I was a teenager, and in retrospect I am deeply grateful. Sadly, for so many children these days, imagination has been either sapped or twisted by our national love affair with television and other visual media. Why bother to think up an adventure when you can simply lie on the couch and be fed one electronically?

My father did not allow music to be played in the house because he said it hurt his ears. So we read. Unlike the books in my uncle Joe's house, which were treated as if they were revered and esteemed companions, the books in our house were treated as neglected foster children. Books teetered on bedside tables and were stacked haphazardly in bookshelves. They lurked behind cushions and piled up on the floor by my father's chair. If we knew nothing else about our parents, we experienced them as readers, and it made us want to do the same.

I remember a woman once lamenting to me over tea that her ten-year-old son never read. When I looked around her living room, I saw an enormous television set and a state-of-the-art stereo system, but nothing, absolutely nothing, to read. Not a book or a magazine or even a newspaper. The poor child, if he had wanted to read, was reduced to scanning the back of the cereal box over breakfast. "But you don't read," I said to her. "So why would he?"

My family took reading for granted. We read fiction and history and poetry. If you had a question, you were encouraged to look it up in a book. My father read the Bible, not because he was in any way a religious man but because he said it was the best book of stories he had ever encountered. We read *Macbeth* out loud with my father assigning the parts. If you happened to pass by his bathroom while he was taking a shower, you heard Hamlet's "O that this too too sallied flesh would melt, thaw and resolve itself into a dew" or "Whether 'tis nobler in the mind to suffer the slings and arrows of outrageous fortune . . . ." Shakespeare for my father was a source of solace and amusement and distraction from daily cares.

Elizabeth Winthrop

Words were precious. I remember how furious he was when advertisers produced the line "Winston tastes good like a cigarette should." "AS!" my father would roar, "as a cigarette should." I hate to think what he would do with the ridiculous proliferation of the word "like" today. I used to charge my children a nickel every time they misused the word, and they would groan and roll their eyes at my old-fashioned ways. My father would have told them that our language is a precious natural resource not to be squandered. He was a man in love with words, and you could not spend much time in his presence without falling in love with words yourself.

So a writing father and a reading family certainly gave me the tools of my trade. But a life with five brothers in postwar Washington gave me even more—adventures to write about. My childhood memories revolve around my brothers.

We children in the family had our own hierarchy, and we knew our places. Joe was boss man, above all, the unquestionable. Ian was the second in command; I was the second second, the henchman. I was always looking for opportunities to displace Ian, to move up in rank, and he was always wary of the attacks from below. Stewart was the much-abused mascot. My younger two brothers, Nick and Andrew, weren't born until much later. Usually Ian and Joe teamed up in any disputes because they were older and they were both boys. Occasionally, Ian sided with me. We were only thirteen months apart and remained the same height through much of our childhood, and sometimes, for a brief moment, the planets seemed to shift and Ian and I would be mysteriously aligned in both our sentiments and our outlook on life. Perhaps we were simply sick of being bossed around by Joe. These moments of partnership rarely lasted long. There was too much at stake, particularly for Ian. He could be accused of siding with a girl; he might even have to give up his place in the line of command. But no matter what happened, we never sided with Stewart. Stewart had a big goofy smile and tightly curled hair in contrast to our dead-straight lank mops. He was a charmer, and grown-ups seemed to go easier on him than on the rest of us. In our exploits, Stewart was merely tolerated.

In the 1950s, my parents bought a weekend house an hour outside of Washington. My father wished us to have some taste of the farm life he had known as a child, and he himself longed for a place to fish and shoot skeet, a place away from the stuffy, provincial politics of the Eisenhower administration. We christened the farm Polecat Park in honor of the family of skunks that lived under the front porch. (In that part of Maryland, a skunk was always known as a polecat.)

Not unlike Washington politics, dynamics in a big family are often a matter of power. Who went first, who knew more, who could order whom around, which one of us had our parents' attention. Many of our power games were played out at Polecat. There is a picture of us stuck in a photo album; the date is 1957 or so. I am nine years old, and I am lying down in the grass on the front lawn with a .22 rifle up to my shoulder. My father looks like a country squire. He is dressed in a tie and jacket, probably because some people are coming for Sunday lunch, but dressed the way he is, he has crouched down next to me to explain the workings of the gun. The paper plate target is white and flaps in the wind. My father has drawn circles on it and numbered each circle. The closer you get to the bull's-eye, the more points you get. Each marksman keeps his own score. In the photo, my brother Ian with his wild blonde hair standing on end is watching me carefully. He has already had his turn because he is older, and we always did things by age—with so many children badgering for turns, it was the simplest way to keep things straight. My brother Stewart looks impatient. He is only six years old and not yet old enough to shoot. He is leaning on one elbow, using my father's broad back as a table. He is too young still to pick up the signals my father gave. "Noli me tangere!" Daddy used to roar in the car going home from the farm. No touching, stop badgering each other, stop fighting in the back seat. But it also applied to him. Don't get too close, don't show me your feelings or probe too deeply for mine. Life, after all, is a matter of facts. My oldest brother, Joe, sets himself apart as usual. He is standing off to one side ostentatiously reading a copy of *Popular Electronics*. He is pretending to be oblivious to what's going on. He already has taken his turn, and he has a look of lofty boredom about him. It was always important for him to establish himself as the oldest, to separate himself from us lowly siblings.

Somebody once said about fiction that God is in the details. I remember details of that funny old farmhouse as vividly today as when we lived there. Since my fiction often springs from the intimate knowledge of a particular setting, it is no surprise that I wrote my first full-length novel, *Walking Away,* about Polecat Park. I remember the

"My grandfather, Joseph Wright Alsop, on his farm in Avon, Connecticut."

cement porch where we would sit in wooden sling-back chairs with our bottoms practically resting on the cement. If you were small, you sank so far down in those chairs that your legs stuck straight out and your feet pointed at the sky. You looked like a *V*. I remember sitting on that porch waiting for the rain to come across the fields, the smell of water hanging in the air, and then the steady thrumming on the red tin roof above our heads. We might have to pull our chairs a little nearer the wall of the house, but we could watch and smell and listen without ever getting wet. The curtain of water surrounding us always made me feel as if we lived behind a waterfall.

My mother took us children to church on Sunday mornings. My father was not a Catholic and did not convert when they married, but he did agree that the children should all be raised Catholic. I remember how jealous I was of him sitting on the porch and reading the newspaper as our car bumped out the road to the small country church with dull priests and wooden pews. When I knelt down, my mouth rested on the rail of the pew ahead of us, and I remember gnawing on it with my front teeth and the satisfying taste of wood varnish in my mouth. I loved the time after church because my mother took us to the local grocery store and allowed us to pick out three different kinds of candy. Then we drove back to the farm and roamed around waiting for the people to arrive from Washington for the usual Sunday lunch party.

The way into the farm was a rutted dirt road, a treacherous affair in any weather, but after a heavy rain, it developed small ponds here and there filled with murky red-brown water. You could watch the cars coming from a long distance across the fields.

"Who's that?" someone would say.

"The Bissells," someone else would answer, and we'd sit and watch as the old beat-up station wagon wended its excruciatingly slow way down the road towards us. On particularly bad days, in an effort to save the axle, the driver, who was usually Mrs. Bissell, would run one wheel up into the fields, and the car would draw inexorably closer looking cockeyed, like a sailboat heeling over in a stiff wind.

After the Bissells would come the others. We were never quite sure who would arrive because my father could never remember exactly whom he had invited for Sunday lunch. Every time another car crested the horizon, we would begin a guessing game as to the number of passengers.

"Blue Buick," my brother would say, "the Evans."

"Yes, I remember now," my father would say. "I must have asked him when we interviewed the secretary of defense last week."

"And the children?" my mother would ask.

"I can't remember."

She would shake her head and go back into the kitchen to scrounge around for the makings of another potato omelet. Grown-ups and children together would tumble out of their cars with a great slamming of doors and "Did you bring a towel for me?" and "God, Stew, you're going to have to do something with that bloody road" and "Let's swim first."

In the warm weather, people changed into bathing suits in whatever upstairs room they found available and made their way down the path my father had cut through the long grass to the pond. The men and women would come

Parents, Stewart and Patricia Alsop, on their wedding day in London, June 1944.

Elizabeth in the third grade, 1956. "I am in the back row, second from right."

trailing down the hill with drinks and cigarettes, talking loudly to each other about politics or the latest scandal in the government. My father would endure a great deal of teasing about the state of his fly rods or his swimming trunks or the pond. The pond was spring-fed, an oval-shaped body of water dammed up at one end and stocked with bass, which we pulled out of it on a regular basis with a fly rod. My father fought a continual battle with the algae which covered the surface of the water in a blue-green scum that became especially noxious in the late summer. The hotter the summer, the thicker the pestilence, as Daddy liked to call it. He rowed himself around and around in a small leaky boat, dragging one of his old black silk socks which had been filled with a green crystallized chemical that seeped slowly out through the thin material of the sock and broke down the algae in some mysterious way.

The thing you most wanted to avoid when swimming in our pond was touching the bottom. The mud felt cold and slimy, and you could imagine things far worse than the algae sucking you under if you weren't careful. It was the kind of pond that invited images of snapping turtles, black snakes, frogs, and fish; and every one of those creatures had been sighted in it at one time or another and was most certainly lurking somewhere just beneath your toes. My father had fashioned a strange facsimile of a raft from a green painted trellis ripped off the side of the porch. This

was attached to a string of canvas-covered rings, the kind that are tossed off ships to drowning people. You walked carefully across this jerry-rigged contraption to a small rickety ladder out at the end. It was important to cross to the ladder when nobody else was coming the other way or else the raft would start to tip back and forth in a precarious manner and you might fall off in the shallow end right into the deepest, ooziest mud in the whole pond. Later in the afternoon when the grown-ups were draped around the lawn finishing off their lunch, the kids would all jump up and down on the raft, trying to knock each other off.

Once you had reached the ladder, you lowered yourself slowly, taking care to avoid splinters and the odd nail here or there that had managed to work itself out of the slimy, water-soaked wood. Then you let go with one hand and collapsed into the dark water. The ladies all shrieked when they pushed off and gave each other reports on the various cold spots and warm spots. "Oh," they'd say with a sigh of relief, "I've found a warm spot. Right here, darling. Isn't it delicious. Don't put your feet down. Oh no, I've floated out of it again."

The teenage boys would rush past and dive off the raft just as the ladies were lowering themselves into the water, and this would make for a great deal of argument and shouts back and forth. If the teenager had done this to a close relative such as his mother or his aunt, he usually stayed underwater and swam like a frog to the far end until his lungs gave out. This way he popped up too far out of reach to be seriously chastised.

With his fly rod balanced across his knees, my father already would have launched himself out into the deepest part of the pond in an old black inner tube; he liked to paddle over and drop his fly in a shady spot under a tall evergreen as far away from the noise and commotion as possible. Those inner tubes entertained us for hours. We threw them out to each other, dove through them, tried to tip a person over when she was innocently floating around in one (but when you were horsing around with an inner tube, you had to be very careful not to scrape any exposed skin on the metal piece used for blowing it up). Whenever one of these black rubber circles sprouted a leak, my father would take it down to the local gas station and get it patched. For some reason, the patches were made of red rubber, and the more a tube got patched, the jauntier it looked.

I do remember one day early on when I did not yet know how to swim. I stood on the grassy shore and watched all those people running off the rickety raft and hurling themselves in the water with such abandon. And I thought that's all swimming is about—courage, a devil-may-care attitude, a daring leap. When nobody was paying any particular attention to me, I walked up to the ladder, let myself down, and simply pushed off for the middle of the pond. And sank. Went down like a stone while the water rushed up into my nose and my toes slid into the slime at the bottom and it was quite clear that I was going to drown. I pushed my arms around the way I had seen the swimmers do up on the surface but to no avail. I did not move in any direction. It would have been easier to walk out of the water. And then up above, someone must have said, "Where's Elizabeth?" And everybody began to look frantically, and someone must have remembered me pushing off the ladder, and suddenly a hand brushed against me. Strong fingers closed around my upper arm, and my father pulled me out of the muck with one swift movement the way you pull a plug out of a drain. The Sunday guests slapped me on the back and wrapped me in towels, and the ladies hugged me against their wet bellies that were

Christmas picture of Elizabeth with her parents and three of her five brothers, 1958.

swathed in flowered, skirted suits. Later, when there were no grown-ups around to hush them, my brothers hooted with laughter at the hopelessness of a sister who thought the only thing you needed to know about swimming was how to get into the water. Starting a new book often feels to me like jumping into the water when you don't know how to swim. No matter how many books I write, each time I start I feel like a beginner again and I wonder if this is the one that will drown me. As Eudora Welty said, "Each story teaches me how to write it but not how to write the next one."

My father used to say that his life at Polecat was a continual war against the elements. And by elements, he meant animals, insects, and reptiles. There were always wasp nests to be batted off the porch and sprayed, stray cats from next door who got chased away by our beagles, rats who lived under the collapsed chicken coop. And snakes. Black snakes. We got rid of the skunks that lived under the front porch, but we never got rid of the snakes. Everybody told us they were harmless, but they didn't look that way. They would surprise you, those snakes. You'd hear a little rustling, and you'd see the grass bending and the thick black body sliding off to seek refuge in some other place when you hadn't even known one was there. They lay in the sun on the tops of rocks near the pond, and they slunk around in the dark places under the barn.

"My father teaching me how to shoot, with three brothers watching."

"Snake," we would scream, and if my father were in earshot, he would come running with his .22 rifle. Once Daddy had shot the snake and turned it over with the toe of his boot and declared it dead, the boys and I would fall to arguing over who got to carry the carcass to the dump. "You got to do it last weekend." "I never get a chance." Daddy would choose one of us, break the barrel, empty the ammunition out of the gun, snap it closed again, and hand it over to the designated pallbearer.

If you were the lucky one, you hunched down and slid the gun under the corpse at the midway point, taking care not to clog the barrel with dirt because Daddy was still watching and he noticed the way you treated his possessions, particularly his guns. You bounced the black body up and down a few times to move it closer to you along the steel carrying stick until you judged the leverage to be right. Then you kept your back straight and your knees bent and lifted ever so carefully, and up would come the snake, draped like a black garland over the gun, and you would set off for the dump with the funeral party, brothers and guests and friends, all the children on the place skipping along next to you waiting for the first twitches. Long after they are dead, snakes keep jerking and shuddering as if their bodies are trying to restart themselves. So soon after you led off, the thick black lifeless rope would suddenly begin to twitch, and if you weren't careful or even if you were, that dead snake would manage to shake itself right off the gun. Then you'd have to lean down and start all over again with the kids behind you saying, "Let me try," "I can do it," "you're no good at this." The dump was not that far away actually, down a little mown path next to the chicken coop, but if the dead body were particularly active, it could take some time to get the snake there. Then the other kids would drop back because this was the moment you'd been waiting for, the whole reason to be the snake carrier. You twisted your body around ever so slowly to move the gun and its cargo back over your shoulder as if you were a fisherman about to cast a spinner, and you held that position for a split second and you prayed the snake wasn't going to slide right down the barrel and end up draped around your neck, and you felt the silence all around you, in the crowd of kids back out of reach and in the woods beyond the dump and even in the dump itself preparing to receive its own, the way the sea waits for the body of a dead sailor. And then you twisted forward with a snap, and if you'd done it right, if the gun swung around fast enough to hold that snake with centrifugal force and then stopped as if surprised at high noon, the black rope body would sail off over the dump in a long, satisfying arc, and behind you, you would hear the sighs from the crowd and you would know you had accorded that snake a fair and decent burial and you would walk proudly back up to the house at the head of the pack of kids to hand the gun over to your father.

Because I was brought up with boys, I was taught the things a man is supposed to know. I can load and shoot a rifle and a shotgun, gut and clean a fish, drive a stick shift, carry the twisting body of a snake to the dump. These are not skills that are of much use in the life of a modern urban woman, but for some inexplicable reason, because I am competent in these ways, I have been willing to try other things I'm not sure I can do. This has come in handy when I negotiate contracts or stand up to speak in front of a large audience. It doesn't mean everything will turn out well or even the way I want it to. It simply means that I'll step up and try where others might hold back. Writing often requires that sense of assurance—some might call it foolishness—that willingness to travel down paths that seem to have no end or at least no connection at all to the main road.

The year I turned eight, our playroom on the second floor above the living room of our house in Washington was requisitioned by the grown-ups. My parents put in a master bedroom, two dressing rooms, a bathroom for themselves, and two doors to close themselves off from the noise of children and maids in the mornings. It was known as "their wing."

In response, Joe went to my father and negotiated with him for the use of the basement. After all, he argued, we children needed a place to play, to set up projects, hang out. Joe expected to have a battle on his hands, but to our surprise, his request was granted without discussion. When my father was working at home, we children knew we were supposed to keep the noise down, but we needed constant reminders. For a brief time, a sign had appeared on my father's office door which read "DO NOT KNOCK UNLESS YOU'RE BLEEDING." This idea of Joe's provided the perfect solution. All our noise and mess would be relegated to the cellar, a part of the house as far away as possible from my father's office. Except for the laundry, a china closet, and a wine cellar, we were given the full run of the place.

The basement was unfinished and filled with narrow, twisting passageways. It reminded me of pictures I had seen of the catacombs. The floors were lined with rough cobblestones, the furnace pumped away in one corner of the first large room, an old stone sink stood in another. There was a drain in the middle of the floor for hosing the place down, but nobody ever did. The rooms were dusty and low ceilinged, and the air smelled of mildew laced with the scent of newly dried clothes when the dryer had been running. It was the kind of hideout kids dreamed about.

Joe was fair. He awarded me a six-by-eight-foot space between two columns in the large furnace room for my dollhouse and Ian a desk in the middle passageway for his woodcarving activities. Joe took the three back rooms for his work. One section was devoted to chemistry, a second to electronic equipment, and a third for storage.

Unlike my father's office door upstairs, Joe's basement door was never closed, and Ian and I often gravitated around the corner to his three rooms because whatever we were doing, he was sure to be cooking up something more interesting. We were careful to stay out of his way except when he needed something. Then Ian and I would fight over which one of us would bring Joe the piece of wire from the supply room or a screwdriver from the desk. He may not have exactly welcomed our constant presence, but he tolerated it. We became a gang of basement ruffians, and he was our noble leader, the father of our downstairs family.

In those days, children were expected to adjust themselves to the schedules and desires of their parents. Ours were busy people. My mother ran a household bursting with children and volunteered for various causes, and my father was often away traveling or interviewing. In a big family like ours, children often raise themselves. We knew it was useless to appeal to our parents for the resolution of daily squabbles, so we made our own rules. And they were imperfect ones.

Because we considered the whole house our stalking plain, we did not knock on doors, ask permission. These transgressions were committed as easily on one another as they were on the adults. We picked up telephone receivers, read other people's mail, poked around in other peoples' closets. If you didn't want your diary read, you'd better hide it. If you didn't want your clothes borrowed, you'd better wear them. If you didn't want your door opened, get a lock. If you didn't want your food speared off your plate, you'd better keep your elbows up and your eyes open. We violated and eavesdropped and trespassed because nobody ever taught us that violating and eavesdropping and trespassing were against the rules. In fact from what we could glean from grown-up conversations, snooping was not only condoned, it was encouraged. The ends justified the means.

Now, looking back, I can see that I developed my own rules, guidelines for keeping myself protected from other gang members whenever that became necessary. Never let down your guard. Always act as if you do know things even when you don't. (Find out the answers secretly later.) Don't ever show your fear. Jump off the high diving board rather than face the humiliation at the bottom of the ladder. Keep it "together" at all times. Anticipate the different crises that might be waiting around the corner. Be prepared to protect yourself, your friends, your pets, your possessions, your territory, your secrets. Get as much on the others as possible. Information is ammunition, and you never know when you might need it.

Of such stuff are writers made.

In Washington in the 1950s, we children had a special fear of the bomb. After all, we lived a couple of miles from the White House and Capitol Hill. If and when the

The pond at Polecat Park with infamous raft and inner tubes.

Senior year at Sarah Lawrence College, 1969.

Soviet Union decided to launch their deadly missiles, the ones we read and heard about daily, we were dead center in their sights. Talk was all of bomb shelters. So it seemed absolutely natural one summer when Joe announced to his little band of basement mercenaries that we were going to dig our own bomb shelter at the top of our hill. He approached my father with this project and was granted permission with a vague wave of the hand. Joe was horrified by my father's cavalier attitude towards the safety of the family. Very well, if our real father wasn't going to make some efforts to protect us then Joe, our downstairs father, would step into the breach.

The project took a number of weeks. Joe designed an elaborate pulley system that ran along a path of trees down our hill to the stream. You filled a bucket with earth, hooked it to the rope, and gave it a shove. The weight of the dirt made the bucket go rocketing down the hill at a great speed until it slammed into a branch and tipped over, spilling the dirt out into a pile. The full bucket going down pulled up an empty one that had been waiting at the bottom of the hill.

Back then, none of the kids in the neighborhood went to camp. They just hung out and rode their bicycles up and down the dead-end lane and waited for someone to think of something to do. The news of the pulley system spread quickly, and soon kids started to troop up our driveway to see what was going on. By the end of the first week, Ian and I were no longer diggers. We were managers who organized the labor force and took in the nickel per day that Joe had determined each worker must pay in order to be allowed to use the bucket system. As soon as one digger got tired, there was a replacement eager to take his place. The pile of dirt at the bottom of the hill soon grew so big that it threatened to dam up our stream, so Joe sent the workers down to spread the dirt up and down the banks.

My parents went away on one of their annual vacations with the Bissells. The other parents in the neighborhood were probably grateful that their kids weren't hanging around the house complaining of the usual summer boredom. Nobody seemed to notice the activity going on just below the driveway wall. At the end of a month, we had dug a fourteen-foot hole and fashioned out a room that could sleep four, back to back. Somewhere Joe laid his hands on a twelve-foot metal ladder, and we threw down some sleeping bags, comic books, and extra food and began to spend nights down in the hole, which Joe continued to insist we call the shelter. Then my parents came home.

They were horrified, not at all happy about the consideration and care we had taken to protect the family from the coming Armageddon. My father seemed far more concerned about the liability provisions in his insurance policy. He hired a carpenter to build a huge cover that no single child or even a pack of children could move by themselves. We were denied any further access. Gradually over the years, all the leaves that were raked off the place were poured down our hole. They molded and compacted into a rich loam, and soon all that was left of our valiant effort was a shallow depression in the earth.

Joe was furious. He stormed around in the basement office for days, and we stayed at arm's length. From that moment on, in his mind and eventually in ours, the grown-ups became the enemy. If there ever had been any doubt in our minds about whose side we were on, it was utterly dispelled that summer of the bomb shelter. It was us against them. All for one and one for all.

Years later, I published a young adult novel called *A Little Demonstration of Affection* in which I described the entire operation of the hole. I changed the circumstances and the emphasis as fiction writers are wont to do. It was not a book about a war between children and grown-ups so much as it was a story about the kind of sexual tension and confusion that can occur around the time of puberty. In my writing, I have often taken an actual experience from my childhood and woven it into a different kind of story. Luckily, I have never run out of childhood experiences from which to draw.

I have found in my eagerness to tell the reader a good story that I sometimes confuse the actual facts of what happened with the requirements of fiction. Did we actually charge the kids who dug the hole? I think so, although I can't be absolutely sure. But whether it's true or not, it reveals character. If we didn't do it, we certainly could have. This is why I have never been that interested in writing a full-length memoir. With fiction, I can mold the memories to make a better story. As Eudora Welty said, "You need to tell the lies of fiction to get to the truth of human nature." I have always cared more about the truth of human nature than I have about getting each and every fact exactly right.

And sometimes fiction can replace memory. Now when I think about my grandmother's house in Avon, Connecticut, I don't remember the real house so much as the one I described in my novel *In My Mother's House*. I don't think so much of the actual people who lived there as I do about the characters I created and placed in that house so that they could work out the daily troubles of their lives. Writing a novel often means that you mourn the death of what truly was at the same time that you welcome the birth of what might have been.

School is mostly a blur to me. I went to an elementary school not far from home through third grade, but I honestly have almost no memories of the place—probably because for so many years, the adventures at home were simply more memorable. From the fourth through the ninth grade, I attended a local Catholic day school. At Stone Ridge, we prayed before and after every class and attended Mass regularly in a small chapel. I liked the mysterious swish of the nuns' black skirts, the flickering candles, the low hum of a Gregorian chant. For a time in the seventh grade, I set up an altar in my room, prayed regularly, and considered joining a convent, but in the end, I found our basement adventures and the lure of spying far more appealing than the contemplative life.

The late fifties and early sixties were the golden days of covert operations for the CIA. Richard Bissell, the mastermind behind the U-2 spy plane and the man responsible for the Bay of Pigs, was one of my father's best friends. Not surprisingly, his son, Richard, was Joe's sidekick. After the betrayal of the bomb shelter, Joe increasingly turned his attention to our own covert actions. He was the downstairs station chief, and we were his operatives. From his basement office, Joe would draw up plans for various projects and deploy us to carry them out. We understood from the beginning that secrecy was vital to our operations. I remember fantasies of holding out until death itself, no matter what tortures would be perpetrated on my body. In the days when I was as steeped in the convent teachings as I was in the loyalties of the basement gang, I often got muddled over which better cause to die for: the children's underground or Catholic martyrdom. It all appealed to my flair for the dramatic.

First, we manufactured and detonated various bombs. Joe miscalculated the fuse on one in the hay barn at Polecat and had to be carried bleeding to the car. He spent quite a few hours in the local hospital while the weekend resident picked bits of small rocks and wood out of his cheek with a pair of tweezers and stitched together the gaping wound on his chin.

The rambling house served our needs. We conducted a relentless search for good hiding places. I came up with the best one, a little rabbit warren of rooms that you accessed through a small door under the liquor cabinet. During dinner parties, I hid in there and scribbled notes on yellow legal pads, but Joe did not like to rely on the vagaries of human behavior. He got electronic. Shipments of materials arrived from various purveyors of electrical equipment. He and Rich huddled together over large sheets of paper anchored with rocks at every corner. They sketched, argued, dispatched us on errands to cut lengths of wire or to measure things. Another headquarters with a tape recorder was set up in Joe's bedroom.

Every time we reached a new goal, Joe escalated the war. He and Rich dropped a microphone down one of the chimneys in the Bissells' house so that they could listen in on the adult conversations, but they were caught. Mr. Bissell was furious. His house on Newark Street was filled with safes and oddly colored telephones that rang at all hours of the night. It must have horrified him to learn that his own son might constitute a breach of security. The boys were admonished, and no doubt with fingers crossed behind their backs, they solemnly promised to reform.

One spring, Joe decided that we should develop our own private telephone system. It was time we watched our own backs, protected our information from the grown-ups, made sure they couldn't listen in on us. It was an indication of the high esteem in which Joe held all our operations that he thought the deputy director of planning for the CIA or the Washington editor of the *Saturday Evening Post* might be the slightest bit interested in what their children had to say to each other. At the time, however, it seemed a perfectly reasonable assessment of the situation.

This was our most ambitious undertaking to date. We were going to run the wiring through the storm sewers of the city to five different houses. Most of them were located on our dead-end street, but one branch went to the Bissells' house on Newark Street, five blocks away up a steep hill. It was decided that Rich would be responsible for getting us in and out of the manholes. Somewhere he had managed to lay his hands on a sizable-looking crowbar. I was selected as the second in command to go with Joe. He had done a test run and discovered that he was too tall to stand straight in the sewers, so he'd built a special wooden platform on wheels that would allow him to scoot along taping the wires to the walls while lying on his back. He needed someone my size to follow with the flashlight, the extra tape, and the roll of wire.

I like to think that it wasn't just my height that made Joe pick me. I had shown a certain reliability in other tight situations. If I felt panicky, I didn't show it. I was not a complainer, nor was I squeamish about dark places, bugs, or rodents, all of which we were likely to encounter.

We lowered ourselves down into the sewers without being seen and made our way slowly up the hill from Porter Street to Ordway. Joe lay on his back on his makeshift dolly and pushed himself along, using first one foot and then the other. He taped the wire on the damp walls of the sewer pipe while I followed along behind carrying the rest of the equipment. We turned right on Newark and

Winthrop with daughter, Eliza, age two.

"Me and all five brothers on summer vacation," 1978.

maneuvered ourselves into position right under the manhole cover opposite the Bissells' house. Everything went according to plan up till that point. I gave the prescribed signal, three knocks on the manhole cover with the butt of the flashlight. Then Joe and I crouched at the bottom of the metal steps to wait. And Rich didn't come.

Cars passed overhead. The manhole cover clanked. We could hear the distant noise of a lawn mower, then a fire engine. Minutes went by. They felt like hours. The only noise in the sewer was the constant drip of water off the walls and the scratching and scrabbling of some rat in the distance. Every so often, the light would catch the glimmer of a slug making its slow patient way up the curved wall. Joe began to panic. He knocked again, then ordered me up next to him on the ladder so we could try and move the cover ourselves. It was hopeless. If Rich didn't come to let us out, there was no way we'd make it out of there.

We must have been down there for an extra two hours. It felt like a lifetime. The flashlight went out. The thin shaft of light that came down through the crowbar holes shifted with the waning of the day. We worried about storms, a sudden flood, the rising water. Joe was sure there was a slug going down his shirt. He jumped at the distant sloshing of the water down the dark tunnel. The more panicky he became, the calmer I grew. At the bottom of the narrow metal stepladder, I pressed my body up against his to try

and stop him from shaking. Finally we heard the slide of the metal bar above us. Joe was the first one out. I followed him, still carrying the extra equipment. Joe and Rich had a huge argument over what had taken Rich so long. It turned out that in all their calculations, they hadn't counted on the next-door neighbor picking that particular afternoon to mow his rather extensive lawn.

By the next week, the phone system was up and running. The wire entered the Bissells' house through a basement window and then ran right up the corner of their dining room through a hole in Rich's floor to his desk. Joe had an elaborate switchboard set up in his room, and bells would start ringing around three in the afternoon when the kids got home from school.

Thinking back on it later, I realized how far out there we had been, how dangerous a caper it really was. Rich was a strange boy, more committed to the cause than to our safety. If rescuing us had meant divulging our secret plan to the enemy, the adults, he might have left us down in the sewers indefinitely.

Sometime late in the summer, the wire gave way. Joe checked all the aboveground connections and found them to be clean. The break was down below, somewhere in the sewers. The kids clamored for him to fix it, but Joe told them to leave him alone, he was too busy, he had other things to do. I knew what he was really saying, but still I

With son, Andrew, 1978.

kept my counsel. Brave as I had been during those long damp hours under the manhole cover, I wasn't eager to repeat the exercise.

Nobody, not even Richard Bissell, Mr. CIA himself, ever knew about the private phone system. It was our pièce de résistance, our crowning achievement. But not long after that Joe left to go to boarding school, and the basement gang disbanded. We'd come to the end of our childhood together.

I was sent to a girls' boarding school in the tenth grade and was perfectly happy to be there, surrounded for the first time by the company of women. My roommate and I sat up late into the night talking, and although we were in danger of discovery by the housemother, at least I knew the room had not been bugged by my brother. I didn't mind the order of the days and the arcane rituals, and I loved the smell of the books in the old paneled library. My grandmother lived five miles in one direction and my aunt and uncle five miles in the other, and although you weren't allowed to visit your parents more than once a term, there seemed to be no rules for more distant relatives, so I was sprung almost every weekend. Senior year I took a creative writing course. The teacher who remains a good friend of mine was tough, but encouraging. I remember a short story I wrote in the style of Saki and another one about an unhappy family based on a painting by Picasso in his blue period.

Sarah Lawrence was a natural college for me because they took creative writing seriously and allowed students to major in it, which meant that at least one-third of my courses would focus on writing. The writing department included Grace Paley, E. L. Doctorow, and Jane Cooper, and I took courses from all of them. In fact, I took just about every fiction writing course I could get into. My senior year, I handed in a short story entitled "The Sewers" based on my underground adventure with Joe, and Jane Cooper suggested I try my hand at children's books. I was wounded by her suggestion at the time, because it implied

that the stories I'd written for adult readers were not as successful. She could not have been more right. After all, I was only twenty. I had barely lived. How could I possibly bring to life the troubles of the married banker or the ailing grandmother or the brassy young working woman, all of whom played leading parts in my stories?

I began writing picture books and submitting them to various publishing houses. They were all rejected, but I received encouraging letters from Charlotte Zolotow, a senior editor at Harper and Row (now HarperCollins). I like to think this interest in my work helped me land a job there as an assistant editor six months after I graduated from college. At Harper, I worked under the legendary Ursula Nordstrom. Maurice Sendak, Arnold and Anita Lobel, Shel Silverstein, and other notables in the field drifted in and out of the office all the time. Once when I was covering for Ursula's assistant on her lunch hour, I picked up the phone and heard a man growl, "Hello, this is Andy White. Is Ursula there?" (E. B. White's nickname was Andy.) I had been trained in my parents' living room to treat famous people as everyday occurrences, so I took a message in a cool, efficient voice. Now I wish I had told him how much I loved *Charlotte's Web*. To this day, I find the first sentence of that novel to be one of the most commanding in English literature. You simply have to keep reading to find out where Pa is going with that ax.

If I learned discipline from my father's example, I practiced it at Harper and Row. In those days, people left their publishing jobs promptly at five o'clock. Every evening once the office had emptied out, I pushed my day work aside and wrote for an hour. By the end of a year, I had produced a number of picture books and a novel. It had a beginning, a middle, an end, and some plausible characters, and Charlotte Zolotow was encouraging. After another six months of rewriting from five to six in the evening, Harper published *Walking Away* in 1973. I quit to write full time.

My daughter, Eliza, was born in 1974 and my son, Andrew, in 1978, and my picture books took on a new immediacy and energy, taken as they were from real-life situations. My old eavesdropping habit surfaced once again. When my daughter was four, I heard her talking to her stuffed animals. "Bear," she announced in a firm voice, "I am going out. You will stay with Mrs. Duck." A pause. "Now stop that terrible crying, Bear," she scolded. "You like Mrs. Duck." I went around the corner and wrote down those lines of conversation in my journal. Eventually they found their way into a book called *Bear and Mrs. Duck.* And Bear proved so beguiling to me and my publisher that I wrote two more books about him and his adventures.

The years my children were growing up proved to be years of great productivity for me as I could witness firsthand the daily dilemmas and trials of childhood. I wrote lots of picture books and some chapter books, and as my children aged so did my characters. In those days, I accepted all challenges, some from editors and many of them of my own creation. If my editor thought I should try a novel in first person, I did. Adaptations of various folktales and Bible stories appealed to my love of language, so I tried my hand at them. After fifteen years of publishing children's books, I finally must have decided I was old enough to write about the adults I had abandoned at the age of twenty, and so I wrote a five-hundred-page historical novel, *In My Mother's House,* which covered almost eighty years of history.

And as all writers do, I often ran into a dead end and had to rethink a project. Frustrated by a realistic picture book that felt heavy-handed, I turned the story into a fantasy novel about a boy named William who travels through time to right a wrong he has committed. This was the first novel that I didn't outline ahead of time, so the characters were free to wander down side paths, to make mistakes, to lead me into new adventures. Not surprisingly, *The Castle in the Attic* remains my best-selling book. I'm sure that's because the reader must sense as I did that the characters' lives are truly happening on the page, and none of us, not the author nor the reader nor the character, knows what's coming next.

So here I am some twenty-six years and more than forty books from my first publication, still practicing my craft, still feeling incredibly fortunate that I can make a living doing what I love. People seem to be fascinated by writers and their lives these days. I never thought about C. S. Lewis and Enid Blyton and Laura Ingalls Wilder when I was reading their stories. I was much more interested in their characters and the world they had created for me to live in. Writers travel and talk to their audiences much more frequently these days. Now when I go around visiting schools and reading in colleges, and people ask me how I got to be a writer, I tell them there is no one answer. So I give them many. I say that you have to live a noticing kind of life, be the kind of person as Henry James said, "on which nothing is lost." I say that you have to be a reader. I say that you have to enjoy your own company and be willing to sit alone in a room for hours on end. I point out that writers never really go on vacation; they take characters and stories with them. I tell them you have to be strong enough to ignore the family critics and the reviewers

"The view down onto the terrace where I could hear every word spoken."

and the worst scourge of the lot—the contemptuous, perfectionist voice inside your own head.

Inevitably, the student then asks me where I get my ideas. They must ask every writer the same question. Perhaps it's because they believe there is some secret formula to writing fiction, some special key that will open the door which separates simply living your life from living your life *and* using that same life as material for stories. I know I used to believe that. Again, I have no simple answer. With picture books, I used to get my ideas from an ancient memory or an incident I witnessed in the playground or a conversation between my four-year-old daughter and her stuffed bear. Now my picture books are triggered more by language: a funny name *(Dumpy La Rue)* or a well-worn phrase *(I'm Going to Tell on You).* I seem to hear whole picture books when other people hear nothing but a cute story or a snatch of small talk.

More often than not, my novels move forward because I know the setting. Let me give you an example. I am writing this piece in the south of France in a house that was built four hundred years ago. The walls are three feet thick, and they keep the house cool while outside, in the hot afternoon sun, the song of the *cigales* creates a constant background serenade. I am here on vacation, but remember we writers never really go on vacation. I am setting some scenes from my new novel in France in 1944, where a character of mine is fighting with the French resistance. Two nights ago I looked down from a narrow slit window in the bedroom to a terrace four stories below, and because of some trick of acoustics, I could hear every word the people were saying. Every syllable of every word. They didn't know I was listening, and they would never have thought to look for a spy so high above them in such a tiny window. The place was an eavesdropper's dream. What if my character were hiding from the Germans and he could look down from this same window and hear them questioning the family below? With that concrete piece of knowledge, a new scene began to form in my head. It will take my characters in new directions, places they might never have gone if I had not been able to stand in my bare feet on that cool stone floor and stare through that narrow window, listening yet again to the rise and fall of voices as people told each other stories.

People have often asked me why I write for so many different ages. It keeps me interested is the simplest reply. Last year I published a novel for adults, *Island Justice,* and soon after that I wrote three picture books. *Island Justice* took me two-and-a-half years from first inkling to final draft. An idea for a picture book may germinate for months or even years, but the actual writing time can be as short as a week, and it feels satisfying after years on one project to be able to finish a book in a matter of days. Each of the audiences I write for presents a different challenge and exercises a different writing muscle. *In My Mother's House,* which spanned three generations of American women, forced me to use all of my plotting and characterization skills, whereas a picture book for young children will remind me to focus on language.

I used to think, although never consciously, that I had to write BIG in order to be taken seriously as a writer for adults. So I chose to work on large stages, either by covering decades of American history *(In My Mother's House)* or by peopling an entire island *(Island Justice).*

Family reunion, Christmas, 1994.

Now I would like to take all the skills I learned in writing my fantasy novels *(The Castle in the Attic* and *The Battle for the Castle)* and bring them to bear on a short novel for adults, one that focuses intensely on two main characters and brings them to life for the reader in a deeper, more layered picture. To put it more simply, I'd like to try using fewer words and making sure that each one counts.

So I continue to challenge myself because as I said before it keeps me interested. What would it be like to write this novel in the first person? I ask myself. Or how would it be to use the voice of an omniscient narrator? Or could this be an epistolary novel? Why not try this picture book in rhyme? And of course, each time I set myself a new task, the excitement propels me along until that inevitable moment when I feel once more like that little girl who jumped into the water and then discovered that she didn't know how to swim. Why did I ever start this? I ask myself. How did I ever think I could make this plot work or that character come to life? But the feeling has become a familiar one, almost an old friend by now. Whenever I sense that I'm out of my depth in the midst of a new novel, then it means the story interests me, and sooner or later, I'll flail my way up through the murky water and back to the surface. I no longer need my father to reach in and pull me out. I've learned how to do it myself.

Writings

FOR CHILDREN; PICTURE BOOKS

Bunk Beds, illustrated by Ronald Himler, Harper, 1972.

That's Mine!, illustrated by Emily McCully, Holiday House, 1976.

Potbellied Possums, illustrated by Barbara McClintock, Holiday House, 1977.

Are You Sad, Mama?, illustrated by Donna Diamond, Harper, 1979.

Journey to the Bright Kingdom, illustrated by Charles Mikolaycak, Holiday House, 1979.

Sloppy Kisses, illustrated by Ann Burgess, Macmillan, 1980.

I Think He Likes Me, illustrated by Denise Saldutti, Harper, 1980.

Katharine's Doll, illustrated by Marylin Hafner, Dutton, 1983.

A Child Is Born: The Christmas Story, illustrated by Charles Mikolaycak, Holiday House, 1983.

Tough Eddie, illustrated by Lillian Hoban, Dutton, 1984.

He Is Risen: The Easter Story, illustrated by Charles Mikolaycak, Holiday House, 1985.

Lizzie and Harold, illustrated by Martha Weston, Lothrop, 1986.

Shoes, illustrated by William Joyce, Harper, 1986.

Maggie and the Monster, illustrated by Tomie dePaola, Holiday House, 1987.

Bear and Mrs. Duck, illustrated by Patience Brewster, Holiday House, 1988.

The Best Friends Club: A Lizzie and Harold Story, illustrated by Martha Weston, Lothrop, 1989.

Sledding, illustrated by Sarah Wilson, Harper, 1989.

Bear's Christmas Surprise, illustrated by Patience Brewster, Holiday House, 1991.

(Adapter) *Vasilissa the Beautiful: A Russian Folktale*, illustrated by Alexander Koshkin, HarperCollins, 1991.

A Very Noisy Girl, illustrated by Ellen Weiss, Holiday House, 1991.

Asleep in a Heap, illustrated by Mary Morgan, Holiday House, 1993.

I'm the Boss, illustrated by Mary Morgan, Holiday House, 1994.

Bear and Roly-Poly, illustrated by Patience Brewster, Holiday House, 1996.

(Adapter) *The Little Humpbacked Horse: A Russian Folktale*, illustrated by Alexander Koshkin, Clarion, 1997.

As the Crow Flies, illustrated by Joan Sandin, Clarion, 1998.

Promises, illustrated by Betsy Lewin, Clarion, in press.

Dumpy La Rue, illustrated by Betsy Lewin, Henry Holt, in press.

Hats, illustrated by Sue Truesdell, Henry Holt, in press.

Squashed in the Middle, Henry Holt, in press.

GOLDEN BOOKS FOR CHILDREN

Shoelace Box, illustrated by Kathy Wibburn, 1984.

The Christmas Pageant, illustrated by Kathy Wibburn, 1984.

Happy Easter, Mother Duck, illlustrated by Diane Dawson Hearn, 1985.

My First Book of the Planets, illustrated by John Nez, 1985.

CHAPTER BOOKS FOR CHILDREN

Belinda's Hurricane, illustrated by Wendy Watson, Dutton, 1984.

Luke's Bully, illustrated by Pat Grant Porter, Viking, 1990.

YOUNG ADULT FICTION

Walking Away, illustrated by Noelle Massena, Harper, 1973.

A Little Demonstration of Affection, Harper, 1975.

Knock, Knock, Who's There?, Holiday House, 1978.

Marathon Miranda, Holiday House, 1979.

Miranda in the Middle, Holiday House, 1980.

The Castle in the Attic, illustrated by Trina Schart Hyman, Holiday House, 1985.

The Battle for the Castle, Holiday House, 1993.

ADULT FICTION

In My Mother's House, Doubleday, 1988.

Island Justice, William Morrow, 1998.

OTHER

Contributor of short stories to periodicals and anthologies. *The Castle in the Attic* and *The Battle for the Castle* were recorded on audiocassette in an unabridged multi-voice dramatization (author as narrator) with Listening Library in 1996 and 1997.

X–Y

XUAN, YongSheng 1952-

Personal

Born July 24, 1952, in Shanghai, China; immigrated to Canada, 1990; son of Xing Kang (a civil engineer) and Bing Xian (Tang) Xuan; married Rong Rong Gu (a restaurant manager); children: Feli. *Education:* Attended Central Institute of Culture, QiDong, China, 1970-73; Central University of Arts and Crafts, Beijing, China, Fine Arts and Crafts certificate, 1985-86; attended University of Regina, Canada, 1993-94.

Addresses

Home—Apartment E5, 4415 Judson Ave., Royal Oak, MI, 48073.

Career

QiDong Arts Factory of China, QiDong, JianShu, China, art designer, 1973-78; Industrial Arts Institute of China, Nan Tong, JianShu, China, master art designer and director, 1978-90; Burant Cabinet and Mill Work, Regina, Saskatchewan, Canada, woodwork designer, carving, and producer, 1990-93; Benchmark Mould Ltd., Windsor, Ontario, Canada, art director and master engraver and finisher, 1994-96; Ford City Business District, Windsor, Ontario, Canada, mural artist, 1998—. Freelance artist and illustrator, 1981—. *Exhibitions:* Solo art exhibition at the Art Gallery of Shanghai, China, 1985; exhibitor at several one-man shows in Regina, Saskatchewan, Canada; art work for *The Rooster's Antlers* exhibited at the Society of Illustrators' Original Art Exhibit, 1999. *Member:* Chinese Arts and Crafts Association.

Awards, Honors

Parents' Choice storybook recommendation, Parents' Choice Foundation, 1998, for *The Laziest Boy in the World;* Notable Children's Trade Book in the Field of Social Studies, National Council for Social Studies-Children's Book Council, 1999, for *Ten Suns.*

Writings

ILLUSTRATOR

Eric A. Kimmel, reteller, *Ten Suns: A Chinese Legend,* Holiday House, 1998.
Lensey Namioka, *The Laziest Boy in the World,* Holiday House, 1998.
Eric A. Kimmel, reteller, *The Rooster's Antlers: A Story of the Chinese Zodiac,* Holiday House, 1999.
(And author) *The Dragon Lover and Other Chinese Proverbs,* Shen's Books, 1999.

OTHER

Contributor of illustrations and writings to numerous publications, including *ShangHai People's Arts Publishing House, Beijing Esperanto Magazine, YuNan Science Magazine, ZheJiang People's Arts Publishing House, Beijing Arts and Crafts Magazine, Beijing People's Arts Publishing House, Beijing Traditional Arts Magazine, JianShu Traditional Arts Magazine, JianShu People's Arts Publishing House, Sinorama Magazine,* and *Cricket* magazine group.

Work in Progress

Two picture books, *The Story of Chopsticks* and *The Story of Noodles;* writing and illustrating eighteen classic Chinese stories for *Sinorama Magazine,* Taiwan; illustrating *That's Ghosts for You,* an anthology of scary stories, for *Cricket* and Fronn Street Books.

Sidelights

Chinese artist and illustrator YongSheng Xuan has been widely praised for his ability to bridge cultural gaps with a unique and compelling style. His illustration work includes the award-winning titles *The Laziest Boy in the World,* written by Lensey Namioka, and *Ten Suns: A Chinese Legend* and *The Rooster's Antlers: A Story of the Chinese Zodiac,* both adapted and retold by Eric A.

YongSheng Xuan

Kimmel. Xuan is also the author and illustrator of *The Dragon Lover and Other Chinese Proverbs.*

Xuan was born in Shanghai, China, in 1952. As a teenager, he studied under famed Chinese sculptor Zhang Chenren. Xuan later worked as an art designer and professional artist, and eventually took advanced fine arts and crafts classes at the Central Arts and Crafts University in Beijing, considered one of the highest art institutes in China.

In 1981 Xuan began contributing artwork to a variety of publications and magazines in China, Japan, Taiwan, and the United States. Since that time his illustrations, paintings, and paper cuts have appeared in *Beijing People's Arts Publishing House, Sinorama Magazine, Cricket,* and many other periodicals.

Xuan and his family immigrated to Canada in 1990. He worked for several years as a woodwork designer and cabinetmaker in Regina, Saskatchewan, then as art director and master engraver and finisher at a production company in Windsor, Ontario. He continued to contribute his work to children's magazines.

In 1998 Xuan illustrated his first North American picture book, *Ten Suns,* retold by Eric A. Kimmel. One of the oldest Chinese legends, *Ten Suns* tells the story of the emperor of the eastern sky, Di Jun, and his ten sons, who are also suns. Each day the emperor's sons take turns walking across the sky from east to west. After many years they tire of following the path alone, and one day, despite their father's warnings, all ten sons make the journey together. Their combined heat scorches the land—crops wither and die, forests burst into flame, and the seas boil. To save the earth and its people, Emperor Di Jun sends the Archer of Heaven to find the suns and shoot all but one from the sky. A *Kirkus Reviews* contributor called Xuan's illustrations "magical" and "as richly crafted and detailed as fine embroidery on Chinese silk."

Xuan next provided artwork for Lensey Namioka's story *The Laziest Boy in the World,* which also appeared in 1998. *Booklist* critic Karen Morgan praised the book as "both fun to read and visually appealing." *The Laziest Boy in the World* tells the story of young Xiaolong, who as a baby is so lazy that he almost never kicks or cries. As he grows older, Xiaolong becomes increasingly spoiled and lazy, until he doesn't even want to play. But when a thief breaks into his home, Xiaolong is finally moved to take action. He thwarts the villain and discovers the satisfaction of a job well done. According to *Horn Book Guide* contributor Minfong Ho, Xuan's vivid illustrations for *The Laziest Boy in the World* are "rich with details of Chinese village life."

The Dragon Lover and Other Chinese Proverbs, published in 1999, was Xuan's first self-illustrated picture book. Written in both English and Chinese, the book includes five traditional Chinese proverbs: "The Lazy Farmer," "The Crane and the Clam," "The Musician and the Water Buffalo," "An Old Horse," and "The Dragon Lover." Each story is illustrated with intricate Chinese-style paper cuts that *Booklist* reviewer Kay Weisman called "striking" and "remarkable."

Works Cited

Ho, Minfong, review of *The Laziest Boy in the World, Horn Book Guide,* July-December, 1998, p. 38.

Morgan, Karen, review of *The Laziest Boy in the World, Booklist,* November 1, 1998, p. 504.

Review of *Ten Suns: A Chinese Legend, Kirkus Reviews,* April 1, 1998, p. 496.

Weisman, Kay, review of *The Dragon Lover and Other Chinese Proverbs, Booklist,* May 15, 1999, p. 1700.

For More Information See

PERIODICALS

Booklist, May 1, 1998, p. 1520.

Bulletin of the Center for Children's Books, July, 1999, p. 1804.

School Library Journal, May, 1998, p. 134.

*   *   *

YOUNG, Karen Romano 1959-

Personal

Born November 21, 1959, in Ithaca, NY; daughter of William S. (a computer consultant) and Carol (a registered nurse; maiden name, Spath) Romano; married Mark C. Young (publisher of the Guiness Book of Records), April 10, 1982; children: Bethany, Sam(uel), Emily. *Education:* Syracuse University, B.S. in Education, 1981. *Politics:* Democrat. *Religion:* Roman Catholic.

Addresses

Home—22 Long Meadow Lane, Bethel, CT 06801. *Agent*—Steven Malk, Writers House, 3368 Governor Dr., #224 F, San Diego, CA 92122. *E-mail*—wrenyoung@aol.com

Career

Scholastic News, New York, NY, writer, assistant and associate editor, 1981-83; freelance writer and editor, 1983—. *Member:* Society of Children's Book Writers and Illustrators, Authors Guild.

Karen Romano Young

Writings

(With Marlene Barron) *Ready, Set, Read and Write: 60 Playful Activities for You and Your Child to Share,* illustrated by Elaine Yabroudy, Wiley, 1995.

(With Marlene Barron) *Ready, Set, Count: 60 Playful Activities for You and Your Child to Share,* illustrated by Elaine Yabroudy, Wiley, 1995.

(With Marlene Barron) *Ready, Set, Cooperate,* Wiley, 1996.

(With Marlene Barron) *Ready, Set, Explore,* Wiley, 1996.

The Ice's Edge: The Story of a Harp Seal Pup, illustrated by Brian Shaw, Soundprints (Norwalk, CT), 1996.

Guinness Record Breakers, Guinness Media, 1997.

The Beetle and Me: A Love Story, (young adult novel), Greenwillow, 1999.

Arctic Investigations: Exploring the Frozen Ocean, Raintree Steck-Vaughn, 1999.

Video, (young adult novel), Greenwillow, 1999.

Work in Progress

Outside In, a young adult novel, due from Greenwillow in 2001, and *Small World: A Book about Maps and Mapmakers,* due from Scholastic in 2001. Research in navigation: sea, air, land.

Sidelights

"These three things happened when I was four years old," Karen Romano Young told *SATA:* "My family moved from Germany back home to the U.S. where everybody spoke English. And I learned to read. And I began to write, not just draw. That year we moved to a town with its own children's library. Can you believe I fell in love with language and stories all at once?

"I have been an avid reader since I was a very young child, and also my parents and grandparents all loved to read to all of us children. There's no better preparation for a writer than so very much joyful reading.

"I always wanted to be a writer and I was always writing something. Along the way I tried art, film, teaching, biology, nursing, library science, marketing, and more. Through a piece of luck—and a friend or two—I found myself walking into an interview at Scholastic. It was my first visit to a children's publishing house. I have never looked back. There could be no greater happiness in work for me than writing books for children—unless one day I woke up with illustrating talent!"

Karen Romano Young's first novel for young adults captured the hearts of critics with its deft blend of romance and coming-of-age themes peopled by surprising and likable characters. In *The Beetle and Me,* fifteen-year-old Daisy sets her heart on restoring the old Volkswagen Beetle rusting in an outbuilding on the family farm, despite the discouragement she receives from the other crack mechanics in her family. *Booklist* reviewer Jean Franklin described the progress of Young's plot as: "Girl risks all to save car; girl loses car; girl gets car back—sort of—and finds her true self." The seven chapters of the novel correspond to seven months in the life of its protagonist, as she stubbornly refuses all offers of help to fix up the car. Daisy endures the disappointment of finding out that the boy she has a crush on is interested in her boisterous cousin, and the realization that Billy, an old friend and fellow car buff, is in love with her. "Young shows many types of love: mature love; intense and unrequited teen love; and steady, slow-growing someday love," observed Cindy

Darling Codell in *School Library Journal,* adding praise for Young's successful creation of "strong, likable female characters who still find men very attractive." Similarly, a reviewer for *Publishers Weekly* predicted that "readers of both sexes are sure to be swept up in the vibrant characterizations, finely nuanced emotions and detailed auto arcana" that comprises the story of *The Beetle and Me.*

In *Video,* Young's second novel for young adults, the author takes a dark turn in plotting. There are repercussions for everyone involved when Eric Gooch decides to secretly videotape fellow classmate Janine Gagnon for his spring term project and discovers that her solitary treks into the wetlands near her home are witnessed by a suspicious older man. The narrative alternates between first-person accounts by Eric and Janine detailing their view of events. "The author creates a compelling picture of Janine as a once popular girl, fallen from favor, and her simultaneous craving for solitude and attention," remarked Sybil Steinberg in *Publishers Weekly.*

Young has also written several activity books with Marlene Barron, including *Ready, Set, Count* and *Ready, Set, Read and Write,* based on the Montessori method, intended for parents of three- to seven-year-olds. *School Library Journal* reviewer Kevin Wayne Booe predicted that "parents will probably have as much fun with these activities as their children will."

Works Cited

Review of *The Beetle and Me, Publishers Weekly,* May 3, 1999, p. 77.

Booe, Kevin Wayne, review of *Ready, Set, Count* and *Ready, Set, Read and Write, School Library Journal,* August, 1996, p. 36.

Codell, Cindy Darling, review of *The Beetle and Me, School Library Journal,* May, 1999, p. 133.

Franklin, Jean, review of *The Beetle and Me, Booklist,* April 15, 1999, p. 1523.

Steinberg, Sybil, review of *Video, Publishers Weekly,* September 13, 1999, p. 85.*